Leadership

Theory and Practice

Richard L. Daft
Owen Graduate School of Management
Vanderbilt University

The Dryden Press
Harcourt Brace College Publishers

Fort Worth   Philadelphia   San Diego   New York   Orlando   Austin   San Antonio
Toronto   Montreal   London   Sydney   Tokyo

Publisher: George Provol
Acquisitions Editor: John Weimeister
Product Manager: Lisé Johnson
Developmental Editor: Tracy Morse
Project Editor: Rebecca Dodson
Art Director: Lora Gray
Production Manager: Darryl King
Cover Image: Chet Phillips

ISBN: 0-03-022417-9

Library of Congress Catalog Card Number:: 98-71914

Address for domestic orders
Harcourt, Inc., 6277 Sea Harbor Drive, Orlando, FL 32887-6777
800-782-4479

Address for international orders
International Customer Service
Harcourt, Inc., 6277 Sea Harbor Drive, Orlando, FL 32887-6777
407-345-3800
(fax) 407-345-4060
(e-mail) hbintl@harcourt.com

Address for editorial correspondence
Harcourt College Publishers, 301 Commerce Street, Suite 3700, Fort Worth, TX 76102

Website address
http://www.harcourtcollege.com

Printed in the United States of America

0 1 2 3 4 5 6 7 8 9   039   13 12 11 10 9 8 7 6 5

Harcourt College Publishers

*To the leaders in academia and business who
so positively influenced my life and career.*

The Dryden Press Series in Management

Anthony, Perrewé, and Kacmar
Strategic Human Resource Management
Second Edition

Bereman, Lengnick-Hall, and Mark
**Compensation Decision Making:
A Computer-Based Approach**
Second Edition

Bergmann, Scarpello, and Hills
Compensation Decision Making
Second Edition

Boone and Kurtz
Contemporary Business
Ninth Edition

Bourgeois
**Strategic Management: From Concept to
Implementation**

Bracker, Montanari, and Morgan
Cases in Strategic Management

Brechner
**Contemporary Mathematics for Business
and Consumers**

Calvasina and Barton
Chopstick Company: A Business Simulation

Costin
Readings in Total Quality Management

Costin
**Managing in the Global Economy:
The European Union**

Costin
Economic Reform in Latin America

Costin
**Management Development and Training:
A TQM Approach**

Costin
**Readings in Strategy and Strategic
Management**

Czinkota, Ronkainen, and Moffett
International Business
Fourth Edition

Czinkota, Ronkainen, Moffett, and Moynihan
Global Business
Second Edition

Daft
Leadership

Daft
Management
Fourth Edition

Daft and Marcic
Understanding Management
Second Edition

DeSimone and Harris
Human Resource Development
Second Edition

Foegen
Business Plan Guidebook
Revised Edition

Gatewood and Feild
Human Resource Selection
Fourth Edition

Gold
**Exploring Organizational Behavior:
Readings, Cases, Experiences**

Greenhaus and Callanan
Career Management
Second Edition

Higgins and Vincze
Strategic Management: Text and Cases
Fifth Edition

Hodgetts
Modern Human Relations at Work
Sixth Edition

Hodgetts and Kroeck
Personnel and Human Resource Management

Hodgetts and Kuratko
Effective Small Business Management
Sixth Edition

Holley and Jennings
The Labor Relations Process
Sixth Edition

Holt
International Management: Text and Cases

Jauch and Coltrin
The Managerial Experience: Cases and Exercises
Sixth Edition

Kindler and Ginsburg
Strategic & Interpersonal Skill Building

Kirkpatrick and Lewis
Effective Supervision: Preparing for the 21st Century

Kuratko and Hodgetts
Entrepreneurship: A Contemporary Approach
Fourth Edition

Kuratko and Welsch
Entrepreneurial Strategy: Text and Cases

Lengnick-Hall, Cynthia, and Hartman
Experiencing Quality

Lewis
Io Enterprises Simulation

Long and Arnold
The Power of Environmental Partnerships

Morgan
Managing for Success

Ryan, Eckert, and Ray
Small Business: An Entrepreneur's Plan
Fourth Edition

Sandburg
Career Design Software

Vecchio
Organizational Behavior
Third Edition

Walton
Corporate Encounters: Law, Ethics, and the Business Environment

Weiss
Business Ethics: A Stakeholder and Issues Management Approach
Second Edition

Zikmund
Business Research Methods
Fifth Edition

My dream for this text is to integrate recent leadership ideas and practices with established research findings in a way that is interesting and valuable to students. The world of leadership is undergoing a revolution. The era of the learning organization has begun, and demands on leaders go well beyond the ideas traditionally taught in courses on management and organizational behavior. The purpose of this book is to expand the treatment and capture the excitement of the subject in a way that will motivate students toward greater leadership.

I have been teaching leadership to students and managers, and have been working with leaders to change their organizations, over the last several years. These experiences have affirmed for me the value of traditional leadership concepts, while highlighting the importance of reaching out to include valuable ideas such as leadership vision, individual courage, ethical and moral issues, leading change, leading a learning organization, the difference between leadership and management, leadership and multiculturalism, a leader's personal capacity for mind, heart (emotion) and spirit, followership, and shaping values and culture. Thus my mission is to integrate timely concepts and models from leadership theory with the practical application of ideas in the real world to provide an up-to-date and valuable leadership resource to instructors and students.

The organization of the book has been influenced by the approach to leadership described by Professor John Kotter of Harvard University in *The Leadership Factor, A Force for Change: How Leadership Differs From Management*, and *Leading Change*. Kotter's approach stresses that leaders differ from managers in the way they set direction, seek alignment between organization and followers, build relationships, and create change. Thus the organization of this book is in seven parts:

1. Introduction to leadership

2. Research perspectives on individual leadership

3. Leader as visionary (setting direction)

4. Leader as social architect (aligning culture, people, and structure)

5. Leader as relationship builder

6. The personal side of leadership

7. Leading change and transformation

The book integrates materials from both micro and macro approaches to leadership, from academia and the real world, and from traditional ideas and recent thinking.

Special Features

This book has a number of special features that are designed to make the material accessible and valuable to students.

Leadership Spotlight This book is loaded with examples woven into the text. Four of these examples are highlighted within each chapter, including the chapter opening examples. The leadership spotlights include Martin Luther King, General George Marshall, Margaret Mead, Phil Knight (Nike), Herb Kelleher (Southwest Airlines), Raoul Wallenberg, Mary Ann Byrnes of Corsair Communications, Grace Pastiak of Tellabs, Les Aberthal of EDS, Orit Gadiesh of Bain & Co., and Pam Coker of Acucobal. The spotlights also include leaders within organizations such as Ford, Royal Dutch Shell, the United States Information Agency, and the U.S. Army. In addition, spotlights describe leaders in new, learning organizations such as David Abrahams of St. Luke's Advertising Agency (England), Lars Kolind of Otico Holding (Denmark), and Dianne Martz of Hemophilia Health Services. These spotlight examples focus on business, education, the military, and not-for-profit organizations.

Living Leadership Each chapter includes a Living Leadership box, that is personal, compelling, real, and inspiring. This box may include a saying from a famous leader, or wisdom from the ages. Examples in the book include "Five Qualities 21st Century Leaders Won't Need," "A Wish for Leaders," "Cultural Norms of Fast Teams," "The Nine Faces of Leadership," excerpts from Nelson Mandela's inaugural speech, "The Ripple Effect," "Polarities," and "Good Leadership." The Living Leadership box provides novel and interesting material to expand the reader's thinking about leadership.

Leader's Bookshelf Each chapter contains a review of a recent book relevant to that chapter's content. The Leader's Bookshelf will connect students to issues and topics being read and discussed in the worlds of academia, business, military, education, and not-for-profit. Examples of these books include *The Way of the Warrior, Everyday Revolutionaries, Managing with the Wisdom of Love, Leadership and the New Sciences, The 9 Natural Laws of Leadership, The Leadership Engine, Leading Change, Organizing Genius, Rewiring the Corporate Brain, Moving Mountains, Built to Last,* and *Maximum Leadership.*

On the Cutting Edge This box highlights a leader doing cutting edge work in an organization, or an organization that is creating cutting edge leaders. These examples describe something extraordinary in contemporary leadership practice. Cutting edge examples include Hard Rock Cafe, Quad/Graphics, Microstrategy, Lucent Technologies, GTO, Black Belt Boss, The Chicago Bulls, and UNUM Life Insurance. These items provide students with insights into cutting edge practices in the world today.

Student Development Each chapter ends with two activities for student development. The first is a personal feedback questionnaire that assesses the student's personal standing with respect to the leadership qualities described in the chapter. These questionnaires were chosen to give students feedback on their personal progress toward leadership. The second item at the end of each chapter is a problem-oriented case that tests the student's ability to apply concepts when dealing with real leadership issues. The case challenges the student's cognitive understanding of leadership ideas while the feedback questionnaire assesses the student's progress as a leader.

Acknowledgments

Textbook writing is a team enterprise. This book has integrated ideas and support from many people whom I want to acknowledge. I especially thank Bob Lengel, at the University of Texas at San Antonio. Bob's enthusiasm for leadership many years ago stimulated me to begin reading, teaching, and training in the area of leadership development. His enthusiasm also led to our collaboration on the book, *Fusion Leadership: Unlocking the Subtle Forces that Change People and Organizations*. I thank Bob for keeping our shared leadership dream alive, which in time enabled me to pursue my dream of writing this leadership textbook.

Here at Vanderbilt, I want to thank Linda Roberts for her ability to plow through the typing and revision of chapters on time every time, and for working on a variety of other tasks to give me time to write. Marty Geisel, the Dean at Owen, maintained a positive scholarly atmosphere and supported me with the time and resources needed to complete this book. I also appreciate the intellectual stimulation and support from friends and colleagues at the Owen School—Bruce Barry, Ray Friedman, Barry Gerhart, Rich Oliver, and Greg Stewart.

I want to acknowledge the reviewers who provided feedback and a very short turnaround. Their ideas helped me improve the book in many areas. Thanks to Bill Bommer—Georgia State University; Nell Hartley—Robert Morris College; and Gregory Manora—Auburn University-Montgomery.

I also want to extend special thanks to my editorial associate, Pat Lane. I could not have undertaken this book without Pat's help. She skillfully drafted materials on a variety of chapters and boxes, found sources, and did an outstanding job with last-minute changes, the copy-edited manuscript, art, and galley proofs. Pat's talent and personal enthusiasm for this text added greatly to its excellence. I also thank Melissa Davis who assisted with several chapters and library research. She, too, with her writing skill and commitment, made a genuine difference to this book.

The editors at Dryden also deserve special mention. John Weimeister, senior acquisitions editor, supported the concept for this book and obtained the resources necessary for its completion. Tracy Morse, developmental editor, provided terrific support for the book's writing, reviews, copy editing, and production.

Finally, I want to acknowledge my loving family. I received much love and support from my wife, Dorothy Marcic, and daughter, Elizabeth, here at home, and appreciate the good feelings and connections with daughters who live elsewhere. On occasion, we have been able to travel, ski, watch a play, or just be together—all of which reconnect me to things that really count.

CONTENTS

PART ONE

Introduction to Leadership
1

Chapter 1

The Importance of Learning Leadership 2
The Nature of Leadership **5**
Definition of Leadership 5
Leadership and the Business of Living **7**
The New Reality for Today's Organizations **8**
From Cherishing Stability to Valuing Change 8
From Control to Empowerment 10
From Competition to Collaboration 10
From Things to Relationships 11
From Uniformity to Diversity 13
Leadership Is Not Automatic **13**
Where Have All the Leaders Gone? **16**
The Leader Within 17
Change Thyself 19
Leadership Can Be Learned **20**
Learning to Lead 20
Learning about Leadership 23

Chapter 2

From Management to Leadership 32
The Nature of Management **35**
The Functions of Management 35
Managerial Roles 36
Comparing Management and Leadership **37**
Providing Direction 39
Alignment 40
Relationships 40
Personal Leadership Qualities 41
Outcomes 45
The Evolution of Leadership **46**
Context of Leadership 46
Framework 47
Implications 51
Rest of the Book 52

PART TWO

**Research Perspectives
on Individual
Leadership
61**

Chapter 3

Traits, Behaviors, and Relationships   62

The Trait Approach   **65**

Behavior Approaches   **69**

Autocratic versus Democratic Leadership   69

Ohio State Studies   72

University of Michigan Studies   73

The Leadership Grid   75

How Grid Styles Emerge   75

Theories of a "High-High" Leader   78

Dyadic Approaches   **80**

Vertical Dyad Linkage Model   80

Leader-Member Exchange (LMX)   82

Partnership Building   82

Systems and Networks   83

Chapter 4

Contingency Approaches   90

The Contingency Approach   **93**

Fiedler's Contingency Model   **94**

Leadership Style   94

Situation   95

Contingency Theory   95

Hersey and Blanchard's Situational Theory   **99**

Path-Goal Theory   **102**

Leader Behavior   103

Situational Contingencies   104

Use of Rewards   106

The Vroom-Jago Contingency Model   **107**

Leader Participation Styles   108

Diagnostic Questions   108

Selecting a Decision Style   109

Substitutes for Leadership   **111**

PART THREE

**Leader as Visionary
121**

Chapter 5

Leadership Vision and Strategic Direction   122

Strategic Leadership   **124**

Leadership Vision   **126**

What Vision Does   127

Common Themes of Vision	130
A Vision Works at Multiple Levels	131
Mission	**133**
Strategy Formulation	**135**
Core Competence	136
Synergy	137
Value Creation	137
Strategy in Action	**138**
The Leader's Contribution	**139**
Stimulating Vision and Action	139
How Leaders Decide	140
The Leader's Impact	**143**

Chapter 6

Leadership Communication	152
How Leaders Communicate	**155**
Management Communication	155
Leader Communication	155
Creating an Open Communication Climate	**156**
Listening and Discernment	**159**
Dialogue	162
Discernment	162
Rich Communication Channels	**164**
Stories and Metaphors	**167**
Symbols and Informal Communication	**169**
Feedback and Learning	**170**
Communication to Develop Followers	171
Organizational Learning	172

PART FOUR

Leader as Social Architect 179

Chapter 7

Shaping Culture and Values	180
Organizational Culture	**183**
What Is Culture?	183
Importance of Culture	184
Culture Strength and Adaptation	**186**
Culture Gap	187
Shaping Culture	**188**
Ceremonies	188
Stories	188

Symbols   190
Specialized Language   190
Selection and Socialization   190
Daily Actions   191
Shaping Values   **192**
The Competing Values Approach   193
Ethical Values in Organizations   **196**
Values-Based Leadership   **197**
Personal Ethics   197
Organizational Structure and Systems   198

Chapter 8

Designing and Leading a Learning Organization   **208**
Efficient Performances Versus Learning Organization   **210**
Organization Structure   **212**
Vertical Structure   212
Horizontal Structure   214
Tasks versus Roles   **215**
Mechanistic and Organic Processes   215
From Routine Tasks to Empowered Roles   216
Systems versus Networks   **217**
Competitive versus Linked Strategy   **218**
Rigid versus Adaptive Culture   **220**
The Leader's Challenge   **222**
Leadership Frames for Learning Organizations   **224**
Structural Frame   224
Human Resource Frame   225
Political Frame   226
Symbolic Frame   226

PART FIVE

Leader as Relationship Builder
235

Chapter 9

Motivation and Empowerment   **236**
Leadership and Motivation   **238**
Intrinsic and Extrinsic Rewards   239
Higher Versus Lower Needs   240
Needs-Based Theories of Motivation   **242**
Hierarchy of Needs Theory   243
Two-Factor Theory   244
Acquired Needs Theory   246

Other Motivational Theories 246
Reinforcement Perspective on Motivation 247
Expectancy Theory 248
The Carrot and Stick Controversy 248
Empowerment 251
Reasons for Empowerment 253
Elements of Empowerment 254
Empowerment Applications 256
Implementing Empowerment 257
Organization-Wide Motivational Programs 258

Chapter 10

Leading Teams 266
Teams in Organizations 268
What Is a Team? 269
Types of Teams 269
Functional Teams 270
Cross-Functional Teams 270
Evolution to Self-Directed Teams 272
Team Leadership 274
The Team Leader's Personal Role 274
Guiding Team Effectiveness 276
Understanding Team Characteristics 278
Size 278
Interdependence 278
Leading Team Dynamics 280
Team Development 280
Team Culture 283
Team Cohesiveness 284
Handling Team Conflict 286
Causes of Conflict 286
Styles to Handle Conflict 287
Other Approaches 288
Leading Global Teams 289

Chapter 11

Leadership and Multiculturalism 298
Multiculturalism Today 302
Definition of Diversity 302
The Reality of Diversity 303

The Need for Organizational Diversity 304
Ways Women Lead 305
Global Diversity 306
The Sociocultural Environment 307
Leadership Implications 310
Challenges Minorities Face 311
Leadership Initiatives toward Multiculturalism 314
Organizational Stages of Diversity Awareness 314
Barriers to Evolution 315
Leadership Solutions 317
Leading Multicultural Organizations 318

PART SIX

The Personal Side of Leadership
329

Chapter 12

Leadership Mind and Heart 330
Leader Capacity versus Competence 333
Charismatic Leadership 334
What Makes a Charismatic Leader? 336
The Black Hat of Charisma 337
Leadership Mind 338
Independent Thinking 338
Open-Mindedness 340
Systems Thinking 341
Mental Models 343
Personal Mastery 344
Leading with Heart—Emotional Intelligence 345
What Are Emotions? 345
The Components of Emotional Intelligence 346
Implications for Leadership 348
Leading with Love versus Leading with Fear 349
Fear in Organizations 349
Bringing Love to Work 350
Why Followers Respond to Love 352

Chapter 13

Courage of Moral Leadership 362
Moral Leadership Today 365
The Ethical Climate in U.S. Business 365
The Leadership Dilemma 366
Becoming a Moral Leader 369
Leadership Control versus Service 371

Authoritarian Management 372
Participative Management 373
Stewardship 373
Servant Leadership 374
Building an Ethical Culture **377**
Leadership Courage **378**
What Is Courage? 379
Moral Courage **383**
Sources of Personal Courage 385

Chapter 14

Followership 394
The Role of Followers **396**
Styles of Followership **397**
The Courageous Follower **400**
Courage to Assume Responsibility 400
Courage to Serve 401
Courage to Challenge 401
Courage to Participate in Transformation 402
Courage to Leave 402
Sources of Follower Courage **403**
Developing Personal Potential **404**
From Dependence to Independence 405
Effective Interdependence 405
Sources of Power **406**
Personal Sources 407
Position Sources 407
Strategies for Effective Followership **407**
Be a Resource for the Leader 408
Help the Leader Be a Good Leader 409
Build a Relationship with the Leader 409
View the Leader Realistically 410
What Followers Want **411**
Building a Community of Followers **411**

PART SEVEN

Leading Change and Transformation
421

Chapter 15

Leading Change 422
Change or Perish **425**
Transactional versus Transformational Leadership **427**
Transactional Leadership 427

Transformational Leadership   427
Leading Major Change   **429**
The Focus of Change   **432**
Creativity   **435**
Leading Creativity in Organizations and People   436
Stages in the Personal Creative Process   439
Leading Culture Change   **441**
Why Do People Resist Change?   441
Overcoming Resistance   442
Culture Change Approaches   443
Total Quality Management   443
Organizational Development   444
Large-Group Interventions   444

Chapter 16

Leader Decision Making, Power, and Influence   **454**
Decision Making   **457**
Two Stages of Decision Making   457
Two Types of Decisions   458
Leader Decisions   **461**
Organizational Decision Making   **462**
Rational Choice versus Political Process   463
Coalition Building   465
Incremental Decisions   467
Combination of Coalition Building and
    Incremental Approaches   468
Decision Mistakes   **468**
Power and Influence   **470**
Five Types of Leader Power   470
Other Sources of Leader Power   471
Asserting Influence   474

Index   **484**

PART ONE

Introduction to Leadership

Chapter 1
The Importance of
Learning Leadership

Chapter 2
From Management to Leadership

1

The Importance of Learning Leadership

- **The Nature of Leadership** 5

- **Leadership and the Business of Living** 7

- **The New Reality for Today's Organizations** 8

- **Leadership Is Not Automatic** 13

- **Where Have All the Leaders Gone?** 16

- **Leadership Can Be Learned** 20

- **On the Cutting Edge: Black Belt Boss** 21

- **Leadership Spotlights:**
  Greyhound Lines, Inc. 14
  EDS 18
  National Training Center 22

- **Leader's Bookshelf:** *Leadership and the New Science* 12

- **Leadership Development: Personal Feedback**
  Tolerance for Ambiguity 27

- **Leadership Development: Case for Analysis**
  Sales Engineering Division 28

Your Leadership Challenge

After reading this chapter, you should be able to:

- Understand the full meaning of leadership and see the leadership potential in yourself and others.

- Recognize and facilitate the five fundamental transformations in today's organizations and leaders.

- Identify the primary reasons for leadership derailment and the new paradigm skills that can help you avoid it.

- Understand how your leadership potential is developed and the stages of development.

- Appreciate the value and potential of learning about leadership.

When Mary Ann Byrnes rose to address the workers seated before her, she looked out over a room full of skeptical faces. These engineers, all men, had spent most of their lives working for a huge defense contractor, California-based TRW, which had just jettisoned them and their project. The government would no longer pay for their services. They had to become civilian workers, making and selling their product in a competitive market, and this small woman was supposed to lead the way.

What kind of civilian market was there for technology designed for government use? One technology developed by TRW's top-secret ESL division could identify the source of electronic transmissions. This technology was valuable to the military because it could pinpoint such things as which particular Soviet submarine issued a transmission. The technology also had significant commercial potential for inhibiting fraudulent cellular-telephone use, since no two cellular phones—like no two military devices—emit the same electronic fingerprint. Corsair Communications was created as a spin-off company, owned 20 percent by TRW, 60 percent by venture capitalists, and 20 percent by its employees. When Byrnes was hired as CEO, Corsair already had a product (although it was far from perfected), a multimillion dollar contract with a cellular carrier, and a group of first-rate engineers. Everything was in place to build the new business—except the glue that would hold it together.

How could Byrnes teach a group of government contract engineers, who were accustomed to working what one called a "10-percent-of-the-day kind of job," to compete as entrepreneurs? Her first step was to visualize the kind of place she wanted Corsair to be and instill enthusiasm throughout the company: "We had some of the smartest scientists in the world," she says. "My job was to make them productive, to help them perfect in a short time what they had not been able to deliver before." Byrnes wanted to create a culture that communicated a sense of shared responsibility and destiny—of everyone pulling together to serve the customer, and sharing in the success or failure of their collaborative efforts. She started by allowing workers to make the decisions they would live with—for example, out of a group of 60 engineers, Byrnes had to narrow it down to 30, so she allowed the engineers themselves to decide who would stay and who would go. Later, she let those who stayed select the new vice president of engineering. She set up cross-functional teams that worked face-to-face with customers and began sharing all company information with employees. Company-wide pizza lunches enhanced communication as well as team spirit. And now, when a big check comes in, employees don't just hear about it—the check gets passed around so everyone can see it, touch it, and realize they had a part in making it happen. The sense of ownership and shared destiny is strengthened because employees themselves own part of the company.

Today, Corsair is thriving and growing rapidly, and most agree it is due to Byrnes' leadership. Corsair's culture has become its major competitive weapon. By trusting her workers and not making all the decisions herself, Byrnes motivates the engineers to get the job done. For example, workers told Byrnes they would need six months to solve one particular technological problem. Despite the competitive pressure to get a product on the market, she took them at their word and told them to get to work. Previously at ESL, managers had insisted they do it in six weeks, and the problem never got solved. At Corsair, the engineers made their six-month deadline, and subsequent goals have been met earlier than projected. The company is growing rapidly, both in profits and number of employees. Byrnes and her workers have created a culture that works. Now, they have to keep it working as the company grows.[1]

You may have heard of Corsair Communications, one of today's thriving high-tech companies, but it is less likely that you've heard of Mary Ann Byrnes, whose leadership is largely responsible for Corsair's success. When we think of leaders in today's world, we often fall back on the "big names" we hear in the news—Bill Clinton or Margaret Thatcher in politics, Jack Welch in business, Oprah Winfrey or Ted Turner in entertainment, Michael Jordan in sports, the late Mother Teresa in charity. But there are leaders working in every organization, large and small. In fact, leadership is all around us every day, in all facets of our lives—our families, schools, communities, churches, social clubs, and volunteer organizations, as well as in businesses. Leadership is not the province of a select few CEOs or business owners; the qualities that make Mary Ann Byrnes a good leader at Corsair Communications are effective whether one is leading a business or a family.

The Nature of Leadership

Before we can examine what makes an effective leader, we need to know what leadership means. Leadership has been a topic of interest to historians and philosophers since ancient times, but it was only around the turn of the century that scientific studies began. Since that time, scholars and other writers have offered more than 350 definitions of the term "leadership," and one authority on the subject has concluded that leadership "is one of the most observed and least understood phenomena on earth."[2] Defining leadership has been a complex and elusive problem largely because the nature of leadership itself is complex. Some have even suggested that leadership is nothing more than a romantic myth, perhaps based in the false hope that someone will come along and solve our problems by force.[3] In recent years, however, much progress has been made in understanding the essential nature of leadership as a real and powerful influence in organizations and societies.

Definition of Leadership

Leadership studies are an emerging discipline and the concept of leadership will continue to evolve. For the purpose of this book, we will focus on a single definition that delineates the essential elements of the leadership process: **Leadership** is an influence relationship among leaders and followers who intend real changes that reflect their shared purposes.[4]

The key elements in this definition are summarized in Exhibit 1.1. Leadership involves influence, it occurs among people, those people intentionally desire significant changes, and the changes reflect purposes shared by leaders and followers. *Influence* means that the relationship among people is not passive; however, also inherent in this definition is the concept that influence is multidirectional and noncoercive. The basic cultural values in North America make it easiest to think of leadership as something a leader does to a follower.[5] However, leadership is reciprocal. In most organizations, superiors influence subordinates, but subordinates also influence superiors. The people involved in the relationship want substantive *changes*—leadership involves creating change, not maintaining the status quo. In addition, the changes sought are not dictated by leaders but reflect *purposes* shared by leaders and followers. Moreover, change is toward an outcome that leader and followers both want, a desired future or shared purpose that motivates them toward this more preferable outcome. Thus leadership involves the influence of people to bring about change toward a desirable future.

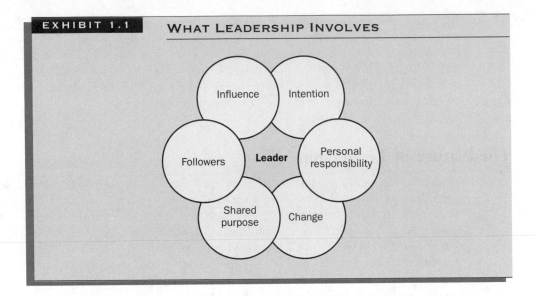

EXHIBIT 1.1   WHAT LEADERSHIP INVOLVES

Also, leadership is a *people* activity and is distinct from administrative paperwork or planning activities. Leadership occurs *among* people; it is not something done *to* people. Since leadership involves people, there must be *followers*. An individual performer who achieves excellence as a scientist, musician, or woodcarver may be a leader in her field of expertise, but is not a leader as it is defined in this book unless followers are involved. Followers are an important part of the leadership process, and leaders are sometimes followers. Good leaders know how to follow, and they set an example for others. The issue of *intention* or will means that people—leader and followers—are actively involved in the pursuit of change toward a desired future. Each person takes *personal responsibility* to achieve the desired future.

One stereotype is that leaders are somehow different, that they are above others; however, in reality, the qualities needed for effective leadership are the same as those needed to be an effective follower.[6] Effective followers think for themselves and carry out assignments with energy and enthusiasm. They are committed to something outside their own self-interest, and they have the courage to stand up for what they believe. Good followers are not "yes people" who blindly follow a leader. Effective leaders and effective followers may sometimes be the same people, playing different roles at different times. At its best, leadership is shared among leaders and followers, with everyone fully engaged and accepting higher levels of responsibility.

In some modern team-based organizations, each team member takes a turn as leader. People who have been team leaders are better followers. Mary Parker Follett wrote nearly half a century ago that "it is of great importance to recognize that leadership is sometimes in one place and sometimes in another."[7] This, along with many of her ideas, was scoffed at by leaders in the 1930s and 1940s but is increasingly appropriate for today's organizations.

Leadership and the Business of Living

Think for a moment about someone you personally have known that you would consider a leader—a grandparent, a teacher, a coach, or even a fellow student. Perhaps you consider yourself a leader, or know that you want to be one. If we stop equating leadership with "greatness" and public visibility, it becomes easier to see our own opportunities for leadership and recognize the leadership of people we interact with every day. Leaders come in all shapes and sizes, and many true leaders are working behind the scenes. Leadership that has big outcomes often starts small.

- In the early 1990s, a small but determined group of political outsiders met in Washington, D.C. and began a campaign to ban land mines. The grassroots movement, spurred by Robert Muller, a Marine veteran who lost the use of his legs during the Vietnam War, seemed to have little chance of influencing anyone at all. Yet six years later, nearly 100 governments signed a treaty that outlaws land mines and requires countries to clean up those already sown. In 1997, the Nobel Peace Prize was awarded to the International Campaign to Ban Landmines, a coalition of organizations from about 60 countries.[8]

- Several years ago, hundreds of unarmed residents of an Argentinean farming village stormed the local police station after officials had refused to search for a missing child who was later found by villagers, raped and strangled. The siege ended only when the provincial government agreed to replace the entire police department, with the villagers allowed to name the new chief.[9] This could not have happened without leadership, and yet no one stepped forward to claim the title of "leader," and no one was able to specifically state who had provided the leadership for this initiative.

- When Jeff Davis moved to Tennessee and offered to volunteer at the Nashville Humane Association, no one ever called him for help—the organization was so understaffed and overwhelmed that it didn't know how to take advantage of the many people wanting to donate their time. Davis took it upon himself to organize a truly useful volunteer program. He created a database of people willing to volunteer, redesigned forms, computerized the mailing list, developed volunteer training, and even designed a Web page. The Association now regularly uses volunteers to do everything from cleaning smelly cages to taking puppies into nursing homes for pet therapy.[10]

- A young graduate student living on a busy street in St. Louis was awakened one Sunday morning by the sound of a car crash. People had complained for years about cars exceeding the speed limit because of a long tempting hill with no traffic lights or stop signs to slow their progress, but no effort had ever been made to change things. Despite her heavy class load and a part-time job, the student spearheaded a grassroots campaign that ultimately resulted in a stop sign that has significantly reduced speeding and traffic accidents.

There are opportunities for leadership all around us that involve influence and change toward a shared future. Without leadership, our families and communities, as well as our organizations, would fall apart. The leaders of tomorrow's organizations will come from anywhere and everywhere, just as they always have. You can start now, wherever you are, to practice leadership in your own life. Leadership is an everyday way of acting and thinking that has little to do with a title or formal position in an organization. As we will discuss in the following section, business leaders will need to understand this tenet more than ever in the world of the 21st century.

The New Reality for Today's Organizations

The Corsair Communications case at the beginning of the chapter illustrates two primary themes. First, organizations are changing. Just as the engineers at Corsair found themselves forced to adapt to a new way of working after the decline of the defense industry, people throughout the business world are feeling the impact of downsizing, outsourcing, globalization, ever-advancing technology, and changing economic, social, and governmental conditions. And, second, it takes strong leaders to effect the changes needed for survival. For example, Roger Hale at LG&E Energy Company of Louisville, Kentucky, and Mark De Michele of Arizona Public Service Company are struggling to keep their organizations competitive in a world of increasing deregulation, the growth of small, independent power producers, strict government mandates, and growing environmental concerns. Where utility companies have traditionally functioned in a protected, regulated environment, Hale predicts a coming "dog-eat-dog" atmosphere for utilities similar to what the telecommunications industry is now experiencing.[11] The environment for all industries is changing fast and leaders are repositioning their organizations for a new reality.

The world today is undergoing a change more profound and far reaching than any experienced since the dawn of the modern age and the scientific revolution about five hundred years ago. Just as society was altered irrevocably in the transition from the agrarian to the industrial age, emerging events are changing the ways we interact with one another in our personal and professional lives. Rapid environmental changes are causing fundamental transformations that have a dramatic impact on organizations and present new challenges for leadership.[12] The transformations represent a shift from a traditional to a new paradigm, as outlined in Exhibit 1.2. A **paradigm** is a shared mind-set that represents a fundamental way of thinking about, perceiving, and understanding our world. The transformations discussed below strike at the very core of how we perceive the world—the beliefs we hold about people, things, and relationships. Effective leaders will respond to this new reality.

From Cherishing Stability to Valuing Change

It is human nature to desire stability in our lives. The medieval idea of order was conceptualized as a "chain of being," a natural ladder that linked all divine and

EXHIBIT 1.2	THE NEW REALITY FOR LEADERSHIP	

OLD Paradigm	NEW Paradigm
Industrial Age	Information Age
Stability	Change
Control	Empowerment
Competition	Collaboration
Things	People and relationships
Uniformity	Diversity

earthly elements; people knew where they fit in the scheme of things. This idea of "a place for everything and everything in its place" is a powerful and comforting one, but it no longer fits reality. Today, the world is in constant motion. The world is characterized more by disorder than by order, and organizations suffer when their leaders cherish stability. In the past, many leaders assumed that if they could just keep things running on a steady, even keel, the organization would be successful. Maintaining stability was considered a cost-saving and energy-efficient way of doing business, and change was perceived to disrupt operations and exhaust resources.[13] However, all we have to do is look around us—at the shifting seasons, the ocean tide, the natural progress of human life—to know that change is inevitable. It actually takes tremendous energy and resources to try to keep things stable. The new paradigm recognizes that, as suggested by the science of chaos theory, we live in a complex world characterized by randomness and uncertainty and that small events often have massive and far-reaching consequences. For example, a seemingly insignificant lawsuit against AT&T some years ago had far-reaching effects, resulting in the emergence of MCI, Sprint, and other long-distance carriers and ultimately creating a whole new world of telecommunications. By the mid-1990s, the company was reminding us in a television commercial that "every day brings the unexpected," ending the commercial with the slogan, "AT&T—Introducing certainty to the uncertain world of business." In this uncertain world, trying to maintain stability is futile.

The system of life—and organizations—is fluid, dynamic, and potentially self-renewing. Today's best leaders are learning to "go with the flow," to accept the inevitability of constant change and recognize change itself as a potential source of energy. They see change as an opportunity for something better, and they cherish not stability but the ongoing development of individual workers and of the organization itself. Beyond accepting change, they embrace and create it, realizing that the benefits associated with stability are a myth, that when things do not change, they die.

From Control to Empowerment

Leaders in powerful positions once thought workers should be told what to do, how to do it, when to do it, and who to do it with. They believed strict control was needed for the organization to function efficiently and effectively. Rigid organizational hierarchies, structured jobs and work processes, and detailed, inviolate procedures let everyone know that those at the top had power and those at the bottom had none. Today, the old assumptions about the distribution of power are no longer valid.

Empowerment has become a worldwide phenomenon. Anyone who's turned on a radio or television in the past few years recognizes that power is being diffused both within and among countries more than ever before. People are demanding empowerment and participation in their lives, including their work, and the emphasis on control and rigidity serves to squelch motivation and morale rather than produce desired results. Today's leaders need to share power rather than hoard it and find ways to increase an organization's brain power by getting everyone in the organization involved and committed.

One reason for this is that knowledge and information, not buildings and machines, have become the primary form of capital. When all the organization needed was workers to run machines eight hours a day, a command and control system generally worked, but the organization received no benefit from employees' minds. Frank Ostroff, who took a summer job at a tire-making factory as a college student, recalled: "We'd spend eight hours a day doing something completely mindless. . . . And then these same people would go home and spend their evenings and weekends rebuilding entire cars from scratch or running volunteer organizations."[14] No longer can organizations afford to have workers check their minds at the door. Success depends on the intellectual capacity of all employees, and leaders have to face a hard fact: Buildings and machines can be owned; people cannot. In the new paradigm, leaders recognize empowerment as what British business consultant and author Charles Handy calls "a moral imperative." Empowerment does not mean that those from on high are graciously handing down power, but that power rightfully belongs to all workers. One of the leader's most challenging jobs is to guide workers in using their own power effectively and responsibly by creating and developing a climate of respect and development for all employees.[15] Power lies more in the strength and quality of relationships rather than in titles, policies, and procedures.

From Competition to Collaboration

The move to empowerment also ties directly into new ways of working that emphasize collaboration over competition and conflict. Some competition can be healthy for an organization, but ideas about the nature of competition are changing. Rather than a struggle to win while someone else loses, organizations and individuals direct their competitive energy toward being the best they can be. Compromise becomes a sign of strength, not weakness. Within organizations, self-directed teams and other forms of horizontal collaboration are eliminating the boundaries between departments and helping to spread knowledge throughout the organization. In addition, there is a growing trend toward reducing boundaries and increasing collaboration with *other* organizations, so that companies think of themselves as teams that create value jointly rather than as autonomous entities in competition with all others.[16] Competition and collaboration often exist simultaneously. For example, in New York City, Time Warner refused to carry Fox's 24-hour news channel on its cable system. The two companies engaged in all-out warfare that included lawsuits and front page headlines. This conflict, however, masked the simple fact that the two companies cannot live without each other. Fox and Time-Warner are wedded to one another in separate business deals around the world and cannot afford to let the local competition in New York upset their interdependence on a global scale.[17]

The move to collaboration presents greater challenges to business leaders than did the old concept of competition. Within the organization, leaders will need to create an environment of teamwork and community that fosters collaboration and mutual support. The call for empowerment, combined with an understanding of organizations as part of a fluid, dynamic, interacting system, makes the use of intimidation and manipulation obsolete as a means of driving the competitive spirit.

From Things to Relationships

The increase in collaboration both within and among organizations reflects another fundamental transformation—a shift from an emphasis on things to an emphasis on relationships. Most of our existing ideas about organizations and leadership are based on an industrial age paradigm that treats the world as a machine that can be taken apart and examined piece by piece—every object can be identified, described, and measured. Broken parts can be fixed or replaced and everything keeps running smoothly. This paradigm has translated into a view of organizations as a conglomeration of "things." The new paradigm, however, takes its cue from quantum physics and ecology, which tell us that some phenomena can be understood only in relation to other phenomena, and that everything is connected to everything else.[18] In this view, the world is perceived as a complex, dynamic system where reality lies not in discrete parts, but in the relationships among them. Thus, leaders will look at their "reality" in a whole new light. Rather than operating on a yes-or-no, black-or-white basis, they will learn to deal with the gray areas—the nuances, subtleties, and possibilities inherent in relationships. Rather than focusing on segments, they will focus on the whole. The dominant image of the organization will be not as a machine, but as a living system or a web of interaction. The Leader's Bookshelf box describes how the new sciences are transforming the view of leadership.

When we think about our personal lives, we have little difficulty understanding that we act and feel differently depending on the situation—who we are with, what we are doing. Yet transferring this understanding to the organization may be one of the greatest challenges for leaders of tomorrow. Whereas objects are concrete and unchanging, relationships are intangible and ever-shifting. It is somehow comforting to conceptualize the organization as a machine where leaders only have to keep it oiled. The reality for today and the 21st century is much more challenging, and much more interesting.

Leadership and the New Science
Margaret J. Wheatley

In searching for a better understanding of organizations and leadership, Margaret Wheatley looked to science for answers. In the world of Newtonian physics, every atom moves in a unique predictable trajectory determined by the forces exerted on it. Prediction and control are accomplished by reducing wholes into discrete parts and carefully regulating the forces that act on those parts. Applied to organizations, this view of the world led to rigid vertical hierarchies, division of labor, task descriptions, and strict operating procedures designed to obtain predictable, controlled results.

Just as Newton's laws broke down as physics explored ever-smaller elements of matter and ever-wider expanses of the universe, rigid, control-oriented organizations don't work well in a world of instant information, constant change, and global competition. The physical sciences responded to the failure of Newtonian physics with a new paradigm called quantum mechanics. Wheatley explores in *Leadership and the New Science* how leaders are re-designing organizations to survive in a quantum world.

Chaos, Relationships, and Fields

From quantum mechanics and chaos theory emerge new understandings of order, disorder, and change. Individual actions, whether by atoms or people, cannot be easily predicted and controlled. Here's why:

- Nothing exists except in relationship to everything else. It is not things, but the relationships among them that are the key determinants of a well-ordered system we perceive. Order emerges through a web of relationships that make up the whole, not as a result of controls on individual parts.
- The empty space between things is filled with fields, invisible material that connects elements together. In organizations, the fields that bind people include vision, shared values, culture, and information.
- Organizations, like all open systems, grow and change in reaction to disequilibrium, and disorder can be a source of new order.

Implications for Leadership

These new understandings provide a new way to see, understand, and lead today's organizations. Wheatley believes the new sciences can influence leaders to:

- Nurture relationships and the fields between people with a clear vision, statements of values, expressions of caring, the sharing of information, and freedom from strict rules and controls.
- Focus on the whole, not on the parts in isolation.
- Reduce boundaries between departments and organizations to allow new patterns of relationships.
- Become comfortable with uncertainty and recognize that any solutions are only temporary, specific to the immediate context, and developed through the relationship of people and circumstances.
- Recognize that healthy growth of people and organizations is found in disequilibrium, not in stability.

Wheatley believes leaders can learn from the new sciences how to lead in today's fast-paced, chaotic world, suggesting that "we can forego the despair created by such common organization events as change, chaos, information overload, and cyclical behaviors if we recognize that organizations are conscious entities, possessing many of the properties of living systems."

Leadership and the New Science, by Margaret J. Wheatley, is published by Berrett-Koehler Publishers.

From Uniformity to Diversity

Many of today's organizations were built on assumptions of uniformity, separation, and specialization. People who think alike, act alike, and have similar job skills are grouped into a department, such as accounting or manufacturing, separate from the remainder of the organization. Homogenous groups find it easy to get along, communicate, and understand one another. The uniform thinking that arises, however, can be a disaster in a world becoming more multi-national and diverse.

Two 20-something-year-old business school graduates saw a niche for a specialized advertising firm. They worked hard, and as the firm grew, they hired more people just like themselves—bright, young, intense college graduates, committed and hard-working. The firm grew to about 20 employees over two and a half years, but the expected profits never materialized. The two entrepreneurs could never get a handle on what was wrong, and the firm slid into bankruptcy. Convinced the idea was still valid, they started over, but with a new philosophy. They sought employees with different ages, ethnic backgrounds, and work experience. People had different styles, yet the organization seemed to work better. People played different roles, and the diverse experiences of the group enabled the firm to respond to unique situations and handle a variety of organizational and personal needs. The advertising firm is growing again, and this time it is also making a profit.

The world is rapidly moving toward diversity at both national and international levels. In the United States, roughly 45 percent of all net additions to the labor force for the next few years will be non-white—half of these will be first-generation immigrants, mostly from Asian and Latin countries. Almost two-thirds will be female. Many business firms are finding they can succeed only by marketing and selling goods and services on a global scale; hence they need multi-national business operations. Bringing diversity into the organization is the way to attract the best human talent and to develop an organizational mind-set broad enough to thrive in a multi-national world.

Leadership Is Not Automatic

As the world changes, organizations are beginning to change in response. Yet we are still in a transition period between the old and the new, and many leaders are caught in midair between the practices and principles that defined the industrial era and the emerging principles of the postmodern world.[19] Attempts to achieve teamwork, empowerment, and diversity in organizations may fail because leaders' as well as workers' beliefs and thought processes are still stuck in the old paradigm that values control, stability, and homogeneity. Managers too often want to treat people the way they treat machines or the bottom line. But the New World asks for a more enlightened approach.

A few clues about the importance of acquiring new paradigm skills were brought to light by the Center for Creative Leadership in Greensboro, North Carolina.[20] The study compared 21 derailed executives with 20 executives who successfully arrived at the top of a company. The derailed managers were successful people who were expected to go far, but they reached a plateau, were fired, or were forced to retire early. They were all bright, worked hard, and excelled in a technical area such as accounting or engineering.

The striking difference between the two groups was the ability to use human skills, the essence of the new paradigm. Only 25 percent of the derailed group were described as being good with people, whereas 75 percent of those who arrived at the top had people skills. The top seven reasons for failure are listed in Exhibit 1.3. Unsuccessful managers were insensitive to others, abrasive, cold, arrogant, untrustworthy, overly ambitious and selfish, unable to delegate or build teams, and unable to acquire appropriate staff to work for them. These managers did not thrive in rapidly changing organizations moving into the new paradigm. For example, one derailed manager was a superb engineer who bogged down in details and tended to lose composure under stress. Another manager was known as cold and arrogant, but once he realized these limits to his career he changed almost over night. He made a genuine effort to learn about collaboration, empowerment, and building relationships—and succeeded.

Leaders will successfully lead organizations when their beliefs are in harmony with the transformations occurring in our world, when they value change over stability, empowerment over control, collaboration over competition, relationships over things, and diversity over uniformity.[21] Many leaders "came of age" in the industrial era and are still acting and thinking based on beliefs associated with an outdated paradigm. The future of Greyhound Bus Lines is in jeopardy because leaders paid lip service to empowerment but acted from their philosophy of narrowness and control.

 LEADERSHIP SPOTLIGHT   **GREYHOUND LINES, INC.**

Everyone agreed that Greyhound Lines had problems. The company was operating on paper-thin margins and could not afford to dispatch nearly empty vehicles or have buses and drivers on call to meet surges in demand. In the terminals, employees could be observed making fun of passengers, ignoring them, and handling their baggage haphazardly. To reduce operating costs and improve customer service, Greyhound's top executives put together a reorganization plan that called for massive cuts in personnel, routes, and services, along with the computerization of everything from passenger reservations to fleet scheduling. They hired a consulting firm specializing in breaking down communication barriers to hold "Breakthrough" seminars, where hundreds of employees participated in role-playing exercises. Inspiring calls for teamwork and customer service began appearing in the company newsletter. Greyhound seemed headed for a turnaround.

In the meantime, as headquarters staff scoured vacant offices for supplies and drivers reported breaking the speed limit to meet new schedules, executives were spending more than $90,000 a month to remodel their offices. Many workers disagreed with the reorganization plan and argued that huge workforce reductions would only exac-

EXHIBIT 1.3	TOP 7 REASONS FOR EXECUTIVE DERAILMENT

1. Insensitive, abrasive, intimidating, bullying style
2. Cold, aloof, arrogant
3. Betrayal of personal trust
4. Overly ambitious, self-centered, thinking of next job, playing politics
5. Specific performance problems with the business
6. Overmanaging: unable to delegate or build a team
7. Unable to select good subordinates

erbate the company's real problem regarding customer satisfaction. Managers in computer programming urged a delay in introducing the computerized reservations system, called Trips, to work out bugs in the highly complex software. The human resources department pointed out that terminal workers generally had less than a high school education and would need extensive technical training before they could use the system. Terminal managers warned that many of Greyhound's low-income passengers didn't have credit cards or even telephones to use Trips. The implementation of the new program was supposed to be a team decision, but when middle managers and other employees spoke up, top executives wouldn't listen or make adjustments, promising that Trips would improve customer service, make ticket buying more convenient, and allow customers to reserve space on specific trips.

A nightmare resulted. The time Greyhound operators spent responding to phone calls dramatically increased. Many callers couldn't even get through because of problems in the new switching mechanism. Most passengers arrived to buy their tickets and get on the bus just as they always had, but the computers were so swamped that it sometimes took 45 seconds to respond to a single keystroke and five minutes to print a ticket. The system crashed so often that agents frequently had to hand-write tickets. Customers stood in long lines, were separated from their luggage, missed connections, and were left to sleep in terminals overnight. Discourtesy to customers increased as a downsized and demoralized workforce struggled to cope with a system they were ill trained to operate. Ridership plunged. As regional rivals continue to pick off Greyhound's dissatisfied customers, the future of the huge bus company remains uncertain.[22]

Although Greyhound's executives touted teamwork and empowerment, they operated from the command and control model. Rather than listening to employees, they made a decision based on their own beliefs and goals. They failed to look at the organization as a dynamic system. Instead, they focused on improving efficiency through computerization while ignoring the complex relationships among the new reservations system, employees, and customers.

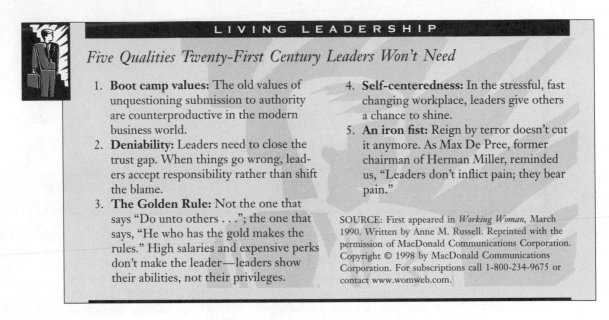

Five Qualities Twenty-First Century Leaders Won't Need

1. **Boot camp values:** The old values of unquestioning submission to authority are counterproductive in the modern business world.
2. **Deniability:** Leaders need to close the trust gap. When things go wrong, leaders accept responsibility rather than shift the blame.
3. **The Golden Rule:** Not the one that says "Do unto others . . ."; the one that says, "He who has the gold makes the rules." High salaries and expensive perks don't make the leader—leaders show their abilities, not their privileges.
4. **Self-centeredness:** In the stressful, fast changing workplace, leaders give others a chance to shine.
5. **An iron fist:** Reign by terror doesn't cut it anymore. As Max De Pree, former chairman of Herman Miller, reminded us, "Leaders don't inflict pain; they bear pain."

SOURCE: First appeared in *Working Woman*, March 1990. Written by Anne M. Russell. Reprinted with the permission of MacDonald Communications Corporation. Copyright © 1998 by MacDonald Communications Corporation. For subscriptions call 1-800-234-9675 or contact www.womweb.com.

A recent study by Korn/Ferry International of changes in the business environment forecasts that the all-powerful, controlling boss—or "controllasaurus"—will be extinct within the next decade.[23] The old ways no longer work and the new ways are just emerging. Everywhere, we hear the cry for leadership.

Where Have All the Leaders Gone?

Just a few decades ago, the business world seemed full of powerful leaders who were capable of taking their organizations to prosperity. When the world was more stable, the control model was productive. Today, it is increasingly counterproductive, and the world is searching for leaders of a new kind.[24] Leaders are moving from being the all-powerful boss and decision-maker to become facilitators, partners, and risk-takers who help others grow, learn, and reach their full potential. The Living Leadership box lists five qualities 21st century leaders *won't* need.

For most of the 20th century, leadership has been equated with good management. However, as we will discuss in Chapter 2, leadership and management are not the same thing. Management focuses on planning and controlling the organization to maintain stability, while leadership focuses on creating a vision for the future and inspiring others to achieve it. Management and leadership are both important to organizations. Traditional management is needed to help meet current obligations to customers, stockholders, employees, and others. But organizations also need strong leadership to visualize the future, motivate and inspire employees, and adapt to changing needs. The problem for today's organizations is that there are too many people doing management, too few providing leadership, and fewer still who have integrated the skills and qualities needed for meeting both leadership and management challenges.

In a survey of executives in successful U.S. companies, nearly two-thirds of the respondents reported that their organizations had too many people who were strong in management but weak in leadership, prompting one researcher to suggest that many of today's corporations are "over-managed and under-led."[25] As illustrated in Exhibit 1.4, today's organizations have insufficient leadership and are particularly bereft of people who can provide both good management and good leadership. What today's organizations need most are more people who can unite the "hard" skills of management with the "soft" skills of leadership.

When the world was stable, good management was often enough to keep organizations healthy and prosperous. Today, organizations more than ever also need good leadership, which requires that leaders develop personal qualities, not just learn a set of skills for planning, organizing, directing, and controlling.

The Leader Within

Teamwork, cooperation, empowerment, employee initiative, and commitment to quality and service cannot be decreed; they are released from within the hearts and minds of workers throughout the organization. Anil Nanji, who was propelled to the top leadership role at Magnet Sales & Manufacturing when his father died of a heart attack, says the most valuable resource at his company is employee energy and spirit. Nanji, whose father "ruled with fear," is creating an environment where workers feel valued and feel that they've accomplished not just the business goals but their own personal goals. Employees are told, "This is where we're going," and they figure out how to get there. Nanji gives credit for the firm's rapid sales growth not to himself, but to Magnet's workers.[26]

To prosper today, organizations need leaders who, like Nanji, can find within themselves the capacity to run an organization. In a complex, rapidly changing environment, it is frequently the absence of a sense of purpose that causes organizations to flounder and employees to lack commitment and enthusiasm. A primary job of a leader is to find the capacity to help create a vision of what the organization can be and what it stands for. At Corsair Communications, described in the opening case, Mary Ann Byrnes stated that when she first came into the company, she had to do only one thing: figure out what kind of place Corsair was going to be. Rather than keeping things as they are, leadership requires imagining, and then creating, what is not. It requires the ability to think creatively, to listen effectively, to change cultures, and to build commitment to the vision. It requires the courage to take risks, to accept responsibility, and to let go and trust others. Instead of treating workers as factors of production, leadership for today's organizations calls for caring about and engaging the whole employee and building a community in which workers can learn and grow. One organization where managers are finding the leader within is EDS, which assembles and operates corporate computer systems and designs Web sites for companies like PepsiCo. Founded by Ross Perot in 1962 as Electronic Data Systems, EDS was sold to General Motors in the mid-1980s and has recently been spun off to shareholders.

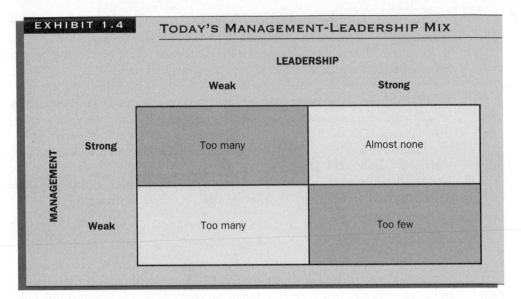

EXHIBIT 1.4 — TODAY'S MANAGEMENT-LEADERSHIP MIX

Based on John P. Kotter, *A Force for Change: How Leadership Differs from Management* (New York: The Free Press, 1990).

LEADERSHIP SPOTLIGHT — **EDS**

A manager who started his career with EDS in 1983 recently said, "I took my personal life underground. We were driven to succeed, a disciplined, well-oiled machine. We grew by leaps and bounds. But we left human carnage in our wake. . . . As I sat in the [EDS leadership program] last week, I visualized myself breaking out of a plaster cast."

He was referring to the program recently set up by CEO Les Alberthal, designed to do no less than remake the souls of the company's 95,000 workers. Alberthal believes EDS, long known for its rigid, hard-driving culture, needs a new kind of leadership for the 21st century. EDS is remaking itself into a network-centric company, redefining itself, in the words of vice chairman Gary Fernandes, "from being a provider of technology services to being a provider of services based on technology." The change may seem subtle, but it basically means that EDS wants to not only run your computers but help redesign your business. EDS can even take over a corporation's purchasing department or run its human resources division. In the new role, EDS has to be a true partner with its customers, not a condescending expert. Alberthal believes when a company is looking for a partner, the most important hiring criterion is listening skills. He knows the leaders of EDS have to be sensitive to customers, employees, and colleagues: "Our business is about making the customer successful and not having all the assets under my control, so leaders are going to have to do more than shout orders. The old command-and-control mind-set is not how we will be successful."

In the new EDS, leadership is spread throughout the organization. The company has moved from a culture where a few top executives made all the decisions to one based on teams arriving at collective decisions. Alberthal is now striving to give each individual worker more power to make decisions at the point of customer contact and he's providing sensitivity training to help them use that power responsibly. He doesn't flinch at criticisms that EDS is going "soft"; he knows that only by listening to feelings and paying attention to relationships can EDS develop the kind of customer intimacy needed in today's world. Senior EDS executives regularly use the expression "S squared equals PS," which translates as "Soft shit equals powerful shit." Heart and soul has become the way to take the company where it wants to go. EDS hasn't given up good management; it is adding good leadership.[27]

Les Alberthal recognizes today's need for greater participation by everyone in the organization, with all employees moving to higher levels of responsibility. And he knows that means connecting with something more than people's heads. After being inaugurated mayor of Lima in 1990, Peruvian talk show host Ricardo Belmont Cassinelli said, "People don't care about having leaders explain things to them. They want to have [leaders who] speak to their hearts."[28] If leading requires speaking to the heart, it also means speaking from the heart, and leaders have to understand their own hearts and minds before they can engage the hearts and minds of others. The essence of leadership is in the hearts of leaders.[29]

Change Thyself

EDS is not the only company recognizing the need for leaders to look within themselves for answers and draw on depths of understanding and meaning they've previously ignored or been unaware of. Various mainstream corporations, including AT&T, PepsiCo, and Aetna, are integrating forms of "introspection training" into their leadership development programs. Books such as *The Fifth Discipline* and *Principle Centered Leadership* encourage leaders to look within, arguing that the unexamined life may not only be "not worth living," but is in today's fast-shifting world, a business liability. AT&T's head of executive training put it this way: "We need our people to act independently, to be accountable and responsible for their own piece of the business. It takes a certain amount of reflection to do that successfully."[30]

Modern society encourages people to follow recipes or guidelines to success, to consult experts to solve problems. When leadership was equated with controlling people to reach a goal, such approaches were helpful. Today, leaders have to serve new roles: to act as a steward rather than a manager or administrator, to suppress ego and allow others to gain credit, to accept personal responsibility, develop relationships, take risks, and become a partner, nurturer and facilitator, all of which requires courage, integrity, and strength from within. Leaders can find only within themselves the forces that make leadership come alive—passion, vision, self-confidence, tolerance for ambiguity and paradox, intuition, and empathy. Leadership is not something we possess; it is something we give from within ourselves.[31]

Today's best leaders ignore quick fixes and practice the basics that rely on ancient wisdom—respect, trust, vision, listening, sensing the environment around them, and acting with courage.[32] They seek to unite mind, body, and spirit within themselves in order to release the potential in others. The Cutting Edge box describes how one leader strives for this integration within himself and in his business.

Leadership Can Be Learned

Leadership involves a complex set of factors, and some people may conclude that leadership is too intangible and mysterious to be learned. However, as Vince Lombardi once said, "Contrary to the opinion of many people, leaders are not born. Leaders are made, and they are made by effort and hard work."[33] Almost anyone has the potential to be a leader. We all have the seeds of leadership within us; our experiences can either kill them or help them to grow. We can either invest in developing leadership qualities or allow those qualities to lie dormant.

Learning to Lead

Today, leadership training is hot. Professional training centers, consultants, business schools, executive programs, and in-house corporate training departments are jumping on the bandwagon as the field of leadership training booms. The proliferation of such programs reflects not only an awareness of the current lack of good leadership but also a new hope for the future. Rather than waiting for heroes to arrive and lead businesses and society through the turbulent years ahead, leaders are being cultivated and nurtured throughout North America and the world.

In recognition that traditional concepts of planning, controlling, and managing "things" cannot solve our problems, most leadership training centers and programs hit hard on people and relationship issues. At leadership training seminars held by EDS, described in the Leadership Spotlight, trainers use "talking hearts" to break through barriers and get leaders in touch with their softer side. Talking hearts are stones in the shape of a heart that you hold in your hand—whoever has the stone has the floor. According to Marsha Clark, head of EDS's training program, "It's about putting your heart in your hand and putting it out for the group to see. . . . If you had a bad morning, or you couldn't start the car, or the kids wouldn't get going, you get to say that."[34] Rodel Inc., a manufacturer in Newark, Delaware, that started its Leadership Intensive Training program as an effort to save the company, uses a similar procedure. At monthly meetings, participants bring progress reports and talk about examples of leadership they've observed in real life. At each meeting is a basket of ping-pong balls, and when a participant's number comes up, he or she gets to tell a story. Facilitators coach participants on how to make a point, recognizing that telling personal stories can be one of the most effective ways of transferring leadership and influencing others.[35] One exercise at the nonprofit Center for Creative Leadership in North Carolina involves trying to persuade a group of people to drink buttermilk that has been injected with green food coloring. Participants try different tactics, many of them manipulative—for example, one person fabricated a story that nuns were tasting but-

Black Belt Boss

Moses Joseph arrives at work at 9:00 A.M., dressed in a business suit and looking like your typical CEO. There's nothing about his demeanor to reveal that he's already meditated, practiced 30 minutes of *kyuku shinkai* karate, run seven miles on the treadmill, had a bi-weekly tennis lesson, and made plans for his afternoon yoga practice. Nothing, perhaps, except his self-confidence, gentleness, and aura of being in control of himself and the world around him.

"Because of karate, everything I do in business and my outside life can be gentle," he says. "I get more out of people by being gentle than by being aggressive." Joseph has had to get plenty out of people since he left a comfortable job in sunny California to try to turn around B-Tree, a Minnetonka, Minnesota-based developer and marketer of machines that test and verify the functions of devices such as heart pacemakers and jetliner controls. He revived the company in six months.

Meditation, he says, helps his mind gain the upper hand over the body—he makes good decisions because he is intensely in tune with the aspect of everything around him. Similarly, karate is designed to bring the mind, body, and spirit together. Even when he's on the treadmill, he's focused inward. Rather than listening to headphones like the joggers next to him at the club, Joseph tunes into his breathing—in through the nose, out through the mouth, in and out . . . a Mystic's Top 40. Joseph also stresses balance in his life by putting family first and business second. He believes you can't be successful at work unless your personal life is in order.

While Joseph wears his gentleness with pride, he points out that it doesn't mean being meek. He constantly makes the connection between conquering an adversary in karate (he's earned a black belt and was a final four contestant in a ferocious fight-to-the-end championship in Tokyo) and conquering a business. In business, as in karate, it's not what you've done but what you do next that counts. Being in tune with his own mind and spirit helps Joseph sense his competitor's next move and know what to do next.

Beyond his own development, Joseph is trying to build a company with the instincts of a karate champion, with each component acting instinctively, swiftly, autonomously, accurately, and dependably to whatever crisis might arise. He keeps all company information—good and bad—in open books and accessible through open doors. He regularly joins employees for a once-a-week bull session at a local pub where they talk not business but fast cars, a sign that the collective mind is relaxed, just the way he wants it. "A company anticipates pain as does a human," he says. "It's threatened by outside forces. But a company that knows its markets, that's gutsy and solid, that has come together such that everyone cares about and believes in one another, that communicates well—and believes in the [leader]—it's hard to make that company feel pain."

SOURCE: Robert A. Mamis, "Black-Belt Boss," *Inc.*, September 1996, 60-64.

termilk to ensure its safety for Bosnian children. Patricia Slaymaker, manager of information protection in Nabisco's information systems unit, says the exercise was an eye-opener: "I learned that I had to let go. I thought I was leading the charge, but instead I was coercing people." The Center is nationally recognized as one of the top leadership training courses. Nearly all of the nation's candidates for brigadier general, including Norman Schwarzkopf, have gone through the program.[36] Another hotbed of new leadership training is the U.S. Army's National Training Center, credited with almost single-handedly transforming the post-Vietnam army.

LEADERSHIP SPOTLIGHT   NATIONAL TRAINING CENTER

t's 5:00 A.M. and Brigadier General William "Scott" Wallace has been up for two hours. Accompanied by senior military officers from 30 nations, he has now made his way to a hill that offers a choice view of today's battle. For 10 days, the thousands of soldiers below have been battling lasers that substitute for real warheads. Now, for the first time, they'll experience live fire—the only way to truly understand the devastation and lethality of modern warfare.

Welcome to the National Training Center, ground zero for army war games. However, NTC is more than that—it is considered by many to be the world's most powerful laboratory for leadership development. Several of America's most forward-thinking companies, including Motorola and General Electric, study it as a source of ideas about leadership and learning. The definitive model at NTC—which applies to business as well as combat—is learning through failure. Over a grueling two-week period, 3,000–5,000 soldiers go head to head with an opposing force of similar size. Some 600 instructors follow the action through 18-hour days, provide personal coaching, and facilitate team meetings as participants struggle to understand what went wrong and how to fix it. For 14 days, every fiber of the organization is stressed to the breaking point—and some of the fibers inevitably break. Those are the areas leaders hone in on during After Action Reviews—the crux of the learning experience, the place where hardship meets insight, where failure meets growth, where everyone grows as leaders. The review process encourages brutal honesty, without regard to rank, enabling both individuals and groups to grow stronger. Day after day, the reviews stress five themes: (1) everyone needs to understand the big picture; (2) everyone needs to think all the time; (3) always put yourself in the shoes of an uncooperative opponent; (4) prepare yourself to the point where nothing can surprise you; and (5) put aside hierarchy, foster self-awareness and self-criticism, and learn to work as a team.

These five themes provide crucial rules not only for war but for business. Two lessons from the National Training Center are particularly appropriate for today. One is that learning requires leaders who coach rather than lecture or yell. At NTC, the role of the facilitators is to make it safe to learn. They never criticize individual performance, and they reinforce the message that the experience is not about success or failure but what each person takes away. Second, a learning mind-set endures beyond the training exercise. During the Gulf War, learning sessions broke out spontaneously, with platoon leaders and soldiers asking what went right, what went wrong, and what could be done better. Business leaders can promote the same kind of continuous learning.[37]

Corporations, like the U.S. Army, are rethinking their approach to leadership training and recommitting themselves to it in a big way. In one recent year, Motorola spent more than $150 million on education, offering at least 40 hours of training to each employee. General Electric spends $500 million annually on training, including sending managers to week-long sessions at its Leadership Development Center. Even more importantly, according to Steve Kerr, director of the Center, training programs are taken directly to workers at their place of business so they can put their leadership ideas directly to work. Kerr credits Jack Welch with having the foresight to invest more than ever in education during the difficult last years of the 1980s.[38]

Increasingly, companies like GE are tying leadership training directly to specific company needs and problems, taking a cue from the Army. Roger Enrico, chairman and CEO of PepsiCo, spends more than 100 days a year personally conducting leadership training—not because it feels good, but because it translates into growth and financial success. Only nine executives at a time attend Enrico's boot camp, called "Building the Business." During a five-day session, they focus on leadership fundamentals and develop a personal vision and action plan for their own individual growth projects. After three months of implementing their plans on the job, the group reconvenes for three days with Enrico to receive coaching, develop personal leadership-improvement plans, and review their successes and failures. It works; one idea that had its genesis in the training program was KFC's Mega-Meal campaign, which led to double digit revenue increases for KFC in all major markets. PepsiCo is now working to spread the leadership development approach throughout the organization. Enrico believes the most important responsibility of a leader is developing other leaders, and his philosophy is cascading down through the company.[39]

Learning about Leadership

It's easy to see how innovative programs like the ones described above can develop leadership qualities because they involve the practice of leadership, not just studying and talking about it. But how can a book or a course about leadership help you be a leader? By exploring leadership in both business and society, students gain an understanding of the importance of leadership to an organization's success, as well as the difficulties and challenges involved in being a leader. Studying leadership can also lead to the discovery of abilities we never knew we had. When students in a leadership seminar at Wharton were asked to pick one leader to represent the class, one woman far outpolled all others. Her leadership was drawn out not in the practice of leadership in student government or volunteer activities, but in a classroom setting.[40] Even for those students who never want to be leaders, who would prefer to "take a back seat" and let someone else take the lead, the study of leadership is still valuable because you will be a better follower for understanding the issues and challenges of leadership.

Acquiring personal leadership competence typically involves progress through four stages, which are illustrated in Exhibit 1.5. Most people start out in stage 1, unconscious incompetence. This means that students don't have any competence with leadership, and they are unaware that they lack competence, probably because they've never tried to be a leader. In a sport like skiing, golf, or tennis, people start out not knowing how good they are until they try. They discover their incompe-

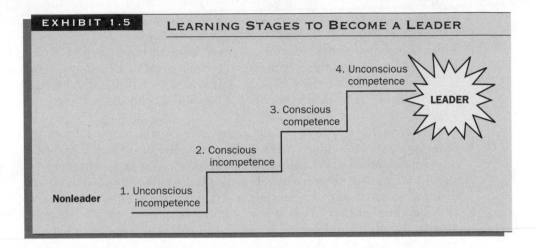

EXHIBIT 1.5 **LEARNING STAGES TO BECOME A LEADER**

4. Unconscious competence

LEADER

3. Conscious competence

2. Conscious incompetence

1. Unconscious incompetence

Nonleader

tence and find they need help to move ahead. By reading books, or taking lessons from a coach or teacher, a potential leader, just like a potential skier or golfer, becomes conscious of what is required to do well. The student can learn about leadership vision, or building a team, just as the athlete can learn about shifting one's weight or keeping one's eye on the ball. This is stage 2, where you become conscious of what is required to do well, but are still personally incompetent. If you have ever tried to swing a golf club or tennis racquet while keeping ten things in your mind at one time and then swing poorly, you understand conscious incompetence.

With practice, your conscious awareness of the correct thing to do will gradually transform into leadership competence. You can learn to visualize a desired future, influence others to engage in that future, and have the courage to take on real change. Stage 3 is where leadership, or a physical sport such as skiing, becomes a real pleasure. You receive positive feedback from your skill and are aware of how well you are doing, which sets up the transition into stage 4. In stage 4, the skills become a part of you. They occur naturally. You no longer have to consciously think about creating a vision; it emerges intuitively.

If you have ever heard the argument that leaders are born rather than made, or that someone is a natural leader, it would mean that they operate in stage 4 without having to go through the first three stages. But this is rare. Most of us have to struggle to awareness of what leadership is about and then become competent through practice and experience. This book helps people achieve stages 2 and 3 in their progress toward becoming a leader. The chapters develop your cognitive understanding of what leaders do. You can build competence by working on the exercises and cases at the end of chapters, and more importantly by applying these concepts in class, in your relationships with others, in student groups, in voluntary organizations, even with friends and family. As you acquire the skills of leadership through your career, you may achieve stage 4, and people may look at you as a natural leader, assuming you had this competence all along.

Summary and Interpretation

This chapter introduced the concept of leadership and explained how individuals can grow as leaders. Leadership is defined as an influence relationship among leaders and followers who intend real changes that reflect their shared purposes. Thus leadership involves people in a relationship, influence, change, a shared purpose of achieving a desired future, and taking personal responsibility to make things happen. Most of us are aware of famous leaders, but most leadership that changes the world starts small and may be reflected in personal frustrations about events that prompt people to initiate change and inspire people to follow them. Your leadership may be expressed in the classroom, your neighborhood, community, or volunteer organization.

The major challenge facing leaders today is the changing world that wants a new paradigm of leadership. The new reality involves the shift from stability to change, from control to empowerment, from competition to collaboration, from focusing on things to building relationships, from uniformity to diversity. These dramatic changes suggest that a control philosophy of leadership based on industrial-age thinking will probably fail. The challenge for leaders is to grow into an information age mind-set that involves the development of "soft" leadership skills that supplement the "hard" skills of management. Organizations, such as EDS, PepsiCo, and the U.S. Army, are undergoing transformation and showing that individuals can become effective leaders. Most people are not born with natural leadership skills, but leadership can be learned by first becoming conscious of leadership qualities and then building personal competence through practical experience.

Key Terms

leadership   **paradigm**

Discussion Questions

1. What do you consider your own strengths and weaknesses for leadership? Discuss your answer with another student.

2. How do you feel about changing yourself first in order to become a leader who can change an organization?

3. Of the elements in the leadership definition as illustrated in Exhibit 1.1, which is the easiest for you? Which is hardest? Explain.

4. What activities should you undertake to improve your leadership capability in areas where you are weak?

5. What does the paradigm shift from control to empowerment mean for you? Discuss.

6. Describe the best leader you have known. How did this leader acquire his or her capability?

7. Why do you think there are so few people who succeed at both management and leadership?

8. Think of a learning activity in which you moved through two or more of the stages shown in Exhibit 1.5. How was moving from unconsciousness to consciousness different from moving from incompetence to competence? Explain.

Leadership Development: Personal Feedback

Tolerance for Ambiguity

Please read each of the following statements carefully. Then rate each of them in terms of the extent to which you either agree or disagree with the statement using the following scale:

Completely Disagree   Neither Agree nor Disagree   Completely Agree

1   2   3   4   5   6   7

Place the number that best describes your degree of agreement or disagreement in the blank to the left of each statement.

_____ 1. An expert who doesn't come up with a definite answer probably doesn't know too much.

_____ 2. I would like to live in a foreign country for a while.

_____ 3. The sooner we all acquire similar values and ideals the better.

_____ 4. A good teacher is one who makes you wonder about your way of looking at things.

_____ 5. I like parties where I know most of the people more than ones where all or most of the people are complete strangers.

_____ 6. Teachers or supervisors who hand out vague assignments give a chance for one to show initiative and originality.

_____ 7. A person who leads an even, regular life, in which few surprises or unexpected happenings arise, really has a lot to be grateful for.

_____ 8. Many of our most important decisions are based upon insufficient information.

_____ 9. There is really no such thing as a problem that can't be solved.

_____ 10. People who fit their lives to a schedule probably miss most of the joy of living.

_____ 11. A good job is one where what is to be done and how it is to be done are always clear.

_____ 12. It is more fun to tackle a complicated problem than to solve a simple one.

_____ 13. In the long run, it is possible to get more done by tackling small, simple problems rather than large and complicated ones.

_____ 14. Often the most interesting and stimulating people are those who don't mind being different and original.

_____ 15. What we are used to is always preferable to what is unfamiliar.

Scoring:

For odd-numbered questions, add the total points. For even-numbered questions, reverse score the answers (7 minus the score), and add the total points. Your score is the total of the even and odd-numbered questions.

Interpretation:

This survey asks 15 questions about personal and work situations with ambiguity. You were asked to rate each situation on a scale of 1 to 7. A perfectly tolerant person would score 15 and a perfectly intolerant person would score 105. Scores ranging from 20 to 80 have been reported, with a mean of 45. Company managers had an average score of about 45, and nonprofit managers had an average score of about 43, although scores in both groups varied widely. Typically, people who are highly tolerant of ambiguity (very low score) will be comfortable in organizations characterized by rapid change, unclear authority, empowerment, and movement toward the new leadership paradigm. People with low tolerance for ambiguity (high score) are comfortable in more stable, well-defined situations. However, individuals can grow in the opposite direction of their score if they so choose.

SOURCE: Paul C. Nutt, "The Tolerance for Ambiguity and Decision Making," The Ohio State University College of Business Working Paper Series, WP88-291, March 1988. Adapted from Stanley Budner, "Intolerance of Ambiguity as a Personality Variable," *Journal of Personality*, 30:1 (March 1962), Table 1, p. 34. Copyright © Blackwell Publishers. Reprinted with permission.

Leadership Development: Case for Analysis

Sales Engineering Division

When DGL International, a manufacturer of refinery equipment, brought in John Terrill to manage its Sales Engineering division, company executives informed him of the urgent situation. Sales Engineering, with 20 engineers, was the highest-paid, best-educated, and least-productive division in the company. The instructions to Terrill: Turn it around. Terrill called a meeting of the engineers. He showed great concern for their personal welfare and asked point blank: "What's the problem? Why can't we produce? Why does this division have such turnover?"

Without hesitation, employees launched a hail of complaints. "I was hired as an engineer, not a pencil pusher." "We spend over half of our time writing asinine reports in triplicate for top management, and no one reads the reports." "We have to account for every penny, which doesn't give us time to work with customers or new developments."

After a two-hour discussion, Terrill began to envision a future in which engineers were free to work with customers and join self-directed teams for product improvement. Terrill concluded he had to get top management off the engineers' backs. He promised the engineers, "My job is to stay out of your way so you can do your work, and I'll try to keep top management off your backs too." He called for the day's reports and issued an order effective immediately that the originals be turned in daily to his office rather than mailed to headquarters. For three weeks, technical reports piled up on his desk. By month's end, the stack was nearly three feet high. During the time no one called for the reports. When other managers entered his office and saw the stack, they usually asked, "What's all this?" Terrill answered, "Technical reports." No one asked to read them.

Finally, at month's end, a secretary from finance called and asked for the monthly travel and expense report. Terrill responded, "Meet me in the president's office tomorrow morning."

The next morning the engineers cheered as Terrill walked through the department pushing a cart loaded with the enormous stack of reports. They knew the showdown had come.

Terrill entered the president's office and placed the stack of reports on his desk. The president and the other senior executives looked bewildered.

"This," Terrill announced, "is the reason for the lack of productivity in the Sales Engineering division. These are the reports your people require every month. The fact that they sat on my desk all month shows that no one reads this material. I suggest that the engineers' time could be used in a more productive manner, and that one brief monthly report from my office will satisfy the needs of the other departments."

Questions

1. Does John Terrill's leadership style fit the definition of leadership in Exhibit 1.1? Explain.

2. With respect to Exhibit 1.2, in what paradigm is Terrill? In what paradigm is headquarters?

3. What approach would you have taken in this situation?

References

[1]Alessandra Bianchi, "Mission Improbable," *Inc.*, September 1996, 69–75.
[2]Warren Bennis and Burt Nanus, *Leaders: The Strategies for Taking Charge* (New York: Harper & Row, 1985), 1; James MacGregor Burns, *Leadership* (New York: Harper & Row, 1978), 2.
[3]J. Meindl, S. Ehrlich, and J. Dukerich, "The Romance of Leadership," *Administrative Science Quarterly*, 30 (1985): 78–102.
[4]Joseph C. Rost, *Leadership for the Twenty-First Century* (Westport, CN: Praeger, 1993), 102.
[5]Peter B. Smith and Mark F. Peterson, *Leadership, Organizations, and Culture: An Event Management Model* (London: Sage Publications, 1988), 14.

[6]Robert E. Kelley, "In Praise of Followers," *Harvard Business Review*, November–December 1988, 142–148.

[7]Mary Parker Follett, quoted in "A Guru Ahead of Her Time," *Nation's Business*, May 1997, 24.

[8]Raymond Bonner, "Small Band Took on Land Mines—And Won," *The Tennessean*, September 21, 1997, 3D, and "Peace Prize Targets U.S. Mine Policy," *The Tennessean*, October 11, 1997, 1A.

[9]Robin Wright and Doyle McManus, *Flashpoints: Promise and Peril in a New World* (New York: Alfred A. Knopf, 1991), 107–110.

[10]Gregg Stuart, "One Person *Can* Make a Difference," *The Critter Chronicle: The Quarterly News Magazine of the Nashville Humane Association*, Spring 1997, 1.

[11]Agis Salpukas, "How a Staid Electric Company Becomes a Renegade," *The New York Times*, December 12, 1993, F10, and Samuel M. DeMarie and Barbara W. Keats, "Deregulation, Reengineering, and Cultural Transformation at Arizona Public Service Company," *Organizational Dynamics* (Winter 1995): 70–76.

[12]Based on Daniel C. Kielson, "Leadership: Creating a New Reality," *The Journal of Leadership Studies* 3, No. 4 (1996): 104–116.

[13]Ibid.

[14]Thomas A. Stewart, "Brain Power: Who Owns It . . . How They Profit From It," *Fortune*, March 17, 1997, 105–110.

[15]Charles Handy, *The Age of Paradox* (Boston: Harvard Business School Press, 1994), 146–147.

[16]Richard L. Daft, *Organization Theory and Design* (Cincinnati, OH: South-Western College Publishing, 1998), 523.

[17]Elizabeth Jensen and Eben Shapiro, "Time Warner's Fight with News Corp. Belies Mutual Dependence," *The Wall Street Journal*, October 28, 1996, A1, A6.

[18]James R. Carlopio, "Holism: A Philosophy of Organizational Leadership for the Future," *Leadership Quarterly* 5, no. 3/4 (1994): 297–307, and Daniel C. Kielson, "Leadership: Creating a New Reality," *The Journal of Leadership Studies* 3, No. 4 (1996): 104–116.

[19]Robert J. Marshak, "Managing in Chaotic Times," in *Managing in the Age of Change: Essential Skills to Manage Today's Diverse Workforce*, Roger A. Ritvo, Anne H. Litwin, and Lee Butler, eds., (Burr Ridge, IL, 1995), 58–66.

[20]Morgan W. McCall, Jr., Michael M. Lombardo, "Off the Track: Why and How Successful Executives Get Derailed" (Technical Report No. 21, Center for Creative Leadership, Greensboro, NC, January 1983); Carol Hymowitz, "Five Main Reasons Why Managers Fail," *The Wall Street Journal*, May 2, 1988.

[21]Rost, *Leadership for the Twenty-First Century*, 100.

[22]Robert Tomsho, "How Greyhound Lines Re-Engineered Itself Right into a Deep Hole," *The Wall Street Journal*, October 30, 1994, A1.

[23]Sharon Nelton, "Leadership for the New Age," *Nation's Business*, May 1997, 18–27.

[24]Genevieve Capowski, "Anatomy of a Leader: Where Are the Leaders of Tomorrow?" *Management Review*, March 1994, 10–17.

[25]This section is based on John P. Kotter, *A Force for Change: How Leadership Differs from Management* (New York: The Free Press, 1990), 3–18.

[26]Nelton, "Leadership for the New Age."

[27]David Kirkpatrick, "This Tough Guy Wants to Give You a Hug," *Fortune*, October 14, 1996, 170–176.

[28]Wright and McManus, *Flashpoints: Promise and Peril in a New World*, 120.

[29]Lee G. Bolman and Terrence E. Deal, "Spirited Leadership," *Leadership Quarterly* 5, No. 3/4 (1994): 309–312.

[30]Stratford Sherman, "Leaders Learn to Heed the Voice Within," *Fortune*, August 22, 1994, 92–100.

[31]Gregory A. Gull, "In Search of Leadership," *Executive Excellence*, December 1994, 16.

[32]Nelton, "Leadership for the New Age."

[33]Quoted in Capowski, "Anatomy of a Leader: Where Are the Leaders of Tomorrow?"

[34]Kirkpatrick, "This Tough Guy Wants to Give You a Hug."

[35]Jay Finegan, "Ready, Aim, Focus," *Inc.*, May 1997, 44–55.

[36]Glenn Rifkin, "Leadership: Can It Be Learned?" *Forbes ASAP*, April 8, 1996, 100–112.

[37]Brian Smale, "Fight. Learn. Lead." *Fast Company*, August/September 1996, 65–70.

[38]Ibid.

[39]Noel M. Tichy and Christopher DeRose, "The Pepsi Challenge: Building a Leader-Driven Organization," *Training and Development*, May 1996, 58–66.

[40]Russell Palmer, "Can Leadership Be Learned?" *Business Today*, Fall 1989, 100–102.

2

From Management to Leadership

- **The Nature of Management**   35
- **Comparing Management and Leadership**   37
- **The Evolution of Leadership**   46
- **Leadership Spotlights:**
  Robert Noyce   38
  The Girl Scout Way   43
  Pratt & Whitney   45
- **Leader's Bookshelf:** *Leadership Is an Art*   42
- **Leadership Development: Personal Feedback**
  Your Leadership Potential   55
- **Leadership Development: Case for Analysis**
  Airstar, Inc.   56

Your Leadership Challenge

After reading this chapter, you should be able to:

1. Understand the traditional functions of management and the roles into which managerial work fits.

2. Recognize the fundamental differences between leadership and management.

3. Understand the crucial importance of providing direction, alignment, relationships, personal qualities, and outcomes.

4. Trace the evolution of leadership through four eras to the facilitating leadership required in many organizations today.

Herb Kelleher, CEO and president of the most consistently profitable airline in the industry, has been seen impersonating Elvis and the Easter bunny, dressed as a leprechaun, and doing the Southwest Shuffle in the persona of Big Daddy-O. Not the typical behavior of your typical CEO, yet most Wall Street analysts credit Southwest Airlines' success to Kelleher's unique personality and style.

What makes Southwest successful, though, is not Kelleher's willingness to impersonate Elvis or dress as a clown. It is his ability to articulate a clear vision for where he wants the company to go and build a bond of loyalty that gets all employees committed to achieving the vision. His antics are only part of how Kelleher strives to keep spirits high and build a culture where—as one employee puts it—"kindness and the human spirit are nurtured." His philosophy is simple but powerful: do what your customers want and be happy in your work. Kelleher thinks the best way to handle stiff competition in the increasingly complex world of business is to get back to the basics. Communication, he says, "must proceed directly from the heart. . . . [it doesn't mean] getting up and giving formal speeches."[1]

Kelleher believes each employee should be treated as an individual, and he's been known to remember the first names of thousands of workers and to visit ill employees from the lowest levels of the company. According to Steve Lewins, a Gruntal & Co. analyst, Kelleher is a powerful leader because he's the kind of person "who will stay out with a mechanic in some bar until four o'clock in the morning to find out what is going on. And then he will fix whatever is wrong." He doesn't just preach the message that front line workers are the heroes of the company; he consistently lives it.

Leadership filters down through the company. Because workers feel valued, they take initiative wherever needed—pilots might man the boarding gate, or ticket agents might find themselves schlepping luggage. When Southwest acquired tiny Morris Air, hundreds of Southwest employees spontaneously began sending cards, candy, and company T-shirts to Morris workers as a way of welcoming them into the fold. Employees express their individual personalities when serving customers. Passengers on a recent Southwest flight, for example, had a bunny-eared flight attendant pop out of an overhead bin to greet them. Strong leadership at Southwest has contributed to unusually good labor-management relations for the company. Southwest has never had a layoff. Kelleher says Southwest has always retained "a patina of spirituality. . . . I feel that you have to be with your employees through all their difficulties, that you have to be interested in them personally."[2]

By being interested in his workers personally, Herb Kelleher has created a company that is tough to beat. Kelleher's leadership makes employees feel valued, and because they care about the company and about each other they put forth their best effort. Poor leadership can have a negative impact on a company. Contrast Kelleher's leadership with that of Frank Lorenzo, former CEO and hatchet man at Continental Airlines. Lorenzo's leadership contributed to employees' *demotivation*. Gregory Brenneman, recruited by new Continental CEO Gordon Bethune to be the airline's chief operating officer, says he was shocked by the demoralized workforce and the degree of rancor that existed between labor and management as a legacy of Lorenzo's reign of terror. The executive suites were kept locked, and top executives' secretaries had buttons under their desks that could be bumped by a knee to call the police. Brenneman and Bethune, who is himself a pilot, are dismantling the destructive culture and assembling a new one. They've set up an 800 number for employee complaints, instituted a profit-sharing plan, and started paying bonuses based on the airline's on-time record. Most importantly, Brenneman and Bethune are visiting employees throughout the company, spreading a message of pride and accountability.[3] Their leadership is helping to put Continental back on the right flight path.

In this chapter, we will explore more closely the characteristics that make people like Herb Kelleher, Gregory Brenneman, and Gordon Bethune effective leaders. In the following section, we will explore the differences between management and leadership and look at some of the personal qualities needed for successful leadership. Then we will trace the evolution of leadership to understand in more detail the need for a new kind of leadership in today's world.

The Nature of Management

Although the terms *leadership* and *management* are often used interchangeably, they are not the same thing. This book is about leadership, so it is important to understand what distinguishes the process of leadership from that of management. Management and leadership can go hand in hand. At Southwest Airlines, described in the opening case, Herb Kelleher is a master leader, yet he also performs many management functions. For example, Kelleher plans strategy, keeps a close eye on costs, and constantly monitors the key industry standard—cost per available seat mile— to make sure Southwest stays a few cents below the pack. Managers may sometimes be leaders and leaders may sometimes be managers, but leadership and management are two different processes.

The Functions of Management

There are two primary ways of looking at management: the functions of management and the roles into which various management activities fit. Exhibit 2.1 illustrates the functional view. **Management** can be defined as the attainment of organizational goals in an effective and efficient manner through planning, organizing, staffing, directing, and controlling organizational resources. Note that leadership is not one of the traditional functions of management.

Planning means defining goals and objectives for the organization, developing strategies, using budgets to allocate resources, and setting policies and procedures. *Organizing* involves work arrangements, establishing organization structure, creating responsibility and authority relationships, and even position descriptions needed to accomplish the plan. It includes the assignment of tasks into departments and the allocation of people and financial resources to various departments. *Staffing* encompasses the recruitment and selection of people for positions, and their instruction and training to help them develop appropriate knowledge and skills. *Directing* is the use of influence and rewards to motivate employees to take desired actions. It also includes delegation, coordination of employees, and managing conflicts. The fifth management function, *controlling*, means developing performance standards, establishing reporting systems, monitoring employees' activities to determine whether the organization is on target towards its goals, and taking corrective action as necessary.

The model of management functions captures some of the broad range of activities managers perform. Some tasks are conceptual, some operational or technical, and others involve people. This approach to management minimizes the relationship of leader and follower, almost as if the organization could be run as a large machine, perhaps the way a ship captain can direct the activities of an oceangoing freighter. This approach to management made a lot of sense under the industrial age paradigm described in Chapter 1. It is also relevant today, but as the world becomes more turbulent, another view of management has emerged.

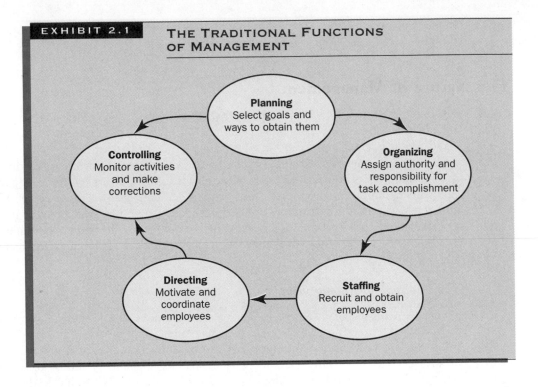

EXHIBIT 2.1 — THE TRADITIONAL FUNCTIONS OF MANAGEMENT

Managerial Roles

Another way of looking at management is based on Henry Mintzberg's observations of the daily activities of managers. He found that the many diverse activities did not always fit the five managerial functions. He proposed that managerial work could be organized into ten managerial roles.[4] A **role** is a set of expectations for a manager's behavior. Mintzberg's roles, outlined in Exhibit 2.2, are divided into three conceptual categories: informational, interpersonal, and decisional. *Informational* roles describe how managers constantly process information. Managers maintain and develop an information network. They seek information from a variety of sources and they also transmit current information to others who can use it, both inside and outside the organization. *Interpersonal* roles pertain to relationships with others, including activities as symbolic head of a group, activities to motivate and develop others, and activities to build relationships with peers. *Decisional* roles pertain to those events about which the manager must make a choice and take action, such as initiating changes, handling problems and negotiating agreements, and allocating resources.

Although the activities of a manager's job are broken down to understand the separate roles, it is important to remember that all of these roles interact in the real world of management. As Mintzberg put it, "The manager who only communicates or only conceives never gets anything done, while the manager who only 'does' ends up doing it all alone."[5] The relative emphasis on each role or each management

EXHIBIT 2.2	MANAGER ROLES	
Category	**Role**	**Activity**
Informational	Monitor	Seek and receive information, scan periodicals and reports, maintain personal contacts.
	Disseminator	Forward information to other organization members; send memos and reports; make phone calls.
	Spokesperson	Transmit information to outsiders through speeches, reports, memos.
Interpersonal	Figurehead	Perform ceremonial and symbolic duties such as greeting visitors, signing legal documents.
	Leader	Direct and motivate subordinates; train, counsel, and communicate with subordinates.
	Liaison	Maintain information links both inside and outside organization; use mail, phone calls, meetings.
Decisional	Entrepreneur	Initiate improvement projects; identify new ideas; delegate idea responsibility to others.
	Disturbance handler	Take corrective action during disputes or crises; resolve conflicts among subordinates; adapt to environmental crises.
	Resource allocator	Decide who gets resources; schedule, budget, set priorities.
	Negotiator	Represent department during negotiation of union contracts, sales purchases, budgets; represent departmental interests.

SOURCES: Adapted from Henry Mintzberg, *The Nature of Managerial Work* (New York: Harper & Row, 1973), 92–93; and Henry Mintzberg, "Managerial Work: Analysis from Observation," *Managerial Science* 18 (1971), B97–B110.

function varies from one manager to another and may depend on many factors, such as the position in the organization and the current needs of the organization in its environment. Many managers have demonstrated strength in the functions of planning, organizing, and controlling, or in informational and decisional roles, but weakness in their ability to lead.

Comparing Management and Leadership

Leadership cannot replace management; it should be in addition to management. Much has been written in recent years about the difference between management and leadership. Unfortunately, with the current emphasis on the need for leadership, managers have gotten a bad name. Jack Welch once commented that at General Electric, it is sometimes "dangerous to call somebody a manager." The term *manager*, he said, has sadly come to mean someone who "controls rather than facilitates, complicates rather than simplifies, acts more like a governor than an accelerator."[6] Managers and leaders are not inherently different types of people. Some people exhibit characteristics of both good management and good leadership, and most managers can develop the qualities needed for effective leadership. Consider the example of the late Robert Noyce, credited with spawning the Silicon Valley.

LEADERSHIP SPOTLIGHT   ROBERT NOYCE

Robert Noyce created a vision that transformed the electronics industry and changed people's lives. After leaving a job with Shockley Semiconductor, where he learned from an unpredictable and often abusive boss how *not* to run an organization of creative people, Noyce and seven other former Shockley employees founded Fairchild Semiconductor, the firm that became the basis for what is now known as Silicon Valley.

Noyce was an electronics wizard who understood the need to carefully manage costs, maintain timetables, and coordinate tasks across departments so that innovative products could be brought to market quickly and efficiently. However, he also knew traditional control-oriented management practices could squelch the creativity and enthusiasm he needed from his workers. He chose instead to give workers freedom to explore, and key people were allowed to take their own lead, developing their own leadership abilities in the process. It was a courageous act, though Noyce looked at it simply as the only decent way to treat people. The primary risk was that his trust would encourage a commitment to innovation rather than a commitment to the firm. Indeed, numerous scientists and engineers left to start up and lead other high-tech firms, eventually leading to Silicon Valley becoming a world center of electronics innovation and new business ventures.

Noyce himself went on to co-found Intel Corporation, then to become president of an emerging 14-firm research consortium. After he suffered a fatal heart attack in June of 1990, one colleague remarked, "His passing left a major leadership void in transforming the semiconductor industry into once again a formidable world competitive power. . . . Noyce had a unique set of skills, which combined technical expertise with management savvy and familiarity with Washington politics."[7] Noyce left a legacy that influenced an entire industry.

Robert Noyce excelled in both management and leadership. He was an electronics wizard with remarkable technical expertise. He capably performed the planning, organizing, and coordinating functions needed to get products out the door and keep costs under control. Yet Noyce was also remarkable for his ability to create a shared vision, provide a clear sense of direction, and energize and empower others to make dreams come true. He had the courage to lead people rather than control them.

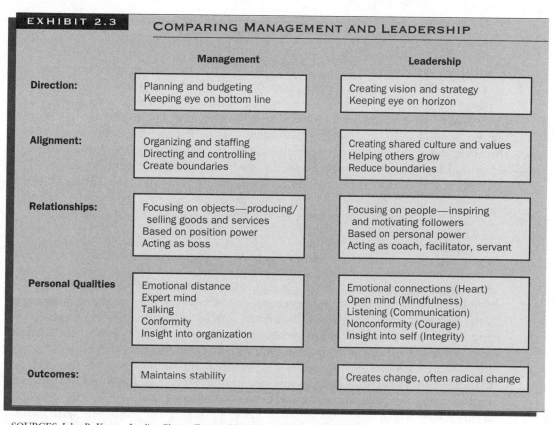

EXHIBIT 2.3 — COMPARING MANAGEMENT AND LEADERSHIP

	Management	Leadership
Direction:	Planning and budgeting Keeping eye on bottom line	Creating vision and strategy Keeping eye on horizon
Alignment:	Organizing and staffing Directing and controlling Create boundaries	Creating shared culture and values Helping others grow Reduce boundaries
Relationships:	Focusing on objects—producing/ selling goods and services Based on position power Acting as boss	Focusing on people—inspiring and motivating followers Based on personal power Acting as coach, facilitator, servant
Personal Qualities	Emotional distance Expert mind Talking Conformity Insight into organization	Emotional connections (Heart) Open mind (Mindfulness) Listening (Communication) Nonconformity (Courage) Insight into self (Integrity)
Outcomes:	Maintains stability	Creates change, often radical change

SOURCES: John P. Kotter, *Leading Change* (Boston, MA: Harvard Business School Press, 1996), 26; Joseph C. Rost, *Leadership for the Twenty-first Century*, (Westport, CN: Praeger, 1993), 149; and Brian Dumaine, "The New Non-Manager Managers," *Fortune*, February 22, 1993, 80–84.

Exhibit 2.3 compares management to leadership in five areas crucial to organizational performance—providing direction, aligning employees, building relationships, personal qualities and leader outcomes.[8]

Providing Direction

Both leadership and management are concerned with providing direction for the organization, but there are differences. Management focuses on establishing detailed plans and schedules for achieving specific results, then allocating resources to accomplish the plan. Leadership calls for creating a compelling vision of the future and developing farsighted strategies for producing the changes needed to achieve that vision. Whereas management calls for keeping an eye on the bottom line and short-term results, leadership means keeping an eye on the horizon and the long-term future.

A **vision** is a picture of an ambitious, desirable future for the organization or team.[9] It can be as lofty as Motorola's aim to "become the premier company in the world" or as down-to-earth as the Swedish company Ikea's simple vision "to provide affordable furniture for people with limited budgets." One owner of a small bakery had a vision to make his company "a showcase, the kind of company which I and all who work there will be proud to say, 'That's my place.'" To be compelling for followers, the vision has to be one they can relate to and share. Few employees can get excited by a vision of creating greater wealth for shareholders. In *Fortune* magazine's study of the "100 Best Companies to Work for in America," two of the recurring traits of great companies were a powerful, visionary leader and a sense of purpose beyond increasing shareholder value. At Medtronic, for example, company leaders stress the vision of "restoring patients to full life." Rather than concentrating on shareholders or doctors, workers at Medtronic are told to focus on the people who will actually have the company's devices implanted inside them. Workers who are inspired and motivated to help sick people get well have made the company's total return to shareholders great too.[10]

Alignment

Management entails organizing a structure to accomplish the plan; staffing the structure with employees; and developing policies, procedures, and systems to direct employees and monitor implementation of the plan. Managers are thinkers and workers are doers. Leadership is concerned instead with communicating the vision and developing a shared culture and set of core values that can lead to the desired future state. This involves others as thinkers, doers, and leaders themselves, fostering a sense of ownership in everyone.[11] Whereas the vision describes the destination, the culture and values help define the journey toward it. Leadership focuses on getting everyone lined up in the same direction. Gertrude Boyle, a housewife and mother who took charge of Columbia Sportswear after her husband's early death, created a comfortable down-to-earth corporate culture that propelled the outdoor clothing manufacturer from sales of $800,000 to just under $300 million. She came into the company with no business experience, but says that, "Running a company is like raising kids. You all have to be in the same line of thinking."[12]

Managers organize by separating people into specialties and functions, with boundaries separating them by department and hierarchical level. Leaders break down boundaries so people know what others are doing, can coordinate easily, and feel a sense of teamwork and equalness for achieving outcomes.

Rather than directing and controlling employees, leadership is concerned with helping others grow so that they can fully contribute to achieving the vision. Whereas the management communication process generally involves providing answers and solving problems, leadership entails asking questions, listening, and involving others. Communicating direction and cultural values in actions as well as words is necessary for leadership to influence the creation of teams or coalitions that understand the vision and support it.[13]

Relationships

In terms of relationships, management focuses on objects such as machines and reports, on taking the steps needed to produce the organization's goods and services. Leadership, on the other hand, focuses on motivating and inspiring people.

Whereas the management relationship is based on formal authority, leadership is a relationship based on personal influence. Formal **position power** means that there is a written, spoken, or implied contract wherein people accept either a superior or subordinate role and see the use of coercive as well as noncoercive behavior as an acceptable way to achieve desired results.[14] For example, in an authority relationship, both people accept that a manager can tell a subordinate to be at work at 7:30 A.M. or her pay will be docked. Leadership, on the other hand, relies on influence, which is less likely to use coercion. Followers are empowered to make many decisions on their own. Leadership strives to make work stimulating and challenging and involves pulling rather than pushing people toward goals. The role of leadership is to attract and energize people, motivating them through identification rather than rewards or punishments.[15] For example, Jean Kvasnica excels as a leader at Hewlett-Packard, where she has no direct reports and doesn't evaluate anyone's performance or recommend raises. According to one team member, she succeeds in motivating people because she has "vision and intense commitment to the successful outcome of a project, but the idea that makes it successful could come from anywhere. She's not selfish about it."[16]

The formal position of authority in the organization is the source of management power, but leadership power comes from the personal characteristics of the leader. Leadership does not require that one hold a formal position of authority, and many people holding positions of authority do not provide leadership. Whereas the manager often thinks of herself as a boss or supervisor, the leader sees herself as a coach or facilitator. The primary concern of a leader is not self, but others, and one of the leader's most important jobs is helping others grow and develop.

The differing source of power is one of the key distinctions between management and leadership. Take away a manager's formal position and will people choose to follow him? Leadership truly depends on who you are rather than on your position or title.

Personal Leadership Qualities

Leadership is more than a set of skills; it relies on a number of subtle personal qualities that are hard to see but are very powerful. These include things like enthusiasm, integrity, courage, and humility. First of all, good leadership springs from a genuine concern for others. This chapter's Leader's Bookshelf considers the leader as a servant of others. The process of management generally encourages emotional distance, but leadership means being emotionally connected to others. Where there is leadership, people become part of a community and feel that they are significant.[17] Leaders suppress their own egos, recognize the contributions of others, and let others know they are valued.

Whereas management means providing answers and solving problems, leadership requires the courage to admit mistakes and doubts, to take risks, to listen, and to trust and learn from others. Emotional connections are risky but necessary for true leadership to happen. George Sparks, a graduate of the Air Force Academy and currently general manager of Hewlett-Packard's measuring-equipment business, says he learned this from a Girl Scout leader.

Leadership Is an Art
Max De Pree

"Leadership is much more of an art, a belief, a condition of the heart, than a set of things to do," writes Max De Pree, author of *Leadership Is an Art*. His book, based on his experiences as CEO of Herman Miller Company, is a guide for practicing leadership, but it doesn't list a set of skills. Instead, De Pree defines leadership as a "covenant," an emotional bond creating mutual trust built on shared goals and values. De Pree believes effective leadership occurs only when there is a sacred relationship between leaders and followers. Some of his major premises about leadership are as follows:

Leadership Begins in the Heart

For De Pree, leadership is a way of life. The leader respects people, believes in the potential of others, understands that beliefs and values precede practice, recognizes the difference between contracts and covenants, and understands that personal relationships count more than formal structure and systems. Only by living these beliefs can leaders truly empower others.

The Leader as Servant

A leader should be a servant and a debtor to the people comprising the organization. "The first responsibility of a leader is to define reality. The last is to say 'thank you.' In between the two, the leader must become a servant and a debtor." For De Pree, leadership is a sacred trust, and leadership and ethics intersect at several primary points:

- Leaders assume stewardship of limited resources and should leave behind them assets and a legacy.
- Leaders help others strive to reach their own potential and explore their leadership abilities. They free people to be their best.
- Leaders subsume their needs to those of their followers and learn how to make a commitment to the common good.
- Leaders appreciate the diversity of people's gifts as the crucial step toward trusting each other.

The Workers' Bill of Rights

De Pree believes that to empower employees, the leader must not only confer the individual's basic human rights but also expand them to include the following: the right to be needed and involved; the right to a covenantal relationship with one's employer; the right to understand and to be accountable; the right to appeal; the right to make a commitment; and the right to affect one's own destiny. By meeting the needs of individuals, leaders help meet the needs of the whole organization.

Realization of Potential Depends on Intimacy

De Pree explores the concept of intimacy with work as that essential, powerful ingredient that precedes commitment, competence, and ownership. Intimacy enables one to realize his or her full potential. Intimacy is the machine operator who knows by virtue of past necessity exactly what makes his machine tick. As De Pree puts it, "Intimacy is at the heart of competence . . . [and it] arises from translating personal and corporate values into daily work practices."

The art of leadership involves "liberating people to do what is required of them in the most effective and humane way possible." The leader as servant removes obstacles that prevent followers from excelling at their jobs and reaching their potential. De Pree's book teaches that "managers who have no beliefs but only understand methodology and quantification are modern-day eunuchs." Yet they can learn to be leaders instead. They can learn to care not just about quality of product or service but also about "the quality of our relationships and the quality of our communications and the quality of our promises to each other."

Leadership Is an Art, by Max De Pree, is published by Doubleday.

LEADERSHIP SPOTLIGHT　　　THE GIRL SCOUT WAY

"The best two days of my career," is how George Sparks describes the time he spent following Frances Hesselbein around. Hesselbein currently runs the Drucker Foundation, a small organization dedicated to sharing the leadership thinking of Peter Drucker with other nonprofits. She began her career 41 years ago as a volunteer Scout leader. She eventually rose to CEO of the Girl Scouts, inheriting a troubled organization of 680,000 people, only 1 percent of whom were paid employees. By the time she retired in 1990, Hesselbein had turned around declining membership, dramatically increased participation by minorities, and replaced a brittle hierarchy with one of the most vibrant organizations in the nonprofit or business world.

Hesselbein describes how she works with others as a circle, in which everyone is included. As Sparks observed her in action, the most compelling quality he noted was her ability to sense people's needs on an emotional level. He explains, "Time and again, I have seen people face two possible solutions. One is 20 percent better, but the other meets their personal needs—and that is the one they inevitably choose." He noticed that Hesselbein would listen carefully and then link people with matching needs and skills, so that their personal needs were met at the same time they were serving the needs of the organization. Hesselbein recognizes that the only way to achieve high performance is through the work of others, and she consistently treats people with care and respect.

Her definition of leadership, she says, was "very hard to arrive at, very painful. . . . [It] is not a basket of tricks or skills. It is the quality and character and courage of the person who is the leader. It's a matter of ethics and moral compass, the willingness to remain highly vulnerable."[18]

As Frances Hesselbein noted, developing leadership qualities can be painful. Abraham Zaleznik has referred to leaders as "twice-born personalities," who struggle to develop their sense of self through psychological and social change.[19] For leadership to happen, leaders have to know who they are and what they stand for. And they remain constant so followers know what to expect. A recent study revealed that people would much rather follow individuals they can count on, even when they disagree with their viewpoint, than people they agree with but who frequently shift their viewpoints or positions.[20] One employee described the kind of person she would follow as this: ". . . it's like they have a stick down through the center of them that's rooted in the ground. I can tell when someone has that. When they're not defensive, not egotistical. They're open-minded, able to joke and laugh at themselves. They can take a volatile situation and stay focused. They bring out the best in me by making me want to handle myself in the same way. I want to be part of their world."[21]

Sixty-seven-year-old Irma Elder illustrates how these qualities are translated into action. She is the first to admit she doesn't know everything. Yet Elder's ability to stand fast in the face of hardship led Troy Ford of Troy, Michigan from the brink of disaster to become one of the most successful groups of Ford dealerships in the

A Wish for Leaders

I sincerely wish you will have the experience of thinking up a new idea, planning it, organizing it, and following it to completion, and then have it be magnificently successful. I also hope you'll go through the same process and have something "bomb out."

I wish you could know how it feels to run with all your heart and lose . . . horribly!

I wish that you could achieve some great good for mankind, but have nobody know about it except you.

I wish you could find something so worthwhile that you deem it worthy of investing your life in it.

I hope you become frustrated and challenged enough to begin to push back the very barriers of your own personal limitations.

I hope you make a stupid mistake and get caught red-handed and are big enough to say those magic words, "I was wrong."

I hope you give so much of yourself that some days you wonder if it's worth all the effort.

I wish for you a magnificent obsession that will give you a reason for living and purpose and direction in life.

I wish for you the worst kind of criticism for everything you do, because that makes you fight to achieve beyond what you normally would.

I wish for you the experience of Leadership.

SOURCE: Earl Reum, "A Wish for Leaders," from *Rainbows of Leadership,* © 1992 Earl Reum. Used with permission.

country. One morning she arrived to find the whole service department flooded from a big rainstorm the night before. The department manager was frantic. Elder felt like hitting the panic button herself, but something inside her said, "Keep smiling, keep calm." To everyone's astonishment, she ordered in a hot breakfast to break the tension and let everyone fuel up before tackling the difficult job ahead.[22]

Like Irma Elder, true leaders draw on a number of subtle but powerful forces within themselves. For example, leaders tend to have an open mind that welcomes new ideas rather than a closed mind that criticizes new ideas. Leaders tend to care about others and build personal connections rather than maintain emotional distance. Leaders listen and discern what people want and need more than they talk to give advice and orders. Leaders are willing to be nonconformists, to disagree and say no when it serves the larger good, and to accept nonconformity from others rather than try to squeeze everyone into the same mind-set. They and others step outside the traditional boundary and comfort zone, take risks, and make mistakes to learn and grow. Moreover, leaders are honest with themselves and others to the point of inspiring trust. They set high moral standards by doing the right thing, rather than just going along with standards set by others.

Leadership causes wear and tear on the individual, because leaders are vulnerable, take risks, and initiate change, which typically encounters resistance. The Living Leadership box describes reasons why leaders need to develop their own personal capacities and qualities to be effective.

Outcomes

The differences between management and leadership create two differing outcomes, as illustrated at the bottom of Exhibit 2.3. Management produces a degree of stability, predictability, order, and efficiency. Thus, good management helps the organization consistently achieve short-term results and meet the expectations of various stakeholders. Leadership, on the other hand, creates change, often to a dramatic degree. Two successful CEOs, Harry Quadracchi of Quad-Graphics and Bill McGowan of MCI, have both independently voiced the opinion that a leader's job is not to be the chief organizer, but the chief disorganizer.[23]

Leadership means questioning and challenging the status quo so that outdated or unproductive norms can be replaced to meet new challenges. Good leadership can lead to extremely valuable change, such as new products or services that gain new customers or expand markets. For example, Edwin Land believed people who enjoyed taking snapshots would like to shorten the time between snapping the picture and gaining the pleasure of seeing it, and the Polaroid camera was born.[24] Thus, although good management is needed to help organizations meet current commitments, good leadership is needed to move the organization into the future.

For much of the 20th century, good management has often been enough to keep organizations healthy, but leaders for the twenty-first century can no longer rely on traditional management practices. Robert Ponchak, a Pratt & Whitney plant manager, saved his job and his factory by making the transition from management to leadership.

LEADERSHIP SPOTLIGHT   **PRATT & WHITNEY**

Several years ago, some Pratt & Whitney executives were saying the company's Maine factory was a dinosaur that ought to be shut down. However, Maine's largest factory was hauled back from the brink with the help of plant manager Robert Ponchak, a 31-year veteran who was on the verge of losing his job. In early 1993, Pratt's manufacturing czar summoned Ponchak to a meeting and showed him the paperwork for an early retirement package, saying, "I'm not sure you can take it to the next level." Ponchak's reply was, "Just you watch me."

For Ponchak—and for the factory—survival meant, first and foremost, learning to take risks. A manager accustomed to keeping things running on an even keel with traditional management techniques, Ponchak had to learn to take chances, let go, and give his workers more freedom and responsibility. One of his first challenges was learning to work cooperatively with a young pup sent from headquarters to be his Number Two. Although the two initially clashed, they learned to work as a team, with each contributing varied strengths. Ponchak also took chances to get workers on the factory floor more involved and committed. Frustrated that workers seemed confused by a new lean production system, he put together a team of factory and front office workers, gave them leave from their regular jobs, and told them to come up with a new job classification system that would link pay to learning the new techniques and skills. Pay increases are now linked not to seniority but to the amount of training workers complete and the degree of responsibility they accept. In addition, a "results-sharing" plan puts extra cash in workers' pockets if the plant exceeds certain targets, such as those for cost-cutting and on-time delivery. "Everybody is trying to cut costs," says Michael Robinson, the plant's new operations manager. "We've got 1,500 people looking at what managers used to look at."

Pratt & Whitney's Maine factory is growing again, and the company holds it up as a model. Factory workers are continuously learning and growing and feel a greater sense of responsibility. Change is embraced rather than feared.[25]

Pratt & Whitney's top executives wanted Ponchak to accept early retirement because they recognized that the Maine factory needed leadership for change in order to survive and thrive in a turbulent environment. However, Ponchak showed that even managers long accustomed to maintaining the status quo can learn to take chances and become leaders.

Society and the world of business are undergoing profound transformations, and organizations face different challenges today than in the past. In the next section, we will briefly examine how organizations have changed over time, and how the concept of leadership has evolved in connection with those changes.

The Evolution of Leadership

Conditions today are changing fast, as we discussed in Chapter 1. Today's leaders find it hard to predict and control what is happening in the world around them or within their own organizations. An executive at a major Italian communications company, STET, recently said, "Our universe is changing every six months. First it is privatization, then deregulation, then technological revolutions, then mergers and strategic alliances. . . . We can no longer plan beyond six months or a year, and frequent discontinuities have become a way of life."[26]

But concepts of leadership emerged during a more stable time, or at least during a time when people believed the world was stable and could be predicted and controlled with logic and rationality. Winston Churchill said that we create our buildings and thereafter our buildings create us. The point is that the structures people create have a reciprocal influence long beyond their useful life. The organizations and concepts of leadership created during a more stable era still shape the design of organizations and the training of managers. The stress between the chaos in the world and the industrial age paradigm held by many organizations and managers means we are at a threshold of breaking with the past as people learn to free themselves from outdated practices and meet new challenges.

Context of Leadership

The evolution of leadership thought and action has unfolded in four eras, which we will discuss by looking at two dimensions: whether leadership works on a *micro* level or a *macro* level, and whether environmental conditions are *stable* or *chaotic*.

Micro versus Macro Leadership Scope   Leadership is directly related to the leader's way of thinking about self, followers, and organizations.[27] The micro side of leadership concerns specific situations, tasks, and individuals. The focus is on one person and one task at a time. The leader has explicit detailed knowledge of work processes and followers' behaviors needed to reach certain goals. The macro side of leadership transcends individuals, groups, and specific situations to focus on whole communities, whole organizations. Macro leadership deals with fundamental ideals, values, and strategies that characterize large groups. It is concerned with purpose, strategy, structure, meaning, and culture.

Stable versus Chaotic Conditions   The stable versus chaotic dimension refers to whether elements in the environment are dynamic. An environment is stable if it remains the same over a number of months or years. People can expect history to repeat itself—what worked yesterday will work again tomorrow. Under chaotic conditions, environmental elements shift abruptly. This can occur when competitors react with aggressive moves and countermoves regarding advertising and new products. For example, only a few years ago, McDonald's seemed unassailable in the fast-food business. Today, however, McDonald's U.S. business is as flat as an all-beef patty, partly due to Burger King's aggressive, upbeat advertising and a string of successful new products like the Big King.[28]

Almost all companies today are operating in a fast-changing environment. As discussed in Chapter 1, today's world is characterized by globalization, hyper-competition, information overload, rapid change, and surprise. Small events can have huge consequences that are difficult or impossible to predict. In chaotic conditions, leaders must learn to support risk, diversity, relationships, collaboration, and learning. Their work involves creating a vision and strategy for change, inspiring and empowering others, and keeping everyone focused on adaptation to changing conditions.

Framework

These two dimensions are combined into a framework for examining the evolution of leadership, as illustrated in Exhibit 2.4. Each cell in the model summarizes an era of leadership thinking that may have been correct for its time, but may be inappropriate for today's fast-changing world.

Macro Leadership in a Stable World   *Era 1* may be conceptualized as pre-industrial and pre-bureaucratic. Most organizations were small and were run by a single individual (usually a man) who many times hired workers because they were friends or relatives, not necessarily because of their skills or qualifications. The size and simplicity of organizations as well as the stable environment made it easy for a single person to have a personal vision, acquire resources, coordinate all activities, and keep things on track. Because the world acted in predictable ways, important resources could be controlled and outcomes predicted. Managers were struggling to learn "administrative principles" by which organizations could be routinized and controlled.

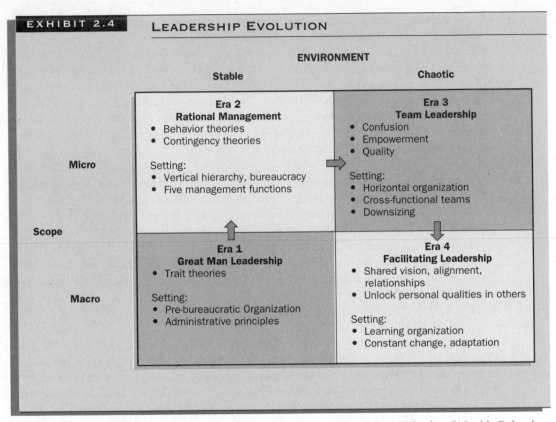

EXHIBIT 2.4   **LEADERSHIP EVOLUTION**

ENVIRONMENT

Stable — Chaotic

Micro

Era 2
Rational Management
- Behavior theories
- Contingency theories

Setting:
- Vertical hierarchy, bureaucracy
- Five management functions

Era 3
Team Leadership
- Confusion
- Empowerment
- Quality

Setting:
- Horizontal organization
- Cross-functional teams
- Downsizing

Scope

Era 1
Great Man Leadership
- Trait theories

Setting:
- Pre-bureaucratic Organization
- Administrative principles

Era 4
Facilitating Leadership
- Shared vision, alignment, relationships
- Unlock personal qualities in others

Setting:
- Learning organization
- Constant change, adaptation

Macro

This is the era of "Great Man" leadership, the granddaddy of leadership concepts. The earliest studies of leadership adopted the belief that leaders were born with certain leadership traits. "Leader" was equated with "hero," a concept particularly engrained in Western culture. Greek mythology, for example, provides us with many examples of the leader as hero. Homer's *Iliad* and *Odyssey* both portray strong leaders as heroes of their people. In organizations, social movements, governments, and the military, leadership was often conceptualized as a single "Great Man" who put everything together. He operated on the macro level, seeing the big picture and how everything fit into a whole. The Great Man focused on developing a vision and strategy and motivating people to achieve the vision. Examples include corporate leaders like Vanderbilt and Carnegie, government leaders like Washington and Lincoln, social leaders like Gandhi and Martin Luther King, Jr., or historical leaders such as Napoleon, Caesar, Richard III, or Henry V.

The dominance of these great figures spurred research into "traits" that comprised a leader. People thought that if traits could be identified, leaders could be predicted or perhaps trained. Despite less relevance for today's rapidly changing world, the concept of the Great Man or the search for traits that make great leaders has not died. Many organizations expect a single, strong leader to come in and "save the day." Studies of strong leaders like Lee Iacocca or Jack Welch often fall back on the idea of the leader as hero rather than considering the complex nature of the leadership process. The Great Man theory and other trait theories that grew out of it are discussed in more detail in Chapter 3.

Micro Leadership in a Stable World   *Era 2* sees the emergence of hierarchy and bureaucracy. Although the world remains stable, organizations have begun to grow large so they require rules and standard procedures to ensure that activities can be performed in an efficient, effective manner. Hierarchy of authority provides a sensible mechanism for supervision and control of workers. Ideas like "scientific" management and functions of management take firm root, based on the principles of engineering efficiency and control. Decisions once based on rules of thumb or tradition are replaced with precise procedures—managers develop standard methods for doing each job, select workers with the appropriate abilities, train workers in the standard methods, and provide wage incentives for workers to accomplish tasks.

This is the era of the "rational manager" who directs and controls others using an impersonal approach. Employees are not expected to think for themselves; they are expected to do as they are told and accomplish specific tasks. The rational manager was well suited to a stable environment in which things could be taken apart and analyzed. The notion of vision or a big idea was reduced to specific data. The focus was on details rather than the big picture. In a stable world, many huge, bureaucratic organizations practically ran themselves; all that was needed was good management to keep things on an even keel.

Leadership scholars during this era put leaders on the academic operating table and dissected them into pieces, hoping to learn how to make companies more efficient. Studies that attempted to determine what specific leadership "behaviors" made subordinates more effective led to various behavioral theories of leadership. In the 1970s, scholars developed "contingency" theories of leadership that determined that behaviors were not the only factors that produced effective outcomes, but considered the situation on which leader behaviors were contingent. The idea that leaders could analyze their situation and tailor their behavior to it was compelling and is the foundation for much leadership training today. Contingency theories are discussed in Chapter 4.

Micro Leadership in a Chaotic World   This era represented the greatest shock to management in North America and Europe. Suddenly the world was no longer stable, and the prized techniques of rational management were no longer working. Following World War II, there was no global competition for U.S. companies. The war had ravaged Europe, the Soviet Union, and Japan. With its technological and manufacturing base intact, the United States enjoyed great economic success with "rational management" practices. Yet, beginning with the OPEC oil embargo of 1972–1973 and continuing with the severe global competition in the 1980s, many managers saw that conditions had become chaotic.

The Japanese began to dominate world commerce with their ideas of team leadership and superb quality products. This became an era of confusion for management that was a time of middle management downsizing, expectations of doing more with less, and of getting greater motivation from employees. Many managers felt overwhelmed as they were expected to abandon the traditional vertical hierarchy and management control and move to the notion of a horizontal organization, with leadership of projects and cross-functional teams, and to learn to empower employees they had previously been expected to limit and control.

Organizations tried team-based approaches, reorganizing, downsizing, and empowerment to improve performance. They became more concerned with quality, experimenting with Japanese management practices. Recognizing the changing work force and the need for new ways of working, they tried to implement programs in teamwork and empowerment.

However, most managers were trapped in old ways of thinking. They had not learned how to give up power, how to act as coaches rather than bosses. A general manager of a radio station recently wrote to a leadership consultant for help with the following predicament: ". . . I want to empower my people, but how can I be sure that the decisions they make are the right ones? I can't be looking over their shoulders all the time."[29] This manager recognizes the need for empowerment, but he's stuck in an old paradigm that says he is the one who has to remain in control. He can't let go. His mind is stuck in Era 2, micro-managing for a stable world, but his organization and its environment have moved on.

Macro Leadership in a Chaotic World *Era 4* represents the **facilitating leader** who has made the leap to giving up control in the traditional sense. Leaders learn to influence others through relationships. Managers learn to think in terms of "control with" others rather than "control over" others. To adapt to a chaotic world, leaders strive to create learning organizations, in which each person is intimately involved in identifying and solving problems so that the organization continues to grow and change to meet new challenges. This requires the full scope of leadership that goes far beyond rational management, or even team leadership. Era 4 leadership is what the majority of this book is about. Leaders learn to "control with" others by building relationships based on a shared vision and shaping the culture that can help achieve it. They develop shared values and outcomes rather than rely on hierarchical control, building whole organizations as communities of shared purpose and information. Leadership in Era 4 requires that leaders develop personal leader qualities and learn to unlock these qualities in others.

Like the "Great Man" of Era 1, Era 4 leaders focus on the big picture, but the image of leader as hero is becoming extinct. In Era 4, the vision is owned not by the leader, but by everyone. Leaders become servants who devote themselves to others and to the organization's vision. They give away power, ideas, and information. One example of an Era 4 leader is George Sztykiel, chairman of Spartan Motors, which builds chassis for fire trucks and motor homes. Sztykiel's attitude is reflected in his statement to new employees: "Welcome. We think this is a good corporation. It is run on the same principles that a family is, because we think that's the most effective way human beings have managed to get along." He adds that, "I am not the boss. I am the number one servant of this corporation."[30] Another company where the idea of leader as hero has died is Lucent Technologies, where Henry

ON THE CUTTING EDGE

Lucent Technologies

Henry Schacht and Richard McGinn might be expected to go at each other's throats after being named to lead Lucent Technologies, Inc., the $21 billion-a-year equipment maker that AT&T spun off a few years ago. Most people at AT&T had expected the top job to go to McGinn, a 27-year veteran of the company who had run Lucent's core business, Network Systems, and won the respect and loyalty of its workers and middle managers. Instead, McGinn had to be content with the Number Two spot, with the top job going to Henry Schacht, an outside director and retired chairman of Cummins Engine.

It wasn't what McGinn had in mind, and he bluntly told his new boss so. Yet, to the amazement of some, McGinn and Schacht are comfortably "leading as equals." While Schacht works Wall Street, McGinn coordinates operations and technology. When one is tied up, the other fills in wherever he's needed. Schacht never talks strategy or gives interviews without McGinn nearby, and when a local newspaper wanted a photo of Schacht alone, he told his public relations department, "That's not acceptable." At public functions, Schacht often defers to McGinn, and McGinn returns the favor.

Schacht practices what he preaches— "We're a team, and we're in this together." He sees himself as a servant of others and the company, and power-sharing is his forte. He co-managed Cummins Engine with a friend, James Henderson, and together they beat back a Japanese challenge in diesel engines and two takeover attempts in the late 1980s. Schacht then retired early so that Henderson could take over the top job and start grooming a younger leader. At Lucent, he sees a big part of his job as "helping to make Rich [McGinn] the best CEO he can be someday."

Together, the two leaders are tackling the huge challenges of making the spinoff successful—and they're doing it by involving everyone in the organization as much as possible. They stage huge pep rallies to boost morale. They let workers in on planning and financial targets. And they've distributed stock options to each worker. To reinforce togetherness, Lucent has no executive dining rooms— Schacht and McGinn stand in line to pay for their lunch just like everyone else and then they generally eat separately with lower-level workers.

Lucent Technologies faces many challenges, but these leaders are creating a culture to help the company face them with strength and solidarity. The two have been referred to as "a mother and a father," working together to lead the organization through turbulent times.

SOURCE: John J. Keller, "An AT&T Outsider and a Veteran Join to Run New Spinoff," *The Wall Street Journal*, October 14, 1996, A1, A9.

Schacht and Richard McGinn are learning to manage as equals, as described in the Cutting Edge box.

Implications

The flow from Great Man leadership to rational management to team leadership to facilitating leadership illustrates the trends in the larger world. The implication is that leadership reflects the era or context of the organization, industry, and society.

For people in organizations, or departments of organizations, that are relatively stable, the rational management approaches, such as behavioral theories of leadership and contingency theories of leadership, have great value. Great man notions of leadership may still be usable for entrepreneurs starting firms, or family-based firms that are not yet large, hierarchical, or bureaucratic.

Most organizations, however, are struggling with the transition from a stable to chaotic environment and the new kinds of leadership qualities needed in this circumstance. Thus, issues of team leadership, empowerment, and working horizontally in organizations are relevant to more and more people. And as organizations struggle to make the transition to being true learning organizations, the notion of facilitating leadership has great value. In a learning organization, leaders find it essential to develop a shared vision and to motivate and align people around that vision through relationships. Leaders can learn to unlock personal qualities and empower others to help the organization adapt to the shifting environment. This book will cover material relevant to all four eras shown in Exhibit 2.4, but special emphasis will be given to ways of dealing with chaotic environmental conditions, and the lessons learned from team leadership in Era 3 and facilitating leadership in our current Era 4.

Rest of the Book

The plan for this book reflects both the management versus leadership discussion summarized in Exhibit 2.3, and the four eras of leadership evolution summarized in Exhibit 2.4. The framework that guides the organization of the book is shown in Exhibit 2.5. Part I introduces leadership, its importance, ways to learn leadership, and the historical transition from leadership to management and back again to leadership. Part II will explore research perspectives on individual leadership, which include the Great Man, trait theories, behavior theories, and contingency theories that evolved through Eras 1 and 2 of stable conditions, particularly in North America. These theories are most relevant to micro leadership that deals with specific tasks and individuals. Then Parts III, IV, and V switch to leadership perspectives in Eras 3 and 4, which reflect leadership as distinct from management. Part III is about leadership vision and communicating the vision. Part IV is about aligning culture and values and the design of a learning organization. Part V is about the leader as relationship builder, which includes motivating and empowering others, leading teams, and embracing human diversity.

Part VI then deals with the personal side of leadership, which is the development of one's own leadership head and heart, understanding moral leadership and courage, and the role of followership. Good leaders make good followers, and followers often display personal leadership skills. The final section, Part VII, brings together all of these ideas for leading change and transformation. These chapters provide a specific model for leading change in organizations and the use of decisions, power, and influence to implement change.

Taken together, the sections and chapters paint a complete portrait of leadership as it has evolved to the present day and describe qualities that are relevant from

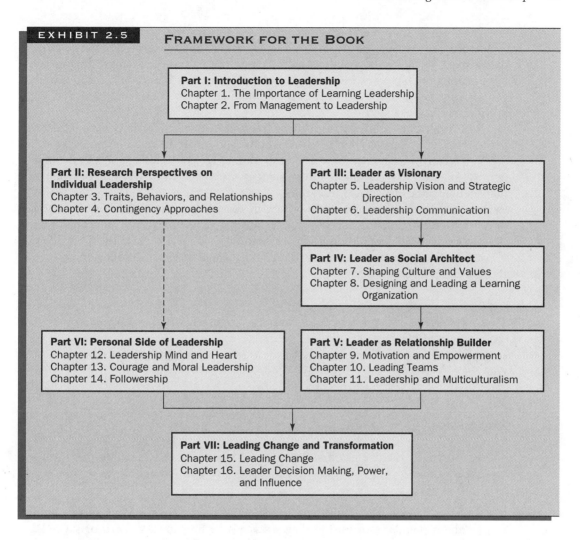

EXHIBIT 2.5 FRAMEWORK FOR THE BOOK

Part I: Introduction to Leadership
Chapter 1. The Importance of Learning Leadership
Chapter 2. From Management to Leadership

Part II: Research Perspectives on Individual Leadership
Chapter 3. Traits, Behaviors, and Relationships
Chapter 4. Contingency Approaches

Part III: Leader as Visionary
Chapter 5. Leadership Vision and Strategic Direction
Chapter 6. Leadership Communication

Part IV: Leader as Social Architect
Chapter 7. Shaping Culture and Values
Chapter 8. Designing and Leading a Learning Organization

Part VI: Personal Side of Leadership
Chapter 12. Leadership Mind and Heart
Chapter 13. Courage and Moral Leadership
Chapter 14. Followership

Part V: Leader as Relationship Builder
Chapter 9. Motivation and Empowerment
Chapter 10. Leading Teams
Chapter 11. Leadership and Multiculturalism

Part VII: Leading Change and Transformation
Chapter 15. Leading Change
Chapter 16. Leader Decision Making, Power, and Influence

today to the future. This book blends systematic research evidence with the real-world impact and experiences for which leadership is essential.

Summary and Interpretation

The most important point of this chapter is that leadership is a distinct focus of study and comprises a distinct set of qualities and skills that can have great impact on others and on organizations and institutions. Leadership is different from management, which is concerned with the five functions of planning, organizing, staffing, directing, and controlling. Research on the roles of management indicate that managers are involved in the areas of informational, interpersonal, and decisional activities. Management strives to maintain stability and improve efficiency.

Leadership, however, is about creating a vision for the future, designing social architecture that shapes culture and values, inspiring and motivating followers, developing personal qualities, and creating change, often dramatic change, to improve organization effectiveness. Leadership can be combined with management to achieve the greatest possible outcomes. Organizations need to be both managed and led, particularly in today's chaotic environment.

The evolution of leadership reflected a shift from stable to chaotic environments. Early leadership perspectives emphasized great men and the traits that enabled them to succeed in government, commerce, the military, or social movements. The next era was rational management that reflected the residue of scientific management and fit vertical hierarchies and bureaucracies. Because of the world's transition to a more chaotic environment in recent years, team leadership became important, with its potential for enabling horizontal organizations. And finally, the most recent era is about facilitating leadership, in which leaders use the skills of vision, alignment, and relationships to unlock personal qualities of followers in adaptive, learning organizations.

Key Terms

management	**vision**	**facilitating leader**
role	**position power**	

Discussion Questions

1. Which of the five original functions of management seems closest to leadership? Why do you think leadership was not considered a management function?

2. Is the "Great Man," or "hero" perspective on leadership alive today? Think about popular movies. Do they stress a lone individual as hero or savior? Give examples.

3. "Leadership is more concerned with people than is management." Do you agree? Discuss.

4. Compare Era 2 of rational management with Era 4 of facilitative leadership. Which approach do you feel most comfortable with for your career?

5. America is considered a highly individualistic society, so the transition to team leadership has been difficult. What do you consider the most difficult part of being in a team?

6. What does "control over" versus "control with" as a philosophy of leadership mean to you? Discuss.

7. What personal capacities should a person develop to be a good leader versus those developed to be a good manager?

8. Is it reasonable to believe that someone can be both a good manager and a good leader? Explain.

Leadership Development: Personal Feedback

Your Leadership Potential

Questions 1–6 below are about you right now. Questions 7–22 are about how you would like to be if you were the head of a major department at a corporation. Answer yes or no to indicate whether the item describes you accurately, or whether you would strive to perform each activity.

Now

1. When I have a number of tasks or homework to do, I set priorities and organize the work to meet the deadlines.

2. When I am involved in a serious disagreement, I hang in there and talk it out until it is completely resolved.

3. I would rather sit in front of my computer than spend a lot of time with people.

4. I reach out to include other people in activities or when there are discussions.

5. I know my long-term vision for career, family, and other activities.

6. When solving problems, I prefer analyzing things to working through a group of people.

Head of Major Department

1. I would help subordinates clarify goals and how to reach them.

2. I would give people a sense of mission and higher purpose.

3. I would make sure jobs get out on time.

4. I would scout for new product or service opportunities.

5. I would use policies and procedures as guides for problem solving.

6. I would promote unconventional beliefs and values.

7. I would give monetary rewards in exchange for high performance from subordinates.

8. I would inspire trust from everyone in the department.

9. I would work alone to accomplish important tasks.

10. I would suggest new and unique ways of doing things.

11. I would give credit to people who do their jobs well.

12. I would verbalize the higher values that I and the organization stand for.

13. I would establish procedures to help the department operate smoothly.

14. I would question the "why" of things to motivate others.

15. I would set reasonable limits on new approaches.

16. I would demonstrate social nonconformity as a way to facilitate change.

Scoring:

Count the number of yes answers to even numbered questions. Count the number of yes answers to odd number questions. Compare the two scores.

Interpretation:

The even numbered items represent behaviors and activities typical of leadership. Leaders are personally involved in shaping ideas, values, vision, and change. They often use an intuitive approach to develop fresh ideas and seek new directions for the department or organization. The odd numbered items are considered more traditional management activities. Managers respond to organizational problems in an impersonal way, make rational decisions, and work for stability and efficiency.

If you answered yes to more even-numbered than odd-numbered items, you may have potential leadership qualities. If you answered yes to more odd-numbered items, you may have management qualities. Leadership qualities can be developed or improved with awareness and experience.

Leadership Development: Case for Analysis

Airstar, Inc.

Airstar, Inc. manufactures, repairs, and overhauls pistons and jet engines for smaller, often privately owned aircraft. The company had a solid niche, and most managers had been with the founder for over 20 years. With the founder's death five years ago, Roy Morgan took over as president at Airstar. Mr. Morgan has called you in as a consultant.

Your research indicates that this industry is changing rapidly. Airstar is feeling encroachment of huge conglomerates like General Electric and Pratt & Whitney, and its backlog of orders is the lowest in several years. The company has always been known for its superior quality, safety, and customer service. However, it has never been under threat before, and senior managers are not sure which direction to take. They have considered potential acquisitions, imports and exports, more research, and additional repair lines. The organization is becoming more chaotic, which is frustrating Morgan and his vice presidents.

Before a meeting with his team, he confides to you, "Organizing is supposed to be easy. For maximum efficiency, work should be divided into simple, logical, routine tasks. These business tasks can be grouped by similar kinds of work characteristics and arranged within an organization under a particularly suited executive. So why are we having so many problems with our executives?"

Morgan met with several of his trusted corporate officers in the executive dining room to discuss what was happening to corporate leadership at Airstar. Morgan went on to explain that he was really becoming concerned with the situation. There have been outright conflicts between the vice president of marketing and the controller over merger and acquisition opportunities. There have been many instances of duplication of work, with corporate officers trying to outmaneuver each other.

"Communications are atrocious," Morgan said to the others. "Why, I didn't even get a copy of the export finance report until my secretary made an effort to find one for me. My basis for evaluation and appraisal of corporate executive performance is fast becoming obsolete. Everyone has been working up their own job descriptions, and they all include overlapping responsibilities. Changes and decisions are being made on the basis of expediency and are perpetuating too many mistakes. We must take a good look at these organizational realities and correct the situation immediately."

Jim Robinson, vice president of manufacturing, pointed out to Morgan that Airstar is not really following the "principles of good organization." "For instance," explained Robinson, "let's review what we should be practicing as administrators." Some of the principles Robinson believed they should be following are:

1. Determine the objectives, policies, programs, and plans that will best achieve the desired results for our company.

2. Determine the various business tasks to be done.

3. Divide the business tasks into a logical and understandable organizational structure.

4. Determine the suitable personnel to occupy positions within the organizational structure.

5. Define the responsibility and authority of each supervisor clearly in writing.

6. Keep the number of kinds of levels of authority at a minimum.

Robinson proposed that the group study the corporate organizational chart, as well as the various corporate business tasks. After reviewing the corporate organizational chart, Robinson, Morgan, and the others agreed that the number and kinds of formal corporate authority were logical and not much different from other corporations. The group then listed the various corporate business tasks that went on within Airstar.

Robinson continued, "How did we ever decide who should handle mergers or acquisitions?" Morgan answered, "I guess it just occurred over time that the vice president of marketing should have the responsibility." "But," Robinson queried, "where is it written down? How would the controller know it?" "Aha!" Morgan exclaimed. "It looks like I'm part of the problem. There isn't anything in writing. Tasks were assigned superficially, as they became problems. This has all been rather informal. I'll establish a group to decide who should have responsibility for what so things can return to our previous level of efficiency."

Questions

1. What is your reaction to this conversation? What would you say to Morgan to help him lead the organization?

2. In what era (Exhibit 2.4) are these managers? Explain.

3. If you were to take over as president of Airstar, what would you do first? Second? Third?

SOURCE: Adapted from Bernard A. Deitzer and Karl A. Shilliff, *Contemporary Management Incidents* (Columbus, OH: Grid, Inc., 1977), 43–46. Reprinted by permission of John Wiley & Sons, Inc.

References

[1] "Southwest Airlines' Herb Kelleher: Unorthodoxy at Work," an interview with William G. Lee, *Management Review*, January 1995, 9–12.

[2] This case is based on Kenneth Labich, "Is Herb Kelleher America's Best CEO?" *Fortune*, May 2, 1994, 44–52; Brenda Paik Sunoo, "How Fun Flies at Southwest Airlines," *Personnel Journal*, June 1995, 62–73; Kristin Dunlap Godsey, "Slow Climb to New Heights: Combine Strict Discipline with Goofy Antics and Make Billions," *Success*, October 1996, 20–26; and "Southwest Airlines' Herb Kelleher: Unorthodoxy at Work," an interview with William G. Lee, *Management Review*, January 1995, 9–12. Direct quotes not otherwise credited are from Labich, "Is Herb Kelleher America's Best CEO?"

[3] Justin Martin, "Tomorrow's CEOs," *Fortune*, June 24, 1996, 76–90.

[4] Henry Mintzberg, *The Nature of Managerial Work* (New York: Harper & Row, 1973), and Lance B. Kurke and Howard E. Aldrich, "Mintzberg Was Right!: A Replication and Extention of *The Nature of Managerial Work*," *Management Science* 29 (1983): 975–984.

[5] Henry Mintzberg, "Rounding Out the Manager's Job," *Sloan Management Review* (Fall, 1994): 11–26.

[6] Martha H. Peak, "Anti-Manager Named Manager of the Year," *Management Review*, October 1991, 7.

[7] Robert E. Coffey, Curtis W. Cook, and Philip W. Hunsaker, *Management and Organizational Behavior* (Burr Ridge, IL: Richard D. Irwin, 1994), 287–288.

[8] This section is based largely on John P. Kotter, *A Force for Change: How Leadership Differs from Management* (New York: The Free Press, 1990), 3–18.

[9] *Leadership, A Forum Issues Special Report* (Boston, MA: The Forum Corporation, 1990), 13.

[10] Charles Handy, *The Age of Paradox* (Boston, MA: Harvard Business School Press, 1994), 278; Ronald B. Lieber, "Why Employees Love These Companies," *Fortune*, January 12, 1998, 72–74.

[11] *Leadership: A Forum Issues Special Report* (Boston, MA: The Forum Corporation, 1990), 15.

[12] James Kaplan, "Amateur's Hour," *Working Woman*, October 1997, 28–33.

[13]John P. Kotter, *Leading Change* (Boston, MA: Harvard Business School Press, 1996), 26.

[14]Joseph C. Rost, *Leadership for the Twenty-First Century* (Westport, CN: Praeger, 1993), 145–146.

[15]Warren Bennis, *Why Leaders Can't Lead* (San Francisco: Jossey-Bass, 1989).

[16]Stratford Sherman, "How Tomorrow's Best Leaders Are Learning Their Stuff," *Fortune*, November 27, 1995, 90–102.

[17]Bennis, *Why Leaders Can't Lead.*

[18]Sherman, "How Tomorrow's Best Leaders Are Learning Their Stuff."

[19]Abraham Zaleznik, "Managers and Leaders: Are They Different?" *Harvard Business Review*, March–April 1992, 126–135.

[20]Bennis, *Why Leaders Can't Lead.*

[21]Sherman, "How Tomorrow's Best Leaders Are Learning Their Stuff."

[22]James Kaplan, "Amateur's Hour," *Working Woman*, October 1997, 28–33.

[23]Oren Harari, "The Essence of Leadership," *Management Review*, November 1991, 63.

[24]Zaleznik, "Managers and Leaders: Are They Different?"

[25]Joseph B. White, "How a Creaky Factory Got Off the Hit List, Won Respect at Last," *The Wall Street Journal*, December 26, 1996, A1, A2.

[26]Personal communication from George Starcher and Dorothy Marcic, 1994.

[27]The discussion of micro and macro is based on Ed Kur, "Developing Leadership in Organizations: A Continuum of Choices," *Journal of Management Inquiry* 4, no. 2 (June 1995): 198–206.

[28]Shelly Branch, "What's Eating McDonald's?" *Fortune*, October 13, 1997, 122–125.

[29]Oren Harari, "Stop Empowering Your People," *Management Review*, February 1997, 48–51.

[30]Edward O. Welles, "The Shape of Things to Come," *Inc.*, February 1992, 66–74.

PART TWO

Research Perspectives on Individual Leadership

Chapter 3
Traits, Behaviors, and Relationships

Chapter 4
Contingency Approaches

3

Traits, Behaviors, and Relationships

- **The Trait Approach**   65

- **Behavior Approaches**   69

- **Dyadic Approaches**   78

- **Leadership Spotlights:**
  J. Robert Oppenheimer   68
  Felton Elementary School   72
  Chrysler Canada   74

- **Leader's Bookshelf:**
  *Moving Mountains: Lessons in Leadership and
       Logistics from the Gulf War*   70

- **Leadership Development: Personal Feedback**
  Assertiveness Questionnaire   86

- **Leadership Development: Case for Analysis**
  Consolidated Products   87

Your Leadership Challenge

After reading this chapter, you should be able to:

- Identify personal traits and characteristics that are associated with effective leaders.

- Recognize autocratic versus democratic leadership behavior and the impact of each.

- Know the distinction between people-oriented and task-oriented leadership behavior and when each should be used.

- Understand how dyadic theories of leadership have broadened the understanding of relationships between leaders and followers, and recognize how to build partnerships for greater effectiveness.

The publication of her book, *Coming of Age in Samoa,* in 1929 brought anthropologist Margaret Mead national recognition at a time when female scholars were a rare commodity. Although she was not yet 30, Mead had already spent extended periods of time studying South Seas cultures, and she focused on nontraditional topics such as puberty and child rearing. The relative liveliness of her subject matter and her straightforward yet engaging prose proved popular among the general public—an audience rarely reached by scholars. Furthermore, Mead revealed a contrast in her book between the carefree, open life of Samoan adolescents and the stormy, rebellious adolescent experience of their U.S. counterparts. The book proposed to Americans that the experience of teenagers was linked to the attitudes and actions of the society that surrounded them. Her popularity with the public enabled her influence to extend beyond academic boundaries and provided the literate society-at-large with a backdrop for examining their own behaviors. In addition, the scientific community took notice of her work because it challenged the prevalent theory that biology determined the behavior of human beings.

Over the course of her career, Mead attracted many followers. Mead advocated new ways of thinking and an interdisciplinary approach to the study of human nature. She became a public figure, an ambassador for anthropology. She published 50 books, gave hundreds of speeches, served on countless panels and committees, and interacted with diverse groups, large and small. She collected friends and followers effortlessly, shaping the behaviors, thinking, and feelings of thousands of individuals.

Throughout her life she pursued the mission that knowledge would unify human nature and validate diverse ways of living. In an effort to transmit the importance of disappearing cultures, she pioneered methods of filming and photographing their rituals and artwork. She also continued to contrast other ways of life with that of the United States. She revealed the Mundugumor and Arapesh cultures, in which men and women were expected to behave the same way, and the Tchambuli culture, in which women were aggressive and men were meek. Studies such as these, like that of the Samoan adolescents, challenged the stereotypes held by Americans regarding such things as gender roles. She showed that disadvantaged groups are not born that way, and that there is no such thing as one "natural" way of life.[1]

As an accessible scholar with a productive career that spanned nearly four decades, Mead led the discipline of anthropology into the public spotlight, altered the way Americans viewed themselves, gave legitimacy to other cultures, gave anthropology additional tools of research, and ultimately influenced the course of scientific thought. Several personal attributes contributed to Mead's ascent to this leadership role. For example, she had the courage to break with tradition by examining topics that others had not considered. Furthermore, Mead's self-confidence was evident in the writing and publication of her first book, which was decidedly challenging to scientific authority and unorthodox in its mass appeal presentation. As the first publication of a young scholar, her Samoan work was a risky endeavor. Yet this book distinguished her from other social scientists. She also had the ability to grasp and remember detailed patterns of culture, a trait that doubtlessly legitimized her expertise to the public when she spoke publicly.

In considering Mead's influence it seems evident that characteristics such as courage, self-confidence, intelligence, and a willingness to take risks are part of the personality that made her a leader. Indeed, personal traits are what captured the imagination of the earliest leadership researchers. Many leaders have possessed traits that researchers believe affected their leadership impact. For example, China's current president, Jiang Zemin, has gained favor since his appointment by his ability to discern the needs of constituents, thereby granting them desired and appropriate resources. Margaret Thatcher, as Prime Minister of Great Britain, was known for her traits of self-confidence, sense of personal identity, and belief in her own philosophy of government.[2]

Moreover, successful leaders display traits through patterns in their behavior. Consequently, many researchers have examined the behavior of leaders to determine what behavioral features comprised leadership style and how particular behaviors related to effective leadership. Later research specified behavior between a leader and each distinct follower, differentiating one-on-one behavior from leader-to-group behavior.

This chapter provides an overview of the initial leadership research in the 20th century. We will examine the evolution of the trait approach and the behavior approach, and introduce the dyadic theory of leadership. The path illuminated by the research into leader traits and behaviors is a foundation for the field of leadership studies and still enjoys remarkable dynamism today for explaining leader success or failure.

The Trait Approach

Early efforts to understand leadership success focused on the leader's personal traits. **Traits** are the distinguishing personal characteristics of a leader, such as intelligence, values, self-confidence, and appearance. Research early in this century examined leaders who had achieved a level of greatness, and hence became known as the Great Man approach. Fundamental to this theory was the idea that some people are born with traits that make them natural leaders. The **Great Man approach** sought to identify the traits leaders possessed that distinguished them from people who were not leaders. Generally, research found only a weak relationship between personal traits and leader success.[3] For example, three football coaches—Tom Osborne at Nebraska, Bobby Bowden at Florida State, and Joe Paterno at Penn State—have different personality traits, but all are successful leaders of their football teams. Indeed, the diversity of traits that effective leaders possess indicates that leadership ability is not necessarily a genetic endowment.

Nevertheless, with the advancement of the field of psychology during the 1940s and 1950s, trait approach researchers began to use aptitude and psychological tests to examine a broad range of personal attributes. Initially, researchers focused on isolating the characteristics that leaders possessed and that non-leaders did not possess. By measuring the traits of successful leaders in correlation to effective leadership, it might be possible to compile a checklist of leadership attributes.

Researchers began by examining personality traits such as creativity and self-confidence, physical traits such as age and energy-level, abilities such as knowledge and fluency of speech, social characteristics such as popularity and sociability, and work-related characteristics such as the desire to excel and persistence against obstacles. Exhibit 3.1 presents a sample of the traits and their respective categories that have comprised trait approach research. Effective leaders were often identified by exceptional follower performance, or by a high status position within an organization and a salary that exceeded that of one's peers.[4]

In a 1948 literature review[5] Stogdill examined over 100 studies based on the trait approach. He uncovered several traits that appeared consistent with effective leadership, including a basic willingness to be in a position of control and dominance over others, and being attuned to the needs of others. While his review revealed that several traits appeared in effective leaders, the importance of a particular trait was often relative to another factor—the situation. Initiative, for example,

EXHIBIT 3.1	PERSONAL CHARACTERISTICS OF LEADERS	
Physical characteristics	**Personality**	**Social characteristics**
Activity	Alertness	Ability to enlist cooperation
Energy	Originality, creativity	Cooperativeness
Social background	Personal integrity, ethical conduct	Popularity, prestige
Mobility	Self-confidence	Sociability, interpersonal skills
Intelligence and ability	**Work-related characteristics**	
Judgment, decisiveness	Achievement drive, desire to excel	Social participation
Knowledge	Drive for responsibility	Tact, diplomacy
Fluency of speech	Responsibility in pursuit of goals	
	Task orientation	

SOURCE: Adapted from Bernard M. Bass, *Stogdill's Handbook of Leadership*, rev. ed., (New York: Free Press, 1981), 75–76. This adaptation appeared in R. Albanese and D. D. Van Fleet, *Organizational Behavior: A Managerial Viewpoint* (Hinsdale, IL: The Dryden Press, 1983).

may contribute to the success of a leader in one situation, but it may be irrelevant to a leader in another situation. Thus, possessing the characteristics identified by Stogdill is no guarantee for success.

Although many researchers desisted their efforts under the trait approach in light of Stogdill's finding that leadership traits were less than universal, other researchers continued with expanded trait lists and research projects. Stogdill's subsequent review 25 years later revealed many of the same traits as well as several new ones that appeared to be consistent with successful leadership.[6] The additional characteristics included, for example, administrative skill, aggressiveness, and independence. However, Stogdill's research again concluded that the value of particular traits varied with the organizational situation. For example, one study suggested the individual traits gain more expression in situations that are ill defined, while highly structured situations inhibit the expression of traits from individual leaders.[7] In other words, the trait of creativity is less viable in a highly bureaucratic organization than in a situation in which an entrepreneur is developing a new business.

Recent researchers still contend that some traits are essential to effective leadership, but only in combination with other factors.[8] The Living Leadership box considers the notion that the traits of an individual have a great bearing on leadership outcomes. Three of the traits deemed essential are self-confidence, honesty, and drive.

Self-Confidence   The trait of **self-confidence** refers to the degree to which one is self-assured in his or her own judgments, decision making, ideas, and capabilities. A leader with a positive self-image, and who displays certainty about his or her own

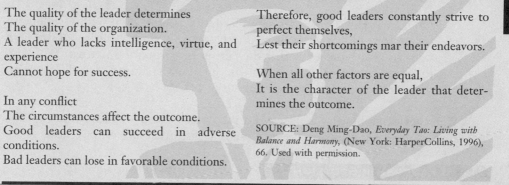

Leader

The quality of the leader determines
The quality of the organization.
A leader who lacks intelligence, virtue, and experience
Cannot hope for success.

In any conflict
The circumstances affect the outcome.
Good leaders can succeed in adverse conditions.
Bad leaders can lose in favorable conditions.

Therefore, good leaders constantly strive to perfect themselves,
Lest their shortcomings mar their endeavors.

When all other factors are equal,
It is the character of the leader that determines the outcome.

SOURCE: Deng Ming-Dao, *Everyday Tao: Living with Balance and Harmony*, (New York: HarperCollins, 1996), 66. Used with permission.

ability, fosters confidence among followers, gains respect and admiration, and meets challenges. The confidence a leader displays and develops creates commitment among followers for the mission at hand.

Active leaders need self-confidence. Leaders initiate changes and they often make decisions without adequate information. Problems are solved continuously. Without the confidence to move forward and believe things will be okay, even if an occasional decision is wrong, leaders could be paralyzed into inaction. Setbacks have to be overcome. Risks have to be taken. Competing points of view have to be managed, with some people left unsatisfied. Self-confidence is the one trait that enables a leader to face all these challenges.[9]

In terms of self-confidence, few leaders display the trait to the degree that Franklin Delano Roosevelt did, even before he became one of the most influential American presidents of the century. While he was still a law clerk, Roosevelt had mapped out his political career and shared his outline with his fellow clerks. Included in his plan were a position in the state legislature, Assistant Secretary of the Navy, becoming Governor, and eventually president of the United States. In retrospect, his self-confidence paid off, and quite accurately as he did, in fact, hold each of those positions despite an unforeseen and crippling bout with polio.[10]

Honesty/Integrity   **Honesty** refers to truthfulness and nondeception. It implies an openness that subordinates welcome. Integrity means that one is whole, so one's actions are in keeping with one's words. By espousing convictions and modeling them through daily action, leaders command respect and loyalty. These virtues are the foundation of trust between leaders and followers. Today people tend to be highly informed and wary of authority and the deceptive use of power. Possessing the traits of honesty and integrity is essential to minimize skepticism and to build productive relationships.

Successful leaders have been found to be highly consistent, doing exactly what they say they will do when they say they will do it. Successful leaders are easy to trust. They have basic principles and consistently apply them. One survey of 1,500 managers asked the values most desired in leaders. Integrity was the most important characteristic. The authors concluded:

> Honesty is absolutely essential to leadership. After all, if we are willing to follow someone, whether it be into battle or into the boardroom, we first want to assure ourselves that the person is worthy of our trust. We want to know that he or she is being truthful, ethical, and principled. We want to be fully confident in the integrity of our leaders.[11]

Consider the following example of a prominent leader of this century to illustrate how the perceived loss of integrity can diminish trust and effectiveness.

LEADERSHIP SPOTLIGHT   J. ROBERT OPPENHEIMER

J. Robert Oppenheimer was a brilliant physicist who directed the Center for Advanced Study and led the Manhattan Project to develop an atomic bomb. His colleagues lauded his performance at Los Alamos, where he was in charge of 4,500 workers involved in the highly technical, top-secret atomic bomb research—a task that was successfully completed. Despite his success in a leadership position of enormous importance, his human sympathies and attempts to educate the public on the possible negative consequences of atomic energy led to a federal hearing to determine his national loyalty. Oppenheimer's public statements were at times complex and confusing, and he seemed as concerned about unity with other countries as with winning wars. He wouldn't apologize for his "mistakes," so the federal inquiry eventually stripped him of his security clearance. Though Oppenheimer continued at the Center, his leadership status was forever diminished. The inquiry caused people throughout the nation to question his integrity and destroyed the trust necessary for him to continue to lead the direction of nuclear arms development for the government.[12]

Drive   **Drive** refers to high motivation that creates a high effort level by a leader. Leaders with drive seek achievement, have energy and tenacity, and are frequently seen to have ambition and initiative to achieve their goals. Leaders rise to the top often because they actively pursue goals. Ambition enables them to set challenging goals and take initiative to achieve those goals.[13]

A strong drive is associated with high energy. Leaders work long hours over many years. They have stamina and are vigorous and full of life in order to handle the pace, the demands, and the challenges of leadership. Leaders often are responsible for initiating new projects as well as guiding projects to successful completion. The following sketch illustrates the kind of drive that predicts successful leadership.

> "I want to be able to demonstrate the things I learned in college and get to the top," said Al, "maybe even be president. I expect to work hard and be at the third level within five years, and to rise to much higher levels in the years beyond. I am specifically working on my MBA to aid in my

advancement. If I am thwarted on advancement, or find the challenges lacking, I'll leave the company."[14]

Traits such as drive, self-confidence and honesty have great value for leaders. A vivid example of how leader traits can be important to success is the Leader's Bookshelf about General Pagonis's experience from the Persian Gulf War. More recently, research has explored how leader behavior contributes to the success or failure of leadership.

Behavior Approaches

The behavior approach says that anyone who adopts the appropriate behavior can be a good leader. Diverse research programs on leadership behavior sought to uncover the behaviors that leaders engage in rather than what traits a leader possesses. Behaviors can be learned more readily than traits, enabling leadership to be accessible to all.

Autocratic versus Democratic Leadership

One study that served as a precursor to the behavior approach recognized autocratic and democratic leadership styles. An **autocratic** leader is one who tends to centralize authority and derive power from position, control of rewards, and coercion. A **democratic** leader delegates authority to others, encourages participation, relies on subordinates' knowledge for completion of tasks, and depends on subordinate respect for influence.

The first studies on these leadership behaviors were conducted at Iowa State University by Kurt Lewin and his associates.[15] The research included groups of children, each with its own designated adult leader who was instructed to act in either an autocratic or democratic style. These experiments produced some interesting findings. The groups with autocratic leaders performed highly so long as the leader was present to supervise them. However, group members were displeased with the close, autocratic style of leadership, and feelings of hostility frequently arose. The performance of groups who were assigned democratic leaders was almost as good, and these groups were characterized by positive feelings rather than hostility. In addition, under the democratic style of leadership, group members performed well even when the leader was absent. The participative techniques and majority rule decision making used by the democratic leader trained and involved the group members so that they performed well with or without the leader present. These characteristics of democratic leadership may partly explain why the empowerment of employees is a popular trend in companies today.

This early work implied that leaders were either autocratic or democratic in their approach. However, further work by Tannenbaum and Schmidt indicated that leadership behavior could exist on a continuum reflecting different amounts of employee participation.[16] Thus, one leader might be autocratic (boss-centered),

Moving Mountains: Lessons in Leadership and Logistics from the Gulf War
Lt. General William G. Pagonis with Jeffrey L. Cruikshank

Moving Mountains presents lessons in leadership gleaned through the author's experience in the Persian Gulf War. Lieutenant General William G. Pagonis led the U.S. Army's 22nd Support Command—the 40,000 men and women who ran the theater logistics for the Persian Gulf War during three phases of operation: Desert Shield (buildup), Desert Storm (ground war), and Desert Farewell (redeployment). It was a remarkable feat by any standard and could not have been accomplished without strong leadership.

The Essential Traits of Leadership
Pagonis believes that to lead successfully, a person must demonstrate two essential and interrelated traits: expertise and empathy.

Expertise
Most leaders first achieve mastery in a particular functional area, such as logistics. Expertise grows out of hard work. Pagonis recalls many instances in his army career where he grumbled his way through an assignment only to realize later how much he'd learned. He chafed at a stint of desk-bound research analyzing logistics-over-the-shore (LOTS) vehicles. Twenty years later, he found himself in charge of a flotilla of LOTS ships, which plied the coast of Saudi Arabia. Because Pagonis had helped specify their design, he knew exactly how to use those vessels. This expertise helped him do his job well and also reinforced his leadership in the eyes of his subordinates.

Empathy
Expertise is not enough—only expertise combined with empathy commands the full respect and trust of followers. To demonstrate empathy, Pagonis recalled his days as a newsboy, when he had to fight the older boys to break into the prime bar and restaurant territory. When Pagonis became one of the "big boys," he empathized with the younger kids based on his recollection of how it felt to get knocked around. He earned a leader's respect by negotiating an arrangement that would give the younger boys a chance to succeed and grow while not cutting too deeply into the profits of the veteran newsboys. Many years later, in the Gulf War, Pagonis found his ability to empathize with Arab customs an "absolutely vital quality."

Pagonis emphasizes that leaders aren't born with these traits. Expertise and empathy are deliberately cultivated. Personal development is the building block of leadership.

The Steps of Leadership
- Know Yourself. Leaders have to know their strengths and weaknesses as well as understand the personal characteristics that make them who they are. For example, Pagonis says that he knows "from years of self-analysis that I am a creature of habit. I love order. . . . This is either a useful trait or a not-so-useful trait, depending on the circumstances."
- Learn How to Listen. Leaders develop good listening skills and put them into practice. As Pagonis says, "There's no magic [to effective listening]. Taking notes can prevent your mind from wandering. Taking a course in listening skills may be a great investment. And, as a wise commanding officer used to say to me, 'Never pass up the opportunity to remain silent.'"
- Understand the Mission. The leader has to know what needs to be accomplished in order to channel his or her expertise effectively. "Knowing oneself is one kind of hard work. Knowing the mission is a different kind of hard work."

Conclusion
Pagonis stresses that leaders must be visible and they must "be real." In addition, each leader can emphasize positive traits in his or her unique personality, such as a sense of humor or a kind disposition, that can help make a genuine connection with followers.

Moving Mountains by Lt. General William G. Pagonis is published by Harvard Business School Press.

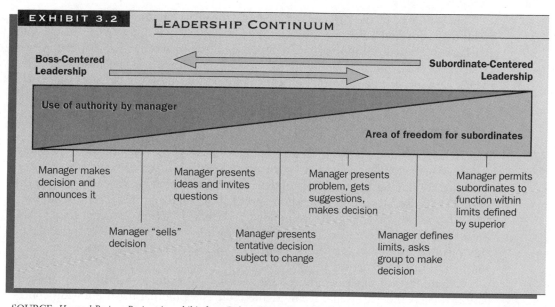

EXHIBIT 3.2 **LEADERSHIP CONTINUUM**

Boss-Centered Leadership ← → Subordinate-Centered Leadership

Use of authority by manager

Area of freedom for subordinates

Manager makes decision and announces it

Manager "sells" decision

Manager presents ideas and invites questions

Manager presents tentative decision subject to change

Manager presents problem, gets suggestions, makes decision

Manager defines limits, asks group to make decision

Manager permits subordinates to function within limits defined by superior

SOURCE: *Harvard Business Review*. An exhibit from Robert Tannenbaum and Warren Schmidt, "How to Choose a Leadership Pattern" (May–June 1973). Copyright © 1973 by the president and Fellows of Harvard College.

another democratic (subordinate-centered), and a third a mix of the two styles. The leadership continuum is illustrated in Exhibit 3.2.

Tannenbaum and Schmidt also suggested that the extent to which leaders should be boss-centered or subordinate-centered depended on organizational circumstances, and that leaders might adjust their behaviors to fit the circumstances. For example, if there is time pressure on a leader or if it takes too long for subordinates to learn how to make decisions, the leader will tend to use an autocratic style. When subordinates are able to learn decision-making skills readily, a participative style can be used. Also, the greater the skill difference, the more autocratic the leader approach, because it is difficult to bring subordinates up to the leader's expertise level.[17] But followers may not be as independent when the leader is autocratic.

For example, Stephen Fleming used an autocratic style as a marketing manager in an oil products company. He was being groomed for a higher position because his department performed so well. However, this meant time spent at meetings away from his group, and performance declined because the subordinates had not learned to function independently. In contrast, Dorothy Roberts, CEO of Echo Scarves, behaves toward people by showing respect and courtesy. Decision making is shared by representatives of design, sales, marketing, and operations. In the traditionally tough fashion industry, her nice-guy leadership behavior permeates the entire company, creating a unique corporate culture that is open, honest, and supportive of employees. Company prosperity is centered on treating people well. Roberts' leadership behavior creates satisfied employees who in turn create satisfied customers, which is certainly correct in her company situation.[18]

The findings of the original Iowa State University studies indicated that leadership behavior had a definite effect on outcomes such as follower performance and satisfaction. Equally important was the recognition that effective leadership was reflected in behavior, not simply by what personality traits a leader possessed. This recognition provided a focus for subsequent studies based on the behavior approach.

Ohio State Studies

Researchers at Ohio State University conducted surveys to establish the dimensions of leader behavior. Narrowing a list of nearly 2,000 leader behaviors into a questionnaire containing 150 examples of definitive leader behaviors, they developed the Leader Behavior Description Questionnaire (LBDQ) and administered it to employees.[19] Hundreds of employees responded to behavior examples according to the degree to which their leaders engaged in the various behaviors. The analysis of ratings resulted in two wide-ranging categories of leader behavior types, later called consideration and initiating structure.

Consideration describes the extent to which a leader is sensitive to subordinates, respects their ideas and feelings, and establishes mutual trust. Showing appreciation, listening carefully to problems, and seeking input from subordinates regarding important decisions are all examples of consideration behaviors.

Initiating structure describes the extent to which a leader is task oriented and directs subordinates' work activities toward goal achievement. This type of leader behavior includes directing tasks, working people hard, planning, providing explicit schedules for work activities, and ruling with an iron hand.

While many leaders fall along a continuum comprising both consideration and initiating structure behaviors, these behavior categories are independent of one another. In other words, a leader can display a high degree of both behavior types, or a low degree of both behavior types. Additionally, a leader might demonstrate high consideration and low initiating structure, or low consideration and high initiating structure behavior. Research indicates that all four of these leader style combinations can be effective.[20] The following example illustrates a leader who demonstrates both high consideration and high initiating structure.

LEADERSHIP SPOTLIGHT   **FELTON ELEMENTARY SCHOOL**

Principal Jessie Sullivan faced a daunting challenge. She was leader of Felton Elementary School in Los Angeles County. Her students were among the poorest in California, with 89 percent qualifying for free lunches, and 86 percent had limited English proficiency. Her first initiative was to work with teachers to set goals for higher academic standards. She also developed teacher committees to establish academic goals and expectations for the children. An example goal for fifth-grade-level reading was: "Students are expected to independently read a wide range of age-appropriate materials; engage in oral discussion with teachers and classmates about stories and books they've read; and make generalizations and begin to judge the validity of the writer's generalizations." Many teachers were skeptical about achieving these goals with disadvantaged students, but agreed to try.

One reason Principal Sullivan won over the teachers was that she included them in each stage of defining goals, implementing goals, and evaluating outcomes. Skepticism and mistrust were removed because she did not force goals onto anyone, enabling teachers to "buy in" to the changes.

What kind of impact has Sullivan's leader behavior had? In only a couple of years, the students who could write a clear and complete summary and explain the theme of a work of literature jumped from 6 percent to 33 percent. Grade-level reading increased from 30 percent to 51 percent of students. Student achievement is clearly up, and Felton Elementary School has also seen a steady improvement in school climate, teaching, and attitude. Leadership by Principal Jessie Sullivan was the most important factor in this school reform.[21]

In this example, Principal Sullivan used initiating structure behavior to clarify goals and set performance standards to be achieved. The high level of initiating structure was essential to move the school toward higher standards. She also demonstrated consideration behavior by anticipating the reaction of teachers and allowing them to participate in how these goals could be met and measured. Thus, Sullivan is a "high-high" leader by exhibiting high levels of both types of leader behaviors.

Additional studies that correlated the two leader behavior types and impact on subordinates initially demonstrated that "considerate" supervisors had a more positive impact on subordinate satisfaction than did "structuring" supervisors.[22] For example, when leader effectiveness was defined by voluntary turnover or amount of grievances filed by subordinates, considerate leaders generated less turnover and grievances. But research that utilized performance criteria, such as group output and productivity, showed leader initiating structure behavior was rated more effective. Other studies involving aircraft commanders and university department heads revealed that leaders rated effective by subordinates exhibited a high level of both consideration and initiating structure behaviors, while leaders rated less effective displayed low levels of both behavior styles.[23]

University of Michigan Studies

Studies at the University of Michigan took a different approach by directly comparing the behavior of effective and ineffective supervisors.[24] The effectiveness of leaders was determined by productivity of the subordinate group. Initial field studies and interviews at various job sites gave way to a questionnaire not unlike the LBDQ, called the Survey of Organizations.[25]

Over time, the Michigan researchers established two types of leadership behavior, each type consisting of two dimensions.[26] First, **employee-centered** leaders display a focus on the human needs of their subordinates. Leader support and interaction facilitation are the two underlying dimensions of employee-centered behavior. This means that in addition to demonstrating support for their subordinates, employee-centered leaders facilitate positive interaction among followers and seek to minimize conflict. The employee-centered style of leadership roughly corresponds to the Ohio State concept of consideration. Jamie Bonini succeeded in his first management position by being an employee-centered leader.

LEADERSHIP SPOTLIGHT　　　CHRYSLER CANADA

Jamie Bonini was a 33-year-old "academic nerd" who was named manager of a large Chrysler manufacturing plant near Windsor Ontario. Being young and less experienced than some of the seasoned staffers who were passed over for the promotion, Bonini knew the first thing he had to do was get on their good side. So he admitted his weakness and asked for their help. Then he focused his attention on the needs of the workers. He taught foremen that intimidation was no longer acceptable. He had the dock heaters repaired to protect the outdoor dock loaders from cold weather. Although he also initiated a needed overhaul of the manufacturing system, Bonini cited the outmoded process as the cause of most errors, not the workers themselves. He united his staff during a retreat in which they went through pole climbing and rope climbing exercises together and led each other around blindfolded, learning to trust. Next, he changed policy to allow workers greater access to phones and even cleaned up the restrooms. The new culture pleased the Canadian Auto Workers Union.

Seeing Bonini, a manager, on the floor among the workers was a strange sight, but a welcome one, as were his technology initiatives, which improved the working conditions and the production process. Bonini is one of a new generation of plant managers who are as quick to apply touchy-feely leadership techniques as they are to use their advanced technical degrees.[27]

Bonini's behavior was that of an employee-centered leader. He demonstrated great concern for managers and employees at the Chrysler plant that he managed. In fact, most of his activities directly addressed the human needs of the workers, whether it was to eliminate the blame for production errors or simply clean the bathrooms.

The **job-centered** leader, on the other hand, directs activities toward efficiency, cost-cutting, and scheduling. Goal emphasis and work facilitation are dimensions of this leadership behavior. By focusing on reaching task goals and facilitating the structure of tasks, job-centered behavior approximates that of initiating structure.

However, unlike the consideration and initiating structure defined by the Ohio State studies, Michigan researchers considered employee-centered leadership and job-centered leadership to be distinct styles in opposition to one another. A leader is identifiable by behavior characteristic of one or the other style, but not both. Another hallmark of later Michigan studies is the acknowledgment that often the behaviors of goal emphasis, work facilitation, support, and interaction facilitation can be meaningfully performed by a subordinate's peers, rather than only by the designated leader. Other people in the group could supply these behaviors, which enhanced performance.[28]

In addition, while leadership behavior was demonstrated to affect the performance and satisfaction of subordinates, performance was also influenced by other factors related to the situation within which leaders and subordinates worked. The situation will be explored in the next chapter.

The Leadership Grid

Blake and Mouton of the University of Texas proposed a two-dimensional leadership theory called **The Leadership Grid** that builds on the work of the Ohio State and Michigan studies.[29] Based on a week-long seminar, researchers rated leaders on a scale of one to nine according to two criteria: the concern for people and the concern for production. The scores for these criteria are plotted on a grid with an axis corresponding to each concern. The two-dimensional model and seven major leadership styles are depicted in Exhibit 3.3.

Team management (9,9) often is considered the most effective style and is recommended because organization members work together to accomplish tasks. *Country club management* (1,9) occurs when primary emphasis is given to people rather than to work outputs. *Authority-compliance management* (9,1) occurs when efficiency in operations is the dominant orientation. *Middle-of-the-road management* (5,5) reflects a moderate amount of concern for both people and production. *Impoverished management* (1,1) means the absence of a leadership philosophy; leaders exert little effort toward interpersonal relationships or work accomplishment. Consider these examples:

Dick Notebaert, CEO of Ameritech Corporation, replaced 60 percent of top executives in a three-year period. In addition, the goals he set challenged people to reach double-digit growth, increase profit percentages, and claim a share of the long-distance telephone services market—high standards for a regional operating service.[30] Conversely, Principal Rob McPhee gave priority to people in devising a school plan for W. P. Wagner High in Edmonton, Alberta, Canada. Students, teachers, parents, and community members all contributed to the development of educational goals. McPhee even made special efforts to include those parents and citizens typically uninvolved in school policy making. Having their input recognized, McPhee reasoned, would inspire people to have a stake in the future of education.[31]

Both styles reflect an integration of the two concerns presented in the grid. Notebaert's leadership style represents a high concern for results working simultaneously with a low concern for others. The reverse is true for McPhee. In each case, both concerns are present, but integrated at different levels.

How Grid Styles Emerge

Grid styles emerge in a relationship when the two concerns meet at the point of interaction with others. This includes any time more than one person is involved in an activity. This involvement doesn't necessarily mean face-to-face meetings or discussions. Grid styles come into play, for example, when a leader considers who to recommend for a promotion, or who to include (or exclude) in a new opportunity. This interaction of concerns where Grid styles emerge is called Interdependence.

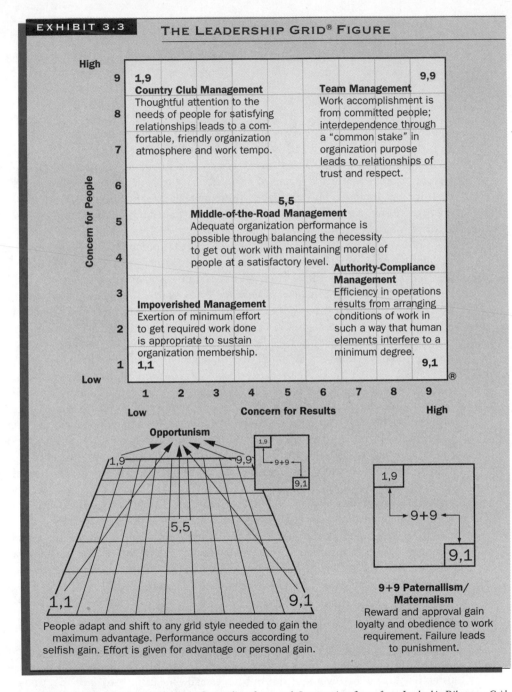

EXHIBIT 3.3 THE LEADERSHIP GRID® FIGURE

SOURCE: The Leadership Grid® figure, Paternalism figure and Opportunism figure from *Leadership Dilemma—Grid Solutions* by Robert R. Blake and Anne Adams McCanse (formerly the Managerial Grid by Robert R. Blake and Jane S. Morton). Houston: Gulf Publishing Company (Grid figure: p. 29, Paternalism figure: p. 30, Opportunism figure: p. 31). Copyright 1991 by Scientific Methods, Inc. Reproduced by permission of the owners.

Interdependence is important because if you *only* think of Grid styles in terms of the independent levels of concerns (people or results), you risk misinterpreting the overall style. For example, in Grid terms, you cannot consider a person's level of concern for people without also considering their related concern for results. The style depends not on the individual levels of concern, but on the levels of concern *interacting*. To illustrate, the high 9 level of concern for people is present in two different Grid styles and the expression of that concern is extremely different in each style. The difference lies in *how* the person expresses the high concern for others in relation to the interdependent concern for results.

Two styles with the same level of concern for people are described below:

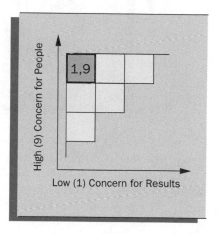

This joining of high concern for people with low concern for results leads to a 1,9 Yield and Comply leader who puts people first in the workplace, even at the expense of achieving sound results. Every action this leader takes is compared against a standard of keeping people happy. This leader is more concerned with maintaining a pleasant environment, even if it means results must suffer. He or she is constantly influenced by the questions, "What will people think? Will this make people angry and disrupt the pleasant environment we enjoy now?"

Even though the concern for people is high in the 1,9 yield and placate style, it takes on a characteristic of hiding and protecting people from unpleasantness. This leader may, for example, decline and hide an opportunity posed to the team because he or she thinks that the mere mentioning may generate conflict, resentment, fears, too much pressure, etc. Instead of posing the opportunity to the team, he or she hides it from members, or presents it in a way that they will accept. "I told them we weren't interested. We would have lost all of the momentum we've made on our current project, and it would be impossible to complete it in time. They weren't in the least upset about it."

Another aspect of this style it that the quest for happiness makes it very difficult for this leader to confront problems because he or she doesn't want to generate conflict. For example, if a team member is abusing policies or taking advantage of other team members, the 1,9 Yield and Comply leader will ignore, make excuses, and dismiss the problem for as long as possible.

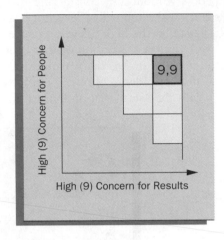

In the 9,9 Contribute and Commit style, the same level of concern for people takes on completely different characteristics as it joins with a high level of concern for results. The emerging style is a leader who encourages and motivates himself and others to achieve excellence. Every action this leader takes is compared against a standard of excellence rather than a standard of making people happy.

The concern for people is the same level for the 9,9 Contribute and Commit styles as in the 1,9 Yield and Comply style, but the difference is the interacting concern for results. When the two high concerns join, the overall style becomes one where happiness and comfort are important, but in relation to also achieving sound results. Happiness is not the overruling priority in this leader. If a person is abusing policies or taking advantage of other team members, the leader will confront the issue for resolution so that it doesn't distract from the team achieving sound results.

Theories of a "High-High" Leader

The leadership styles described by the researchers at Ohio State, University of Michigan, and University of Texas pertain to variables that roughly correspond to one another: consideration and initiating structure; employee-centered and job-centered; concern for people and concern for production, as illustrated in Exhibit 3.4. The research into the behavior approach culminated in two predominate types of leadership behaviors—people-oriented and task-oriented.

The findings about two underlying dimensions and the possibility of leaders rated high on both dimensions raises four questions to think about. The first is whether these two dimensions are the most important behaviors of leadership. Certainly, these two behaviors are important. They capture fundamental, underlying

EXHIBIT 3.4	THEMES OF LEADER BEHAVIOR RESEARCH	
	People-Oriented	**Task-Oriented**
Ohio State University	Consideration	Initiating Structure
University of Michigan	Employee-Centered	Job-Centered
University of Texas	Concern for People	Concern for Production

aspects of human behavior that must be considered for organizations to succeed. One reason why these two dimensions are compelling is that the findings are based on empirical research, which means that researchers went into the field to study real leaders across a variety of settings. When independent streams of field research reach similar conclusions, they probably represent a fundamental theme in leadership behavior. Concern for task and concern for people must be shown toward followers at some reasonable level, either by the leader or by other people in the system. While these are not the only important behaviors, as we will see throughout this book, they certainly require attention.

The second question is whether people orientation and task orientation exist together in the same leader, and how. The Grid theory argues that yes, both are present when people work with or through others to accomplish an activity. Although leaders may be high on either style, there is considerable belief that the best leaders are high on both behaviors. Principal Sullivan, described in the Leadership Spotlight, is an example of success on both dimensions. How does a leader achieve both behaviors? Some researchers argue that "high-high" leaders alternate the type of behavior from one to the other, showing concern one time and task initiation another time.[32] Another approach says that effective "high-high" leaders encompass both behaviors simultaneously in a fundamentally different way than people who behave in one way or the other. For example, when initiating the change described in the Leadership Spotlight, Principal Sullivan helped set challenging but realistic goals for student performance and also consulted teachers about ways to achieve those goals. A task-oriented leader might set difficult goals and simply pressure subordinates to improve quality. A person-oriented leader might ignore student achievement scores and simply seek improvement by consulting with teachers and building positive relationships with them. The "high-high" leaders seem to have a knack for displaying concern for both people and production in the majority of their behaviors.[33]

The third question is whether a "high-high" leadership style is universal or situational. Universal means that the behavior will tend to be effective in every situation, while situational means the behavior succeeds only in certain settings. Research has indicated some degree of universality with respect to people-oriented and task-oriented behavior. In other words, the leader behavior of concern for people tended to be related to higher employee satisfaction and fewer personnel problems across a wide variety of situations. Likewise, task-oriented behavior was associated with higher productivity across a large number of situations.

The fourth question concerns whether people can actually change themselves into leaders high on people and/or task-orientation. In the 1950s and 1960s, when the Ohio State and Michigan studies were underway, the assumption of researchers was that the behaviors of effective leaders could be emulated by anyone wishing to become an effective leader. In general it seems that people can learn new leader behaviors, as described in Chapter 1. There is a general belief that "high-high" leadership is a desirable quality, because the leader will meet both needs simultaneously. Despite the research indicating that "high-high" leadership is not the only effective style, researchers have looked to this kind of leader as a candidate for success in a wide number of situations. However, as we will see in the next chapter, the next generation of leadership studies refined the understanding of situations to pinpoint more precisely when each type of leadership behavior is most effective.

Dyadic Approaches

Dyadic theorists believe that trait and behavior theories oversimplify the relationship between leaders and subordinates. Dyadic theorists focus on the concept of exchange between a leader and a follower, a relationship known as a dyad. **Dyadic theory** involves a perspective that examines why leaders have more influence over and greater impact on some followers than on other followers. Dyadic theorists argue that leaders do not uniformly broadcast a trait such as self-confidence or a behavior such as people-orientation that is received equally by each subordinate. The dyadic view argues that a single leader will form different relationships with different followers. For example, interviewing subordinates of a single leader will reveal different descriptions of the same person, with some descriptions being positive and some negative. To understand leadership in this perspective, a closer look at the specific relationship in each leader-subordinate dyad is necessary.[34]

The first dyadic theory was introduced nearly 25 years ago and has been steadily revised ever since. The development of this viewpoint is illustrated in Exhibit 3.5. The first stage was the awareness of a relationship between a leader and each subordinate, rather than between a leader and a group of subordinates. The second stage examined specific attributes of the exchange between leader and subordinate. The third stage explored whether leaders could intentionally develop partnerships with each subordinate, and the fourth stage expanded the view of dyads to include larger systems and networks.

Vertical Dyad Linkage Model

The **Vertical Dyad Linkage (VDL) model** argues for the importance of the dyad formed by a leader with each member of the subordinate group. Initial findings indicated that subordinates provided very different descriptions of the same leader. For example, subordinates might report a leader, and their relationship with the leader, as having a high degree of mutual trust, respect, and obligation. These high-quality relationships might be characterized as high on both people and task orientation.

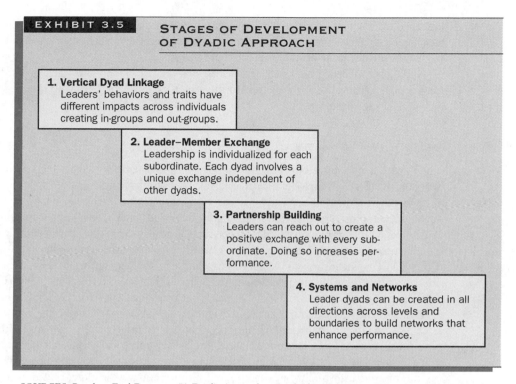

EXHIBIT 3.5 STAGES OF DEVELOPMENT OF DYADIC APPROACH

1. **Vertical Dyad Linkage**
Leaders' behaviors and traits have different impacts across individuals creating in-groups and out-groups.

2. **Leader–Member Exchange**
Leadership is individualized for each subordinate. Each dyad involves a unique exchange independent of other dyads.

3. **Partnership Building**
Leaders can reach out to create a positive exchange with every subordinate. Doing so increases performance.

4. **Systems and Networks**
Leader dyads can be created in all directions across levels and boundaries to build networks that enhance performance.

SOURCES: Based on Fred Danereau, "A Dyadic Approach to Leadership: Creating and Nurturing This Approach Under Fire," *Leadership Quarterly* 6, No. 4 (1995), 479–490, and George B. Graen and Mary Uhl-Bien, "Relationship-Based Approach to Leadership: Development of Leader-Member Exchange (LMX) Theory of Leadership Over 25 Years: Applying a Multi-level, Multi-domain Approach," *Leadership Quarterly* 6, No. 2 (1995), 219–247.

Other subordinates reported a low-quality relationship with the leader, such as having a low degree of trust, respect, and obligation. These subordinates perceived the leader as being low on important leadership behaviors.

Based on these two extreme exchange patterns, subordinates were found to exist in an "in-group" or an "out-group" in relation to the leader. The subordinates who rated the leader highly had developed close relationships with the leader and often became assistants who played key roles in the functioning of the work unit. Out-group members were not key players in the work unit. Because of these differences, individuals often fell into subgroups, which might be considered supporters and opponents of the leader. Some subordinates were getting their needs met, while others were not. These differences were based on the dyad between the leader and each subordinate. The in-group had high access to the leader, while the out-group members tended to be passive and did not have positions of influence or access to the leader. In-group members expressed greater mutual influence and collaborative effort with the leader, and they had opportunities to receive greater rewards and perform additional duties. Out-group members tended not to experience positive leader relationships and influence, and the leader was more likely to use formal authority and coercive behavior on these subordinates. In-group members typically received more attention, more approval, and probably more status, but they were also expected to be loyal, committed, and productive.

Thus, by focusing on the relationship between a leader and each subordinate, the Vertical Dyad Linkage research found great variance of leader style and impact within a group of subordinates.

Leader-Member Exchange

Stage two in the development of the dyad theory explored the leader-member exchange (LMX) in more detail, discovering that the impact on outcomes depended on how the leader-member exchange process developed over time. Studies evaluating characteristics of the LMX relationship explored such things as communication frequency, value agreement, characteristics of followers, job satisfaction, performance, job climate, and commitment. Overall, these studies found that the quality of the LMX relationship was substantially higher for in-group members. Moreover, a high-quality relationship was associated with higher satisfaction and performance. High-quality LMX relationships had very positive outcomes for leaders, followers, work units, and the organization in general.

LMX theorists identified three stages dyad members went through in their working relationship. In the initial stage, the leader and follower, as strangers, tested each other to identify what kinds of behaviors were comfortable. The relationship was negotiated informally between each follower and the leader. The definition of each group member's role defined what the member and leader expected the member to do. Next, as the leader and member became acquainted, they engaged in shaping and refining the roles they would play together. Finally, in the third stage, as the roles reached maturity, the relationship attained a steady pattern of behavior. Leader-member exchanges were difficult to change at this point. The exchange tended to determine in-group and out-group status.

Partnership Building

In this third phase of research, the focus was on whether leaders could develop effective relationships with a large number of subordinates. The emphasis was on how a leader might work with each subordinate on a one-on-one basis to develop a partnership. The emphasis was not on how or why discrimination among subordinates occurred, but on how to develop beneficial relationships with everyone. Effective leaders could provide all employees access to high-quality leader-member exchanges, thereby providing a more equitable environment and greater benefits to leaders, followers, and the organization.

In this view, the leader views each person independently, and may treat each individual in a different but positive way. Sometimes called *individualized leadership*, leaders can actively develop positive relationships with each subordinate, although the positive relationship will have a different form for each person. For example, one person might be treated with "consideration," another with "initiating structure," depending on what followers need to feel involved and to succeed.

In cases where leaders were trained to offer the opportunity for a high-quality relationship to all of their subordinates, the followers who accepted the offer improved their performance dramatically. The implications of this finding are that true performance and productivity gains can be achieved by having the leader develop positive relationships one-on-one with each subordinate. As these relationships matured, the entire work group became more productive, and the payoffs were tremendous. Leaders could count on followers to provide the assistance needed for high performance, and followers participated in and influenced decisions. Leaders provided support, encouragement, and training, and followers responded with high performance. In some sense, leaders were meeting both the personal and work-related needs of each subordinate, one at a time. The Cutting Edge box describes how leaders at General Electric's Plastics division used an innovative approach to promote the idea of partnership among all employees.

Systems and Networks

The final stage of this work suggests that leader dyads can be expanded to larger systems. Rather than focusing on leaders and subordinates, a systems-level perspective examines how dyadic relationships can be created across traditional boundaries to embrace a larger system. This larger network for the leader may cut across work unit, functional, divisional, and even organizational boundaries. In this view, leader relationships are not limited to subordinates, but include peers, teammates, and other stakeholders relevant to the work unit. To this point, there has been little systematic research of a broader systemic view of dyadic relationships. But the theory suggests the need for leaders to build networks of one-to-one relationships and to use their traits and behaviors selectively to create positive relationships with as many people as possible. A large number of people thereby can be influenced by the leader, and these stakeholders will contribute to the success of the work unit.

Summary and Interpretation

The point of this chapter is to understand the importance of traits and behaviors in the development of leadership theory and research. Traits include self-confidence, honesty, and drive. A large number of personal traits and abilities distinguish successful leaders from non-leaders, but traits themselves are not sufficient to guarantee effective leadership. The behavior approach explored autocratic versus democratic leadership, consideration versus initiating structure, employee-centered versus job-centered leadership, and concern for people versus concern for production. The theme of people versus tasks runs through this research, suggesting these are fundamental behaviors through which leaders meet followers' needs. There has been some disagreement in the research about whether a specific leader is either people- or task-oriented or whether they can be both. Today, the consensus is that leaders can achieve a "high-high" leadership style.

GE Plastics/Borg Warner

GE Plastics, with headquarters in Pittsfield, Massachusetts, has recognized the importance of partnership for a long time, but it took on new urgency after the company purchased a long-time rival, Borg-Warner Chemicals, based in Parkersville, West Virginia. Many Borg-Warner employees still considered GE "the competition" and didn't feel like a part of the company—and what's more, they weren't sure they wanted to.

Company leaders wanted a way to get employees throughout the organization acting like partners, without regard to department or hieararchical levels. They considered the former types of team-building activities they had used—rowing events, donkey races, wilderness experiences—and realized what they really needed was an event that would make a lasting impression on employees while serving a larger purpose and creating something of enduring value. The decision was made that employees would renovate five non-profit facilities, using many of GE's materials, borrowing equipment when possible, and purchasing other supplies and tools in the local community. Teams were carefully formed to give employees a chance to meet and work with new people, combine executives with lower-level workers, and, above all, mix former Borg-Warner employees with GE workers. In one 12-hour day, 30 teams completely renovated the run-down Copley Family YMCA, located in a low-income San Diego neighborhood riddled with gangs and drugs. They scraped and painted walls, cleaned graffiti, laid tile, replaced windows, landscaped the grounds, and even restored a 20-year-old mural covering a two-story outer wall. In the process, people had a chance to begin developing one-on-one relationships with fellow workers from different areas and levels of the company.

Teams had arrived at the site ready to compete with one another, but as the day wore on they noticed something different about this exercise—they wanted *all* the teams to win, and any team that finished its project first gladly pitched in to help others. The final effect on the community was impressive, but what was most phenomenal was the impact on employees. The feelings of accomplishment and camaraderie were more than executives had ever hoped for, and the event proved to be the turning point in the integration of GE Plastics and Borg-Warner employees. After a day of pounding nails and painting walls, they shed their rivalries to become partners working toward a common cause they all felt proud of. As one former Borg-Warner employee said, ". . . any questions I had about whether or not this was the kind of company I wanted to work for were gone, absolutely. For us to be able to pull this off and to want to do this really made all the difference."

SOURCE: David Bollier, "Building Corporate Loyalty While Rebuilding the Community," *Management Review*, October 1996, 17–22.

Another approach was the dyad between a leader and each follower. Followers have different relationships with the leader, and the ability of the leader to develop a positive relationship with each subordinate contributes to team performance. The leader-member exchange theory says that high-quality relationships have a positive outcome for leaders, followers, work units, and the organization. Leaders can attempt to build individualized relationships with each subordinate as a way to meet needs for both consideration and structure.

The historical development of leadership theory presented in this chapter introduces some important ideas about leadership. While certain personal traits and abilities constitute a greater likelihood for success in a leadership role, they are not in themselves sufficient to guarantee effective leadership. Rather, behaviors are equally significant, as outlined by the research at several universities. Therefore, the style of leadership demonstrated by an individual greatly determines the outcome of the leadership endeavor. Often, a combination of styles is most effective. To understand the effects of leadership upon outcomes, the specific relationship behavior between a leader and each follower is also an important consideration.

Key Terms

traits	autocratic	job-centered leader
Great Man approach	democratic	The Leadership Grid
self-confidence	consideration	dyadic theory
honesty	initiating structure	vertical dyad linkage model
drive	employee-centered	

Discussion Questions

1. Compare and contrast the two traits in Pagonis's *Moving Mountains* to people- and task-oriented leader behaviors described in this chapter.

2. Suggest some personal traits of leaders you have known. Which traits do you believe are most valuable? Why?

3. What is the difference between trait theories and behavioral theories of leadership?

4. Would you prefer working for a leader who has a "consideration" or an "initiating-structure" leadership style? Discuss the reasons for your answer.

5. The Vertical Dyad Linkage model suggests that followers respond individually to the leader. If this is so, what advice would you give leaders about displaying people-oriented versus task-oriented behavior?

6. Does it make sense to you that a leader should develop an individualized relationship with each follower? Explain advantages and disadvantages to this approach.

7. Why would subordinates under a democratic leader perform better in the leader's absence than would subordinates under an autocratic leader?

8. Which type of leader—task-oriented or people-oriented—do you think would have an easier time becoming a "high-high" leader? Why?

Leadership Development: Personal Feedback

Assertiveness Questionnaire

For each statement below, decide which of the following answers best applies to you. Place the number of the answer to the left of the statement.

1. Never true; 2. Sometimes true; 3. Often true; 4. Always true

_____ 1. I respond with more modesty than I really feel when my work is complimented.

_____ 2. If people are rude, I will be rude right back.

_____ 3. Other people find me interesting.

_____ 4. I find it difficult to speak up in a group of strangers.

_____ 5. I don't mind using sarcasm if it helps me make a point.

_____ 6. I ask for a raise when I feel I really deserve it.

_____ 7. If others interrupt me when I am talking, I suffer in silence.

_____ 8. If people criticize my work, I find a way to make them back down.

_____ 9. I can express pride in my accomplishments without being boastful.

_____ 10. People take advantage of me.

_____ 11. I tell people what they want to hear if it helps me get what I want.

_____ 12. I find it easy to ask for help.

_____ 13. I lend things to others even when I don't really want to.

_____ 14. I win arguments by dominating the discussion.

_____ 15. I can express my true feelings to someone I really care for.

_____ 16. When I feel angry with other people, I bottle it up rather than express it.

_____ 17. When I criticize someone else's work, they get mad.

_____ 18. I feel confident in my ability to stand up for my rights.

SOURCE: Douglas T. Hall, Donald D. Bowen, Roy J. Lewicki, and Francine S. Hall, *Experiences in Management and Organizational Behavior*, 2nd ed. (New York: John Wiley & Sons, 1982), 101. Reprinted by permission of John Wiley & Sons, Inc.

Scoring

These questions are designed to assess aggressive, passive, and assertive behavior. Sum your answers to items 2, 5, 8, 11, 14, and 17. This is your "aggressive" score. Sum your answers to items 1, 4, 7, 10, 13, and 16 for your "passive" score. Your "assertive" score is the total for items 3, 6, 9, 12, 15, and 18.

Aggressive Score =   Passive Score =   Assertive Score=

Assertiveness is considered to be more effective leadership behavior than either aggressive or passive behavior. Passive behavior tends to be associated with conflict avoidance, suppressing one's own needs, wanting the approval of others, and being inhibited and submissive. These traits are not considered effective for leadership.

Aggressive behavior is the opposite of passiveness. Aggressive people are self-centered, have little concern for the feelings or rights of others, and tend to be domineering and pushy. This behavior seems effective for getting things done, but frequently creates resistance and resentment.

Assertive behavior is considered the most effective for leadership. Assertive people ask for what they want, say what they believe, and stand up for their rights in a way that others can accept. The quality of assertiveness means being straightforward yet open to the needs of others. Assertiveness strikes the correct balance between being too dominant and too "soft," which are not effective ways to influence others.

Leadership Development: Case for Analysis

Consolidated Products

Consolidated Products is a medium-sized manufacturer of consumer products with nonunionized production workers. Ben Samuels was a plant manager for Consolidated Products for 10 years, and he was very well liked by the employees there. They were grateful for the fitness center he built for employees, and they enjoyed the social activities sponsored by the plant several times a year, including company picnics and holiday parties. He knew most of the workers by name, and he spent part of each day walking around the plant to visit with them and ask about their families or hobbies.

Ben believed that it was important to treat employees properly so they would have a sense of loyalty to the company. He tried to avoid any layoffs when production demand was slack, figuring that the company could not afford to lose skilled workers that are so difficult to replace. The workers knew that if they had a special problem, Ben would try to help them. For example, when someone was injured but wanted to continue working, Ben found another job in the plant that the person could do despite having a disability. Ben believed that if you treat people right, they will do a good job for you without close supervision or prodding. Ben applied the same principle to his supervisors, and he mostly left them alone to run their departments as they saw fit. He did not set objectives and standards for the plant, and he never asked the supervisors to develop plans for improving productivity and product quality.

Under Ben, the plant had the lowest turnover among the company's five plants, but the second worst record for costs and production levels. When the company was acquired by another firm, Ben was asked to take early retirement, and Phil Jones was brought in to replace him.

Phil had a growing reputation as a manager who could get things done, and he quickly began making changes. Costs were cut by trimming a number of activities such as the fitness center at the plant, company picnics and parties, and the human relations training programs for supervisors. Phil believed that human relations training was a waste of time; if employees don't want to do the work, get rid of them and find somebody else who does.

Supervisors were instructed to establish high-performance standards for their departments and insist that people achieve them. A computer monitoring system was introduced so that the output of each worker could be checked closely against the standards. Phil told his supervisors to give any worker who had substandard performance one warning, then if performance did not improve within two weeks, to fire the person. Phil believed that workers don't respect a supervisor who is weak and passive. When Phil observed a worker wasting time or making a mistake, he would reprimand the person right on the spot to set an example. Phil also checked closely on the performance of his supervisors. Demanding objectives were set for each department, and weekly meetings were held with each supervisor to review department performance. Finally, Phil insisted that supervisors check with him first before taking any significant actions that deviated from established plans and policies.

As another cost-cutting move, Phil reduced the frequency of equipment maintenance, which required machines to be idled when they could be productive. Since the machines had a good record of reliable operation, Phil believed that the current maintenance schedule was excessive and was cutting into production. Finally, when business was slow for one of the product lines, Phil laid off workers rather than finding something else for them to do.

By the end of Phil's first year as plant manager, production costs were reduced by 20 percent and production output was up by 10 percent. However, three of his seven supervisors left to take other jobs, and turnover was also high among the machine operators. Some of the turnover was due to workers who were fired, but competent machine operators were also quitting, and it was becoming increasingly difficult to find any replacements for them. Finally, there was increasing talk of unionizing among the workers.

SOURCE: Reprinted with permission from Gary Yukl, *Leadership in Organizations* Fourth Edition (Englewood Cliffs, NJ: Prentice Hall, 1998), 66–67.

Questions

1. Compare the leadership traits and behaviors of Ben Samuels and Phil Jones.

2. Which leader do you think is more effective? Why? Which leader would you prefer to work for?

3. If you were Phil Jones' boss, what would you do now?

References

[1]Howard Gardner, *Leading Minds: An Anatomy of Leadership* (New York: Basic Books, 1995).

[2]James Cox, "Jian Hoping for Historic U.S. Visit Next Week," *USA Today*, October 20, 1997; Gardner, *Leading Minds*.

[3]G.A. Yukl, *Leadership in Organizations* (Englewood Cliffs, NJ: Prentice-Hall, 1981); and S.C. Kohs and K.W. Irle, "Prophesying Army Promotion," *Journal of Applied Psychology* 4 (1920), 73–87.

[4]Yukl, *Leadership in Organizations*, 254.

[5]R.M. Stogdill, "Personal Factors Associated with Leadership: A Survey of the Literature," *Journal of Psychology* 25 (1948), 35–71.

[6]R.M. Stogdill, *Handbook of Leadership: A Survey of the Literature* (New York: Free Press, 1974).

[7]D.G. Winter, "Leader Appeal, Leader Performance, and Motive Profiles of Leaders and Followers: A Study of American Presidents and Elections, *Journal of Personality and Social Psychology* 52 (1987), 196–202; and R.E. Donley and D.G. Winter, "Measuring Motives of Public Officials at a Distance: An Exploratory Study of American Presidents," *Behavioral Science* 15 (1970), 227–236.

[8]Edwin Locke and Associates, *The Essence of Leadership* (New York: Lexington Books, 1991).

[9]Shelley A. Kirkpatrick and Edwin A. Locke, "Leadership: Do Traits Matter?" *Academy of Management Executives* 5(2): 48–60 (1991).

[10]Howard Gardner, *Leading Minds: An Anatomy of Leadership* (New York: Basic Books, 1995).

[11]James M. Kouzes and Barry Z. Posner, *Credibility: How Leades Gain and Lose It, Why People Demand It* (San Francisco: Jossey-Bass Publishers, 1993), 14.

[12]Gardner, *Leading Minds: An Anatomy of Leadership.*

[13]This discussion is based on Kirkpatrick and Locke, "Leadership: Do Traits Matter?"

[14]A. Howard and D.W. Bray, *Managerial Lives in Transition: Advancing Age and Changing Times* (New York: Guilford Press, 1988).

[15]K. Lewin, "Field Theory and Experiment in Social Psychology: Concepts and Methods," *American Journal of Sociology* 44 (1939): 868–896; K.Lewin and R. Lippet, "An Experimental Approach to the Study of Autocracy and Democracy: A Preliminary Note," *Sociometry* 1 (1938): 292–300; and K. Lewin, R. Lippett, and R.K. White, "Patterns of Aggressive Behavior in Experimentally Created Social Climates," *Journal of Social Psychology* 10 (1939): 271–301

[16]R. Tannenbaum and W.H. Schmidt, "How to Choose a Leadership Pattern," *Harvard Business Review* 36 (1958), 95–101.

[17]F.A. Heller and G.A. Yukl, "Participation, Managerial Decision-Making and Situational Variables," *Organizational Behavior and Human Performance* 4 (1969) 227–241.

[18]Patricia O'Toole, "How Do You Build a $44 Million Company? By Saying Please," *Working Woman,* April 1990, 88–92.

[19]J.K. Hemphill and A.E. Coons, "Development of the Leader Behavior Description Questionnaire," in *Leader Behavior: Its Description and Measurement,* Eds. R. M. Stogdill and A.E. Coons (Columbus, OH: Ohio State University, Bureau of Business Research, 1957).

[20]P.C. Nystrom, "Managers and the High-High Leader Myth," *Academy of Management Journal* 21 (1978), 325–331; and L.L. Larson, J.G. Hunt and Richard N. Osborn, "The Great High-High Leader Behavior Myth: A Lesson from Occam's Razor," *Academy of Management Journal* 19 (1976), 628–641.

[21]Jessie Sullivan and Claude Goldenburg, "Using Goals to Drive School Reform," *The Education Digest* (November 1996), 12–15.

[22]E.W. Skinner, "Relationships Between Leadership Behavior Patterns and Organizational-Situational Variables," *Personnel Psychology* 22 (1969), 489–494; and E.A. Fleishman and E.F. Harris, "Patterns of Leadership Behavior Related to Employee Grievances and Turnover," *Personnel Psychology* 15 (1962), 43–56.

[23]A.W. Halpin and B.J. Winer, "A Factorial Study of the Leader Behavior Descriptions," in R.M. Stogdill and A.E. Coons, eds., *Leader Behavior: Its Descriptions and Measurement,* (Columbus, OII: Ohio State University, Bureau of Business Research, 1957); and J.K. Hemphill, "Leadership Behavior Associated with the Administrative Reputations of College Departments," *Journal of Educational Psychology* 46 (1955): 385–401.

[24]R. Likert, "From Production- and Employee-Centeredness to Systems 1-4," *Journal of Management* 5 (1979), 147–156.

[25]J. Taylor and D. Bowers, *The Survey of Organizations: A Machine Scored Standardized Questionnaire Instrument,* (Ann Arbor, MI: Institute for Social Research, University of Michigan, 1972).

[26]D.G. Bowers and S.E. Seashore, "Predicting Organizational Effectiveness with a Four-Factor Theory of Leadership," *Administrative Science Quarterly* 11 (1966), 238–263.

[27]Gabriella Stern, "Shifting Gears," *The Wall Street Journal,* April 21, 1997.

[28]Bowers and Seashore, "Predicting Organizational Effectiveness with a Four-Factor Theory of Leadership."

[29]Robert Blake and Jane S. Mouton, *The Managerial Grid III* (Houston: Gulf, 1985).

[30]Peter Elstom, "Telecom's Pit Bull," *Business Week,* July 1, 1996.

[31]Rob McPhee, "Orchestrating Community Involvement," *Educational Leadership* 53 (December/January 1996), 71–76.

[32]J. Misumi, " The Behavioral Science of Leadership: An Interdisciplinary Japanese Research Program," (Ann Arbor, MI: University of Michigan Press, 1985).

[33]Fleishman and Harris, "Patterns of Leadership Behavior Related to Employee Grievances and Turnover"; and Misumi, "The Behavioral Science of Leadership: An Interdisciplinary Japanese Research Program."

[34]This discussion is based on Fred Danereau, "A Dyadic Approach to Leadership: Creating and Nurturing This Approach Under Fire," *Leadership Quarterly* 6, No. 4 (1995), 479-490, and George B. Graen and Mary Uhl-Bien, "Relationship-Based Approach to Leadership: Development of Leader Member Exchange (LMX) Theory of Leadership Over 25 Years: Applying a Multi-Level Multi-Domain Approach," *Leadership Quarterly* 6, No. 2 (1995), 219-247.

4

Contingency Approaches

- **The Contingency Approach**   93

- **Fiedler's Contingency Model**   94

- **Hersey and Blanchard's Situational Theory**   99

- **Path-Goal Theory**   102

- **The Vroom-Jago Contingency Model**   107

- **Substitutes for Leadership**   111

- **Leadership Spotlights:**
  Plastic Lumber Company   96
  Sunbeam-Oster   100
  McGuffey's   107
  Ko-Rec-Type   111

- **Leader's Bookshelf:**
  Maximum Leadership: The World's Leading CEOs Share Their Five Strategies for Success   105

- **Leadership Development: Personal Feedback**
  T-P Leadership Questionnaire: An Assessment of Style   115

- **Leadership Development: Case for Analysis**
  Alvis Corporation   117

Your Leadership Challenge

After reading this chapter, you should be able to:

- Understand how leadership is often contingent on people and situations.

- Apply Fiedler's contingency model to key relationships among leader style, situational favorability, and group task performance.

- Apply Hersey and Blanchard's situational theory of leader style to the level of follower readiness.

- Explain the path-goal theory of leadership.

- Use the Vroom-Jago model to identify the correct amount of follower participation in specific decision situations.

- Understand how to use the power of situational variables to substitute for or neutralize the need for leadership.

At Sterling Information Group, employees are encouraged to develop interests outside the office instead of working long hours, and saving overtime costs isn't the reason. Co-founders of the software consulting firm, Chip Wolfe and Dan Thibodeau, remember their days as corporate employees unfavorably. Based on inspiration from Dr. Seuss's *If I Ran the Zoo,* the leadership duo sought to create a unique culture. They pay hourly wages rather than salaries so the incentive for management to overwork employees is reduced. Wolfe and Thibodeau believe overworked employees are not happy employees.

They also give five weeks of annual leave for employees to use at their own discretion. When two employees became fathers, they were allowed more time off to spend with their new infants. Employees devise their own schedules, including the option to telecommute. This flexibility extends without limits so long as workers attend meetings, let people know where they are, follow up with customers and coworkers, and ensure the best interests of clients, coworkers, and themselves. One employee explains that Sterling "doesn't expect you to be here at eight and look busy."

In addition to the enormous flexibility in work schedules, the leaders allot a full 50 percent of profits to employees as a bonus, and they dump clients that make unreasonable demands on employees. Furthermore, because employee jobs vary according to project, the company has little reliance on job titles, preferring instead a "flat" organizational structure.

Employee benefits go far beyond traditional medical, dental, and long-term disability coverage, and the co-leaders have stood by their guarantee of no layoffs for the 11 years the company has been operating. Not surprisingly, the turnover rate is only 11 percent in a very competitive market for qualified employees. With people hard to find, Wolfe and Thibodeau have managed a growth of 50 percent for each of the past five years, and net profit has doubled the average for the software consulting industry.[1]

The leadership style of Wolfe and Thibodeau is successful because of the enormous demand for the highly trained people they employ; without giving employees great benefits and autonomy and responsibility, Sterling Information Group could not retain workers who inspire clients to return. Indeed, 90 percent of the customer base is comprised of repeat business, a substantial savings for the marketing department. Giving employees the opportunity to create a healthy balance between professional life and family life creates a desirable atmosphere in which to work. This attracts the best people in a tight labor market and results in a growing organization.

By contrast, as owner of two R.F. Moeller Jeweler stores in Minnesota, Mark Moeller makes enormous demands on his employees, who have to be accessible around the clock, buy their own lap top computers, and dare not bend the rules. Moeller insists that his high expectations be shared by employees. Demands are so high that over half of the newly hired resign in less than a year. In an industry dominated by chain stores, discount giants, and the spreading reach of home shopping networks, Moeller's strict standards reflect the aggressiveness that has propelled his family stores into the commercial jewelry fray.[2]

Both R.F. Moeller and Sterling are successful companies, and yet the leadership styles of Moeller and the team of Wolfe and Thibodeau are dramatically different. Moeller seems task-oriented while Wolfe and Thibodeau display a strong people orientation. This difference points to what researchers of leader traits and leader behaviors eventually discovered: many different leadership styles are effective. What, then, determines the success of a leadership style?

In the above example, the *situation* of each organization was very different. Moeller had to stand out against the looming commercial jewelry giants; Wolfe and Thibodeau had to attract and retain top notch workers in a field characterized as an "employees' market." The differences in the organizational situations faced by these leaders guided their leadership style choices, and both styles achieved success.

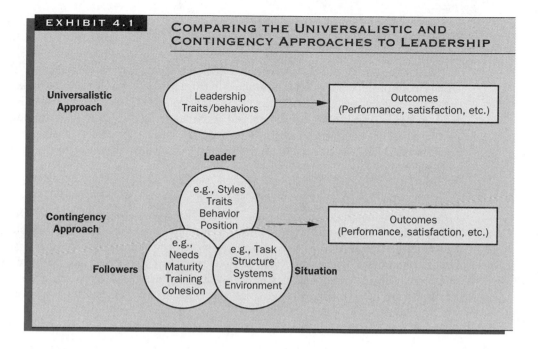

EXHIBIT 4.1

COMPARING THE UNIVERSALISTIC AND CONTINGENCY APPROACHES TO LEADERSHIP

This chapter explores the relationship between leadership effectiveness and the situation in which leadership activities occur. We will discuss the elements of leader, follower, and situation, and the impact each has upon the others. We will closely examine the theories that define how leadership styles, follower attributes, and organizational characteristics fit together to enable successful leadership.

The Contingency Approach

The failure to find universal leader traits or behaviors that would always determine effective leadership led researchers in a new direction. While leader behavior was still examined, the central focus of the new research was the situation in which leadership occurred. The basic tenet of this focus was that behavior effective in some circumstances may be ineffective under different conditions. Thus, the effectiveness of leader behavior is *contingent* upon organizational situations. Aptly called contingency approaches, these theories explain the relationship between leadership styles and effectiveness in specific situations.

The universalistic approach as described in Chapter 3 is compared to the contingency approach used in this chapter in Exhibit 4.1. In the previous chapter, researchers were investigating traits or behaviors that could improve performance and satisfaction in any or all situations. They sought universal leadership traits and behaviors. **Contingency** means that one thing depends on other things, and for a leader to be effective there must be an appropriate fit between the leader's behavior and style and the conditions in the situation. A leadership style that works in one situation may not work in another situation. There is not one best way of leadership. Contingency means "it depends."

The contingencies most important to leadership as shown in Exhibit 4.1 are the situation and followers. Research implies that situational variables such as task, structure, and environment are important to leadership style, just as we saw in the examples of Wolfe and Thibodeau compared to Moeller in the opening examples. The nature of followers has also been identified as a key contingency. Thus the needs, maturity, and cohesiveness of followers make a significant difference to the best style of leadership.

Several models of situational leadership have been developed. The Contingency Model developed by Fiedler and his associates, the Situational Theory of Hersey and Blanchard, Path-Goal Theory, the Vroom-Jago Model of Decision Participation, and the Substitutes for Leadership concept will all be described in this chapter. The **contingency approaches** seek to delineate the characteristics of situations and followers and examine the leadership styles that can be used effectively. Assuming that a leader can properly diagnose a situation and muster the flexibility to behave according to the appropriate style, successful outcomes are highly likely.

Fiedler's Contingency Model

An early extensive effort to link leadership style with organizational situation was made by Fiedler and his associates.[3] The basic idea is simple: Match the leader's style with the situation most favorable for his or her success. **Fiedler's contigency model** was designed to enable leaders to diagnose both leadership style and organizational situation.

Leadership Style

The cornerstone of Fiedler's theory is the extent to which the leader's style is relationship-oriented or task-oriented. A *relationship-oriented leader* is concerned with people. Like the consideration style described in Chapter 3, a relationship-oriented leader establishes mutual trust and respect, and listens to employee's needs. A *task-oriented leader* is primarily motivated by task accomplishment. Similar to the initiating structure style described earlier, a task-oriented leader provides clear directions and sets performance standards.

Leadership style was measured with a questionnaire known as the least preferred coworker (LPC) scale. The LPC scale has a set of 16 bipolar adjectives along an 8-point scale. Examples of the bipolar adjectives used by Fiedler on the LPC scale follow:

open – – – – – – – guarded

quarrelsome – – – – – – – harmonious

<pre>
    efficient – – – – – – – – inefficient
 self-assured – – – – – – – – hesitant
       gloomy – – – – – – – – cheerful
</pre>

If the leader describes the least preferred coworker using positive concepts, he or she is considered relationship-oriented; that is, a leader who cares about and is sensitive to other people's feelings. Conversely, if a leader uses negative concepts to describe the least preferred coworker, he or she is considered task-oriented; that is, a leader who sees other people in negative terms and places greater value on task activities than on people.

Situation

Fiedler's model presents the leadership situation in terms of three key elements that can be either favorable or unfavorable to a leader: the quality of leader-member relations, task structure, and position power.

Leader-member relations refers to group atmosphere and members' attitudes toward and acceptance of the leader. When subordinates trust, respect, and have confidence in the leader, leader-member relations are considered good. When subordinates distrust, do not respect, and have little confidence in the leader, leader-member relations are poor.

Task structure refers to the extent to which tasks performed by the group are defined, involve specific procedures, and have clear, explicit goals. Routine, well-defined tasks, such as those of assembly-line workers, have a high degree of structure. Creative, ill-defined tasks, such as research and development or strategic planning, have a low degree of task structure. When task structure is high, the situation is considered favorable to the leader; when low, the situation is less favorable.

Position power is the extent to which the leader has formal authority over subordinates. Position power is high when the leader has the power to plan and direct the work of subordinates, evaluate it, and reward or punish them. Position power is low when the leader has little authority over subordinates and cannot evaluate their work or reward them. When position power is high, the situation is considered favorable for the leader; when low, the situation is unfavorable.

Combining the three situational characteristics yields a list of eight leadership situations, which are illustrated in Exhibit 4.2. Situation I is most favorable to the leader because leader-member relations are good, task structure is high, and leader position power is strong. Situation VIII is most unfavorable to the leader because leader-member relations are poor, task structure is low, and leader position power is weak. Other octants represent intermediate degrees of favorableness for the leader.

Contingency Theory

When Fiedler examined the relationships among leadership style, situational favorability, and group task performance, he found the pattern shown in Exhibit 4.3. Task-oriented leaders are more effective when the situation is either highly favorable or

EXHIBIT 4.2	FIEDLER'S CLASSIFICATION OF SITUATION FAVORABLENESS							
	Very Favorable		**Intermediate**				**Very Unfavorable**	
Leader-Member Relations	Good	Good	Good	Good	Poor	Poor	Poor	Poor
Task Structure	High		Low		High		Low	
Leader Position Power	Strong	Weak	Strong	Weak	Strong	Weak	Strong	Weak
Situations	I	II	III	IV	V	VI	VII	VIII

SOURCE: Fred E. Fiedler, " The Effects of Leadership Training and Experience: A Contingency Model Interpretation," *Administrative Science Quarterly* 17 (1972), 455. Reprinted by permission of *Administrative Science Quarterly*.

highly unfavorable. Relationship-oriented leaders are more effective in situations of moderate favorability.

The task-oriented leader excels in the favorable situation because everyone gets along, the task is clear, and the leader has power; all that is needed is for someone to take charge and provide direction. Similarly, if the situation is highly unfavorable to the leader, a great deal of structure and task direction is needed. A strong leader defines task structure and can establish authority over subordinates. Because leader-member relations are poor anyway, a strong task orientation will make no difference to the leader's popularity.

The relationship-oriented leader performs better in situations of intermediate favorability because human relations skills are important in achieving high group performance. In these situations, the leader may be moderately well liked, have some power, and supervise jobs that contain some ambiguity. A leader with good inter-personal skills can create a positive group atmosphere that will improve relation-ships, clarify task structure, and establish position power.

A leader, then, needs to know two things in order to use Fiedler's Contingency Theory. First, the leader should know whether he or she has a relationship- or task-oriented style. Second, the leader should diagnose the situation and determine whether leader-member relations, task structure, and position power are favorable or unfavorable.

Using the incorrect style for the situation can cause problems, as Alan Robbins discovered at Plastic Lumber Company.

LEADERSHIP SPOTLIGHT   **PLASTIC LUMBER COMPANY**

Alan Robbins intentionally put his factory in a gritty downtown neighborhood in Akron, Ohio. He considers himself an enlightened employer who wants to give people—even those who have made serious missteps—a chance to prove

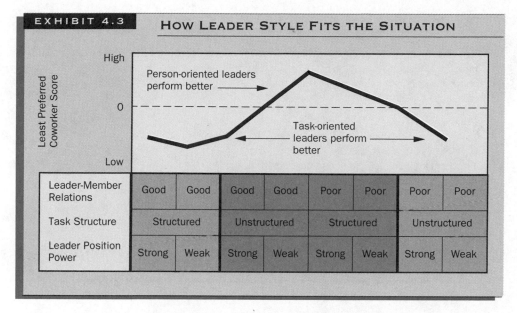

EXHIBIT 4.3   HOW LEADER STYLE FITS THE SITUATION

Leader-Member Relations	Good	Good	Good	Good	Poor	Poor	Poor	Poor
Task Structure	Structured		Unstructured		Structured		Unstructured	
Leader Position Power	Strong	Weak	Strong	Weak	Strong	Weak	Strong	Weak

SOURCE: Fred E. Fiedler, " The Effects of Leadership Training and Experience: A Contingency Model Interpretation," *Administrative Science Quarterly* 17 (1972), 455. Reprinted by permission of *Administrative Science Quarterly*.

themselves. Plastic Lumber Company converts old milk and soda bottles into fake lumber. Robbins employs about 50 workers and offers everyone full health insurance.

When he started the company, Robbins wanted to be both a boss and a friend to his workers. He would sometimes break out cold beers for everyone at the end of a shift or grant personal loans to employees in a financial bind. He stressed the idea of teamwork and spent lots of time running ideas by workers on the factory floor. He resisted the idea of drug testing, partly because of the expense and partly because it showed distrust. Besides, he couldn't imagine workers would show up drunk or on drugs when they knew they'd be operating dangerous machinery.

He was wrong. Robbins' relationship-oriented style didn't work in the situation he was operating in. The low-skilled workers, many from low-income drug-infested neighborhoods, weren't ready for the type of freedom Robbins granted them. Workers were frequently absent or late without calling, showed up under the influence, and started fights on the factory floor. The turning point came for Robbins when he finally dismissed two workers for fighting. One was roaming the factory looking for the other with an iron pipe in his hand. Today, Robbins has given up his ideals of being a pal. "I'm too busy just trying to make sure they show up," he says.[4]

Robbins' leadership at Plastic Lumber was unsuccessful because he used a relationship-oriented style in an unfavorable situation. Because of their life circumstances, many of those he hired were naturally distrustful, thus leader-member

The following points out that behavior that persists can be a disadvantage by ultimately resulting in the opposite of what the individual is striving for:

Polarities

All behavior consists of opposites or polarities. If I do anything more and more, over and over, its polarity will appear. For example, striving to be beautiful makes a person ugly, and trying too hard to be kind is a form of selfishness.

Any over-determined behavior produces its opposite:

- An obsession with living suggests worry about dying.

- True simplicity is not easy.
- Is it a long time or short time since we last met?
- The braggart probably feels small and insecure.
- Who would be first ends up last.

Knowing how polarities work, the wise leader does not push to make things happen, but allows process to unfold on its own.

SOURCE: John Heider, *The Tao of Leadership: Leadership Strategies for a New Age* (New York: Bantam Books, 1986), 3. Copyright © 1985 Humanic Ltd., Atlanta, GA. Used with permission.

relations were poor. Although Robbins had high formal power, many workers had poor work ethics and little respect for authority. Robbins' failure to provide rules, guidelines, and direction weakened his authority in their view. In the early days, workers believed they could get away with anything because of Robbins' easygoing style. Today, Robbins is developing a more task-oriented style, including putting together a comprehensive rules and policy manual and requiring drug tests of all new workers.

An important contribution of Fiedler's research is that it goes beyond the notion of leadership styles to show how styles fit the situation. On the other hand, the model has also been criticized,[5] although new research has continued to improve the model.[6] Using the LPC score as a measure of relationship- or task-oriented behavior seems simplistic to some observers, and how the model works over time is unclear. For instance, if a task-oriented leader is matched with an unfavorable situation and is successful, the organizational situation is likely to improve and become a situation more appropriate for a relationship-oriented leader. For example, after turning around a troubled Giddings & Lewis, and spawning a steady climb in earnings and sales over a six year period, William J. Fife, Jr., was asked to resign as director of the machine company. At Giddings, the situation improved, and the leadership needs of the organization changed. With an improved business climate, Fife's direct, quick-fix aggression became abrasive. Because the company was out of jeopardy, positive leader-member relations were more important to the organization. Creating enemies among subordinates and micromanaging every detail no longer made sense after the turn-around succeeded. Fife's extreme task-oriented leadership no longer suited the situation.[7] The Living Leadership box underscores the disadvantages of persisting in a behavior style despite the processes of change.

Hersey and Blanchard's Situational Theory

The **situational theory** developed by Hersey and Blanchard is an interesting extension of the leadership grid outlined in Chapter 3. This approach focuses on the characteristics of followers as the important element of the situation, and consequently of determining effective leader behavior. The point of Hersey and Blanchard is that subordinates vary in readiness level. People low in task readiness, because of little ability or training, or insecurity, need a different leadership style than those who are high in readiness and have good ability, skills, confidence, and willingness to work.[8]

The relationship between leader style and follower readiness is summarized in Exhibit 4.4. The upper part of the exhibit indicates the style of the leader, which is based on a combination of relationship behavior and task behavior. The bell-shaped curve is called a prescriptive curve, because it indicates when each leader style should be used. The four styles are telling (S1), selling (S2), participating (S3), and delegating (S4).

Telling (S1) is a very directive style. It involves giving explicit direction about how tasks should be accomplished. Mickey Drexler, president of The Gap clothing stores, provides his employees with specific guidelines for how all merchandise is to be displayed, and he monitors stores to ensure consistency.

Selling (S2) involves providing direction, but also includes seeking input from others before making decisions. George Bush was a consummate S2 leader. For example, before and during the Gulf War, Bush gathered input from the military and world leaders, which he used to make decisions.

Participating (S3) is a style that focuses on supporting the growth and improvement of others by guiding skill development and acting as a resource for advice and information. Sam Walton, founder of Wal-Mart, maximized his human resources by insisting on communication in all directions and enabling decision making opportunities for all employees.

Delegating (S4) is a style that affords little direction and little support. Under such conditions, employees assume responsibility for their work—and for the success of their organization. Ted Turner gives free reign to employees of Cable Network News (CNN) because their vested interest keeps them on the competitive edge.[9]

The appropriate style depends on the development or readiness of followers, indicated in the lower part of Exhibit 4.4. R1 is low readiness and R4 represents high readiness. The telling style is for low-readiness subordinates, because people are unable or unwilling to take responsibility for their own task behavior. The selling and participating styles work for followers with moderate readiness, and delegating is appropriate for employees with high readiness.

This contingency model is easier to understand than Fiedler's model, because it focuses only on the characteristics of followers, not those of the larger situation. The leader should evaluate subordinates and adopt whichever style is needed. The Cutting Edge box describes how a classroom teacher learned to work with followers at varying degrees of readiness.

The style can be tailored to individual subordinates similar to the leader-member exchange theory described in Chapter 3. If one follower is at a low level of

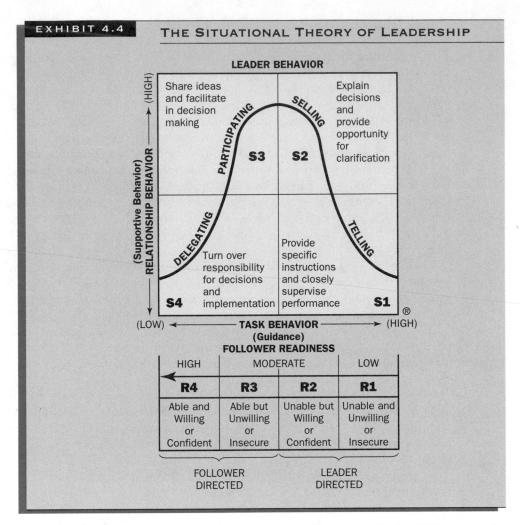

EXHIBIT 4.4 — THE SITUATIONAL THEORY OF LEADERSHIP

readiness, the leader must be very specific, telling them exactly what to do, how to do it, and when. For a follower high in readiness, the leader provides a general goal and sufficient authority to do the task as the follower sees fit. Leaders can carefully diagnose the readiness level of followers and then tell, sell, participate, or delegate. Consider the two contrasting styles in the following example.

LEADERSHIP SPOTLIGHT　　　**SUNBEAM-OSTER**

As CEO of Sunbeam-Oster, Paul B. Kazarian dictated the production schedule, withheld resources for product development, and controlled the daily operation of the company. Kazarian was very effective in saving Sunbeam-Oster from

ON THE CUTTING EDGE

Leadership in the Classroom

Classroom teachers face one of the toughest leadership challenges around. Carole McGraw, who has taught in Detroit, Michigan schools for 28 years, describes what a seasoned teacher sees when she walks into the classroom: "A ubiquitous sea of easily recognizable faces. There's Jamie, whose eyes glow with enthusiasm for learning. And Terrell, who just came from the crib after having no breakfast, no supervision of his inadequate homework, and a chip on his shoulder because he needed to flip hamburgers 'til 10 o'clock at night. . . . And Matt, who slumps over his desk, fast asleep from the Ritalin he took for a learning disorder that was probably misdiagnosed to correct a behavior problem. . . ." And on and on.

McGraw diagnosed what teenagers have in common to find the best way to help students of such varying degrees of readiness learn. She realized that all teenagers are exposed to countless hours of MTV, television programs, CDs, and disc jockeys. They spend a lot of time playing sports, eating junk food, talking on the phone, playing computer games, going to the movies, reading pop magazines, hanging out with peers, and avoiding adults. After considering this, McGraw developed her teaching method focused on three concepts: painless, interesting, and enjoyable. Students in McGraw's biology class now do almost all of their work in labs or teamwork sessions. During the labs, a captain is selected and she, not McGraw, is the boss. In teams, students select a viable problem to investigate and then split up the work and conduct research in books, on computers, and using laboratory supplies. Teams also spend a lot of time engaged in dialogue and brainstorming. McGraw will throw out an idea and let the students take off with it. She tells them there is always more than one way to look at an idea or problem and stresses that she's there to learn from their efforts too. Most of the tests are open-book and open-notes, and she also uses oral quizzes to discuss important topics from the textbook.

McGraw's teaching method combines telling and participating. Students are provided with direction about certain concepts, vocabulary words, and so forth that they must master, along with guidelines for doing so. However, most of her leadership focuses on supporting students as they learn and grow on their own. Does McGraw's innovative approach work? Sixty percent of the students get a grade of A and all score fairly well on objective tests McGraw gives after the teamwork is complete. Students from her classes score great on standardized tests like the SAT because they not only accumulate a lot of knowledge but also gain self-confidence and learn how to think on their feet. "All the stress my kids lived with for years disappears," McGraw says. "My classroom buzzes with new ideas and individual approaches."

SOURCE: Carole McGraw, "Teaching Teenagers? Think, Do, Learn," *Education Digest*, February 1998, 44–47.

chapter 11 bankruptcy, but within a short time his style was alienating executives. He was controlling things so tightly those executives did not have enough autonomy to make decisions, nor could they develop new products or build plants needed for the future. So, despite a healthy financial outlook, the board fired Kazarian based on complaints by executives.

The new CEO, Roger W. Schipke, valued his own autonomy and did not deny autonomy to his employees. The household-products market was constantly in flux and his managers had developed the capability to respond with their own initiatives. Schipke did not interfere with the work of his managers. The new production schedules and product designs testify to Schipke's confidence in the skills and decisions of his workforce. Indeed innovative products now give the company a competitive edge and allow expansion into additional markets.[10]

Kazarian had imposed a telling (S1) style of leadership upon a workforce that needed direction, but only for a short time. Schipke's participative style (S3) gave much more support to employee ideas. When employees develop a higher-level of readiness, they benefit from support, not directives.

When Jack Johnson became manager of a forklift plant, he assumed a participative style of leadership with the idea that the foreman under him was able to continue the high production levels of the past. However, production decreased, while the number of errors increased. Jack was forced to reexamine the situation and decide upon a new course of action. First, he determined the readiness level of the foreman. Since the foreman had not solved the problem, nor sought Jack's assistance in doing so, Jack determined a lack of commitment, thus a low level of readiness. He focused his next encounter with the foreman upon the task of decreasing errors only, delineated what the foreman must do, and closely monitored the progress of the foreman. Though difficult, Jack went from a participating (S3) leadership style appropriate for a higher level of readiness, to one for a low level of readiness, telling (S1).[11]

In this example the performance of the subordinate determined leadership style. Since the level of readiness for the foreman was low, Jack was able to gain control of the task and ensure a more effective outcome by assuming the style necessary to lead a low-readiness subordinate.

Path-Goal Theory

Another contingency approach to leadership is called the path-goal theory.[12] According to the **path-goal theory,** the leader's responsibility is to increase subordinates' motivation to attain personal and organizational goals. As illustrated in Exhibit 4.5, the leader increases follower motivation by either (1) clarifying the follower's path to the rewards that are available or (2) increasing the rewards that the follower values and desires. Path clarification means that the leader works with subordinates to help them identify and learn the behaviors that will lead to successful task accomplishment and organizational rewards. Increasing rewards means that the leader talks with subordinates to learn which rewards are important to them—that is, whether they desire intrinsic rewards from the work itself or extrinsic rewards such as raises or promotions. The leader's job is to increase personal payoffs to subordinates for goal attainment and to make the paths to these payoffs clear and easy to travel.[13] This model is called a contingency theory because it consists of three sets of contingencies—leader style, followers and situation, and the rewards to meet followers'

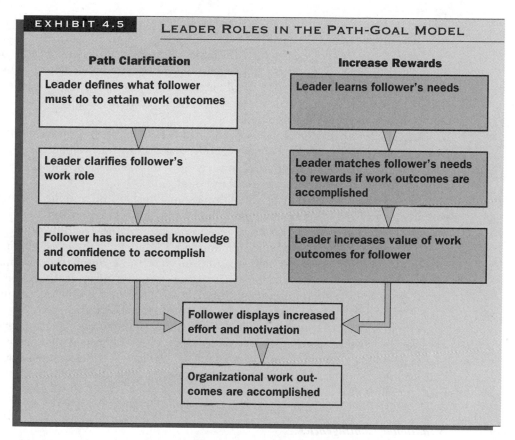

EXHIBIT 4.5 LEADER ROLES IN THE PATH-GOAL MODEL

Path Clarification

Leader defines what follower must do to attain work outcomes

Leader clarifies follower's work role

Follower has increased knowledge and confidence to accomplish outcomes

Increase Rewards

Leader learns follower's needs

Leader matches follower's needs to rewards if work outcomes are accomplished

Leader increases value of work outcomes for follower

Follower displays increased effort and motivation

Organizational work outcomes are accomplished

SOURCE: Based on Bernard M. Bass, "Leadership: Good, Better, Best," *Organizational Dynamics* 13 (Winter 1985), 26–40.

needs.[14] Whereas the Fiedler theory described earlier made the assumption that new leaders could take over as situations change, in the path-goal theory leaders change their behaviors to match the situation.

Leader Behavior

The path-goal theory suggests a fourfold classification of leader behaviors.[15] These classifications are the types of behavior the leader can adopt and include supportive, directive, achievement-oriented, and participative styles.

Supportive leadership shows concern for subordinates' well-being and personal needs. Leadership behavior is open, friendly, and approachable, and the leader creates a team climate and treats subordinates as equals. Supportive leadership is similar to the consideration or people-oriented leadership described earlier.

Directive leadership tells subordinates exactly what they are supposed to do. Leader behavior includes planning, making schedules, setting performance goals and behavior standards, and stressing adherence to rules and regulations. Directive leadership behavior is similar to the initiating structure or task-oriented leadership style described earlier.

Participative leadership consults with subordinates about decisions. Leader behavior includes asking for opinions and suggestions, encouraging participation in decision making, and meeting with subordinates in their workplaces. The participative leader encourages group discussion and written suggestions, similar to the S3 style in the Hersey and Blanchard model.

Achievement-oriented leadership sets clear and challenging goals for subordinates. Leader behavior stresses high-quality performance and improvement over current performance. Achievement-oriented leaders also show confidence in subordinates and assist them in learning how to achieve high goals.

To illustrate achievement-oriented leadership, consider the training of army officers in the ROTC. This training goes far beyond how to command a platoon. It involves the concepts of motivation, responsibility, and the creation of a team in which decision making is expected of everyone. Fundamentally, this training will enable officers to respond to any situation, not just those outlined in the manual. Thus achievement-oriented leadership is demonstrated: the set goals are challenging, require improvement, and demonstrate confidence in the abilities of subordinates—on the part of the future officers and the army who trains them.[16]

The four types of leader behavior are not considered ingrained personality traits as in the earlier trait theories; rather, they reflect types of behavior that every leader is able to adopt, depending on the situation. The Leader's Bookshelf also suggests that leaders consciously choose a leadership style that is suitable for their organization's circumstances.

Situational Contingencies

The two important situational contingencies in the Path-Goal Theory are (1) the personal characteristics of group members and (2) the work environment. Personal characteristics of subordinates are similar to Hersey and Blanchard's readiness level and include such factors as ability, skills, needs, and motivations. For example, if an employee has a low level of ability or skill, the leader may need to provide additional training or coaching in order for the worker to improve performance. If a subordinate is self-centered, the leader may use monetary rewards to motivate him or her. Subordinates who want clear direction and authority require a directive leader to tell them exactly what to do. Craft workers and professionals, however, may want more freedom and autonomy and work best under a participative leadership style.

The work environment contingencies include the degree of task structure, the nature of the formal authority system, and the work group itself. The task structure is similar to the same concept described in Fiedler's contingency theory; it includes the extent to which tasks are defined and have explicit job descriptions and work procedures. The formal authority system includes the amount of legitimate power used by leaders and the extent to which policies and rules constrain employees' behavior. Work-group characteristics are the educational level of subordinates and the quality of relationships among them.

Maximum Leadership: The World's Leading CEOs Share Their Five Strategies for Success
Charles M. Farkas and Philippe De Backer

According to Charles M. Farkas and Philippe De Backer, successful leaders around the world adopt leadership approaches that reflect the needs of the organization, not the personality of the leader. From interviews with 161 top leaders on six continents, including such companies as Nestlé, Gillette, Tenneco, and Dell Computer, Farkas and De Backer concluded that leaders can use five distinct leadership approaches to add value to their organizations. Although styles may overlap, most leaders focus on only one or two. Thus, regardless of personality, successful leaders demonstrate the knack for determining the style that is suitable for their particular organizational circumstances.

Five Strategies for Success

The five distinct approaches adopted by successful leaders are:

1. *The Strategic Approach*: The leader focuses on a vision of the organization's future and systematically maps out how to get there. A leader using this approach tries to see the big picture and may spend up to 80 percent of his or her time on external matters such as customers, competitors, technological advances, and market trends.

2. *The Human Assets Approach*: The leader cultivates empowered people through organizational policies and programs; rewards those who act; builds relationships; and focuses on shared values. These leaders spend most of their time in personnel-related activities because they consider the growth and development of employees their primary responsibility.

3. *The Expertise Approach*: The leader focuses the organization on a specific expertise that identifies the company's competitive edge. Most of this leader's time is spent cultivating and continually improving this expertise throughout the organization, such as studying new technological research, analyzing competitors' products, and meeting with engineers and customers.

4. *The Box Approach*: The leader who uses this approach concentrates on building a set of rules, systems, and procedures to control behavior and outcomes within well-defined boundaries. These leaders spend a lot of time looking at and correcting deviations from organizational controls, such as a project behind deadline or quarterly results below expectations.

5. *The Change Approach*: The leader focuses on significant organizational change. The leader who uses this approach sees his or her most critical role as creating an environment of continual reinvention, even if it causes mistakes and temporarily hurts financial performance. These leaders encourage risk taking, and they spend most of their time communicating directly with a wide range of stakeholders—customers, investors, suppliers, and employees at all organizational levels.

A Leadership Framework

The authors emphasize that leadership style is a matter of informed choice, often requiring leaders to inhibit their personalities or develop traits they don't already have. By answering questions about an organization's maturity, competitive advantage, technology, and human assets, a leader can determine which style will most effectively add value. Although the five leadership approaches are not recipes for success, they provide structure for the leader's role, and each can be powerful when used in the right circumstances.

Maximum Leadership: The World's Leading CEOs Share Their Five Strategies for Success, by Charles M. Farkas and Philippe De Backer, is published by Henry Holt & Company.

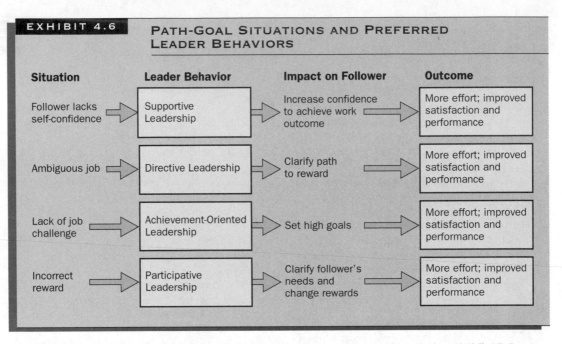

EXHIBIT 4.6 PATH-GOAL SITUATIONS AND PREFERRED LEADER BEHAVIORS

Situation	Leader Behavior	Impact on Follower	Outcome
Follower lacks self-confidence	Supportive Leadership	Increase confidence to achieve work outcome	More effort; improved satisfaction and performance
Ambiguous job	Directive Leadership	Clarify path to reward	More effort; improved satisfaction and performance
Lack of job challenge	Achievement-Oriented Leadership	Set high goals	More effort; improved satisfaction and performance
Incorrect reward	Participative Leadership	Clarify follower's needs and change rewards	More effort; improved satisfaction and performance

SOURCE: Adapted with permission from Gary A. Yukl, *Leadership in Organizations* Fourth Edition (Englewood Cliffs, NJ: Prentice-Hall, 1998).

Use of Rewards

Recall that the leader's responsibility is to clarify *the path to rewards* for subordinates or to increase *the amount of rewards* to enhance satisfaction and job performance. In some situations, the leader works with subordinates to help them acquire the skills and confidence needed to perform tasks and achieve rewards already available. In others, the leader may develop new rewards to meet the specific needs of a subordinate.

Exhibit 4.6 illustrates four examples of how leadership behavior is tailored to the situation. In the first situation, the subordinate lacks confidence, thus, the supportive leadership style provides the social support with which to encourage the subordinate to undertake the behavior needed to do the work and receive the rewards. In the second situation, the job is ambiguous, and the employee is not performing effectively. Directive leadership behavior is used to give instructions and clarify the task so that the follower will know how to accomplish it and receive rewards. In the third situation, the subordinate is unchallenged by the task; thus, an achievement-oriented behavior is used to set higher goals.

This clarifies the path to rewards for the employee. In the fourth situation, an incorrect reward is given to a subordinate, and the participative leadership style is used to change this. By discussing the subordinate's needs, the leader is able to identify the correct reward for task accomplishment. In all four cases, the outcome of fitting the leadership behavior to the situation produces greater employee effort by either clarifying how subordinates can receive rewards or changing the rewards to fit their needs. Leaders learn what rewards are valued by employees when they listen, as Keith Dunn discovered at McGuffey's.

Keith Dunn, owner of McGuffey's restaurants, offered dental insurance to retain quality employees. Still, his company lost money and experienced a 220 percent turnover rate. Then he tied compensation to his employees' performance. By getting more financial rewards, he reasoned, his employees would work harder and better. He initiated competitions between employee teams, and gave quarterly bonus incentives for managers who reached high goals. Nothing changed. He instituted "rap sessions" to find out why. No one attended.

It was no coincidence that Dunn's presence at his restaurants suffered as other things competed for his attention. After a long while, at the end of a trail of demoralized employees and resentful managers, Dunn finally heard when an assistant manager told him that nobody liked the contests because the same team kept winning. Then Dunn realized that he had not been listening to his employees but simply burdening them with untenable programs and ideas. Now employees are devising their own incentives for performance. Turnover has plummeted to less than 60 percent, and the profit margin looks more hopeful than it has in years.

Initially, Dunn neither clarified the path to rewards nor provided desired rewards. Only by utilizing a participating style of leadership did Dunn learn about his employees and what they wanted from their jobs. Only with this new knowledge could provisions for those desires be made.[17]

Path-goal theorizing can be complex, but much of the research on it has been encouraging.[18] Using the model to specify relationships and make exact predictions about employee outcomes may seem difficult at first, but the four types of leader behavior and the ideas for fitting them to situational contingencies provide a useful way for leaders to think about motivating subordinates.

The Vroom-Jago Contingency Model

The **Vroom-Jago Contingency Model** shares some basic principles with the previous models, yet it differs in significant ways as well. This model focuses specifically on varying degrees of participative leadership, and how each level of participation influences quality and accountability of decisions. A number of situational factors shape the likelihood that either a participative or autocratic approach will produce the best outcome.

This model starts with the idea that a leader faces a problem that requires a solution. Making decisions to solve the problem may be made by a leader alone, or through inclusion of a number of followers.

The Vroom-Jago model is very applied, which means it tells the leader precisely the correct amount of participation by subordinates to use in making a particular decision.[19] This approach helps the leader gauge the appropriate amount of participation for subordinates. It has three major components: leader participation styles, a set of diagnostic questions with which to analyze a decision situation, and a series of decision rules.

Leader Participation Styles

The model employs five levels of subordinate participation in decision making ranging from highly autocratic to highly democratic, as illustrated in Exhibit 4.7. Autocratic leadership styles are represented by AI and AII, consulting styles by CI and CII, and a group decision by G. The five styles fall along a continuum, and the leader should select one depending on the situation. If the situation warrants, the leader could make the decision alone, (AI), share the problem with subordinates individually (CI), or let group members made the decision (G).

Diagnostic Questions

How does a leader decide which of the five decision styles to use? The appropriate degree of the decision style to use? The appropriate degree of decision participation depends on the responses to eight diagnostic questions. These questions deal with the problem, the required level of decision quality, and the importance of having subordinates commit to the decision.

1. **Quality Requirement (QR):** *How important is the quality of this decision?* If a high-quality decision is important for group performance, the leader has to be actively involved.

2. **Commitment Requirement (CR):** *How important is subordinate commitment to the decision?* If implementation requires that subordinates commit to the decision, leaders should involve the subordinates in the decision process.

3. **Leader's Information (LI):** *Do I have sufficient information to make a high-quality decision?* If the leader does not have sufficient information or expertise, the leader should involve subordinates to obtain that information.

4. **Problem Structure (ST):** *Is the decision problem well structured?* If the problem is ambiguous and poorly structured, the leader will need to interact with subordinates to clarify the problem and identify possible solutions.

5. **Commitment Probability (CP):** *If I were to make the decision by myself, is it reasonably certain that my subordinates would be committed to the decision?* If subordinates typically go along with whatever the leader decides, their involvement in the decision process will be less important.

6. **Goal Congruence (GC):** *Do subordinates share the organizational goals to be attained in solving this problem?* If subordinates do not share the goals of the organization, the leader should not allow the group to make the decision alone.

EXHIBIT 4.7		FIVE LEADER DECISION STYLES
	Decision Style	**Description**
Highly Autocratic	**AI**	You solve the problem or make the decision yourself using information available to you at that time.
	AII	You obtain the necessary information from your subordinates and then decide on the solution to the problem yourself.
	CI	You share the problem with relevant subordinates individually, getting their ideas and suggestions without bringing them together as a group. Then you make the decision.
	CII	You share the problem with your subordinates as a group, collectively obtaining their ideas and suggestions. Then you make the decision.
Highly Democratic	**G**	You share a problem with your subordinates as a group. Your role is much like that of chairman. You do not try to influence the group to adopt "your" solution, and you are willing to accept and implement any solution that has the support of the entire group.

Note: A = autocratic; C = consultative; G = group.
SOURCE: Reprinted from Victor H. Vroom and Arthur G. Jago, *The New Leadership: Managing Participation in Organizations* (Englewood Cliffs, NJ: Prentice-Hall, 1988). Copyright 1987 by V. H. Vroom and A. G. Jago.

7. **Subordinate Conflict (CO):** *Is conflict over preferred solutions likely to occur among subordinates?* Disagreement among subordinates can be resolved by allowing their participation and discussion.

8. **Subordinate Information (SI):** *Do subordinates have enough information to make a high-quality decision?* If subordinates have good information, then more responsibility for the decision can be delegated to them.

These questions seem detailed, but they quickly narrow the options and point to the appropriate level of group participation in the decision.

Selecting a Decision Style

The decision flowchart in Exhibit 4.8 allows a leader to adopt a participation style by answering the questions in sequence. The leader begins at the left side of the chart with question QR: How important is the quality of the decision? If the answer is high, then the leader proceeds to question CR: How important is subordinate commitment to the decision? If the answer is high, the next question is LI: Do I have sufficient

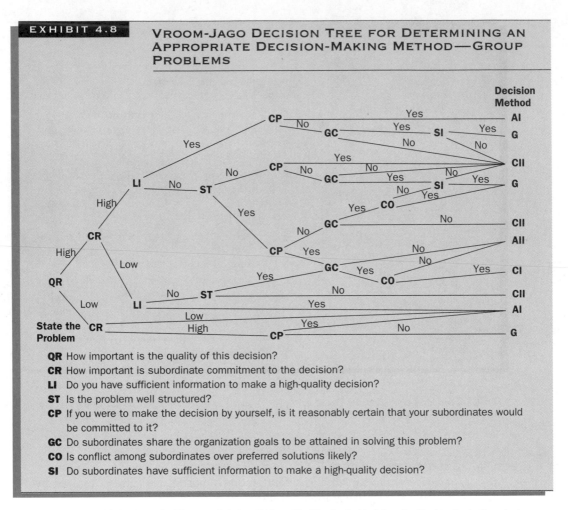

EXHIBIT 4.8

VROOM-JAGO DECISION TREE FOR DETERMINING AN APPROPRIATE DECISION-MAKING METHOD—GROUP PROBLEMS

QR How important is the quality of this decision?

CR How important is subordinate commitment to the decision?

LI Do you have sufficient information to make a high-quality decision?

ST Is the problem well structured?

CP If you were to make the decision by yourself, is it reasonably certain that your subordinates would be committed to it?

GC Do subordinates share the organization goals to be attained in solving this problem?

CO Is conflict among subordinates over preferred solutions likely?

SI Do subordinates have sufficient information to make a high-quality decision?

SOURCE: Reprinted from Victor H. Vroom and Arthur G. Jago, *The New Leadership: Managing Participation in Organizations* (Englewood Cliffs, NJ: Prentice-Hall, 1988). Copyright 1987 by V. H. Vroom and A. G. Jago.

information to make a high-quality decision? If the answer is yes, the leader proceeds to answer question CP because question ST is irrelevant if the leader has sufficient information to make a high-quality decision. Leaders can quickly learn to use the basic model to adapt their styles to fit their decision problem and the situation.

Several decision styles are equally acceptable in many situations. When this happens, Vroom and Jago note that the autocratic style saves time without reducing decision quality or acceptance. However, in today's changing workplace, where employees are often demanding more participation, leaders should try to involve subordinates in decision making whenever possible.

The decision tree model has been criticized as being less than perfect,[20] but it is useful to decision makers, and the body of supportive research is growing.[21]

Leaders make timely, high-quality decisions when following the model. One application of the model occurred at Barouh-Eaton Allen Corporation.

LEADERSHIP SPOTLIGHT   KO-REC-TYPE

Barouh-Eaton Allen started prospering when owner Vic Barouh noticed that a typist kept a piece of white chalk by her machine. To erase an error, she would lightly rub over it with the chalk. It took several passes, but the correction was neatly made. Barouh's company already made carbon paper, so he tried rubbing chalk on one side of a sheet of paper, putting the paper between the error and typewriter, and striking the same key. Most of the error disappeared under a thin coating of chalk dust. Thus, Ko-Rec-Type was born. Demand for the product was enormous, and the company prospered.

Then IBM invented the self-correcting typewriter. Within two days after IBM's announcement, nearly 40 people told Barouh that the company was in trouble. Nobody was going to buy Ko-Rec-Type again.

Barouh bought a self-correcting typewriter, took it to the plant, called everybody together, and told them what they had to do. To survive, the company had to learn to make this ribbon. They also had to learn to make the cartridge that held the ribbon, because cartridges could not be purchased on the market. They also had to learn to make the spools that held the tape. They had to learn to make the ink, the machine that puts on ink, injection molding to make the spools, and so on. It was an enormous challenge. Barouh got everyone involved regardless of position.

To everyone's astonishment, the company produced its first self-correcting ribbon in only six months. Moreover, it was the only company in the world to produce that product. Barouh later learned that it took IBM six years to make its self-correcting ribbon. With the new product, sales remained high, and the company avoided disaster.[22]

The Vroom-Jago model shows that Vic Barouh used the correct leader decision style. Moving from left to right in Exhibit 4.8, the questions and answers are as follows. **(QR)** *How important is the quality of this decision?* Definitely high. **(CR)** *How important is subordinate commitment to the decision?* Importance of commitment is probably low, because subordinates had a great deal of respect for Barouh and would do whatever he asked. **(LI)** *Did Barouh have sufficient information to make a high-quality decision?* Definitely no. **(ST)** *Is the problem well structured?* Definitely no. The remaining questions are not relevant because at this point the decision tree leads directly to the CII decision style. Barouh should have used a consultative decision style by having subordinates participate in problem discussions as a group—which he did.

Substitutes for Leadership

The contingency leadership approaches considered so far have focused on the leader's style, the follower's nature and the situation's characteristics. The final contingency approach suggests that situational variables can be so powerful that they actually substitute for or neutralize the need for leadership.[23] This approach outlines those organizational settings in which task-oriented and people-oriented leadership styles are unimportant or unnecessary.

Exhibit 4.9 shows the situational variables that tend to substitute for or neutralize leadership characteristics. A **substitute** for leadership makes the leadership style unnecessary or redundant. For example, highly educated, professional subordinates who know how to do their tasks do not need a leader who initiates structure for them and tells them what to do. In addition, long-term education often develops autonomous, self-motivated individuals. Thus, task-oriented and people-oriented leadership is substituted by professional education and socialization.[24]

A **neutralizer** counteracts the leadership style and prevents the leader from displaying certain behaviors. For example, if a leader is physically removed from subordinates, the leader's ability to give directions to subordinates is greatly reduced. Kinko's, a nationwide copy center, includes numerous locations widely scattered across regions. Managers enjoy very limited personal interaction due to the distances between stores. Thus, their ability to both support and direct is neutralized.

Situational variables in Exhibit 4.9 include characteristics of the followers, the task, and the organization itself. For example, when subordinates are highly professional, both leadership styles are less important. The employees do not need either direction or support. With respect to task characteristics, highly structured tasks substitute for a task-oriented style, and a satisfying task substitutes for a people-oriented style. In other words, when a task is highly structured and routine, like a cash auditor, the leader should provide personal consideration and support that is not provided by the task. Satisfied people don't need as much consideration. Likewise with respect to the organization itself, group cohesiveness substitutes for both leader styles. For example, the relationship that develops among air-traffic controllers and jet fighter pilots is characterized by high stress interactions and continuous peer training. This cohesiveness provides support and direction that substitutes for formal leadership.[25] Formalized rules and procedures substitute for leader task orientation, because the rules tell people what to do. Physical separation of leader and subordinate neutralizes both leadership styles.

The value of the situations described in Exhibit 4.9 is that they help leaders avoid leadership overkill. Leaders should adopt a style with which to complement the organizational situation. For example, the work situation for bank tellers provides a high level of formalization, little flexibility, and a highly structured task. The head teller should not adopt a task-oriented style, because the organization already provides structure and direction. The head teller should concentrate on a people-oriented style. In other organizations, if group cohesiveness or previous training meets employee social needs, the leader is free to concentrate on task-oriented behaviors. The leader can adopt a style complementary to the organizational situation to ensure that both task needs and people needs of followers are met.

Recent studies examined how substitutes (the situation) can be designed to have more impact than leader behaviors on such outcomes as subordinate satisfaction.[26]

EXHIBIT 4.9	SUBSTITUTES AND NEUTRALIZERS FOR LEADERSHIP		
Variable		Task-Oriented Leadership	People-Oriented Leadership
Organizational variables:	Group cohesiveness	Substitutes for	Substitutes for
	Formalization	Substitutes for	No effect on
	Inflexibility	Neutralizes	No effect on
	Low positional power	Neutralizes	Neutralizes
	Physical separation	Neutralizes	Neutralizes
Task characteristics:	Highly structured task	Substitutes for	No effect on
	Automatic feedback	Substitutes for	No effect on
	Intrinsic satisfaction	No effect on	Substitutes for
Follower characteristics:	Professionalism	Substitutes for	Substitutes for
	Training/experience	Substitutes for	No effect on
	Low value of rewards	Neutralizes	Neutralizes

The impetus behind this research is the idea that substitutes for leadership can be designed in organizations in ways to complement existing leadership, act in the absence of leadership, and otherwise provide more comprehensive leadership alternatives. For example, Paul Reeves, a foreman at Harmon Auto Parts, shared half-days with his subordinates during which they helped him perform his leader tasks. After Reeves' promotion to middle management, his group no longer required a foreman. Followers were trained to act on their own.[27] Thus, a situation in which follower ability and training were highly developed created a substitute for leadership.

The ability to utilize substitutes to fill leadership "gaps" is often advantageous to organizations. Indeed, the fundamental assumption of substitutes-for-leadership researchers is that effective leadership is the ability to recognize and provide the support and direction not already provided by task, group, and organization.

Summary and Interpretation

The most important point in this chapter is that situational variables affect leadership outcomes. The contingency approaches were developed to systematically address the relationship between a leader and the organization. The contingency approaches focus on how the components of leadership style, subordinate characteristics, and situational elements impact one another. Fiedler's contingency model,

Hersey and Blanchard's situational theory, the path-goal theory, and substitutes for leadership each examine how different situations call for different styles of leadership behavior.

According to Fiedler, leaders can determine if the situation is favorable to their leadership style. Task-oriented leaders tend to do better in very easy or very difficult situations, while person-oriented leaders do best in situations of intermediate favorability. Hersey and Blanchard contend that leaders can adjust their task or relationship style to accommodate the readiness level of their subordinates. The path-goal theory states that leaders can use a style that appropriately clarifies the path to desired rewards. The Vroom-Jago model indicates that leaders can choose a participative decision style based on contingencies such as quality requirement, commitment requirement, or the leader's information. Leaders can analyze each situation to determine the appropriate involvement of subordinates. Finally, substitutes-for-leadership recommends that leaders adjust their style to provide resources not otherwise provided in the organizational situation.

By discerning the characteristics of tasks, subordinates, and organizations, leaders can determine the style that increases the likelihood of effective leadership outcomes. Therefore effective leadership is about developing diagnostic skills and being flexible in your leadership behavior.

Key Terms

contingency	situational theory	substitute
contingency approaches	path-goal theory	neutralizer
Fiedler's contingency model	Vroom-Jago model	

Discussion Questions

1. Consider Fiedler's theory as illustrated in Exhibit 4.2. How often do you think very favorable, intermediate, or very unfavorable situations occur to leaders in real life? Discuss.

2. Do you think leadership style is fixed and unchangeable or flexible and adaptable? Why?

3. Consider the leadership position of the managing partner in a law firm. What task, subordinate, and organizational factors might serve as substitutes for leadership in this situation?

4. Compare Fiedler's contingency model with the path-goal theory. What are the similarities and differences? Which do you prefer?

5. Think of a situation in which you worked. At what level of readiness (R1 to R4) would you rate yourself and coworkers? Did your leader use the correct style according to the Hersey and Blanchard model?

6. Think back to teachers you have had, and identify one each who fits a supportive style, directive style, participative style, and achievement-oriented style according to the path-goal theory. Which style did you find most effective? Why?

7. Do you think leaders should decide on a participative style based on the most "efficient" way to reach the decision? Should leaders sometimes let people participate for other reasons?

8. Consider the situational characteristics of group cohesiveness, organizational formalization, and physical separation. How might each of these substitute for or neutralize task-oriented or people-oriented leadership? Explain.

Leadership Development: Personal Feedback

T-P Leadership Questionnaire: An Assessment of Style

The following items describe aspects of leadership behavior. Respond to each item according to the way you would most likely act if you were a leader of a work group. Circle whether you would most likely behave in the described way: always (A), frequently (F), occasionally (O), seldom (S), or never (N).

1. I would most likely act as the spokesperson of the group. A F O S N

2. I would encourage overtime work. A F O S N

3. I would allow members complete freedom in their work. A F O S N

4. I would encourage the use of uniform procedures. A F O S N

5. I would permit members to use their own judgment in solving problems. A F O S N

6. I would stress being ahead of competing groups. A F O S N

7. I would speak as a representative of the group. A F O S N

8. I would needle members for greater effort. A F O S N

9. I would try out my ideas in the group. A F O S N

10. I would let members do their work the way they think best. A F O S N

11. I would be working hard for a promotion. A F O S N

12. I would tolerate postponement and uncertainty. A F O S N

13. I would speak for the group if there were visitors present. A F O S N

14. I would keep the work moving at a rapid pace. A F O S N

15. I would turn the members loose on a job and let them
    go for it.   A F O S N

16. I would settle conflicts when they occurred in the group.   A F O S N

17. I would get swamped by details.   A F O S N

18. I would represent the group at outside meetings.   A F O S N

19. I would be reluctant to allow the members any freedom
    of action.   A F O S N

20. I would decide what should be done and how it should
    be done.   A F O S N

21. I would push for increased production.   A F O S N

22. I would let some members have authority that I could keep.   A F O S N

23. Things would usually turn out as I had predicted.   A F O S N

24. I would allow the group a high degree of initiative.   A F O S N

25. I would assign group members to particular tasks.   A F O S N

26. I would be willing to make changes.   A F O S N

27. I would ask the members to work harder.   A F O S N

28. I would trust the group members to exercise good
    judgment.   A F O S N

29. I would schedule the work to be done.   A F O S N

30. I would refuse to explain my actions.   A F O S N

31. I would persuade others that my ideas are to their advantage. A F O S N

32. I would permit the group to set its own pace.   A F O S N

33. I would urge the group to beat its previous record.   A F O S N

34. I would act without consulting the group.   A F O S N

35. I would ask that group members follow standard rules
    and regulations.   A F O S N

Scoring   T _____   P _____

The T-P Leadership Questionnaire is scored as follows:

a. Circle the item number for items 8, 12, 17, 18, 19, and 35.

b. Write the number 1 in front of *circled item numbers* to which you
   responded S (seldom) or N (never).

c. Also write a number 1 in front of *item numbers not circled* if you responded A (always) or F (frequently).

d. Circle the number 1s that you have written in front of the following items: 3, 5, 8, 10, 15, 18, 19, 22, 24, 26, 28, 30, 32, 34, and 35.

e. Count the circled number 1s. This is your score for concern for people. Record the score in the blank following the letter P at the end of the questionnaire.

f. *Count uncircled number 1s.* This is your score for concern for task. Record this number in the blank following the letter T.

Interpretation

Some leaders deal with people needs, leaving task details to subordinates. Other leaders focus on specific details with the expectation that subordinates will carry out orders. Depending on the situation, both approaches may be effective. The important issue is the ability to identify relevant dimensions of the situation and behave accordingly. Through this questionnaire, you can identify your relative emphasis on two dimensions of leadership: task orientation (T) and people orientation (P). These are not opposite approaches, and an individual can rate high or low on either or both.

What is your leadership orientation? What would you consider an ideal leader situation for your style?

SOURCE: The T-P Leadership Questionnaire was adapted by J. B. Ritchie and P. Thompson in *Organization and People* (New York: West, 1984). Copyright 1969 by the American Educational Research Association. Adapted by permission of the publisher from "Toward a Particularistic Approach to Leadership Style: Some Findings" by T.J. Sergiovanni, AERA 6 (1), 62-79, 1969.

Leadership Development: Case for Analysis

Alvis Corporation

Kevin McCarthy is the manager of a production department in Alvis Corporation, a firm that manufactures office equipment. After reading an article that stressed the benefits of participative management, Kevin believes that these benefits could be realized in his department if the workers are allowed to participate in making some decisions that affect them. The workers are not unionized. Kevin selected two decisions for his experiment in participative management.

The first decision involved vacation schedules. Each summer the workers were given two weeks vacation, but no more than two workers can go on vacation at the same time. In prior years, Kevin made this decision himself. He would first ask the workers to indicate their preferred dates, and he considered how the work would be affected if different people were out at the same time. It was important to plan a vacation schedule that would ensure adequate staffing for all of the essential operations performed by the department. When more than two workers wanted the same time period, and they had similar skills, he usually gave preference to the workers with the highest productivity.

The second decision involved production standards. Sales had been increasing steadily over the past few years, and the company recently installed some new equipment to increase productivity. The new equipment would allow Kevin's department to produce more with the same number of workers. The company had a pay incentive system in which workers received a piece rate for each unit produced above a standard amount. Separate standards existed for each type of product, based on an industrial engineering study conducted a few years earlier. Top management wanted to readjust the production standards to reflect the fact that the new equipment made it possible for the workers to earn more without working any harder. The savings from higher productivity were needed to help pay for the new equipment.

Kevin called a meeting of his 15 workers an hour before the end of the workday. He explained that he wanted them to discuss the two issues and make recommendations. Kevin figured that the workers might be inhibited about participating in the discussion if he were present, so he left them alone to discuss the issues. Besides, Kevin had an appointment to meet with the quality control manager. Quality problems had increased after the new equipment was installed, and the industrial engineers were studying the problem in an attempt to determine why quality had gotten worse rather than better.

When Kevin returned to his department just at quitting time, he was surprised to learn that the workers recommended keeping the standards the same. He had assumed they knew the pay incentives were no longer fair and would set a higher standard. The spokesman for the group explained that their base pay had not kept up with inflation and the higher incentive pay restored their real income to its prior level.

On the vacation issue, the group was deadlocked. Several of the workers wanted to take their vacations during the same two-week period and could not agree on who should go. Some workers argued that they should have priority because they had more seniority, while others argued that priority should be based on productivity, as in the past. Since it was quitting time, the group concluded that Kevin would have to resolve the dispute himself. After all, wasn't that what he was being paid for?

SOURCE: Reprinted with permission from Gary Yukl, *Leadership in Organizations* Fourth Edition (Englewood Cliffs, NJ: Prentice Hall, 1998), 147-148.

Questions

1. Analyze this situation using the Hersey-Blanchard model and the Vroom-Jago model. What do these models suggest as the appropriate leadership or decision style? Explain.

2. Evaluate Kevin McCarthy's leadership style before and during his experiment in participative management.

3. If you were Kevin McCarthy, what would you do now? Why?

References

[1]Harvey Meyer, "A Tale of 2 Bosses," *Journal of Business Strategy*, November/December 1996, 46–51.

[2]Meyer, "A Tale of 2 Bosses."

[3]Fred E. Fiedler, "Assumed Similarity Measures as Predictors of Team Effectiveness," *Journal of Abnormal and Social Psychology* 49 (1954), 381–388; F.E. Fiedler, *Leader Attitudes and Group Effectiveness* (Urbana, IL: University of Illinois Press, 1958); and F.E. Fiedler, *A Theory of Leadership Effectiveness* (New York: McGraw-Hill, 1967).

[4]Timothy Aeppel, "Personnel Disorders Sap a Factory Owner of His Early Idealism," *The Wall Street Journal*, January 14, 1998, A1, A14.

[5]R. Singh, "Leadership Style and Reward Allocation: Does Least Preferred Coworker Scale Measure Tasks and Relation Orientation?" *Organizational Behavior and Human Performance* 27 (1983), 178–197; and D. Hosking, "A Critical Evaluation of Fiedler's Contingency Hypotheses," *Progress in Applied Psychology* 1 (1981), 103–154.

[6]Roya Ayman, M.M. Chemers, and F. Fiedler, "The Contingency Model of Leadership Effectiveness: Its Levels of Analysis," *Leadership Quarterly* 6 (2):147–167 (1995).

[7]Robert L. Rose, "Sour Note," *The Wall Street Journal*, June 22, 1993.

[8]Paul Hersey and Kenneth H. Blanchard, *Management of Organizational Behavior: Utilizing Human Resources*, 4th Ed. (Englewood Cliffs, NJ: Prentice-Hall, 1982).

[9]These examples are adapted from *Soundview: Executive Book Summaries*, 16 (7): 3–4, (July 1994).

[10]Gail DeGeorge, "Why Sunbeam Is Shining Brighter," *Business Week*, August 29, 1994, 74–75.

[11]Adapted from Oliver Niehouse, "The Strategic Nature of Leadership," *Management Solutions*, July 1987, 27–34.

[12]M.G. Evans, "The Effects of Supervisory Behavior on the Path-Goal Relationship," Organizational Behavior and Human Performance 5 (1970), 277–298; M.G. Evans, "Leadership and Motivation: A Core Concept," *Academy of Management Journal* 13 (1970), 91–102; and B.S. Georgopoulos, G.M. Mahoney, and N.W. Jones, "A Path-Goal Approach to Productivity," *Journal of Applied Psychology* 41 (1957), 345–353.

[13]Robert J. House, "A Path-Goal Theory of Leadership Effectiveness," *Administrative Science Quarterly* 16 (1971), 321–338.

[14]M.G. Evans, "Leadership," in *Organizational Behavior*, ed. S. Kerr (Columbus, OH: Grid, 1974), 230–233.

[15]Robert J. House and Terrence R. Mitchell, "Path Goal Theory of Leadership," *Journal of Contemporary Business* (Autumn 1974), 81–97.

[16]Dyan Machan, "We're Not Authoritarian Goons," *Forbes*, October 24, 1994, 264–268.

[17]Joshua Hyatt, "The Odyssey of an Excellent Man," *Inc.*, February 1989, 63–69.

[18]Charles Greene, "Questions of Causation in the Path-Goal Theory of Leadership," *Academy of Management Journal* 22 (March 1979), 22–41; and C.A. Schriesheim and Mary Ann von Glinow, "The Path-Goal Theory of Leadership: A Theoretical and Empirical Analysis," *Academy of Management Journal* 20 (1977), 398–405.

[19]V.H. Vroom and Arthur G. Jago, *The New Leadership: Managing Participation in Organizations* (Englewood Cliffs, NJ: Prentice-Hall, 1988).

[20]R.H.G. Field, "A Test of the Vroom-Yetton Normative Model of Leadership," *Journal of Applied Psychology* (October 1982), 523–532; and R.H.G. Field, "A Critique of the Vroom-Yetton Contingency Model of Leadership Behavior," *Academy of Management Review* 4 (1979), 249–251.

[21]Jennifer T. Ettling and Arthur G. Jago, "Participation Under Conditions of Conflict: More on the Validity of the Vroom-Yetton Model," *Journal of Management Studies* 25 (1988), 73–83; Madeline E. Heilman, Harvey A. Hornstein, Jack H. Cage, and Judith K. Herschlag, "Reactions to Prescribed Leader Behavior as a Function of Role Perspective: The Case of the Vroom-Yetton Model," *Journal of Applied Psychology*

(February 1984), 50–60; and Arthur G. Jago and Victor H. Vroom, "Some Differences in the Incidence and Evaluation of Participative Leader Behavior," *Journal of Applied Psychology* (December 1982), 776–783.

[22]Tom Richman, "One Man's Family," *Inc.*, November 1983, 151–156.

[23]S. Kerr and J.M. Jermier, "Substitutes for Leadership: Their Meaning and Measurement," *Organizational Behavior and Human Performance* 22 (1978), 375–403; and Jon P. Howell and Peter W. Dorfman, "Leadership and Substitutes for Leadership Among Professional and Nonprofessional Workers," *Journal of Applied Behavioral Science* 22 (1986), 29–46.

[24]J.P. Howell, D.E. Bowen, P.W. Doreman, S. Kerr, and P.M. Podsakoff, "Substitutes for Leadership: Effective Alternatives to Ineffective Leadership," *Organizational Dynamics* (Summer 1990), 21–38.

[25]Howell, et al., "Subsitutes for Leadership: Effective Alternatives to Ineffective Leadership."

[26]P.M. Podsakoff, S.B. MacKenzie, and W.H. Bommer, "Transformational Leader Behaviors and Substitutes for Leadership as Determinants of Employee Satisfaction, Commitment, Trust, and Organizational Behaviors," *Journal of Management*, 22 (2) (1996), 259–298.

[27]Howell, et al., "Substitutes for Leadership."

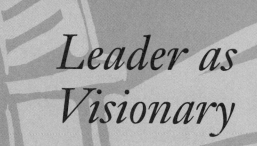

PART THREE

Leader as Visionary

Chapter 5
Leadership Vision and
Strategic Direction

Chapter 6
Leadership Communication

Leadership Vision and Strategic Direction

- **Strategic Leadership**   124

- **Leadership Vision**   126

- **Mission**   133

- **Strategy Formulation**   135

- **Strategy in Action**   138

- **The Leader's Contribution**   139

- **The Leader's Impact**   143

- **Leadership Spotlights:**
  Walt Disney   130
  Amgen   136
  Boy Scouts of America   141

- **Leader's Bookshelf:**
  Built to Last: Successful Habits of Visionary Companies   134

- **Leadership Development: Personal Feedback**
  Visionary Leadership   146

- **Leadership Development: Case for Analysis**
  Metropolis Police Department   148

Your Leadership Challenge

After reading this chapter, you should be able to:

- Explain the relationship among vision, mission, strategy, and implementation mechanisms.

- Create your personal leadership vision.

- Use the common themes of powerful visions and apply what good visions can do.

- Understand how leaders formulate and implement strategy.

- Apply the elements of effective strategy.

Nike CEO Phil Knight has always believed in taking risks. In the 1960s, he turned the sleepy footwear industry upside down by acting on the belief that joggers would pay premium prices for high-quality running shoes. When shoe sales slowed during the 1980s, the company saturated the airwaves with cutting-edge commercials that featured major athletes, appealing to a passion for sports rather than focusing on Nike's products. Today, Nike has moved beyond shoes into a wide range of sports apparel and equipment, as well as producing major events like golf tournaments and soccer matches. By pursuing a strategy of continuous reinvention, Nike has remained successful and profitable in a volatile industry.

"We're constantly reviewing how the world has changed and how we're reacting to it," Knight says. Despite this passion for continuous renewal, Nike's strategies have always

been guided by the same basic philosophy, the emotional experience of competition: winning and crushing competitors. This philosophy permeates the entire company. At company headquarters, giant photos of Nike heroes cover the walls, bronze plaques of athletes hang along the Nike Walk of Fame, and buildings honor outstanding athletes like Michael Jordan and John McEnroe. The company culture supports and rewards employees who are aggressive and competitive.

Nike has thrived for years on its vision to "crush the enemy." First, it set out to beat Adidas and within a decade all but destroyed the former market leader. Unexpectedly, Reebok gained ground and became a target worthy of Nike's competitive drive. Today, Nike commands 40 percent of the athletic shoe business compared to Reebok's 16 percent. Although Nike is clearly the Goliath of sporting equipment today, Adidas is making a surprising comeback, helping to keep Nike's competitive juices flowing. Says Sonny Vaccaro, the promoter who discovered Michael Jordan for Nike, but is now helping Adidas make a comeback: "Does Phil Knight want me dead? You bet."[1]

Regardless of Nike's past success, Phil Knight is constantly looking forward. An important part of a leader's job is to set a course toward the future and get everyone in the organization moving in the same direction. Employee motivation and energy are crucial to the success of all organizations; the role of leadership is to focus everyone's energy on the same path. For Phil Knight, this means focusing employees on defeating a common enemy. At City Bank, the predecessor of Citicorp, it meant energizing employees to make the company "the most powerful, the most serviceable, the most far-reaching world financial institution that has ever been." That vision, articulated in 1915 by a small regional bank, motivated and inspired generations of workers until it was eventually achieved.[2]

One of leadership's primary functions is to create a compelling vision and develop a strategy to achieve it. Traditionally, in more stable times, top leaders defined the vision and organized human and material resources to achieve it. In today's era of turbulent change, everyone in an organization must understand and support the vision so they can adapt their behaviors to achieving it.

In this chapter, we will first provide an overview of the leader's role in creating the organization's future. Then, we examine what vision is, the underlying themes that are common to effective visions, and how vision works on multiple levels. The distinction between vision and the organization's mission will also be explained. We will discuss how leaders formulate vision and strategy and the leader's contribution to actually achieving the vision. The last section discusses the impact this leadership has on organizations.

Strategic Leadership

Superior organizational performance is not a matter of luck. It is determined largely by choices leaders make. Top leaders, like Phil Knight at Nike, are responsible for knowing the organization's environment, considering what it might be like in five or ten years, and setting a direction for the future that everyone can believe in. In

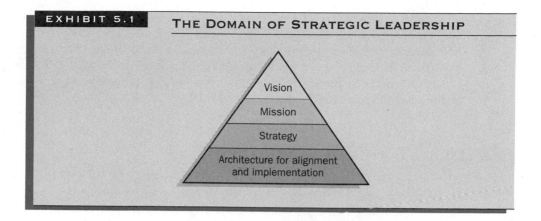

EXHIBIT 5.1 THE DOMAIN OF STRATEGIC LEADERSHIP

Vision

Mission

Strategy

Architecture for alignment
and implementation

a fast-changing world, leaders are faced with a bewildering array of complex, ambiguous information, and no two leaders will see things the same way or make the same choices.

The complexity of the environment and the uncertainty of the future can overwhelm an executive. Thus, many are inclined to focus on internal organizational issues where they feel they have more control. They tend to concentrate on short-term results rather than taking the long-term view. One study found that, on average, senior executives in today's organizations spend less than 3 percent of their energy on building a corporate perspective for the future, and in some companies, the average is less than 1 percent.[3]

The first, essential step to remaining competitive is to develop an understanding of the trends and discontinuities that can be used to gain an edge. Companies like Nike, Harley Davidson, Home Depot, and Champion Enterprises have gained a competitive edge by either inventing new industries or totally reinventing existing ones. Champion was going broke selling inexpensive factory-built houses. CEO Walter Young, Jr., says, "People thought we were in the trailer park business. It was a real perception problem." Young decided to rewrite the rules of the manufactured housing industry. Today, Champion builds full-size houses in its factories and offers customers options like porches, skylights, and whirlpool baths.[4]

Thinking about how to meet future customer needs is more important now than ever. Globalization, deregulation, advancing technology, and changing demographics and lifestyles are profoundly altering the way businesses are perceived and operate. The world in 2010 will be different from the world of today, and leaders are responsible for determining how their organizations can fit into that world. No organization can thrive for long without a clear viewpoint and framework for the future.

Exhibit 5.1 illustrates the levels that make up the domain of strategic leadership. **Strategic leadership** is responsible for the relationship of the external environment to choices about vision, mission, strategy, and their implementation.[5] At the top of Exhibit 5.1 is a clear, compelling vision of where the organization wants to be in five to ten years. The vision reflects the environment and works in concert with the company's mission--its core values, purpose, and reason for existence. Strategy provides direction for translating the vision into action and is the basis for the development of specific mechanisms to help the organization achieve goals. Strategies are intentions, whereas implementation is through the basic organization architecture (structure, incentives) that makes things happen. Each level of the hierarchy in Exhibit 5.1 supports the level above it. Each part of this framework will be discussed in the remainder of this chapter.

Leadership Vision

A vision can be thought of as a dream for the future. Rebekka Weinstein, the daughter of an entrepreneur, has grown up with the dream of going into business for herself, of not being "harnessed and restricted by the corporate world." Her dream motivated her to study hard and achieve high academic honors at Richardson High School in Texas, which in turn enabled her to win a scholarship that will help finance her studies at Brown University. Moreover, Rebekka has already started her own jewelry-making business, creating custom pieces for individuals and selling original designs through the museum store at the Dallas Museum of Art and through a few independent retailers.[6] Rebekka's dream has played a powerful role in motivating her behavior and guiding her decisions and actions. Rebekka's dream is a personal one, but if her vision becomes a reality, she will someday have to create a vision that will inspire and motivate her employees as well as herself.

For organizations, a **vision** is an attractive, ideal future that is credible yet not readily attainable. A vision is not *just* a dream—it is an ambitious view of the future that everyone in the organization can believe in, one that can realistically be achieved, yet offers a future that is better in important ways than what now exists. In the 1950s, Sony Corporation wanted to "[b]ecome the company most known for changing the worldwide poor-quality image of Japanese products."[7] It may be hard to believe today, but in the 1950s this was a highly ambitious goal. Sometimes visions are brief, compelling, and slogan-like, easily communicated to and understood by everyone in the organization. For example, Coca-Cola's "A Coke within arm's reach of everyone on the planet" and Komatsu's "Encircle Caterpillar" serve to motivate all workers. The Cutting Edge box describes the vision for a young company called Microstrategy.

As these visions illustrate, a vision presents a challenge—it is an ambitious view of the future that requires employees to give their best. The City Bank vision mentioned earlier is another example: considering its size and strength at the time, City Bank's vision to become the most far-reaching bank in the world was highly ambitious, but it was eventually attained. Bill Gates at Microsoft has been talking about "a personal computer on every desk in every home" for 20 years—long before most people knew how to turn one on.[8]

In Exhibit 5.2, vision is shown as a guiding star, drawing everyone in the organization along the same path toward the future. Taking the organization on this path requires leadership. Compare this to rational management (as described in Chapter 2), which leads to the status quo. When employees have a guiding vision, everyday

ON THE CUTTING EDGE

Microstrategy

When Michael Saylor started Microstrategy back in 1989, no one thought it would amount to much. Saylor was 24 years old and just out of the Massachusetts Institute of Technology. Eight years later, the company had more than 400 employees and was bringing in around $50 million in revenues a year.

Saylor has an ambitious, almost radical vision: to bring all sorts of data directly to the public—to allow the man or woman on the street to wander through the databases of life, finding whatever information they need directly at the source. He believes we will all eventually be able to sit in front of our personal computers and ask questions of any database around the world.

Microstrategy's specialty is relational online analytical processing, or ROLAP, which answers questions by analyzing very large data sets. Companies want to tie their computer systems into huge networks that integrate databases: customer records, transactions, sales calls, receipts, employee records, and so forth. All that data is useful only to the extent that it can be accessed and made pertinent to everyone who has a stake in it. Even in large marketing companies, it is difficult to get answers to fairly simple questions, such as how sales of a particular product are doing against the budget in each region. Microstrategy's software is already helping companies make their data useful to employees as well as suppliers and customers.

The visionary next step is open public access to big databases. Although there are tricky, unresolved questions about privacy and proprietary rights to information, Saylor believes in his vision and believes there are significant economic and social benefits to be gained from open access. He doesn't blink an eye when he talks about building the next billion-dollar software company based on the idea. Saylor has already mapped out every step of the company's long-term strategy for converting his vision into reality. Some people may think he's nuts, but Saylor doesn't care. No one ever built a billion-dollar company by thinking small.

SOURCE: Stewart Alsop, "Now I Know How a Real Visionary Sounds," *Fortune*, September 8, 1997, 161–162.

decisions and actions throughout the organization respond to current problems and challenges in ways that move the organization toward the future rather than maintain the status quo.

What Vision Does

Vision works in a number of important ways. An effective vision provides a link between today and tomorrow, serves to energize and motivate employees toward the future, provides meaning for people's work, and sets a standard of excellence in the organization.[9]

Vision Links the Present to the Future Vision connects what is going on right now with what the organization aspires to. A vision is always about the future, but it begins with the here and now. In organizations, the pressures to meet deadlines, make the big sale, solve immediate problems, and complete specific projects are very

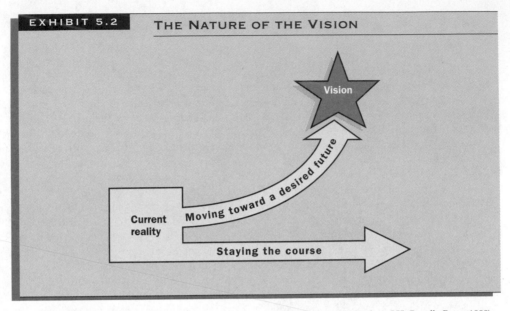

EXHIBIT 5.2 — THE NATURE OF THE VISION

SOURCE: Based on William D. Hitt, *The Leader-Manager: Guidelines for Action* (Columbus, OH: Battelle Press, 1988).

real. The problem for today's organizations is that managers spend most of their time dealing with current problems and little time contemplating and visualizing the future. Some have suggested that today's leaders need "bifocal vision," the ability to take care of the needs of today and meet current obligations while also aiming toward dreams for the future.[10] The ability to operate on both levels can be seen in a number of successful companies, such as DuPont. Top executives routinely review short-term operational goals with managers throughout the company, reflecting a focus on the present. However, DuPont has succeeded over the long haul because of its leaders' ability to look to the future and shift gears quickly to take advantage of new opportunities. Since its beginning, DuPont's business portfolio has shifted from gunpowder to specialty chemicals, and today, the company is moving into biotechnology and life sciences.[11]

Vision Energizes People and Garners Commitment People want to feel enthusiastic about their work. A powerful vision frees people from the mundane by providing them with a challenge worthy of their best efforts. Many people commit their time and energy voluntarily to causes they believe in—a political campaign, the animal rights movement, environmental causes. These same people often leave their energy and enthusiasm at home when they go to work, because they don't have anything to inspire them. Employees are not generally willing to make emotional commitments just for the sake of increasing profits and enhancing shareholder wealth. Vision needs to transcend the bottom line because people are willing, and even eager, to commit to something truly worthwhile, something that makes life better for others or improves their communities.[12] At Schlage Lock Company, for

LIVING LEADERSHIP

Vision's Offspring

A compelling vision inspires and nurtures three qualities, here personified as individuals. Do you think followers would benefit from contact with the following "people" in an organization?

Clarity

My visits to Clarity are soothing now. He never tells me what to think or feel or do but shows me how to find out what I need to know . . . he presented me with a sketchbook and told me to draw the same thing everyday until the drawing started to speak to me.

Commitment

Commitment has kind eyes. He wears sturdy shoes. . . . You can taste in [his] vegetables that the soil has been cared for. . . . He is a simple man, and yet he is mysterious. He is more generous than most people. His heart is open. He is not afraid of life.

Imagination

Some people accuse Imagination of being a liar. They don't understand that she has her own ways of uncovering the truth. . . . Imagination has been working as a fortuneteller in the circus. She has a way of telling your fortune so clearly that you believe her, and then your wishes start to come true. . . . Her vision is more complex, and very simple. Even with the old stories, she wants us to see what has never been seen before.

SOURCE: J. Ruth Gendler, *The Book of Qualities* (New York: Harper & Row, 1988). Used with permission.

example, employee enthusiasm is spurred by a vision to "make the world more secure" by becoming the dominant lock supplier in the United States by the year 2000.[13]

Vision Gives Meaning to Work   People have always needed to find meaning and dignity in their work. People love having a larger purpose for what they do, and they want to feel pride in their work. Consider three stonecutters talking about their jobs. The first stonecutter says, "I'm cutting stone," the second says, "I'm carving a cornerstone," and the third says, "I'm building a cathedral." The third stonecutter saw the vision that gave his work larger meaning.[14]

Vision Establishes a Standard of Excellence   Vision provides a measure by which employees can gauge their contributions to the organization. Most workers welcome the chance to see how their work fits into the whole. Think of how frustrating it is to watch a movie when the projector is out of focus. Today's complex, fast-changing business environment often seems just like that—out of focus.[15] A vision is the focus button. It clarifies an image of the future and lets people see how they can contribute. For example, salespeople at Nordstrom have a clear picture of superior customer service, so they can see how to serve customers better. A vision presents a challenge, asks people to go where they haven't gone before. Thus, it encourages workers to take risks and find new ways of doing things. The Living Leadership box discusses three qualities a powerful vision can inspire.

A good vision brings out the best by speaking to the hearts of employees, letting them be a part of something bigger than themselves. Consider how Walt Disney painted a picture of Disneyland that unified and energized employees.

Walt Disney created a clear picture of what he wanted Disneyland to be. His vision translated hopes and dreams into words and allowed employees to help create the future. Notice how the vision says nothing about making money—the emphasis is on a greater purpose that all employees could believe in.

> "The idea of Disneyland is a simple one. It will be a place for people to find happiness and knowledge. It will be a place for parents and children to spend pleasant times in one another's company, a place for teachers and pupils to discover greater ways of understanding and education. Here the older generation can recapture the nostalgia of days gone by, and the younger generation can savor the challenge of the future. Here will be the wonders of Nature and Man for all to see and understand. Disneyland will be based upon and dedicated to the ideals, the dreams, and hard facts that have created America. And it will be uniquely equipped to dramatize these dreams and facts and send them forth as a source of courage and inspiration for all the world. Disneyland will be something of a fair, an exhibition, a playground, a community center, a museum of living facts, and a showplace of beauty and magic. It will be filled with the accomplishments, the joys and hopes of the world we live in. And it will remind us and show us how to make these wonders part of our lives."[16]

A clear, inspiring picture such as that painted by Walt Disney can have a powerful impact on people. His vision gave meaning and value to workers' activities. Painting a clear picture of the future is a significant responsibility of leaders, yet it cannot always be the leader's alone. To make a difference, a vision can be widely shared and is often created with the participation of others. Every good organizational vision is a shared vision. There are a number of other common themes that are found in powerful or transforming visions like the one for Disneyland.

Common Themes of Vision

Five themes are common to powerful, effective visions: they have broad, widely shared appeal; they help organizations deal with change; they encourage faith and hope for the future; they reflect high ideals; and they define both the organization's destination and the basic rules to get there.

Vision Has Broad Appeal   One theme common to effective visions is a focus on people. Although it may be obvious that a vision can be achieved only through people, many visions fail to adequately involve employees. The vision cannot be the property of the leader alone.[17] The ideal vision is identified with the organization as a whole, not with a single leader or even a top leadership team. It "grabs people in the gut" and motivates them to work toward a common end.[18] It allows each individual to act independently but in the same direction.

Vision Deals with Change   Visions that work help the organization achieve bold change. Vision is about action and challenges people to make important changes toward a better future. Change can be frightening, but a clear sense of direction helps people face the difficulties and uncertainties involved in the change process.

Vision Encourages Faith and Hope   Vision exists only in the imagination—it is a picture of a world that cannot be observed or verified in advance. The future is shaped by people who believe in it, and a powerful vision helps people believe that they can be effective, that there is a better future they can move to through their own commitment and actions. Vision is an emotional appeal to our fundamental human needs and desires—to feel important and useful, to believe we can make a real difference in the world.[19] John F. Kennedy's vision for NASA to send a man to the moon by the end of the 1960s was so powerful that hundreds of thousands of people throughout the world believed in a future they couldn't see.[20]

Vision Reflects High Ideals   Good visions are idealistic. Vision has power to inspire and energize people only when it paints an uplifting future. When Kennedy announced the "man on the moon" vision, NASA had only a small amount of the knowledge it would need to accomplish the feat. Giro Sport Design, a young, small company that manufactures bicycle products, wants to "become the Nike of the cycling industry." When the vision was first described in the early 1990s, it reflected idealistic dreams of the future, such as: "We will receive unsolicited phone calls and letters from customers who say, 'Thank you for being in business; one of your helmets saved my life.'"[21]

Vision Defines the Destination and the Journey   A good vision for the future includes specific outcomes that the organization wants to achieve. It also incorporates the underlying values that will help the organization get there. For example, Giro wants to be to the bicycling industry what Nike is to athletic shoes, but it doesn't want to do so "at any cost." Giro's complete vision statement is based on a set of guiding principles that emphasize making a positive impact on society.[22] As another example, a private business school might specify certain outcomes such as a top 20 ranking, placing 90 percent of students in summer internships, and getting 80 percent of students into jobs by June of their graduating year. Yet in the process of reaching those specific outcomes, the school wants to increase students' knowledge of business, values, and teamwork, as well as prepare them for lifelong learning. Additionally, the vision may espouse underlying values such as no separation between fields of study or between professors and students, a genuine concern for students' welfare, and adding to the body of business knowledge. A good vision includes both the desired future outcomes and the underlying values that set the rules for achieving them.[23]

A Vision Works at Multiple Levels

Many people think of a vision as being for the company as a whole, but visions for divisions, departments, and individuals are powerful too. The CEO of an effective company develops a vision for the organization, and at the same time a project team leader five levels beneath the CEO can develop a vision with team members for a new product they are working on. Leaders of functional departments, divisions, and teams can use vision with the same positive results as do top leaders of an organization.

Consider the facility manager for a large corporation. His department received requests to fix toilets and air conditioners. The manager took this to mean that people cared about their physical space, which became the basis for his vision to "use physical space to make people feel good." People in his department started planting flowers outside office windows and created an internal environment that lifted people's spirits.[24] In innovative companies, every group or department creates its own vision, as long as the vision is in line with the overall company's direction. At the Ritz-Carlton hotel chain, each department in each hotel develops its own vision statement. The engineering department for the Amelia Island, Florida, hotel came up with its statement partly because it appealed to everyone's sense of humor. One engineer, who helped draft the statement, "to boldly go where no hotel has gone before—free of all defects," says, "it made us laugh. But the more we got to talking about it, the more we liked it."[25] At Ritz-Carlton hotels, people in the parking garage, housekeeping, and the front desk all wrestle with their purpose, and develop a shared vision for their future.

A clear mental picture of how to do something successfully is a tremendous advantage. When individuals have a clear vision, they become effective as leaders. Without the vision, a person's work in the moment may be disconnected from the higher mission.

Perhaps Vince Lombardi, renowned coach of the Green Bay Packers, said it best. As quoted by John Madden, "The best coaches know what the end results look like. . . . If you don't know what the end result is supposed to look like, you can't get there. All the teams basically do the same things. . . . But the bad coaches don't know what the hell they want. The good coaches do."[26] Successful individuals, just like successful leaders, have developed a clear mental picture of their vision and how to achieve it. People who do not have this clear vision of the future and how to achieve it have less chance for success.

When a vision for the organization as a whole is shared among individuals and departments, it has real impact. Therefore top leaders' real work is to share the vision with others, and to help them to develop their part of the vision so that everyone has the picture. As Peter Senge said in *The Fifth Discipline*, a shared vision changes people's relationship with the organization. It creates a common identity and allows each employee to look at a manager and think of "our company" rather than "their company." The vision becomes the common thread connecting people, involving them personally and emotionally in the organization.[27]

When every person understands and embraces a vision, the organization becomes self-adapting. Although each individual acts independently, everyone is working in the same direction. In the new sciences, this is called the principle of self-reference. **Self-reference** means that each element in a system will serve the mission of the whole system when the elements are imprinted with an understanding of the mission of the whole. Thus the vision serves to direct and control people for the good of themselves and the organization.

To develop a shared vision, leaders share their personal visions with others and encourage others to express their dreams for the future. This requires openness, good listening skills, and the courage to connect with others on an emotional level. Good leaders give up the idea that vision emanates from only the top. A leader's ultimate responsibility is to be in touch with the hopes and dreams that drive employees and find the common ground that binds personal dreams into a shared vision for the organization. As one successful CEO put it, "My job, fundamentally, is listening to what the organization is trying to say, and then making sure it is forcefully articulated."[28]

Mission

Mission is not the same thing as a company's vision, although the two work together. The **mission** is the organization's core broad purpose and reason for existence. It defines the company's core values and reason for being, and it provides a basis for creating the vision. Whereas vision is an ambitious desire for the future, mission is what the organization "stands for" in a larger sense. James Collins compares Zenith and Motorola to illustrate how knowing what the organization stands for helps companies adapt and grow. Both Zenith and Motorola were once successful makers of televisions. Yet while Zenith stayed there, Motorola continued to move forward— to making microprocessors, integrated circuits, and numerous other products—and became one of the most highly regarded companies in the country. The difference is that Motorola defined its mission as "applying technology to benefit the public," not as "making television sets."[29] Visions for the future should change and grow continuously, whereas the mission itself should persist in the face of change, as discussed in the Leader's Bookshelf. The mission defines the enduring character, values, and purpose of the organization.

Typically the mission is made up of two critical parts: the core values and the core purpose. The *core values* guide the organization "no matter what." As Ralph Larsen, CEO of Johnson & Johnson, explains it, "The core values embodied in our credo might be a competitive advantage, but that is not *why* we have them. We have them because they define for us what we stand for, and we would hold them even if they became a competitive *dis*advantage in certain situations."[30] Johnson & Johnson's core values led the company, for example, to voluntarily remove Tylenol from the market after the cyanide poisoning of some Tylenol capsule users, even though this act cost the company more than $100 million.

The mission also includes the company's *core purpose*. An effective purpose statement doesn't just describe products or services, it captures people's idealistic motivations for why the organization exists. For 3M, it is "To solve unsolved problems innovatively"; for Merck, "To preserve and improve human life." Merck illustrates how a specific vision grows out of the company's mission and works together with it:

We will be the first drug maker with advanced research in every disease category. Our research will be as good as the science being done anywhere in the world. Our drugs won't be used by a single person who doesn't need

Built to Last: Successful Habits of Visionary Companies
James C. Collins and Jerry I. Porras

In a six-year study comparing 18 companies that have experienced long-term success with 18 similar companies that have not performed as well, James Collins and Jerry Porras found a key determining factor in the successful companies to be a culture in which employees share such a strong sense of purpose that they know in their hearts what is right for the company. *Built to Last* describes how companies such as 3M, Boeing, Wal-Mart, Merck, Nordstrom, Hewlett-Packard, and others have successfully adapted to a changing world without losing sight of the core values that guide the organization. Collins and Porras found that the successful companies were guided by a "core ideology"—values and a sense of purpose that go beyond just making money and that provide a guide for employee behavior.

Timeless Fundamentals

The book offers four key concepts that show how leaders can contribute to building successful companies.

- Be a Clock Builder, Not a Time Teller. Products and market opportunities are vehicles for building a great organization, not the other way around. Visionary leaders concentrate on building adaptive cultures and systems that remain strong despite changes in products, services, or markets.

- Embrace the "Genius of the AND". Successful organizations simultaneously embrace two extremes, such as continuity and change, stability and revolution, predictability and chaos.
- Preserve the Core/Stimulate Progress. The core ideology is balanced with a relentless drive for progress. Successful companies set ambitious goals and create an atmosphere that encourages experimentation and learning.
- Seek Consistent Alignment. Strive to make all aspects of the company work in unison with the core ideology. At Disneyland, employees are "cast members" and customers are "guests." Hewlett-Packard's policies reinforce its commitment to respect for each individual.

Conclusion

Built to Last offers important lessons on how leaders can build organizations that stand the test of time. By concentrating on the timeless fundamentals, organizations can adapt and thrive in a changing world.

Built to Last: Successful Habits of Visionary Companies, by James C. Collins and Jerry I. Porras, is published by HarperCollins.

them. Merck will continue to grow on a steady basis, bringing forth worthwhile products. . . .[31]

Discovery Toys, based in Martinez, California, sold $93 million in toys and kid-related products in a recent year, and has 30,000 distributors in the United States and Canada. However, according to CEO Lane Nemeth, the company's purpose isn't to sell toys; it is to be a parent educator. Discovery exists for the higher purpose of helping parents experience the joys and realize the benefits of playing with their children: "That's how kids learn; that's what keeps communication and social life alive."[32]

EXHIBIT 5.3	HALLMARK'S MISSION STATEMENT

This is Hallmark

We believe:

That our *products* and *services* must enrich people's lives
and enhance their relationships.

That *creativity and quality*—in our concepts, products
and services—are essential to our success.

That the *people* of Hallmark are our company's most valuable resource.

That distinguished *financial performance* is a must, not as an end in itself,
but as a means to accomplish our broader mission.

That our *private ownership* must be preserved.

The values that guide us are:

Excellence in all we do.

Ethical and moral conduct at all times.

Innovation in all areas of our business as a means of attaining and sustaining leadership.

Corporate social responsibility to Kansas City and to each community
in which we operate.

These beliefs and values guide our business strategies, our corporate behavior, and our
relationships with suppliers, customers, communities, and each other.

SOURCE: Patricia Jones and Larry Kahaner, *Say It and Live It: 50 Corporate Mission Statements That Hit the Mark* (New York: Currency Doubleday, 1995).

Many companies have mission statements that define what they stand for, including their core values and core purpose. Exhibit 5.3 shows the mission statement for Hallmark. Some companies also include the specific vision for the future as a part of their mission statements. However, it is important to remember that the vision continually grows and changes, while the mission endures. It serves as the glue that holds the organization together in times of change and guides strategic choices and decisions about the future.

Strategy Formulation

Strong missions and guiding visions are important, but they are not enough alone to make strong, powerful organizations. For organizations to succeed, they need ways to translate vision, values, and purpose into action, which is the role of strategy. Formulating strategy is the hard, serious work of taking a specific step toward the future. **Strategic management** is the set of decisions and actions used to formulate and implement specific strategies that will achieve a competitively superior fit between the organization and its environment so as to achieve organizational goals.[33] It is the leader's job to find this fit and translate it into action.

Strategy can be defined as the general plan of action that describes resource allocation and other activities for dealing with the environment and helping the organization attain its goals. In formulating strategy, leaders ask questions such as "Where is the organization now? Where does the organization want to be? What changes and trends are occurring in the competitive environment? What courses of action can help us achieve our vision?" Developing effective strategy requires actively listening to people both inside and outside the organization, as well as examining trends and discontinuities in the environment. At Amgen, the key to innovative strategy was listening in new and different ways.

LEADERSHIP SPOTLIGHT   AMGEN

Drug companies generally succeed or fail based on only a handful of blockbuster drugs. Amgen, with a 68 percent average annual return over the past decade, has only two drugs on the market—one for dialysis patients and one that is an immune-system booster to help people fight infections. However, each of these drugs brings in a billion dollars a year. Amgen succeeds with an unconventional strategy.

Most pharmaceutical companies are basically market-driven. They see that a large number of people have a particular disease, so they begin research to meet the need. Amgen, however, heard things differently. Rather than start with the disease and work backwards, the company takes the opposite strategy—to take brilliant science and find unique uses for it. Amgen's immune-system booster, for example, helps to keep the side effects of chemotherapy from killing cancer patients.

Starting with the science enables Amgen to create the future. The company focuses its energy on what it does best—high-quality scientific research. Amgen also has collaborative arrangements with about 200 colleges and universities, allowing the company to take advantage of some of the best medical research. One of those collaborations may lead to the next blockbuster drug. A professor at Rockefeller University recently discovered a gene—now licensed by Amgen—that may hold the key to fighting obesity. With people in the United States alone spending more than $30 billion a year to shed pounds, that kind of science could really pay off.[34]

Like Amgen, most successful companies develop strategies based on what they do uniquely well within the environment. Strategy necessarily changes over time to fit environmental conditions. To remain competitive, leaders develop company strategies that focus on three qualities: core competencies, developing synergy, and creating value for customers.

Core Competence

An organization's **core competence** is something the organization does extremely well in comparison to competitors. Leaders try to identify the organization's unique strengths—what makes their organization different from others in the industry. A core competence may be in the area of superior research, as at Amgen pharmaceutical company, mastery of a technology, cost efficiency, or customer service. At Chelsea Milling Co. in Chelsea, Michigan, Howard "Howdy" Holmes, a former racecar driver, is leading a total, irrevocable shake-up of the family firm. He believes new strategies are needed to keep Chelsea, best known for its pocket-sized blue and white boxes of Jiffy cake mix, competitive in the coming years. Holmes is modernizing the factory, revising internal procedures, and expanding the product line to include fruit-flavored muffin mixes, "just-add-water" buttermilk pancake mix, and six-packs of mixes designed to get Jiffy into warehouse clubs like Sam's. Yet he isn't changing the basics of what the company does best—keep costs low and provide inexpensive, instant baking mixes that can cost one-third to one-half less than Betty Crocker or Duncan Hines. Except for a new Web site, the company still doesn't spend a cent on advertising, but has annual sales of $90 million.[35]

Chase Brass Industries, the largest brass rod manufacturer in the United States, pursued a strategy of diversification to grow and expand its markets. Chase began its transformation from a manufacturer of brass rods to an engineered metals company by following its core competence of highly efficient production processes. In late 1996, Chase Brass bought steel tubing manufacturer UNR-Levitt, and is considering expanding into aluminum, plastics, and ceramics. Each of these materials involves similar production processes and employee skills so that competencies are transferable across product lines. The addition of Levitt increased net sales for Chase by more than $49 million.[36]

Synergy

Synergy occurs when organizational parts interact to produce a joint effect that is greater than the sum of the parts acting alone. As a result the organization may attain a special advantage with respect to cost, market power, technology, or employee skills. Synergy can also be obtained by good relations between suppliers and customers and by strong alliances between companies. For example, Erie Bolt, a small Erie, Pennsylvania company, teamed up with 14 other area companies to give itself more muscle in tackling competitive global markets. Team members share equipment, customer lists, and other information that enable each small company to go after more business than it ever could without the team approach.[37]

Value Creation

Focusing on core competencies and attaining synergy helps companies create value for their customers. **Value** can be defined as the combination of benefits received and costs paid by the customer.[38] A product that is low cost but does not provide benefits is not a good value. For example, People Express Airlines initially made a splash with ultra-low prices, but travelers couldn't tolerate the airline's consistently late takeoffs at any price.[39] Delivering value to the customer is at the heart of strategy. McDonald's made a thorough study of how to use its core competencies to create better value for customers. This analysis resulted in the introduction of "Extra

Value Meals" and the decision to open restaurants in different locations, such as inside Wal-Mart and Sears stores.[40]

Strategy in Action

Strategy formulation integrates knowledge of the environment, vision, and mission with the company's core competence in a way to achieve synergy and create value for customers. When these elements are brought together, the company has an excellent chance to succeed in a competitive environment. But to do so, leaders have to ensure that strategies are implemented—that actual behavior within the organization reflects the desired direction.

Strategy is implemented through specific mechanisms, techniques, or tools for directing organizational resources to accomplish strategic goals. This is the basic architecture for how things get done in the organization. Some people argue that **strategy implementation** is the most important as well as the most difficult part of strategic management.[41] Strategy implementation involves using several tools or parts of the organization that can be adjusted to put strategy into action. Strong leadership is one of the most important tools for strategy implementation. Leaders motivate and influence others to adopt the behaviors needed for the new strategy. For example, the manager of a department store might implement a strategy of increased sales by using leadership to pump up morale, encouraging aggressive selling, being physically present on the sales floor, and by speaking about the high sales goals to employees at every opportunity.

Strategy is also implemented through elements such as structural design, pay or reward systems, budget allocations, and organizational rules, policies, or procedures. For example, at ConAgra, maker of Healthy Choice and Banquet brands, CEO Philip B. Fletcher made changes to incentive pay systems and computerized the company's information systems to encourage commitment to a new strategy of cooperation and efficiency.[42] Another company reorganized its workforce into teams, each responsible for all details of a product for a single customer. Each group was a separate structural unit that could do whatever was necessary to adapt to changes in the product or customer. Dedicating these resources to customers provided extraordinary service.

Leaders are responsible for making decisions about changes in structure, systems, policies, and so forth, to support the company's strategic direction. Exhibit 5.4 shows a simplified continuum illustrating how structural organizing may be related to strategy implementation. If an organization pursues a strategy of internal efficiency to offer customers lower costs than competitors, the organization might be designed with a traditional, hierarchical structure. Today, however, more organizations are recognizing a need for a strategy of greater innovation and flexibility. Because of the need for increased horizontal collaboration and communication, leaders are shifting to structures based on horizontal teams rather than vertical hierarchies.

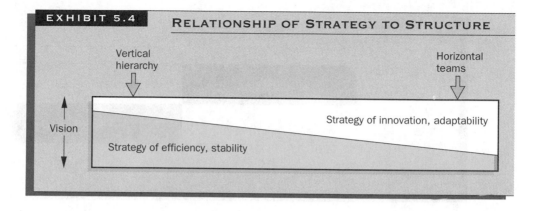

EXHIBIT 5.4   RELATIONSHIP OF STRATEGY TO STRUCTURE

Vertical hierarchy

Horizontal teams

Vision

Strategy of innovation, adaptability

Strategy of efficiency, stability

The Leader's Contribution

Although good leadership for today's organizations calls for actively involving everyone in the organization, leaders are still ultimately responsible for establishing organizational direction through vision and strategy. When leadership fails to provide direction, organizations flounder. For example, McDonald's is a well-managed company, but recently franchisees, who have seen per-store profits sink as much as 30 percent in the 1990s, blamed the decline on the failure of leaders to provide vision and strategy. Among the quotes in a recent survey was one that pleaded for "long-term focus on direction and identity of McDonald's, rather than expensive knee-jerk changes." McDonald's is still a powerful company, yet some observers agree that recently leaders may have failed to provide the strategic direction the company needs to remain competitive over the long haul.[43] One of the most critical jobs of the leader is deciding the vision for the future and linking the future with strategic actions.

Stimulating Vision and Action

In the waiting lounge of a fine lakeside restaurant a sign reads, "Where there is no hope in the future, there is no power in the present." The owner explains its presence there by telling the story of how his small, picturesque village with its homes and businesses was sacrificed to make way for a flood-control project. After losing their fight to reverse the decision, most business leaders simply let their businesses decline and die. Soon, the only people who came to the village did so to eat at the cheery little diner, whose owner became the butt of jokes because he continued to work so hard. Everyone laughed when he chose to open a larger and fancier restaurant on the hill behind the village. Yet, when the flood-control project was finally completed, he had the only attractive restaurant on the edge of a beautiful, newly constructed lake that drew many tourists. Anyone could have found out, as he did, where the edge of the lake would be, yet most of the business owners had no vision

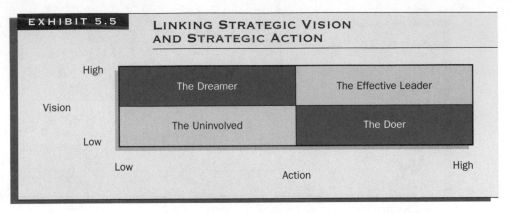

EXHIBIT 5.5 LINKING STRATEGIC VISION AND STRATEGIC ACTION

SOURCE: Based on William D. Hitt, *The Leader-Manager: Guidelines for Action* (Columbus, OH: Battelle Press, 1988), 7.

for the future. The restaurant owner had a vision and he took action on it. Hopes and dreams for the future are what keep people moving forward. However, for leaders to make a real difference, they have to link those dreams with strategic actions. An old English churchyard saying applies to organizations as it does to life:

> Life without vision is drudgery.
> Vision without action is but an empty dream.
> Action guided by vision is joy and the hope of the earth.[44]

Exhibit 5.5 illustrates four possibilities of leadership in providing direction. Four types of leader are determined based on their attention to vision and attention to action. The person who is low both on providing vision and stimulating action is uninvolved, not really a leader at all. The leader who is all action and little vision is a Doer. He or she may be a hard worker and dedicated to the job and the organization, but the Doer is working blind. Without a sense of purpose and direction, activities have no real meaning and do not truly serve the organization, the employees, or the community. The Dreamer, on the other hand, is good at providing a big idea with meaning for self and others. This leader may effectively inspire others with a vision, yet he or she is weak on implementing strategic action. The vision in this case is only a dream, a fantasy, because it has little chance of ever becoming reality. To be an Effective Leader, one both dreams big *and* transforms those dreams into significant strategic action.

How Leaders Decide

To determine strategic direction for the future, leaders look inward, outward, and forward. Leaders scan both the internal and external organizational environment to identify trends, threats, and opportunities for the organization. Consider how top leaders of the Boy Scouts of America considered changes and trends in the environment to develop a strategic plan.

LEADERSHIP SPOTLIGHT   BOY SCOUTS OF AMERICA

Led by chief Scout executive Jere Ratcliffe, a man described by colleagues as a "strategic visionary," the Boy Scouts of America organization is implementing its first-ever comprehensive national strategic plan. Taking to heart the Scout motto, "Be Prepared," leaders of the 89-year-old organization have carefully considered the changing internal and external environment to prepare the Boy Scouts for survival in the 21st century.

Leaders began formulating the new strategy by looking at where the organization is now and where it needs to go in the future. Environmental trends of particular concern to the Scouts organization are a population shift to urban areas, increased demands on volunteers and potential volunteers, and a general decrease in charitable giving. The Boy Scouts, with its emphasis on camping and other outdoor activities, has traditionally appealed to white middle-class youngsters in smaller towns and rural areas. However, 70 percent of the growth in the youth population over the next decade will be among minorities and families living in urban areas. In addition, changing social and economic conditions have led to a decrease in the number of volunteers. Today, many people who might be excellent, ethical volunteers hesitate to take on the responsibility of Scout leadership in an era when charges of child abuse are rampant. In addition, those adults who would make the best leaders have many more demands on their time today than they did 20 years ago. National leaders recognized that they must come up with new ways to recruit volunteer leaders as well as attract minority members and those in urban areas.

Putting strategy into action for the Boy Scouts means placing emphasis on growth and development in urban centers, with new kinds of services targeted toward the concerns of urban youth. Two aspects of this emphasis are a crime prevention program to serve urban areas and a program called Operation First Class that strives to recruit volunteer leaders from diverse economic, ethnic, and social backgrounds as well as sponsors for troops in urban areas. Another plan for recruiting leaders is through a college intern program, developed with the assistance of the University of Boston and The Walt Disney Co. In addition, the strategic plan includes a public relations element aimed at finding strong volunteers as well as selling communities and potential troop sponsors on the importance of supporting scouting. Several councils have reported increased financial support as a result of P.R. efforts.

Ratcliffe knows the heart of the Scouts organization is on the local and regional, rather than the national, level. However, for the organization to continue to thrive in a changing world, he felt top leaders should "develop a vision of the future and a plan to shepherd this organization of a million volunteer leaders moving in the [same] direction. . . ."[45]

Leaders such as Jere Ratcliffe recognize that organizations need both a broad and inspiring vision and an underlying plan for how to achieve it. To decide and map a strategic direction, leaders strive to develop industry foresight based on trends in technology, demographics, government regulation, and lifestyles that will help them identify new competitive advantages.[46]

One approach leaders take in setting a course for the future is through hard analysis. Situation analysis, for example, includes a search for SWOT—strengths, weaknesses, opportunities, and threats that affect organizational performance. Leaders using situation analysis obtain external information from a variety of sources, such as customers, government reports, suppliers, consultants, or association meetings. They gather information about internal strengths and weaknesses from sources such as budgets, financial ratios, profit and loss statements, and employee surveys. Another formula often used by companies is a five-force analysis developed by Michael Porter, who studied a number of businesses and proposed that strategy is often the result of five competitive forces: potential new entrants into an industry; the bargaining power of buyers; the bargaining power of suppliers; the threat of substitute products; and rivalry among competitors. By carefully examining these five forces, leaders can develop effective strategies to remain competitive.

Vision and strategy have to be based on a solid factual foundation, but too much rationality can get in the way of creating a compelling vision. When leaders rely solely on formal strategic planning, competitor analysis, or market research, they miss new opportunities. For example, when Ted Turner first talked about launching a 24-hour news and information channel in the 1970s, many dismissed him as delusional. Every source of conventional wisdom, from market research to broadcast professionals, said the vision was crazy and bound to fail. Yet Turner looked at emerging social and demographic trends, listened to his intuition, and launched a global network that generates 35 percent gross margins.[47] Sony has long been known for creating the future. As Sony's visionary leader Akio Morita puts it, "Our plan is to lead the public with new products rather than ask them what kinds of products they want. The public does not know what is possible, but we do."[48]

To formulate a vision, leaders also look inward to their hopes and dreams. Foresight and the ability to see future possibilities emerge not just from traditional strategic planning tools and formulas, but from curiosity, instinct and intuition, emotions, deep thinking, personal experience, and hope. To develop foresight, leaders view the world with a wide-angle lens, capturing bits and pieces of subtle information without shutting it off with "yeah, but" preconceptions.[49] Charles Wang, founder and CEO of Computer Associates, is constantly telling employees, "Stand on your head! Stand on your head!" meaning obliterate your preconceptions and see things in a new way. Sam Walton's version was "Swim upstream."[50]

Another good reason for not relying too heavily on rational analysis is that rationality can kill a vision. Overly rational people have a hard time letting go and dreaming big. At Sewell Village Cadillac in Dallas, antique lamps are used instead of fluorescent lights. The expensive fixtures don't make sense in a rational, economic sense, but the setting captures people's imaginations, making the dealership seem special. To connect with people's deeper yearning for something great, vision can transcend the rational. Although it is based on reality, it comes from the heart rather than the head. One writer has suggested that leaders take a tip from Helen Keller, who was blind and deaf since early childhood and in order to see had to go out and touch the world, relying on instinct, emotion, and cues from others.[51]

The Leader's Impact

When leaders link vision and strategy, they can make a real difference for their organization's future. A leader's greatest discretion is often over strategic vision and strategic action. Research has shown that strategic thinking and planning for the future can positively affect a company's performance and financial success.[52] Another study has shown that as much as 44 percent of the variance in profitability of major firms may be attributed to strategic leadership.[53] For example, when Richard Teerlink took over as CEO of Harley Davidson, he saw the strategic opportunity to revive customers' emotional connections with the struggling company: "We symbolize the feeling of freedom and independence that people want in this stressful world." By capitalizing on the nostalgia of biking, creating the Harley Owners Group (HOG for short), and slapping the Harley logo on merchandise from deodorant to throw pillows, Teerlink revolutionized the company, translating an emotional bond into steadily increasing profits.[54]

One way leader impact has been evaluated is to examine whether top executive turnover makes a difference. Several studies of chief executive turnover have been conducted, including a sample of 167 corporations studied over a 20-year period, 193 manufacturing companies, a large sample of Methodist churches, and retail firms in the United Kingdom.[55] These studies found that leader succession was associated with improved profits and stock prices and, in the case of churches, with improved attendance, membership, and donations. Although good economic conditions and industry circumstances play a part in improved performance for any organization, the top leader had impact beyond these factors. Overall, when research has been carefully done, typically top leader succession explains from 20 percent to 45 percent of the variance in organizational outcomes.[56]

More recent research has explored the notion of top leadership teams, as opposed to an individual executive. The makeup of the top leadership group is believed to affect whether an organization develops organizational capability and the ability to exploit strategic opportunities. A team provides diverse aptitudes and skills to deal with complex organizational situations. Many researchers believe the configuration of the top leadership team to be more important for organizational success than the characteristics of a single CEO. For example, the size, diversity, attitudes, and skills of the team affect patterns of communication and collaboration, which in turn affect company performance.[57]

The emerging focus on teams is more realistic in some ways than focusing on individual leadership. In a complex environment, a single leader cannot do all things. An effective team may have a better chance of identifying and implementing a successful strategy, of discerning an accurate interpretation of the environment, and of developing internal capability based on empowered employees and a shared vision. Without a capable and effectively interacting top leadership team, a company may not adapt readily in a shifting environment. Although research in the area of leader impact is still relatively limited, it does seem to affirm the belief that the choices leaders make have significant impact on an organization's performance.

Summary and Interpretation

Leaders establish organizational direction through vision and strategy. They are responsible for studying the organization's environment, considering how it may be different in the future, and setting a direction everyone can believe in. The shared vision is an attractive, ideal future for the organization that is credible yet not readily attainable. A clear, powerful vision links the present and the future by showing how present actions and decisions can move the organization toward its long-range goals. Vision energizes employees and gives them an inspiring picture of the future to which they are eager to commit themselves. The vision can also give meaning to work and establish a standard of excellence by presenting a challenge that asks all workers to give their best.

The mission includes the company's core values and its core purpose or reason for existence. Visions for the future change, whereas the mission should persist, as does the enduring character of the organization.

Strategy is the serious work of figuring out how to translate vision and mission into action. Strategy is a general plan of action that describes resource allocation and other activities for dealing with the environment and helping the organization reach its goals. Like vision, strategy changes, but successful companies develop strategies that focus on core competence, develop synergy, and create value for customers. Strategy is implemented through the systems and structures that are the basic architecture for how things get done in the organization.

Leaders decide on direction through rational analysis as well as intuition, personal experience, and hopes and dreams. Leaders make a real difference for their organization only when they link vision to strategic action, so that vision is more than just a dream. Superior organizational performance is not a matter of luck. It is determined by the decisions leaders make.

Key Terms

strategic leadership	strategic management	value
vision	strategy	strategy formulation
self-reference	core competence	strategy implementation
mission	synergy	

Discussion Questions

1. A management consultant said that strategic leaders are concerned with vision and mission, while strategic managers are concerned with strategy. Do you agree? Discuss.

2. A vision can apply to an individual, a family, a college course, a career, or decorating an apartment. Think of something you care about for which you want the future to be different from the present and write a vision statement for it.

3. If you worked for a company like Microsoft that has a strong vision for the future, how would that affect you compared to working for a company that did not have a vision?

4. Do you agree with the principle of self-reference? In other words, do you believe if people know where the organization is trying to go, they will make decisions that support the desired organizational outcome?

5. What does it mean to say that the vision can include a description of both the journey and the destination?

6. Many visions are written and hung on a wall. Do you think this type of vision has value? What would be required to imprint the vision within each person?

7. What is the difference between mission and vision? Can you give an example of each?

8. What is the difference between synergy and value creation with respect to strategy?

9. Strategic vision and strategic action are both needed for an effective leader. Which do you think you are better at doing? Why?

10. If a new top leader is hired for a corporation, and performance improves, to what extent do you think the new top leader was responsible compared to other factors? To what extent do you think a new coach is responsible if her basketball team did better after she took over?

Leadership Development: Personal Feedback

Visionary Leadership

Think about a situation in which you either assumed or were given a leadership role in a group. Imagine your own behavior as leader. To what extent does each of the following statements characterize your leadership?

> 1 = very little
> 2
> 3 = a moderate amount
> 4
> 5 = very much

_____ 1. I have a clear understanding of where we are going.

_____ 2. I work to get others to be committed to our desired future.

_____ 3. I paint an interesting picture for my group.

_____ 4. I get the group to work together for the same outcome.

_____ 5. I initiate discussion with others about the kind of future I would like us to create together.

_____ 6. I clearly and repeatedly communicate a positive outlook for the group's future.

_____ 7. I look ahead and forecast what I expect in the future.

_____ 8. I show others how their interests can be realized by working toward a common vision.

_____ 9. I am excited and enthusiastic about future possibilities.

_____ 10. I make certain that the activities I manage are broken down into manageable chunks.

_____ 11. I seek future challenges for the group.

_____ 12. I spend time and effort making certain that people adhere to the values and outcomes that have been agreed on.

_____ 13. I inspire others with my ideas for the future.

_____ 14. I give special recognition when others' work is consistent with the vision.

Scoring

The odd-numbered questions pertain to creating a vision for the group. The even-numbered questions pertain to implementing the vision. Calculate your score for each set of questions. Which score is higher? Compare your scores with other students.

Interpretation

This questionnaire pertains to two dimensions of visionary leadership. Creating the vision is whether you think about the future, whether you are excited about the future, and whether you engage others in the future. Implementing the vision is about the extent to which you communicate, allocate the work, and provide rewards for activities that achieve the vision. Which of the two dimensions is easiest for you? Are your scores consistent with your understanding of your own strengths and weaknesses? What might you do to improve your scores?

Leadership Development: Case for Analysis

Metropolis Police Department

You are in a hotel room watching the evening news as a local reporter interviews people who complain about abuse and mistreatment by police officers. These reports have been occurring in the news media with increasing frequency over the last three years. Some observers believe the problem is the police department's authoritarian style. Police managers encourage paramilitary values and a them-against-us attitude. The police orientation has been towards a spit-and-polish force that is efficient and tolerates no foolishness. The city believes that a highly professional, aloof police force is the best way to keep the city under control. Training emphasizes police techniques, the appropriate use of guns, and new technology, but there is no training on dealing with people. Several citizens have won large lawsuits against the police force, and many suits originated with minority groups. Critics believe the police chief is a major part of the problem. He has defended the rough actions of police officers, giving little public credence to complaints of abuse. He resists the community-oriented, people-friendly attitudes of other city departments. The chief has been considered insensitive toward minorities and has been heard to make disparaging public comments about African Americans, women, and Hispanics.

One vocal critic alleges that police brutality depends upon the vision and moral leadership set by the chief of police and lays responsibility for incidents of abuse on the current chief. Another critic believes there is a relationship between his intemperate remarks and the actions of police officers.

The reason you are in Metropolis, watching the news in a hotel room, is that you have been invited to interview for the job of police chief. The mayor and selected council members are preparing to fire the chief and name a replacement. You are thinking about what you would do if you took the job.

Questions

1. Identify themes that you would like to make a part of your vision for the police department.

2. If you get the job, how will you gain acceptance for your vision? How will you implement changes that will support the new vision and values?

3. Would you relish the challenge of becoming police chief of Metropolis? Why or why not?

References

[1]Gary Hamel, "Killer Strategies That Make Shareholders Rich," *Fortune,* June 23, 1997, 70–84; James C. Collins and Jerry I. Porras, "Building Your Company's Vision," *Harvard Business Review* September–October 1996, 65–77; and Charles P. Wallace, "Adidas: Back in the Game," *Fortune*, August 18, 1997, 176–182.

[2]Collins and Porras, "Building Your Company's Vision."

[3]Gary Hamel and C.K. Prahalad, "Seeing the Future First," *Fortune*, September 5, 1994, 64–70.

[4]Hamel, "Killer Strategies."

[5]Ray Maghroori and Eric Rolland, "Strategic Leadership: The Art of Balancing Organizational Mission with Policy, Procedures, and External Environment," *The Journal of Leadership Studies* no. 2 (1997), 62–81.

[6]Suzanne Martin, "Family Inspires a Bright Future for Young Entrepreneur," *Self-Employed America* September–October 1997, 12–13.

[7]Collins and Porras, "Building Your Company's Vision."

[8]Stewart Alsop, "Now I Know How a Real Visionary Sounds," *Fortune*, September 8, 1997, 161–162.

[9]This section is based on Burt Nanus, *Visionary Leadership* (San Francisco: Jossey-Bass, 1992), 16–18; and Richard L. Daft and Robert H. Lengel, *Fusion Leadership: Unlocking the Subtle Forces That Change People and Organizations* (San Francisco: Berrett-Koehler, 1998).

[10]Oren Harari, "Looking Beyond the Vision Thing," *Management Review*, June 1997, 26–29; and William D. Hitt, *The Leader-Manager: Guidelines for Action* (Columbus, OH: Battelle Press, 1988), 54.

[11]Nancy Chambers, "The Really Long View," *Management Review*, January 1998, 11-15, and Arie de Geus, "The Living Company," *Harvard Business Review*, March–April 1997, 51-59.

[12]Nanus, *Visionary Leadership*, 16.

[13]James C. Collins and Jerry I. Porras, "Organizational Vision and Visionary Organizations," *California Management Review* (Fall 1991), 30–52.

[14]Daft and Lengel, *Fusion Leadership.*

[15]James M. Kouzes and Barry Z. Posner, *The Leadership Challenge: How to Get Extraordinary Things Done in Organizations* (San Francisco: Jossey-Bass, 1988), 98.

[16]B. Thomas, *Walt Disney: An American Tradition* (New York: Simon & Schuster, 1976), 246–247.

[17]Marshall Sashkin, "The Visionary Leader," in Jay Conger and Rabindra N. Kanungo, eds., *Charismatic Leadership: The Elusive Factor in Organizational Effectiveness* (San Francisco: Jossey-Bass, 1988), 122–160.

[18]Collins and Porras, "Organizational Vision and Visionary Organizations," 31.

[19]Nanus, *Visionary Leadership*, 26; John W. Gardner, "Leadership and the Future," *The Futurist* May–June 1990, 9–12; and Warren Bennis and Burt Nanus, *Leaders: The Strategies for Taking Charge* (New York: Harper & Row, 1985), 93.

[20]Gardner, "Leadership and the Future."

[21]Collins and Porras, "Organizational Vision and Visionary Organizations."

[22]*Ibid.*

[23]Daft and Lengel, *Fusion Leadership.*

[24]Kouzes and Posner, *The Leadership Challenge*, 82.

[25]Alan Farnham, "State Your Values, Hold the Hot Air," *Fortune* (April 19, 1993), 117–124.

[26]Kouzes and Pozner, *The Leadership Challenge*.

[27]This section is based on Peter M. Senge, *The Fifth Discipline: The Art and Practice of the Learning Organization* (New York: Doubleday Currency, 1990), 205–225.

[28]Senge, *The Fifth Discipline*, 218.

[29]James Collins, "It's Not What You Make, It's What You Stand For," *Inc.*, October 1997, 42–45.

[30]Collins, and Porras, "Building Your Company's Vision," 65–77.

[31]*Ibid.*

[32]Duncan Maxwell Anderson, "An Empire at Home: Discovery Toys Thrives on the Renaissance of Family Life," *Success*, June 1995, 24–26.

[33]John E. Prescott, "Environments as Moderators of the Relationship between Strategy and Performance," *Academy of Management Journal* 29 (1986), 329–346.

[34]Ronald B. Lieber, "Smart Science," *Fortune*, June 23, 1997, 73.

[35]Gabriella Stern, "Race Car Driver Goes Home, Sets New Course for Bake-Mix Concern," *The Wall Street Journal*, February 19, 1997, A1, A6.

[36]Gail Dutton, "What Business Are We In?" *Management Review*, September 1997, 54–57.

[37]John S. DeMott, "Company Alliances for Market Muscle," *Nation's Business*, February 1994, 52–53.

[38]Gregory M. Bounds, Gregory H. Dobbins, and Oscar S. Fowler, *Management: A Total Quality Perspective* (Cincinnati, OH: South-Western College Publishing, 1995), 244.

[39]Michael Treacy, "You Need a Value Discipline—But Which One?" *Fortune*, April 17, 1995, 195.

[40]Michael A. Hitt, R. Duane Ireland, and Robert Hoskisson, *Strategic Management: Competitiveness and Globalization* (St. Paul, MN: West, 1995), 238.

[41]L.J. Bourgeois, III and David R. Brodwin, "Strategic Implementation: Five Approaches to an Elusive Phenomenon," *Strategic Management Journal* 5 (1984), 241–264; and Anil K. Gupta and V. Govindarajan, "Business Unit Strategy, Managerial Characteristics, and Business Unit Effectiveness at Strategy Implementation," *Academy of Management Journal* (1984), 25–41.

[42]Greg Burns, "How a New Boss Got ConAgra Cooking Again," *Business Week*, July 25, 1994, 72–73.

[43]Shelly Branch, "What's Eating McDonald's?" *Fortune*, October 13, 1997, 122–125.

[44]Quoted in Pat McHenry Sullivan, "Finding Visions for Work and Life," *Spirit at Work* April 1997, 3.

[45]Rick Mullin, "Reorienting the Boy Scouts," *Journal of Business Strategy*, July/August 1996, 21–27.

[46]Hamel and Prahalad, "Seeing the Future First."

[47]Oren Harari, "Catapult Your Strategy Over Conventional Wisdom," *Management Review* October 1997, 21–24.

[48]Hamel and Prahalad, "Seeing the Future First."

[49]Harari, "Catapult Your Vision."

[50]Richard Teitelbaum, "Tough Guys Finish First," *Fortune*, July 21, 1997, 82–84; Harari, "Catapult Your Strategy."

[51]Pat McHenry Sullivan, "Finding Visions for Work and Life," 3.

[52]C. Chet Miller and Laura B. Cardinal, "Strategic Planning and Firm Performance: A Synthesis of More than Two Decades of Research," *Academy of Management Journal* 37, no. 6 (1994), 1649–1665.

[53]Sydney Finkelstein and Donald C. Hambrick, *Strategic Leadership: Top Executives and Their Effect on Organizations* (St. Paul, MN: West, 1996), 23.

[54]Hamel, "Killer Strategies."

[55]Stanley Lieberson and James F. O'Connor, "Leadership and Organizational Performance: A Study of Large Corporations," *American Sociological Review* 37 (1972), 119; Nan Weiner and Thomas A. Mahoney, "A Model of Corporate Performance as a Function of Environmental, Organizational, and Leadership Influences," *Academy of Management Journal* 24 (1981), 453–470; Ralph A. Alexander, "Leadership: It Can Make a Difference," *Academy of Management Journal* 27 (1984), 765–776; and Alan Berkeley Thomas, "Does Leadership Make a Difference to Organizational Performance?" *Administrative Science Quarterly* 33 (1988), 388–400.

[56]David G. Day and Robert G. Lord, "Executive Leadership and Organizational Performance: Suggestions for a New Theory and Methodology," *Journal of Management* 14 (1988), 453–464.

[57]Ken G. Smith, Ken A. Smith, Judy D. Olian, Henry P. Sims, Jr., Douglas P. O'Bannon, and Judith A. Scully, "Top Management Team Demography and Process: The Role of Social Integration and Communication," *Administrative Science Quarterly* 39 (1994), 412–438.

6

Leadership Communication

- **How Leaders Communicate** 155

- **Creating an Open Communication Climate** 156

- **Listening and Discernment** 159

- **Rich Communication Channels** 164

- **Stories and Metaphors** 167

- **Symbols and Informal Communication** 169

- **Feedback and Learning** 170

- **Leadership Spotlights:**
  Synergex 158
  ATI Medical, Inc. 166
  U.S. Army 172

- **Leader's Bookshelf:**
  The Way of the Warrior: Business Tactics and Techniques from History's Twelve Greatest Generals 157

- **Leadership Development: Personal Feedback**
  Listening Self-Inventory 174

- **Leadership Development: Case for Analysis**
  The Superintendent's Directive 175

Your Leadership Challenge

After reading this chapter, you should be able to:

- Know how to act as a communication champion rather than just as an information processor.

- Use key elements of effective listening and understand why listening is important to leader communication.

- Recognize and apply the difference between dialogue and discussion.

- Select an appropriate communication channel for your leadership message.

- Use communication feedback and realize its importance for leadership.

In December of 1955 Martin Luther King, Jr., was installed as president of the new Montgomery Improvement Association. That same evening, he was called upon to address a crowd of thousands regarding the bus boycott that had begun only days earlier. In his impromptu speech, King reminded his audience of Rosa Parks' arrest and conviction for refusing to give up her bus seat to a white person. He commended her integrity; her action was a move toward justice and reflected a belief that all Americans are entitled to basic rights and privileges. King pointed out that the bus boycott was a means of protest with similar integrity. The boycott was nonviolent, it required patience, and it rested on the expectation of equal treatment of all people—values King had preached in his sermons as a minister.

King described the audience to whom he was speaking as people "tired of being pushed out of the glittering sunlight of life's July, and left standing amidst the chill of an alpine November." The audience rallied in agreement, and under King's guidance 50,000 Montgomery, Alabama citizens participated in the boycott for the duration of the protest despite the fact that most of those same citizens needed to ride the buses to get to and from work.

King's actions over the next several months were a witness of his sincerity to the protestors. He was the first to be arrested for participating in the boycott. His home was bombed the same day as his arrest. To these tribulations he declared his determination inviolate. The boycott continued.

After nearly a year of protest, the U.S. Supreme Court ruled that Alabama's segregation laws were indeed unconstitutional. The boycott ended in victory. King declared the verdict a leap of progress for the entire American population.[1]

What made King's first public role in a political drama so powerful that it ignited the support of thousands? How did King manage to maintain the support of so many people over a long period of hardship? Much of King's impact occurred the moment he gave his first speech. With his initial words, King created the parameters of a social movement. First, he stood before the crowd and directed their collective attention to the immediate situation—Parks' action and the decision to boycott. Then he defined the significance of the boycott by comparing it to the incident on the bus—in effect, every boycotter was Rosa Parks. He also discerned that the audience was tired of injustice. He described this point of critical mass with a metaphor contrasting summer sunshine with winter winds. This metaphor made the experience of racism tangible, felt upon the skin of each person in the crowd.

King was thrust into a position of leadership where others looked to him for direction and inspiration. As he endured arrest and violence against his family without changing course, he symbolized his message of determination in the face of hardship. He communicated with both words and actions a vision and possibility of equality. King's followers wanted a future based on basic religious values and American ideals, a future King motivated them to work for and helped them see. For thousands, Martin Luther King, Jr. created a purpose and an identity that had not existed before.

A leader must successfully communicate his or her vision to others for it to make any difference. Successful communication is not achieved simply by telling others what you want them to know, but involves a wide range of activities and tools for getting a vision into the consciousness of numerous followers. Like King, a leader can direct the attention of followers to what is significant, define the higher meaning of actions and attitudes, and be aware of the symbolic messages conveyed by his or her own behavior, appearance, and personal expressions of the vision.

Successful leader communication also includes deceptively simple components, such as actively listening to others. Today's fast-paced environment does not always provide the time for the listening and reflection that good communication requires.[2] For example, a recent study showed that while leaders at a majority of companies agree that communication is a priority, less than half bother to tailor their messages to employees, customers, or suppliers, and even fewer seek feedback from those constituencies. Furthermore, investors appear to have a better idea of the vision and mission of companies than do employees.[3]

To create a desired future for an organization, communication is essential because the leader must *share* the vision to get the desired outcomes. This chapter will describe the tools that overcome the communication deficit pervading today's organizations and the broader social world. These tools will be presented along with their leadership application in organizations.

How Leaders Communicate

Communication is a process by which information and understanding are transferred between a sender and a receiver. The sender is anyone who wishes to convey an idea or concept to others, impart information, or express a thought or emotion. The receiver is the person to whom the message is sent. Potential communication errors exist when sending and receiving messages, because knowledge, attitudes, and background act as filters and create "noise" when translating from words into meaning. Feedback from the receiver to the sender enables the sender to determine whether the receiver correctly interpreted the message. The process of sending, receiving, and feedback underlies both management and leader communications.

Management Communication

The manager's role is that of "information processor." Managers spend some 80 percent of each working day in communication with others.[4] In other words, 48 minutes of every hour are spent in meetings, on the telephone, or talking informally with others. Managers scan their environments for important written and personal information, gathering facts and data, which in turn is then sent to subordinates and others who can use it. A manager then receives subordinate messages and feedback to see if "noise" interfered with translation, and determines whether to modify messages for accuracy.

Managers have a huge communication responsibility directing and controlling an organization. Communication effectiveness lies in accuracy of formulation, with less "noise" as one determinant of success. Managers communicate facts, statistics, and decisions. Effective managers establish themselves at the center of information networks to facilitate the completion of tasks. Leadership communication, however, serves a different purpose.

Leader Communication

While leader communication includes such components as sending and receiving, it is different from management communication. Leaders often communicate the big picture—the vision—rather than facts and pieces of information. Whereas a manager acts as an information processor to disseminate data accurately, a leader can be seen as a communication champion.[5] A **communication champion** is philosophically grounded in the belief that communication is essential to pursuing the organizational vision. Learning, problem solving, decision-making, and strategizing are

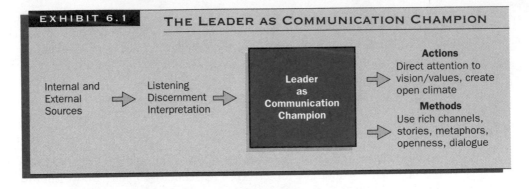

EXHIBIT 6.1 THE LEADER AS COMMUNICATION CHAMPION

Internal and External Sources ⇒ Listening Discernment Interpretation ⇒ Leader as Communication Champion ⇒ **Actions** Direct attention to vision/values, create open climate ⇒ **Methods** Use rich channels, stories, metaphors, openness, dialogue

all oriented around and stem from the vision. Furthermore, communication champions visibly and symbolically engage in communication-based activities. Whether they walk around asking and answering questions or thoughtfully listen to a subordinate's problem, the actions of champions convey a commitment to communication. Communicating vision is not only about formal speeches and motivating people. It is about drawing the vision to the forefront in people's minds during day-to-day interactions and activities. Leaders build a shared vision by communicating with words and actions every day.

Exhibit 6.1 shows the leader-as-communication-champion model. Through the efforts of listening with pure concentration on the needs of others, and the discernment of underlying messages, leaders gather what they need to communicate. Active listening requires that leaders temporarily drop their personal agendas and give their attention to speakers. Discernment involves recognizing the needs that followers, for whatever reason, are unable to articulate.

Leader communication actions include directing others' attention toward the vision and values of an organization. Leaders can use many communication methods including rich channels of communication, stories, metaphors, informality, openness, and dialogue. For example, in communicating his message about the federal budget, President Reagan spoke of a trillion dollars in terms of stacking it next to the Empire State Building. Framed this way, the message redefined the meaning of a trillion dollars, and took on a new reality for the audience. Historical and contemporary leaders as diverse as Reagan, Martin Luther King, Jr., Napoleon, Bill Gates, and Norman Schwartzkopf all share the ability to powerfully communicate their messages to followers and others. This chapter's Leader's Bookshelf examines how the world's greatest military commanders have used the skill of communication to its greatest effect.

Creating an Open Communication Climate

Open communication means sharing all types of information throughout the company, especially across functional and hierarchical levels. Open communication runs counter to the traditional flow of selective information downward from supervisors

The Way of the Warrior: Business Tactics and Techniques from History's Twelve Greatest Generals

James Dunnigan and Daniel Masterson

In *The Way of the Warrior*, lessons of a dozen of the world's greatest military commanders—from Alexander the Great to Norman Schwarzkopf—are applied to the contemporary business world. According to authors James Dunnigan and Daniel Masterson, whether embroiled in the conquest of the Persian Empire or the process of a merger, a leader faces challenges that require vision, communication, and other timeless skills. For example, the authors point out that, "Leaders who fail to communicate fail. If there is one skill that all Great Captains use, and use to greatest effect, it is communication."

History's Great Warriors

The book provides clear, to-the-point histories of each military commander and his time. Some of the 12 leaders profiled in *The Way of the Warrior* are:

1. Alexander the Great.   Twenty-four hundred years ago Alexander the Great led Greek forces to conquer the much larger Persian Empire. Although he was Macedonian, Alexander had embraced Greek culture, and part of his vision was to spread it throughout the vast territory. He took charge of his own "public relations," writing letters to the folks back in Greece as well as carefully crafting directives to his new Persian subjects.

2. Julius Caesar.   The authors show how Caesar deliberately molded public opinion and motivated his armies through his speeches, debates, and writings. Caesar excelled at oratory and rhetoric, a valuable skill in an era when "skillfully wielded words were often mightier than brute force." Caesar's great talents were, however, applied primarily in the raw pursuit of personal wealth and power, leading to ruin for himself and the empire.

3. Ulysses S. Grant.   The leader of the victorious Union Army in the American Civil War was known for his focus, persistence, and ability to remain calm under stressful situations. An important trait was his skill at written communication, which was of tremendous importance during the Civil War because orders often had to be carried over long distances. He handled the job of writing communications personally—stating clearly the final objective of the order, outlining the details he considered most important, and then leaving the rest up to his subordinates.

4. Norman Schwarzkopf.   A master of spoken communication, General Norman Schwarzkopf showed off his skills to perfection during the Gulf War briefings. What made the briefings so well received was their directness, simplicity, and truthfulness, laced with Schwarzkopf's unique style of humor. He used the same approach in speaking to his troops, which he did as often as possible. Schwarzkopf was also powerful in dealing with the press, realizing that if he didn't tell the story, someone else would—and probably in a way he wouldn't like. Schwarzkopf's communication fostered admiration, respect, and loyalty from subordinates and superiors alike.

Timeless Techniques

Dunnigan and Masterson say all Great Captains cultivate similar strengths. They learn to communicate with purpose, act with courage, take risks, and lead by example. The techniques used by the 12 military commanders in *The Way of the Warrior* are just as effective for business leaders—as the authors put it, ". . . if a general or manager can lead, all else becomes possible."

The Way of the Warrior, by James Dunnigan and Daniel Masterson, is published by St. Martin's Press.

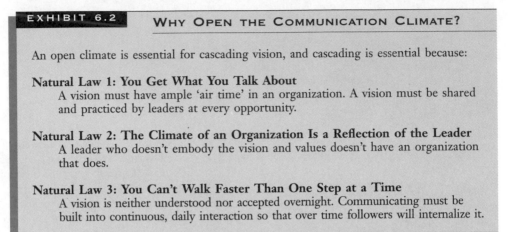

EXHIBIT 6.2   WHY OPEN THE COMMUNICATION CLIMATE?

An open climate is essential for cascading vision, and cascading is essential because:

Natural Law 1: You Get What You Talk About
A vision must have ample 'air time' in an organization. A vision must be shared and practiced by leaders at every opportunity.

Natural Law 2: The Climate of an Organization Is a Reflection of the Leader
A leader who doesn't embody the vision and values doesn't have an organization that does.

Natural Law 3: You Can't Walk Faster Than One Step at a Time
A vision is neither understood nor accepted overnight. Communicating must be built into continuous, daily interaction so that over time followers will internalize it.

SOURCE: Based on Bob Wall, Robert S. Sloum, and Mark R. Sobol, *Visionary Leader* (Rocklin, CA: Prima Publishing, 1992), 87–89.

to subordinates. But to transmit the vision, leaders want communication to flow in all directions. Eliminating the conventional boundaries and directions of communication enables leaders to convey a higher mission and establish followers' understanding of it. In an open climate, the communication "cascades" through an organization, immersing members in the vision.[6]

It is important that leaders actually embrace the ideas they communicate. When leaders truly believe in an idea, they want to share it with others, and their actions will match their words. Consistent and frequent communication brings follower understanding and acceptance. With fewer boundaries and constraints, the opportunity for communication increases. Leaders seize every opportunity to stress the vision and values to followers. Exhibit 6.2 discusses further how these factors make an open climate essential for leader communication.

An open communication climate encompasses the recent trend toward "open book management," in which financial information is shared with and explained to all employees to engender an attitude of ownership. Leslie Fishbein, president of Kacey Fine Furniture, opened the financial books to all 170 employees based on the belief that "information helps people make decisions that are good for the company."[7] When an employee understands the effect of purchases on profits, for example, he or she makes more informed decisions. Consider the results of a leader using open communication at Synergex.

LEADERSHIP SPOTLIGHT   SYNERGEX

Michele C. Wong, president of the software company Synergex, believes that sharing information is the responsibility of every member of the organization. Her employees hold open forums in which they ask questions and congratulate one another. The chief financial officer provides statements of the company's finances to all employees each month. Employees are kept abreast of Synergex people and products through a newsletter. Employees also use a computer database network to post recent communications with customers and suppliers for all to read. Departments discuss their goals at team meetings, and share their activities with other departments in the learning-at-lunch program. The informal skills-sharing sessions foster everything from professional development to at-home projects.

Letting company information flow freely in all directions among all ranks, says Wong, has made Synergex more efficient, increased morale, and kept skilled, professional workers on board. Open communication began at Synergex when the company faced a financial crisis and employees suggested an open forum to air problems and discuss solutions. Leaders wisely agreed and within a year, Synergex was celebrating financial success. Open communication at Synergex has enabled happier, more knowledgeable employees who provide superior customer service.[8]

The employees at Synergex understand how their actions affect the company. By having full information, Synergex employees are more aware of their place in the organizational portrait, which makes them more effective followers.

Communication across boundaries also enables leaders to hear what followers have to say. The same perspectives batted back and forth between the same panel of supervisors do not lead to effective change, nor to the creation of an exceptional vision. New voices and new conversations involving a broad spectrum of members revitalize and enhance communication.[9] Cross-departmental problem-solving teams brought body shop workers and sales reps together at Childress Buick/Kia Company. The new conversations produced an increase in referrals from the shop to the sales force for new car purchases. Overall customer satisfaction is now over 95 percent. Rusty Childress has also successfully broken down traditional departmental barriers with informal meetings, electronic newsletters, frequent surveys, and recognition boards. These open communication lines are simple and inexpensive, yet together they serve as a relentless source of vision, focus, remedies, suggestions, sharing, brainstorming, and praise for everyone.[10] Open communication goes in all directions and includes all members. Kim Polese, president and CEO of Marimba, refuses to miss any of the software company's "All-Hands Meetings." Why? Because, Polese claims, "It's my chance to learn from the entire staff." As a leader, Polese benefits from the face-to-face discussion of the concerns of every employee.[11]

Followers need to see the vision and values enacted by their leaders before they can accept what leaders want to convey. Thus, open communication not only improves the operations of an organization, but it provides a foundation for a leader to communicate vision, values, and other vital big picture information.

Listening and Discernment

One of the most important tools in a leader's communication tool kit is listening, both to customers and subordinates. Many leaders now believe that important infor-

EXHIBIT 6.3	TEN KEYS TO EFFECTIVE LISTENING	
Keys	**Poor Listener**	**Good Listener**
1. Listen actively	Is passive, laid back	Asks questions; paraphrases what is said
2. Find areas of interest	Tunes out dry subjects	Looks for opportunities, new learning
3. Resist distractions	Is easily distracted	Fights distractions; tolerates bad habits; knows how to concentrate
4. Capitalize on the fact that thought is faster than speech	Tends to daydream with slow speakers	Challenges, anticipates, summarizes; listens between lines to tone of voice
5. Be responsive	Is minimally involved	Nods; shows interest, positive feedback
6. Judge content, not delivery	Tunes out if delivery is poor	Judges content; skips over delivery errors
7. Hold one's fire	Has preconceptions; argues	Does not judge until comprehension is complete
8. Listen for ideas	Listens for facts	Listens to central themes
9. Work at listening	No energy output; faked attention	Works hard; exhibits active body state, eye contact
10. Exercise one's mind	Resists difficult material in favor of light, recreational material	Uses heavier material as exercise for the mind

SOURCE: Adapted from Sherman K. Okum, "How to Be a Better Listener," *Nation's Business* (August 1975), 62; and Philip Morgan and Kent Baker, "Building a Professional Image: Improving Listening Behavior," *Supervisory Management* (November 1985), 34–38.

mation flows from the bottom up, not top down, and that a crucial component of leadership is to listen effectively.[12] A listener is responsible for message reception, which is a vital link in the communication process. **Listening** involves the skill of grasping and interpreting a message's genuine meaning. Only then can a leader's response be on target. Listening is an activity; it requires attention, energy, and skill.

Many people do not listen effectively. They concentrate on formulating what they are going to say next rather than on what is being said to them. Our listening efficiency, as measured by the amount of material understood and remembered by subjects 48 hours after listening to a 10-minute message, is, on average, no better than 25 percent.[13]

What constitutes good listening? Exhibit 6.3 gives 10 keys to effective listening and illustrates a number of ways to distinguish a bad listener from a good one. A good listener finds areas of interest, is flexible, works hard at listening, and uses thought speed to mentally summarize, weigh, and anticipate what the speaker says.

The act of good listening affirms others, builds trust, and suppresses personal

ON THE CUTTING EDGE

Springfield Remanufacturing Corp.

Quite by chance did CEO Jack Stack learn that leaders within Springfield Remanufacturing Corp. (SRC) were not listening to workers. By participating in an outside poll, employees revealed how low their morale had become. For example, in the Heavy-Duty division, 43 percent felt that their opinions did not count; 48 percent felt they had no chance to rise in rank; 62 percent claimed that no one had consulted them about their personal development. Stack was stunned. Despite the outward success of the division, it was clear that workers were perceiving SRC from a different perspective. So Stack began to listen.

One worker who tested products revealed that he had been complaining about a faulty specification setting for two years to no avail. Stack saw that no one had heard these people.

The division was fraught with problems that were solved easily and quickly, such as machine setting adjustments, but the damage done to employee morale required real changes to resolve. An employee satisfaction committee was installed comprising 18 shop-floor volunteers. Using the same poll questions that initially revealed worker dissatisfaction, SRC leaders began to audit the division with the goal of reducing to zero the percentage of demoralized employees. By routinizing the act of "listening" through the committee resource and the audits, Stack envisions a more satisfied workforce.

SOURCE: Jack Stack, "Measuring Morale," *Inc.*, January 1997, 29–30.

judgments that shape perceptions. Merrill Lynch superbroker Richard F. Green explained the importance of listening to his success: "If you talk, you'll like me. If I talk, I'll like you—but if I do the talking, my business will not be served."[14] By not interrupting people when they talk, and by not plying them with his business agenda, Green builds long-term relationships with his clients.

Being a good listener expands a leader's role in the eyes of others; it deepens the relationship between a leader and a follower. When Sunrise at Queen Anne retirement home came under new ownership, manager Dory Parker asked residents what changes they wanted to see take place. She addressed many of the responses immediately, such as purchasing additional handrails. By listening to the needs of residents, and subsequently responding to those needs, Parker decreased residents' anxiety and strengthened their trust in her leadership.[15] She became a caregiver to their needs. This transformation is what leader listening—indeed, communication—is all about.

Active listening is necessary not only during times of change, but is a daily, ongoing part of a leader's communication. Norm Brodsky is convinced that if you do not listen to customers, you cannot possibly meet their needs. At CitiStorage, Brodsky's archive-retrieval business, he regularly gives his customers exactly what they ask for, despite having to change his system. Customers are often surprised by his agreeability because they are used to business leaders who try to tell customers what they want. Like Green, Brodsky approaches potential clients without a business agenda and does not formulate his sales pitch until he fully understands their needs.[16]

The characteristics of good listening hold true for communication within organizations as well. The Cutting Edge box details how not listening to employees affects morale, and how SRC measured its listening skills by assessing employee satisfaction. The connection between personal satisfaction and being listened to, whether one is a customer or an employee, is not a mystery. When people sense that they have been heard they simply feel better. Few things are as maddening to people as ignored requests or being told they can't be accommodated, signals that nobody is listening. Furthermore, when leaders don't listen, it sends the signal, "you don't matter" to organization members, thus decreasing their commitment and motivation.

Listening is a requirement for leader communication, for doing better work, and for enabling others to do better work. Tom Peters, the famous management author and consultant, says that executives can become good listeners by observing the following: Effective listening is engaged listening; ask dumb questions; break down barriers by participating with employees in casual get-togethers; force yourself to get out and about; provide listening forums; take notes; promise feedback—and deliver.[17]

Dialogue

Dialogue is what you get when active listening spreads throughout an organization. A dialogue occurs when a group of good listeners convene. The "roots of dialogue" are *dia* and *logos*, which can be thought of as *stream of meaning*. In **dialogue,** people together create a stream of shared meaning that enables them to understand each other and share a view of the world.[18] People may start out as polar opposites, but by talking authentically to one another, they discover their common ground, common issues, and common dreams on which they can build a better future. An absence of prejudgments, personal agendas, and right answers are characteristic of participants who engage in a dialogue. Participants in a dialogue do not presume to know the outcome nor do they sell their convictions. Participants bring only uncertainty; they have no "right' answer or solution because it has yet to be discovered.

Exhibit 6.4 illustrates the distinctions between a dialogue and a discussion. A dialogue's focus is to reveal feelings and build common ground, with more emphasis on inquiry than advocacy. A discussion explores opposition by individuals who advocate their positions and convince others to adopt those positions. While both forms of communication can result in change, a discussion is resolved by logic or "beating down" opponents. The result of a discussion is limited to the topic deliberated. The result of a dialogue is marked by group unity, shared meaning, and transformed mind-sets. This kind of result is far reaching. A new, common mind-set is not the same thing as agreement, because it creates a reference point from which subsequent communication can start. As new and deeper solutions are developed, a trusting relationship is built among communicators, and this is important to all communication episodes that follow. Dialogue thus transforms communication and, by extension, the organization.[19]

Discernment

One of the most rewarding kinds of listening involves **discernment**. By this kind of listening a leader detects the unarticulated messages hidden below the surface of spo-

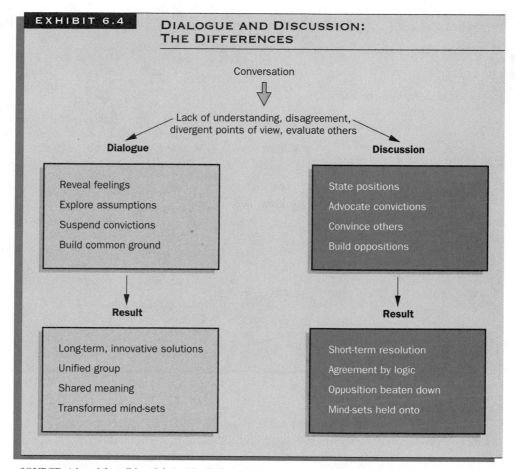

EXHIBIT 6.4

DIALOGUE AND DISCUSSION: THE DIFFERENCES

Conversation

Lack of understanding, disagreement, divergent points of view, evaluate others

Dialogue

Reveal feelings

Explore assumptions

Suspend convictions

Build common ground

Result

Long-term, innovative solutions

Unified group

Shared meaning

Transformed mind-sets

Discussion

State positions

Advocate convictions

Convince others

Build oppositions

Result

Short-term resolution

Agreement by logic

Opposition beaten down

Mind-sets held onto

SOURCE: Adapted from Edgar Schein, "On Dialogue, Culture, and Organization Learning," *Organizational Dynamics* (Autumn 1993), 46.

ken interaction, complaints, behavior, and actions. A discerning leader pays attention to patterns and relationships underlying the organization and those it serves. The Living Leadership box discusses discernment as the essence of leadership.

Richard Teerlink, CEO of Harley-Davidson, used discernment to help turn around the company. Through the innovative Harley Owners Group (HOG) rallies, Teerlink has the opportunity to mingle with many of the 360,000 members nationwide. He attends the rallies, talks with owners, listens to what they have to say, and takes note of the ideas they toss his way. Teerlink thus determined how to give more people a reason to use Harley products. He discerned that people really seek relief from the stresses of daily life when they buy a Harley. The company is selling a sense of freedom and independence more than providing motorcycles and related products. This feeling of escaping the daily grind was not something stated to him

Discerning Feelings

Caotang said:

There is essentially nothing to leadership but to carefully observe people's conditions and know them all, in both upper and lower echelons.

When people's inner conditions are thoroughly understood, then inside and outside are in harmony. When above and below communicate, all affairs are set in order. This is how leadership is made secure.

If the leader cannot minutely discern people's psychological conditions, and the feeling of those below is not communicated above, then above and below oppose each other and matters are disordered. This is how leadership goes to ruin.

It may happen that a leader will presume upon intellectual brilliance and often hold to biased views, failing to comprehend people's feelings, rejecting community counsel and giving importance to his own authority, neglecting public consideration and practicing private favoritism—all of this causes the road of advance in goodness to become narrower and narrower, and causes the path of responsibility for the community to become fainter and fainter.

Such leaders repudiate whatever they have never before seen or heard, and become set in their ways, to which they are habituated and by which they are veiled. To hope that the leadership of people like this would be great and far-reaching is like walking backward trying to go forward.

SOURCE: Thomas Cleary, translator, *Zen Lessons: The Art of Leadership* (Boston, Mass.: Shambhala Publications 1989), 83–84.

by the latest customer, but something Teerlink was able to discern from what he encountered by strolling among and listening to rally members.[20]

A leader hears the undercurrents that have yet to emerge and acknowledges them in executing his or her vision.[21] Remember how Martin Luther King, Jr. discerned a readiness to fight injustice in his audience, a frustration just beginning to surface to which he subsequently gave definition and organization? His was an act of discernment.

Rich Communication Channels

A **channel** is a medium by which a communication message is carried from sender to receiver. Leaders have a choice of many channels through which to communicate to subordinates. A leader may discuss a problem face-to-face, use the telephone, write a memo or letter, use e-mail, or put an item in a newsletter, depending on the nature of the message. Recent research has attempted to explain how managers select communication channels to enhance communication effectiveness.[22] The research has found that channels differ in their capacity to convey information. Just as a pipeline's physical characteristics limit the kind and amount of liquid that can be

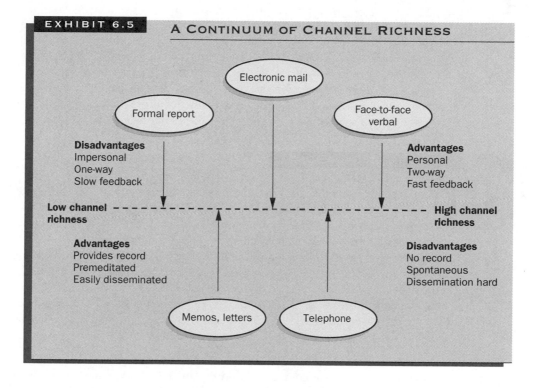

EXHIBIT 6.5   **A CONTINUUM OF CHANNEL RICHNESS**

Electronic mail

Formal report

Face-to-face verbal

Disadvantages
Impersonal
One-way
Slow feedback

Advantages
Personal
Two-way
Fast feedback

Low channel richness   -   **High channel richness**

Advantages
Provides record
Premeditated
Easily disseminated

Disadvantages
No record
Spontaneous
Dissemination hard

Memos, letters

Telephone

pumped through it, a communication channel's physical characteristics limit the kind and amount of information that can be conveyed among people. The channels available to leaders can be classified into a hierarchy based on information richness. **Channel richness** is the amount of information that can be transmitted during a communication episode. The hierarchy of channel richness is illustrated in Exhibit 6.5.

The richness of an information channel is influenced by three characteristics: (1) the ability to handle multiple cues simultaneously; (2) the ability to facilitate rapid, two-way feedback; and (3) the ability to establish a personal focus for the communication. Face-to-face discussion is the richest medium, because it permits direct experience, multiple information cues, immediate feedback, and personal focus. Face-to-face discussions facilitate the assimilation of broad cues and deep, emotional understanding of the situation. For example, Tony Burns, CEO of Ryder Systems, Inc., likes to handle things face-to-face: "You can look someone in the eyes. You can tell by the look in his eyes or the inflection of his voice what the real problem or question or answer is."[23] Telephone conversations and interactive electronic media, such as voice mail and electronic mail, while increasing the speed of communications, lack the element of "being there." Eye contact, gaze, blush, posture, and body language cues are eliminated. Therefore a leader's ability to listen actively or discern is diminished. In recognition of the need for channel richness, electronic communication is improving the immediacy of "being there" through video conferencing.

Written media that are personalized, such as notes and letters, can be personally focused but they convey only the cues written on paper and are slow to provide feedback. Impersonal written media, including fliers, bulletins, and standard computer reports, are the lowest in richness. The channels are not focused on a single receiver, use limited information cues, and do not permit feedback. Paul Stevenson, president and CEO of ATI Medical, Inc. banned the practice of writing memos to encourage employees to use rich communication channels.

LEADERSHIP SPOTLIGHT　　　ATI MEDICAL, INC.

Paul Stevenson felt that memos substituted for human interaction and wasted valuable decision making time. Stevenson claimed, "We want to instill the idea of doing, rather than writing." He attributes the company's yearly increase in sales to the productive and timely personal interactions that have resulted from the no-memo policy.

Nevertheless, as ATI Medical grew to 41 offices and 300 employees, Stevenson was compelled to accommodate some written communication. However, his policy modifications are limited to areas that do not compromise the use of rich channels. Announcements notifying workers of a price change, for example, must be directed to entire departments, never to individuals. Individual communication still requires a personal encounter.[24]

Lacking memos as a communication channel, ATI employees must communicate in person to get their ideas out, and they build strong relationships with one another in the process. Leaders recognize that innovation and teamwork are the by-products of using rich channels.

However, it is important for leaders to understand that each communication channel has advantages and disadvantages, and that each can be an effective means of communication in the appropriate circumstances.[25] Channel selection depends on whether the message is routine or nonroutine. Routine communications are simple and straightforward, such as the ATI price change. Routine messages convey data or statistics or simply put into words what people already understand and agree on. Routine messages can be efficiently communicated through a channel lower in richness. Written communications also are effective when the audience is widely dispersed or when the communication is "official" and a permanent record is required.[26] On the other hand, nonroutine messages typically concern issues of change, conflict, or complexity that have great potential for misunderstanding. Nonroutine messages often are characterized by time pressure and surprise. Leaders can communicate nonroutine messages effectively only by selecting a rich channel.

Consider a CEO trying to work out a press release with public relations people about a plant explosion that injured 15 employees. If the press release must be ready in three hours, the communication is truly nonroutine and forces a rich information exchange. The group will meet face-to-face, brainstorm ideas, and provide rapid feedback to resolve disagreement and convey the correct information. If the CEO has three days to prepare the release, less information capacity is needed. The

CEO and public relations people might begin developing the press release with an exchange of memos and telephone calls.

The leadership key is to select a channel to fit the message. During a major acquisition, one firm elected to send senior executives to all major work sites, where 75 percent of the acquired workforce met the officials in person. The results were well worth the time and expense of the personal appearances. Participating leaders claimed that the workers saw them as understanding and willing to listen—people they would not mind working for.[27] The choice of these leaders to use a rich channel for their nonroutine message was a wise one. Indeed, leader communication by its nature is largely comprised of nonroutine messages. While leaders maximize the use of all channels, they do not let anything substitute for the rich face-to-face channel when important issues are at stake.

Sometimes a channel conveys more than the simple message content, a symbolic meaning to the receiver of which the leader must be aware. In other words, members of an organization attach meaning to the channel itself. Reports and memos—low richness channels—typically convey formality and legitimize a message. Personal visits from a leader or other rich channels are seen as a sign of teamwork.[28] The very modes of communication, then, are symbolic, as when students gauge the importance of a topic based on the amount of time a professor spends talking about it, or when an individual experiences indignation at receiving a "Dear John" letter instead of having a relationship end in person.

Stories and Metaphors

Communication encounters can be further enriched by leaders who are conscious of the language they use, and the definitions and context they create with their language. When Federal Express acquired its airfreight rival, Flying Tiger Lines, Inc., the careers and trust of employees in both firms were at stake. Chairman Fred Smith and Chief Operating Officer Jim Barksdale chose the word "merger" rather than "acquisition" to define the situation to 35,000 employees. This simple language choice defined the importance of both workforces to the endeavor, easing concerns over job security from the beginning.[29]

Choosing the best terminology is but one way leaders can enrich their communication. It is in the leader's purview to direct followers' attention to the values that underlie the organization, to define the meaning of situations and objectives, and to give visionary messages in ways that make them palpable and meaningful to organizational members. People seek meaning in their daily work and want to understand their role in the larger context of the organization. It is up to leaders to provide that context for followers, to frame activity with discrete meaning.[30] By using language rich in metaphor and storytelling, leaders can make sense of situations in ways that will be understood similarly throughout the organization.

Consider the meaning conveyed by a leader telling followers: "Every morning in Africa, a gazelle wakes up. It knows it must outrun the fastest lion or it will be killed. Every morning in Africa, a lion wakes up. It knows it must run faster than the slowest gazelle or it will starve. It doesn't matter whether you're a lion or a gazelle—when the sun comes up, you'd better be running."[31]

A conscious use of metaphors often results in a story. At baked goods manufacturer Rhino Foods, Ted Castle involved his workers in the company's bottom line with the metaphor and story that business is a game, complete with winners, losers, and scores. The financial "score card" determines whether Rhino wins or loses. At the end of each month, Castle awards bonus checks when Rhino "wins" against the competition. Castle is convinced that the 600 percent increase in revenues and profits is the direct result of the game.[32] A game does not have the same meaning as work; a new structure and motivation to win are built into the metaphor of a game. When Brian Ruder, president of Heinz USA, told his workers "Ketchup is finger paint for kids; we're not building intercontinental ballistic missiles here," he focused the organization on maximizing the playful side of the product.[33] In this context, workers are encouraged to have fun, be innovative, and so they go about their work differently.

David Armstrong, president of Armstrong International, wrote *Management by Storying Around* because of the way people listened to his minister's stories each Sunday.[34] Even when people had heard a story many times, their attention perked up. Armstrong saw that people loved to hear stories and decided to use stories to enhance his leadership impact. He used stories to replace rules and regulations. He told a story about an individual traveling for the company who spent money just the way he did at home. This story replaced Armstrong International's travel and entertainment expense rulebook. Stories eventually replaced the entire policy manual at Armstrong.

One of the most compelling stories used by Armstrong to shape corporate culture was about the decision not to expand the plant in the direction of the property lived on by Fred Kemp. The building committee recommended a new plant right next to the old one. The layout would be efficient. All that was needed was to buy the home of Fred Kemp, in his mid-70s, a retired Armstrong employee. As the story goes:

> The President vetoed the plan.
>
> "Fred has lived in the house forever," he said. "His children grew up there and it really is the only place he's ever called home. I know he loves that place. We bought it from him years ago when it looked like we'd have to expand on to his property someday. But when we bought it, I promised he could stay there as long as he liked. Making him move now might upset him to the point where it shortens his life. We'll build a new plant on the other side of the property."[35]

This story vividly illustrates to everyone who hears it that human values outweigh planned efficiency at Armstrong International.

Evidence for the compatibility of stories with human thinking was demonstrated by a study at the Stanford Business School.[36] The point was to convince MBA students that a company practiced a policy of avoiding layoffs. For some students, only a story was used. For others, statistical data were provided that showed little turnover compared to competitors. For other students, statistics and stories were combined, and yet other students were shown the company's policy statement. Of all these approaches, students presented with the story alone were most convinced about the avoiding layoff policy.

Symbols and Informal Communication

Martin Luther King, Jr. was a symbol to the Montgomery, Alabama boycotters. King himself stood for something abstract, a commitment. That King was impervious to bombs and arrests communicated something to his followers—perseverance and possibility. His actions held important meanings to supporters and adversaries alike.

Leaders are watched, and their appearance, behavior, actions, and attitudes are symbolic to others. Symbols are a powerful tool for communicating what is important. Therefore, leaders are aware of what they signal to others in addition to verbal messages. Indeed, **nonverbal communication,** that is, messages transmitted through action and behavior, accounts for over one half of the entire message received in a personal encounter.[37] People interpret leader actions as symbols, just as they attach meaning to words. By closing the door to his or her office a leader conveys inaccessibility. Conversing from behind a desk denotes authority, while a side-by-side seating arrangement suggests equality and teamwork.[38]

In interpreting a leader's nonverbal cues, followers determine the extent to which a leader's actions correspond with his or her verbal messages. Research suggests that if there is a discrepancy between a person's verbal and nonverbal communication, the nonverbal is granted more weight by the interpreter.[39] For example, a whole week after delivering an impassioned software development pitch to a group of investors, Michael Damphousse still had no takers. It wasn't until he took the advice of a friend and quit his job that $150,000 rolled in for his start-up project.[40] Verbally, Damphousse communicated effectively, but investors considered his recent promotion within his firm to mean that he wasn't committed to the project. His resignation corresponded to his verbal message, prompting the investors to reconsider.[41]

Leaders use actions to symbolize their vision and their commitment to it. They draw attention to specific values and ideas. For example, in order to underscore the importance of his open-door policy, former Centennial Medical Center president, Bill Arnold, hung his office door from the ceiling of his lobby.[42]

Informal communication is built into an open communication climate and includes interactions that go beyond formal, authorized channels. Informal communication is important not only because it can be symbolic of leader vision, but also because it has great impact on participants. For example, consider how much more memorable the quarterly results were for Mattel employees when CEO John Amerman used a rap song to deliver them instead of a memo.[43] Another example of informal communication is "management by wandering around (MBWA)" presented in the books *In Search of Excellence* and *A Passion for Excellence*.[44] MBWA means that leaders leave their offices and speak directly to employees as they work. These impromptu encounters send positive messages to followers. In addition, the communication is richer, therefore likely to make a lasting impression in both directions. When E. Grady Bogue became interim chancellor at Louisiana State University, one of the first things he did was walk through the departments on campus. He wound up in the biology building, where he enjoyed an extended tour of the facility by a faculty member he ran across. Bogue remarked that he learned an enormous amount about the university operations and the strengths and weaknesses of the biology program that was "more direct, personal and meaningful than any written communication might have conveyed."[45] Thus, both leaders and followers benefit from informal channels.

Feedback and Learning

When a leader listens, chooses channels, directs attention, or creates a story, he or she does so with a desired outcome in mind. A leader must decide to what extent the desired outcome is reflected in his or her message. Whether it is an expression of company values, a quarterly financial report, or work performance, an outcome can be evaluated for the reflection of leader intent and objective. **Feedback** occurs when a leader uses evaluation and communication to help individuals and the organization learn and improve.

Feedback is an essential tool for leadership communication.[46] As an evaluation, feedback enables leaders to determine if they have been successful or unsuccessful in communicating with others. Feedback is crucial for the closure of a communication loop. This is not to say that communication ends with feedback, but that only by evaluating the success of a communication can leaders reformulate and increase the effectiveness of subsequent messages, signals, and organizational practices. By understanding feedback as a process of communication with a systematic improvement component, leaders can increase their communication effectiveness, and use this awareness to develop followers and improve the organization. The result of feedback is change—change in the follower and change in the organization.

The feedback process involves four elements, as illustrated in Exhibit 6.6. **Observations** are visible occurrences, either subordinate behavior or results of organizational activity. An **assessment** is the interpretation of observed behaviors, an evaluation of the results in terms of vision and goals. A **consequence** refers to the outcome of what was observed, and can include both actual consequences and the consequences possible if no change takes place. **Development** refers to the sustainment or improvement of behaviors. Leaders communicate what they observe, how they assess it, what consequences it has, and how to effectively address the observed behavior and consequence. Each element is communicated from the leader to the individual or organization.[47]

Furthermore, the development becomes an observation in the next communication loop. For example, a leader who observes development and assesses it positively may consequently promote the responsible subordinate. Thus, feedback

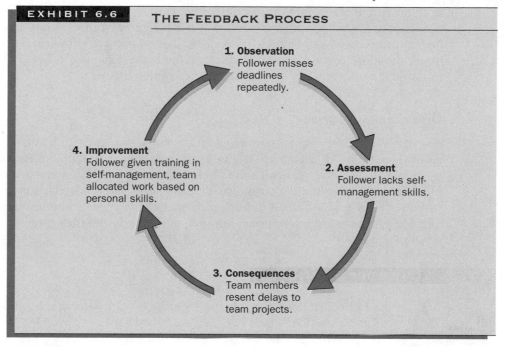

EXHIBIT 6.6   **THE FEEDBACK PROCESS**

1. Observation
Follower misses deadlines repeatedly.

2. Assessment
Follower lacks self-management skills.

3. Consequences
Team members resent delays to team projects.

4. Improvement
Follower given training in self-management, team allocated work based on personal skills.

SOURCE: Adapted from Mary Mavis, "Painless Performance Evaluations," *Training and Development*, October 1994, 40–44.

enables communication to form a continuous loop. Leaders employ these elements to provide feedback that facilitates growth for followers and organizations.

Despite the importance of feedback to leadership communication, often it is neglected. Remember the research presented at the beginning of this chapter that found even as most companies feel that communication is a priority, few of them utilize feedback to employees in their communication process. Indeed, operationalizing feedback can seem daunting because it potentially involves many sources. A single individual might receive feedback from supervisors, coworkers, and customers. Leaders focus feedback on both the individual and organization; they use it to develop the capacities of followers, and to teach the organization how to better reach its objectives.

Communicating to Develop Followers

Generally people enjoy neither receiving nor giving evaluative feedback. To receive criticism makes people defensive, and to give criticism makes people responsible for their judgments and leaves them open to fire. There are several ways for leaders to optimize the use of feedback and yet minimize the "conflict" that it typically connotes, such as using a previously accepted goal to support leader assessment.[48]

But primarily, a leader must clarify for everyone involved the purpose of the feedback—to congratulate efforts and outcomes that support the shared vision and to improve the efforts and outcomes that do not. Thus, leaders can recognize the opportunity for both positive and negative evaluations. Communication that is limited to moments of shortcoming runs the risk of demoralizing followers. Furthermore, the more communication takes place, the better-equipped followers become to do their work, which is a significant source of development.

Organizational Learning

Just as feedback is a communication tool for developing followers, it is also an important means by which organizations can learn from their mistakes and improve the work they do. Leaders who enlist the whole organization to review the outcomes of its activities can quickly discover what does and does not work. This provides an additional source of information for leaders in creating and communicating vision. The U.S. Army uses organizational feedback in significant ways to promote whole-system learning.

LEADERSHIP SPOTLIGHT   **U.S. ARMY**

At the National Training Center near Death Valley, U.S. Army troops engage in a simulated battle: the "enemy" has sent unmanned aerial vehicles (UAV) to gather targeting data. When the troops fire upon the UAVs, they reveal themselves to the "opposition forces" hidden nearby, and are defeated. Now that the exercise is over, the real learning begins. Unit members and their superiors hold "after action reviews." After reviewing the ingredients of this battle, General William Hartzog suggested that decoy UAVs might be just the thing to get an enemy to reveal his location. His observation amounts to a lesson for the entire Army.

This process of weeding out mistakes, of innovating, and of learning from experience is known in the Army as a lessons-learned system. A systematic review of action after it has taken place yields a lesson, whether it is the application of a high-tech UAV or simply how to mask a vehicle using terrain. The Army stockpiles lessons such as these and disseminates them throughout the combat forces.

The lessons do not come just from the training ground. The Center for Army Lessons Learned (CALL) sends experts to soldiers in the field to conduct after action reviews. The resulting lessons are collected. In 1994, CALL compiled 26 lessons in Haiti for the incoming replacement troops, who confronted 23 of the scenarios within the first few months. Fortunately, they had learned what to do. In Bosnia the following year, lessons were sent to all units every 72 hours—and shared with the multinational peace keepers.

The Army has come to depend on the results of the lessons-learned system for organizational learning. A case study by the Harvard Business School concluded that the process is what enables the Army to minimize mistakes and create success in an efficient way.[49]

In this example the organization is learning by communicating feedback about the consequences of field operations. Compiling what is learned and using communication feedback creates an improved organization. The success of the Army's system for organizational learning has inspired corporations to adopt after action reviews. Bill Goodspeed, of J. M. Huber Corporation's wood-products division, claims to see concrete results after only two months of after action reviews with customers.[50]

Communication feedback is dynamic and continuous. It serves to develop followers and organizations, giving closure to each innovation within an organization, and enhancing performance with each subsequent loop. Leaders cannot guide their organizations effectively, nor can they fully communicate without feedback. As asserted by long-time university leader E. Grady Bogue, "Leaders are teachers. Teachers are learners."[51]

Summary and Interpretation

Effective communication is a vital element of leadership. Leaders make choices about how to communicate with others. In an organization, the shift to open communication is far reaching in its effect. An open climate paves the way for more opportunities to communicate with followers; more practice at listening actively and discerning the messages waiting to emerge; more opportunities to use rich channels; more chances to repeat the leader's vision through informal communication and symbolic actions. In addition, a conscious choice to communicate through stories, metaphors, and meaningful language enables a leader to direct attention to specific ideas, define the parameters of organizational values, and have longer lasting impact on followers. Finally, using feedback as an essential tool for communication provides the leader a means by which to develop followers and transform organizations.

Key Terms

communication	discernment	observations
communication champion	channel	assessment
open communication	channel richness	consequence
listening	nonverbal communication	development
dialogue	feedback	

Discussion Questions

1. How do you think typical leadership communication differs from management communication?

2. If you were to evaluate an organization based upon the degree of open communication climate, what things would you look for? Discuss.

3. A manager in a communication class remarked, "Listening seems like minimal intrusion of oneself into the conversation, yet it also seems like more work." Do you agree or disagree? Discuss.

4. How does dialogue differ from discussion? Give an example of each from your experience.

5. Some senior executives believe they should rely on written information and computer reports because these yield more accurate data than face-to-face communications do. Do you agree?

6. Why is "management by wandering around" considered effective communication?

7. If you were to communicate symbolically with your team to create a sense of trust and team work, what would you do?

8. Is speaking accurately or listening actively the more important communication skill for leaders? Discuss.

Leadership Development: Personal Feedback

Listening Self-Inventory

Go through the following questions, filling in yes or no next to each question. Mark each as truthfully as you can in light of your behavior in the last few meetings or gatherings you attended.

_____ 1. I frequently attempt to listen to several conversations at the same time.

_____ 2. I like people to give me only the facts and then let me make my own interpretation.

_____ 3. I sometimes pretend to pay attention to people.

_____ 4. I consider myself a good judge of nonverbal communications.

_____ 5. I usually know what another person is going to say before he or she says it.

_____ 6. I usually end conversations that don't interest me by diverting my attention from the speaker.

_____ 7. I frequently nod, frown, or whatever to let the speaker know how I feel about what he or she is saying.

_____ 8. I usually respond immediately when someone has finished talking.

_____ 9. I evaluate what is being said while it is being said.

_____ 10. I usually formulate a response while the other person is still talking.

_____ 11. The speaker's "delivery" style frequently distracts me from the content.

_____ 12. I usually ask people to clarify what they have said rather than guess at the meaning.

_____ 13. I make a concerted effort to understand other people's points of view.

_____ 14. I frequently hear what I expect to hear rather than what is actually said.

_____ 15. Most people feel that I have understood their point of view even when we disagree.

Scoring

The correct answers according to communication theory are as follows: No for questions 1, 2, 3, 5, 6, 7, 8, 9, 10, 11, 14. Yes for questions 4, 12, 13, 15.

Interpretation

If you missed only one or two questions, you strongly approve of your own listening habits and you are on the right track to becoming an effective listener in your role as leader. If you missed three or four questions, you have uncovered some doubts about your listening effectiveness, and your knowledge of how to listen has some gaps. If you missed five or more questions, you probably are not satisfied with the way you listen, and your followers and coworkers may not feel you are a good listener either. Work on improving your active listening skills.

Leadership Development: Case for Analysis

The Superintendent's Directive

Educational administrators are bombarded by possible innovations at all educational levels. Programs to upgrade math, science, and social science education, state accountability plans, new approaches to administration, and other ideas are initiated by teachers, administrators, interest groups, reformers, and state regulators. In a school district, the superintendent is the key leader; in an individual school, the principal is the key leader.

In the Carville City School District, Superintendent Porter has responsibility for 11 schools—eight elementary, two junior high and one high school. After attending a management summer course, Porter sent an e-mail directive to each principal stating that every teacher in their building was required to develop a set of performance objectives for each class they taught. These objectives were to be submitted one month after the school opened, and copies were to be forwarded to the superintendent's office. Porter also wrote that he had hired the consultant who taught the summer management course to help teachers write objectives during their annual opening in-service day of orientation work.

Mr. Weigand, Principal of Earsworth Elementary School, sent his teachers the following memo: "Friends, Superintendent Porter has asked me to inform you that written performance objectives for your courses must be handed in one month from today. This afternoon at the in-service meeting, you will receive instruction in composing these objectives."

In response, one teacher sent a note asking, "Is anything wrong with our teaching? Is this the reason we have to spend hours writing objectives?"

Another teacher saw Weigand in the hall and said, "I don't see how all this objectives business will improve my classroom. It sounds like an empty exercise. In fact, because of the time it will take me to write objectives, it may hurt my teaching. I should be reading on new developments and working on lesson plans."

In response to these and other inquiries, Principal Weigand announced to the teachers with a follow-up memo, "I was told to inform all of you to write performance objectives. If you want to talk about it, contact Dr. Porter."

Questions

1. Evaluate the communications of Porter and Weigand. To what extent do they communicate as leaders? Explain.

2. How would you have handled this if you were Superintendent Porter?

3. How would you have handled the communication if you were the principal of Earsworth Elementary School? Why?

SOURCE: Based on Robert C. Mills, Alan F. Quick, and Michael P. Wolfe, *Critical Incidents in School Administration* (Midland, MI: Pendell Publishing Co., 1976).

References

[1] Howard Gardner, *Leading Minds: An Anatomy of Leadership* (New York: Basic Books, 1995), 204–208.

[2] Cynthia Crossen, "Blah, Blah, Blah," *The Wall Street Journal*, July 10, 1997.

[3] Peter Lowry and Byron Reimus, "Ready, Aim, Communicate," *Management Review*, July 1996.

[4] Henry Mintzberg, *The Nature of Managerial Work* (New York: Harper & Row, 1973).

[5] Mary Young and James E. Post, "Managing to Communicate, Communicating to Manage: How Leading Companies Communicate with Employees," *Organizational Dynamics* (Summer 1993), 31–43; and Warren Bennis and Burt Nanus, *Leaders: The Strategies for Taking Charge* (New York: Harper & Row, 1985).

[6] Bob Wall, Robert S. Solum, and Mark R. Sobal, *Visionary Leader* (Rocklin, CA: Prima Publishing, 1992).

[7] Stephanie L. Gruner, "Why Open the Books?" *Inc.*, November 1996, 95.

[8] Roberta Maynard, "Managing Your Small Business," *Nation's Business*, September 1997, 4.

[9] Gary Hamel, "Killer Strategies That Make Shareholders Rich," *Fortune*, June 23, 1997, 70–84.

[10] John Kerr, "The Informers," *Inc.*, March 1995, 50–61.

[11] Matt Goldberg, "How Marimba Keeps in Step," *Fast Company*, June/July 1997, 34.

[12] C. Glenn Pearce, "Doing Something About Your Listening Ability," *Supervisory*

Management, March 1989, 29–34; and Tom Peters, "Learning to Listen," *Hyatt Magazine*, Spring 1988, 16–21.

[13]Gerald M. Goldhaber, *Organizational Communication*, 4th ed. (Dubuque, IA: Wm. C. Brown, 1980), 189.

[14]Monci Jo Williams, "America's Best Salesman," *Fortune*, October 26, 1987, 122–134.

[15]Sharon Nelton, "Face to Face," *Nation's Business*, November 1995, 18–25.

[16]Norm Brodsky, "Listen and Learn," *Inc.*, March 1997, 33–35.

[17]Tom Peters, "Learning to Listen."

[18]David Bohm, *On Dialogue* (Ojai, CA: David Bohm Seminars, 1989).

[19]Glenna Gerard and Linda Teurfs, "Dialogue and Organizational Transformation," in *Community Building: Renewing Spirit and Learning in Business*, Kazimierz Gozdz, ed. (New Leaders Press, 1995).

[20]R.B.L., "Selling the Sizzle," *Fortune*, June 23, 1997, 80.

[21]Joseph Jaworski, *Synchronicity: the Inner Path of Leadership* (San Francisco, CA.: Berrett-Koehler Publishers, Inc, 1996).

[22]Robert H. Lengel and Richard L. Daft, "The Selection of Communication Media as an Executive Skill," *Academy of Management Executive* 2 (August 1988), 225–232; and Richard L. Daft and Robert Lengel, "Organizational Information Requirements, Media Richness and Structural Design," *Managerial Science* 32 (May 1986), 554–572.

[23]Ford S. Worthy, "How CEOs Manage Their Time," *Fortune*, January 18, 1988, 88–97.

[24]"Enforcing a No-Memo Policy," *Small Business Report*, July 1988, 26–27.

[25]Ronald E. Rice, "Task Analyzability, Use of New Media, and Effectiveness: A Multi-Site Exploration of Media Richness," *Organizational Science* 3, No. 4 (November 1994), 502–527.

[26]Richard L. Daft, Robert H. Lengel, and Linda Klebe Trevino, "Message Equivocality, Media Selection and Manager Performance: Implications for Information Systems," *MIS Quarterly* 11 (1987), 355–368.

[27]Young and Post, "Managing to Communicate, Communicating to Manage."

[28]Jane Webster and Linda Klebe Trevino, "Rational and Social Theories as Complementary Explanations of Communication Media Choices: Two Policy Capturing Studies," *Academy of Management Journal*, December 1995, 1544–1572.

[29]Young and Post, "Managing to Communicate, Communicating to Manage."

[30]Linda Smircich and Gareth Morgan, "Leadership: The Management of Meaning," *Journal of Applied Behavioral Science* 18, November 3, 1982, 257–273.

[31]Nancy K. Austin, "Just Do It," *Working Woman* (April 1990), 78–80, 126.

[32]Christopher Caggiano, "The Profit-Promoting Daily Score Card," *Inc.*, May 1994, 101–103.

[33]Justin Martin, "Tomorrow's CEOs," *Fortune*, June 24, 1996, 76–90.

[34]David Armstrong, *Managing by Storying Around: A New Method of Leadership* (New York: Doubleday Currency, 1992).

[35]Ibid.

[36]J. Martin and M. Powers, "Organizational Stories: More Vivid and Persuasive than Quantitative Data," in B.M. Staw, ed., *Psychological Foundations of Organizational Behavior* (Glenview, IL: Scott Foresman, 1982), 161–168.

[37]Albert Mehrabian, *Silent Messages* (Belmont, CA: Wadsworth, 1971); and Albert Mehrabian, "Communicating Without Words," *Psychology Today*, September 1968, 53–55.

[38]Arthur H. Bell, *The Complete Manager's Guide to Interviewing* (Homewood, IL: Richard D. Irwin, 1989).

[39]I. Thomas Sheppard, "Silent Signals," *Supervisory Management*, March 1986, 31–33.

[40]Welles, "Why Every Company Needs a Story."

[41]Ibid.

[42]Nancy K. Austin, "Wacky Management Ideas that Work," *Working Woman*, November 1991, 42–44.

[43]Peter Richardson and D. Keith Denton, "Communicating Change," *Human Resource Management* (Summer 1996), 203–216.

[44]Thomas H. Peters and Robert J. Waterman, Jr., *In Search of Excellence* (New York: Harper & Row, 1982); and Tom Peters and Nancy Austin, *A Passion for Excellence: The Leadership Difference* (New York: Random House, 1985).

[45]Grady Bogue, *Leadership by Design: Strengthening Integrity in Higher Education* (San Francisco, CA: Jossey-Bass, Inc., 1994), 81.

[46]John C. Kunich and Richard I. Lester, "Leadership and the Art of Feedback: Feeding the Hands that Back Us," *The Journal of Leadership Studies*, Vol. 3(4), (1996), 3–22.

[47]Mary Mavis, "Painless Performance Evaluations," *Training & Development*, October 1994, 40–44.

[48]R. Hughes, R. Ginnett, and R. Curphy, Leadership: *Enhancing the Lessons of Experience* (Homewood, IL: Irwin, 1993), 209–215.

[49]Thomas E. Ricks, "Army Devises System to Decide What Does, and Does Not, Work," *The Wall Street Journal*, May 23, 1997, A1.

[50]Ricks, "Lessons Learned."

[51]Bogue, *Leadership by Design*, 143.

PART FOUR

Leader as Social Architect

Chapter 7
Shaping Culture and Values

Chapter 8
Designing and Leading a
Learning Organization

7

Shaping Culture and Values

- **Organizational Culture**   183

- **Culture Strength and Adaptation**   186

- **Shaping Culture**   188

- **Shaping Values**   192

- **Ethical Values in Organizations**   196

- **Values-Based Leadership**   197

- **Leadership Spotlights:**
  Merck   185
  Bob Kierlin   191
  Rhone-Poulenc   195

- **Leader's Bookshelf:**
  Leading Change: The Argument for Values-Based Leadership   199

- **Leadership Development: Personal Feedback**
  Culture Preference Inventory   202

- **Leadership Development: Case for Analysis:**
  Acme and Omega   204

Your Leadership Challenge

After reading this chapter, you should be able to:

- Understand why shaping culture is a critical function of leadership.

- Know characteristics of an adaptive as opposed to an unadaptive culture.

- Understand and apply how leaders shape culture and values through cere-monies, stories, symbols, language, selection and socialization, and daily actions.

- Identify the cultural values associated with adaptability, achievement, clan, and bureaucratic cultures and the environmental conditions associated with each.

- Use the concept of values-based leadership.

"Everyone will think differently about the planet in the year 2000," says David Abraham of St. Luke's, a small advertising agency on the edge of London's Bloomsbury district. "We'll no longer be seen as all that revolutionary." What's so revo-lutionary about St. Luke's today is that the agency preaches—and practices—a gospel of total ethics and common owner-ship. St. Luke's employees own the company—all of it—and every person holds equal shares, from the person who answers the phone to the creative director. St. Luke's calls itself a com-munications resource office, not an ad agency. Its mission is to produce honest, ethical advertising that represents a com-pany's Total Role in Society, which is an evaluation of the organization among the totality of its stakeholders: employ-ees, customers, shareholders, the community, the environ-ment, vendors, competitors, the families of employees, etc.

St. Luke's was once the London office of Chiat/Day, the agency known for the Energizer bunny. When communications conglomerate Omnicom bought the struggling agency and announced plans to merge Chiat/Day with a larger agency, Andy Law, managing director of the London office, knew it spelled spiritual death to his employees. After buying the London office from Omnicom, Law called in all the employees to let them decide their own future. The biggest concerns were that employees wanted to work for a company that embodied their own personal values and they wanted a concrete mechanism for universal commitment and contribution. Taking his cue from Aristotle's ethics, within a few weeks of buying the company, Law gave it away to the employees.

At St. Luke's, ethics is a requirement, not an option. St. Luke's creates advertising based on the premise that an organization's interaction with all its stakeholders is its most powerful communications medium. The physical layout at St. Luke's reflects the company's values. Employees have traded desks and personal workspaces for "brand rooms," large client-specific glass-enclosed conference rooms where teams meet for each account to generate ideas and store work-in-progress. Employees eat lunch together, play Ping-Pong, or crawl out the window to enjoy a moment of sunshine on the rooftop. There are no trophies or awards lining the walls and shelves at St. Luke's. The company has never won any advertising awards for the simple reason that they refuse to enter any contests.

After only a year in business, St. Luke's was generating annual billings of around $72 million and was the fastest growing agency in London. In a recent survey asking London's art directors and copywriters where they would most like to work, tiny St. Luke's came in third. Law believes people want to work for a company they can be proud of, and he and his employees have created a distinctive culture at St. Luke's that emphasizes self-motivation, personal growth, and integrity in all actions. "We've created this company to live beyond us," says Law. "We're just renting resources. Remember that we're a collective here—everybody is equal. What's disappeared are ego and greed. . . ."[1]

St. Luke's has definite values that make it unique in the advertising industry. In addition, employees go away once a year to "reinvent" the company, applying its basic values and beliefs to their current needs and interests. Andy Law, the firm's leader, sees his job as helping keep the cultural values relevant to today and the people of St. Luke's.

Leaders align people by influencing organizational culture and shaping the environment that influences morale and performance. The nature of the culture is highly important because it impacts a company for better or worse. Southwest Airlines and Starbucks have often attributed their success to the cultures their leaders helped create. IBM and Kodak, on the other hand, have faced major problems as a result of the company culture, and leaders are changing those cultures to remain competitive in today's environment.

This chapter explores ideas about organizational culture and values, and the role of leaders in shaping them. The first section will describe the nature of corporate culture and its importance to organizations. Then we turn to a consideration of how shared organizational values can help the organization stay competitive and how leaders influence organizational culture. Leaders emphasize specific cultural values depending on the organization's situation. The final section of the chapter will briefly discuss ethical values in organizations and examine how values-based leadership shapes an ethical atmosphere.

Organizational Culture

The concept of organizational culture is fairly recent. It became a topic of significant concern in the United States during the early 1980s, primarily due to an interest in learning why U.S. corporations were not performing as well as their counterparts in Japan. Observers and researchers thought that the national culture and corporate culture could explain differences in performance.[2] Leaders now understand that when a company's culture fits the needs of its external environment and company strategy, employees can create a company that is tough to beat.[3]

What Is Culture?

Culture can be defined as the set of key values, assumptions, understandings, and ways of thinking that is shared by members of an organization and taught to new members as correct.[4] At its most basic, culture is a pattern of shared assumptions about how things are done in an organization. This pattern is invented or learned as organizational members cope with internal and external problems and in turn is taught to new members as the correct way to perceive, think, and feel in relation to those problems.[5]

Culture can be thought of as consisting of three levels, as illustrated in Exhibit 7.1, with each level becoming less obvious.[6] At the surface level are visible artifacts such as manner of dress, patterns of behavior, physical symbols, organizational ceremonies, and office layout, all the things one can see, hear, and observe by watching members of the organization. The open office layout at St. Luke's, with no personal desks or workspaces, is an example of a visible manifestation of culture. At a deeper level are the expressed values and beliefs, which are not observable but can be discerned from how people explain and justify what they do. These are values that members of the organization hold at a conscious level. At 3M, for example, all employees consciously know that innovation is highly valued and rewarded in the company's culture.

Some values become so deeply embedded in a culture that organizational members may not be consciously aware of them. These basic, underlying assumptions are the deepest essence of the culture. At 3M, these assumptions might include (1) that individual employees are the source of all innovation, (2) that each individual must think for himself and do what he thinks is right, even if it means defying supervisors, and (3) that organization members are part of a family and will take care of and support each other in taking risks.[7] Assumptions generally start out as expressed values, but over time they become more deeply embedded and less open to question—organization members take them for granted and often are not even aware of the assumptions that guide their behavior, language, and patterns of social interaction.

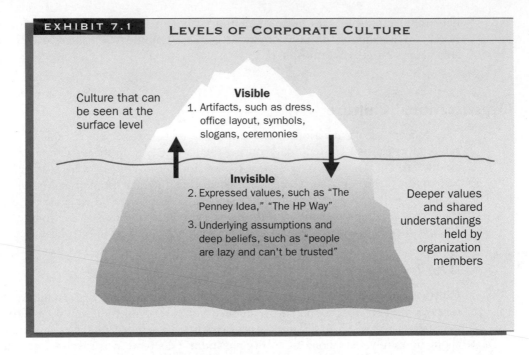

EXHIBIT 7.1   LEVELS OF CORPORATE CULTURE

Culture that can be seen at the surface level

Visible
1. Artifacts, such as dress, office layout, symbols, slogans, ceremonies

Invisible
2. Expressed values, such as "The Penney Idea," "The HP Way"
3. Underlying assumptions and deep beliefs, such as "people are lazy and can't be trusted"

Deeper values and shared understandings held by organization members

Importance of Culture

When people are successful at what they undertake, the ideas and values that led to that success become institutionalized as part of the organization's culture.[8] Culture gives employees a sense of organizational identity and generates a commitment to particular values and ways of doing things. Culture serves two important functions in organizations: (1) it integrates members so that they know how to relate to one another, and (2) it helps the organization adapt to the external environment.

Internal Integration   Culture helps members develop a collective identity and know how to work together effectively. It is culture that guides day-to-day working relationships and determines how people communicate in the organization, what behavior is acceptable or not acceptable, and how power and status are allocated. Culture can imprint a set of unwritten rules inside employees' minds, which can be very powerful in determining behavior, thus affecting organizational performance.[9] Comparative studies of traditional American management practices and Japanese management methods suggest that the relative success of Japanese firms in the 1980s can be partly explained by strong corporate cultures in the Japanese firms that emphasized team collaboration based on employee participation, open communication, security, and equality.[10]

At NASA, Dan Goldin wanted to change the way people worked together in order to break down resistance to change, reduce costs, and build new space satellites in months or years rather than decades. He initiated new internal values for

NASA by setting up teams to conduct bottom-up reviews of all NASA activities, and he worked to give field stations power to make their own decisions, be creative, and take action rather than waiting for decisions from headquarters.[11] At Merck, Ray Gilmartin also focused on changing the culture for more effective internal integration.

LEADERSHIP SPOTLIGHT　　MERCK

When Ray Gilmartin, an outsider to the pharmaceutical industry, arrived at Merck, his first goal was to halt the exodus of top executives, build morale, and change the turf-conscious culture to one focused on teamwork and participation.

Gilmartin started by interviewing each of the top 40 or so managers, asking them how they thought the company's major problems could be resolved. Based on those interviews, he created a broad-based, 12-member committee that would end Merck's long-standing leadership by a tiny cadre. He then employed a series of team-building strategies intended to promote a cooperative spirit and eliminate backstabbing and jockeying for position, which had become a hallmark of Merck's working relationships. Off-site retreats each year reduce barriers among departments and build mutual confidence. In addition, Gilmartin has held regular breakfast meetings with staffers to restore morale and foster a new atmosphere of collegiality. At every turn, he pushes employees to air problems and debate issues without regard for hierarchy. He unlocked the doors to the executive suite to show employees they had access to the top leadership group.

Gilmartin says the way he operates is "to be receptive to other people's ideas and to basically respect what they do. I get a lot in return." At Merck, what he has gotten in return is performance. Sales and income have shot upward. Perhaps more importantly, top research and management talent is committed once again.[12]

By shifting cultural values related to internal integration from backstabbing to cooperation and power sharing, Gilmartin has put Merck back on the path to success and profitability.

External Adaptation　Culture also determines how the organization meets goals and deals with outsiders. The right cultural values can help the organization respond rapidly to customer needs or the moves of a competitor. Culture can encourage employee commitment to the core purpose of the organization, its specific goals, and the basic means used to accomplish goals.

The culture should embody the values and assumptions needed by the organization to succeed in its environment. If the competitive environment requires extraordinary customer service, for example, the corporate culture should encourage good service. Nordstrom has built so strong a culture around the concept of extraordinary customer service that the entire employee manual is a 5 × 8 inch card that reads "Rule #1: Use your good judgment in all situations. There will be no additional rules."[13] Nordstrom gives its 40,000 employees the responsibility and the authority to do whatever is needed to best serve the customer. At Nucor, a $25 billion steelmaker with headquarters in Charlotte, North Carolina, the culture encourages and rewards continuous experimentation and risk, which gives the company a significant advantage over competitors. Nucor's conversion cost—the cost of turning a ton of scrap into a ton of finished steel—is around $50 to $75 lower than competitors, making it a low-cost producer in the industry. This competitive advantage has come from a series of small improvements effected by workers who are constantly tinkering with new ways of doing things. As one plant manager says, "Half the time I don't know who's doing what out there."[14]

Cultures are important because they bind employees together, making the organization a community rather than just a collection of isolated individuals. However, for the organization to stay healthy and profitable, the culture should encourage adaptation to the external environment. As we will discuss in the following section, a strong organizational culture can have either positive or negative outcomes.

Culture Strength and Adaptation

A strong organizational culture can have a powerful impact, although not necessarily always a positive one. **Culture strength** refers to the degree of agreement among employees about the importance of specific values and ways of doing things. If widespread consensus exists, the culture is strong and cohesive; if little agreement exists, the culture is weak.[15]

A strong culture can increase employee cohesion and commitment to the values, goals, and strategies of the organization. However, research at Harvard into some 200 corporate cultures found that a strong culture does not ensure success unless it also encourages a healthy adaptation to the external environment.[16] A strong culture that does not encourage adaptation can be more damaging to an organization than having a weak culture. Consider the example of Merry-Go-Round, a once-ubiquitous presence in malls across America. It was *the* place where trendy teens of the 1980s bought their clothes, from knock-offs of the leather jacket featured in Michael Jackson's *Beat It* video to Madonna-style black bustiers. Leonard "Boogie" Weinstein, who founded the chain, created a strong, arrogant, happy-go-lucky corporate culture, often hiring people in his own image—street-smart kids with a good feel for fashion trends. When a combination of changes in the fashion industry led to a drastic decline in sales, the chain confronted the critical shifts in the market with arrogance and clung to its big-bet mentality of the 1980s. Because of the strong, insular culture, Merry-Go-Round didn't adapt to the changing environment. Store managers simply weren't able to consider doing things any other way. By the mid-1990s, the nationwide chain was dead.[17]

As illustrated in Exhibit 7.2, adaptive corporate cultures have different values and behavior from unadaptive cultures. In adaptive cultures, leaders are concerned with customers and those internal people, processes, and procedures that bring about useful change. In the unadaptive cultures, leaders are concerned with themselves or their own special projects, and their values tend to discourage risk-taking and

EXHIBIT 7.2	ADAPTIVE VERSUS UNADAPTIVE CULTURE	
	Adaptive Organizational Culture	**Unadaptive Organizational Culture**
Visible Behavior:	Leaders pay close attention to all their constituencies, especially customers, and initiate change when needed to serve their legitimate interests, even if it entails taking some risks.	Managers tend to behave somewhat insularly, politically, and bureaucratically. As a result, they do not change their strategies quickly to adjust to or take advantage of changes in their business environments.
Expressed Values:	Leaders care deeply about customers, stockholders, and employees. They also strongly value people and processes that can create useful change (e.g., leadership initiatives up and down the management hierarchy).	Managers care mainly about themselves, their immediate work group, or some product (or technology) associated with that work group. They value the orderly and risk-reducing management process much more highly than leadership initiatives.
Underlying Assumption:	Serve whole organization, trust others.	Meet own needs, distrust others.

SOURCE: Reprinted with the permission of The Free Press, a division of Simon & Schuster from *Corporate Culture and Performance* by John P. Kotter and James L. Heskett. Copyright © 1992 by Kotter Associates, Inc. and James L. Heskett.

change. Thus, a strong culture is not enough, because an unhealthy culture may encourage the organization to march resolutely in the wrong direction. Healthy cultures help companies adapt to the external environment.

Culture Gap

An organization's culture may not always be in alignment with the needs of the external environment. The values and ways of doing things may reflect what worked in the past, as they did at Merry-Go-Round. The difference between desired and actual values and behaviors is called the **culture gap**.[18] Organizations can be much more effective when the culture fits the external environment.

Culture gaps can be immense, particularly in the case of mergers. Despite the popularity of mergers and acquisitions as a corporate strategy, many fail. Almost one-half of all acquired companies are sold within five years, and some experts claim that 90 percent of mergers never live up to expectations.[19] One reason for this is the difficulty of integrating cultures. When Harty Press acquired Pre-Press Graphics to move their company into the digital age, the two cultures clashed from the beginning. Executives initially focused on integrating the acquired firm's financial systems and production technologies, but their failure to pay attention to culture seriously damaged the company. According to general manager Michael Platt, "I thought all that stuff people said about culture when it came to mergers was a bunch of fluff—until it happened." Organizational leaders should remember that the human systems—in particular the habits and values of corporate culture—are what make or break any change initiative.[20] The problem of integrating cultures increases in scope and complexity with global companies and cross-cultural mergers or acquisitions.

Culture gaps can also exist in companies that have not gone through a merger. The Cutting Edge box describes how Chuck Mitchell closed the culture gap at GTO, Inc., a nearly-bankrupt maker of automatic gate openers in Tallahassee, Florida. The example also illustrates how the leader plays the significant role in shaping organizational culture.

Shaping Culture

Leaders use a number of techniques to create and maintain strong, healthy cultures that provide smooth internal integration as well as enable the organization to adapt to the needs of the external environment. Leaders can use organizational rites and ceremonies, stories, symbols, and specialized language to instill cultural values. In addition, they can emphasize careful selection and socialization of new employees to keep cultures strong. Perhaps most importantly, leaders signal the cultural values they want to instill in the organization through their day-to-day actions.

Ceremonies

A **ceremony** is a planned activity that makes up a special event and is generally conducted for the benefit of an audience. Leaders can schedule ceremonies to provide dramatic examples of what the company values. Ceremonies reinforce specific values, create a bond among employees by allowing them to share an important event, and anoint and celebrate employees who symbolize important achievements.[21]

A ceremony often includes the presentation of an award. At Mary Kay Cosmetics, one of the most effective companies in the world at using ceremonies, leaders hold elaborate award ceremonies at an annual event called "Seminar," presenting gold and diamond pins, furs, and pink Cadillacs to high-achieving sales consultants. The most successful consultants are introduced by film clips like the ones used to present political nominees.[22] These ceremonies recognize and celebrate high-performing employees and help bind sales consultants together. Even when they know they will not personally be receiving awards, consultants look forward to Seminar all year because of the emotional bond it creates with others.

Stories

A **story** is a narrative based on true events that is repeated frequently and shared among employees. Stories are told to new employees to illustrate the company's primary values and used by leaders to keep values alive and provide a shared understanding among workers.

ON THE CUTTING EDGE

Transforming an Unadaptive Culture

When Chuck Mitchell took over at GTO, a small company that makes automatic gate openers, the company was in serious trouble. Average monthly sales were $35,000 short of the break-even point. Most suppliers would send goods only on a C.O.D. basis. Mitchell realized that the most damaging inefficiencies were not in the company's products or processes, but in the hearts of its workers.

Morale was terrible on the shop floor, and no one seemed to feel any commitment to the company or to their fellow workers. The previous CEO had insisted that being a good leader meant that he bicycled through the plant daily, barking epithets at workers, ordering them to work faster, or scolding them for filing claims on the company's health insurance policy. Mitchell knew that to survive, the company had to tap into the inner reserves of its workers. His opening speech amounted to a plea for help. Then, one by one, he trotted employees into his office and listened to what they had to say. They didn't say much at first, but as Mitchell began acting on minor suggestions, more and more people were willing to open up. He went out and bought coffee and sugar, for example, which the previous CEO had refused to provide for workers because he didn't drink it. One worker suggested that GTO expand its product line and carry items made by other companies—today, only about a third of the products GTO sells are actually made there. Concerns over the minimal health insurance plan led to changes in the policy. This doubled the company's cost, but Mitchell believes "making people comfortable frees them to come up with ideas for making this business better. I need their help."

To promote a sense of ownership, 5 percent of net profits are put aside in a profit-sharing plan. Mitchell freely gives employees keys to the building and tells them they can use GTO tools to do weekend projects like car repair. And whenever an employee needs to buy a part, Mitchell hands over a blank check. He knows there's a risk in such freedom. Yet he also knows that "any company in which there isn't trust is a company with one hand tied behind its back."

GTO has seen big changes. Largely thanks to employee suggestions, sales increased by 10 percent, and net profit went up from -$311,287 in 1993 to $475,821 in 1994. The number of employees who submit substantive ideas for improvement has tripled. What matters most to Chuck Mitchell is that GTO workers have started creating a culture to care about each other and the company, helping the organization adapt and grow.

SOURCE: Joshua Hyatt, "Real-World Reengineering," *Inc.*, April 1995, 40–53.

Nordstrom uses storytelling of above-and-beyond-the-call-of-duty acts, which the company calls "heroics," to emphasize the importance of customer service. One such example is the story about Van Mensah, a native of Ghana who sells men's tailored clothing in Pentagon City, Virginia. One day, Mensah received a letter from a customer in Sweden who had purchased $2,000 worth of shirts and ties. The letter explained that he had mistakenly washed 12 shirts in hot water, causing them to shrink, and he wanted to know if Mensah had any suggestions to help him out of his predicament. Mensah immediately called the customer in Sweden and informed him that a dozen new shirts—in the same size, style, and colors—were being mailed out that day, compliments of the company. Nordstrom's leaders encourage any employee who witnesses a colleague performing a "heroic" to write the story up and submit it to top executives.[23]

In some cases, stories may not be supported by facts, but they are consistent with the values and beliefs of the organization. At Nordstrom, for example, leaders do not deny the story about a customer who got his money back on a defective tire, even though Nordstrom does not sell tires. The story reinforces the company's no-questions-asked return policy.[24]

Symbols

Another tool for conveying cultural values is the symbol. A **symbol** is an object, act, or event that conveys meaning to others. In a sense, stories and ceremonies are symbols, but physical artifacts can be used by leaders to symbolize particular values. For example, at MasterBrand Industries, president Randall Larrimore wanted to break down the emotional walls that isolated departments and develop a team culture in the organization. When he realized many of the managers were uncertain of their ability to lead such a change process, he gave them a motivational speech and then symbolized the message by giving each manager a copy of *Oh, The Places You'll Go* by Dr. Seuss.[25]

Specialized Language

Language can shape and influence organizational values and beliefs. Leaders sometime use slogans or sayings to express key corporate values. Slogans can easily be picked up and repeated by employees. For example, at Speedy Muffler in Canada, the saying, "At Speedy, you're somebody," applies to customers and employees alike. Leaders at Sequins International, where 80 percent of workers are Hispanic, had W. Edwards Deming's words, "You don't have to please the boss; you have to please the customer," embroidered in Spanish on the pockets of workers' jackets.[26]

Leaders also express and reinforce cultural values through written public statements, such as corporate mission statements or other formal statements that express the core values of the organization. Eaton Corporation developed a philosophy statement, called "Excellence Through People," which includes values such as encouraging employee involvement in all decisions, regular face-to-face communication between executives and employees, emphasizing promotion from within, and always focusing on the positive behavior of workers.[27] Levi Strauss's set of "corporate aspirations" is intended by leaders to stress teamwork, trust, diversity, recognition, ethics, and empowerment.[28]

Selection and Socialization

Selection and socialization of new employees helps maintain specific cultural values. At Procter & Gamble, leaders assign new employees to minor tasks while they question their old beliefs, values, and behavior so that they have room to assimilate the values and beliefs of P&G. Through extensive training, new recruits constantly hear about the company's values and overarching purpose, about watershed events in the company's history, and about exemplary individuals who represent important cultural values.[29]

Companies with strong, healthy cultures, such as Southwest Airlines and Nordstrom, often have careful and rigorous hiring practices. At Southwest, prospective employees are subjected to extensive interviewing, sometimes even by Southwest's regular customers, so that only those who fit the culture are hired. Southwest looks first and foremost for a sense of humor. At Nordstrom, "niceness" is an important cultural value. "We can hire nice people and teach them to sell," retired co-chairman Bruce Nordstrom likes to say, "but we can't hire salespeople and teach them to be nice."[30]

Daily Actions

Ceremonies, stories, slogans, and symbols are useless if leaders don't signal and support important cultural values through their daily actions. Employees learn what is valued most in a company by watching what attitudes and behaviors leaders pay attention to and reward, how leaders react to organizational crises, and whether the leader's own behavior matches the espoused values.[31] At Levi Strauss, for example, managers' bonus pay, which can be two-thirds of their total compensation, is tied explicitly to how well they follow the corporate aspirations in their daily work. Because leaders at Levi Strauss create linkages between stated values, training, everyday action, and appraisal and reward systems, employees rely on the aspirations as a standard of behavior.

Good leaders recognize how carefully they are watched by employees. One senior executive told a story of how employees always knew in advance when someone was about to be laid off in his company. He finally picked up on the pattern. Employees noticed that the executive always dressed in his favorite pink shirt and matching tie when layoffs were to be announced. The story of Bob Kierlin, CEO of Fastenal, illustrates clearly that the leader's greatest impact on culture comes from what he or she does on a day-by-day basis.

 LEADERSHIP SPOTLIGHT   **BOB KIERLIN**

Inc. magazine recently referred to Bob Kierlin, the top leader of Fastenal Co. of Winona, Minnesota, as "the cheapest CEO in America." It may sound like a dubious honor, but Kierlin runs a national powerhouse that operates 560 stores in 48 states, Canada, and Puerto Rico. The company sells and custom manufactures nuts and bolts, safety supplies, tools, and other industrial products. Despite Kierlin's "cheapness," Fastenal is a growing company because it invests wisely in new equipment and technology. In addition, Fastenal's employees are happy and feel a strong commitment to the company.

Bob Kierlin is the kind of guy who just loves a bargain. He clips coupons from the Sunday paper, eats McDonald's Extra Value Meals, drives an Oldsmobile, and has taken home the same $120,000 yearly paycheck for the last decade. He buys his suits used from the manager of a men's clothing store for around $60 each. Fastenal's culture very much reflects Kierlin's values—scratch pads are made from glue and used paper, annual reports are produced in-house for 40 cents a copy, and the warehouse shelving was bought used for 25 cents on the dollar.

Kierlin himself sets the example daily. Rather than flying to a conference in Chicago, he and the chief financial officer drove five and a half hours in a van, saving Fastenal hundreds of dollars. They lunched at A&W on burgers and root beer for $5 each and spent the night in a suburb to avoid high city prices—they even shared a room. Top executives have no special privileges. Kierlin fights for a good parking space just like anyone else in the company. Until recently, he shoveled snow at corporate headquarters and sorted the mail himself. That kind of social leveling has created a bond between workers and executives that most companies can only dream of. Workers respect Kierlin—he treats everyone the same, whether you're a janitor or a vice president, and he comes in at 6 A.M. and works as hard as anyone in the company. They also share the cultural values Kierlin models every day—not just the value of a buck, but the importance of being fair and treating everyone as an equal. Because of a profit-sharing plan, they know that cutting costs fattens everyone's paycheck, but the quality of their relationships is just as important.

Kierlin doesn't see anything unusual about his leadership or his company's culture—he thinks it's just good, old-fashioned common sense.[32]

A culture of frugality and fairness is powerful at Fastenal, not just because it saves money. The company's constant obsession with costs promotes a kind of attentiveness to the mundane that inevitably improves quality. In addition, the culture spreads accountability and responsibility everywhere—at Fastenal, you never call somebody else to fix a problem, you fix it yourself. The culture is strong primarily because the company's top leaders live the cultural values every day.

Leaders can also change unadaptive cultures by their actions. On his first day as new chief at IBM, Lou Gerstner called a dozen top executives into his office and asked them to write a five-page report answering such questions as "What business are you in? Who are your customers? What are your strengths and weaknesses?" He asked for the report in two days. In a company known for meetings steeped in ritual, requiring extensive and elaborate preparations and accompanied by massive reports in blue binders, the message was clear: It was no longer business as usual at Big Blue.[33]

Through ceremonies, stories, symbols, language, hiring and training practices, and their own behavior, leaders influence culture. When culture change is needed to adapt to the environment or bring about smoother internal integration, leaders are responsible for instilling new cultural values. Changing cultures is not easy, but through their words, and particularly their actions, leaders let other members know what really counts in the company.

Shaping Values

Today's leaders recognize the importance of shared values and invest time in thinking about and discussing them. **Values** are the enduring beliefs that have worth, merit, and importance for the organization. Changes in the nature of work, as well as the increasing diversity in the workforce, have made the topic of values one of considerable concern to leaders. They are faced with such questions as, "How can I determine what cultural values are important? Are some values 'better' than others? How can the organization's culture help us be more competitive?"

The Competing Values Approach

In considering what values are important for the organization, leaders consider the external environment and the company's vision and strategy. Cultures can vary widely across organizations; however, organizations within the same industry often reveal similar values because they are operating in similar environments.[34] Key values should embody what the organization needs to be effective. For example, if the competitive environment requires flexibility and responsiveness, the culture should value adaptability. Rather than looking at values as either "good" or "bad," leaders look for the right combination. The correct relationship among cultural values, organizational strategy, and the external environment can enhance organizational performance.

Studies of culture and effectiveness have suggested that the fit among environment, strategy, and values is associated with four categories of culture, which are illustrated in Exhibit 7.3. The differences are based on two dimensions: (1) the extent to which the external environment requires flexibility or stability and (2) the extent to which the strategic focus is internal or external. Together the dimensions form four quadrants, each representing a cultural category with emphasis on specific values.[35]

The four culture categories are Adaptability, Achievement, Clan, and Bureaucratic. An organization may have cultural values that fall into more than one category, or even into all categories. However, successful organizations with strong cultures will lean more toward one particular cultural category. For example, Fastenal, described in the previous section, clearly values economy, listed in the bureaucratic culture category. However, its overall set of values places it more clearly in the clan culture category because of its strong emphasis on fairness, social equality, and caring for people.

Adaptability Culture   The **adaptability culture** is characterized by strategic leaders encouraging values that support the organization's ability to interpret and translate signals from the environment into new behavior responses. Employees have autonomy to make decisions and act freely to meet new needs, and responsiveness to customers is highly valued. Leaders also actively create change by encouraging and rewarding creativity, experimentation, and risk-taking. Nucor Steel, described earlier, is an example of an adaptability culture, where leaders encourage experimentation and taking risks as an everyday way of life. 3M also succeeds with an adaptability culture. The company's values promote individual initiative, risk-taking, and entrepreneurship. Leaders have employees take a class where they are told to pursue their ideas even if it means defying their supervisors.[36]

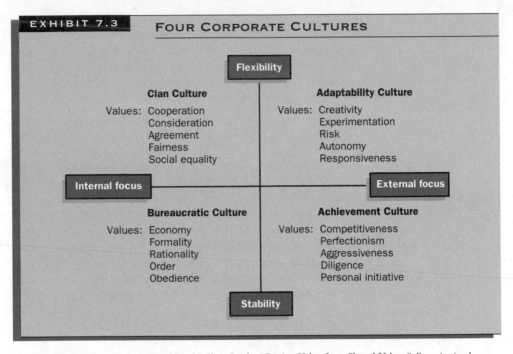

EXHIBIT 7.3   FOUR CORPORATE CULTURES

SOURCES: Based on Paul McDonald and Jeffrey Gandz, "Getting Value from Shared Values," *Organizational Dynamics* 21, No. 3 (Winter 1992), 64–76; Deanne N. Den Hartog, Jaap J. VanMuijen, and Paul L. Koopman, "Linking Transformational Leadership and Organizational Culture," *The Journal of Leadership Studies* 3, No. 4 (1996), 68–83; Daniel R. Denison and Aneil K. Mishra, "Toward a Theory of Organizational Culture and Effectiveness," *Organizational Studies* 6, No. 2 (March—April 1995), 204–223; Robert Hooijberg and Frank Petrock, "On Cultural Change: Using the Competing Values Framework to Help Leaders Execute a Transformational Strategy," *Human Resource Management* 32, No. 1 (1993), 29–50; R.E. Quinn, *Beyond Rational Management: Mastering the Paradoxes and Competing Demands of High Performance* (San Francisco: Jossey-Bass, 1988).

Achievement Culture   The **achievement culture** is characterized by a clear vision of the organization's goals, and leaders focus on the achievement of specific targets such as sales growth, profitability, or market share. An organization concerned with serving specific customers in the external environment but without the need for flexibility and rapid change is suited to the achievement culture. This is a results-oriented culture that values competitiveness, aggressiveness, personal initiative, and the willingness to work long and hard to achieve results. An emphasis on winning is the glue that holds the organization together.[37]

A good example of an achievement culture is PepsiCo, where former CEO Wayne Calloway set a vision to be the best consumer products company in the world. He set back-breaking standards and raised them methodically each year. Executives who met high performance standards were generously rewarded—first-class air travel, company cars, stock options, bonuses, and rapid promotion. Tough annual performance reviews were designed to weed out the weak and reward the strong.[38]

Clan Culture   The **clan culture** has an internal focus on the involvement and participation of employees to rapidly meet changing expectations from the external environment. More than any other, this culture places value on meeting the needs of employees. These organizations are generally friendly places to work and employees may seem almost like a family. Leaders emphasize cooperation, consideration of both employees and customers, and avoiding status differences. Leaders put a premium on fairness and reaching agreement with others. One company that achieves success with a clan culture is Southwest Airlines. Southwest believes if it takes care of its employees, they will in turn take care of customers. CEO Herb Kelleher knows many employees by name and everyone feels comfortable just calling him "Herb" rather than "Mr. Kelleher." Colleen Barrett, Southwest's number two executive, often invites workers to picnics at her home. Employees get Christmas cards signed "Herb and Colleen." Southwest is like a family, and employees care about each other and the company, a focus that has helped the airline adapt to stiff competition and changing markets.[39]

Bureaucratic Culture   The **bureaucratic culture** has an internal focus and consistency orientation for a stable environment. The culture supports a methodical, rational, orderly way of doing business. Following the rules and being thrifty are valued. The organization succeeds by being highly integrated and efficient.

Safeco Insurance has functioned well with a bureaucratic culture. Employees take their coffee breaks at an assigned time, and a dress code specifies white shirts and suits for men and no beards. However, employees like this culture—reliability is highly valued and extra work isn't required. The bureaucratic culture works for the insurance company, and Safeco succeeds because it can be trusted to deliver on insurance policies as agreed.[40] In today's fast-changing world, very few organizations operate in a stable environment, and most leaders are shifting away from bureaucratic cultures because of a need for greater flexibility.

Each of the four cultures can be successful. The relative emphasis on various cultural values depends on the organization's strategic focus and on the needs of the external environment. It is the responsibility of leaders to ensure that organizations don't get "stuck" in cultural values that worked in the past but are no longer successful. This chapter's Living Leadership box on page 197 highlights the importance of adaptability. As environmental conditions change, leaders work to instill new cultural values to help the organization meet new needs. Consider the example of Rhone-Poulenc, the U.S. subsidiary of France's leading chemical and pharmaceutical manufacturer.

LEADERSHIP SPOTLIGHT   **RHONE-POULENC**

Until the early 1990s, Rhone-Poulenc operated quite successfully with a bureaucratic culture. However, after years of steady growth and a number of acquisitions, the company found that its culture, which emphasized internal efficiency and consistency in following established policies and procedures, was no longer suitable to meet the demands of the rapidly changing global environment in which the company operated. CEO Peter Neff began changing organizational values toward an adaptability culture emphasizing the importance of employee flexibility, creativity, and responsiveness to the external environment.

According to Neff, to remain competitive in an ever-changing global world, "You need an atmosphere of openness and respect, you need to let people make mistakes, and you need to reward risk-taking." Under Neff's leadership, Rhone-Poulenc has broken down the walls between functional departments and set up teams of employees empowered to solve problems and encouraged to take risks. Neff has created a culture in which change is embraced rather than feared.

A basic cultural assumption at Rhone-Poulenc is that all employees want to do a good job and want to make a contribution to the organization. Ideas, big or small, are valued. The company has a spot-bonus program for employees who display creativity in their jobs and each year officially recognizes and celebrates one or more of its teams for innovativeness. Managers at the company view their role as enabling each employee to do and be their best and to continue to learn and grow. "Our success depends on people," says Neff, ". . . on our ability to tap the collective wisdom—that is, the accumulated judgments, perceptions, experiences, intuition, and intelligence—of all our employees."[41]

Rhone-Poulenc's new culture leads not only to breakthrough products but also to continuous learning, ensuring that the company can continue to adapt in response to the global environment.

Ethical Values in Organizations

Of the values that make up an organization's culture, ethical values are considered highly important for leaders. Leaders have made ethical standards part of the formal policies and informal cultures of many organizations. Some companies, such as St. Luke's, described in the opening case, place significant emphasis on ethics. Dollar General Corp. also emphasizes ethics in its business conduct. The company is infused with the small town values of CEO Cal Turner and distributes wallet-sized cards to all employees that tell them about Dollar General's commitment to hard work and moral integrity. After an experimental learning center and store the company built in a public housing development in Nashville was looted and burned, Dollar General immediately began reinvesting time and money in rebuilding the center, despite warnings from observers that the same thing could happen again. The center provides GED training and job skills to low-income residents, and offers people a "way out" of poverty, because leaders like Cal Turner have the courage to uphold the company's stated ethical values.[42]

Ethics is difficult to define in a precise way. In general, **ethics** is the code of moral principles and values that governs the behavior of a person or group with respect to what is right or wrong. Ethics sets standards as to what is good or bad

LIVING LEADERSHIP

Flexible or Rigid

The ability to embrace change is characteristic of growth and vibrancy. This metaphor illustrates that organizations should remain adaptable:

At birth, a person is flexible and flowing. At death, a person becomes rigid and blocked. Consider the lives of plants and trees: during their time of greatest growth, they are relatively tender and pliant. But when they are full grown or begin to die, they become tough and brittle.

The tree which has grown up and become rigid is cut into lumber. . . .

Whatever is flexible and flowing will tend to grow. Whatever is rigid and blocked will atrophy and die.

SOURCE: John Heider, *The Tao of Leadership: Leadership Strategies for a New Age* (New York: Bantam Books, 1985), 151. Copyright © 1985 Humanic Ltd., Atlanta, GA. Used with permission.

in conduct and decision making.[43] Many people believe that if you are not breaking the law, then you are behaving in an ethical manner, but ethics often go far beyond the law.[44] The law arises from a set of codified principles and regulations that are generally accepted in society and are enforceable in the courts. Ethical standards for the most part apply to behavior not covered by law. Although current laws often reflect minimum moral standards, not all moral standards are codified into law. The morality of aiding a drowning person, for example, is not specified by law.

The standards for ethical conduct are embodied within each employee as well as within the organization itself. In a recent survey about unethical conduct in the workplace, more than half of the respondents cited poor leadership as a factor.[45] Leaders can create and sustain a climate that emphasizes ethical behavior for all employees.

Values-Based Leadership

Ethical values in organizations are developed and strengthened primarily through **values-based leadership,** a relationship between leaders and followers that is based on shared, strongly internalized values that are advocated and acted upon by the leader.[46] Leaders influence ethical values through their personal behavior as well as through the organization's systems and policies.

Personal Ethics

Employees learn about values from watching leaders. Values-based leaders generate a high level of trust and respect from employees, based not just on stated values but on the courage, determination, and self-sacrifice they demonstrate in upholding those values. When leaders are willing to make personal sacrifices for the sake of values, employees become more willing to do so. At Eastman Kodak, for example, CEO George Fisher has emphasized his commitment to corporate social responsibility by linking a portion of his own pay to social factors.[47]

For organizations to be ethical, leaders need to be openly and strongly committed to ethical conduct. Several factors contribute to an individual leader's ethical stance. Every individual brings a set of personal beliefs, values, personality characteristics, and behavior traits to the job. The family backgrounds and spiritual beliefs of leaders often provide principles by which they conduct business. Personality characteristics such as ego strength, self-confidence, and a strong sense of independence may enable leaders to make ethical decisions even if those decisions might be unpopular.

One important personal factor is the leader's stage of moral development, which affects an individual's ability to translate values into behavior.[48] For example, some people make decisions and act only to obtain rewards and avoid punishment for themselves. Others learn to conform to expectations of good behavior as defined by society. This means willingly upholding the law and responding to the expectations of others. At the highest level of moral development are people guided by high internal standards. These are self-chosen ethical principles that don't change with reward or punishment. Leaders can strive to develop higher moral principles so that their daily actions reflect important ethical values. When faced with difficult decisions, values-based leaders know what they stand for, and they have the courage to act on their principles. As discussed in the Leader's Bookshelf box, organizational success in a time of rapid change calls for values-based leadership.

In a study of ethics policy and practice in successful, ethical companies such as Boeing, Chemical Bank, General Mills, GTE, Xerox, Johnson & Johnson, and Hewlett-Packard, no point emerged more clearly than the crucial role of top leaders.[49] Leaders set the tone for an organization's ethics through their own actions.

Organizational Structure and Systems

Leaders also influence ethical values through formal systems, programs, and policies. Formal systems that have effectively influenced organizational ethics are codes of ethics, ethical structures, training programs, and disclosure mechanisms.

Code of Ethics　A **code of ethics** is a formal statement of the company's ethical values. It communicates to employees what the company stands for. Codes of ethics state the values and behavior that are expected and those that will not be tolerated. A study by the Center for Business Ethics found that 90 percent of *Fortune* 500 companies and almost half of all other companies now have codes of ethics.[50] When leaders support and enforce these codes, they can uplift a company's ethical climate.

Some companies include ethics as a part of broader statements that also define their mission. These statements generally define ethical values as well as corporate culture and contain language about company responsibility, quality of product, and treatment of employees. For example, Northern Telecom's *Code of Business Conduct*, which is provided to all employees and is also available on the Internet, is a set of

Leading Change: The Argument for Values-Based Leadership
James O'Toole

James O'Toole begins his argument for values-based leadership by describing how the four American presidents carved at Mt. Rushmore—George Washington, Thomas Jefferson, Abraham Lincoln, and Theodore Roosevelt—led by example and trust rather than command and fear. These leaders, he says, inspired followers to accompany them through periods of tremendous, often painful, change based on their integrity and strength of character. They genuinely cared about the welfare of followers, listened to them, and showed them respect.

Rushmorean Change

Guiding an organization through major change requires leadership based on moral courage, trust, respect, and service to others. O'Toole profiles a number of modern examples of "Rushmorean" leaders, such as Max De Pree, former CEO of Herman Miller, Corning CEO James R. Houghton, and Frances Hesselbein, former head of the Girl Scouts. He found that successful change led by these and other values-based leaders shares several characteristics:

- *The change has top leadership support.* Leaders make a long-term commitment to the hard work involved, including a commitment to change their own behavior to facilitate the transformation. James Houghton began the revitalization of Corning by changing himself. Soon after instituting a total quality program, it became clear that someone had made a very costly mistake. Houghton's first response was to shout, "Who did it?" Then he caught himself, apologized, and calmly asked, "How did it happen and how can we fix it?"
- *The specifics of change are not imposed from the top.* Leaders don't dictate change; they create conditions that allow productive change to happen. Followers at all levels participate in making decisions. For example, Frances Hesselbein proposed that five-year-olds from single-parent households be included as members (the minimum age for Girl Scouts was six). Most of the councils opposed the plan, so Hesselbein began working with the few councils who agreed with her and left the others alone. Within a year, two-thirds of the councils had adopted the new plan.
- *Change is holistic.* Leaders recognize the complex interrelationship of parts of the organization. All parts, such as strategies, reward systems, and training programs, are interlinked so that change in one area requires changes in others. At Motorola, Robert Galvin taught workers to understand how their individual and group decisions affect the whole, and he made significant changes in reward systems so that employees directly benefit from active participation in decision making.
- *Change is ongoing.* Values-based leaders instill a culture of continuous renewal. The process of change becomes institutionalized so that the organization keeps pace with changes in the environment and stakeholder needs.

Making the Moral Choice

Rushmorean change results from values-based leadership. O'Toole emphasizes that values-based leaders make a choice to respect followers, listen to them, faithfully represent them, keep promises made to them, and do what is best for them. Even in times of crisis, they follow moral guidelines of integrity and trust, recognizing that although amoral leadership may lead to short-term success, it damages the organization in the long run.

Leading Change: The Argument for Values-Based Leadership, by James O'Toole, is published by Jossey-Bass Publishers and Ballantine Books.

guidelines and standards that illustrates how the company's mission and core values translate into ethical business practices.

Structure   Ethical structure represents the various positions or programs an organization uses to encourage ethical behavior. One example is an ethics committee— a group of employees appointed to oversee the company's ethics. The committee provides rulings on questionable ethical issues. An ethics **ombudsperson** is a single person given the responsibility of the corporate conscience who hears and investigates complaints and points out potential ethics failures to top leaders.

Many organizations today are setting up ethics departments with full-time staff. These offices, such as the one at Northrup Grumman, work more as counseling centers than police departments. They are charged with helping employees deal with day-to-day ethical problems or questions. The offices also provide training based on the organization's code of ethics or business conduct, so that employees can translate the values into daily behavior.[51]

Training   To make sure ethical issues are considered in daily actions, leaders often implement training programs to supplement a written code of ethics. Texas Instruments developed an eight-hour ethics-training course for all employees. In addition, leaders incorporate ethics into every course the company offers.[52]

Companies with a strong commitment to ethical values, like Texas Instruments, make ethical issues a part of all training. Starbucks Coffee uses new employee training to begin instilling values such as taking personal responsibility, treating everyone with respect, and doing the right thing even if others disagree with you.[53] Levi Strauss also includes ethics in its training programs, and the leadership training course in particular stresses the importance of honesty, fairness, and personal integrity.

Disclosure Mechanisms   Finally, leaders can support employees who do the right thing and voice their concerns about unethical practices. One important step is to develop policies about **whistle-blowing,** employee disclosure of illegal or immoral practices on the part of the organization. It can be risky for employees to blow the whistle—they can lose their jobs, be transferred to lower-level positions, or be ostracized by coworkers.

Leaders set the standard for how whistle-blowers are treated. If the organization genuinely wants to maintain ethical standards, whistle-blowers are valued and leaders make dedicated efforts to protect them.[54] Leaders can create a climate where people feel free to point out problems without fear of punishment. In addition, they can set up hot lines to give employees a confidential way to report problems, and then make sure action is taken to investigate reported concerns.

In summary, leaders can create an ethical climate for the organization through systems and programs such as codes of ethics, ethics committees or offices, training programs, and mechanisms to protect whistle-blowers. Leaders instill and encourage ethical values most clearly through their own personal actions. Organizations can be ethical only when leaders are ethical.

Summary and Interpretation

Leaders influence organizational culture and ethical values. Culture is the set of key values, assumptions, and ways of thinking that is shared by members of an organization and taught to new members as correct. Culture serves two critically important functions—to integrate organizational members so they know how to relate to one another and to help the organization adapt to the environment. Strong, adaptive cultures have a positive impact on organizational outcomes. A culture gap exists when an organization's culture is not in alignment with the needs of the external environment. Leaders use ceremonies, stories, symbols, specialized language, selection, and socialization to influence cultural values. In addition, leaders shape cultural values most strongly through their daily actions.

Leaders consider the external environment and the company's vision and strategy in determining which values are important for the organization. Four types of culture may exist in organizations: Adaptability, Achievement, Clan, and Bureaucratic. Each type emphasizes different values, although organizations may have values that fall into more than one category.

Of the values that make up an organization's culture, ethical values are among the most important. Ethics is the code of moral principles and values that governs the behavior of a person or group with respect to what is right or wrong. Leaders shape ethical values through values-based leadership, including their own personal behavior as well as the organization's systems and policies. Leaders' personal beliefs and level of moral development influence their personal ethics. For organizations to be ethical, leaders have to be openly and strongly committed to ethical conduct in their daily actions. Leaders can also influence ethical values in the organization through codes of ethics, ethics committees or ombudspersons, training programs, and disclosure mechanisms to support employees who voice concerns about ethical practices.

Key Terms

culture	values	ethics
culture strength	adaptability culture	values-based leadership
culture gap	achievement culture	code of ethics
ceremony	clan culture	ombudsperson
story	bureaucratic culture	whistle-blowing
symbol		

Discussion Questions

1. Describe the culture for an organization you are familiar with. Identify the physical artifacts and underlying values and assumptions. What did you learn?

2. Discuss how a culture could have either positive or negative consequences for an organization.

3. What is a culture gap? What are some techniques leaders might use to influence and change cultural values when necessary?

4. Compare and contrast the achievement culture with the clan culture. What are some possible *disadvantages* of having a strong clan culture? A strong achievement culture?

5. Which do you think is more important for improving ethical values in an organization: a code of ethics, leader behavior, or employee training? Discuss.

6. In which of the four types of culture (adaptability, achievement, clan, bureaucratic) might you expect to find the greatest emphasis on ethical issues? Why?

7. If a leader directs her health care company to reward hospital managers strictly on hospital profits, is the leader being ethically responsible? Discuss.

8. What is meant by the idea that culture helps a group or organization solve the problem of internal integration?

Leadership Development: Personal Feedback

Culture Preference Inventory

The inventory below consists of 14 sets of four responses that relate to typical values or situations facing leaders in organizations. Although each response to a question may appear equally desirable or undesirable, your assignment is to "rank" the 4 responses in each row according to your preference. Think of yourself as being in charge of a major department or division in an organization. Rank the responses in each row according to how much you would like each one to be a part of your department. There are no correct or incorrect answers; the scores simply reflect your preferences for different responses.

Rank each of the four in each row using the following scale. You must use all four numbers for each set of four responses.

1. Would not prefer at all

2. Would prefer on occasion

4. Would prefer often

8. Would prefer most of all

	I		II		III		IV
1.	___ Aggressiveness	___	Cost-efficiency	___	Experimentation	___	Fairness
2.	___ Perfection	___	Obedience	___	Risk-taking	___	Agreement
3.	___ Pursue future goals	___	Solve current problems	___	Be flexible	___	Develop people's careers
4.	___ Apply careful analysis	___	Rely on proven approaches	___	Look for creative approaches	___	Build consensus
5.	___ Initiative	___	Rationality	___	Responsiveness	___	Collaboration
6.	___ Highly capable	___	Productive and accurate	___	Receptive to brainstorming	___	Committed to the team
7.	___ Be the best in our field	___	Have secure jobs	___	Recognition for innovations	___	Equal status
8.	___ Decide and act quickly	___	Follow plans and priorities	___	Refuse to be pressured	___	Provide guidance and support
9.	___ Realistic	___	Systematic	___	Broad and flexible	___	Sensitive to the needs of others
10.	___ Energetic and ambitious	___	Polite and formal	___	Open-minded	___	Agreeable and self-confident
11.	___ Use key facts	___	Use accurate and complete data	___	Use broad coverage of many options	___	Use limited data and personal opinion
12.	___ Competitive	___	Disciplined	___	Imaginative	___	Supportive
13.	___ Challenging assignments	___	Influence over others	___	Achieving creativity	___	Acceptance by the group
14.	___ Best solution	___	Good working environment	___	New approaches or ideas	___	Personal fulfillment
	___		___		___		___

Scoring: Add the points in each of the four columns— I, II, III, IV. The sum of the point columns should be 220 points. If your sum does not equal 210 points, check your answers and your addition.

Interpretation

The scores represent your preference for I, Achievement culture; II, Bureaucratic culture; III, Adaptability culture; and IV, Clan culture. Your personal values are consistent with the culture for which you achieved the highest score, although all four sets of values exist within you just as they exist within an organization. The specific values you exert as a leader may depend on the group situation, particularly the needs of the external environment. Compare your scores with other students and discuss their meaning. Are you pleased with your preferences? Do you think your scores accurately describe you?

SOURCE: Adapted from Alan J. Rowe and Richard O. Mason, *Managing with Style: A Guide to Understanding, Assessing, and Improving Decision Making* (San Francisco: Jossey-Bass, 1987).

Leadership Development: Case for Analysis

Acme and Omega

Acme Electronics and Omega Electronics both manufacture integrated circuits and other electronic parts as subcontractors for large manufacturers. Both Acme and Omega are located in Ohio and often bid on contracts as competitors. As subcontractors both firms benefited from the electronics boom of the 1980s, and both looked forward to growth and expansion. Acme has annual sales of about $100 million dollars and employs 950 people. Omega has annual sales of $80 million and employs about 800 people. Acme typically reports greater net profits than Omega.

The president of Acme, John Tyler, believed that Acme was the far superior company. Tyler credited his firm's greater effectiveness to his managers' abilities to run a "tight ship." Acme had detailed organization charts and job descriptions. Tyler believed that everyone should have clear responsibilities and narrowly defined jobs, which generates efficient performance and high company profits. Employees were generally satisfied with their jobs at Acme, although some managers wished for more empowerment opportunities.

Omega's president, Jim Rawls, did not believe in organization charts. He believed organization charts just put artificial barriers between specialists who should be working together. He encouraged people to communicate face-to-face rather than with written memos. The head of mechanical engineering said, "Jim spends too much time making sure everyone understands what we're doing and listening to suggestions." Rawls was concerned with employee satisfaction and wanted everyone to feel part of the organization. Employees were often rotated among departments so they would be familiar with activities throughout the organization. Although Omega wasn't as profitable as Acme, they were able to bring new products on stream more quickly, work bugs out of new designs more accurately, and achieve higher quality because of superb employee commitment and collaboration.

It is the end of May, and John Tyler, president of Acme, has just announced the acquisition of Omega Electronics. Both management teams are proud of their cultures and have unflattering opinions of the other's. Each company's customers are rather loyal, and their technologies are compatible, so Tyler believes a combined company will be even more effective, particularly in a time of rapid change in both technology and products.

The Omega managers resisted the idea of an acquisition, but the Acme president is determined to unify the two companies quickly, increase the new firm's marketing position, and revitalize product lines—all by year end.

Questions

1. Using the competing values model, what type of culture (adaptability, achievement, clan, bureaucratic) would you say is dominant at Acme? At Omega? What is your evidence?

2. Is there a culture gap? Which type of culture do you think is most appropriate for the newly merged company? Why?

3. If you were John Tyler, what techniques would you use to integrate and shape the cultures to overcome the culture gap?

SOURCE: Adapted from John F. Veiga, "The Paradoxical Twins: Acme and Omega Electronics," in John F. Veiga and John N. Yanouzas, *The Dynamics of Organization Theory* (St. Paul: West, 1984), 132–138; and "Alpha and Omega," Harvard Business School Case 9-488-003, published by the President and Fellows of Harvard College, 1988.

References

[1] Stevan Alburty, "The Ad Agency to End All Ad Agencies," *Fast Company* (December–January 1997), 116–124.

[2] Edgar H. Schein, "Organizational Culture," *American Psychologist* 45, No. 2 (February 1990), 109–119.

[3] Yoash Wiener, "Forms of Value Systems: A Focus on Organizational Effectiveness and Culture Change and Maintenance," *Academy of Management Review* 13 (1988), 534–545; V. Lynne Meek, "Organizational Culture: Origins and Weaknesses," *Organization Studies* 9 (1988), 453-473; and John J. Sherwood, "Creating Work Cultures with Competitive Advantage," *Organizational Dynamics*, Winter 1988, 5–27.

[4] W. Jack Duncan, "Organizational Culture: Getting a 'Fix' on an Elusive Concept," *Academy of Management Executive* 3 (1989), 229-236; Linda Smircich, "Concepts of Culture and Organizational Analysis," *Administrative Science Quarterly* 28 (1983), 339–358; and Andrew D. Brown and Ken Starkey, "The Effect of Organizational Culture on Communication and Information," *Journal of Management Studies* 31, No. 6 (November 1994), 807–828.

[5] Schein, "Organizational Culture."

[6] This discussion of the levels of culture is based on Edgar H. Schein, *Organizational Culture and Leadership*, 2nd ed. (San Francisco: Jossey-Bass, 1992), 3–27.

[7] Schein, "Organizational Culture," 113.

[8] John P. Kotter and James L. Heskett, *Corporate Culture and Performance* (New York: The Free Press, 1992), 6.

[9] Peter B. Scott-Morgan, "Barriers to a High-Performance Business," *Management Review*, July 1993, 37–41.

[10]William Ouchi, *Theory Z: How American Business Can Meet the Japanese Challenge* (Reading, MA: Addison-Wesley, 1979); and R. Pascale and A. Athos, *The Art of Japanese Management* (New York: Simon & Schuster, 1981).

[11]David C. Morrison, "NASA's Big Bang," *Government Executive*, February 1993, 16–19, 39–41.

[12]Joseph Weber, "Mr. Nice Guy with a Mission," *Business Week*, November 25, 1996, 132–142.

[13]Robert Specter, "The Nordstrom Way," *Corporate University Review*, May/June 1997, 24–25, 66.

[14]Edward O. Welles, "Bootstrapping for Billions," *Inc.*, September 1994, 78-82.

[15]Bernard Arogyaswamy and Charles M. Byles, "Organizational Culture: Internal and External Fits," *Journal of Management* 13 (1987), 647–659.

[16]Kotter and Heskett, *Corporate Culture and Performance*.

[17]Justin Martin, "The Man Who Boogied Away a Billion," *Fortune*, December 23, 1996, 89–100.

[18]Ralph H. Kilmann, Mary J. Saxton, Roy Serpa, and Associates, *Gaining Control of the Corporate Culture* (San Francisco: Jossey-Bass, 1985).

[19]Oren Harari, "Curing the M&A Madness," *Management Review*, July/August 1997, 53–56; Morty Lefkoe, "Why So Many Mergers Fail," *Fortune*, June 20, 1987, 113–114.

[20]Edward O. Welles, "Mis-Match," *Inc.* (June 1994), 70–79; Thomas A. Stewart, "Rate Your Readiness to Change," *Fortune*, February 7, 1994, 106–110.

[21]Harrison M. Trice and Janice M. Beyer, "Studying Organizational Culture Through Rites and Ceremonials," *Academy of Management Review* 9 (1984), 653–669.

[22]Alan Farnham, "Mary Kay's Lessons in Leadership," *Fortune*, September 20, 1993, 68–77.

[23]Specter, "The Nordstom Way."

[24]Joan O'C. Hamilton, "Why Rivals Are Quaking As Nordstrom Heads East," *Business Week*, June 15, 1987, 99-100.

[25]Patrick Flanagan, "The ABCs of Changing Corporate Culture," *Management Review*, July 1995, 57–61.

[26]Barbara Ettorre, "Retooling People and Processes," *Management Review*, June 1995, 19–23.

[27]Gerald E. Ledford, Jr., Jon R. Wendenhof, and James T. Strahley, "Realizing a Corporate Philosophy," *Organizational Dynamics* 23, No. 3, (Winter 1995), 5–19.

[28]Stratford Sherman, "Levi's: As Ye Sew, So Shall Ye Reap," *Fortune*, May 12, 1997, 104–116.

[29]Richard Pascale, "Fitting New Employees into the Company Culture," *Fortune*, May 28, 1984, 28–39; and Richard Pascale, "The Paradox of 'Corporate Culture': Reconciling Ourselves to Socialization," *California Management Review* 27 (Winter 1985), 26–41.

[30]Brenda Paik Sunoo, "How Fun Flies at Southwest," *Personnel Journal*, June 1995, 62–73; Specter, "The Nordstrom Way."

[31]Deanne N. Den Hartog, Jaap J. Van Muijen, and Paul L. Koopman, "Linking Transformational Leadership and Organizational Culture," *The Journal of Leadership Studies* 3, No. 4 (1996), 68–83; and Schein, "Organizational Culture."

[32]Marc Ballon, "The Cheapest CEO in America," *Inc.*, October 1997, 53–61.

[33]Steve Lohr, "On the Road with Chairman Lou," *The New York Times*, June 26, 1994, Section 3, 1.

[34]Jennifer A. Chatman and Karen A. Jehn, "Assessing the Relationship Between Industry Characteristics and Organizational Culture: How Different Can You Be?" *Academy of Management Journal* 37, No. 3 (1994), 522–553.

[35]Paul McDonald and Jeffrey Gandz, "Getting Value from Shared Values, *Organizational Dynamics* 21, no. 3 (Winter 1992), 64-76; Daniel R. Denison and Aneil K. Mishra, "Toward a Theory of Organizational Culture and Effectiveness," *Organization Science* 6, No. 2 (March-April 1995), 204–223.

[36]Thomas A. Stewart, "3M Fights Back," *Fortune*, February 5, 1996, 94–99.

[37]Robert Hooijberg and Frank Petrock, "On Cultural Change: Using the Competing Values Framework to Help Leaders Execute a Transformational Strategy," *Human Resource Management* 32, No. 1 (1993), 29–50.

[38]Brian Dumaine, "Those High Flying PepsiCo Managers," *Fortune*, April 10, 1989; L. Zinn, J. Berry, and G. Burns, "Will the Pepsi Brass Be Drinking Hemlock?" *Business Week*, July 25, 1994, 31; and S. Lubove, "We Have a Big Pond to Play In," *Forbes*, September 12, 1993, 216–224.

[39]Scott McCartney, "Airline Industry's Top-Ranked Woman Keeps Southwest's Small-Fry Spirit Alive," *The Wall Street Journal*, November 30, 1995, B1.

[40]Carey Quan Jelernter, "Safeco: Success Depends Partly on Fitting the Mold," *Seattle Times*, June 5, 1986, D8.

[41]Michael A. Verespej, "Lead, Don't Manage," *IW*, 4 (March 1996), 55–60.

[42]Michael Davis, "Dollar General Jobs Offer 'A Way Out'," *The Tennessean*, June 15, 1996, 1E; Lisa Benavides, "Workplace Ethics a Way of Life for Christians," *The Tennessean*, October 19, 1997, 1E; and Candy McCampbell, "Dollar General Wins Award," *The Tennessean*, April 19, 1997, 1E.

[43]Gordon F. Shea, *Practical Ethics* (New York: American Management Association, 1988); and Linda Klebe Trevino, "Ethical Decision Making in Organizations: A Person-Situation Interactionist Model," *Academy of Management Review* 11 (1986), 601–617.

[44]Dawn-Marie Driscoll, "Don't Confuse Legal and Ethical Standards," *Business Ethics*, July/August 1996, 44.

[45]Alison Boyd, "Employee Traps—Corruption in the Workplace," *Management Review*, September 1997, 9.

[46]Robert J. House, Andre Delbecq and Toon W. Taris, "Value Based Leadership: An Integrated Theory and an Empirical Test" (Working Paper).

[47]"Best Moves of 1995," *Business Ethics*, January/February 1996, 23.

[48]Lawrence Kohlberg, "Moral Stages and Moralization: The Cognitive-Developmental Approach," in *Moral Development and Behavior: Theory, Research, and Social Issues*, T. Likona, ed. (New York: Holt, Rinehart & Winston, 1976), 31–53; and Jill W. Graham, "Leadership, Moral Development, and Citizenship Behavior," *Business Ethics Quarterly* 5, No. 1, (January 1995), 43–54.

[49] "Corporate Ethics: A Prime Business Asset," The Business Roundtable, 200 Park Avenue, Suite 2222, New York, NY 10166, February 1988.

[50]Carolyn Wiley, "The ABCs of Business Ethics: Definitions, Philosphies, and Implementation," *IM*, January–February 1995, 2-27.

[51]Beverly Geber, "The Right and Wrong of Ethics Offices," *Training*, October 1995, 102–118.

[52]Mark Henricks, "Ethics in Action," *Management Review*, January 1995, 53–55.

[53]Jennifer Reese, "Starbucks: Inside the Coffee Cult," *Fortune*, December 9, 1996, 190–200.

[54]Eugene Garaventa, "*An Enemy of the People* by Henrik Ibsen: The Politics of Whistle-Blowing," *Journal of Management Inquiry* 3, No. 4 (December 1994), 369–374; and Marcia P. Miceli and Janet P. Near, "Whistleblowing: Reaping the Benefits," *Academy of Management Executive* 8, No. 3 (1994), 65–74.

8

Designing and Leading a Learning Organization

- **Efficient Performance versus Learning Organization**   210

- **Organization Structure**   212

- **Tasks versus Roles**   215

- **Systems versus Networks**   217

- **Competitive versus Linked Strategy**   218

- **Rigid versus Adaptive Culture**   220

- **The Leader's Challenge**   222

- **Leadership Frames for Learning Organizations**   224

- **Leadership Spotlights:**
  American Express Financial Advisors   213
  Lynn Mercer   216
  Visa International   221

- **Leader's Bookshelf:**
  The Boundaryless Organization: Breaking the Chains of Organizational Structure   223

- **Leadership Development: Personal Feedback**
  Your Leadership Orientation   228

- **Leadership Development: Case for Analysis**
  The Fairfax County Social Welfare Agency   230

Your Leadership Challenge

After reading this chapter, you should be able to:

- See the basic differences between organizations designed for efficient performance and those designed for learning and adaptability.

- Recognize how leaders build learning organizations through changes in structure, tasks, systems, strategy, and culture.

- Know when and how horizontally-organized structures provide advantages over vertical, functionally organized ones.

- Distinguish between tasks and roles and how each impacts employee satisfaction and organizational performance.

- Apply the concept of linked strategy.

- Recognize your own natural leadership frame of reference and how you can expand your perspective.

Lars Kolind, head of the Danish company Oticon Holding A/S, believes a primary job of leadership is to keep things disorganized. Oticon makes hearing aids, hardly the sort of business where you'd expect to find people talking about revolution. But according to Kolind, "Hearing aids are not the core of what this company is about. It's about something more fundamental. It's about the way people perceive work."

There is no formal organization at Oticon—no organization chart, no departments, no functions, no titles, and no permanent desks. All vestiges of an organizational hierarchy have disappeared. All 150 employees have mobile workstations and are constantly forming and reforming into self-directed teams that work on specific projects. Their desks are wheeled caddies with room for hanging folders, a few binders, and maybe a family photo or two. Everyone has a mobile phone because employees are on the move. Oticon's Think Tank uses new technology to support shared creativity. The large, computer-filled conference room includes groupware systems for electronic brainstorming. Groupware also allows technical manuals to be written collaboratively—10 people may simultaneously work on the same document. According to Kolind, the technology speeds up the intellectual processes, enabling the company to accomplish in a day what it once did in a week.

In addition, Oticon's employees are highly productive because each project feels like the company and the project leader feels like the CEO. Project leaders (basically anyone with a compelling idea) compete to attract the people and resources needed to deliver results. And deliver they do. Oticon is the fastest-growing hearing aid producer in the world and within the past five years has introduced at least 10 major product innovations, including the world's first digital hearing aid. Yet, although the company is developing products twice as fast as other companies, the atmosphere at Oticon is surprisingly relaxed. Conflict is at a minimum because when employees move around and sit next to different people they learn to respect what others do.

Kolind thinks the organization of the future will liberate employees to grow personally and professionally and to become more creative and action-oriented. At Oticon, the future is now. Says Kolind, "We give people the freedom to do what they want."[1]

Organizations, like biological species, must adapt in order to survive. In a stable environment, many companies developed into highly structured systems with strong vertical hierarchies, specialized jobs, and formal information and control systems. However, these organizations do not work in today's fast-shifting environment, and many leaders are struggling to transform their organizations into more flexible systems capable of continuous learning and adaptation. This chapter examines elements of organization design by looking at traditional organizations that were designed for efficient production, in comparison with new organizational forms that emphasize flexibility and rapid response. We will examine five elements of organization design—structure, tasks, systems, strategy, and culture. Then we will turn to a discussion of the various frames of reference leaders use to think about designing learning organizations. Each frame of reference has strengths and weaknesses, and effective leaders strive for a balanced perspective so that all the needs of the organization are met.

Efficient Performance versus Learning Organization

As discussed in Chapter 1, fundamental societal transformations are having a dramatic impact on organizations. When the business environment was stable, leaders emphasized stability within organizations. They worked to direct and control organizational resources toward attaining specific goals. Routine, specialized jobs and standardized control procedures were effective in organizations based on mass-production technology. Today, however, organizations designed strictly for efficient performance are often not effective. Knowledge and information are more important than production machinery, and organizations need employees' minds as much as their physical labor.

Many leaders are redesigning their companies toward something called the **learning organization,** one in which everyone is engaged in identifying and solving problems. This enables the organization to continuously experiment, improve, and increase its capability. The learning organization is based on equality, open information, little hierarchy, and a shared culture that encourages adaptability and enables the organization to seize opportunities and handle crises. In the learning organization, leaders emphasize employee empowerment and encourage collaboration across departments and with other organizations. The essential value is problem solving, in contrast to the traditional organization designed for efficient performance.

The Living Leadership box offers a lesson for leaders who want to develop learning organizations.

Exhibit 8.1 compares organizations designed for efficient performance with those designed for continuous learning by looking at five elements of organization design: structure, tasks, systems, strategy, and culture. Each of these five elements will be discussed in detail in the following sections.[2] The efficient performance organization is based on a hard, rational model and is characterized by a vertical structure, formalized systems, routine tasks, competitive strategy, and a rigid culture. The learning organization, on the other hand, emerges from a soft, intuitive perspective of organizations. Structures are more horizontal than vertical and employees are empowered to act independently and creatively rather than performing routine standardized jobs. Systems are fluid, based on networks of shared information. Strategy emerges from collaborative links within and among organizations, and the culture encourages experimentation and adaptability.

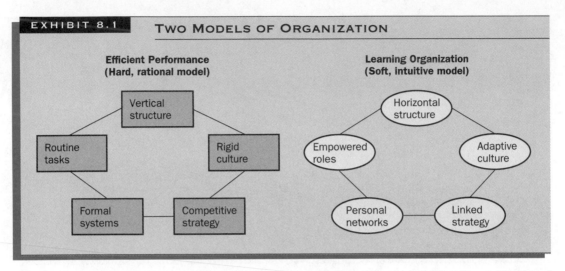

SOURCE: Adapted from David K. Hurst, *Crisis and Renewal: Meeting the Challenge of Organizational Change* (Boston, MA: Harvard Business School Press, 1995).

Organization Structure

The traditional organization structure, shaped like a pyramid with the CEO at the top and everyone else in layers down below, is a legacy that dates back nearly a century.[3] These vertical structures are effective in stable times. However, they become a liability in a fast-changing environment. Hierarchical, vertical structures create distance between managers and workers and build walls between departments; they do not allow for the fast, coordinated response often needed in today's world. Many of today's organizations are shifting toward horizontal structures based on work processes rather than departmental functions. Exhibit 8.2 shows a simple illustration of the change from the vertical to the horizontal organization. Most companies are somewhere in the middle of the evolutionary scale; few companies have shifted to an organization structure based entirely on horizontal processes.[4]

Vertical Structure

Traditionally, the most common organizational structure has been one in which activities are grouped together by common function from the bottom to the top of the organization, as shown in part A of Exhibit 8.2. For example, all engineers are located in one department, and the vice president of engineering is responsible for all engineering activities. The same is true for manufacturing, accounting, and research and development. Generally little collaboration occurs across departments, and employees are committed to achieving the goals of their own functional units. The whole organization is coordinated and controlled through the vertical hierarchy, with decision making authority residing with upper-level managers.

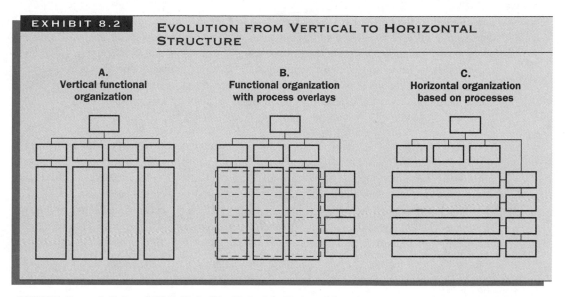

EXHIBIT 8.2

EVOLUTION FROM VERTICAL TO HORIZONTAL STRUCTURE

A.
Vertical functional organization

B.
Functional organization with process overlays

C.
Horizontal organization based on processes

SOURCE: George Stalk, Jr. and Jill E. Black, "The Myth of the Horizontal Organization," *Canadian Business Review* (Winter 1994), 26–31.

The vertical, functionally organized structure can be quite effective. It promotes efficient production and in-depth skill development of employees. Hierarchy of authority provides a sensible mechanism for supervision and control in a large, complex organization. However, in a rapidly changing environment, the vertical hierarchy becomes overloaded. Decisions pile up and top executives cannot respond quickly enough to threats or opportunities. Poor coordination among departments inhibits innovation. Today, the vertical hierarchy is beginning to break down in many organizations. Some, like Oticon, have done away with departments, titles, and organization charts altogether. Others have maintained elements of a traditional structure but have found ways to increase horizontal collaboration and communication across departments. Consider the case of American Express Financial Advisors.

 LEADERSHIP SPOTLIGHT   **AMERICAN EXPRESS FINANCIAL ADVISORS**

Although American Express Financial Advisors (AEFA) was basking in the glow of 21 percent annual earnings growth, the company's leaders realized earnings did not tell the whole story. The heavy attrition of AEFA's 8,000 independent financial planners and changes in the financial services industry that could threaten client-retention were danger signs that needed to be addressed. AEFA's top leaders set out to redesign the organization to promote strong horizontal coordination.

Front-line teams set up around core processes are the foundation of AEFA's new organizational structure. Leaders also recognized that stronger horizontal coordination was needed in the executive office as well. Therefore, the position of general sales manager was dropped, and those duties are now shared by seven senior executives. Each has a vertical responsibility, but each also "owns" a process that horizontally spans the organization—for example, client acquisition or account management. Below the senior managers, 180 divisions have been reconfigured into 45 clusters led by group vice presidents who also own horizontal processes, such as planner integration.[5]

American Express Financial Advisors sells financial products such as insurance, mutual funds, and investment certificates. But its redesign highlights *how* the company sells these products, with teams of empowered workers focused on building relationships with customers. Although the organization retains some elements of a vertical, functional structure, emphasis is on horizontal collaboration to promote better and faster communication within the company and with clients. In the learning organization, horizontal teams are the basic building block of the structure.

Horizontal Structure

In learning organizations, the vertical structure that created distance between the top and the bottom of the organization is disbanded. Structure is created around workflows or processes rather than departmental functions, and processes are based on meeting customer needs. The vertical hierarchy is flattened, with perhaps only a few senior executives in traditional support functions such as finance and human resources, as illustrated in part C of Exhibit 8.2. Traditional management tasks are delegated to the lowest level.

Self-directed teams are the fundamental unit in a learning organization. **Self-directed teams** are made up of employees with different skills who rotate jobs to produce an entire product or service. They also deal directly with customers, making changes and improvements as they go along. Team members have the authority to make decisions about new ways of doing things. In learning organizations, bosses are practically eliminated, with team members taking responsibility for training, safety, scheduling vacations, and decisions about work methods, pay and reward systems, and coordination with other teams. Boundaries between departments are reduced because teams include members from several functional areas. In some cases, such as Oticon, boundaries are entirely eliminated because there are no functional departments.

Boundaries between organizations also become more permeable. Companies are collaborating in unprecedented ways to share resources and exploit opportunities. Emerging organizational forms, such as the network organization and virtual organization, are horizontal teams of companies rather than teams of individuals. Much like building blocks, parts can be added or taken away to meet changing needs.[6] In a network structure, a company keeps key activities in-house and then outsources other functions, such as sales, accounting, and manufacturing, to partner organizations or individuals. For example, TopsyTail, Inc., started by 37-year-old Tomima Edmark to produce and sell the hair care gadget she invented, grew to an $80 mil-

lion company with only two full-time employees. The company's production partners include a toolmaker, two injection molders, a package designer, a logo designer,
freelance photographers, and a printer. TopsyTail also outsources packaging and
shipping to three fulfillment houses, television commercials to a video production
company, customer mailings to a mailing list firm, and publicity to a public relations
firm. Four distributing companies sell TopsyTail products in the United States,
Canada, Mexico, the Pacific Rim, Europe, and South Africa. The company's employees focus on finding the right partners and then managing relationships horizontally.[7]

Tasks versus Roles

Another response to today's rapidly changing environment is the amount of formal
structure and control placed on employees in the performance of their work. A **task**
is a narrowly defined piece of work assigned to a person. In a stable environment,
tasks tend to be rigidly defined and employees generally have little say over how
they do their jobs. A **role** is a part in a social system. A role has discretion and
responsibility, such as the role of mother in a family or manager in an organization.
An organizational role is an opportunity to use one's discretion and ability to achieve
an outcome. In chaotic environments, employees need more freedom and responsibility to make decisions and react quickly to changing conditions. One way of considering the distinction between organizations designed for task performance and
those designed for learning is through the concept of mechanistic versus organic
work processes.

Mechanistic and Organic Processes

Tom Burns and G. M. Stalker use the terms *mechanistic* and *organic* to explain organizational responses to the external environment.[8] When the external environment
is stable, the tasks tend to be mechanistic—that is, characterized by rigid rules, formal procedures, and a clear hierarchy of authority with decisions made at the top.
Tasks are rigidly defined and are broken down into specialized, separate parts, as in
a machine. Knowledge and control of tasks are centralized at the top of the organization, and employees are expected to do as they are told, not to make decisions
about how to do it. In rapidly changing environments, on the other hand, tasks tend
to be much looser, free flowing, and adaptive. Burns and Stalker use the term *organic*
to characterize this type of organization. Leaders push authority and responsibility
down to lower level employees, encouraging them to take care of problems by working with one another and with customers. Teamwork is highly valued and there are
few strict rules and procedures for how things should be done. Thus, the organization is more fluid and able to adapt to changes in the environment.[9]

Mechanistic tasks are characteristic of the efficient performance organization.
The clearest example is a mass-production assembly line, where jobs are structured by standardization and division of labor into small, specialized tasks that are

governed by formal rules and procedures. Workers perform the same small job repetitively, thus little education or experience is needed. Employees are not expected to think for themselves or make any decisions about how they do their jobs. Routine tasks provide little satisfaction for employees, but structuring work into small, specialized tasks made sense in an era of mass-production manufacturing. It was an efficient way of getting the work done, and specialized techniques and procedures ensured reliable performance.

From Routine Tasks to Empowered Roles

Learning organizations use an organic form, an organizational architecture that is fluid and adaptable, with less clear job responsibilities and authority pushed down to the lowest level.[10] Employees play a role in the department or team, and roles are adjusted or redefined through employee interaction within and among teams. There are few rules and procedures, and knowledge and control of tasks are located with workers rather than top executives. Each individual is encouraged to experiment, learn, and solve problems within the team.

The idea of encouraging employees to participate fully in the organization is called empowerment. **Empowerment** means sharing power with everyone in the organization so they can act more freely to accomplish their jobs. At Hampton Inns, for example, employees are empowered to make their own decisions and do whatever is necessary to honor the company's "100% Satisfaction Guarantee." In one instance, a business traveler had forgotten to bring a tie and the stores were not yet open. The desk clerk drove home and returned with one of his own ties for the guest to wear to an important meeting.[11] The trend today is clearly toward moving power out of the executive suite and into the hands of lower-level workers. Many of today's organizations are knowledge- and information-based rather than machine-based. Knowledge work relies on project teams and cross-functional collaboration that is inherently resistant to formal authority. Employees are also better educated and more willing to question their leaders. In the emerging learning organization, the leader's role is to give workers the information they need and the right to act on it.[12] At Lucent Technologies, plant manager Lynn Mercer has shifted the traditional machine-based assembly line to a system based on teamwork, empowerment, and shared information.

 LEADERSHIP SPOTLIGHT   **LYNN MERCER**

Phillip Dailey strings cables inside a steel box the size of a refrigerator—a digital transmitting station for cellular phone systems. Studying a bottleneck along the assembly line one day, Dailey realized a way to increase output by 33 percent. He didn't have to talk to his bosses about his insight; he simply recruited temporary workers from other teams and made it happen.

Lynn Mercer, plant manager at Lucent Technologies' factory in Mount Olive, New Jersey, distributes authority three levels down because she believes those people know the job better than she does. In two years, the factory's self-directed workforce of 480 employees hasn't missed a single delivery deadline, and total labor costs represent an exceedingly low 3 percent of product cost. Teams elect their own leaders to oversee quality, training, scheduling, and coordination with other teams. They all follow a one-page list of "working principles," but teams are continually altering the manufacturing process and even the product design itself. The process is so fluid that none of the manufacturing equipment is bolted to the floor. Engineers and assemblers constantly bat around ideas, and the professional staff cubicles sit right next to the assembly cells to promote constant interaction. According to production manager Steve Sherman, "We solve problems in hallways rather than conference rooms."

The factory is flooded with information because Mercer believes that's how any complex system balances itself. Every single procedure is written down, but procedures are constantly changing—any worker can propose changing any procedure in the plant, subject to ratification by those whose work it affects. Operating statistics are displayed everywhere. Anyone with a few spare minutes consults an "urgents board" listing orders that are behind schedule, so they can jump in where they're most needed. Assemblers also work directly with customers by attending trade shows and installation sites as well as giving tours of the plant.

Yearly bonuses, based equally on individual achievement and team performance, can be equivalent to 15 percent of regular pay. However, for workers, the greatest motivator is that they have a role in shaping the organization. "This business has been handed to us," says technician Tom Guggiari. "This business is ours."[13]

Although many companies, like Lucent Technologies, are implementing empowerment programs, they are empowering workers to varying degrees.[14] When employees are fully empowered, they are given larger roles with decision-making authority and control over how they do their own jobs, as well as the power to influence and change such areas as organizational goals, structures, and reward systems. Few organizations have moved to this level of empowerment. One that has is W. L. Gore and Associates (makers of Gore-Tex), which has been referred to as a "company built of self-leaders." The company operates with no hierarchy, job titles, or formal budgets. Emphasis is on teamwork, mutual support, equality, freedom, independent effort, and commitment to the total organization rather than to narrowly defined tasks, jobs, or functional departments.[15] W. L. Gore & Associates has remained highly successful and profitable under this empowered system for more than 30 years.

However, empowerment programs are difficult to implement in established organizations where they destroy traditional hierarchies and upset the familiar balance of power. Most organizations begin with small steps and gradually increase the degree of authority and power delegated to lower employees. The use and implementation of empowerment programs is explored in more detail in Chapter 9.

Systems versus Networks

In young, small organizations, communication is generally informal and face-to-face. There are few formal control and information systems because leaders of the

· company work closely with employees in the day-to-day operation of the business. Because the organization is small, it is easy for everyone to know what is going on. As organizations grow larger, they establish formal systems to manage the growing amount of complex information. In addition, information is increasingly used for control purposes, to detect deviations from established standards and goals.[16] Extensive formal reporting systems allow leaders to monitor operations on an ongoing basis and help them make decisions and maintain steady performance.

The danger is that formal systems become so entrenched that information no longer filters down to the people on the front lines who can use it to do their jobs better and serve customers. The informal grapevine often survives as a remnant of the days when information was freely shared among all employees, but its functioning is hampered by the lack of opportunity for personal interaction.[17] The learning organization strives to return to the condition of a young, entrepreneurial company in which all employees have complete information about the company so that they can identify needs and act quickly. The learning organization is based on personal networks of information. People serve on teams and talk to whoever has the information they need. Learning organizations practice open-book management, which means data about budgets, profits, expenses, and other financial matters is freely available to anyone. The learning organization also encourages open communication as described in Chapter 6. Ideas are shared throughout the organization and may be implemented anywhere. At Oticon, for example, all incoming mail is scanned into a computer, and, with few exceptions, anyone can read anyone else's mail. The same applies to financial documents. In addition, learning organizations maintain open lines of communication with customers, suppliers, and even competitors. Bringing outside organizations into communication networks enhances learning capability as well as the potential to better serve customers.

In the learning organization, top executives no longer hoard information to make decisions and control the organization. Leaders encourage open communication and dialogue throughout the organization and with other companies. However, in large and complex organizations, communication on a face-to-face level is often impossible to achieve. New information technology has enhanced the possibilities for keeping people in worldwide organizations in touch. Networked computers and intranets can change the locus of knowledge by getting information to people who really need it. The Cutting Edge box describes how one company uses information technology to share information, promote trust and teamwork, and spread knowledge and power down to the front lines.

Competitive versus Linked Strategy

In traditional organizations, top executives are responsible for strategy. Strategy is seen as something that is formulated and imposed on the organization. Leaders think about how the organization can best respond to competitors, cope with difficult environmental changes, and effectively use available resources. Research has shown that strategic planning positively affects an organization's performance.[18] Therefore, top

ON THE CUTTING EDGE

Buckman Laboratories International

Bob Buckman believes the front line and the bottom line have everything to do with each other. "The basic philosophy," he says, "is, 'How do we take this individual and make him bigger, give him power?' How? Connect him to the world." Buckman Laboratories' knowledge-sharing network, called K'Netix, keeps the company's international workforce connected with one another and brings all of the organization's brainpower to bear in serving each customer.

Buckman Laboratories, a $270 million company with 1,200 people in 80 countries, makes more than 1,000 different specialty chemicals in eight factories around the world. The company competes in a variety of businesses, often with companies three to five times its size. Buckman has an edge because any of its employees can tap into a worldwide knowledge resource—a steady stream of information about products, markets, customers, and opportunities, keeping the company so tuned in to customers that it can anticipate their needs. Companies such as AT&T, 3M, International Paper Company, and USWest have made pilgrimages to this small, Memphis, Tennessee-based company to learn how knowledge can be used as a critical corporate asset.

When Bob Buckman took over Buckman Laboratories after the death of his father, he knew he wanted to create a new kind of organization. His father had epitomized the traditional pyramid-style leader, overseeing every decision, sales order, check, or memorandum. Buckman wanted to turn the organization upside down, putting the customer on top and giving front line workers the information and power to actively satisfy customer needs. "I realized that if I can give everybody complete access to information about the company, then I don't have to tell them what to do all the time," says Buckman. "The organization starts moving forward of its own initiative."

Today, the knowledge network has become the basis of the organization. Anything is discussable, and anyone can participate. At the heart of knowledge-sharing is a commitment to and respect for each individual. For example, the first proposition of the Buckman Code of Ethics is "that the company is made up of individuals—each of whom has different capabilities and potentials—all of which are necessary to the success of the company." The open sharing of information promotes trust, which in turn promotes wider sharing of information. For example, one lengthy online discussion tackled the issue of a special bonus award given each year to salespeople who record the largest year-to-year percentage sales growth. For weeks, salespeople from around the world shared opinions and argued directly with Buckman about why the current award was unfair and how it might be changed to be more equitable.

Buckman admits that getting people to share information in the beginning was difficult because employees had learned to hoard knowledge as a source of power. Now, at Buckman Labs, power comes from being a source of knowledge, sharing whatever you know with others.

SOURCE: Glenn Rifkin, "Nothing But Net," *Fast Company* (June—July 1996), 118–127.

executives often engage in formal strategic planning exercises or hire strategic planning experts to help keep the organization performing well.

In learning organizations, however, strategy emerges bottom up as well as top down. Chapter 5 discussed many of the elements of strategy in detail. A strong, shared vision is the basis for the emergence of strategy in a learning organization. When all employees are linked with the vision, their accumulated actions contribute to strategy development. Since many employees are in touch with customers, suppliers, and new technologies, they identify needs and solutions and are linked into strategy making.

Strategy can also emerge from partnership linkages with suppliers, customers, and even competitors. Learning organizations have permeable boundaries and are often linked with other companies, giving each organization greater access to information about new strategic needs and directions.[19] Organizations become collaborators more than competitors, experimenting to find the best way to learn and adapt. Some companies, such as Chevron, Springfield Remanufacturing, and Andersen Windows, encourage a regular free exchange of information with other organizations, allowing teams to visit and observe their "best practices." These cutting-edge companies believe the best way to keep their organizations competitive is through a mutual sharing of ideas.[20] Some medium-size companies go even further in forming strategy together. For example, the CEO of Advanced Circuit Technologies in Nashua, New Hampshire, formed a coalition of 10 electronics firms to jointly package and market non-competing products. Member companies still conduct their own business, but they now can adopt a strategy of bidding on projects larger than they could deliver individually, and ask partners for services they can't do themselves. The coalition landed a job with Compaq Corporation to design and build a specialized computer board that none of the companies could have handled alone.[21]

Rigid versus Adaptive Culture

As we discussed in Chapter 7, for an organization to stay healthy, its culture should encourage adaptation to the external environment. A danger for many successful organizations is that the culture becomes set. When organizations are successful, the values, ideas, and practices that helped attain the success become institutionalized. However, as the environment changes, those values may become detrimental to future performance. Many organizations become victims of their own success, clinging to outdated and even destructive values and behaviors because of rigid cultures that do not encourage adaptability and change.

One of the most important qualities for a learning organization to have is a strong, adaptive organizational culture. The learning organization reflects the values of adaptive cultures discussed in Chapter 7. In addition, a learning organization culture often incorporates the following values.

1. *The whole is more important than the part and boundaries between parts are minimized.*[22] People in the learning organization are aware of the whole system, how everything fits together, and the relationships among various organizational parts. Therefore, everyone considers how their actions affect other elements of the organization. The emphasis on the whole reduces boundaries both within the organization and with other companies. The

free flow of people, ideas, and information allows coordinated action and continuous learning.

2. *Equality is a primary value.* The culture of a learning organization creates a sense of community, compassion, and caring for one another. Each person is valued and the organization becomes a place for creating a web of relationships that allows people to develop to their full potential. Activities that create status differences are discarded. At Tyson Foods, former CEO Donald Tyson showed up at the office in the same brown uniform his workers wore, with "Don" embroidered on the shirt pocket. His successor has continued the tradition. At a company like Intel, everyone, including CEO Andrew Grove, works in small, open cubicles.[23] The learning organization also does away with status symbols such as executive dining rooms and reserved parking places. The emphasis on treating everyone with care and respect creates a climate of safety and trust that allows experimentation, frequent mistakes, and failures that enable learning.

3. *The culture encourages change, risk-taking, and improvement.* A basic value is to question the status quo, the current way of doing things. Constant questioning of assumptions opens the gates to creativity and improvement. The culture rewards and celebrates the creators of new ideas, products, and work processes, as well as sometimes rewarding those who fail in order to learn and grow and to symbolize the importance of taking risks. As Marc Sokol, vice president of advanced technology at Computer Associates International, puts it, "Computer Associates tends to reward people who push the envelope. The thing is, if you push the envelope, sometimes it rips."[24]

In a learning organization, the culture encourages openness, boundarylessness, equality, continuous improvement, and change. No company represents a perfect example of a learning organization, but one excellent example of an organization that is built on the concept of a fluid, living system is Visa International. You've heard of the credit card, but have you heard of the company?

 LEADERSHIP SPOTLIGHT   **VISA INTERNATIONAL**

Visa International was set up nearly 25 years ago to be a company without any of the ordinary rules of organizations. Early in his career, Visa founder Dee Hock walked away from a number of fast-track jobs at leading financial companies, each time "raging that the hierarchical, rule-following, control-everything organizations" stifled employee creativity and initiative and prohibited companies from responding to new challenges.

Hock wanted to create an organization based on biological concepts and metaphors, not on the command and control model that had developed to support the industrial revolution. He designed Visa to be highly decentralized and highly collaborative. Visa is a nonstock, for-profit membership corporation with ownership in the form of nontransferable rights of participation. Authority, initiative, decision-making, and wealth are all pushed out to the periphery of the organization, to the member financial institutions. Members are fierce competitors—they, not Visa, issue the credit cards so they're constantly going after each other's customers. However, members also have to cooperate. It is this harmonious blend of cooperation and competition that has enabled the system to expand worldwide in the face of different currencies, languages, legal codes, cultures, customs, and political philosophies. A "one-best-way" of doing business dictated from headquarters could never have accomplished this. According to Hock, "the organization had to be based on biological concepts to evolve, in effect, to invent and organize itself." Visa, he says, "like the body, the brain, and the biosphere, [is] largely self-organizing." Hock coined the word "chaordic" to describe the kind of organization needed in today's fast-paced environment. A chaordic organization encourages as much competition and initiative as possible throughout the organization, while at the same time building in mechanisms for cooperation and order.

Hock believes leaders should understand that they "work for" those people who are often mislabeled "subordinates." His philosophy is that, to create learning organizations, leaders should lead themselves, lead those with authority over them, and lead their peers, and they should free the people they "work for" to do the same.[25]

Visa International works without a hierarchy or rigid organization chart. Unlike the old-style pyramidal organization, Visa is a confederation of companies that virtually organizes itself. The organization itself is almost invisible—it is difficult to answer questions such as who runs the company, who makes the decisions, even where company headquarters are located.[26] Founder Dee Hock believes the better an organization is, the less visible it is, and he created Visa to be an adaptive, free-flowing, continuously changing system, always capable of responding to new challenges, threats, and opportunities.

The Leader's Challenge

Leaders in learning organizations face a mighty challenge: to maintain efficient performance and become a learning organization at the same time. Companies must maintain an efficient performance remnant of traditional vertical organizations because they have a responsibility to both shareholders and employees to be competitive and profitable. This is achieved by balancing the hard and soft aspects of organizational design. For example, as discussed in the Leader's Bookshelf, the boundaries in traditional organizations limit learning and change. Thus, leaders can work to replace the sense of concrete walls both vertically and horizontally with permeable boundaries. Also, organizations need mechanisms for controlling and directing resources, but leaders can build mechanisms that are based on shared purpose, common assumptions, and trust. Leaders can support order and change, competition and collaboration.

The Boundaryless Organization: Breaking the Chains of Organizational Structure
Ron Ashkenas, Dave Ulrich, Todd Jick, and Steve Kerr

The authors of this book challenge leaders to become "boundary-aware," stressing that fluid boundaries both within and between organizations are necessary to achieve the speed, flexibility, integration, and innovation critical to company success. Today's leaders can find the right balance of permeability for their organizations. *The Boundaryless Organization* uses case studies of well-known companies such as General Electric and SmithKline Beecham to illustrate the importance of creating boundaryless behavior in four essential areas.

Four Boundaries That Block Success

The authors describe four types of boundaries, examine the impact of each, and offer questionnaires, checklists, and mini-models that can help leaders create crossboundary linkages.

- Vertical Boundaries: Four critical dimensions required to span vertical boundaries are information sharing, building competence, delegating authority, and distributing rewards.
- Horizontal Boundaries: The best way to permeate horizontal boundaries is by focusing on the customer; teams should be formed and re-formed as needed to serve customers.
- External Boundaries: To create essential relationships with customers, suppliers,

regulators, and other organizations, companies can determine where opportunities exist for collaboration and align and integrate systems, structures, and processes.
- Geographic Boundaries: To attain globalization, companies must be committed to spanning geographic boundaries, identifying challenges and opportunities in the international marketplace, and recalibrating human resource practices and other organizational systems and processes.

Conclusion

The authors acknowledge that boundaries are necessary and will always exist, but they argue that traditional boundaries within and between organizations are dysfunctional in today's complex world. The two chapters on creating permeable boundaries between organizations are particularly useful because these boundaries are the least understood by most leaders. As the authors put it: "Boundaryless behavior is not about eliminating all administrative procedures and rules . . . it is about substituting permeable structures for concrete walls."

The Boundaryless Organization, by Ron Ashkenas, Dave Ulrich, Todd Jick, and Steve Kerr, is published by Jossey-Bass.

In the hard, rational view of organizations designed for efficient performance, the leadership model is that of a commander who sets goals, makes decisions, and gives clear, specific instructions for who is to do what and when. David Hurst describes the leadership model in a learning organization as "that of the shepherd, who follows his flock watchfully as it meanders along the natural contours of the land. He carries the weak and collects the strays, for they all have a contribution to make. This style may be inefficient, but it is effective. The whole flock reaches its destination at more or less the same time."[27] To keep learning alive, leaders can build a shared vision, help people see the whole system, design horizontal structures, reduce boundaries, initiate change, and expand the opportunity for employees to shape the future.[28] To promote the change and continuous learning needed in a fast-shifting environment, leaders can challenge assumptions and structures that are no longer appropriate for today's world.[29]

Leadership Frames for Learning Organizations

A **frame** is a perspective from which a leader views the world. The concept of organizational frames calls attention to the way people use their personal frames of reference to gather information and make decisions. Each leader uses a frame of reference to make sense of the world. Most people are stuck in a limited frame of reference based upon their past experience. To enrich a leader's ability to make better decisions with respect to learning organizations, it is helpful to broaden the frames they use to see the organization and make decisions. Failures occur when leaders are unable to see the world from a different perspective and therefore are unable to help the organization adapt to a changing environment.

When leaders can "reframe," they are able to look at old problems in a new light. Broadening one's frame of reference allows leaders a greater variety of approaches to solving problems. There are four perspectives or frames of reference through which leaders can view the organization as a whole—structural, human resource, political, and symbolic. These frames of reference determine how situations are defined and what actions are taken.[30] Clinging to a single vantage point is like imprisoning one's self in a frustrating, self-made, and narrow intellectual jail cell.[31] The learning organization requires that a leader see through all four frames. Each frame, to be discussed in detail in the remainder of this chapter, represents a side of the learning organization that requires leadership attention. By understanding how frames of reference affect leader perception, judgment, and behavior, leaders can expand their capability to respond to all of a learning organization's needs.

The four frames are illustrated in Exhibit 8.3 as a set of stairsteps. Leaders often begin with a limited structural perspective of the organization and develop the other frames of reference based on their own personal development and their experience with the organization. One study found the structural frame of reference was used about 60 percent of the time, while the symbolic frame was used only about 20 percent of the time.[32] Effective leaders balance their view of the organization by becoming aware of all four frames of reference, the importance of each, and how using multiple frames can facilitate a learning organization that is also efficient and productive.

Structural Frame

The organization as machine is the dominant image in the structural frame of reference. Leaders strive for machine-like efficiency and make decisions based on eco-

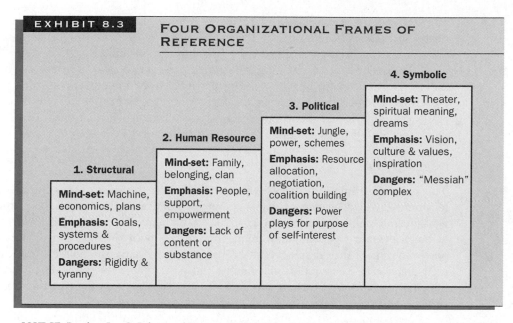

EXHIBIT 8.3 FOUR ORGANIZATIONAL FRAMES OF REFERENCE

SOURCE: Based on Lee G. Bolman and Terrence E. Deal, *Reframing Organizations* (San Francisco: Jossey-Bass, 1991); and Bolman and Deal, "Leadership and Management Effectiveness: A Multi-Frame, Multi-Sector Analysis," *Human Resource Management* 30, No. 4 (Winter 1991), 509–534. Thanks to Roy Williams for suggesting the stair sequence.

nomic efficiency. Plans and goals are the primary tools of management. Structure, plans, and rationality are needed in learning organizations, although not to the exclusion of other frames.

The **structural frame** of reference places emphasis on goal setting and clarifying job expectations as a way to provide order, efficiency, and continuity. Leaders emphasize clear job descriptions, specific policies and procedures, and the view of the organization as a rational system. Leaders value hard data and analysis, keep an eye on the bottom line, and stress adherence to accepted standards, conformity to rules, and the creation of administrative systems as a way to bring order and logic to the organization. Clarity of direction and control of results are important characteristics in this frame, and the organization is usually designed in hierarchical fashion. Carried to an extreme, the structural frame of reference leads to rigidity and even tyranny among leaders, who will quote the rules and insist that they be followed to the letter.[33]

Human Resource Frame

According to the **human resource frame** of reference, people are the organization's most valuable resource. This frame defines problems and issues in interpersonal terms and looks for ways to adjust the organization to meet human needs. Leaders value relationships and feelings, lead through empowerment and support, and encourage open communication, teamwork, and the development of others. This frame of reference can also lead to ineffectiveness, however, if leaders are wishy-washy and always bending to the whims of others, in essence using caring and participation as an excuse to avoid hard leadership responsibility.[34]

Effective leaders use the human resource perspective to involve others and give them opportunities for personal and professional development. They value people, are visible and accessible, and serve others. The images in this view are a sense of family, belonging, and the organization as a clan. Effective relationships are essential in a learning organization.

Political Frame

The **political frame** of reference views organizations as arenas of ongoing conflict or tension over the allocation of scarce resources. Political leaders spend their time networking and building alliances and coalitions to influence decisions. These leaders strive to build a power base, and they frequently exercise both personal and organizational power to achieve their desired results. Carried to an extreme, the political frame of reference can lead to deception, dishonesty, and power plays for purposes of individual self-interest. However, effective political leaders typically use their negotiating, bargaining, and coalition-building skills to serve organizational needs.[35]

Power and politics are an important, although often hidden, part of the learning organization. In the absence of structure, people rely on personal networking to accomplish their tasks. Leaders build alliances and coalitions among employees and other stakeholders to build shared vision and common ground. The mind-set in the political frame is to be aware of the organization as a jungle. Power is a reality, and schemes are a part of things. Embracing this frame, although not to the exclusion of the other frames, is important to leader success in the ambiguity of a learning organization.

Symbolic Frame

To use full leadership potential requires that leaders also develop a fourth frame of reference—the **symbolic frame,** which sees "a chaotic world in which meaning and predictability are social creations, and facts are interpretive rather than objective."[36] The organization is perceived as a system of shared meanings and values. These leaders use rituals, ceremonies, stories, and other symbols to create and reinforce a corporate culture. The symbolic leader focuses on shared vision, culture, and values in leading the organization and frequently inspires people to higher levels of performance and commitment. The danger of relying too heavily on the symbolic frame is that leaders may develop a "messiah" complex. The focus shifts to the leader rather than the organization and all its employees. Symbols can also be used for dishonest, unethical, and self-serving purposes.

Symbolic leaders are effective when they articulate a vision that is widely shared and understood, and when they support the deepest values and concerns of their followers. The leader thinks in terms of the organization as theater, is concerned with spirit and meaning, and with harnessing people's dreams.

Each of the four frames illustrated in Exhibit 8.3 provides significant possibilities for enhancing leadership effectiveness, but by itself is incomplete in a true learning organization. Leaders can understand their own natural frame of reference and recognize its limitations. In addition, they can learn to integrate multiple frames to fully use their leadership potential. The complex nature of a learning organization requires that all four frames come into play. As Bolman and Deal state it, "Wise leaders understand their own strengths, work to expand them, and build teams that together can provide leadership in all four modes—structural, human resource, political, and symbolic."[37]

Summary and Interpretation

Leaders can design learning organizations using the five elements of structure, tasks, systems, strategy, and culture. For many of today's companies, these elements developed during a time when environments were stable and organizations were based primarily on mass-production technology. Characteristics such as a strong vertical hierarchy, specialized routine jobs, formal information and control systems, a directed competitive strategy, and a strong internal culture helped organizations perform efficiently and consistently. However, these organizations may no longer work in today's chaotic world.

Many leaders are transforming their organizations into something called the learning organization, a fluid, flexible system almost like a biological entity, capable of continuous learning and adaptability. Vertical structures and functional boundaries are replaced by self-directed teams organized around work processes. Boundaries between organizations are also becoming permeable, as even competitors collaborate to share resources and exploit new opportunities. In a learning organization, responsibility and authority are pushed down to the lowest level. Strategy, rather than being directed top-down as in a traditional organization, can emerge from anywhere in the learning organization. In addition, learning organizations develop cultural values that emphasize adaptation and change.

The challenge for today's leaders is to balance a hard model of efficient organizations with a softer model of the learning organization. One consideration for leaders is the frame of reference they use to view the organization and its needs. Frames of reference determine how situations are defined and what actions are taken. There are four frames of reference leaders may use: structural, human resource, political, and symbolic. Most leaders rely heavily on one or the other, but they can learn to use multiple frames of reference to expand their leadership potential and better meet the needs of the organization.

Key Terms

learning organization	empowerment	political frame
self-directed team	frame	symbolic frame
task	structural frame	
role	human resource frame	

Discussion Questions

1. Would you like to work at an organization such as Oticon, described in the opening chapter case? Why or why not?

2. What are the primary differences between a traditional, functionally-organized company and the horizontally-organized learning organization?

3. Discuss the primary reasons so many of today's organizations are empowering lower level workers.

4. Discuss how bringing other organizations into a company's information network might contribute to strategy.

5. Why are cultural values of minimal boundaries and equality important in a learning organization compared to an efficient performance organization?

6. Which organizational frame of reference do you most identify with? How do you think this frame of reference could be beneficial or detrimental to your leadership capability?

7. Discuss why symbolic leadership needs to be balanced by other leadership perspectives in order to meet organizational needs.

8. What is the difference between a task and a role? Between formal systems and personal networks? Discuss.

Leadership Development: Personal Feedback

Your Leadership Orientation

This questionnaire asks you to describe yourself as a leader. For each item, give the number "4" to the phrase that best describes you, "3" to the item that is next best on down to "1" for the item that is least like you.

1. My strongest skills are

    _____ a. analytical skills.

    _____ b. interpersonal skills.

    _____ c. political skills.

    _____ d. flair for drama.

2. The best way to describe me is

    _____ a. technical expert.

    _____ b. good listener.

_____ c. skilled negotiator.

_____ d. inspirational leader.

3. What has helped me the most to be successful is my ability to

_____ a. make good decisions.

_____ b. coach and develop people.

_____ c. build strong alliances and a power base.

_____ d. inspire and excite others.

4. What people are most likely to notice about me is my

_____ a. attention to detail.

_____ b. concern for people.

_____ c. ability to succeed in the face of conflict and opposition.

_____ d. charisma.

5. My most important leadership trait is

_____ a. clear, logical thinking.

_____ b. caring and support for others.

_____ c. toughness and aggressiveness.

_____ d. imagination and creativity.

6. I am best described as a(n)

_____ a. analyst.

_____ b. humanist.

_____ c. politician.

_____ d. visionary.

Scoring

Compute your scores as follows:

Structural = 1a + 2a + 3a + 4a + 5a + 6a = _____

Human Resource = 1b + 2b + 3b + 4b + 5b+ 6b = _____

Political = 1c + 2c + 3c + 4c + 5c + 6c = _____

Symbolic = 1d + 2d + 3d + 4d + 5d + 6d = _____

Interpretation

The Leadership Orientation instrument reveals your leadership preferences for the four frames of reference associated with a learning organization. The higher the score, the greater your preference. Compare your scores to other people. What have you learned about your leader frames for leading within a learning organization?

SOURCE: Leadership Framework, 440 Boylston Street, Brookline, MA 02146, (1988). All rights reserved..

Leadership Development: Case for Analysis

The Fairfax County Social Welfare Agency

The Fairfax County Social Welfare Agency was created in 1965 to administer services under six federally funded social service grants:

- The Senior Citizens' Development Grant (SCD).

- The Delinquent Juvenile Act Grant (DJA).

- The Abused Children's Support Grant (ACS).

- The Job Development and Vocational Training Grant (JDVT).

- The Food Stamp Program (Food).

- The Psychological Counseling and Family Therapy Fund (Counseling).

The agency's organizational structure evolved as new grants were received and as new programs were created. Staff members—generally the individuals who had written the original grants—were assigned to coordinate the activities required to implement the programs. All program directors reported to the agency's executive director, Wendy Eckstein, and had a strong commitment to the success and growth of their respective programs. The organizational structure was relatively simple, with a comprehensive administrative department handling client records, financial records, and personnel matters. (See organizational chart on page 231.)

The sense of program "ownership" was intense. Program directors jealously guarded their resources and only reluctantly allowed their subordinates to assist on other projects. Consequently, there was a great deal of conflict among program directors and their subordinates.

The executive director of the agency was concerned about increasing client complaints regarding poor service and inattention. Investigating the matter, Eckstein discovered the following.

1. Staff members tended to "protect" their clients and not refer them to other programs, even if another program could provide better services.

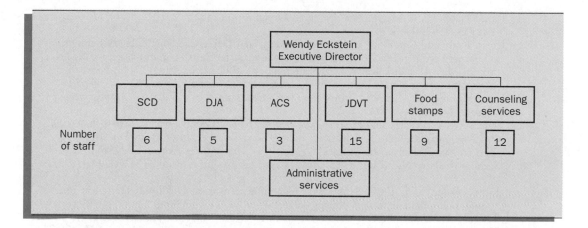

2. There was a total absence of integration and cooperation among program directors.

3. Programs exhibited a great deal of duplication and redundancy; program directors acquired administrative support for their individual programs.

Eckstein concluded that the present client or program-based structure no longer met the agency's needs. A major reorganization of this county social welfare agency is being considered.

Questions

1. Refer back to Exhibit 8.1. What elements of the agency could be causing the problems?

2. What "frames" are dominant in the agency? What frames are missing?

3. If you were Eckstein, how would you lead the agency toward becoming more of a learning organization? Discuss.

SOURCE: "The Fairfax County Social Welfare Agency," in *1998-99 Annual Editions: Management*, Fred Maidment, ed., (Guilford, CN: Dushkin/McGraw-Hill, 1998), 78. Used with permission.

References

[1]Polly LaBarre, "This Organization is Disorganization," *Fast Company*, June–July 1996, 77.
[2]Based on David K. Hurst, "Of Boxes, Bubbles, and Effective Management," *Harvard Business Review*, May–June 1984, 78–88; and *Crisis and Renewal: Meeting the Challenge of Organizational Change* (Boston, MA: Harvard Business School Press, 1995), 32–52.
[3]Alan Webber, "The Best Organization is No Organization," *USA Today*, March 6, 1997, 13A.
[4]George Stalk, Jr. and Jill E. Black, "The Myth of the Horizontal Organization," *Canadian Business Review*, Winter 1994, 26–31.

[5]Rahul Jacob, "The Struggle to Create an Organization for the 21st Century," *Fortune*, April 3, 1995, 9–99.

[6]Kevin Kelly and Otis Port, with James Treece, Gail DeGeorge, and Zachary Schiller, "Learning from Japan," *Business Week*, January 27, 1992, 52–60; and Gregory G. Dess, Abdul M.A. Rasheed, Kevin J. McLaughlin, and Richard L. Priem, "The New Corporate Architecture," *Academy of Management Executive* 9, No. 3 (1995), 7–20.

[7]Echo Montgomery Garrett, "Innovation + Outsourcing = Big Success," *Management Review*, September 1994, 17–20.

[8]Tom Burns and G.M. Stalker, *The Management of Innovation* (London: Tavistock, 1961).

[9]John A. Coutright, Gail T. Fairhurst, and L. Edna Rogert, "Interaction Patterns in Organic and Mechanistic Systems," *Academy of Management Journal* 32 (1989), 773–802.

[10]Stanley F. Slater "Learning to Change," *Business Horizons*, November–December 1995, 13–20.

[11]Jules Sowder, "The 100% Satisfaction Guarantee: Ensuring Quality at Hampton Inn," *National Productivity Review*, Spring 1996, 53–66.

[12]Thomas A. Stewart, "Get with the New Power Game," *Fortune*, January 13, 1997, 58–62.

[13]Thomas Petzinger, Jr. "How Lynn Mercer Manages a Factory That Manages Itself," *The Wall Street Journal*, March 7, 1997, B11.

[14]Robert C. Ford and Myron D. Fottler, "Empowerment: A Matter of Degree," *Academy of Management Executive* 9, No. 3 (1995), 21–31.

[15]Sanjay Goel, Charles C. Manz, Christopher P. Neck, and Heidi M. Neck, "Beyond Traditional Leadership: Leading Others to Lead Themselves," *The Journal of Leadership Studies* 2, No. 1 (1995), 81–92; Ford and Fottler, "Empowerment: A Matter of Degree."

[16]Hurst, *Crisis and Renewal*, 44.

[17]Ibid.

[18]C. Chet Miller and Laura B. Cardinal, "Strategic Planning and Firm Performance: A Synthesis of More than Two Decades of Research," *Academy of Management Journal* 37, No. 6 (1994), 1649–1665.

[19]Marc S. Gerstein and Robert B. Shaw, "Organizational Architectures for the Twenty-First Century," in David A. Nadler, Marc S. Gerstein, Robert B. Shaw, and Associates, eds., *Organizational Architecture: Designs for Changing Organizations* (San Francisco: Jossey-Bass, 1992), 263–274.

[20]Justin Martin, "Are You as Good as You Think You Are?" *Fortune*, September 30, 1996, 142–152.

[21]Jessica Lipnack and Jefferey Stamps, "One Plus One Equals Three," *Small Business Reports*, August 1993, 49–58.

[22]Mary Anne DeVanna and Noel Tichy, "Creating the Competitive Organization of the Twenty-First Century: The Boundaryless Corporation," *Human Resource Management* 29 (Winter 1990), 455–471; and Fred Kofman and Peter M. Senge, "Communities of Commitment: The Heart of Learning Organizations," *Organizational Dynamics* 22, No. 2 (Autumn 1993), 4–23.

[23]Stewart, "Get with the New Power Game."

[24]Jenny C. McCune, "Making Lemonade," *Management Review*, June 1997.

[25]Mitchell Waldrop, "The Trillion-Dollar Vision of Dee Hock," *Fast Company*, October–November 1996, 75–86.

[26]Webber, "The Best Organization Is No Organization."

[27]Hurst, "Of Boxes, Bubbles, and Effective Management."

[28]Peter M. Senge, "The Leader's New Work: Building Learning Organizations," *Sloan Management Review*, Fall 1990, 7–22.

[29]Slater, "Learning to Change."

[30]Based on Lee G. Bolman and Terrence E. Deal, *Reframing Organizations: Artistry, Choice, and Leadership* (San Francisco: Jossey-Bass, 1991), and "Leadership and Management Effectiveness: A Multi-Frame, Multi-Sector Analysis," *Human Resource Management* 30, No. 4 (Winter 1991), 509–534.

[31]Bolman and Deal, *Reframing Organizations.*

[32]Bolman and Deal, "Leadership and Management Effectiveness."

[33]Richard D. Heimovics, Robert D. Herman, and Carole L. Jurkiewicz Couglin, "Executive Leadership and Resource Dependence in Nonprofit Organizations: A Frame Analysis," *Public Administration Review* 53, No. 5 (September–October 1993), 419–427.

[34]Bolman and Deal, *Reframing Organizations,* 431.

[35]Jeffrey Pfeffer, *Managing with Power: Politics and Influence in Organizations* (Boston, MA: Harvard Business School Press, 1992); and Peter Moroz and Brian H. Kleiner, "Playing Hardball in Business Organizations," *IM,* January–February 1994, 9–11.

[36]Bolman and Deal, "Leadership and Management Effectiveness," 512.

[37]Bolman and Deal, *Reframing Organizations,* 445.

PART FIVE

Leader as Relationship Builder

Chapter 9
Motivation and Empowerment

Chapter 10
Leading Teams

Chapter 11
Leadership and Multiculturalism

Motivation and Empowerment

- **Leadership and Motivation**   238

- **Needs-Based Theories of Motivation**   242

- **Other Motivational Theories**   246

- **The Carrot and Stick Controversy**   248

- **Empowerment**   251

- **Organization-Wide Motivational Programs**   258

- **Leadership Spotlights:**
  Outback Steakhouse   245
  Lantech Corporation   250
  The USS *Missouri*   254

- **Leader's Bookshelf:** *The Living Company: Habits for Survival in a Turbulent Business Environment*   241

- **Leadership Development: Personal Feedback**
  Motivation Assumptions   260

- **Leadership Development: Case for Analysis**
  The Parlor   261

Your Leadership Challenge

After reading this chapter, you should be able to:

- Recognize and apply the difference between intrinsic and extrinsic rewards.

- Motivate others by meeting their higher level needs.

- Apply needs-based theories of motivation.

- Implement individual and system-wide rewards.

- Avoid the disadvantages of "carrot and stick" motivation.

- Implement empowerment by providing the five elements of information, knowledge, discretion, meaning, and rewards.

Sequins International, Inc., based in Woodside, NY, faces brutal competition, particularly from factories in China and India, where women and children hand sew sequins for meager wages, producing $100 million in wholesale goods annually. To compete, Sequins used machines that were first developed in the 1940s. The machines saved labor but created other problems: Repetitive motions caused muscle pains as well as mind-numbing boredom. With funding from the Ergonomics Project, administered by the International Ladies Garment Workers' Union, Sequins International redesigned the machines to reduce the physical stresses. At the same time, inspections and tasks that were once performed separately were integrated into the line workers job. This gave workers increased task involvement and a greater stake in quality control.

Because many of the people in Sequins' largely Hispanic workforce have poor English skills, the company offers English lessons three times a week during lunch hours. Classes in mathematics and statistical process control are also available to help train operators for new tasks. Two teams, one for products and one for customer support, provide operators with ongoing feedback and training.

These improvements in job design and motivation dramatically increased worker satisfaction. As a result, absenteeism is down two and one-half times in some departments. In addition, Sequins International has reduced the cost of producing a unit of goods by 30 percent and realized 30 percent cuts in cycle time, inventory, and overhead.[1]

The improvements at Sequins International occurred because its leaders found ways to meet the needs of workers. Increased involvement in job design, outside classes, and less physical strain created a workforce that was more innovative and positive. The leaders of Sequins gave more to their workers, which in turn helped the company achieve its goals. The leaders' ability to motivate workers paid off for everyone.

This chapter will explore motivation in organizations and examine how leaders can bring out the best in organizational followers. We will examine the difference between intrinsic and extrinsic rewards and how they meet the needs of followers. Individuals have both lower and higher needs they want satisfied, and there are different methods of motivation to meet those needs. The chapter presents several theories of motivation, with particular attention to the differences between leadership and conventional management methods for creating a motivated workforce. The final sections of the chapter explore empowerment and other recent motivational tools that do not rely on traditional reward and punishment methods.

Leadership and Motivation

Most of us get up in the morning, go to school or work, and behave in ways that are predictably our own. We usually respond to our environment and the people in it with little thought as to why we work hard, enjoy certain classes, or find some recreational activities so much fun. Yet all these behaviors are motivated by something. **Motivation** refers to the forces either internal or external to a person that arouse enthusiasm and persistence to pursue a certain course of action. Employee motivation affects productivity, and so part of a leader's job is to channel followers' motivation toward the accomplishment of the organization's vision and goals.[2] The study of motivation helps leaders understand what prompts people to initiate action, what influences their choice of action, and why they persist in that action over time.

Exhibit 9.1 illustrates a simple model of human motivation. People have basic needs, such as for food, recognition, or monetary gain, that translate into an internal tension that motivates specific behaviors with which to fulfill the need. To the extent that the behavior is successful, the person is rewarded when the need is satisfied. The reward also informs the person that the behavior was appropriate and can be used again in the future.

The importance of motivation, as illustrated in Exhibit 9.1, is that it can lead to behaviors that reflect high performance within organizations. One recent study found that high employee motivation and high organizational performance and prof-

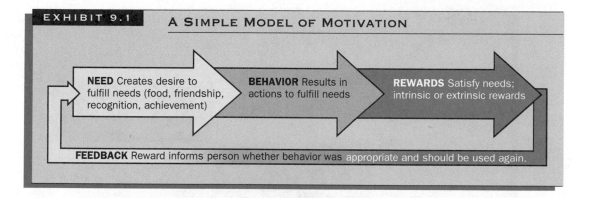

EXHIBIT 9.1   A SIMPLE MODEL OF MOTIVATION

NEED Creates desire to fulfill needs (food, friendship, recognition, achievement)

BEHAVIOR Results in actions to fulfill needs

REWARDS Satisfy needs; intrinsic or extrinsic rewards

FEEDBACK Reward informs person whether behavior was appropriate and should be used again.

its go hand-in-hand.[3] Leaders may use motivation theory to help satisfy followers' needs and simultaneously encourage high work performance. When workers are not motivated to achieve organizational goals, the fault is often the leader's.

Intrinsic and Extrinsic Rewards

Rewards can be either intrinsic or extrinsic, system-wide or individual. Exhibit 9.2 illustrates the categories of rewards, combining intrinsic and extrinsic rewards with those that are applied system-wide or individually.[4] **Intrinsic rewards** are the internal satisfactions a person receives in the process of performing a particular action. Solving a problem that benefits others may fulfill a personal mission or the completion of a complex task may bestow a pleasant feeling of accomplishment. An intrinsic reward is internal and under the control of the individual, such as to engage in task behavior to satisfy a need for competency and self-determination.

Conversely, **extrinsic rewards** are given by another person, typically a supervisor, and include promotions and pay increases. Because they originate externally as a result of pleasing others, extrinsic rewards compel individuals to engage in a task behavior for an outside source that provides what they need, such as money to survive in modern society. Consider, for example, the different motivation for polishing a car if it belongs to you versus if you work at a car wash. Your good feelings from making your own car shine would be intrinsic. However, buffing a car that is but one of many in a day's work requires the extrinsic reward of a paycheck.[5]

Rewards can be given system-wide or on an individual basis. **System-wide rewards** apply the same to all people within an organization or within a specific category or department. **Individual rewards** may differ among people within the same organization or department. An extrinsic, system-wide reward could be insurance benefits or vacation time available to an entire organization or category of people, such as those who have been with the organization for two years or more. An intrinsic, system-wide reward would be the sense of pride that comes from within by virtue of contributing to a "winning" organization. An extrinsic, individual reward is a promotion or a bonus check. An intrinsic, individual reward would be a sense of self-fulfillment that an individual derives from his or her work. It is the intrinsic rewards—both system-wide and individual—that leaders work to enable subordinates

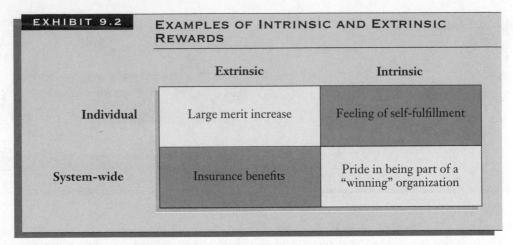

EXHIBIT 9.2	EXAMPLES OF INTRINSIC AND EXTRINSIC REWARDS	
	Extrinsic	**Intrinsic**
Individual	Large merit increase	Feeling of self-fulfillment
System-wide	Insurance benefits	Pride in being part of a "winning" organization

SOURCE: Adapted from Richard M. Steers, Lyman W. Porter, and Gregory A. Bigley, *Motivation and Leadership at Work*, 6th ed. (New York: McGraw-Hill, 1996), 498. Reprinted with permission of the McGraw-Hill Companies.

to achieve. A leader creates an environment that brings out the best in people. When leaders put the development of people before profits, they help organizations thrive over the long term, as discussed in the Leader's Bookshelf box.

Higher Versus Lower Needs

Intrinsic rewards appeal to the "higher" needs of individuals, such as accomplishment, competence, fulfillment, and self-determination. Extrinsic rewards appeal to the "lower" needs of individuals, such as material comfort and basic safety and security. Exhibit 9.3 outlines the distinction between conventional management and leadership approaches to motivation based on people's needs. Conventional management approaches often appeal to an individual's lower, basic needs and rely on extrinsic rewards and punishments—carrot and stick methods—to motivate subordinates to behave in desired ways. These approaches are effective, but they are based on controlling the behavior of people by manipulating their decisions about how to act. The higher needs of people may be unmet in favor of utilizing their labor in exchange for external rewards. Under conventional management, people perform adequately to receive the "carrot," or avoid the "stick," since they will not necessarily derive intrinsic satisfaction from their work.

Leaders often try to motivate others by providing them with the opportunity to satisfy higher needs, and thus become intrinsically rewarded. Remember that the source of an intrinsic reward is internal to the follower. When leaders empower followers, that is, allow them freedom to determine their own actions, subordinates reward themselves intrinsically for good performances. They may become creative, innovative, and develop a greater commitment to their objectives. So motivated, they often achieve their best possible performance.

The Living Company: Habits for Survival in a Turbulent Business Environment
Arie de Geus

Arie de Geus says that most companies do not survive the upheavals of change and competition over the long haul because leaders focus on assets rather than real people. Most major corporations survive for only about 40 years, but there are some remarkable companies that have withstood the test of centuries. The author studied 27 companies scattered throughout North America, Europe, and Japan that range in age from 100 to 700 years, including DuPont, W. R. Grace, Kodak, Mitsui, and Siemens. These *living companies*, he says, have a personality that allows them to "evolve harmoniously."

In his book, *The Living Company: Habits for Survival in a Turbulent Business Environment*, de Geus argues that employee motivation—or "the amount that people care, trust, and engage themselves at work"—has a direct effect on the bottom line as well as the most direct effect of any factor on a company's expected lifespan. He points out that a single-minded focus on profits can kill a company. In living companies, leaders follow a different philosophy.

Living Company Leadership
Leaders in living companies set priorities that allow people to grow as part of a community held together by trust and common values. Four priorities are:

- *Leaders make a commitment to people before assets.* The traditional management priorities are inverted, so that leaders value employees rather than buildings, equipment, and products. Living companies don't scuttle people to save plants and machinery.
- *Leaders loosen controls and give people space to develop new ideas.* They put a respect for innovation before the devotion to policy and procedure. Employees in living companies have the freedom to take risks without fear of punishment for failures.
- *Leaders organize for learning.* "Birds that flock learn faster," says de Geus. "So do organizations that encourage flocking behavior." Skunkworks—separate innovation groups free of company control—are an example of how to encourage interaction among creative, curious employees so they can learn together. Living companies also invest heavily in training programs that bring together people from diverse cultural backgrounds and professional disciplines.
- *Leaders put the perpetuation of the human community before all other concerns.* In living companies, employees are bound together by strong bonds of shared values, mutual trust, sharing, and caring. They understand that in exchange for their effort and commitment, the company will help them develop their potential.

Conclusion
Money is not considered a positive motivator in living companies. If pay is insufficient, employees will be dissatisfied, but giving more money doesn't motivate people to give more to the company. In living companies, employees are committed because they feel they belong to a community that cares about them as individuals.

The Living Company, by Arie de Geus, is published by Harvard Business School Press.

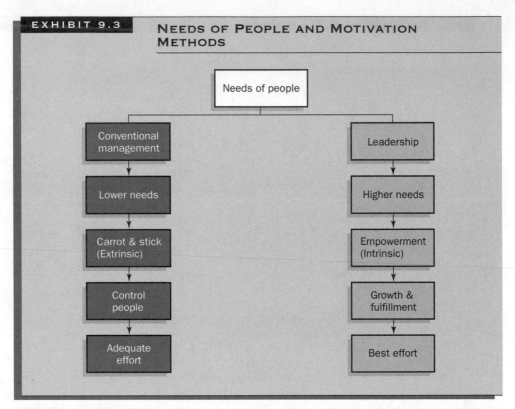

EXHIBIT 9.3 NEEDS OF PEOPLE AND MOTIVATION METHODS

SOURCE: Adapted from William D. Hitt, *The Leader-Manager: Guidelines for Action* (Columbus, OH: Battelle Press, 1988), 153.

Ideally, work behaviors should satisfy a follower's lower and higher needs as well as serve the mission of the organization. Unfortunately, this is often not the case. The leader's motivational role, then, is to create a situation that integrates the needs of people—especially higher needs—and the fundamental objectives of the organization.

Needs-Based Theories of Motivation

Needs-based theories emphasize the needs that motivate people. At any point in time, people have basic needs such as those for food, achievement, or monetary reward. These needs are the source of an internal drive that motivates behavior to fulfill the needs. An individual's needs are like a hidden catalog of the things he or she wants and will work to get. To the extent that leaders understand worker needs, they can design the reward system to reinforce employees for directing energies and priorities toward attainment of shared goals.

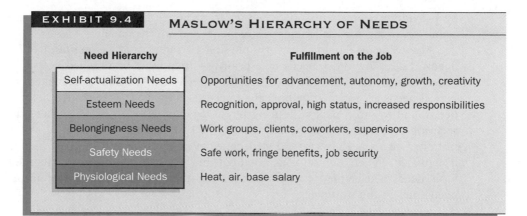

EXHIBIT 9.4   MASLOW'S HIERARCHY OF NEEDS

Need Hierarchy	Fulfillment on the Job
Self-actualization Needs	Opportunities for advancement, autonomy, growth, creativity
Esteem Needs	Recognition, approval, high status, increased responsibilities
Belongingness Needs	Work groups, clients, coworkers, supervisors
Safety Needs	Safe work, fringe benefits, job security
Physiological Needs	Heat, air, base salary

Hierarchy of Needs Theory

Probably the most famous needs-based theory is the one developed by Abraham Maslow.[6] Maslow's **hierarchy of needs theory** proposes that humans are motivated by multiple needs and those needs exist in a hierarchical order, as illustrated in Exhibit 9.4, wherein the higher needs cannot be satisfied until the lower needs are met. Maslow identified five general levels of motivating needs.

Physiological   The most basic human physiological needs include food, water, and sex. In the organizational setting, these are reflected in the needs for adequate heat, air, and base salary to ensure survival.

Safety   Next is the need for a safe and secure physical and emotional environment and freedom from threats—that is, for freedom from violence and for an orderly society. In an organizational workplace, safety needs reflect the needs for safe jobs, fringe benefits, and job security.

Belongingness   People have a desire to be accepted by their peers, have friendships, be part of a group, and be loved. In the organization, these needs influence the desire for good relationships with coworkers, participation in a work team, and a positive relationship with supervisors.

Esteem   The need for esteem relates to the desires for a positive self-image and for attention, recognition, and appreciation from others. Within organizations, esteem needs reflect a motivation for recognition, an increase in responsibility, high status, and credit for contributions to the organization.

Self-Actualization   The highest need category, self-actualization, represents the need for self-fulfillment: developing one's full potential, increasing one's competence, and becoming a better person. Self-actualization needs can be met in the organization by providing people with opportunities to grow, be empowered and creative, and acquire training for challenging assignments and advancement.

According to Maslow's theory, physiology, safety, and belonging are *deficiency* needs. These low-order needs take priority—they must be satisfied before higher-order, or growth needs, are activated. The needs are satisfied in sequence: physiological needs are satisfied before safety needs, safety needs are satisfied before social needs, and so on. A person desiring physical safety will devote his or her efforts to securing a safer environment and will not be concerned with esteem or self-actualization. Once a need is satisfied, it declines in importance and the next higher need is activated. When a union wins good pay and working conditions for its members, basic needs will be met; union members may then want to have social and esteem needs met in the workplace.

Two-Factor Theory

Frederick Herzberg developed another popular theory of motivation called the *two-factor theory*.[7] Herzberg interviewed hundreds of workers about times when they were highly motivated to work and other times when they were dissatisfied and unmotivated to work. His findings suggested that the work characteristics associated with dissatisfaction were quite different from those pertaining to satisfaction, which prompted the notion that two factors influence work motivation.

The two-factor theory is illustrated in Exhibit 9.5. The center of the scale is neutral, meaning that workers are neither satisfied nor dissatisfied. Herzberg believed that two entirely separate dimensions contribute to an employee's behavior at work. The first dimension, called **hygiene factors,** involves the presence or absence of job dissatisfiers, such as working conditions, pay, company policies, and interpersonal relationships. When hygiene factors are poor, work is dissatisfying. This is similar to the concept of deficiency needs described by Maslow. Good hygiene factors remove the dissatisfaction, but they do not in themselves cause people to become highly satisfied and motivated in their work.

The second set of factors does influence job satisfaction. **Motivators** fulfill high-level needs and include achievement, recognition, responsibility, and opportunity for growth. Herzberg believed that when motivators are present, workers are highly motivated and satisfied. Thus, hygiene factors and motivators represent two distinct factors that influence motivation. Hygiene factors work in the area of lower-level needs, and their absence causes dissatisfaction. Unsafe working conditions or a noisy working environment will cause people to be dissatisfied; but their correction will not cause a high level of work enthusiasm and satisfaction. Higher-level motivators such as challenge, responsibility, and recognition must be in place before employees will be highly motivated to excel at their work.

The implication of the two-factor theory for leaders is clear. The leader's role is to go beyond the removal of dissatisfiers to the use of motivators to meet higher-level needs and propel employees toward greater achievement and satisfaction. Consider how leaders at Outback Steakhouse strive to meet workers' higher-level needs.

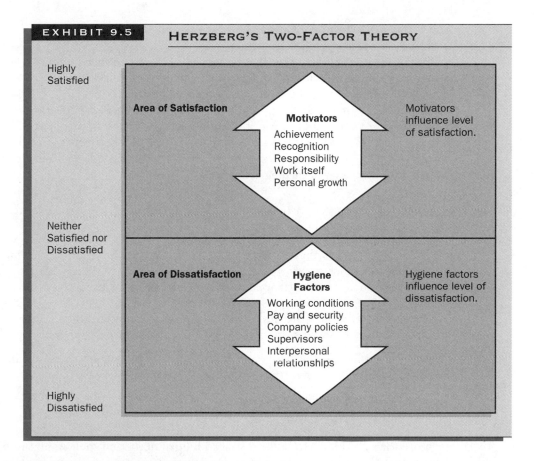

EXHIBIT 9.5 — **HERZBERG'S TWO-FACTOR THEORY**

Highly Satisfied

Area of Satisfaction

Motivators
Achievement
Recognition
Responsibility
Work itself
Personal growth

Motivators influence level of satisfaction.

Neither Satisfied nor Dissatisfied

Area of Dissatisfaction

Hygiene Factors
Working conditions
Pay and security
Company policies
Supervisors
Interpersonal relationships

Hygiene factors influence level of dissatisfaction.

Highly Dissatisfied

LEADERSHIP SPOTLIGHT   **OUTBACK STEAKHOUSE**

With their years of experience in the restaurant business, Robert Basham, Timothy Gannon, and Chris Sullivan, founders of Outback Steakhouse, were acutely aware of the hygiene factors in the food-service industry. While the average restaurant is designed to maximize the number of customers at the expense of the food preparation area, Outback's leaders put the emphasis on providing the best possible space for servers and kitchen staff to do their jobs effectively, even at peak business times. Outback's policy of serving dinner only and its maximum five-day workweek give managers and staff time for a life outside the restaurant, which cuts down on employee turnover. Each server handles only three tables at a time, ensuring first-class service to customers and higher tips for servers.

Outback uses ownership to motivate managers. After making a $25,000 investment and signing a five-year contract, Outback managers receive 10 percent of the earnings of their restaurants each month. This provides the average manager with a total income of about $118,600 per year, far above the rest of the industry. In addition, managers receive about 4,000 shares of stock, which are vested at the end of five years. Hourly staff also participate in a stock ownership plan.

Managers are further motivated by the level of responsibility Outback leaders bestow on them. Restaurant managers have the authority to make their own decisions rather than merely implement decisions dictated by headquarters.

Has Outback's motivational approach worked? In December of 1994, six years after its launch, there were 210 Outback Steakhouses, with revenues estimated at $554 million, up from $347.5 million the year before. As Timothy Gannon put it, "We believe if you treat employees as if you were one of them and give them the right environment, they will blow you away with their performance."[8]

Acquired Needs Theory

Another needs-based theory was developed by David McClelland. The **acquired needs theory** proposes that certain types of needs are acquired during an individual's lifetime. In other words, people are not born with these needs but may learn them through their life experiences.[9] Three needs are most frequently studied.

> *Need for achievement*—the desire to accomplish something difficult, attain a high standard of success, master complex tasks, and surpass others.

> *Need for affiliation*—the desire to form close personal relationships, avoid conflict, and establish warm friendships.

> *Need for power*—the desire to influence or control others, be responsible for others, and have authority over others.

For more than 20 years, McClelland studied human needs and their implications for management. People with a high need for achievement tend to enjoy work that is entrepreneurial and innovative. People who have a high need for affiliation are successful "integrators," whose job is to coordinate the work of people and departments.[10] Integrators include brand managers and project managers, positions that require excellent people skills. A high need for power often is associated with successful attainment of top levels in the organizational hierarchy. For example, McClelland studied managers at AT&T for 16 years and found that those with a high need for power were more likely to pursue a path of continued promotion over time.

Needs-based theories focus on underlying needs that motivate how people behave. The hierarchy of needs theory, the two-factor theory, and the acquired needs theory all identify the specific needs that motivate people. Leaders can work to meet followers' needs and hence elicit appropriate and successful work behaviors.

Other Motivational Theories

Reinforcement and expectancy approaches to motivation are characterized by extrinsic rewards and punishments, sometimes called the "carrot and stick" approach.[11]

The behavior that produces a desired outcome is rewarded with "carrots," such as a pay raise or a promotion. Conversely, undesirable or unproductive behavior brings the "stick," such as a demotion or withholding a pay raise. Carrot and stick approaches tend to focus on lower needs, although higher needs can sometimes also be met.

Reinforcement Perspective on Motivation

The reinforcement approach to employee motivation sidesteps the deeper issue of employee needs described in the needs-based theories. **Reinforcement theory** simply looks at the relationship between behavior and its consequences by changing or modifying followers' on-the-job behavior through the appropriate use of immediate rewards or punishments.

Behavior modification is the name given to the set of techniques by which reinforcement theory is used to modify behavior. The basic assumption underlying behavior modification is the **law of effect,** which states that positively reinforced behavior tends to be repeated, and behavior that is not reinforced tends not to be repeated. **Reinforcement** is defined as anything that causes a certain behavior to be repeated or inhibited. Tools of reinforcement include positive reinforcement, punishment, and extinction.[12]

Positive reinforcement is the administration of a pleasant and rewarding consequence following a behavior. A good example of positive reinforcement is immediate praise for an employee who arrives on time or does a little extra in his or her work. The pleasant consequence will increase the likelihood of the excellent work behavior occurring again.

Punishment is the imposition of unpleasant outcomes on an employee. Punishment typically occurs following undesirable behavior. For example, a supervisor may berate an employee for performing a task incorrectly. The supervisor expects that the negative outcome will serve as a punishment and reduce the likelihood of the behavior recurring. The use of punishment in organizations is controversial and often criticized because it fails to indicate the correct behavior.

Extinction is the withdrawal of a positive reward, meaning that behavior is no longer reinforced and hence is less likely to occur in the future. If a perpetually tardy employee fails to receive praise and pay raises, he or she will begin to realize that the behavior is not producing desired outcomes. The behavior will gradually disappear if it is continually not reinforced.

Some executives use reinforcement theory very effectively to shape employees' behavior. Jack Welch, chairman of General Electric, always made it a point to reinforce behavior. As an up-and-coming group executive, Welch used positive reinforcement with purchasing agents by having someone telephone him whenever an agent got a price concession from a vendor. Welch would stop whatever he was doing and call the agent to say, "That's wonderful news; you just knocked a nickel off the price of steel." He would also sit down and scribble out a congratulatory note to the agent. The effective use of positive reinforcement and the heightened motivation of purchasing employees marked Jack Welch as executive material in the organization.[13]

Expectancy Theory

Expectancy theory suggests that motivation depends on individuals' mental expectations about their ability to perform tasks and receive desired rewards. Expectancy theory is associated with the work of Victor Vroom, although a number of scholars have made contributions in this area.[14] Expectancy theory is concerned not with understanding types of needs but with the thinking process that individuals use to achieve rewards. Consider Betty Bradley, a university student with a strong desire for an A on her accounting exam. Betty's motivation to study for the exam will be influenced by her expectation that hard study will truly lead to an A on the exam. If Betty believes she cannot get an A on the exam, she will not be motivated to study exceptionally hard.

Expectancy theory is based on the relationship among the individual's effort, the possibility of high performance, and the desirability of outcomes following high performance. In order to be motivated, Betty must want a high grade and must believe that putting effort into her task—studying—will lead her to a high performance on the test.

Like the path-goal theory of leadership described in Chapter 4, expectancy theory is personalized to subordinates' needs and goals. A leader's responsibility is to help followers meet their needs while attaining organizational goals. One employee may want to be promoted to a position of increased responsibility, and another may want a good relationship with peers. To increase motivation, leaders can increase followers' expectancy by clarifying individual needs, providing the desired outcomes, and ensuring that individuals have the ability and support needed to attain their desired outcomes.

An example of expectancy theory at work occurs at Lincoln Electric Co., where leaders cite the expectation of rewards for hard work as the reason their four plants have remained competitive for a century. The 2,000 workers are paid by the piece and receive no vacation or sick pay. Wages are based on ratings of skill, effort, and responsibility for each job. Employees know they must produce quality goods in order to make any money. In addition to keeping the company's absenteeism at half the national average, the reinforcement system enables employees at Lincoln to earn up to three times that of their counterparts at other companies. Sometimes year-end bonuses exceed $20,000. However, it does take the right attitude and set of expectations to work at Lincoln. "I think of myself as an entrepreneur," said one 17-year piecework veteran. "I'm CEO of my own operation, and I try to find the quickest way to make a quality product for my company."[15]

The Carrot and Stick Controversy

Reward and punishment motivation practices dominate organizations; as many as 94 percent of companies in the United States engage in practices that reward performance or merit with pay.[16] In addition, many companies regard their incentive programs as successful. For example, U.S. Healthcare, a health maintenance organization (HMO), pays physicians who meet performance goals up to an additional 28 percent of their regular monthly premium. This HMO earned the highest quality care rating of any in the United States.[17]

Despite the testimonies of numerous organizations that enjoy successful incentive programs, the arguments against the efficacy of carrot and stick methods are growing. Critics argue that extrinsic rewards are neither adequate nor productive motivators and may even work against the best interest of organizations. Reasons for this criticism include the following.

1. *Extrinsic rewards diminish intrinsic rewards.* The motivation to seek an extrinsic reward, whether a bonus or approval, leads people to focus on the reward, rather than on the work they do to achieve it.[18] Reward seeking of this type necessarily diminishes the intrinsic satisfaction people receive from the process of working, from the actual activities. When people lack intrinsic rewards in their work, their performance levels out; it stays just adequate to reach the reward. In the worst case, people perform hazardously, such as covering up an on-the-job accident to get a bonus based on a safety target. In addition, with extrinsic rewards, individuals tend to attribute their behavior to extrinsic rather than intrinsic factors, diminishing their own contributions.[19]

2. *Extrinsic rewards are temporary.* Bestowing people with outside incentives might ensure short-term success, but not long-term quality.[20] The success of reaching immediate goals is quickly followed by the development of unintended consequences. Because people are focusing on the reward, the work they do holds no interest for them, and without interest in their work, the potential for exploration, innovation, and creativity disappears.[21] The current deadline may be met, but better ways of working will not be discovered.

3. *Extrinsic rewards assume people are driven by lower needs.* The perfunctory rewards of praise and pay increases tied only to performance presumes that the primary reason people initiate and persist in actions is to satisfy lower needs. However, behavior is also based on yearning for self-expression, and on self-esteem, self-worth, feelings, and attitudes. A survey of employees at *Fortune* magazine's "100 Best Companies to Work For in America" found that the majority mentioned intrinsic rather than extrinsic rewards as their motivation. Although many of these workers had been offered higher salaries elsewhere, they stayed where they were because of such motivators as a fun, challenging work environment; flexibility that provided a balance between work and personal life; and the potential to learn, grow, and be creative.[22] Offers of an extrinsic reward do not encourage the myriad behaviors that are motivated by people's need to express elements of their identities. Extrinsic rewards focus on the specific goals and deadlines delineated by incentive plans rather than enabling people to facilitate their vision for a desired future, that is, to realize their possible higher need for growth and fulfillment.[23]

4. *Organizations are too complex for carrot and stick approaches.* The current organizational climate is marked by uncertainty and high interdependence among departments and with other organizations. In short, the relationships and the accompanying actions that comprise organizations are overwhelmingly complex.[24] By contrast, the carrot and stick plans are very simple, and the application of an overly simplified incentive plan to a highly complex operation usually creates a misdirected system.[25] Extrinsic motivators wind up rewarding behaviors that are the opposite of what the organization wants and needs. While managers may espouse long-term growth, they wind up rewarding quarterly earnings; thus, workers are motivated to act for quick returns for themselves. Consider this chapter's Living Leadership box.

5. *Carrot and stick approaches destroy people's motivation to work as a group.* Extrinsic rewards and punishments create a culture of competition versus a culture of cooperation.[26] In a competitive environment, people see their goal as individual victory, as making others appear inferior. Thus, one person's success is a threat to another's goals. Furthermore, sharing problems and solutions is out of the question when coworkers may use your weakness to undermine you, or when a supervisor might view the need for assistance as a disqualifier for rewards. The organization is less likely to achieve excellent performance from employees who are mistrustful and threatened by one another. In contrast, replacing the carrot and stick with methods based on meeting higher as well as lower needs enables a culture of collaboration marked by compatible goals; all the members of the organization are trying to achieve a shared vision. Without the effort to control behavior individually through rigid rewards, people can see coworkers as part of their success. Each person's success is mutually enjoyed because every success benefits the organization. When leaders focus on higher needs they can make everyone feel valued, which facilitates excellent performance.

The conflicts that arose among the workers at Lantech illustrate how the competition for rewards led to the demise of collaboration. Luckily, the leaders understood how to fix the problem.

LEADERSHIP SPOTLIGHT   **LANTECH CORPORATION**

Patrick Lancaster III is convinced that the negative consequences on Lantech of incentive pay programs are greater than any motivational benefit. For nearly three decades, Lancaster has adopted, modified, and abandoned various incentive programs at his packaging machine manufacturing company. His first plan involved a bonus pool from which employees were rewarded based upon evaluations of one another's performance. The first six months saw a rapid rise in productivity. However, stress, insecurity, and the competition for the bonus pool took its toll; productivity fell steadily. Too much focus by employees on the reward and the threat of a bad evaluation from a fellow worker compromised their ability to cooperate and perform together. Then Lancaster rewarded several division managers with profit percentages based on their division sales growth. One of the unforeseen consequences of this plan was a sudden over-concern with tasks believed to directly increase sales growth. The quality of customer service diminished because it wasn't rewarded directly. Moreover, managers started fighting to attribute expenses to other divisions in order to maximize their own profit. One argument was about where to bill the toilet paper used in the common areas. Lancaster was spending 95 percent of his time resolving conflicts rather than serving clients.

Lancaster also tried linking rewards to sales-calls-per-day. He discovered, however, that even when the call records had not been "inflated," the employees believed everyone else was doing so anyway. Eventually, Lancaster realized that most workers simply resented the manipulation implicit in the attempt to control their behavior with rewards.[27]

Now Lantech operates with a very simple profit sharing plan. Everyone shares in the overall success of Lantech. According to Lancaster, the difference now is that he does not consider the plan a motivation incentive. He attributes Lantech's success to the feelings of accomplishment, job satisfaction, and empowerment that his associates receive from the positive culture he has sought to engender at Lantech.[28]

Some incentive programs are successful, especially when the people involved are actually motivated by money and lower needs. One way for leaders to address the carrot and stick controversy is to understand a programs' strengths and weaknesses and acknowledge the positive but limited effects of extrinsic motivators. A leader also appeals to the higher needs of people, and no subordinate should have work that does not offer some self-satisfaction as well as a yearly pay raise. Furthermore, rewards can be directly linked to behavior promoting the higher needs of both individuals and the organization, such as rewarding quality, long-term growth, or a collaborative culture.[29]

Empowerment

One way leaders can meet the higher motivational needs of subordinates is to shift power down from the top of the organizational hierarchy and share it with subordinates. They can decrease the emphasis on incentives designed to affect and control subordinate behavior and instead attempt to share power with organizational members to achieve shared goals. **Empowerment** is power sharing, the delegation of power or authority to subordinates in the organization.[30] In addition to delegating power, leaders can provide subordinates with the knowledge of how their jobs are relevant to the organization's performance and mission. This connection between job and mission gives subordinates a direction within which to act. The process of empowering subordinates hinges on providing them with this directed autonomy.[31] For example, Hewlett-Packard decentralized power by devising worldwide, cross

On the Folly of Rewarding A While Hoping for B

Managers who complain about the lack of motivation in workers might do well to examine whether the reward system encourages behavior different from what they are seeking. People usually determine which activities are rewarded and then seek to do those things, to the virtual exclusion of activities not rewarded. Nevertheless, there are numerous examples of fouled-up systems that reward unwanted behaviors, while the desired actions are not being rewarded at all.

In sports, for example, most coaches stress teamwork, proper attitude, and one-for-all spirit. However, rewards are usually distributed according to individual performance. The college basketball player who passes the ball to teammates instead of shooting will not compile impressive scoring statistics and will be less likely to be drafted by the pros. The big-league baseball player who hits to advance the runner rather than to score a home run is less likely to win the titles that guarantee big salaries. In universities, a primary goal is the transfer of knowledge from professors to students; yet professors are rewarded primarily for research and publication, not for their commitment to good teaching. Students are rewarded for making good grades, not necessarily for acquiring knowledge, and may resort to cheating rather than risk a low grade on their college transcript.

In business, there are often similar discrepancies between the desired behaviors and those rewarded. For example see the table below.

What do a majority of managers see as the major obstacles to dealing with fouled-up reward systems?

1. The inability to break out of old ways of thinking about reward and recognition. This includes entitlement mentality in workers and resistance by management to revamp performance review and reward systems.
2. Lack of an overall systems view of performance and results. This is particularly true of systems that promote subunit results at the expense of the total organization.
3. Continuing focus on short-term results by management and shareholders.

Motivation theories must be sound because people do what they are rewarded for. But when will organizations learn to reward what they say they want?

SOURCE: Steven Kerr, "An Academy Classic: On the Folly of Rewarding A, while Hoping for B," and "More on the Folly," *Academy of Management Executive* 9, no. 1 (1995), 7–16.

Managers hope for	But they reward
Teamwork and collaboration	The best individual performers
Innovative thinking and risk taking	Proven methods and not making mistakes
Development of people skills	Technical achievements and accomplishments
Employee involvement and empowerment	Tight control over operations and resources
High achievement	Another year's routine effort
Commitment to quality	Shipping on time, even with defects
Long-term growth	Quarterly earnings

functional teams. Each team has the autonomy to react rapidly to changing customer needs.[32] The autonomy of empowered employees creates flexibility that is an enormous advantage for a company.[33]

Reasons for Empowerment

What are the organizational advantages of having empowered workers? One study suggests that empowering workers enables leaders to create a unique organization with superior performance capabilities.[34] The strategic advantages are intimately linked to the motivation that empowerment unleashes among employees, and by extension, the overall effort of an organization.

First, empowerment provides strong motivation because it meets the higher needs of individuals. Research indicates that individuals have a need for self-efficacy, which is the capacity to produce results or outcomes, to feel they are effective.[35] Most people come into an organization with the desire to do a good job, and empowerment enables leaders to release the motivation already there. The employee reward is intrinsic—a sense of personal mastery and competence.

Second, empowerment actually increases the total amount of power in an organization. To say that leaders give power away to subordinates is something of a misnomer; leaders actually share power, creating a bigger overall power base. Simply put, if everyone in the organization has power, then the organization is more powerful.[36] The freedom from over-control allows subordinates to utilize their talents and abilities in ways that were otherwise constrained. Empowered employees use more of themselves to do their jobs.

For example, when Robin Landew Silverman and her husband made the painful decision to move their clothing store from downtown Grand Forks, North Dakota, to a suburban location, they knew they would need the full commitment of their staff. The Silvermans had always called the shots, but the move was a tremendous project that they couldn't lead alone. By giving up full control of the operation, the Silvermans gave their employees the opportunity to utilize themselves in new ways. "Skills emerged that we didn't know people had," recalls Robin. For example, a timid secretary became a dynamic bid researcher, and a marketing manager demonstrated a talent for interior design. The previous leadership of the Silvermans had amounted to "juggling crises," which gave way to shared power and company-wide participation.[37]

Third, leaders benefit from the additional capabilities employee participation brings to the organization. For one thing, leaders can devote more time to vision and the big picture. For another, empowerment takes the pressure off because subordinates are able to respond quicker and better to the markets they serve.[38] Front-line workers often have a better understanding than do leaders of how to improve a work process, satisfy a customer, or solve a production problem.

An interesting example of a leader who recognized the value of empowering front-line workers so they can better do their jobs is Admiral William F. "Bull" Halsey.

LEADERSHIP SPOTLIGHT   THE USS *MISSOURI*

obert Roddewig recalls being an 18-year-old radioman serving under Admiral William F. Halsey aboard the USS *Missouri*, deep in the Pacific Theater of Operations during World War II:

It required keen concentration to find our signal and stay on it while totally ignoring all the "trash." One evening I was copying KCT with the usual Japanese garbage jamming my frequency. . . .

Then a loud voice behind me asked, "Are they jamming our station?"

"Yes, sir," I replied, my concentration broken. I hit the space bar on the mill several times to indicate missed letters. I found the signal again.

"Are you able to copy it?" The voice again. I hit the space bar several more times before finding my signal once more. "Will you be able to get enough for us?" And the space-bar routine again. But this time I blurted out, "Shut up!"

When the transmission was complete, I pulled the message from the machine . . . . turned in my seat—and looked up at four stars on each lapel of a brown shirt. I had just met Admiral Halsey.

"Sir, are you the one I told to shut up?"

"Yes, lad," he blared. . . .

[Then he] began to pace the floor. "Lad," he bellowed, "when I come into this radio shack and speak to you while you are on that radio, YOU DO NOT TELL ME TO SHUT UP! DO YOU UNDERSTAND?"

"Yes sir, I understand." I was frozen at attention and, I am certain, tears were welling in my eyes.

Then, stopping in front of me and looking me straight in the eye, he went on in a calm and friendly voice. "If I or anyone else ever bothers you while you are on that radio, you do not tell them to shut up. What you do tell them is GET THE HELL OUT OF HERE AND THAT'S AN ORDER."[39]

Elements of Empowerment

Five elements must be in place before employees can be truly empowered to perform their jobs successfully: information, knowledge, discretion, meaning, and rewards.[40]

1. *Employees receive information about company performance.* In companies where employees are fully empowered, such as Semco S/A, Brazil's largest manufacturer of marine and food processing equipment, no information is secret. At Semco, every employee is given access to the books and any other information, including executive salaries. To show they're serious about sharing information, Semco leaders work with the labor union to

train its workers—even messengers and cleaning people—to read balance sheets and cash flow statements.

2. *Employees receive knowledge and skills to contribute to company goals.* Companies train employees to have the knowledge and skills they need to personally contribute to company performance. Knowledge and skills lead to competency—the belief that one is capable of accomplishing one's job successfully.[41] For example, regular quality awareness workshops are held at Chrysler Canada's assembly plant in Bramalea, Ontario, so that employees can initiate quality improvements on their own.

3. *Employees have the power to make substantive decisions.* Many of today's most competitive companies are giving workers the power to influence work procedures and organizational direction through quality circles and self-directed work teams. At Prudential Insurance Company's Northeastern Group Operations, teams made up of clerical, processing, technical, and quality control specialists are empowered to approve claims up to a dollar amount representing 95 percent of all claim submissions. Another team decided employees could save the company money by processing claims from home. Workers, free to set their own hours, are setting new records for productivity.[42] The Cutting Edge box describes how a school superintendent improved performance by empowering students, teachers, and parents to make substantive decisions.

4. *Employees understand the meaning and impact of their jobs.* Empowered employees consider their jobs important and personally meaningful and see themselves as influential in their work roles.[43] Understanding the connection between one's day-to-day activities and the overall vision for the organization gives a subordinate a sense of direction, an idea of what his or her job means. It enables employees to fit their actions to the vision and have an active influence upon the outcome of their work.[44] Furthermore, the work they do contributes to the overarching purpose and goals of the organization. For example, Xerox gives its workers what the company calls "line of sight" training, in which employees familiarize themselves with how their job fits into upstream and downstream activities, all the way to the customer. The training helps empowered employees make better decisions that contribute to the company's overall goals.[45]

5. *Employees are rewarded based on company performance.* Two of the ways in which organizations can financially reward employees based on company performance are through profit sharing and employee stock ownership plans (ESOPs). At W.L. Gore & Associates, makers of Gore-Tex, compensation takes three forms—salary, profit sharing, and an associates stock ownership program.[46] Contrary to conventional carrot and stick plans, these rewards focus on the performance of the group rather than individuals. Furthermore, rewards are just one component of empowerment, rather than the sole basis of motivation.

The Revolution at Hunterdon High

According to Ray Farley, "Once you put people in charge of their own destiny and say, 'Here's where you need to go if you want to be ready for the future,' the rest just happens." Farley has turned some of the traditional power of a school superintendent over to teams of students, teachers, and parents. Now, they are the ones who decide what gets taught, who gets hired, and what the school calendar looks like.

Hunterdon High School's teams found ways to equip the school with PCs, video facilities, ISDN lines, fiber-optic cables—the works—for $40,000 per classroom. Hunterdon also has a student-run FM radio station, a television studio, a telephone in every classroom, and a state-of-the-art instructional media center. Each classroom is linked to the school library, to the Internet, and to a host of other databases. Suburban Hunterdon High is also linked electronically to four inner-city New Jersey Schools, including Asbury Park High. Students at the two schools collaborate to produce a poetry magazine in real time.

At Hunterdon, attendance by both students and teachers is up, as is the number of students making it onto the honor roll and the number of graduates going on to college. Results are also beginning to be seen at Asbury Park since Farley began his revolution of empowerment. According to Dan Murphy, Asbury Park's principal, "One year ago we had two computers hooked up to the Internet. Right now, technicians are setting up 200 computers, providing them all with access . . . . And all of this is just the tip of the iceberg. It's unbelievable."

At the heart of Ray Farley's vision is that students should be responsible for their own learning. At Hunterdon, students even write their own lesson plans. "You have to make available all the technology you can get your hands on," says Farley. "And then you have to do one more thing—you have to trust them."

SOURCE: Nicholas Morgan, "Fast Times at Hunterdon High," *Fast Company*, February/March 1998, 42, 44.

Empowerment Applications

Many of today's organizations are implementing empowerment programs, but they are empowering workers to varying degrees. At some companies, empowerment means encouraging employee ideas while managers retain final authority for decisions; at others it means giving front-line workers almost complete power to make decisions and exercise initiative and imagination.[47]

Current methods of empowering workers fall along a continuum as shown in Exhibit 9.6. The continuum runs from a situation where front-line workers have no discretion (such as on a traditional assembly line) to full empowerment where workers even participate in formulating organizational strategy An example of full empowerment is when self-directed teams are given the power to hire, discipline, and dismiss team members and to set compensation rates. Few organizations have moved to this level of empowerment. As stated above, leaders at W.L. Gore and Associates fully empower employees. The company, which operates with no titles, hierarchy, or any of the conventional structures associated with a company of its size, has remained highly successful and profitable under this empowered system for more than 30 years. The culture emphasizes teamwork, mutual support, freedom, moti-

Motivation and Empowerment • 257

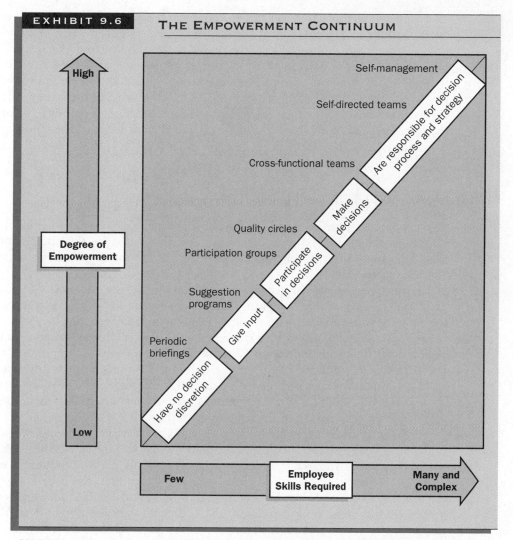

EXHIBIT 9.6   THE EMPOWERMENT CONTINUUM

SOURCES: Based on Robert C. Ford and Myron D. Fottler, "Empowerment: A Matter of Degree," *Academy of Management Executive* 9, No. 3 (1995), 21–31; Lawrence Holpp, "Applied Empowerment," *Training* (February 1994), 39–44; and David P. McCaffrey, Sue R. Faerman, and David W. Hart, "The Appeal and Difficulties of Participative Systems," *Organization Science* 6, No. 6 (November—December 1995), 603–627.

vation, independent effort, and commitment to the total organization rather than to narrow jobs or departments.[48]

Implementing Empowerment

Empowerment programs can be difficult to implement in established organizations because they destroy hierarchies and upset the familiar balance of power. A study of *Fortune* 1000 companies found that the empowerment practices that have diffused most widely are those that redistribute power and authority the *least*, for example, quality circles or job enrichment, because managers can keep decision authority.[49] Also, workers sometimes balk at the added responsibility freedom brings. Most organizations begin with small steps. For example, at Recyclights, a small Minneapolis-based company that recycles fluorescent lights, CEO Keith Thorndyke first gave employees control of their own tasks. As employees' skills grew, they developed a greater interest in how their jobs fit into the total picture. Thorndyke recognized that workers wanted to shape corporate strategy, so he engaged their participation in company goal setting.[50]

Organization-Wide Motivational Programs

Leaders can motivate organizational members using other recent programs that are more than the carrot and stick approaches described earlier in this chapter, but less than full empowerment: employee ownership, paying for knowledge, gainsharing, and job enrichment.

Employee ownership occurs on two levels. First, the processes of empowerment can result in a psychological commitment to the mission of an organization whereby members act as "owners" rather than employees. Secondly, by owning stock in the companies for whom they work, individuals are motivated to give their best performances. Chemical Banking Corporation gave its workers the option to buy 500 shares of its stock at $40.50, and the option to cash in when the stock increases 10 to 20 points. The workers' vested interest in seeing the stock rise motivates them to perform well. Additionally, stock options give workers a sign that their employer acknowledges each person's role in the organization.[51]

Pay for knowledge programs base an employee's salary on the number of task skills he or she possesses. Employees are motivated to acquire more skills to increase their salaries. A workforce in which individuals skillfully perform numerous tasks is more flexible and efficient. Many workers at Com-Corp Industries have worked their way up the corporate ladder by acquiring additional skills. Judi Sandbrook began as a receptionist, went back to school, and eventually became Director of Human Resources. Com-Corp rewards its employees for acquired skills by promoting them to higher paying positions and reimbursing their tuition. [52]

Gainsharing is a method of encouraging teamwork among employees by rewarding groups for reaching productivity improvement goals. At Carrier, a heating and cooling systems manufacturer, workers participate in the Improshare program. When workers produce more quality products per hour than in their benchmark year, the labor cost savings are split in half between the company and all of the employees. This proves to be a compelling incentive for teamwork. For example, in order to ensure their weekly share, employees worked through the night to recover from a broken water main. [53]

Job enrichment incorporates high-level motivators into the work, including job responsibility, recognition, and opportunities for growth, learning, and achievement. In an enriched job, the employee controls resources needed to perform well and makes decisions on how to do the work. One way to enrich an oversimplified job is to enlarge it, that is, to extend the responsibility to cover several tasks instead of only one.

Enriching jobs lead to greater motivation and job satisfaction. For example, at AES, the workers do much more than produce electricity. Volunteer teams at the plant level oversee public relations, project finance, human resources, operations, and purchasing. In short, workers effectively perform a wide range of tasks. "It makes work a lot more fun," says CEO Dennis W. Bakke. "Fun is when you're intellectually excited."[54]

Summary and Interpretation

This chapter introduced a number of important ideas about motivating people in organizations. Individuals are motivated to act to satisfy a range of needs. The leadership approach to motivation tends to focus on the higher needs of employees. The role of the leader is to create a situation in which followers' higher needs and the needs of the organization can be met simultaneously.

Needs-based theories focus on the underlying needs that motivate how people behave. Maslow's hierarchy of needs proposes that individuals satisfy lower needs before they move on to higher needs. Herzberg's two-factor theory holds that dissatisfiers must be removed, and motivators then added to satisfy employees. McClelland asserted that people are motivated differently depending on which needs they have acquired. The reinforcement perspective proposes that behavior can be modified by the use of rewards and punishments. Expectancy theory is based on the idea that a person's motivation is contingent upon his or her expectations that a given behavior will result in rewards.

Although carrot and stick methods of motivation are pervasive in North American organizations, many critics argue that extrinsic rewards undermine intrinsic rewards, bring about unintended consequences, are too simple to capture organizational realities, and replace workplace cooperation with unhealthy competition.

An alternative approach to carrot and stick motivation is that of empowerment, by which subordinates know the direction of the organization and have the autonomy to act as they see fit to go in that direction. Leaders provide employees with the knowledge to contribute to the organization, the power to make consequential decisions, and the necessary resources to do their jobs. Empowerment typically meets the higher needs of individuals. Other organization-wide motivational programs include employee ownership, pay-for-knowledge, gainsharing, and job enrichment.

Key Terms

motivation	motivators	punishment
intrinsic rewards	acquired needs theory	extinction
extrinsic rewards	reinforcement theory	expectancy theory
system-wide rewards	behavior modification	empowerment

individual rewards	law of effect	employee ownership
hierarchy of needs theory	reinforcement	pay for knowledge
hygiene factors	positive reinforcement	gainsharing
job enrichment		

Discussion Questions

1. Describe the kinds of needs that people bring to an organization.

2. What is the relationship among needs, rewards, and motivation?

3. What do you see as the leader's role in motivating others in an organization?

4. Do you believe it is possible to increase the total amount of power in an organization? Discuss.

5. What is the carrot and stick approach? Do you think that it should be minimized in organizations? Why?

6. What are the features of the reinforcement and expectancy theories that make them seem like carrot and stick methods for motivation? Why do they often work in organizations?

7. What are advantages of an organization with empowered employees?

8. Would you rather work for a leader who has a high need for achievement, high need for affiliation, or high need for power? Why?

Leadership Development: Personal Feedback

Motivation Assumptions

You are the leader of a department of 15 people. Answer each of the following questions according to how you think you would act. Do *not* answer what you want for yourself, but what you want to provide your people—from 1 (very unimportant) to 7 (very important).

_____ 1. The feeling of self-esteem a person gets from being in the job.

_____ 2. The opportunity for personal growth and development in the job.

_____ 3. The prestige of the job inside the company (that is, regard received from others in the company).

_____ 4. The opportunity for independent thought and action in the job.

_____ 5. The feeling of security in the job.

_____ 6. The feeling of self-fulfillment a person gets from being in the position (that is, the feeling of being able to use one's own unique capabilities, realizing one's potential).

_____ 7. The prestige of the job outside the company (that is, the regard received from others not in the company).

_____ 8. The feeling of worthwhile accomplishment in the job.

_____ 9. The opportunity in the job to give help to other people.

_____ 10. The opportunity in the job for participation in the setting of goals.

_____ 11. The opportunity in the job for participation in the determination of methods and procedures.

_____ 12. The authority connected with the job.

_____ 13. The opportunity to develop close friendships in the job.

Scoring

When you have completed the questionnaire, score it as follows:

Rating for question 5 = _____. Divide by 1 = _____ security.
Rating for questions 9 and 13 = _____. Divide by 2 = _____ social.
Rating for questions 1, 3, and 7 = _____. Divide by 3 = _____ esteem.
Rating for questions 4, 10, 11 and 12 = _____. Divide by 4 = _____ autonomy.
Rating for questions 2, 6 and 8 = _____. Divide by 3 = _____ self-actualization.

Interpretation

Your scores represent your leader preferences for meeting employee needs of security, social, esteem, autonomy, and self-actualization. Compare your scores with the scores of others. What kind of situation with what kinds of followers will suit your preferences?

SOURCE: Lyman W. Porter, *Organizational Patterns of Managerial Job Attitudes* (New York: American Foundation for Management Research, 1964), 17, 19.

Leadership Development: Case for Analysis

The Parlor

The Parlor, a local franchise operation located in San Francisco, serves sandwiches and small dinners in an atmosphere reminiscent of the "roaring twenties." Period fixtures accent the atmosphere and tunes from a mechanically driven, old-time player piano greet one's ears upon entering. Its major attraction, however, is a high quality, old-fashioned soda fountain that specializes in superior ice cream sundaes and sodas. Fresh, quality sandwiches are also a popular item. Business has grown steadily during the seven years of operation.

The business has been so successful that Richard Purvis, owner and manager, decided to hire a parlor manager so that he could devote more time to other business interests. After a month of quiet recruitment and interviewing, he selected Paul McCarthy whose prior experience included the supervision of the refreshment stand at one of the town's leading burlesque houses.

The present employees were unaware of McCarthy's employment until his first day on the job, when he walked in unescorted (Purvis was out of town) and introduced himself.

During the first few weeks, he evidenced sincere attempts at supervision and seemed to perform his work efficiently. According to his agreement with Purvis, he is paid a straight salary plus a percentage of the amount he saves the business monthly, based on the previous month's operating expenses. All other employees are on a straight hourly rate.

After a month on the job, McCarthy single-mindedly decided to initiate an economy program assured to increase his earnings. He changed the wholesale meat supplier and lowered both his cost and product quality in the process. Arbitrarily, he reduced the size and portion of everything on the menu, including those fabulous sundaes and sodas. He increased the working hours of those on the minimum wage and reduced the time of those employed at a higher rate. Moreover, he eliminated the fringe benefit of one dollar meal credit for employees who work longer than a five-hour stretch, and he cut out the usual 20 percent discount on anything purchased by the employees.

When questioned by the owner about the impact of his new practices, McCarthy swore up and down that there would be no negative effect upon the business. Customers, though, have begun to complain about the indifferent service of the female waitresses and the sloppy appearance of the male soda fountain clerks—"Their hair keeps getting in the ice cream." And there has been almost a complete turnover among the four short-order cooks who work two to a shift.

Ron Sharp, an accounting major at the nearby university, has been a short-order cook on the night shift for five months prior to McCarthy's arrival. Conscientious and ambitious, Ron enjoys a fine work record, and even his new boss recognizes Ron's superiority over the other cooks—"The best we got."

Heavy customer traffic at the Parlor has always required two short-order cooks working in tandem on each shift. The work requires a high degree of interpersonal cooperation in completing the food orders. An unwritten and informal policy is that each cook would clean up his specific work at closing time.

One especially busy night, Ron's fellow cook became involved in a shouting match with McCarthy after the cook returned five minutes late from his shift break. McCarthy fired him right on the spot and commanded him to turn in his apron. This meant then that Ron was required to stay over an extra half-hour to wash the other fellow's utensils. He did not get to bed until 3 A.M. But McCarthy wanted him back at the store at

9 A.M. to substitute for a daytime cook whose wife reported him ill. Ron was normally scheduled to begin at 4 P.M. However, when Ron arrived somewhat sleepily at 10 A.M. (and after an 8 A.M. accounting class), McCarthy was furious. He thereupon warned Ron, "Once more and you can look for another job. If you work for me, you do things my way or you don't work here at all." "Fine with me," fired back Ron as he slammed his apron into the sink. "You know what you can do with this job!"

The next day, McCarthy discussed his problems with the owner. Purvis was actually very upset. "I can't understand what went wrong. All of a sudden, things have gone to hell."

SOURCE: Bernard A. Deitzer and Karl A. Schillif, *Contemporary Incidents in Management* (Columbus, OH: Grid, Inc., 1977), 167–168. Reprinted by permission of John Wiley & Sons, Inc.

Questions

1. Contrast the beliefs about motivation held by Purvis and McCarthy.

2. Do you consider either Purvis or McCarthy a leader? Discuss.

3. What would you do now if you were in Purvis' position? Why?

References

[1] Barbara Ettorre, "Retooling People and Processes," *Management Review*, June 1995, 19–23.

[2] Richard M. Steers and Lyman W. Porter, Eds., *Motivation and Work Behavior*, 3rd ed. (New York: McGraw-Hill, 1983); Don Hellriegel, John W. Slocum, Jr., and Richard W. Woodman, *Organizational Behavior*, 7th ed. (St. Paul, MN: West, 1995), 170; and Jerry L. Gray and Frederick A. Starke, *Organizational Behaviors: Concepts and Applications*, 4th ed. (New York: Macmillan, 1988), 104–105.

[3] Linda Grant, "Happy Workers, High Returns," *Fortune*, January 12, 1998, 81.

[4] Richard M. Steers, Lyman W. Porter, and Gregory A. Bigley, *Motivation and Leadership at Work*, 6th ed. (New York: McGraw-Hill, 1996), 496–498.

[5] Steven Bergals, "When Money Talks, People Walk," *Inc.*, May 1996, 25–26.

[6] Abraham F. Maslow, "A Theory of Human Motivation," *Psychological Review*, 50 (1943): 370–396.

[7] Frederick Herzberg, "One More Time: How Do You Motivate Employees?" *Harvard Business Review* (January—February 1968), 53–62.

[8] Jay Finegan, "Unconventional Wisdom," *Inc.* (December 1994), 44–58.

[9] David C. McClelland, *Human Motivation* (Glenview, IL: Scott Foresman, 1985).

[10] David C. McClelland, "The Two Faces of Power," in *Organizational Psychology*, ed. D.A. Colb, I.M. Rubin, and J.M. McIntyre (Englewood Cliffs, NJ: Prentice-Hall, 1971), 73–86.

[11] See Alfie Kohn, "Why Incentive Plans Cannot Work," *Harvard Business Review*, September-October 1993, 54–63; and A. J. Vogl, "Carrots, Sticks, and Self-Deception," (an interview with Alfie Kohn) *Across the Board*, January 1994, 39–44.

[12] H. Richlin, *Modern Behaviorism* (San Francisco: Freeman, 1970); and B.F. Skinner, *Science and Human Behavior* (New York: Macmillan, 1953).

[13] Tom Peters and Nancy Austin, *A Passion for Excellence: The Leadership Difference* (New York: Random House, 1985), 267.

[14] Victor H. Vroom, *Work and Motivation* (New York: Wiley, 1969); B.S. Gorgopoulos,

G.M. Mahoney, and N. Jones, "A Path-Goal Approach to Productivity," *Journal of Applied Psychology* 41 (1957), 345–353; and E.E. Lawler III, *Pay and Organizational Effectiveness: A Psychological View* (New York: McGraw-Hill, 1981).

[15]Anita Lienert, "A Dinosaur of A Different Color," *Management Review*, February 1995, 24–29.

[16]A.J. Vogl, "Carrots, Sticks, and Self-Deception," (an interview with Alfie Kohn), *Across the Board*, January 1994, 39–44.

[17]James M. Kouzes and Barry Z. Posner, *The Leadership Challenge* (San Francisco, CA: Jossey-Bass, 1995).

[18]Vogl, "Carrots, Sticks, and Self-Deception," 40; and Alfie Kohn, "Incentives Can Be Bad for Business," *Inc.*, January 1998, 93–94.

[19]Jerry L. Gray and Frederick A. Starke, *Organizational Behavior: Concepts and Applications*, 4th ed. (New York, NY: Merrill, 1988).

[20]Richard M. Steers, Lyman W. Porter, and Gregory A. Bigley, *Motivation and Leadership at Work*, 6th ed. (New York: McGraw-Hill, 1996), 512.

[21]Steers, Porter, and Bigley, *Motivation and Leadership at Work*, 517; Vogl, "Carrots, Sticks, and Self-Deception," 40.

[22]Ibid., 154–157; Anne Fisher, "The 100 Best Companies to Work for in America," *Fortune*, January 12, 1998, 69–70.

[23]William D. Hitt, *The Leader-Manager: Guidelines for Action* (Columbus, OH: Battelle Press, 1988), 153.

[24]Steers, Porter and Bigley, *Motivation and Leadership at Work*, 520–525.

[25]Vogl, "Carrots, Sticks, and Self-Deception," 43.

[26]James M. Kouzes and Barry Z. Posner, *The Leadership Challenge* (San Francisco, CA: Jossey-Bass, 1995), 153.

[27]Patrick R. Lancaster III, "Incentive Pay Isn't Good for Your Company," *Inc.*, September 1994, 23–24; Peter Nulty, "Incentive Pay Can Be Crippling," *Fortune*, November 13, 1995, 235.

[28]Peter Nulty, "Incentive Pay Can Be Crippling," *Fortune*, November 13, 1995, 235.

[29]Kouzes and Posner, *The Leadership Challenge*, 282.

[30]Edwin P. Hollander and Lynn R. Offerman, "Power and Leadership in Organizations," *American Psychology* 45 (February 1990), 179–189.

[31]Robert C. Ford and Myron D. Fottler, "Empowerment: A Matter of Degree," *Academy of Management Executive* 9, (1995), 21–31.

[32]Alan Deutschman, "How H-P Continues to Grow and Grow," *Fortune*, May 2, 1994, 90.

[33]David P. McCaffrey, Sue R. Faerman and David W. Hart, "The Appeal and Difficulties of Participative Systems," *Organization Science* 6, No. 6 (November—December 1995), 603–627.

[34]David E. Bowen and Edward E. Lawler III, "Empowering Service Employees," *Sloan Management Review* (Summer 1995), 73–84.

[35]Jay A. Conger and Rabindra N. Kanungo, "The Empowerment Process: Integrating Theory and Practice," *Academy of Management Review* 13 (1988): 471–482.

[36]Arnold S. Tannenbaum and Robert S. Cooke, "Organizational Control: A Review of Studies Employing the Control Graph Method," in Cornelius J. Lamners and David J. Hickson, eds., *Organizations Alike and Unalike* (Boston: Rutledge and Keegan Paul, 1980), 183–210.

[37]Robin Landew Silverman, "A Moving Experience," *Inc.*, August 1996, 23–24.

[38]McCaffrey, Faerman and Hart, "The Appeal and Difficulties of Participative Systems."

[39]Robert Roddewig, "Bull Session," *American Heritage*, September 1997, 28–30.

[40]Bowen and Lawler, "Empowering Service Employees."

[41]Gretchen Spreitzer, "Social Structural Characteristics of Psychological Empowerment," *Academy of Management Journal* 39 No. 2. (April 1996), 483–504.

[42]Peter C. Fleming, "Empowerment Strengthens the Rock," *Management Review*, December 1991, 34–37.

[43]Gretchen M. Spreitzer, "Psychological Empowerment in the Workplace: Dimensions, Measurement, and Validation," *Academy of Management Journal* 38, No. 5 (October 1995), 1442.

[44]Gretchen Spreitzer, "Social Structural Characteristics of Psychological Empowerment."

[45]Bowen and Lawler, "Empowering Service Employees."

[46]Frank Shipper and Charles C. Manz, "Employee Self-Management Without Formally Designated Teams: An Alternative Road to Empowerment," *Organizational Dynamics* (Winter 1992), 48–61.

[47]Robert C. Ford and Myron D. Fottler, "Empowerment: A Matter of Degree," *Academy of Management Executive* 9, No. 3 (1995), 21–31.

[48]Ibid.

[49]McCaffrey, Faerman and Hart, "The Appeal and Difficulties of Participative Systems,"

[50]Michael Barrier, "The Changing Face of Leadership," *Nation's Business*, January 1995, 41–42.

[51]Kerry Capell, "Options for Everyone," *Business Week*, July 22, 1996, 80–88.

[52]Teri Lammers Prior, "If I Were President," *Inc.*, April 1995, 56–61; and Nancy J. Perry, "Here Comes Richer, Riskier Pay Plans," *Fortune*, December 19, 1988, 50–58.

[53]Shawn Tully, "Your Paycheck Gets Exciting," *Fortune*, November 1, 1993, 83–98.

[54]Alex Markels, "A Power Producer Is Intent on Giving Power to Its People," *The Wall Street Journal*, July 3, 1995, A1.

10

Leading Teams

- **Teams in Organizations**   268
- **Types of Teams**   269
- **Team Leadership**   274
- **Understanding Team Characteristics**   278
- **Leading Team Dynamics**   280
- **Handling Team Conflict**   286
- **Leading Global Teams**   289
- **Leadership Spotlights:**
  Whole Foods Market Inc.   274
  Athletic Team Interdependence   279
  BP Norge   282
  Southwest Airlines   286
- **Leader's Bookshelf:** *Organizing Genius: The Secrets of Creative Collaboration*   271
- **Leadership Development: Personal Feedback**
  Team Cohesiveness   291
- **Leadership Development: Case for Analysis**
  Valena Scientific Corporation   293

Your Leadership Challenge

After reading this chapter, you should be able to:

- Turn a group of individuals into a collaborative team that achieves high performance through shared mission and collective responsibility.

- Develop and apply the personal qualities of effective team leadership.

- Understand and handle the stages of team development and forms of interdependence.

- Guide cultural norms and values to influence team cohesiveness.

- Handle conflicts that inevitably arise among members of a team.

Several years ago when the United States Information Agency (USIA) faced severe budget cuts, its response was to create another bureau. However, this bureau was unlike anything seen before in "government work." The traditional bureaucratic hierarchy with layers of authority on top of one another was obliterated. USIA's new Bureau of Information (the I Bureau) is made up of 21 self-directed workteams. The reorganization of the agency's information programs wiped out branches and divisions, downgraded managers, cut supervisory levels, and abolished the positions of deputies and special assistants.

Traditionally, USIA managers had spent their time issuing orders and "breathing down people's necks" to make sure decisions from the top were implemented. Today, teams iron out problems and make decisions together.

Authority is no longer derived from title, and leadership is based on the ability to create an environment that brings out the best in workers. In discussing his role as team leader compared to the old-style manager, Bill Peters said, "It came to me [the other day] that the team is the leader, not me. That is what we are striving for. As team leader, I don't try to second-guess team members or the team. We try hard to reach consensus and find out whether everyone can live with a decision."[1]

The team-based approach has given the I Bureau greater flexibility to respond to challenges and enhanced the motivation and commitment of workers. Teams come up with new ideas and new ways to do their work. Few employees feel any desire to return to the old hierarchy, but the transition to teams was not easy, especially for managers who had to give up power and authority. As Bob Fulton, Associate Director for the I Bureau put it, many managers "learned all their behaviors from working in the old hierarchy. People now have to think of themselves differently. Leadership is more difficult now, when authority is more ambiguous."[1]

A quiet revolution has been occurring in organizations across the country. From the assembly line to the executive suite, from large businesses such as Exxon and Volvo to government organizations like USIA , teams are becoming the basic building block of organizations. The use of teams has increased dramatically in response to new competitive pressures and the need for flexibility and speed. One survey found that within three years, the number of *Fortune* 1000 companies using work-teams increased by almost 20 percent, and teamwork has become the most frequent topic taught in company training programs. In a study of 109 Canadian organizations, 42 percent reported widespread team-based activity and only 13 percent reported little or no team activity.[2]

Teams present greater leadership challenges and opportunities than does the traditional hierarchical organization. Every team member has to develop some leadership capability. This chapter explores team leadership in today's organizations. We will define various types of teams, examine the personal changes people make to become good team leaders, and discuss how leaders can help teams be more effective. Then we examine such characteristics as team size, interdependence, cohesiveness, and culture. We will also look at the role of leadership in guiding team development and handling conflict. The final section of the chapter will briefly discuss the emergence of global teams and the role of information technology in expanding teamwork options.

Teams in Organizations

The concept of teamwork is a fundamental change in the way work is organized. More and more companies are recognizing that the best way to meet the challenges of higher quality, faster service, and total customer satisfaction is through an aligned, coordinated, and committed effort by all employees.[3] At the Frito-Lay plant in Lubbock, Texas, team members handle everything from potato processing to equipment maintenance. Each team has authority to select new hires, determine crew scheduling, and discipline team members who are not pulling their load. The four owners of Crescent Manufacturing in Fremont, Ohio, run their company as a team, switching jobs among themselves as the company's needs change. At Massachusetts General Hospital, the emergency-trauma team performs so smoothly that the team switches leaders seamlessly, depending on the crisis at hand. With each new emergency, direction may come from a doctor, intern, nurse, or technician—whoever is particularly experienced with the problem.[4]

Teams such as the one at Massachusetts General are self-directed and anyone may assume a leadership role. Others, such as the teams at the I Bureau, operate without a hierarchy but have designated team leaders who play a central role in guiding the team's work. Still other teams function within the traditional vertical hierarchy. In this section, we will first define teams and examine the types of teams that exist in organizations.

What Is a Team?

A **team** is a unit of two or more people who interact and coordinate their work to accomplish a specific goal.[5] This definition has three components. First, teams are made up of two or more people. Teams can be large, but most have fewer than 15 people. Second, people in a team work together regularly. People who do not interact regularly, such as those waiting in line at the company cafeteria or riding together in the elevator, do not comprise a team. Third, people in a team share a goal, whether it be to build a car, design a new laptop computer, or write a textbook. Today's students are frequently assigned to complete assignments in teams. In this case, the shared goal is to complete the task and receive an acceptable grade.

A team is a group of people, but the two are not equal. A professor, coach, or employer can put together a *group* of people and never build a *team*. The sports world is full of stories of underdog teams that have won championships against a group of players who were better individually but did not make up a better team.[6] The team concept implies a sense of shared mission and collective responsibility. Exhibit 10.1 lists the primary differences between groups and teams. A team achieves high levels of performance through shared leadership, purpose, and responsibility by all members working toward a common goal. Teams are characterized by equality; in the best teams, there are no individual "stars" and everyone sublimates individual ego to the good of the whole. The Leader's Bookshelf examines some characteristics of great teams.

Types of Teams

Many types of teams can exist within organizations. We will look at three important types of teams: functional teams, cross-functional teams, and self-directed teams.

EXHIBIT 10.1	DIFFERENCES BETWEEN GROUPS AND TEAMS
Group	**Team**
Has a designated, strong leader	Shares or rotates leadership roles
Individual accountability	Mutual and individual accountability (accountable to each other)
Identical purpose for group and organization	Specific team vision or purpose
Performance goals set by others	Performance goals set by team
Works within organizational boundaries	Not inhibited by organizational boundaries
Individual work products	Collective work products
Organized meetings, delegation	Mutual feedback, open-ended discussion, active problem-solving

SOURCES: Based on Jon R. Katzenbach and Douglas K. Smith, "The Discipline of Teams," *Harvard Business Review* (March–April 1995), 111–120; and Milan Moravec, Odd Jan Johannessen, and Thor A. Hjelmas, "Thumbs Up for Self-Managed Teams," *Management Review* (July–August 1997), 42–47 (chart on 46).

Functional Teams

A **functional team** is part of the traditional vertical hierarchy. This type of team is made up of a supervisor and his or her subordinates in the formal chain of command. Sometimes called a *vertical team* or a *command team*, the functional team may in some cases include three or four levels of hierarchy within a department. Typically, a functional team makes up a single department in the organization. For example, the quality control department at Blue Bell Creameries in Brenham, Texas, is a functional team that tests all incoming ingredients to make sure only the best products go into the company's ice cream. A financial analysis department, a human resources department, and a sales department are all functional or vertical teams. Each is created by the organization within the vertical hierarchy to attain specific goals through members' joint activities. Functional teams exist in most organizations, but they are on the decline as companies look for ways to better serve customers and increase speed, flexibility, and quality.

Cross-Functional Teams

As the name implies, **cross-functional teams** are made up of members from different functional departments within the organization. Employees are generally from about the same hierarchical level in the organization, although cross-functional teams sometimes cross vertical as well as horizontal boundaries. Cross-functional teams typically have a specific team leader and lead change projects, such as creating a new product in a manufacturing organization or developing an interdisciplinary curriculum in a middle school. Cross-functional teams are generally involved

Organizing Genius: The Secrets of Creative Collaboration
Warren Bennis and Patricia Ward Biederman

This book is a systematic examination of seven successful teams, including the Disney animation team that created movies such as *Snow White and the Seven Dwarfs* and members of the Manhattan Project that built the atomic bomb. Warren Bennis and Patricia Biederman describe how the creative collaboration of team members resulted in great achievement. Based on their analysis of these seven teams, the authors provide 15 clues to leaders for how to turn a group of people into a team that achieves extraordinary results through collaboration. They argue that the greatest achievements come from creative alliances—teams of leaders—rather than from "triumphant individuals."

Take Home Lessons

Bennis and Biederman summarize the essential conditions for what they call "Great Groups." Leaders can improve team performance by creating teams based on these clues. A sample of the take-home lessons the authors offer include:

> *Greatness starts with superb people.* Superb means much more than being good at what one does. For superb people, solving problems and finding new ways to do things are as natural and necessary as breathing. Recruiting these original and tenacious people is the first step toward creating a Great Group.
> *Great Groups and great leaders create each other.* The contribution of the leader is to create and maintain an environment in which the group can achieve greatness. Through serving the group, leaders find their own greatness. *Great Groups think they're on a holy mission.*

Members are working toward a crucial, collective purpose that transforms a mere job into a crusade. In a Great Group, the mission instills meaning into every action.
A Great Group is an island—but with a bridge to the mainland. Great Groups tend to be physically and psychologically removed from the world around them. They're free from the distractions, but able to tap into necessary resources. They typically create a culture of their own, in which an original brand of fun, games, and commitment prevails.
Great Groups see themselves as winning underdogs. The energy and joy that characterize a Great Group stem from a self-image of the team as a wily upstart that will snatch the prize from a powerful, favored competitor.

No Heroes

Great Groups differ from a collection of great individuals. Although every great group is great in its own way, Bennis and Biederman provide a summary of the essential ingredients for creating and maintaining a team of leaders—one that can make things happen and create a lasting impact without a single hero. Members of such teams don't talk about who gets the credit for what. They remember the camaraderie, the joy, the excitement of pushing back the boundaries and collaboratively doing something superbly well.

Organizing Genius: The Secrets of Creative Collaboration, by Warren Bennis and Patricia Ward Biederman, is published by Addison-Wesley Publishing Company, Inc.

in projects that affect several departments and therefore require that many views be considered. For example, at GE Lighting Co. in Cleveland, Ohio, a cross-functional team with members from information technology, finance, and several other

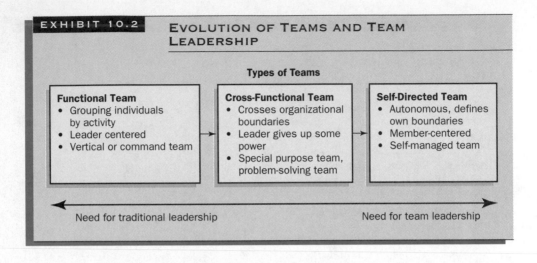

EXHIBIT 10.2 — EVOLUTION OF TEAMS AND TEAM LEADERSHIP

Types of Teams

Functional Team
- Grouping individuals by activity
- Leader centered
- Vertical or command team

Cross-Functional Team
- Crosses organizational boundaries
- Leader gives up some power
- Special purpose team, problem-solving team

Self-Directed Team
- Autonomous, defines own boundaries
- Member-centered
- Self-managed team

Need for traditional leadership ◄─────────────────────► Need for team leadership

departments oversaw an ambitious systems-integration project that spanned operations in the United States and Canada. Coca-Cola Fountain Manufacturing Baltimore Syrup Operation uses cross-functional teams to work on projects such as uniform, vacation, and compensation policies.[7]

Cross-functional teams facilitate information sharing across functional boundaries, generate suggestions for coordinating the departments represented, develop new ideas and solutions for existing organizational problems, and assist in developing new practices or policies. The members of one type of cross-functional team, the *problem-solving* or *process-improvement* team, meet voluntarily to discuss ways to improve quality, efficiency, and the work environment. Their recommendations are proposed to top executives for approval. Another type of cross-functional team is the *special purpose* team, which is created outside the formal organization structure to undertake a project of special importance or creativity. McDonald's assigned E. J. (Bud) Sweeney to lead a special purpose team to create the Chicken McNugget. The team was separated from the formal organization to give it the autonomy to innovate successfully. Members perceived themselves as a separate entity.[8] Cross-functional teams are often an organization's first step toward greater employee participation and empowerment. These teams may gradually evolve into self-directed teams, which represent a fundamental change in how work is organized.

Evolution to Self-Directed Teams

Exhibit 10.2 illustrates the evolution of teams and team leadership. The functional team represents grouping individuals by common skill and activity within the traditional structure. Leadership is based on the vertical hierarchy. In cross-functional teams, members have more freedom from the hierarchy, but the team typically is still leader-centered and leader-directed. The leader is most often assigned by the organization and is usually a supervisor or manager from one of the departments represented on the team. Leaders do, however, have to give up some of their control and power at this stage in order for the team to function effectively.

In the highest stage of evolution, team members work together without the direction of managers, supervisors, or assigned team leaders.[9] Self-directed teams are member- rather than leader-centered and directed. Hundreds of companies, including Westinghouse Electric Company, Chrysler, Wilson Golf Ball, Edy's Grand Ice Cream, and Tennessee Eastman Chemical, are trying self-directed teams as a way to increase the participation and enthusiasm of lower-level workers. Self-directed teams enable workers to feel challenged, find their work meaningful, and develop a strong sense of identity with the organization.[10]

Self-directed teams typically consist of 5 to 20 members who rotate jobs to produce an entire product or service or at least one complete aspect or portion of a product or service (e.g., engine assembly, insurance claim processing).[11] Self-directed teams often are long-term or permanent in nature and they typically include three elements:

1. The team includes workers with varied skills and functions and the combined skills are sufficient to perform a major organizational task, thereby eliminating barriers among departments and enabling excellent coordination.

2. The team is given access to resources such as information, financial resources, equipment, machinery, and supplies needed to perform the complete task.

3. The team is empowered with decision-making authority, which means that members have the freedom to select new members, solve problems, spend money, monitor results, and plan for the future.

In self-directed teams, members take over duties such as scheduling work or vacations, ordering materials, and evaluating performance. Teams work with minimum supervision, and members are jointly responsible for conflict resolution and decision making. Many self-directed teams elect one of their own to serve as team leader, and the leader may change each year. Some teams function without a designated leader, so anyone may play a leadership role depending on the situation. In either case, equality and empowerment are key values in organizations based on self-directed teams. When Eastman Chemical reorganized into self-directed teams, the company referred to its new organization chart as "the pizza chart" because it looks like a round pizza with slices of pepperoni on top. Each slice of pepperoni on the pizza represents a self-directed team that is responsible for a specific work flow, such as cellulose technology. The white space between the circles reflects where the interaction among teams should take place. As Ernest W. Deavenport, Jr., the "head pepperoni," says, "We did it in circular form to show that everyone is equal in the organization. No one dominates the other."[12]

Organizations are integrating a variety of team approaches into their operations. One organization that has always been based on teamwork is Whole Foods Market.

LEADERSHIP SPOTLIGHT   WHOLE FOODS MARKET INC.

Whole Foods Market, the largest natural foods grocer in the United States, has turned empowerment, autonomy, and teamwork into a highly profitable business model. As recently as 1991, Whole Foods Market had barely a dozen stores in three states. Today, it has the clout of a nationwide chain, with 43 stores in 10 states from California to New England, revenues of $500 million, and net profits double the industry average.

The Whole Foods Market culture is based on decentralized teamwork. Each store is an autonomous profit center made up of an average of 10 self-directed teams—grocery, produce, and so forth. Teams—and only teams—have the power to approve new hires for full-time jobs. Store leaders screen candidates and recommend them for a job on a specific team, but it takes a two-thirds vote of the team to approve the hire. Teams set high standards and they routinely reject candidates.

Company leaders believe the first prerequisite of teamwork is trust. Trust starts with the hiring vote. In addition, Whole Foods Market supports teamwork with wide-open information on financial and operational systems. Sensitive figures on store sales, team sales, profit margins, and even yearly salaries and bonuses are available to any employee. Executive salaries are limited to no more than eight times the average wage. According to CEO John Mackey, open information keeps everyone "aligned to the vision of shared fate. . . . If you're trying to create a high-trust organization, an organization where people are all-for-one and one-for-all, you can't have secrets."[13]

At Whole Foods Market, Eastman Chemical, and other companies, the development of a smoothly functioning team-based organization requires a significantly different approach to leadership than that used in traditional hierarchical organizations. In the following section, we explore the challenges facing team leaders.

Team Leadership

There are two key aspects of team leadership. First are the personal qualities team leaders need. Second is how leaders use team characteristics and processes to guide team effectiveness.

The Team Leader's Personal Role

Successful teams begin with confident and effective team leaders. However, leading a team requires a shift in mind-set and behavior for those who are accustomed to working in traditional organizations where managers make the decisions. Most people can learn the new skills and qualities needed for team leadership, but it is not always easy. To be effective team leaders, people have to be willing to change themselves, to step outside their comfort zone and let go of many of the assumptions that have guided their behavior in the past. Here we will discuss five changes leaders can make to develop a foundation for effective team leadership.

Learn to relax and admit your ignorance. Team leaders don't have to know everything, and they can't always be in control. To be effective, team leaders let go of two counterproductive beliefs that are a legacy of the command-and-control system:

- If you don't know, don't ask.

- Don't look vulnerable.

Effective team leaders *do* ask—they aren't afraid to show that they don't know everything and they openly admit their mistakes as well as their fears. Although it is hard for many traditional managers to believe, admitting and learning from mistakes earns the respect of team members faster than almost any other behavior.[14] Being open and vulnerable also serves to build trust and improve team relationships.

In many cases, team leaders don't fully understand their teammates' jobs. For example, Eric Doremus spent seven years in marketing at Honeywell before being asked to lead a team of engineers developing data storage systems for Northrop Grumman's B2 bomber. He knew he would never have the technical skills of the engineers on the team, so he had to determine how he could make a contribution. "My most important task," he says, "was not figuring out everybody's job. It was to help this team feel as if they owned the project by getting them whatever information, financial or otherwise, they needed. I knew that if we could all charge up the hill together, we would be successful." Doremus was right, and his leadership helped the team meet its goal and deliver the new system right on time.[15] For traditional managers who have spent years pretending they have all the answers, hiding their mistakes, and feeling in control, the move to team leader can be frightening. The first step to becoming effective in the new role is to let go and relax. Then, leaders can determine their own strengths and how those strenghts can benefit the team.

Take care of team members. The leader sets the tone for how team members treat one another and their customers. Rather than always thinking about oneself and how to get the next promotion or salary increase, effective team leaders spend their time taking care of team members. Most team members share the critically important needs for recognition and support.[16] Leaders frequently overlook how important it is for people to feel that their contribution is valued, and they may especially forget to acknowledge the contributions of lower level support staff. One woman who has held the same secretarial position for many years attributes her high enthusiasm to her team leader: "For the last several years, our team of four has reported to him. At the end of each day—no matter how hectic or trying things have been—he comes by each of our desks and says, 'Thank you for another good day.'"[17]

Team members also need to feel that their leader will go to the wall for them and back them up. Top executives expect the team leader to represent the organization's needs to the team. However, the leader is also responsible for representing the team's needs to the organization, getting the team what it needs to effectively do the job, and being a champion for the team. Leaders take the heat so team members don't have to.

Communicate. Good communication skills are essential for team leadership—but this doesn't mean just learning how to express oneself clearly. It means, first and foremost, learning to listen. Effective team leaders ask more questions than they answer. By asking the right questions, leaders help team members solve problems and make decisions. In addition, leaders help team members focus on the issues, encourage balanced participation in team meetings, summarize differences and agreements, and brainstorm alternative ideas, all of which require careful listening.[18]

Learn to truly share power. Team leaders embrace the concept of teamwork in deeds as well as words. This means sharing power, information, and responsibility. It requires leaders to have faith that team members will make the best decisions, even though those decisions might not be the ones the leader would have made. It is not always easy for a leader to let go and trust the team, as the leader of a sales team discovered. Having received a limited number of much-coveted tickets to a golf outing, he turned them over to the team, with the suggestion that they give one of the tickets to a manager from another department. When the team decided to give the tickets to exceptionally hardworking team members instead, the leader exploded. After he saw and admitted his mistake, and openly discussed it with the team, the sales team pulled together again.[19]

Effective team leaders recognize that it is example, not command, that holds a team together. They learn that helping team members be happier and more productive means thinking less about what they can do and more about what they can stop doing.[20]

Recognize the importance of shared purpose and values. Building a team means creating a community united by shared values and commitment. It is at heart a spiritual undertaking.[21] To promote teamwork, leaders use ritual, stories, ceremonies, and other symbolism to create meaning for team members and give them a sense of belonging to something important. The importance of vision and of shaping organizational culture and values was discussed in Chapters 5 and 7, and these issues strongly apply to team leadership. To create a team—a community of equals—the leader sublimates his own ego and helps others do so. Phil Jackson understood this aspect of team leadership when he took over as head coach of the Chicago Bulls, as described in the Cutting Edge box. Team leaders are responsible for facilitating a team vision and culture that works within and becomes a part of the larger organizational culture. Teams are successful only if they serve the organization's needs. In addition to developing personal qualities, team leaders work to ensure that the team's efforts benefit the organization.

Guiding Team Effectiveness

A number of factors are associated with workteam effectiveness, as illustrated in Exhibit 10.3. **Team effectiveness** can be defined as achieving four performance outcomes—innovation/adaptation, efficiency, quality, and employee satisfaction.[22] Innovation/adaptation means the degree to which teams impact the organization's abil-

ON THE CUTTING EDGE

The Chicago Bulls

In the ego-driven world of professional sports, Phil Jackson seems almost without ego. When Jackson was named head coach of the Chicago Bulls in 1989, he wanted to weave together his two greatest passions—basketball and spiritual exploration. His leadership approach, based on Native American and Eastern thought, stresses awareness, compassion, and the importance of selfless team play to achieve victory. He teaches his players to let the 'me' become the servant of the 'we.' As Jackson puts it, "I knew the only way to win consistently was to give everybody—from the starters to the number 12 player on the bench—a vital role on the team and inspire them to be acutely aware of what was happening, even when the spotlight was on somebody else."

Jackson's first challenge was to win Michael Jordan over to the vision of selfless team play. Rather than trying to coax his star player to produce more, the way most coaches do, Jackson was asking his star to produce less, to take fewer shots and give up the ball more, to sublimate his own ego and forego some individual accomplishments for the sake of teamwork. Jordan's response to this request—showing more concern for the team than for his own personal glory—demonstrated why he was the team's informal leader.

Unlike many business leaders who approach building a team as an experiment in social engineering, Jackson recognizes that the essence of teamwork is interconnectedness and selflessness in action. He wants his team members to feel intimately connected to one another and to feel that they are engaged in something sacred. "People need to be able to share a certain amount of 'heart space' in their work world," he says. Jackson refers to the Bulls' team room in the Berto Center in Deerfield, Illinois, as "the room where the spirit of the team takes form."

By focusing on the spirit of the team rather than on individual players, Jackson cultivates everyone's leadership abilities and gives everyone the freedom to realize their full potential.

SOURCE: Brian S. Moskal, "Running with the Bulls," *IW*, January 8, 1996, 26–34.

ity to rapidly respond to environmental needs and changes. Efficiency pertains to whether the team helps the organization attain goals using fewer resources. Quality refers to achieving fewer defects and exceeding customer expectations. Satisfaction pertains to the team's ability to maintain employee commitment and enthusiasm by meeting the personal needs of its members.

Performance is influenced by team characteristics, including the type of team (functional, cross-functional, or self-directed), the size of the team, and the degree of team interdependence. These characteristics influence team dynamics, which in turn affect performance outcomes. Team leaders should understand and handle the stages of team development, cultural norms and values, and team cohesiveness and conflict. Performance outcomes are influenced by the ability of leaders to guide teams through these processes in a positive manner.

Team leaders influence the factors described in Exhibit 10.3. We have already discussed the types of teams and personal qualities needed for team leadership. In the following sections, we will examine size and interdependence of teams and internal team dynamics.

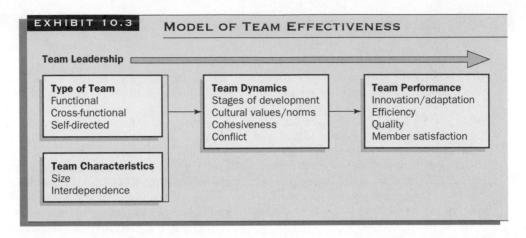

EXHIBIT 10.3 MODEL OF TEAM EFFECTIVENESS

Team Leadership →

Type of Team
Functional
Cross-functional
Self-directed

Team Characteristics
Size
Interdependence

Team Dynamics
Stages of development
Cultural values/norms
Cohesiveness
Conflict

Team Performance
Innovation/adaptation
Efficiency
Quality
Member satisfaction

Understanding Team Characteristics

Teams in organizations have certain characteristics that are important to team dynamics and performance. Two characteristics of particular concern to leaders are team size and interdependence.

Size

The ideal size of workteams is thought to be seven, although variations from 5 to 12 are associated with high performance. These teams are large enough to take advantage of diverse skills, yet small enough to permit members to feel an intimate part of a community. Even teams of much greater size can be effective, and information technology has contributed to the ability of larger teams to maintain close contact, interact regularly, and share information. In general, however, as a team increases in size it becomes harder for each member to interact with and influence the others.

A summary of research on size suggests that small teams show more agreement, ask more questions, and exchange more opinions. Members want to get along with one another. Small teams report more satisfaction and enter into more personal discussions, and members feel a greater sense of cohesiveness and belonging. Large teams (generally defined as 12 or more) tend to have more disagreements and differences of opinion. Subgroups often form and conflicts among them may occur. Demands on leaders are greater in large teams because there is less member participation. Large teams also tend to be less friendly and members do not feel that they are part of a cohesive community.[23] As a general rule, it is more difficult to satisfy members' needs in large teams, forcing leaders to work harder to keep members focused and committed to team goals.

Interdependence

Interdependence means the extent to which team members depend on each other for information, resources, or ideas to accomplish their tasks. Tasks such as performing surgery or directing military operations, for example, require a high degree of interaction and exchange, whereas tasks such as assembly-line manufacturing require very little.[24]

Three types of interdependence can affect teams: pooled, sequential, and reciprocal.[25]

In **pooled interdependence,** the lowest form of interdependence, members are fairly independent of one another in completing their work, participating *on* a team, but not *as* a team.[26] They may share a machine or a common secretary, but most of their work is done independently. An example might be a sales team, with each salesperson responsible for his or her own sales area and customers, but sharing the same appointment secretary. Salespersons need not interact to accomplish their work and little day-to-day coordination is needed.[27]

Sequential interdependence is a serial form wherein the output of one team member becomes the input to another team member. One member must perform well in order for the next member to perform well, and so on. Because team members have to exchange information and resources and rely upon one another, this is a higher level of interdependence. An example might be an engine assembly team in an automobile plant. Each team member performs a separate task, but his work depends on the satisfactory completion of work by other team members. Regular communication and coordination is required to keep work running smoothly.

The highest level of interdependence, **reciprocal interdependence,** exists when team members influence and affect one another in reciprocal fashion. The output of team member A is the input to team member B, and the output of team member B is the input back again to team member A. Reciprocal interdependence characterizes most teams performing knowledge-based work. Writing a technical manual, for example, rarely moves forward in a logical, step-by-step fashion. It is more like "an open-ended series of to-and-fro collaborations, iterations, and reiterations" among team members.[28] The emergency trauma team at Massachusetts General Hospital mentioned earlier is another good example of reciprocal interdependence. Team members provide a variety of coordinated services in combination to a patient. Intense coordination is needed and team members are expected to "cover" their teammates, adjusting to each individual's strengths and weaknesses and to the changing demands of the specific problem at hand. On reciprocal teams, each individual member makes a contribution, but only the team as a whole "performs."[29]

According to a study of athletic teams, baseball, football, and basketball have differences that clearly illustrate these three levels of interdependence.

LEADERSHIP SPOTLIGHT　　　**ATHLETIC TEAM INTERDEPENDENCE**

Baseball, football, and basketball differ significantly in the degree of interdependence among team players. Baseball is low in interdependence, football is medium, and basketball is high.

An old baseball saying is, "Up at bat, you're totally alone." In baseball, interdependence among team players is low and can be defined as pooled. Each member acts independently, taking a turn at bat and playing his or her own position. When interaction does occur, it is only between two or three players, as in a double play. Players often practice and develop their skills individually and each strives to be successful as an individual. As Pete Rose put it, "Baseball is a team game, but nine men who reach their individual goals make a nice team."

In football, interdependence tends to be sequential. The line first blocks the opponents to enable the backs to run or pass. Plays are performed sequentially from first down to fourth down. Each player has an assignment that fits together with the assignments of other team members, and the various assignments are coordinated to achieve victory.

Basketball represents the highest level of interdependence and tends to be reciprocal. The game is free flowing, and the division of labor is less precise than in other sports. Each player is involved in both offense and defense. The ball flows back and forth among players, and teammates must learn to adapt to the flow of the game and to one another as events unfold. Phil Jackson of the Chicago Bulls says each game of basketball is like a riddle and the players in the thick of the action are the ones who have to solve it.

Interdependence among players is a primary difference among these three sports. Baseball is organized around an autonomous individual, football around groups that are sequentially interdependent, and basketball around the free flow of reciprocal players.[30]

Leaders are responsible for facilitating the degree of coordination and communication needed among team members, depending on the level of team interdependence. True team leadership is most important when interdependence is high. Studies have found that empowering the team to make decisions and take action is especially important to high performance when team interdependence is high. However, for teams with low interdependence, traditional leadership, individual rewards, and granting authority and power to individuals rather than the team may be appropriate.[31]

Leading Team Dynamics

In this section, we will discuss team dynamics and interactions that change over time and can be influenced by team leaders. These include the stages of team development, culture, and cohesiveness. Team conflict will be discussed in the next section.

Team Development

After a team has been created, it goes through distinct stages of development.[32] Effective team leaders realize that new teams are different from mature teams. If you have participated in teams to do class assignments, you probably noticed that the team changed over time. In the beginning, members have to get to know one another, establish some order, divide responsibilities, and clarify tasks. These activities help members become part of a smoothly functioning team. The challenge for

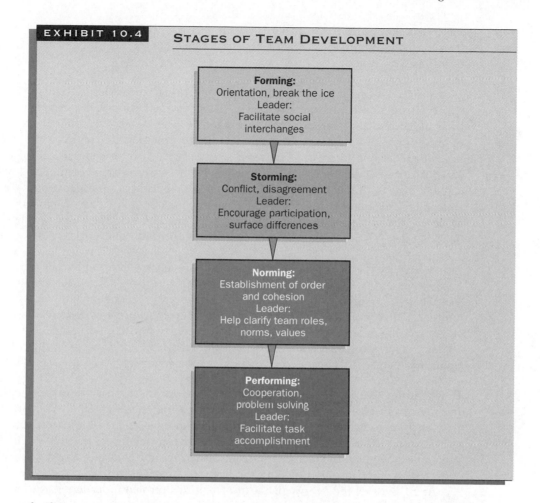

EXHIBIT 10.4 **STAGES OF TEAM DEVELOPMENT**

Forming:
Orientation, break the ice
Leader:
Facilitate social
interchanges

Storming:
Conflict, disagreement
Leader:
Encourage participation,
surface differences

Norming:
Establishment of order
and cohesion
Leader:
Help clarify team roles,
norms, values

Performing:
Cooperation,
problem solving
Leader:
Facilitate task
accomplishment

leaders is to recognize the stages of development and help teams move through them successfully.

Research suggests that teams develop over several stages. One model describing these stages is shown in Exhibit 10.4. These four stages typically occur in sequence, although there can be overlap. Each stage confronts team members and leaders with unique problems and challenges.

Forming The **forming** stage of development is a period of orientation and getting acquainted. Team members find out what behavior is acceptable to others, explore friendship possibilities, and determine task orientation. Uncertainty is high because no one knows what the ground rules are or what is expected of them. Members will usually accept whatever power or authority is offered by either formal or informal leaders. The leader's challenge at this stage of development is to facilitate communication and interaction among team members to help them get acquainted and establish guidelines for how the team will work together. It is important at this stage that the leader try to make everyone feel comfortable and like a part of the team. Leaders can draw out shy or quiet team members to help them establish relationships with others.

Storming   During the **storming** stage, individual personalities emerge more clearly. People become more assertive in clarifying their roles. This stage is marked by conflict and disagreement. Team members may disagree over their perceptions of the team's mission or goals. They may jockey for position or form subgroups based on common interests. The team is characterized by a general lack of unity and cohesiveness. It is essential that teams move beyond this stage or they will never achieve high performance. The leader's role is to encourage participation by each team member and help them find their common vision and values. Members need to debate ideas, surface conflicts, disagree with one another, and work through the uncertainties and conflicting perceptions about team tasks and goals.

Norming   At the **norming** stage, conflict has been resolved and team unity and harmony emerge. Consensus develops as to who the natural team leaders are and members' roles are clear. Team members come to understand and accept one another. Differences are resolved and members develop a sense of cohesiveness. This stage typically is of short duration and moves quickly into the next stage. The team leader should emphasize openness within the team and continue to facilitate communication and clarify team roles, values, and expectations.

Performing   During the **performing** stage, the major emphasis is on accomplishing the team's goals. Members are committed to the team's mission. They interact frequently, coordinate their actions, and handle disagreements in a mature, productive manner. Team members confront and resolve problems in the interest of task accomplishment. At this stage, the team leader should concentrate on facilitating high task performance and helping the team self-manage to reach its goals.

At BP Norge, the Norwegian arm of British Petroleum, leaders had to understand the stages of team development in order to defuse negative employee reactions to the company's transition to self-directed teams.

BP Norge wanted to dismantle its hierarchy and switch to a team-based organization in order to increase flexibility, speed up decision making, reduce costs and cycle time, and increase innovation. However, early efforts to introduce self-directed teams at the company failed, and employees were left disillusioned and skeptical. Leaders needed a way to work through resistance and negativity barriers, reenergize the workforce, and help the existing work groups develop into true self-directed teams.

The company's solution was to hold a series of workshops and meetings to discuss the self-directed team concept and educate employees about the stages of team development. At BP Norge, the four stages of team development were called denial, resistance, exploration, and commitment. In the *denial* stage (similar to forming), employees idealized the past and resisted mutual accountability. Relationships were characterized by politeness as people explored what was expected of them in their new roles. The *resistance* stage (storming) was marked by anxiety, anger, depression, apathy, and conflict. BP Norge's *exploration* stage straddled the storming and the norming stages in our model. There was still some confusion, but teams were letting go of old values and ideas and incorporating new ones. The final stage, *commitment*, is analogous to the performing stage in our model. The focus here was on a common purpose and approach and the complete movement from "I" to "we." Team members accepted the concept of mutual responsibility and accountability and focused on performance and task accomplishment.

Because team leaders understood the stages of team development, they were able to recognize what was happening as normal and take a nonjudgmental "this is where we are in the process" attitude rather than a "this will never work" attitude. Thus, leaders guided the development of teams as a natural process that involved self-discovery, exploration of new ideas, and the opportunity to grow and develop.[33]

Team Culture

Another important aspect of team dynamics is the development of team values and norms. A team **norm** is a standard of conduct that is shared by team members and guides their behavior.[34] Leaders shape team cultural values and norms to define the boundaries of acceptable behavior and provide a frame of reference as to what is right or wrong. The Living Leadership box describes the norms that developed for a project team at Cambridge Technology Partners.

Cultural values and norms begin to develop in the first interactions among members of a new team.[35] Leaders facilitate values and norms in three primary ways: critical events, primacy, and symbols and explicit statements.

Critical Events Norms and values often arise around the way in which members respond to critical events.[36] One example occurred when Arthur Schlesinger, who had serious reservations about the Bay of Pigs invasion, was pressured by Attorney General Robert Kennedy not to raise his objections to President Kennedy. This critical incident helped create a norm in which team members refrained from expressing disagreement with the president. Any critical incident can lead to the creation of norms, values, and beliefs that guide team members' behavior.

Primacy Primacy means that the first behaviors that occur in a team often set a precedent for later team expectations. The first team meeting at a paper manufacturing plant set an unproductive norm regarding employee participation. The team leader raised an issue and turned it over to the team for discussion. As members offered solutions and alternatives, the leader responded to each with a friendly, "Yes, but what if . . ." response. As team members began trying to guess what solution the leader wanted, the leader began asking more and more leading questions to help them arrive at that solution. The pattern became so ingrained that team members dubbed staff meetings the "Guess What I Think" game.[37]

LIVING LEADERSHIP

Cultural Norms of Fast Teams

Project teams at Cambridge Technology Partners have to work fast, but few have ever worked as fast as the team that recently introduced a new customer-management application for AT&T. Team leader Tammy Urban says the team values and norms contributed to its ability to bring the project together so quickly. She cites four principles of fast teams.

1. *Let the group make its own rules.* Let everyone have a say in how they're going to work together. As a team, agree on "boundaries," such as what the core working hours will be, times of the day when jokes and playing around are acceptable and times when they're not, etc.
2. *Speak up early and often.* Team members should ask for advice and help when they need it. Urban's team adopted a two minute rule—if someone is stuck on a problem, they shouldn't remain stuck more than two minutes without asking for help from other team members.
3. *Learn as you go.* At the end of each phase of a project, team members should openly and honestly assess what worked and what didn't.
4. *Fast has to be fun.* It's important for team members to invest as much energy in keeping each other pumped up as in pumping out the work. Members of Urban's team went on regular team outings to throw darts or shoot pool. The personal connections outside the workplace helped team members feel more relaxed with one another when things got hectic on the project.

SOURCE: "Four Rules for Fast Teams," in Eric Matson, "Speed Kills the Competition," *Fast Company* (August-September 1996), 84–90, (87).

Symbols and Explicit Statements   Leaders or team members can use symbols as well as explicit statements to instill norms and values, as we discussed in Chapter 7 on organizational culture. At Hewlett-Packard's North American distribution organization, a team led by Mei-Lin Cheng and Julie Anderson used symbolism to instill a team norm to keep trying and learning a little bit every day. A team member suggested that the team's work reminded him of the movie *Groundhog Day*, in which Bill Murray plays a character who relives one day of his life over and over. He had to figure out how to do things right that one day so he can get to the next day of his life. Each time the day began again in the movie, his clock radio played Sonny & Cher's "I Got You Babe." The song became a metaphor for HP's team and leaders started playing it at 8:30 each morning.[38]

Explicit statements are probably the most effective way for leaders to change norms in an established team. When Richard Boyle at Honeywell wanted to develop a more relaxed, casual atmosphere, he wrote a memo called "Loosening Up the Tie." The explicit statement officially relaxed the excessive formality, gradually creating a new norm.

Team Cohesiveness

Team **cohesiveness** is defined as the extent to which members stick together and remain united in the pursuit of a common goal.[39] Members of highly cohesive teams are committed to team goals and activities, feel that they are involved in something significant, and are happy when the team succeeds. Members of less cohesive teams are less concerned about the team's welfare. Cohesiveness is generally considered an attractive feature of teams.

Determinants of Cohesiveness Leaders can use several factors to influence team cohesiveness. One is team *interaction*. The greater the amount of contact between team members and the more time they spend together, the more cohesive the team. Through frequent interaction, members get to know one another and become more devoted to the team. Another factor is *shared mission and goals*. When team members agree on purpose and direction, they will be more cohesive. The most cohesive teams are those that feel they are involved in something immensely relevant and important—that they are embarking on a journey together that will make the world better in some way. An aerospace executive, recalling his participation in an advanced design team, put it this way: "We even walked differently than anybody else. We felt we were way out there, ahead of the whole world."[40] A third factor is *personal attraction* to the team, meaning members find their common ground and have similar attitudes and values and enjoy being together. Members like and respect one another.

The organizational context can also affect team cohesiveness. When a team is in moderate *competition* with other teams, its cohesiveness increases as it strives to win. Finally, *team success* and the favorable evaluation of the team's work by outsiders add to cohesiveness. When a team succeeds and others in the organization recognize this success, members feel good and their commitment to the team will be higher.

Consequences of Team Cohesiveness The consequences of team cohesiveness can be examined according to two categories: morale and performance. As a general rule, employee *morale* is much higher in cohesive teams because of increased communication, a friendly atmosphere, loyalty, and member participation in decisions and activities. High team cohesiveness has almost uniformly positive effects on the satisfaction and morale of team members.[41]

With respect to team *performance*, it seems that cohesiveness and performance are generally positively related, although research results are mixed. Cohesive teams can sometimes unleash enormous amounts of employee energy and creativity. One explanation for this is the research finding that working in a team increases individual motivation and performance. *Social facilitation* refers to the tendency for the presence of other people to enhance an individual's motivation and performance. Simply interacting with others has an energizing effect.[42] In relation to this, one study found that cohesiveness is more closely related to high performance when team interdependence is high, requiring frequent interaction, coordination, and communication, as discussed earlier in this chapter.[43]

Another factor influencing performance is the relationship between teams and top leadership. One study surveyed more than 200 workteams and correlated job performance with cohesiveness.[44] Highly cohesive teams were more productive when team members felt supported by organizational leaders and less productive when they sensed hostility and negativism from leaders. The support of leaders contributes to the development of high performance norms, whereas hostility leads to team norms and goals of low performance. At Southwest Airlines, highly cohesive teams are supported by top leaders.

LEADERSHIP SPOTLIGHT   **SOUTHWEST AIRLINES**

At Southwest Airlines, teamwork is built through the Crew Resource Management (CRM) program, implemented by the aviation industry to reduce air carrier accidents. The program is derided by employees at many airlines as *Cockpit* Resource Management, since the attitude of most airlines is that flight safety is in the hands of the pilot.

Not so at Southwest. The successful airline, under the leadership of Herb Kelleher, focuses on teams, not individuals, as the driving force behind the company. The entire team is responsible for flight safety, from flight attendants and pilots to ground crews and baggage handlers. Training emphasizes communication and mutual understanding of each team member's role in ensuring a safe flight. Each member understands the time constraints, expectations, and particular problems of other workers. For example, dispatchers observe pilots in flight simulation training and pilots learn about the time constraints of baggage handlers.

Southwest's top leadership has demonstrated total commitment to team training and responsibility since the CRM program began in 1985. The combination of team cohesiveness and leadership support has made Southwest's workers the most productive in the industry and the company a benchmark for flight safety.[45]

Handling Team Conflict

The final characteristic of team dynamics is team conflict. Of all the skills needed for effective team leadership, none is more important than handling the conflicts that inevitably arise among members. Conflict can arise between members of a team or between one team and another.

Conflict refers to hostile or antagonistic interaction in which one party attempts to thwart the intentions or goals of another. Conflict is natural and occurs in all teams and organizations. However, too much conflict can be destructive, tear relationships apart, and interfere with the healthy exchange of ideas and information needed for team development and cohesiveness.[46]

Causes of Conflict

Leaders can be aware of several factors that cause conflict among individuals or teams. Whenever teams compete for scarce resources, such as money, information, or supplies, conflict is almost inevitable. Conflicts also emerge when task responsibilities are unclear. People may disagree about who has responsibility for specific tasks or who has a claim on resources, and leaders help members reach agreement. Another rea-

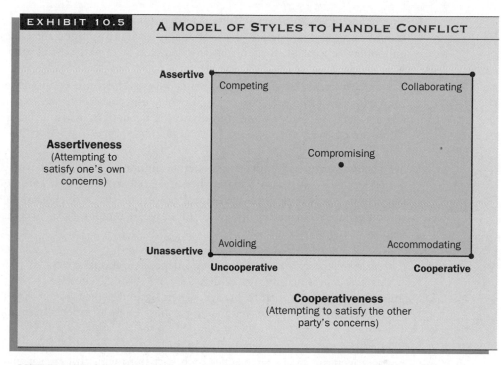

EXHIBIT 10.5   A MODEL OF STYLES TO HANDLE CONFLICT

Assertive
Competing   Collaborating

Assertiveness
(Attempting to
satisfy one's own
concerns)
                          Compromising

Unassertive
Avoiding   Accommodating
Uncooperative   Cooperative

Cooperativeness
(Attempting to satisfy the other
party's concerns)

SOURCE: Adapted from Kenneth Thomas, "Conflict and Conflict Management," in *Handbook of Industrial and Organizational Behavior*, ed. M.D. Dunnette (New York: John Wiley, 1976), 900. Used by permission of Marvin D. Dunnette.

son for conflict is simply because individuals or teams are pursuing conflicting goals. For example, individual salespeople's targets may put them in conflict with one another and with the sales manager. Finally, it sometimes happens that two people simply do not get along with one another and will never see eye to eye on any issue. Personality clashes are caused by basic differences in personality, values, and attitudes. When Reed Breland became a team facilitator at Hewlett-Packard's financial services center in Colorado Springs, he noticed immediately that one team was in constant turmoil. "It was a classic case of personality conflict," he says. "When two people on an eight-person team don't get along, believe me, it's disruptive." After trying for nine months to work out the conflicts, Breland reassigned team members, who did just fine in other assignments where they did not interact.[47]

Styles to Handle Conflict

Teams as well as individuals develop specific styles for dealing with conflict, based on the desire to satisfy their own concerns versus the other party's concerns. Exhibit 10.5 describes five styles of handling conflict. How an individual approaches conflict is measured along two dimensions: *assertiveness* versus *cooperation*. Effective leaders and team members vary their style to fit a specific situation, as each style is appropriate in certain cases.[48]

1. The *competing style*, which reflects assertiveness to get one's own way, should be used when quick, decisive action is vital on important issues or unpopular actions, such as during emergencies or urgent cost cutting.

2. The *avoiding style*, which reflects neither assertiveness nor cooperativeness, is appropriate when an issue is trivial, when there is no chance of winning, when a delay to gather more information is needed, or when a disruption would be costly.

3. The *compromising style* reflects a moderate amount of both assertiveness and cooperativeness. It is appropriate when the goals on both sides are equally important, when opponents have equal power and both sides want to split the difference, or when people need to arrive at temporary or expedient solutions under time pressure.

4. The *accommodating style* reflects a high degree of cooperativeness, which works best when people realize that they are wrong, when an issue is more important to others than to oneself, when building social credits for use in later discussions, or when maintaining cohesiveness is especially important.

5. The *collaborating style* reflects both a high degree of assertiveness and of cooperativeness. This style enables both parties to win, although it may require substantial dialogue and negotiation. The collaborating style is important when both sets of concerns are too important to be compromised, when insights from different people need to be merged into an overall solution, or when the commitment of both sides is needed for a consensus.

Other Approaches

The various styles of handling conflict discussed above are especially effective for an individual to use when he or she disagrees with another. But what can a team leader do when conflict erupts among others? Research suggests several techniques that help resolve conflicts among people or teams.

Vision A compelling vision can pull people together. A vision is for the whole team and cannot be attained by one person. Its achievement requires the cooperation of conflicting parties. To the extent that leaders can focus on a larger team or organizational vision, conflict will decrease because the people involved see the big picture and realize they must work together to achieve it.

Bargaining/Negotiating Bargaining and negotiating mean that the parties engage one another in an attempt to systematically reach a solution. They attempt logical problem-solving to identify and correct the conflict. This approach works well if the individuals can set aside personal animosities and deal with conflict in a businesslike way.

Mediation   Using a third party to settle a dispute involves mediation. A mediator could be a supervisor, another team leader, or someone from the human resources department. The mediator can discuss the conflict with each party and work toward a solution. If a solution satisfactory to all parties cannot be reached, the parties may be willing to turn the conflict over to the mediator and abide by his or her solution.

Facilitating Communication   One of the most effective ways to reduce conflict is to help conflicting parties communicate openly and honestly. As conflicting parties exchange information and learn more about one another, suspicions diminish and teamwork becomes possible. A particularly promising avenue for reducing conflict is through dialogue, as discussed in Chapter 6. Dialogue asks that participants suspend their attachments to their own viewpoint so that a deeper level of listening, synthesis, and meaning can evolve from the interaction. Individual differences are acknowledged and respected, but rather than trying to figure out who is right or wrong, the parties search for a joint perspective.

Each of these approaches can be helpful in resolving conflicts between individuals or teams. Effective leaders use a combination of these on a regular basis—such as articulating a larger vision and continuously facilitating communication—to keep conflict at a minimum while the team moves forward.

Leading Global Teams

The reality of today's world has led many organizations to establish global workteams. **Global teams,** also called *transnational teams*, are workteams made up of members whose activities span multiple countries. For example, Heineken formed a 13-member team representing five countries to explore the question of how the company's production facilities throughout Europe could best be configured to cope with new challenges.[49]

Information technology is a key component in global teams. With what economist William Knoke, author of *Bold New World*, calls "the technology of placelessness," it no longer matters whether team members are down the hall or across the hemisphere. For example, lengthy phone calls, frequent e-mail, and weekly video conferences provided the lifeline between global team members creating Texas Instruments C82 digital signal processor.[50]

Global teams bring new challenges to the concept of teamwork. Leaders of global teams have to coordinate across time, distance, and culture. In some cases, they lead teams in which members speak different languages, use different technologies, and have different cultural beliefs about authority, time, and decision making. Global team leaders have to be flexible and culturally astute, able to deal with differences without compromising any team member's integrity.[51] One model for global team effectiveness, called the GRIP model, suggests that leaders focus on developing common understanding in four critical areas: goals, relationships, information, and work processes, thus helping the team "get a grip" on its collaborative work at a high level.[52] The need for and use of global teams is likely to grow. Leaders can learn to blend diverse backgrounds and interests into a teamwork culture focused on serving the organization's international goals.

Summary and Interpretation

The important point of this chapter is that teams are a reality in most organizations, and leaders are called upon to facilitate teams rather than manage direct report subordinates. Functional teams typically are part of the traditional organization structure. Cross-functional teams, including problem-solving teams, process-improvement teams, and special purpose teams, often represent an organization's first move toward greater team participation. Cross-functional teams may evolve into self-directed teams, which are member- rather than leader-centered and directed.

Successful teams begin with effective team leaders. People typically have to change themselves to become effective team leaders. Five principles that provide a foundation for team leadership are: relax and admit mistakes; take care of team members; communicate; truly share power; and recognize the shared-values nature of teamwork. Several other factors are associated with team effectiveness, such as the type of team, size, and interdependence, as well as team cohesiveness, culture, conflict, and stages of development.

All teams experience some conflict because of scarce resources, ambiguous responsibilities, faulty communication, goal conflicts, power and status differences, or personality clashes. Handling team conflict is one of the most important skills of team leadership. Leaders face even greater challenges with global teams because leaders have to coordinate across time, distance, and culture. One model suggests that leaders focus on four critical areas in leading global teams: goals, relationships, information, and work processes. The need for and use of global teams will likely grow in the coming years.

Key Terms

team	pooled interdependence	performing
functional team	sequential interdependence	norm
cross-functional team	reciprocal interdependence	cohesiveness
self-directed team	forming	conflict
team effectiveness	storming	global team
interdependence	norming	

Discussion Questions

1. What is the difference between a "team" and a "group"? Describe personal experience with each.

2. What is the difference between a cross-functional team and a self-directed team?

3. Why might a person need to go through significant personal changes to be an effective team leader? What are some of the changes required?

4. Describe the three levels of interdependence. Is team leadership more difficult under low or high interdependence? Discuss.

5. What are the stages of team development? How can a team leader best facilitate the team at each stage?

6. Think about a team or group of which you have been a member, either at work or at your university. Can you identify some of the team's cultural norms and values?

7. Discuss the relationship between team cohesiveness and performance.

8. What style of handling conflict do you typically use? Can you think of instances where a different style might have been more productive?

Leadership Development: Personal Feedback

Team Cohesiveness

Part I

Think about a student group with which you worked over several weeks. Answer the questions below as they pertain to the functioning of that group.

Disagree Strongly			**Agree Strongly**	
1	2	3	4	5

1. Group meetings were held regularly and everyone attended.
   1   2   3   4   5

2. We talked about and shared the same goals for group work and grade.
   1   2   3   4   5

3. We spent most of our meeting time talking business, but discussions were open-ended and active.
   1   2   3   4   5

4. We talked through any conflicts and disagreements until they were resolved.
   1   2   3   4   5

5. Group members listened carefully to one another.
   1   2   3   4   5

6. We really trusted each other, speaking personally about what we really felt.
   1   2   3   4   5

7. Leadership roles were rotated and shared, with people taking initiative at appropriate times for the good of the group.
   1   2   3   4   5

8. Each member found a way to contribute to the final work product.
   1   2   3   4   5

9. I was really satisfied being a member of the group.
   1   2   3   4   5

10. We freely gave each other credit for jobs well done.
    1   2   3   4   5

11. Group members gave and received feedback to help the group do better.
    1   2   3   4   5

12. We held each other accountable; each member was accountable to the group.
    1   2   3   4   5

13. Group members really liked and respected each other.
    1   2   3   4   5

Total Score _____

Part II

Reread the questions, this time placing a check mark by each one for which you consciously contributed to improving the group dynamic. Give yourself one point for each check mark.

Total Score _____

Scoring and Interpretation

The questions here are about team cohesiveness. For Part I, if you scored 52 or greater, your group experienced authentic teamwork. Congratulations. If you scored between 39 and 51, there was a positive group identity that might have been developed even further. If you scored between 26 and 38, group identity was weak and probably not very satisfying. If you scored below 26, it was hardly a group at all, resembling more a loose collection of individuals.

For Part II, if you scored 3 or fewer, you weren't taking a strong leadership role in building team cohesiveness. If you scored 6 or higher, you were playing a significant role in building cohesiveness.

Remember, teamwork doesn't happen by itself. Members like you have to understand what a team is and then work to make it happen. What can you do to make a student group more like a team? Do you have the courage to take the initiative?

Leadership Development: Case for Analysis

Valena Scientific Corporation

Valena Scientific Corporation (VSC) is a large manufacturer of health care products. The health care market includes hospitals, clinical laboratories, universities, and industries. Clinical laboratories represent 52 percent of VSC's sales. Laboratories are located in hospitals and diagnostic centers where blood tests and urine analyses are performed for physicians. Equipment sold to laboratories can range from a five-cent test tube to a $195,000 blood analyzer.

By 1980, the industry experienced a move into genetic engineering. Companies such as Genentech Corporation and Cetus Scientific Laboratories were created and staffed with university microbiologists. These companies were designed to exploit the commercial potential for gene splicing.

Senior executives at VSC saw the trend developing and decided to create a Biotech Research Program. Skilled microbiologists were scarce, so the program was staffed with only nine scientists. Three scientists were skilled in gene splicing, three in recombination, and three in fermentation. The specialties reflected the larger departments to which they were assigned. However, they were expected to work as a team on this program. Twenty technicians were also assigned to the program to help the scientists.

Senior management believed that the biotech research program could be self-managed. For the first 18 months of operation, everything went well. Informal leaders emerged among the scientists in gene splicing, recombination, and fermentation. These three informal leaders coordinated the work of the three groups, which tended to stay separate. For example, the work typically started in the gene-splicing group, followed by work in recombination, and then in fermentation. Fermentation was used to breed the bacteria created by the other two groups in sufficient numbers to enable mass production.

During the summer of 1983, the biotech research program was given a special project. Hoffman-LaRoche was developing leukocyte interferon to use as a treatment against cancer. VSC contracted with Hoffman-LaRoche to develop a technique for large-scale interferon production. VSC had only six months to come up with a production technology. Scientists in each of the subgroups remained in their own geographical confines and began immediately to test ideas relevant to their specialty. In September, the informal group leaders met and discovered that each group had taken a different research direction. Each of the subgroups believed their direction was best and the informal leaders argued vehemently for their positions, rather than change to another direction. Future meetings were conflict-laden and did not resolve the issues. As management became aware of the crisis, they decided to appoint a formal leader to the program.

On November 15, a Stanford professor with extensive research experience in recombinant DNA technology was hired. His title was Chief Biologist for the Biotech Research Program, and all project members reported to him for the duration of the interferon project.

The chief biologist immediately took the nine scientists on a two-day retreat. He assigned them to three tables for discussions, with a member from each subgroup at each table, so they had to talk across their traditional boundaries. He led the discussion of their common ground as scientists, and of their hopes and vision for this project. After they developed a shared vision, the group turned to scientific issues and in mixed groups discussed the ideas that the VSC subgroups had developed. Gradually, one approach seemed to have more likelihood of success than the others. A consensus emerged, and the chief biologist adopted the basic approach that would be taken in the interferon project. Upon their return to VSC, the technicians were brought in and the scientists explained the approach to them. At this point, each subgroup was assigned a set of instructions within the overall research plan. Firm deadlines were established based upon group interdependence. Weekly progress reports to the chief biologist were required from each group leader.

Dramatic changes in the behavior of the scientists were observed after the two-day retreat. Communication among groups became more common. Problems discovered by one group were communicated to other groups so that effort was not expended needlessly. Subgroup leaders coordinated many problems among themselves. Lunch and coffee gatherings that included several members of the subgroups began to appear. Group leaders and members often had daily discussions and cooperated on research requirements. Enthusiasm for the department and the interferon project was high, and cohesion seemed especially strong.

SOURCE: Adapted from *Organization Theory and Design*, 5th ed. by Richard Daft, 474–477. Copyright 1995 West Publishing. Used by permission of South-Western College Publishing, a division of International Thomson Publishing Inc., Cincinnati, Ohio 45227.

Questions

1. Was the research program a group or team? What type of team were they (functional, cross-functional, self-directed)? Explain.

2. Did the interdependence among the subgroups change with the interferon project? What were the group norms before and after the retreat?

3. What factors account for the change in cohesiveness after the chief biologist took over?

References

[1]Mark A. Abramson, "First Teams," *Government Executive*, May 1996, 53–58.

[2]Susan G. Cohen, Gerald E. Ledford, Jr., and Gretchen M. Spreitzer, "A Predictive Model of Self-Managing Work Team Effectiveness," *Human Relations* 49, No. 5 (1996), 643–676; "Training in the 1990s," *The Wall Street Journal*, March 1, 1990, B1; Patricia Booth, "Embracing the Team Concept," *Canadian Business Review* (Autumn 1994), 10–13.

[3]Jeffrey Pfeffer, "Producing Sustainable Competitive Advantage through the Effective Management of People," *Academy of Management Executive* 9, No. 1 (1995), 55–72.

[4]Wendy Zellner, "No More Same Ol'-Same Ol'," *Business Week*, October 17, 1994, 95–96; Michael Barrier, "However You Slice It," *Nation's Business*, June 1996, 16; Kenneth Labich, "Elite Teams Get the Job Done," *Fortune*, February 19, 1996, 90–99.

[5]Carl E. Larson and Frank M. J. LaFasto, *Team Work* (Newbury Park, CA: Sage, 1989).

[6]Lee G. Bolman and Terrence E. Deal, "What Makes a Team Work?" *Organizational Dynamics*, August 1992, 34–44.

[7]Laton McCartney, "A Team Effort," *IW*, December 18, 1995, 65–72; Sandra N. Phillips, "Team Training Puts Fizz in Coke Plant's Future," *Personnel Journal* (January 1996), 87–92.

[8]Larson and LaFasto, *Team Work*.

[9]Pierre van Amelsvoort and Jos Benders, "Team Time: A Model for Developing Self-Directed Work Teams," *International Journal of Operations and Production Management* 16, No. 2 (1996), 159–170.

[10]Jeanne M. Wilson, Jill George, and Richard S. Wellins, with William C. Byham, *Leadership Trapeze: Strategies for Leadership in Team-Based Organizations* (San Francisco: Jossey-Bass, 1994).

[11]Booth, "Embracing the Team Concept."

[12]John A. Byrne, "The Horizontal Corporation," *Business Week*, December 20, 1993, 76–81.

[13]Charles Fishman, "Whole Foods Is All Teams," *Fast Company*, April/May 1996, 102–109.

[14]Wilson, et. al., *Leadership Trapeze*, 14.

[15]Susan Caminiti, "What Team Leaders Need to Know," *Fortune*, February 20, 1995, 93–100.

[16]Based on Mark Sanborn, *TeamBuilt: Making Teamwork Pay* (New York: MasterMedia Limited, 1992), 99–101.

[17]Sanborn, *TeamBuilt: Making Teamwork Pay*, 100.

[18]Lawrence Holpp, "New Roles for Leaders: An HRD Reporter's Inquiry," *Training & Development*, March 1995, 46–50.

[19]J. Thomas Buck, "The Rocky Road to Team-Based Management," *Training & Development*, April 1995, 35–38; Wilson, et. al., *Leadership Trapeze*, 15–16.

[20]Lee G. Bolman and Terrence E. Deal, "What Makes a Team Work?"; Stratford Sherman, "Secrets of HP's 'Muddled' Team," *Fortune*, March 18, 1996, 116–120.

[21]Based on Bolman and Deal, "What Makes a Team Work?"

[22]Dexter Dunphy and Ben Bryant, "Teams: Panaceas or Prescriptions for Improved Performance," *Human Relations* 49, No. 5 (1996), 677–699; and Cohen, Ledford, and Spreitzer, "A Predictive Model of Self-Managing Work Team Effectiveness."

[23]For research findings on group size, see M. E. Shaw, *Group Dynamics*, 3rd ed. (New York: McGraw-Hill, 1981); G. Manners, "Another Look at Group Size, Group Problem-Solving and Member Consensus," *Academy of Management Journal* 18 (1975), 715–724; and Albert V. Carron and Kevin S. Spink, "The Group Size-Cohesion Relationship in Minimal Groups," *Small Group Research* 26, No. 1 (February 1995), 86–105.

[24]Stanley M. Gully, Dennis J. Devine, and David J. Whitney, "A Meta-Analysis of Cohesion and Performance: Effects of Level of Analysis and Task Interdependence," *Small Group Research* 26, No. 4 (November 1995), 497–520.

[25]James Thompson, *Organizations in Action* (New York: McGraw-Hill, 1967).

[26]Peter F. Drucker, *Managing in a Time of Great Change* (New York: Truman Talley Books/Dutton, 1995), 98.

[27]Ibid.

[28]Thomas A. Stewart, "The Great Conundrum—You vs. the Team," *Fortune*, November 25, 1996, 165–166.

[29]Labich, "Elite Teams"; and Drucker, *Managing in a Time of Great Change*, 101.

[30]Robert W. Keidel, "Team Sports Models as a Generic Organizational Framework," *Human Relations* 40 (1987), 591–612; Robert W. Keidel, "Baseball, Football, and Basketball: Models for Business, *Organizational Dynamics* (Winter 1984), 5–18; Richard L. Daft and Richard M. Steers, *Organizations: A Micro-Macro Approach* (Glenview, IL: Scott, Foresman, 1986); and Peter M. Drucker, *Managing in a Time of Great Change*, 97–102.

[31]Liden, Wayne, and Bradway, "Connections Make the Difference."

[32]Kenneth G. Koehler, "Effective Team Management," *Small Business Report*, July 19, 1989, 14–16; Connie J.G. Gersick, "Time and Transition in Work Teams: Toward a New Model of Group Development," *Academy of Management Journal* 31 (1988), 9–41; and John Beck and Neil Yeager, "Moving Beyond Myths," *Training & Development*, March 1996, 51–55.

[33]Milan Moravec, Odd Jan Johannessen, and Thor A. Hjelmas, "Thumbs Up for Self-Managed Teams," *Management Review*, July-August 1997, 42–47.

[34]Cohen, Ledford, and Spreitzer, "A Predictive Model of Self-Managing Work Team Effectiveness."

[35]Kenneth Bettenhausen and J. Keith Murnighan, "The Emergence of Norms in Competitive Decision-Making Groups," *Administrative Science Quarterly* 30 (1985), 350–372.

[36]Edgar H. Schein, "Organizational Culture," *American Psychologist* 45, No. 2 (February 1990), 109–119.

[37]Wilson, et. al., *Leadership Trapeze*, 12.

[38]Sherman, "Secrets of HP's 'Muddled' Team."

[39]Carron and Spink, "The Group Size-Cohesion Relationship in Minimal Groups."

[40]Harold J. Leavitt and Jean Lipman-Blumen, "Hot Groups," *Harvard Business Review*, (July-August 1995), 109–116.

[41]Dorwin Cartwright and Alvin Zander, *Group Dynamics: Research and Theory*, 3rd ed. (New York: Harper & Row, 1968); Eliot Aronson, *The Social Animal* (San Francisco: W. H. Freeman, 1976); and Thomas Li-Ping Tang and Amy Beth Crofford, "Self-Managing Work Teams," *Employment Relations Today* (Winter 1995/96), 29–39.

[42]Tang and Crofford, "Self-Managing Work Teams."

[43]Gully, Devine, and Whitney, "A Meta-Analysis of Cohesion and Performance: Effects of Level of Analysis and Task Interdependence."

[44]Stanley E. Seashore, *Group Cohesiveness in the Industrial Work Group* (Ann Arbor, Mich.: Institute for Social Research, 1954).

[45]Connie Bovier, "Teamwork: The Heart of the Airline," *Training*, June 1993, 53–58; and Tang and Crofford, "Self-Managing Work Teams," 34–35.

[46]Kenneth G. Koehler, "Effective Team Management"; and Dean Tjosvold, "Making Conflict Productive," *Personnel Administrator* 29 (June 1984), 121.

[47]Caminiti, "What Team Leaders Need to Know."

[48]This discussion is based on K. W. Thomas, "Towards Multidimensional Values in Teaching: The Example of Conflict Behaviors," *Academy of Management Review* 2 (1977), 487.

[49]Mary O'Hara-Devereaux and Robert Johansen, *Globalwork: Bridging Distance, Culture, and Time* (San Francisco: Jossey-Bass, 1994); Charles C. Snow, Scott A. Snell, Sue Canney Davison, and Donald C. Hambrick, "Use Transnational Teams to Globalize Your Company," *Organizational Dynamics* 24, No. 4 (Spring 1996), 50–67.

[50]James Daly, "Digital Cowboys," *Forbes ASAP*, February 26, 1996, 62.

[51]Sylvia Odenwald, "Global Work Teams," *Training and Development*, February 1996, 54–57.

[52]O'Hara-Devereaux and Johansen, *Globalwork: Bridging Distance, Culture, and Time*, 227–228.

11

Leadership and Multiculturalism

- **Multiculturalism Today**   302

- **Ways Women Lead**   305

- **Global Diversity**   306

- **Challenges Minorities Face**   311

- **Leadership Initiatives Toward Multiculturalism**   314

- **Leadership Solutions**   317

- **Leadership Spotlights:**
  Grace Pastiak   305
  Ralston Purina Company   310
  Leadership Education for Asian Pacifics, Inc.   312
  Denny's   319

- **Leader's Bookshelf:** *Everyday Revolutionaries: Working Women and the Transformation of American Life*   301

- **Leadership Development: Personal Feedback**
  A Passive Bias Quiz   323

- **Leadership Development: Case for Analysis**
  Northern Industries   324

Your Leadership Challenge

After reading this chapter, you should be able to:

- Apply an awareness of the dimensions of diversity and multicultural issues in your everyday life.

- Encourage and support diversity to meet organizational needs.

- Consider the role of cultural values and attitudes in determining how to deal with employees from different cultures or ethnic backgrounds.

- Reduce the difficulties faced by minorities in organizations.

- Break down your personal barriers that may stand in the way of enhancing your level of diversity awareness and appreciation.

At Ford's assembly plant in Avon Lake, Ohio, Deborah S. Kent's vision for her job as plant manager is to treat people the way she wants to be treated. Kent is the first woman—and the only African American woman—to head a vehicle assembly plant for Ford. Her duties include managing two shifts with a total of almost 4,000 workers, overseeing the annual production of 216,035 Ford Econoline vans and 115,184 Mercury Villager and Nissan Quest mini-vans at a pace of up to 56 vehicles an hour on an assembly line that stretches 19.5 miles.

One way top leaders in the U.S. auto industry are working to regain the industry's competitive edge and reputation for quality is by using a more diverse workforce. As aging factory workers retire, companies are recruiting a wider range of workers whose brainpower and diverse ideas give the company an edge in the fierce global market. Kent's leadership style is appropriate for just such an organization. Because she is open to all opinions and accessible to all workers, Kent quickly became an energizing force among both peers and subordinates at the Avon Lake factory. When she talks to people, she says, "Give me some feedback and some eye contact. Don't look away from me and say 'Okay, we have to do this because she says so.' Let's talk about it."

Kent spends a great part of her time walking the assembly line, learning from the workers who do the job every day. As plant manager, she's often called upon to make spur-of-the-moment decisions with millions of dollars weighing in the balance. She relies on her gut instincts, on her 17 years of experience in the auto industry—where she worked her way up through every phase of the job—and on what she learns from workers. As she puts it, "It does no good to have a diverse workforce if you don't listen to their opinions and thoughts. I treat people the way I want to be treated."[1]

Leaders at Ford aren't the only people who recognize the value of diversity. Approximately 18 car companies, especially those from Japan and Germany, have established design centers in Los Angeles because of the area's Anglo-Afro-Latino-Asian ethnic mix. Companies that sell cars all over the world use Los Angeles as a multicultural proving ground.[2]

Multiculturalism is a fact of life for today's organizations. The U.S. population, the workforce, and the customer base are changing dramatically in terms of national origin as well as age, race, gender, sexual orientation, and physical ability. In addition, attitudes toward cultural differences have changed significantly over the past few decades. In the past, the United States was seen as a "melting pot" where people of different national origins, races, ethnicity, and religions came together and blended to resemble one another. Opportunities for advancement in society and in organizations favored people who fit easily into the mainstream culture. Many times immigrants chose desperate measures, such as changing their last names, abandoning their native languages, and sacrificing their own unique cultures. People were willing to assimilate in order to get ahead.

Today, however, the burden of adaptation rests more on the organization than on the individual. People of different races, nationalities, genders, sexual orientations, religions, and so forth, are no longer willing to give up or hide their own values, beliefs, and ways of doing things in order to "fit in." The social landscape of the United States has changed dramatically over the past several decades. This chapter's Leader's Bookshelf examines the role of women in this transformation.

In addition to the increasing heterogeneity in the U.S. population, organizations increasingly operate multinationally. Some large U.S. companies, like Johnson & Johnson, Gillette, Corning, Coca-Cola, and Xerox, now generate more than half their revenues outside the United States, and both Ford Motor Company and Matsushita Electric employ nearly half their workers outside their respective borders.[3] Moreover, even small organizations are becoming enmeshed with competitors, suppliers, and customers from all over the world.

Successful leaders in an increasingly multicultural world have a responsibility to acknowledge and value cultural differences and understand how diversity affects

Everyday Revolutionaries: Working Women and the Transformation of American Life
Sally Helgesen

Sally Helgesen boldly claims that women are the driving force in the transformation of American society. In this study of the lives of women in Naperville, Illinois, Helgesen argues that the life choices women have made over the past few decades have radically changed the workplace, the community, and the nation. Thus, any woman who has ever entered the workforce is an "everyday revolutionary."

Helgesen contrasts domesticity, work, social and religious life, and family composition in 1990s Naperville with William Whyte's classic 1957 study of nearby Park Forest, Illinois. Whyte's "Organization Man" was a wing-tipped, suited junior executive living in a community characterized by sameness, from family configuration to worship, commuting patterns, cars, houses, and leisure activities. The new typical American, Helgesen asserts, is the working woman, whose choices have contributed to the significant diversity that permeates suburban America.

From Well-Defined to Ill-Defined

The society of the Organization Man was characterized by predictable adult life stages and similar choices and experiences of everyone, particularly those of the same age. Today, the well-defined lives of the Organization Man and his neighbors have lost their predictability and given way to lives that individuals find difficult to categorize.

- *The end of uniformity.* Domestic life is more heterogeneous than ever, with a combination of single parents, childless couples, blended families, and a greater range of ages at which marriage and childbearing occur. Careers are also no longer characterized by stable, linear progress. Women are often in and out of the workforce, and they garner skills and contacts in their communities during their years at home that contribute

to the opportunities that arise and the path careers follow.

- *The end of time.* When women entered the workforce in significant numbers, the amount of time for other endeavors necessarily dwindled. The pace of business and the demands of multiple life spheres mean that every minute must count. Increasingly particularized needs have given rise to niche products and services, which expand women's options but also increase the time needed to make purchasing decisions.

- *The beginning of opportunity.* The erosion of exclusive male privilege and the increasing need for expert talent and knowledge-based work have given women more opportunities than ever before. Women's concerns have contributed to the work-from-home options made available by an increasing number of employers. The disintegration of the distinction between work and home provides women with an opportunity to manage their tasks in a way that is most coherent for them.

Transformations

The participation of women in the economy has brought about a number of transformations in the basic social organizations of homes, families, and workplaces. Women's approach to work has traditionally been very different, says Helgesen, because they have not been socialized as the Organization Man was. Indeed, the practical approach of women to organizing tasks and the necessity to accommodate women's needs has resulted in a social landscape that is radically different from the predictable, patterned life stages of 1950s society.

Everyday Revolutionaries: Working Women and the Transformation of American Life, by Sally Helgesen, is published by Doubleday.

organizational operations and outcomes.[4] This chapter explores the topic of diversity and multiculturalism. We will first define diversity and explore the need for diversity in today's organizations. Then we will look at new styles of leadership and the multicultural challenges brought about by globalization. We will also examine some of the specific challenges facing minority employees and leadership initiatives for supporting and valuing multiculturalism in the workplace.

Multiculturalism Today

At Rotoflow, a southern California company that manufactures giant turbines used in the natural gas industry, Australian-born president Frank Van Gogh counts 30 nationalities among his 200 employees. "We are an international business," says Van Gogh, "and the [multicultural] workforce we found here has become our great strength." For example, Van Gogh believes a recent order out of Korea is a direct result of the company's Korean-American salesman who speaks fluent Korean.[5] Rotoflow represents both the challenge of diversity and its value for today's organizations.

Definition of Diversity

Workforce diversity means the hiring and inclusion of people with different human qualities or who belong to various cultural groups. From the perspective of individuals, **diversity** means including people different from themselves along dimensions such as age, ethnicity, gender, or race. It is important to remember that diversity includes everyone, not just racial or ethnic minorities.

Several important dimensions of diversity are illustrated in Exhibit 11.1. This "diversity wheel" shows the myriad combinations of traits that make up diversity. The inside wheel represents primary dimensions of diversity, which include inborn differences or differences that have an impact throughout one's life.[6] Primary dimensions are core elements through which people shape their self-image and world view. These dimensions are age, race, ethnicity, gender, mental or physical abilities, and sexual orientation. Turn the wheel and these primary characteristics match up with various secondary dimensions of diversity.

Secondary dimensions can be acquired or changed throughout one's lifetime. These dimensions tend to have less impact than those of the core but nevertheless affect a person's self-definition and worldview and have an impact on how the person is viewed by others. For example, Vietnam veterans may have been profoundly affected by their military experience and may be perceived differently from other people. An employee living in a public housing project will be perceived differently from one who lives in an affluent part of town. Secondary dimensions such as work style, communication style, and educational or skill level are particularly relevant in the organizational setting.[7] The challenge for organizational leaders is to recognize that each person can bring value and strengths to the workplace based on his or her own unique combination of diversity characteristics.

EXHIBIT 11.1 | **THE DIVERSITY WHEEL**

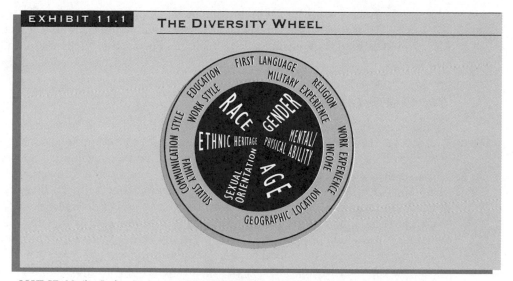

SOURCE: Marilyn Loden, *Implementing Diversity* (Homewood, IL: Irwin, 1996). Used with permission.

The Reality of Diversity

Attitudes toward diversity are changing partly because they have to —organizations are recognizing and welcoming cultural differences as a result of significant changes in our society, including globalization and the changing workforce.[8] The average worker is older now, and many more women, people of color, and immigrants are entering the workforce. Estimates are that through the year 2000, roughly 45 percent of all net additions to the labor force will be non-white, with half of them first generation immigrants and almost two-thirds female. White males, the majority of workers in the past, already make up less than half the U.S. workforce, and white, native-born males are expected to contribute only 15 percent of new entrants to the workforce through the year 2000. Studies also project that in the twenty-first century Asian Americans, African Americans, and Hispanics will make up 85 percent of the U.S. population growth and constitute about 30 percent of the total workforce.[9]

The other factor contributing to increased acceptance of diversity is globalization. In today's world, ideas, capital investments, products, services, and people flow freely and rapidly around the world. Even small organizations are affected. Montague Corporation produces unique folding mountain bikes, which are designed in Cambridge, Massachusetts, made in Taiwan, and sold largely in Europe. Some large multinational corporations, including Canada's Northern Telecom, U.S.-based Coca-Cola, Switzerland's Nestlé, and France's Carrefour (the retailer that invented the hypermarket concept), all get a large percentage of their sales from outside their home countries. In this global environment, foreign-born people with global experience have been appointed to lead such U.S. companies as Ford, Gerber, NCR, and Heinz, and almost every employee is dealing with a wider range of cultures than ever before.[10] For example, a Digital Equipment Corporation factory near Boston that produces keyboards for Digital's computers, employs people from 44 countries who speak 19 languages. When plant managers issue written announcements, they are printed in English, French, Spanish, Chinese, Portuguese, Vietnamese, and Haitian Creole.[11]

The Need for Organizational Diversity

Top leaders of organizations are responding to diversity and new attitudes for a number of reasons beyond the simple fact that shifting demographics make it necessary to do so. There is no question that the workforce is changing and organizations have to change to reflect the new workforce composition. However, there are a number of other reasons leaders need to incorporate and support diversity.

Organizations use internal diversity to meet the needs of diverse customers. Culture plays an important part in determining the goods, entertainment, social services, and household products that people use and buy. A Glass Ceiling commission study noted that two out of every three people in the United States are minority-group members or females or both, so organizations are recruiting minority employees who can understand how diverse people live and what they want and need.[12] Diverse employees can also help an organization build better relationships with customers.

A second need for diversity is to develop employee and organizational potential. When organizations support diversity, people feel valued for what they can bring to the organization, which leads to higher morale. It can also produce better relationships at work when employees develop the skills to understand and accept cultural differences. In addition, the presence of people with different cultural values and languages develops greater organizational flexibility.

By seriously recruiting and valuing individuals without regard to race, nationality, gender, age, sexual preference, or physical ability, organizations can attract and retain the best human talent. The labor market is growing smaller—one estimate is that by the turn of the century there will be four to five million fewer entry level workers than in 1990. Organizations looking for the best people will have fewer options, and the labor pool will be more diverse.[13]

Finally, diversity within the organization provides a broader and deeper base of experience for problem solving, creativity, and innovation. Diversity of thought is essential to the learning organization, which we described in Chapter 8. Recall that a learning organization is based on teams of empowered workers that cross functional boundaries. Everyone is engaged in identifying and solving problems. Competitive pressures are challenging all leaders to create organizational environments that foster and support creative thinking and sharing of diverse viewpoints. Diverse groups tend to be more creative than homogeneous groups in part because of the different perspectives people can bring to the problem or issue. One study reported that companies that are high on creativity and innovation have a higher percentage of women and non-white male employees than less innovative companies.[14]

One aspect of diversity that is of particular interest in relation to the emerging learning organization is the way in which women's style of leadership may differ from men's. As women move into higher positions in organizations, it has been observed that they often use a style of leadership that is highly effective in today's turbulent, multicultural environment.[15]

Ways Women Lead

Leadership qualities traditionally associated with white, American-born males include aggressiveness or assertiveness, rational analysis, and a "take charge" attitude. Male leaders tend to be competitive and individualistic and prefer working in vertical hierarchies. They rely on formal authority and position in the organization in their dealings with subordinates.

Although women may also demonstrate these qualities, research has found that in general, women tend to be more concerned with consensus building, inclusiveness, participation, and caring. Female leaders such as Linda Johnson Rice, president and CEO of Johnson Publishing Company, which owns *Ebony*, *Jet*, and Fashion Fair Cosmetics, are often more willing to share power and information, to empower employees, and to strive to enhance workers' feelings of self-worth. As Rice puts it, "It is the creative process that I find stimulating, sitting down and letting ideas flow among the different groups. I love the interaction with people."[16]

Professor and author Judy B. Rosener has called this style **interactive leadership**.[17] The leader favors a consensual and collaborative process, and influence derives from relationships rather than position power and authority. Some psychologists have suggested that women may be more relationship-oriented than men because of different psychological needs stemming from early experiences. This difference between the relationship orientations of men and women has sometimes been used to suggest that women cannot lead effectively because they fail to exercise power. However, whereas male leaders may associate effective leadership with a top-down command-and-control process, women's interactive leadership seems appropriate for the future of diversity and learning organizations. Grace Pastiak provides an excellent example of the interactive leadership style.

 LEADERSHIP SPOTLIGHT   **GRACE PASTIAK**

"I have the bias that people do better when they are happy," says Grace Pastiak, director of manufacturing for a division of Tellabs, Inc., a maker of sophisticated telephone equipment in Lisle, Illinois. "The old style of beating on people to get things done does not work."

Pastiak has shown that factories can function effectively without relying on the traditional command structure. Regarded as an effective leader by both subordinates and bosses, Pastiak manages a 170-person workforce that meets production targets 98 percent of the time. Compare that to an industry standard of around 90 percent. She does so without seeming to be preoccupied with output, attendance, and cost reports, focusing instead on worker empowerment and involvement. She is in constant and direct communication with people on the plant floor and develops self-reliance and a sense of responsibility in teams of line workers. According to Tom Sharpe and Tim Murphy, two of her subordinates, Pastiak throws most of the problem-solving directly to workers on the factory floor. "We get daily reports on why things did not ship," says Sharpe. "Usually it is for a reason out of our control. If it is within our control, we fix it and then cut the boss in on what we have done."

Tellabs' workers are productive largely because Pastiak emphasizes that every worker matters, and she invests a great deal of time in employee training and development. For example, she takes two full days each month to teach a course called Total Quality Commitment. About a dozen workers at a time are taken from their usual jobs to attend the hour-long sessions. Despite the loss of production time, Pastiak considers it time well spent. "I cannot think of anything more important that I should be doing than empowering people. I want them to have a sense of accomplishment."[18]

Although Grace Pastiak believes an interactive, nurturing style of leadership is essential for today's organizations, she doesn't believe this style is gender-specific.

The values associated with interactive leadership, such as inclusion, relationship building, and caring, are generally considered "feminine" values, but they are emerging as valuable qualities for both male and female leaders in the twenty-first century.[19] Many of the "new ideas" being touted by management consultants and business authors have been practiced as a normal way of working by women leaders and business owners for years.

As illustrated in Exhibit 11.2, one recent survey of followers rated women leaders significantly higher than men on several characteristics that are crucial for developing fast, flexible, learning organizations. Female leaders were rated as having more idealized influence, providing more inspirational motivation, and being more individually considerate.[20] *Idealized influence* means followers identify with and want to emulate the leader; the leader is trusted and respected, maintains high standards, and is considered to have power because of who she is rather than what position she holds. *Inspirational motivation* is derived from the leader who appeals emotionally and symbolically to employees' desire to do a good job and help achieve organizational goals. *Individual consideration* means each follower is treated as an individual but all are treated equitably; individual needs are recognized and assignments are delegated to followers to provide learning opportunities. *Intellectual stimulation* means questioning current methods and challenging employees to think in new ways. In addition, women leaders were judged by subordinates as more effective and satisfying to work for and were considered able to generate extra levels of effort from employees.

Again, the interactive leadership style is not exclusive to women. Any leader can learn to adopt a more inclusive style by developing the skills and attention to nonverbal behavior, listening, empathy, cooperation, and collaboration.[21]

Global Diversity

One of the most rapidly increasing sources of diversity in North American organizations is globalization, which means hiring employees in many countries. Some

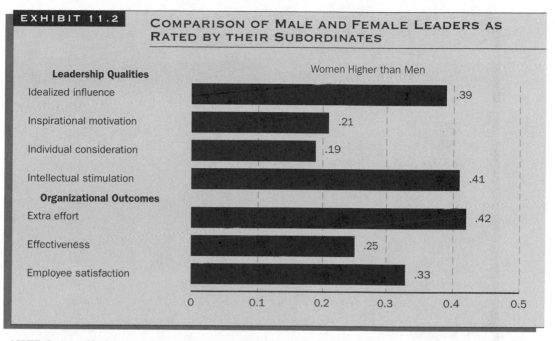

EXHIBIT 11.2

COMPARISON OF MALE AND FEMALE LEADERS AS RATED BY THEIR SUBORDINATES

NOTE: Ratings of leaders were on a scale of 1-5. Women leaders were rated higher, on average, by the amount indicated for each item.
SOURCE: Based on Bernard M. Bass and Bruce J. Avolio, "Shatter the Glass Ceiling: Women May Make Better Managers," *Human Resource Management* 33, No. 4 (Winter 1994), 549–560.

have estimated that by the year 2000, half of the world's assets will be controlled by multinational corporations.[22] Globalization means that organizations are confronting diversity issues across a broader stage than ever before. To handle the challenges of global diversity, leaders can develop cross-cultural understanding, the ability to build networks, and the understanding of geopolitical forces. Two significant aspects of global diversity are the sociocultural environment and communication differences.

The Sociocultural Environment

Social and cultural factors are even more perplexing than political and economic factors in foreign countries. For organizations operating globally, cultural differences may provide more potential for difficulties and conflicts than any other source. For example, although an alliance between Northwest Airlines and KLM Dutch Airlines was highly successful from a financial perspective, it was referred to in the press as a "marriage from hell" because of conflicts based on a clash of cultures. "It's the European way versus the American way," said KLM President Pieter Bouw. The Dutch collect modest salaries, disdain glitz, and believe in minimizing debt and investing for the long haul, while the American owners of Northwest draw huge salaries, live in Beverly Hills mansions, and believe risky on-the-edge dealmaking is the right way to run a business.[23]

EXHIBIT 11.3	RANK ORDERINGS OF 10 COUNTRIES ALONG FOUR DIMENSIONS OF NATIONAL VALUE SYSTEM			
Country	**Power[a]**	**Uncertainty[b]**	**Individualism[c]**	**Masculinity[d]**
Australia	7	7	2	5
Costa Rica	8 (tie)	2 (tie)	10	9
France	3	2 (tie)	4	7
West Germany	8 (tie)	5	5	3
India	2	9	6	6
Japan	5	1	7	1
Mexico	1	4	8	2
Sweden	10	10	3	10
Thailand	4	6	9	8
United States	6	8	1	4

[a]1 = highest power distance
10 = lowest power distance
[b]1 = highest uncertainty avoidance
10 = lowest uncertainty avoidance

[c]1 = highest individualism
10 = highest collectivism
[d]1 = highest masculinity
10 = highest femininity

SOURCE: From Dorothy Marcic, *Organizational Behavior and Cases*, 4th ed. (St. Paul, MN: West, 1995). Based on Geert Hofstede, *Culture's Consequences* (London: Sage Publications, 1984); and *Cultures and Organizations: Software of the Mind* (New York: McGraw-Hill, 1991).

National cultures are intangible, pervasive, and difficult to comprehend. However, it is imperative that leaders in international organizations understand local cultures and deal with them effectively.

Social Value Systems Research done by Geert Hofstede on IBM employees in 40 countries discovered that mind-set and cultural values on issues such as individualism versus collectivism strongly influence organizational and employee relationships and vary widely among cultures.[24] Exhibit 11.3 shows examples of how countries rate on four significant dimensions.

Power distance High **power distance** means people accept inequality in power among institutions, organizations, and individuals. Low power distance means people expect equality in power. Countries that value high power distance are Malaysia, the Philippines, and Panama. Countries that value low power distance include Denmark, Austria, and Israel.

Uncertainty avoidance High **uncertainty avoidance** means that members of a society feel uncomfortable with uncertainty and ambiguity and thus support beliefs and behavior that promise certainty and conformity. Low uncertainty avoidance means that people have a high tolerance for the unstructured, the unclear, and the unpredictable. High uncertainty avoidance cultures include Greece, Portugal, and Uruguay. Singapore and Jamaica are two countries with low uncertainty avoidance values.

Individualism and collectivism **Individualism** reflects a value for a loosely knit social framework in which individuals are expected to take care of themselves. **Collectivism** is a preference for a tightly knit social framework in which people look out for one another and organizations protect their members' interests. Countries with individualist values include the United States, Great Britain, and Canada. Countries with collectivist values are Guatemala, Ecuador, and Panama.

Masculinity and femininity **Masculinity** reflects a preference for achievement, heroism, assertiveness, work centrality, and material success. **Femininity** reflects the values of relationships, cooperation, group decision making, and quality of life. Japan, Austria, Mexico, and Germany are countries with strong masculine values. Countries with strong feminine values include Sweden, Norway, Denmark, and the former Yugoslavia. Both men and women subscribe to the dominant value in masculine or feminine cultures.

Social values influence leadership style and organizational functioning. For example, in Germany and other central European countries, leaders strive to run their organizations as impersonal, well-oiled machines. In Taiwan, Hong Kong, and Singapore, leaders perceive the organization as a large family and emphasize cooperation through networks of personal relationships.[25]

Other Cultural Characteristics Other cultural characteristics that can affect international leadership are language, religion, attitudes, social organization, and education. Some countries, such as India, are characterized by *linguistic pluralism*, meaning several languages are spoken there. Other countries may rely heavily on spoken rather than written language. Religion includes sacred objects, philosophical attitudes toward life, taboos, and rituals. Attitudes toward time, space, authority, and achievement can all affect organizations. People from urban cultures tend to follow rigid time schedules, for example, while those from rural cultures are less concerned with clock-time, which can lead to disputes regarding tardiness. In some cultures, the amount of space an employee is given to work in is a status symbol, while other cultures treat space as inconsequential. Elements of social organization include kinship and families, status systems, and opportunities for social mobility. For example, leadership in Japan is a way to move up in the social "pecking order." Age commands more status and respect in Europe and the Middle East than in the United States.[26]

Leaders working in a global context have found that these cultural differences cannot be ignored. Those doing business in the Czech Republic are learning the impact of social and cultural factors on organizations.

For U.S. and other Western businesses, the Czech Republic represents a market brimming with unmet needs. Kmart, Procter & Gamble, Otis Elevator, and other companies have made significant investments there. McDonald's has opened at least 15 restaurants there since the early 1990s. Philip Morris is exporting cigarettes to the huge Russian market from its large Czech factories.

Ralston Purina Company invested more than $10 million for a controlling interest in the Czech Republic's household battery-making monopoly. The Americans found the Czechs very willing and able to implement an overhaul of the antiquated production facilities, but they hadn't prepared for the cultural differences. For one thing, the Americans were bothered by the heavy smoking among the company's 350 employees and the photos of naked women liberally pasted all over the factory. After telling workers that this would not be acceptable in America, plant manager Richard N. Chenail remembers the polite but firm response: "We've only just gotten our freedom. We're not about to give it up yet." Western companies have had to adapt to local conditions to be successful. For example, advertising that would be considered "politically incorrect" in the United States is quite successful in the Czech Republic.

Even more troublesome for Ralston and other companies are the language barriers and the work attitudes left over from communist times: a high rate of absenteeism, a general unwillingness to take responsibility, and less interest in producing profits. "It's not laziness," says Ralston Purina's Laurent Claizergues, "just old habits."[27]

Many organizations have discovered, as Ralston Purina did, that cultural differences create more barriers than any other factor to successful communication and collaboration in organizations. Consider one of the most ambitious cross-cultural projects of all time, a joint venture among Siemens AG of Germany, Toshiba Corporation of Japan, and the U.S. corporation IBM. Brought together to develop a revolutionary memory chip, scientists from the three companies soon found themselves in the midst of a culture clash. The Japanese, who like to work in large, informal groups, found it almost painful to have to schedule meetings in small, individual offices. The Germans were appalled by the offices, saying no one in their country would be asked to work in an office without a window. IBMers complained that the Germans planned too much and that the Japanese wouldn't make a decision. Working through these cultural differences has been the greatest challenge of the Triad project.[28]

Leadership Implications

Leaders can be aware of cultural and subcultural differences in order to lead effectively in a multicultural environment. Chapter 4 examined contingency theories of leadership that explain the relationship between leader style and a given situation. It is important for leaders to recognize that culture impacts both style and the leadership situation. For example, in cultures with high uncertainty avoidance, a leadership situation with high task structure as described in Chapter 4 is favorable, but those in low uncertainty avoidance cultures prefer less structured work situations.

In addition, how behavior is perceived differs from culture to culture. To criticize a subordinate in private directly is considered appropriate behavior in individualistic societies such as the United States. However, in Japan, which values collectivism over individualism, the same leader behavior would be seen as inconsiderate. Japanese employees lose face if they are criticized directly by a supervisor. The expectation is that people will receive criticism information from peers rather than directly from the leader.[29] Research into how the contingency models apply to cross-cultural situations is sparse. However, all leaders need to be aware of the impact culture may have and consider cultural values in their dealings with employees.

Challenges Minorities Face

Valuing diversity and enabling all individuals to develop their unique talents is difficult to achieve. **Ethnocentrism,** the belief that one's own culture and subculture are inherently superior to other cultures, is a natural tendency of most people.[30] Moreover, the organizational climate in the United States still tends to reflect values, behaviors, assumptions, and expectations based on the experience of a rather homogeneous, white, middle-class male workforce. Many leaders relate to people in the organization as if everyone shares similar values, beliefs, motivations, and attitudes about work and life. This assumption is typically false even when dealing with people who share the same cultural background. Ethnocentric viewpoints combined with a standard set of cultural assumptions and practices create a number of challenges for minority employees and leaders.

Unequal Expectations/Difference as Deficiency   The one-best-way approach leads to a mind-set that views difference as deficiency or dysfunction.[31] The experience of most career women and minorities is that no matter how many college degrees they earn, how many hours they work, how they dress, or how much effort and enthusiasm they invest, they are never perceived as "having the right stuff." For example, a Hispanic executive, in discussing the animosity he experienced in one job, said, "The fact that I graduated first in my class didn't make as much difference as the fact that I looked different."[32] If the standard of quality were based, for instance, on being white and male, anything else would be seen as deficient. This dilemma is often difficult for white men to understand because most of them are not intentionally racist and sexist. Many men feel extremely uncomfortable with the prevailing attitudes and stereotypes, but don't know how to change them. These attitudes are deeply rooted in our society as well as in our organizations. For example, although there has been much progress in recent years, it is often considered "news" when a woman or minority is elected governor, promoted to general in the army, or named CEO of a major corporation. Simple phrases we hear everyday, such as "a black lawyer" or "a woman doctor" imply that lawyers and doctors are expected to be white men.

Women and minorities generally feel that they are not evaluated by the same standards as their male counterparts. For example, where having a family is often considered a plus for a male executive, it is perceived as a hindrance for a woman who wants to reach the top. One term heard frequently is the *mommy track*, which implies that a woman's commitment to her children limits her commitment to the company or her ability to handle the rigors of corporate leadership.[33]

Living Biculturally Research on differences between whites and blacks has focused on issues of biculturalism and how it affects employees' access to information, level of respect and appreciation, and relation to superiors and subordinates. **Biculturalism** can be defined as the sociocultural skills and attitudes used by racial minorities as they move back and forth between the dominant culture and their own ethnic or racial culture.[34] More than 90 years ago, W.E.B. Du Bois referred to this as a "double-consciousness. . . . One always feels his twoness—an American, a Negro; two souls, two thoughts, two unreconciled strivings. . . ."[35] In general, African Americans feel less accepted in their organizations, perceive themselves to have less discretion on their jobs, receive lower ratings on job performance, experience lower levels of job satisfaction, and reach career plateaus earlier than whites.

Racism in the workplace often shows up in subtle ways—the disregard by a subordinate for an assigned chore; a lack of urgency in completing an important assignment; the ignoring of comments or suggestions made at a meeting. Black and other minority leaders often struggle daily with the problem of delegating authority and responsibility to employees who show them little respect. Such groups also struggle with biculturalism as well. They find themselves striving to adopt behaviors and attitudes that will help them be successful in the white-dominated corporate world while at the same time maintaining their ties to their ethnic community and culture. J.D. Hokoyama started a nonprofit organization to teach Asian Americans how to be bicultural.

LEADERSHIP SPOTLIGHT

LEADERSHIP EDUCATION FOR ASIAN PACIFICS, INC.

Asian Americans who aspire to leadership positions are often frustrated by the stereotype that they are hard workers but not executive material. Many times Asian Americans are perceived as too quiet or not assertive enough. One Chinese American woman says her boss claimed she wasn't strong enough for an executive-level job because she didn't raise her voice in discussions as he did.

J. D. Hokoyama, a 47-year-old Japanese American, started a nonprofit organization to try to change these perceptions. Hokoyama runs workshops to alert Asian Americans to the ways in which their communication style may hold them back in the American workplace. Participants are taught to use more eye contact, start more sentences with "I," and use more assertive body language. Many Asian Americans are offended by the implication that they should abandon their cultural values to succeed. Hokoyama, however, looks at this as a way to help more Asian Americans adjust their style so they can move into leadership positions. Pauline Ho, a senior technical staff member at Sandia National Laboratories, agrees. She has seen the obstacles her parents and other immigrants faced and knows how difficult it is to succeed in the mainstream culture: "They want to get ahead, but they don't understand what they should be doing."

Hokoyama says Asian Americans and other minorities should not have to give up their own culture; however, he believes that only by understanding the differences between Asian values and mainstream American values can more Asians and Asian Americans move into leadership positions.[36]

The workshops offered by Leadership Education for Asian Pacifics, Inc. are a sad commentary on the opportunities for minorities in America's organizations. Many minorities feel they have a chance for career advancement only by becoming bicultural or abandoning their native cultures altogether. Culturally-sensitive leadership can work to remove these barriers.

The Glass Ceiling   Another issue is the **glass ceiling,** an invisible barrier that separates women and minorities from top leadership positions. They can look up through the ceiling, but prevailing attitudes are invisible obstacles to their own advancement. Evidence of the glass ceiling is the distribution of women and minorities, who are clustered at the bottom levels of the corporate hierarchy. A recent Glass Ceiling Commission study reports that women and minorities hold only 5 percent of senior-level jobs in organizations. White males still hold more than 50 percent of all administrative and management-level positions, with blacks holding less than 7 percent and Hispanics only 5 percent.[37] Women and minorities also earn substantially less. Black male employees earn 24 to 27 percent less than what their white counterparts earn, even when educational levels are similar. Women earn considerably less than their male peers, with black women earning the least. As women move up the career ladder, the wage gap widens; at the level of vice-president, a woman's average salary is 42 percent less than her male counterpart.[38]

The glass ceiling persists because top-level corporate culture in most organizations still evolves around traditional management thinking, a vertical hierarchy populated by white, American-born males, who often hire and promote people who look, act, and think like them. Although hiring and promotion patterns are well intended, women and minority employees may be relegated to less visible positions and projects; hence, their work fails to come to the attention of top executives. Recent research has suggested the existence of "glass walls" that serve as invisible barriers to important lateral movement within the organization. Glass walls bar experience in areas such as line supervision or general management that would enable women and minorities to advance to senior-level positions.[39] In general, women and minorities feel that they must work harder and perform at higher levels than their white male counterparts in order to be noticed, recognized, fully accepted, and promoted.

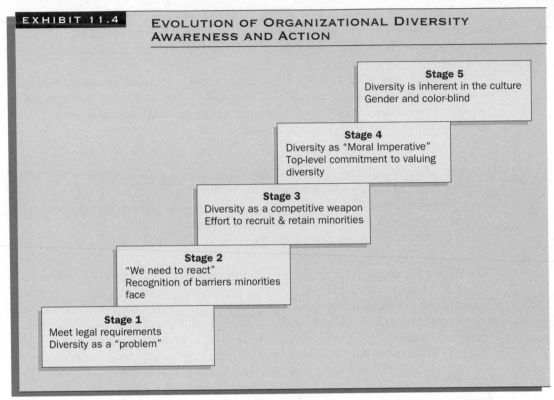

EXHIBIT 11.4   EVOLUTION OF ORGANIZATIONAL DIVERSITY AWARENESS AND ACTION

Stage 5
Diversity is inherent in the culture
Gender and color-blind

Stage 4
Diversity as "Moral Imperative"
Top-level commitment to valuing diversity

Stage 3
Diversity as a competitive weapon
Effort to recruit & retain minorities

Stage 2
"We need to react"
Recognition of barriers minorities face

Stage 1
Meet legal requirements
Diversity as a "problem"

SOURCE: Adapted from AMERICA'S COMPETITIVE SECRET: UTILIZING WOMEN AS A MANAGEMENT STRATEGY, p.142 by Judy B. Rosener. Copyright © 1995 by J.B. Rosener. Used by permission of Oxford University Press, Inc.

Leadership Initiatives toward Multiculturalism

One goal for today's learning organizations is to ensure that *all* employees—women, ethnic and racial minorities, gay people, the disabled, the elderly, as well as white males—are given equal opportunities in the workplace.[40] Strong, culturally-sensitive leadership can move organizations toward multiculturalism, where all people are valued and respected for the unique abilities they can bring to the workplace.

Organizational Stages of Diversity Awareness

Organizations as well as individuals vary in their sensitivity and openness to other cultures, attitudes, values, and ways of doing things. Exhibit 11.4 shows a model of five organizational stages of diversity awareness and action.[41] The continuum ranges from meeting the minimum legal requirements regarding affirmative action and sexual harassment to valuing diversity as an inherent part of the organizational culture.

Stage 1 organizations and leaders consider themselves successful if their legal record is good. Women and minorities are viewed primarily as a "problem" that must be dealt with, and typically there are only a few minorities in executive-level jobs to meet legal requirements. At Stage 2, leaders become aware that women and minorities face challenges not faced by white males, and that higher absenteeism and turnover rates among minorities are detrimental to the organization. However, awareness is seldom translated into action until the organization moves into Stage 3. Leaders become proactive, and acknowledge that addressing issues of gender, race, disability, etc., is important not just for the minority employees but for the health of the organization. They recognize that women and minorities can bring needed insight into developing and marketing products for new customers, so they look for ways to attract and retain high-quality minority employees. In Stage 3 organizations, more women and minorities make it to high-level positions and the organization begins providing some diversity awareness training to all employees. The motivation for diversity at Stage 3 is to remain competitive.

When the organization reaches Stage 4, there is a top-level leadership commitment to broad equality and community. Leaders rectify the undervaluation and underutilization of women and minorities. Top leaders allocate significant resources for diversity training and other programs to bring about organizational change. A genuine attempt is made to develop policies and practices that are inclusive rather than exclusive, and executives at all levels are generally required to provide evidence that they are recruiting, retaining, and promoting quality female and minority employees. Stage 4 leaders believe valuing differences is the right thing to do morally as well as for economic reasons. UNUM Life Insurance Company of America, described in the Cutting Edge box, illustrates the evolution of a company to Stage 4 of diversity awareness.

Stage 5 organizations are gender- and color-blind. All employees are judged on their competence, and stereotypes and prejudices are completely erased. No group of employees feels different or disadvantaged. This stage represents the ideal organization. Although it may seem unreachable, many of today's best organizations are striving to reach this stage.

Barriers to Evolution

Leaders face a number of personal and organizational barriers to achieving a high level of diversity awareness, acceptance, and appreciation.[42] Four of these barriers are discussed below.

Ethnocentrism   Recall that ethnocentrism is the belief that one's own group and subculture are inherently superior to other groups and cultures. Viewing one's own culture as the best culture is a natural tendency among most people and contributes to cultural cohesiveness. However, ethnocentrism makes it difficult to value diversity because it tends to produce a monoculture, a culture that accepts only one way of doing things and one set of values and beliefs. The goal for organizations seeking cultural diversity is to develop *ethnorelativism*, or the belief that all groups, cultures, and subcultures are inherently equal.

Stereotypes and Prejudice   Carried to an extreme, ethnocentrism becomes outright prejudice, which is perhaps the single biggest obstacle to providing equal

UNUM Life Insurance Company of America

Portland, Maine, where UNUM Life Insurance has its headquarters, may not be as ethnically diverse as New York or Los Angeles, but that hasn't kept the company from taking workplace diversity seriously. UNUM has taken a long hard look at itself and made significant changes in the way it deals with a multicultural workforce.

According to Sandy Bishop, manager of UNUM's diversity program, prior to 1989 the company viewed diversity as a matter of complying with EEO and affirmative action laws (Stage 1 of diversity awareness). Even though the company worked hard to bring women and minorities into the organization, executives began to recognize that UNUM had extremely high turnover among these groups. The organization began looking inward and recognized pressures that minority groups were feeling (Stage 2).

In Stage 3 of diversity awareness, UNUM decided that having a diverse workforce was critical to the organization's success. "We built a business case for it," says Bishop. "We wanted our business environment to mirror our world, the people we were insuring." UNUM's proactive program began simply with the human resources staff developing a diversity philosophy. Senior executives, the majority of whom were white males, began meeting regularly with representatives of minority groups. What the executives discovered shocked them—that minority groups felt so out of place that they tried to "hide" in the organization. Following surveys and dialogues

that brought together various ethnic groups to discuss issues, top leaders made a commitment to full-scale cultural and organizational change (Stage 4). One effort is a three-day diversity workshop held each year to help employees build what the company calls "cultural competence." A company newsletter focuses on diversity issues, and an education committee offers "Lunch and Learn" talks about diversity. UNUM has also formed a Diversity Board made up of members from five affinity groups identified within the organization—people of color, women, people with disabilities, gays/lesbians, and older workers. Significantly, UNUM's president is also a member of the board, which meets monthly to look at "systematic changes within the organization" to encourage and support diversity.

UNUM is still early in Stage 4 of diversity awareness, and results are difficult to measure. However, Bishop sees the change in employees. For example, some recently questioned whether it was okay to play Christmas music on the phone lines since Christmas isn't a holiday that all religious groups celebrate. Bishop doesn't mind seeing workers throughout the company taking on her role in asking such questions. "My goal," she says, "is to do such a good job that I'll eliminate the need for my job." If she manages to do that, UNUM will have made it to Stage 5 of diversity awareness.

SOURCE: Jenny C. McCune, "Diversity Training: A Competitive Weapon," *Management Review* (June 1996), 25–28.

opportunities for women and minorities. *Prejudice* can be defined as the tendency to view people who are different from the mainstream in terms of sex, race, ethnic background, or physical ability as being deficient. Prejudice is the assumption, without evidence, that minorities are inherently inferior, less competent at their jobs, and less suitable for leadership positions. Recent surveys have found that stereotypes are still prevalent in our society, and prejudice is a contributing factor in most other barriers to accepting and valuing diversity in the workplace.[43]

The "White Male" Club   The work environment for many minorities is lonely, unfriendly, and stressful, which is partly attributed to the so-called white male club. Particularly in executive level positions, women and minorities are heavily outnumbered by white men, many of whom treat them differently from the way they treat their white male colleagues. Women and minorities may be excluded from social functions, lunches, and even regular office banter. In addition, there are few role models or mentors for women and minorities trying to reach senior level positions. Minorities feel they have no one to talk to about their fears, their mistakes, and even their ideas for the organization. If they try to fit into the white male club they are often rejected, yet if they remain isolated, they are perceived as aloof and arrogant.

The Paradox of Diversity   Leaders also face a significant challenge in simultaneously promoting diversity and maintaining a strong, unified corporate culture.[44] Homogeneous cultures provide a firmer basis for building a strong culture, which is considered critical to organizational success. One reason is that, in general, people feel more comfortable and satisfied dealing with others who are like themselves. Also, in many communities, ethnic groups still do not interact socially, and this carries over into unfamiliarity and discomfort in the workplace. Diverse ethnic groups within a work environment can be competitive with and even antagonistic toward one another, and the time and energy leaders spend dealing with interpersonal issues dramatically increases in a diverse environment. Leaders have to work harder than ever to unite employees around a common purpose while also allowing individual differences to flourish.

Actual Cultural Differences   Finally, real cultural differences can cause problems in the workplace. As we discussed earlier in the chapter, culture influences attitudes toward such things as time, physical space, and authority. Leaders may face enormous challenges in relating to employees from different cultures. For example, most organizations will not accept routine tardiness or absenteeism from employees simply because their time orientation is culturally different from the mainstream values.

As another example of how cultural differences complicate leadership, one supervisor declined a gift from a new employee, an immigrant who wanted to show gratitude for her job. He was concerned about ethics and explained the company's policy about not accepting gifts. The employee was so insulted that she quit, even though she desperately needed the work.[45] The potential for communication difficulties is much greater in heterogeneous groups, leading to misunderstandings, conflict, and anxiety for leaders as well as employees.

Leadership Solutions

In the past, the pressure to change has been on the new employee coming into the workplace. Today, however, the idea that culturally diverse individuals have to assimilate into the mainstream culture is dead. The pressure is now on organizations to change, and strong leadership is needed. Many of today's leaders have had little experience with multiculturalism and are unprepared to deal with emerging diversity in the workplace. The benefits of diversity are not automatic, and working with people different from oneself can be difficult and frustrating. Without strong leadership, increased cultural diversity can lead to decreased work effort and lower organizational performance. The Living Leadership box urges leaders to first clear their own minds of prejudice.

Leading Multicultural Organizations

To successfully lead in multicultural organizations, leaders must develop personal characteristics that support diversity. Four characteristics have been identified as important for leadership of multicultural organizations.[46]

- A personal, long-range vision that recognizes and supports a diverse organizational community. Leaders should have long-term plans to include employees of various cultures at all levels of the organization. In addition, they express the vision through symbols and rituals that reinforce the value of a diverse workforce.

- A broad knowledge of the dimensions of diversity and awareness of multicultural issues. Multicultural leaders need a basic knowledge of the primary dimensions of diversity as discussed earlier in this chapter: age, race, ethnicity, gender, mental or physical abilities, and sexual orientation, as well as some understanding of secondary dimensions. Knowledge is also put into action through the use of inclusive language and showing respect for cultural differences.

- An openness to change themselves. Leaders in multicultural organizations encourage feedback from their employees, can accept criticism, and are willing to change their behavior.

- Mentoring and empowerment of diverse employees. Leaders take an active role in creating opportunities for all employees to use their unique abilities. They also offer honest feedback and coaching as needed, and they reward those in the organization who show respect to culturally different employees.

Once leaders examine and change themselves, they can lead change in the organization. In the following sections, we will briefly discuss two major actions that can help organizations stretch to accommodate and support increasing cultural diversity: changing corporate culture and providing diversity training.

Changing Corporate Culture Creating and communicating a shared vision and values for the organization becomes even more critical in an organization made up of diverse individuals with differing beliefs, ideas, and ways of thinking and behaving. Leaders are also challenged to ensure that the organizational culture is contin-

LIVING LEADERSHIP

Good Leadership

Lingyuan said:

"Good leaders make the mind of the community their mind, and never let their minds indulge in private prejudices. They make the eyes and ears of the community their eyes and ears, and never let their eyes and ears be partial.

"Thus are they ultimately able to realize the will of the community and comprehend the feelings of the community.

"When they make the mind of the community their own mind, good and bad are to the leaders what good and bad are to the community. Therefore the good is not wrongly so, and the bad is unmistakably so.

"Then why resort to airing what is in your own mind, and accepting the flattery of others?

"Once you use the community's ears and eyes for your ears and eyes, then the people's perceptivity is your own—thus it is so clear nothing is not seen, nothing is not heard.

"So then why add personal views and stubbornly invite hypocrisy and deception from others?

"When they expressed their own hearts and added their own views, the accomplished sages were striving to find their own faults, to have the same wishes as the people of the community, and to be without bias."

SOURCE: Thomas Cleary, trans., *Zen Lessons: The Art of Leadership* (Boston: Shambhala Press, 1989), 45-46. Used with permission.

ually open to new and different ideas and ways of doing things, while maintaining a focus on the common purpose and vision.[47]

Today's organizational cultures for the most part reflect the white male model of doing business. As a result of this mismatch between the dominant culture and the growing employee population of minorities and women, many employees' talents and abilities are not being fully used. Chapter 7 described how leaders shape culture and values. An adaptive culture is one that helps the organization survive and prosper in an increasingly diverse world. Leaders can begin by actively using symbols for new values, such as encouraging and celebrating the promotion of minorities. They also examine the unwritten rules and assumptions in the organization. What are the values that exemplify the existing culture? What are the myths and stereotypes about minorities? Are unwritten rules communicated from one person to another in ways that exclude women and minority workers?

Top leadership support is critical to changing the corporate culture to one that values diversity. After Flagstar Companies, the parent company of Denny's, paid $54 million to settle two civil rights class action suits, new Chairman and CEO James B. Adamson issued a clear mandate: "If you discriminate, you're history."

LEADERSHIP SPOTLIGHT   DENNY'S

Only a few years ago, some Denny's managers routinely barred black customers and asked minority diners to prepay their dinner bills. Only one of the chain's franchises was minority-owned. Today, a sweeping cultural overhaul has transformed Denny's and its parent company, Flagstar. The top leadership committee, once made up of all white men, now includes a Hispanic American male, two white women, and a black woman who is specifically responsible for diversity initiatives. Store managers' pay is linked directly to diversity goals, and 27 franchises are now owned by African Americans.

Flagstar's CEO, James Adamson, sets the tone for the cultural change. For example, he recently fired off a letter to the local newspaper protesting its use of a stereotypical illustration of a black waitress. He's revised systems and procedures and made diversity issues a top priority. At the home office, African Americans now make up 17 percent of Flagstar's executives, and minority purchasing contracts exceed $50 million. Adamson knows it's only a start and that cultural transformation doesn't happen overnight. However, he won't tolerate any vestige of the status quo that accepted prejudice as natural and right. Any evidence of bigotry at Flagstar and Denny's today brings immediate termination; a monitor tracks all civil rights charges; and each restaurant has to post the number of complaints from minority customers. When asked how to end racism, Adamson says, "You hit people in the face, and then it becomes natural."[48]

Diversity Awareness Training Many organizations, including GTE, Xerox, Mobil Oil, Towers Perrin, and Texaco, provide **diversity awareness training** to help employees become aware of their own cultural boundaries, their prejudices and stereotypes, so they can learn to work together successfully. Leaders in these companies understand that their future competitiveness may depend on how well they handle diversity issues.[49]

People vary in their sensitivity and openness to other cultures and ways of doing things. Exhibit 11.5 shows a model of five stages of individual diversity awareness, which are roughly comparable to the organizational stages shown in Exhibit 11.4. The continuum ranges from a defensive, ethnocentric attitude to a complete understanding and acceptance of people's differences. The model can help leaders assess their own and employees' openness to change. People at different levels may require different kinds of training. A primary aim of diversity awareness training is to help people recognize that their own hidden and overt biases direct their thinking about specific individuals and groups. Diversity awareness programs also focus on helping people of varying backgrounds communicate effectively with one another and understand the language and context used in dealing with people from other cultural groups. One of the most important aspects of diversity training is to bring together people of differing perspectives so that they can engage in learning new interpersonal communications skills.

Diversity presents many challenges, yet it also provides leaders with an exciting opportunity to build organizations as integrated communities in which all people feel encouraged, respected, and committed to common purposes and goals. The learning organization described in Chapter 8 depends on a sense of equality and community, which means people are able to communicate openly and honestly with

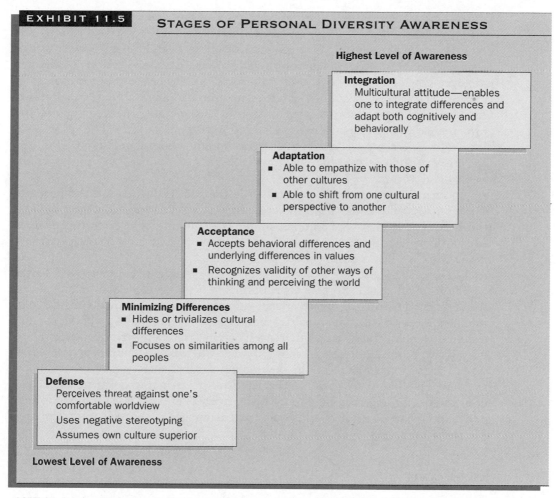

EXHIBIT 11.5 — **STAGES OF PERSONAL DIVERSITY AWARENESS**

Highest Level of Awareness

Integration
Multicultural attitude—enables one to integrate differences and adapt both cognitively and behaviorally

Adaptation
- Able to empathize with those of other cultures
- Able to shift from one cultural perspective to another

Acceptance
- Accepts behavioral differences and underlying differences in values
- Recognizes validity of other ways of thinking and perceiving the world

Minimizing Differences
- Hides or trivializes cultural differences
- Focuses on similarities among all peoples

Defense
Perceives threat against one's comfortable worldview
Uses negative stereotyping
Assumes own culture superior

Lowest Level of Awareness

SOURCE: Based on M. Bennett, "A Developmental Approach to Training for Intercultural Sensitivity," *International Journal of Intercultural Relations* 10 (1986), 179–196.

one another and maintain their unique identities while also being firmly committed to something larger than individual interests.

Summary and Interpretation

The main point of this chapter is that multiculturalism is a fact of life in today's world, and leaders can create change in organizations to keep up. The U.S. population, the workforce, and the customer base are changing. In addition, people of different national origins, races, and religions are no longer willing to be assimilated into the mainstream culture. Organizations are also operating in an increasingly global world, which means dealing with diversity on a broader stage than ever before.

Dimensions of diversity are both primary, such as age, gender, and race, and secondary, such as education, marital status, and religion. There are several reasons why organizations are recognizing the need to value and support diversity. Diversity helps organizations build better relationships with diverse customers and helps develop employee potential. Diversity provides a broader and deeper base of experience for creativity and problem solving, which is essential to building learning organizations. One aspect of diversity of particular interest for the emerging learning organization is women's style of leadership, referred to as interactive leadership. The values associated with interactive leadership, such as inclusion, relationship-building, and caring, are emerging as valuable qualities for both male and female leaders in the twenty-first century.

Another important idea in this chapter is global diversity. Leaders can be aware of the impact culture may have and consider cultural differences in their dealings with followers. Within organizations, people who do not fit the mainstream white, U.S.-born, male culture face a number of challenges, including unequal expectations, the need to live biculturally, and the glass ceiling.

Organizations generally evolve through stages of diversity awareness and action, ranging from minimum efforts to meet affirmative action guidelines to valuing diversity as an integral part of organizational culture. The barriers to successful evolution include ethnocentrism, prejudice, the so-called "White Male" club, the paradox of diversity, and actual cultural differences. Strong, culturally-sensitive leadership is the only way organizations can move through the stages of diversity awareness. Leaders first change themselves by developing personal characteristics that support diversity. They use these personal characteristics to change the organization. The ultimate goal for leaders in the twenty-first century is to build organizations as integrated communities in which all people feel encouraged, respected, and committed to common purposes and goals.

Key Terms

workforce diversity	individualism	ethnocentrism
diversity	collectivism	biculturalism
interactive leadership	masculinity	glass ceiling
power distance	femininity	diversity awareness training
uncertainty avoidance		

Discussion Questions

1. How might a leader's role and responsibility change as a company becomes more diverse? Explain.

2. How might diversity within the organization ultimately lead to better problem solving and greater creativity?

3. What is interactive leadership and why may this approach be increasingly important in the twenty-first century?

4. Discuss ways in which low uncertainty avoidance as a social value among followers could affect their interaction with leaders who display high uncertainty avoidance.

5. What is the glass ceiling and why does it persist in organizations?

6. What is the paradox of diversity and how could it be a barrier to valuing and supporting diversity within organizations?

7. In preparing organizations to accept and value diversity, do you think leaders should focus primarily on changing the underlying culture or on diversity awareness training? Discuss.

8. Recall a company you worked for. At what stage of diversity awareness (Exhibit 11.4) was it? Explain.

Leadership Development: Personal Feedback

A Passive Bias Quiz

	Yes	No
1. What you notice first about people around you are the characteristics that make them different from you.	_____	_____
2. You make it a general rule never to discuss the subject of race, ethnicity, politics, age, religion, gender, and sexuality when you are at work.	_____	_____
3. When others make bigoted remarks or jokes, you either laugh or say nothing because you don't want to seem sensitive or self-righteous.	_____	_____
4. When you see media that are targeted at an ethnic, gender, or religious group that you do not represent, you usually ignore them.	_____	_____
5. When you look for a mentor or protégé, you pick someone like yourself.	_____	_____
6. If someone tells you about a cultural difference that you have never heard of, you rarely ask questions.	_____	_____
7. You are affiliated with organizations that practice subtle discrimination, but you say nothing because you didn't create the rules.	_____	_____

	Yes	No

8. Before you hire someone for a position, you have a vague picture in mind of what the ideal candidate would look like. _____ _____

9. Your conversations make use of phrases like "you people" or "our kind." _____ _____

10. You avoid talking about cultural differences when dealing with people different from you because you're afraid of saying the wrong thing. _____ _____

11. When complimenting someone from a different background, you might tell them, "You are nothing like the others" or "I really don't think of you as a _____." _____ _____

12. There are people in your organization whom you like and respect but whom you would feel uncomfortable introducing to your family or close friends. _____ _____

Scoring:

Give yourself five points for each "yes" answer.

Interpretation:

The appropriate score for today's world is "0." However, if you scored less than 20, you're probably making a good attempt to eliminate personal passive bias. A score of 20 to 40 means you need to watch it—you reveal passive bias that is inappropriate in organizations and society. If you scored more than 40, your level of bias could get you into trouble. You should definitely consider ways to become more diversity aware and culturally sensitive.

SOURCE: Adapted from the book *Proversity: Getting Past Face Values and Finding the Soul of People* by Lawrence Otis Graham (John Wiley & Sons, 1997). Used with permission of Lawrence Otis Graham.

Leadership Development: Case for Analysis

Northern Industries

Northern Industries asked you, a consultant in organizational change and diversity management, to help them resolve some racial issues that, according to president Jim Fisher, are "festering" in their manufacturing plant in Springfield, Massachusetts. Northern Industries is a family-owned enterprise that manufactures greeting cards and paper and plastic holiday decorations. It employs 125 people full time, including African Americans and Asians. About 80 percent of the full-time workforce is female. During the peak production months of September and January (to produce orders primarily for Christmas/Hanukah and Mother's Day) the company runs a second shift and adds about 50 part-time workers, most of whom are women and minorities.

All orders are batch runs made to customer specifications. In a period of a week, it is not unusual for 70 different orders to be filled requiring different paper stocks, inks, plastics, and setups. Since these orders vary greatly in size, the company has a long-term policy of giving priority to high-volume customers and processing other orders on a first-come first-served basis. Half a dozen of the company's major customers have been doing business with Northern for more than 20 years, having been signed on by Jim Fisher's father (now retired).

To begin your orientation to the company, Fisher asks his Production Manager, Walter Beacon, to take you around the plant. Beacon points out the production areas responsible for each of the various steps in the manufacture of a greeting card, from purchasing to printing to quality control and shipping. The plant is clean, but the two large printing rooms, each the workplace for about 25 workers, are quite noisy. You catch snatches of the employees' conversations there, but you cannot figure out what language they are speaking. In the shipping and receiving department you notice that most workers are black, perhaps African American. Beacon confirms that eight out of ten of the workers in that department are black males, and that their boss, Adam Wright, is also African American.

It has been previously arranged that you would attend a meeting of top management in order to get a flavor of the organizational culture. The president introduces you as a diversity consultant and notes that several of his managers have expressed concerns about potential racial problems in the company. He says, "Each of the minority groups sticks together. The African Americans and Orientals rarely mix. Recently there has been a problem with theft of finished product, especially on the second shift, and we had to fire a Thai worker." Fisher has read a lot lately about "managing diversity" and hopes you will be able to help the company. Several managers nod their heads in agreement.

Fisher then turns his executive team to its daily business. The others present are the general manager, personnel manager (the only woman), sales manager, quality control manager, production manager (Beacon), and the shipping and receiving manager (the only non-white manager). Soon an angry debate ensues between the sales and shipping/receiving managers. It seems that orders are not being shipped quickly enough, according to the sales manager, and several complaints have been received from smaller customers about the quality of the product. The shipping/receiving manager argues that he needs more hands to do the job, and that the quality of incoming supplies is lousy. While this debate continues, the other managers are silent and seemingly uncomfortable. Finally one of them attempts to break up the argument with a joke about his wife. Fisher and the other men laugh loudly, and the conversation shifts to other topics.

Questions

1. What recommendations would you make to Northern's leaders to help them move toward successfully managing diversity issues?

2. If you were the shipping and receiving or personnel manager, how do you think you would feel about your job? Discuss some of the challenges you might face at Northern.

3. Refer to Exhibit 11.5. Based on the information in the case, at what stage of personal diversity awareness do leaders at Northern seem to be? Discuss.

References

[1] Lena Williams, "A Silk Blouse on the Assembly Line? (Yes, the Boss's)," *The New York Times*, February 5, 1995, Business Section, 7.

[2] Kurt Anderson, "California Dreamin'," *Time*, September 23, 1991, 38–42.

[3] Richard A. Luecke, *Scuttle Your Ships before Advancing, and Other Lessons from History on Leadership and Change for Today's Managers* (New York: Oxford University Press, 1994), 108–109.

[4] Frances J. Milliken and Luis I. Martins, "Searching for Common Threads: Understanding the Multiple Effects of Diversity in Organizational Groups," *Academy of Management Review* 21, no. 2 (1996): 402–433.

[5] Louis Uchitelle, "The New Faces of U. S. Manufacturing," *The New York Times*, July 3, 1994, Sec. 3, 1, 6.

[6] Marilyn Loden and Judy B. Rosener, *Workforce America!* (Homewood, IL: Business One Irwin, 1991); and Marilyn Loden, *Implementing Diversity* (Homewood, IL: Irwin, 1996).

[7] Milliken and Martins, "Searching for Common Threads."

[8] C. Keen, "Human Resource Management Issues in the '90s," *Vital Speeches* 56, no. 24 (1990): 752–754.

[9] Gilbert W. Fairholm, *Leadership and the Culture of Trust* (Westport, CN: Praeger, 1994), 184.

[10] Alan Farnham, "Global—or Just Globaloney?" *Fortune*, June 27, 1994, 97–100; William C. Symonds, Brian Bremner, Stewart Toy, and Karen Lowry Miller, "The Globetrotters Take Over," *Business Week*, July 8, 1996, 46–48; Carla Rapoport, "Nestlé's Brand Building Machine," *Fortune*, September 19, 1994, 147–156; and "Execs with Global Vision," *USA Today*, International Edition, February 9, 1996, 12B.

[11] Joel Dreyfuss, "Get Ready for the New Workforce," *Fortune*, April 29, 1990, 165–181.

[12] Sharon Nelton, "Nurturing Diversity," *Nation's Business*, June 1995, 25–27.

[13] Fairholm, *Leadership and the Culture of Trust*, 185.

[14] Taylor H. Cox, *Cultural Diversity in Organizations* (San Francisco: Berrett-Koehler, 1994).

[15] Judy B. Rosener, *America's Competitive Secret: Women Managers* (New York: Oxford University Press, 1995), and "Ways Women Lead," *Harvard Business Review*, November—December 1990, 119–125; Sally Helgesen, *The Female Advantage: Women's Ways of Leadership* (New York: Currency/Doubleday, 1990); Joline Godfrey, "Been There, Doing That," *Inc.*, March 1996, 21–22; Chris Lee, "The Feminization of Management," *Training*, November 1994, 25–31; and Bernard M. Bass and Bruce J.

Avolio, "Shatter the Glass Ceiling: Women May Make Better Managers," *Human Resource Management* 33, no. 4 (Winter 1994): 549–560.

[16]Dawn Hill, "Women Leaders Doing It Their Way," *New Woman*, January 1994, 78.

[17]Based on Judy B. Rosener, *America's Competitive Secret: Women Managers* (New York: Oxford University Press, 1997), 129–135.

[18]John Holusha, "Grace Pastiak's 'Web of Inclusion,'" *The New York Times*, May 5, 1991, Section 3, 1, 6.

[19]Sally Helgesen, *The Female Advantage: Women's Ways of Leadership* (New York: Doubleday Currency, 1990).

[20]Bass and Avolio, "Shatter the Glass Ceiling."

[21]M. Fine, F. Johnson, and M. S. Ryan, "Cultural Diversity in the Workforce," *Public Personnel Management* 19 (1990): 305–319; and Hill, "Women Leaders Doing It Their Way," *New Woman*.

[22]Joel Dreyfuss, "Get Ready for the New Work Force," *Fortune*, April 23, 1990, 165–181; and Ronald E. Dulek, John S. Fielden, and John S. Hill, "International Communication: An Executive Primer," *Business Horizons*, January—February 1991, 20–25.

[23]Shawn Tully, "Northwest and KLM—The Alliance from Hell," *Fortune*, June 24, 1996, 64–72.

[24]Geert Hofstede, "The Interaction between National and Organizational Value Systems," *Journal of Management Studies* 22 (1985): 347–357, and "The Cultural Relativity of the Quality of Life Concept," *Academy of Management Review* 9 (1984): 389–398.

[25]Geert Hofstede, "Cultural Constraints in Management Theories," excerpted in Dorothy Marcic and Sheila M. Puffer, *Management International: Cases, Exercises, and Readings* (St. Paul, MN: West Publishing, 1994), 24.

[26]Fairholm, *Leadership and the Culture of Trust*, 187–188.

[27]Burton Bollag, "Walking the Line . . .," *Across the Board*, July/August 1995, 37–41.

[28]E. S. Browning, "Computer Chip Project Brings Rivals Together, But the Cultures Clash," *The Wall Street Journal*, May 3, 1994, A1.

[29]Harry C. Triandis, "The Contingency Model in Cross-Cultural Perspective," in Martin M. Chemers and Roya Ayman, eds., *Leadership Theory and Research: Perspectives and Directions* (San Diego, CA: Academic Press, Inc., 1993), 167–188; and Peter B. Smith and Mark F. Peterson, *Leadership, Organizations, and Culture: An Event Management Model* (London: Sage, 1988).

[30]G. Haight, "Managing Diversity," *Across the Board* 27, no. 3 (1990): 22–29.

[31]This section is based on Rosener, *America's Competitive Secret*, 33–34.

[32]Ann Morrison, *The New Leaders: Guidelines on Leadership Diversity in America* (San Francisco: Jossey-Bass, 1992), 37.

[33]Deborah L. Jacobs, "Back from the Mommy Track," *The New York Times*, October 9, 1994, F1, F6.

[34]Robert Hooijberg and Nancy DeTomaso, "Leadership In and Of Demographically Diverse Organizations," *Leadership Quarterly* 7, no. 1 (1996): 1–19.

[35]W. E. B. DuBois, *The Souls of Black Folks* (Chicago: Chicago University Press, 1903), quoted in Hooijberg and DiTomaso, "Leadership in and of Demographically Diverse Organizations."

[36]Vivian Louie, "For Asian-Americans, A Way to Fight a Maddening Stereotype," *The New York Times*, August 8, 1993, 9.

[37]Michele Galen with Ann Therese Palmer, "Diversity: Beyond the Numbers Game," *Business Week*, August 14, 1995, 60–61.

[38]C. Solomon, "Careers under Glass," *Personnel Journal* 69, no. 4 (1990), 96–105; and *Population Profile of the United States 1995*, U. S. Department of Commerce, Bureau of the Census, July 1995.

[39]Julie Amparano Lopez, "Study Says Women Face Glass Walls as Well as Glass Ceiling," *The Wall Street Journal*, March 3, 1992, B1, B2; and Joann S. Lublin, "Women at Top

Still Are Distant from CEO Jobs," *The Wall Street Journal*, February 28, 1996, B1, B8.

[40]Renee Blank and Sandra Slipp, "The White Male: An Endangered Species?" *Management Review*, September 1994, 27–32; and Sharon Nelton, "Nurturing Diversity," *Nation's Business*, June 1995, 25–27.

[41]Rosener, *America's Competitive Secret*, 142–148.

[42]Based on Fairholm, *Leadership and the Culture of Trust*, 189–192; Cox, *Cultural Diversity in Organizations*; and Ann M. Morrison, *The New Leaders: Guidelines on Leadership Diversity in America* (San Francisco: Jossey-Bass, 1992), 29–56.

[43]Morrison, *The New Leaders*, 35.

[44]Based on Nicholas Imparato and Oren Harari, *Jumping the Curve: Innovation and Strategic Choice in an Age of Transition* (San Francisco: Jossey-Bass, 1994), 186–203.

[45]Lennie Copeland, "Learning to Manage a Multicultural Workforce," *Training*, May 25, 1988, 48–56.

[46]Martin M. Chemers and Roya Ayman, *Leadership Theory and Research: Perspectives and Directions* (San Diego, CA: Academic Press, 1993), 209.

[47]Fairholm, *Leadership and the Culture of Trust*, 194.

[48]Nicole Harris, "A New Denny's—Diner by Diner," *Business Week*, March 25, 1996, 166–168.

[49]Jenny C. McCune, "Diversity Training: A Competitive Weapon," *Management Review*, June 1996, 25–28.

PART SIX

The Personal Side of Leadership

Chapter 12
Leadership Mind and Heart

Chapter 13
Courage and Moral Leadership

Chapter 14
Followership

12

Leadership Mind and Heart

- **Leader Capacity versus Competence** 333

- **Charismatic Leadership** 334

- **Leadership Mind** 338

- **Leading with Heart—Emotional Intelligence** 345

- **Leading with Love versus Leading with Fear** 349

- **Leadership Spotlights:**
  Orit Gadiesh   335
  Sears   343
  The United States Army   347

- **Leader's Bookshelf:** *Rewiring the Corporate Brain: Using the New Science to Rethink How We Structure and Lead Organizations* 339

- **Leadership Development: Personal Feedback**
  Emotional Intelligence   355

- **Leadership Development: Case for Analysis**
  The USS *Florida*   356

Your Leadership Challenge

After reading this chapter, you should be able to:

- Apply aspects of charismatic leadership by pursuing a vision or idea that you care deeply about and want to share with others.

- Engage in independent thinking by staying mentally alert, thinking critically, and being mindful rather than mindless.

- Start to break out of categorized thinking patterns and open your mind to new ideas and multiple perspectives.

- Begin to apply systems thinking, mental models, and personal mastery to your activities at school or work.

- Exercise emotional intelligence in your relationships, including being self-aware, managing your emotions, motivating yourself, displaying empathy, and applying social skills.

- Apply the difference between motivating others based on fear and motivating others based on love.

Pamela Coker's company, Acucobol, Inc. went from a six-person start-up to an international software company with annual sales of over $4 million in just 40 months. Profits have been flowing steadily since the twelfth month of operation. When asked about the secret to Acucobol's success, Coker cites her philosophy: "Love your customers, employees, shareholders, vendors, and community . . . and the profits will follow."

Love and business are two words that aren't often heard together, but Coker firmly believes they should be. She thinks letting customers know you love them develops a high level of trust that is crucial for long-term success.

Acucobol's customers develop commercial applications for software in areas such as payroll, inventory control, and fleet maintenance, using ACUCOBOL-85, a new version of COBOL. What's different about Acucobol's product is its ability to interact with more than 500 platforms (different types of computers and operating systems). Acucobol people spend hours communicating with customers so that technical problems can be solved quickly and smoothly. They demonstrate caring and respect for customers by going beyond standard business practices. Every customer gets a call once a month just to ask if there's anything Acucobol can do to help them out. A couple of times a year, Acucobol mails every customer a gift to express appreciation for their business. A yearly conference allows customers and employees to talk about problems and new products.

Acucobol's employees are committed to showing care and respect for customers because company leaders show care and respect for employees. Coker is committed to creating a work environment where employees can "learn, make mistakes, grow, excel, and prosper." She stresses the importance of caring about employees as persons—which means caring about their health, their families, their personal problems, and their dreams, as well as their work and career goals. Flexible hours allow workers to have personal time when they most need it and encourages them to best use their time at work. Regular company-sponsored events include friends and families. These events develop camaraderie, openness, and trust, which Coker believes lead to greater productivity. Although she believes loving employees leads to greater productivity and greater profits for shareholders, she emphasizes that the primary goal is not making money: "I am committed to helping every Acucobol employee attain his or her dreams."[1]

Pamela Coker is not the only business leader talking about building work relationships based on caring, trust, and respect. Peter Drucker, a writer who is widely read by practicing managers, has been stressing the importance of people and relationships for years. Wayne Calloway, former CEO of PepsiCo, when asked the secret to his company's competitiveness, once said, "The three Ps: people, people, people." Even Jack Welch, CEO of General Electric, who was once called the toughest boss in America, has mandated that he and his senior executives must get softer, more human, and more collegial.[2] Many organizations have a growing appreciation for the fact that the strength of relationships with employees, customers, suppliers, and competitors is just as important as formal rules, contracts, plans, and even profits. In a time of rapid change, leaders focus on personal relationships as a way to bind people together.

Making relationships rather than rules and schedules a priority is not easy for traditional managers who have been accustomed to thinking emotions should be left outside the company gate. However, smart leaders are increasingly aware that human emotion is the most basic force in organizations and that acknowledging and respecting employees as whole people can enhance organizational performance. People cannot be separated from their emotions, and it is through emotion that leaders generate employee commitment to shared vision and mission, values and culture, and caring for the work and each other.

This chapter and the next explore current thinking about the importance of leaders becoming whole people by exploring the full capacities of their mind and spirit. By doing so, they help others reach their full potential and contribute fully to the organization. We will first examine what we mean by leader capacity and explore the concept of charismatic leadership. Then we will discuss the role of the mind by examining leadership qualities such as independent thinking, an open mind, and systems thinking. Then we take a closer look at human emotion as illustrated in the leadership concept of emotional intelligence and the emotions of love versus fear in leader-follower relationships. In the next chapter we will turn to spirit as reflected in moral leadership and courage.

Leader Capacity versus Competence

Traditionally, effective leadership, like good management, has been thought of as competence in a set of skills; once these specific skills are acquired, all one has to do to succeed is put them into action. However, as we all know from personal experience, effectively working with other people requires much more than practicing specific, rational skills; it often means drawing on subtle aspects of ourselves—our thoughts, beliefs, or feelings—and appealing to those aspects in others. As discussed in the Living Leadership box, FedEx specifies nine qualities that make a person a good leader, all of which draw on personal capabilities rather than skills competence. Particularly in today's rapidly changing environment, skills competence is no longer enough. While organizational issues such as production schedules, structure, finances, costs, profits, and so forth are important, in a time of uncertainty and change organizations need more. Key issues include how to give people a sense of meaning and purpose when major shifts occur almost daily; how to make employees feel valued and respected in an age of downsizing and job uncertainty; and how to keep morale and motivation high in the face of rapid change and the stress it creates.

In this chapter, rather than discussing competence, we will explore a person's *capacity* for mind and heart. Whereas competence is limited and quantifiable, capacity is unlimited and defined by the potential for expansion and growth.[3] **Capacity** means the potential each of us has to do more and be more than we are now. Leadership capacity goes beyond learning the skills for organizing, planning, or controlling others. It also involves something deeper and more subtle than the leadership traits and styles we discussed in Chapters 3 and 4. Living, working, and leading based on our capacity means using our whole selves, including intellectual, emotional, and spiritual abilities and understandings. A broad literature has emphasized that being a whole person means operating from mind, heart, spirit, and body.[4] Although we can't "learn" capacity the way we learn a set of skills, we can expand and develop leadership capacity. For example, just as the physical capacity of our lungs is increased through regular aerobic exercise, the capacities of the mind, heart, and spirit can be expanded through conscious development and regular use. This chapter will focus on the leadership capacities of mind and heart.

The Nine Faces of Leadership

According to FedEx, its best leaders have nine personal attributes in common. The FedEx leadership curriculum, which takes up to 14 months to complete, first asks aspiring leaders to consider their interest in and capability for leadership, and uses a system for rating aspiring leaders according to the following nine faces of leadership.

1. **Charisma.** Instills faith, respect, and trust. Has an ability to see what others need to consider. Conveys a strong sense of purpose and vision.
2. **Individual consideration.** Coaches, advises, and teaches people. Listens actively. Supports and assists newcomers.
3. **Intellectual stimulation.** Gets others to use reasoning and evidence. Enables others to think about old problems in new ways, question their assumptions, and rethink ideas they've never questioned before.
4. **Courage.** Willing to stand up for ideas and beliefs, even if they are unpopular. Does not give in to pressure or the opinions of others. Does what's right for the organization and its employees, even if it causes personal hardship.
5. **Dependability.** Follows through and keeps commitments. Can be counted on. Takes responsibility for actions and accepts responsibility for mistakes. Able to work independently.
6. **Flexibility.** Works well in shifting environments. Able to handle more than one problem at a time. Changes course when the situation warrants it.
7. **Integrity.** Does what is morally and ethically right and acts as a consistent role model. Does not abuse power or privileges of position.
8. **Judgment.** Makes sound and objective evaluations of alternative courses of actions. Puts facts together rationally and realistically. Uses logic, analysis, and comparison, as well as past experience and information to consider present decisions.
9. **Respect for others.** Honors others. Does not belittle the opinions, ideas, suggestions, or work of other people, regardless of their status or position.

SOURCE: Heath Row, "Is Management for Me? That Is the Question." *Fast Company* (February/March 1998), 50–52.

Charismatic Leadership

Charismatic leadership has long been of interest to researchers studying political leadership, social movements, and religious cults. In recent years, attention has been given to the impact of charismatic leadership in organizations. Charisma is difficult to define, but involves mental and emotional intensity. It has been called "a fire that ignites followers' energy and commitment, producing results above and beyond the call of duty."[5] **Charismatic leaders** have the ability to inspire and motivate people to do more than they would normally do, despite obstacles and personal sacrifice. In describing the charismatic leader, one business writer says, "He persuades people—subordinates, peers, customers, even the S.O.B. you both work for—to do things they'd rather not. People charge over the hill for him. Run through fire. Walk barefoot on broken glass. He doesn't demand attention, he commands it."[6]

Charismatic leaders have an impact on people because they appeal to both the heart and the mind. They may speak emotionally about putting themselves on the line for the sake of a mission. When Arthur Martinez took over as CEO of Sears in 1992, he knew he was facing big problems to rescue its sinking retail unit. To lure top talent, Martinez put himself in the role of evangelist, enrolling people in a mission. He met personally with almost every applicant for senior level positions and told them, "This is one of the greatest adventures in business history. . . . You have to be courageous, filled with self-confidence. If we do it, we'll be wealthier, yes. But more than that, we'll have incredible psychic gratification. How can you not do it?" Martinez assembled one of the best executive teams in retailing, persuading some people who previously had no interest in changing jobs.[7] Used wisely and ethically, charisma can lift the entire organization's level of performance. Charismatic leaders can raise people's consciousness about new possibilities and motivate them to transcend their own interests for the sake of the team, department, or organization. Bain & Company Chairman Orit Gadiesh illustrates the emotional appeal of the charismatic leader.

LEADERSHIP SPOTLIGHT　　　ORIT GADIESH

The first thing a new client may notice about Orit Gadiesh, chair of management consulting firm Bain & Co., is that her skirt starts about eight inches above the knee. Or maybe that her hair viewed from the side and back is magenta. Or perhaps her long red fingernails make the first impression. She seems out of place chairing one of the most secretive firms in a low-key industry, but thanks to Gadiesh's leadership, revenues at Bain & Co. are increasing 25 percent a year.

The "Orit mystique" is well known around Boston, where Bain is located, and throughout the consulting industry. According to Bain managing director Tom Tierney, her charisma comes mainly from an intense passion about being true to herself and to the client. For Gadiesh, business success isn't systematic; it's about pulling emotional levers. She's always willing to challenge the status quo, disagree with others, and stand up for her opinions. Being around her loosens people up and increases their energy level. She challenges employees as well as clients with thoughtful questions that encourage them to think in new ways and imagine new possibilities. However, it may be her ability to empathize with others that makes her so successful. According to James Morgan, CEO of Philip Morris USA, one of Bain's clients, "Orit has that talent for making you feel you're the most important person in the room. She bleeds your blood."[8]

Orit Gadiesh galvanizes people to action by operating from her heart as well as her mind. Herb Kelleher, chairman and CEO of Southwest Airlines, is another leader who is well known for inspiring employees with his unconventional approach, helping to make the airline consistently profitable. In what he has called "management by fooling around," Kelleher motivates employees to break the rules, maintain their individuality, and have fun. It's a style that has made Southwest's workers the most productive in the industry.[9] Not everyone will develop the personal appeal of Gadiesh or Kelleher. However, charisma can be developed by pursuing activities you really love and feel strongly about. U.S. Army Major General John H. Stanford referred to this aspect of charisma when questioned about leadership development:

> When anyone asks me that question, I tell them I have the secret to success in life. The secret to success is stay in love. Staying in love gives you the fire to really ignite other people, to see inside other people, to have a greater desire to get things done than other people. A person who is not in love doesn't really find the kind of excitement that helps them to get ahead and lead others and to achieve. I don't know any other fire, any other thing in life that is more exhilarating and is more positive a feeling than love is.[10]

Leaders who really love what they do have a magical quality of charisma. Charismatic leaders are pursuing a vision, idea, project, or activity that they genuinely care about. They are engaging their emotion in everyday work life, which makes them energetic, enthusiastic, and attractive to others. Finding exhilaration from one's life work is a basic premise of leadership.

What Makes a Charismatic Leader

In today's turbulent business environment, there is increased interest in how charismatic leaders build emotional attachment and commitment among followers. A number of studies have identified the unique qualities of charismatic leaders, documented the impact they have on followers, and described the behaviors that help them achieve remarkable results.[11] Exhibit 12.1 compares distinguishing characteristics of charismatic and noncharismatic leaders.[12]

Charismatic leaders create an atmosphere of change and articulate an idealized vision of a future that is significantly better in some way than what now exists. They have an ability to communicate complex ideas and goals in clear, compelling ways, so that everyone from the vice-president to the janitor can understand and identify with their message. Charismatic leaders inspire followers with an abiding faith even if the faith cannot be translated into specific goals that can be easily attained. The faith itself becomes a "reward" to followers. Martin Luther King's "I Have a Dream" speech is an example of how leaders can motivate followers by inspiring hope and faith in a better future.[13] Charismatic leaders also act in unconventional ways and use unconventional means to transcend the status quo and create change. They may sometimes seem like oddballs, but this image only enhances their appeal.

Charismatic leaders earn followers' trust by being willing to incur great personal risk. Putting themselves on the line affirms charismatic leaders as passionate advocates for their vision. According to a personal friend of the King family, Martin Luther King received death threats against himself and his family almost every day during the civil rights movement.[14] By taking risks, leaders can enhance their emotional appeal to followers. Michael Jordan is a good example of how the nerve to take great personal risks can enhance charisma and likability. Jordan temporarily left a career as a highly successful basketball player to flounder in the game of baseball.

EXHIBIT 12.1	DISTINGUISHING CHARACTERISTICS OF CHARISMATIC AND NONCHARISMATIC LEADERS	
	Noncharismatic Leaders	**Charismatic Leaders**
Likableness:	Shared perspective makes leader likable	Shared perspective and idealized vision make leader likable and an honorable hero worthy of identification and imitation
Trustworthiness:	Disinterested advocacy in persuasion attempts	Passionate advocacy by incurring great personal risk and cost
Relation to status quo:	Tries to maintain status quo	Creates atmosphere of change
Future goals:	Limited goals not too discrepant from status quo	Idealized vision that is highly discrepant from status quo
Articulation:	Weak articulation of goals and motivation to lead	Strong and inspirational articulation of vision and motivation to lead
Competence:	Uses available means to achieve goals within framework of the existing order	Uses unconventional means to transcend the existing order
Behavior:	Conventional, conforms to norms	Unconventional, counter-normative
Influence:	Primarily authority of position and rewards	Transcends position; personal power based on expertise and respect and admiration for the leader

SOURCE: Jay A. Conger and Rabindra N. Kanungo and Associates, *Charismatic Leadership: The Elusive Factor in Organizational Effectiveness* (San Francisco: Jossey-Bass Publishers, 1988), 91.

Quaker Oats, which pays Jordan to promote Gatorade, surveyed consumers daily during Jordan's baseball career, and his emotional appeal never wavered. In fact, most people identified more personally with Jordan because he seemed more "human."[15] Another characteristic of charismatic leaders is that people like and identify with the leader and want to be like her or him. The final characteristic of charismatic leaders is that their source of influence comes from personal power as opposed to authority of position. Followers respect and admire the leader because of his or her knowledge, enthusiasm, or personal character. Charismatic leadership transcends formal organizational position because the leader's influence is based on personal qualities rather than the power and authority granted by the organization.

The Black Hat of Charisma

Most researchers agree that charisma can be a curse as well as a blessing. Leaders such as Winston Churchill, John F. Kennedy, and Mohandas Gandhi exhibited tremendous charisma. So did leaders such as Adolf Hitler, Charles Manson, and Idi Amin. Charisma isn't always used to benefit the group, organization, or society. It can also be used for self-serving purposes, which leads to deception, manipulation, and exploitation of others.

One explanation for the distinction between charisma that results in positive outcomes and that which results in negative outcomes relates to the difference between "personalized" leaders and "socialized" leaders.[16] Leaders who respond to organizational problems in terms of their own emotional needs rather than the needs of the whole group often act in ways that can have disastrous consequences for others. Personalized charismatic leaders are characterized as self-aggrandizing, nonegalitarian, and exploitative, whereas socialized charismatic leaders are empowering, egalitarian, and supportive. Personalized behavior is based on intensely caring about self; socialized behavior is based on enthusiastically valuing others. Studies have shown that personalized charismatic leaders can have a significant detrimental impact on long-term organizational performance. Leaders who have been consistently successful in improving organizational performance exhibit a pattern of socialized behavior.[17]

Leadership Mind

One mark of charismatic leaders is that they question the status quo, look for new ideas, and encourage novel solutions. They think "outside of the box" and encourage others to think. Issues of mind are more critical to effective leadership than ever. The Leader's Bookshelf argues that the standard business-world model of thinking is inadequate for today's constantly changing world.

The leader's mind can be developed beyond the nonleader's in five critical areas: independent thinking; open mindedness; systems thinking; mental models; and personal mastery.

Independent Thinking

Independent thinking means questioning assumptions and interpreting data and events according to one's own beliefs, ideas, and thinking, not according to preestablished rules, routines, or categories defined by others. People who think independently are willing to stand apart, to have opinions, to say what they think, and to determine a course of action based on what they personally believe rather than on what other people think. To think independently means staying mentally alert, thinking critically, being mindful rather than mindless. **Mindfulness** can be defined as the process of continuously reevaluating previously learned ways of doing things in the context of evolving information and shifting circumstances.[18] It is the opposite of mindlessness, which means blindly accepting rules and labels created by others. Mindless people let others do the thinking for them.

In the chaotic world of organizations, everything is constantly changing. What worked in one situation may not work the next time. In these conditions, mental laziness and accepting others' answers can hurt the organization and all

Rewiring the Corporate Brain: Using the New Science to Rethink How We Structure and Lead Organizations
Danah Zohar

In *Rewiring the Corporate Brain*, Danah Zohar says leaders must go beyond rationality and develop new models of thinking to cope with today's environment. She asserts that many organizations never achieve needed transformation because leaders are stuck in old ways of thinking that stifle the organization's capacity for fundamental change. She proposes a model for leadership based on "quantum thinking"—a new paradigm based on eight principles that help organizations function "at the creative edge of what is and what might be."

Eight Principles of Quantum Organizations

1. *The quantum organization is holistic.* Leaders engage in systems thinking and build infrastructures that encourage and develop relationships between leaders and employees, employees and colleagues, divisions and functional groups, and the organization and its environment.
2. *The organization is flexible and responsive.* Leaders understand that ambiguity, complexity, and rapid change dominate events both inside and outside the organization and design infrastructures that allow the organization to evolve.
3. *The organization is bottom-up, self-organizing, and emergent.* Leaders create systems that nourish human and organizational creativity. They minimize boundaries and facilitate the free flow of information and ideas. Parts of the organization (whether individuals, teams, or divisions) are free to rearrange themselves as needed to meet new conditions.
4. *The organization thrives on diversity.* There is no "one best way" in the quantum organization. Leaders encourage diversity of people and ideas. "My way" gives way to shared vision, shared opportunity, and shared responsibility.

5. *The quantum organization operates like a jazz jam session.* In a jam session, there is no set score and no conductor, but rather an evolving background theme and an emergent whole that organizes the parts. Quantum organizations allow different questions to be asked, different goals considered, different products or functions imagined.
6. *The quantum organization is playful.* Leaders encourage playfulness and reward risk-taking, recognizing that people and organizations learn and change by being curious and taking chances.
7. *The quantum organization is "deeply green."* Leaders are concerned with the organization's human environments as well as its societal, cultural, and natural environments.
8. *The quantum organization is vision-centered and values-driven.* Leaders understand that people seek meaning in their work and need to dream big dreams. They create organizations as living systems that are always reaching beyond themselves to new possibilities.

The Leadership Challenge
Leaders who want to develop quantum organizations face a number of challenges. The first is to shift to a new-paradigm mind-set and be able to lead both those who thrive on uncertainty and change and those who fear it. According to Zohar, there is no quick fix, no short route to transformation. "Real change must issue from those deep levels of our human being where we are in touch with meaning and value. It is not something we can do in order to 'beat the hell out of the competition.'"

Rewiring the Corporate Brain, by Danah Zohar, is published by Berrett-Koehler Publishers.

its members. Leaders apply critical thinking to explore a situation, problem, or question from multiple perspectives and integrate all the available information into a possible solution. When leaders think critically, they question all assumptions, vigorously seek divergent opinions, and try to give balanced consideration to all alternatives.[19] Thinking independently and critically is hard work, and most of us can easily relax into temporary mindlessness, accepting black and white answers and relying on standard ways of doing things. Leaders need to stay mentally alert, keep thinking, and keep asking questions.

Open-Mindedness

One approach to independent thinking is to try to break out of the mental boxes, the categorized thinking patterns we have been conditioned to accept as correct. Mind potential is released when we open up to new ideas and multiple perspectives, when we can get outside our mental box. John Keating, the private school teacher portrayed in the movie *Dead Poets Society*, urged his students to stand on their desks to get a new perspective on the world: "I stand on my desk to remind myself we must constantly look at things a different way. The world looks different from here."

The power of the conditioning that guides our thinking and behavior is illustrated by what has been called the Pike Syndrome. In an experiment, a northern pike is placed in one half of a large glass-divided aquarium, with numerous minnows placed in the other half. The hungry pike makes repeated attempts to get the minnows, but succeeds only in battering itself against the glass, finally learning that reaching the minnows is futile. The glass divider is then removed, but the pike makes no attempt to attack the minnows because it has been conditioned to believe that reaching them is impossible. When people assume they have complete knowledge of a situation because of past experiences, they exhibit the Pike Syndrome, a rigid commitment to what was true in the past and a refusal to consider alternatives and different perspectives.[20]

Leaders have to forget many of their conditioned ideas to be open to new ones. This openness—putting aside preconceptions and suspending beliefs and opinions—can be referred to as "beginner's mind." Whereas the expert's mind rejects new ideas based on past experience and knowledge, the beginner's mind reflects the openness and innocence of a young child just learning about the world. Nobel prize-winning physicist Richard Feynman, one of the most original scientific minds of the twentieth century, illustrates the power of the beginner's mind. Feynman's IQ was an unremarkable 125. The heart of his genius was a childlike curiosity and a belief that doubt was the essence of learning and knowing. Feynman was always questioning, always uncertain, always starting over, always resisting any authority that prevented him from doing his own thinking and exploring.[21]

Effective leaders strive to keep open minds and cultivate an organizational environment that encourages curiosity. They understand the limitations of past experience and reach out for diverse perspectives. For example, one leader had a personal board of directors, each of whom had opinions different from himself, that he would consult on important issues. Talking with them broadened his mind-set to encompass issues far beyond his own thinking. Some companies, such as Southwest Airlines, Quad/Graphics, and Manco, make curiosity and interest in learning a more important hiring criterion than experience or expertise. Leaders can also support and reward people who are willing to ask questions, stretch boundaries, experiment, and keep learning. At Manco, an adhesives company, employees can enroll in any outside course they choose, whether it's business management or basketweaving, and be reimbursed as long as they pass the course. CEO Jack Krahl's rationale is that, "It lets people know . . . that one of the highest values at Manco is to be curious and to allow curiosity to take place."[22]

Bernard Bass, who has studied charismatic and transformational leadership, talks about the value of intellectual stimulation—which means arousing followers' thoughts and imagination as well stimulating their ability to identify and solve problems creatively.[23] People admire leaders who challenge them to think and learn, to break out of the box of conditioned thinking and be open to new, inspiring ideas and alternatives.

Systems Thinking

Peter Senge, author of *The Fifth Discipline*, argued that leaders in learning organizations must acquire five competencies. Two of these—shared vision and team learning—were explored in Chapters 5 and 10. The other three are to develop the mental capabilities of systems thinking, mental models, and personal mastery.[24]

Systems thinking means seeing patterns in the organizational whole instead of just the parts, and learning to reinforce or change system patterns. Traditional managers have been trained to solve problems by breaking things down into discrete pieces, and the success of each piece is believed to add up to the success of the whole. But it is the *relationship* among the parts that form the whole that counts. Systems thinking enables leaders to look for patterns of movement over time and focus on the qualities of rhythm, flow, direction, shape, and networks of relationships that accomplish the work of an organization. Systems thinking is a mental discipline and framework for seeing patterns and interrelationships.

It is important to see organizational systems as a whole because of their complexity. Complexity can overwhelm managers, undermining confidence. When leaders can see the structures that underlie complex situations, they can facilitate improvement. But it requires a focus on the big picture. Leaders can develop what David McCamus, former Chairman and CEO of Xerox Canada, calls "peripheral vision" the ability to view the organization through a wide-angle lens, rather than a telephoto lens, so that they perceive how their decisions and actions affect the whole.[25]

An important element of systems thinking is to discern circles of causality. Senge argues that reality is made up of circles rather than straight lines. For example, Exhibit 12.2 shows circles of influence for producing new products. In the circle on the left, a high-tech firm grows rapidly by pumping out new products quickly. New products increase revenues, which enable the further increase of the R&D budget to add more new products.

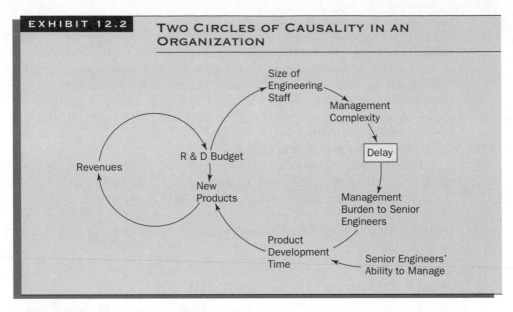

EXHIBIT 12.2 **TWO CIRCLES OF CAUSALITY IN AN ORGANIZATION**

SOURCE: From *The Fifth Discipline: The Art and Practice of the Learning Organization* by Peter M. Senge, 97. Copyright © 1990 by Peter M. Senge. Used by permission of Doubleday, a division of Bantam Doubleday Dell Publishing Group, Inc..

But another circle of causality is being influenced as well. As the R&D budget grows, the engineering and research staff increases. The burgeoning technical staff becomes increasingly hard to manage. The management burden falls on senior engineers, who provide less of their time for developing new products, which reduces product development time. The slowing of product development time has a negative impact on new products, the very thing that created organizational success. Maintaining product development time in the face of increasing management complexity depends upon senior engineers' management ability. Thus, understanding the circle of causality enables leaders to allocate resources to the training and development of engineering leadership as well as directly to new products. Without an understanding of the system, top leaders would fail to understand why increasing R&D budgets can actually increase product development time and reduce the number of new products coming to market.

The other element of systems thinking is learning to influence the system with reinforcing feedback as an engine for growth or decline. In the example of new products, after managers see how the system works, they can allocate revenues to speed new products to market, either by hiring more engineers, or by training senior engineers in management and leadership skills. They can guide the system when they understand it conceptually. Without this kind of understanding, managers will hit blockages in the form of seeming limits to growth, and resistance to change because the large complex system will appear impossible to manage. Systems thinking is a significant solution.

Mental Models

Mental models are the deep-seated assumptions, beliefs, blind spots, biases, and prejudices that determine how leaders make sense of the world.[26] Mental models govern the actions leaders take in response to situations. Someone who has the assumption that people are untrustworthy will act very differently in a situation than someone who assumes people are trustworthy. When leaders are not aware of their own biases and mental models, they have the potential to make serious mistakes. In a time of rapid change, many leaders are still trapped in mental models based on circumstances that no longer exist. For example, American auto manufacturers lost 38 percent of the U.S. market to Japanese and German automakers because they failed to recognize that public preference had shifted from car style and status to quality and economy. Researcher Ian Mitroff studied General Motors and recognized that leaders were operating on a set of assumptions that had been the company's "magic formula for success" for many years:[27]

> Styling is more important than quality. The American market is isolated from the world. Workers do not affect productivity or quality.

GM leaders regarded their assumptions as fixed truths rather than as temporary ideas that worked well under particular conditions. Only after enormous losses did GM executives begin to question whether their mental models fit the reality of the new marketplace.

To help organizations survive in today's rapidly changing global environment, leaders have to break out of outdated mental models or paradigms. What worked yesterday may not work today. Following conventional wisdom about "how things have always been done" is a sure route to failure. The following example illustrates the impact a top leader's mental model can have on the organization.

LEADERSHIP SPOTLIGHT   SEARS

Sears was getting crushed by the competition and losing billions of dollars in 1992 when CEO Ed Brennan recruited Arthur Martinez to head the retail unit. Martinez, now CEO of Sears, rejuvenated the company with a strategy Brennan, a third-generation Sears merchant, had long resisted: closing the catalogue division, shutting 113 unprofitable stores, and focusing on a new target customer: women.

A *Fortune* interview that asked the same questions of the old and new CEOs revealed just how different their assumptions and beliefs were. Brennan was rooted in a mental model that seemed outdated for Sears' new environment. He focused on male-oriented businesses such as hardware, tools, and automotive. Martinez recognized that in most cases women were making the purchasing decisions. He allocated $4 billion to make the stores more appealing to female customers, revamped advertising, and moved furniture and hardware to freestanding stores to make room for more apparel and cosmetics. Brennan refused to acknowledge mistakes and problems that hurt the company. Today, Sears is thriving by focusing on retail, yet Brennan insisted that his earlier strategy of adding a financial services supermarket made up of Dean Witter, Discover Card, Coldwell Banker, and Allstate Insurance was not a mistake. When questioned about a scandal involving 72 Sears tire and auto centers that defrauded customers with unnecessary repairs, Brennan assumed that Sears "never lost the good will of the American consumer." Martinez, on the other hand, believed that the scandal hurt the company's image and provided potential for a tremendous breakdown of trust with customers.

Perhaps the most telling difference between Brennan and Martinez concerns their assumptions about what makes a good organizational leader. Brennan responded with one simple word: "Conviction." Martinez disagreed. "I can only tell you what has served me well," he said. "And that is a very open attitude. A willingness to try things, to let people try things. . . . And not treating mistakes as fatal."[28]

Personal Mastery

Peter Senge uses the term *personal mastery* to describe the discipline of personal growth and learning, of mastering yourself in a way that facilitates your leadership and achieves desired results.[29] Organizations can grow and learn only when the people who make up the organization are growing and learning.

Personal mastery embodies three qualities—personal vision, facing reality, and holding creative tension. First, leaders engaged in personal mastery know and clarify what is important to them. They focus on the end result, the vision or dream that motivates them and their organization. They have a clear vision of a desired future, and their purpose is to achieve that future. One element of personal mastery, then, is the discipline of continually focusing and defining what one wants as their desired future and vision.

Second, facing reality means a commitment to the truth. Leaders are relentless in uncovering the mental models that limit and deceive themselves and are willing to challenge assumptions and ways of doing things. These leaders are committed to the truth, and will break through denial of reality in themselves and others. Their quest for truth leads to a deeper awareness of themselves and of the larger systems and events within which they operate. Commitment to the truth enables them to deal with reality, which increases the opportunity to achieve the results they seek.

Third, often there is a large gap between one's vision and the current situation. The gap between the desired future and today's reality, say between the dream of starting a business and the reality of having no capital, can be discouraging. But the gap is the source of creative energy. Acknowledging and living with the disparity between the truth and the vision, and facing it squarely, is the source of resolve and creativity to move forward. The effective leader resolves the tension by letting the vision pull reality toward it, in other words, by reorganizing current activities to work toward the vision. The leader works in a way that moves things toward the vision. The less effective way is to let reality pull the vision downward toward it. This means lowering the vision, such as walking away from a problem or settling for less than desired. Settling for less releases the tension, but also engenders mediocrity. Leaders with personal mastery learn to accept both the dream and the reality simultaneously, and to close the gap by moving the organization toward the dream.

All five elements of mind are interrelated. Independent thinking and open-mindedness improve systems thinking, expand mental models, and enable personal mastery. Since they are all interdependent, leaders working to improve even one element of their mental approach can move forward in a significant way toward mastering their mind and becoming an effective leader.

Leading with Heart—Emotional Intelligence

Willis T. White, Jr., president and CEO of West Coast Valet Service, a commercial dry cleaning and laundry service in Burlingame, California, gives emotions a high priority in running his business. "When people are stressed, when people are frustrated, it's hard to get any input from them and it's hard to get any productivity," he says. "You might see the quantity, but you don't get the quality."[30] White is among a growing number of leaders who recognize that emotions play a critical role in the workplace. In recent years, psychologists and other researchers have broadened our understanding of how emotional understanding and skills impact our success and happiness in our work as well as personal lives. Leaders can acknowledge, harness, and direct the power of emotions to improve employee satisfaction, morale, and motivation, as well as to enhance organizational effectiveness.

What Are Emotions?

There are hundreds of emotions and more subtleties of emotion than there are words to explain them. Some researchers accept eight categories or "families" of emotions, as illustrated in Exhibit 12.3.[31] These categories do not resolve every question about how to categorize emotions, and scientific debate continues. The argument for there being a set of core emotions is based partly on the discovery that specific facial expressions for four of them (fear, anger, sadness, and enjoyment) are universally recognized. People in cultures around the world have been found to recognize these same basic emotions when shown photographs of facial expressions. The primary emotions and some of their variations follow.

Anger: fury, outrage, resentment, exasperation, indignation, animosity, annoyance, irritability, hostility, violence.

Sadness: grief, sorrow, gloom, melancholy, self-pity, loneliness, dejection, despair, depression.

Fear: anxiety, apprehension, nervousness, concern, consternation, wariness, edginess, dread, fright, terror, panic.

Enjoyment: happiness, joy, relief, contentment, delight, amusement, pride, sensual pleasure, thrill, rapture, gratification, satisfaction, euphoria.

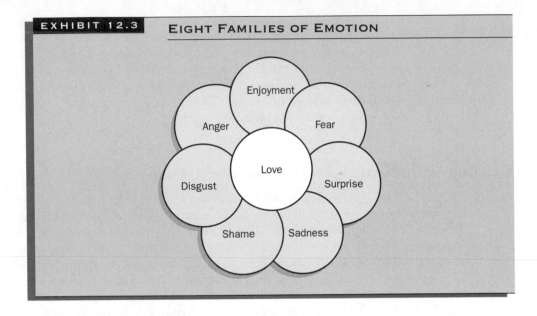

EXHIBIT 12.3   EIGHT FAMILIES OF EMOTION

Love: acceptance, respect, friendliness, trust, kindness, affinity, devotion, adoration, infatuation.

Surprise: shock, astonishment, amazement, wonder.

Disgust: contempt, disdain, scorn, abhorrence, aversion, distaste, revulsion.

Shame: guilt, embarrassment, chagrin, remorse, humiliation, regret, mortification, contrition.

Leaders who are attuned to their own feelings and the feelings of others can use their understanding to enhance the organization. The first step to developing what psychologist Daniel Goleman calls "emotional intelligence" is to be consciously aware of the kinds of emotions people have and how those emotions may manifest themselves.

The Components of Emotional Intelligence

Five basic components of emotional intelligence are important to organizational leaders.[32]

Self-awareness, which is the basis for all the other components, means being aware of what you are feeling, being conscious of the emotions within yourself. People who are in touch with their emotions are better able to guide their own lives. Leaders can be in touch with their emotions in order to interact effectively and appreciate emotions in others. Leaders with a high level of self-awareness learn to trust their "gut feelings" and realize that these feelings can provide useful information about difficult decisions. Answers are not always clear as to whether to propose a major deal, let an employee go, reorganize a business, or revise job responsibilities. When the answers are not available from external sources, leaders have to rely on their own feelings.

Managing emotions is the second key component, which means the leader is able to balance his or her own moods so that worry, anxiety, fear, or anger do not get in the way of what needs to be done. Leaders who can manage their emotions perform better because they are able to think clearly. Managing emotions does not mean suppressing or denying them but understanding them and using that understanding to deal with situations productively.[33] Leaders first recognize a mood or feeling, think about what it means and how it affects them, and then choose how to act.

Motivating oneself is the ability to be hopeful and optimistic despite obstacles, setbacks, or even outright failure. This ability is crucial for pursuing long-term goals in life or in business. Martin Seligman, a professor of psychology at the University of Pennsylvania, once advised the MetLife insurance company to hire a special group of job applicants who tested high on optimism but failed the normal sales aptitude test. Compared to salespeople who passed the regular aptitude test but scored high on pessimism, the "optimistic" group made 21 percent more sales in their first year and 57 percent more in the second.[34]

Empathy, the fourth component, means being able to put yourself in someone else's shoes, to recognize what others are feeling without them needing to tell you. Most people never tell us what they feel in words but rather in tone of voice, body language, and facial expression. Empathy is built from self-awareness; being attuned to one's own emotions makes it easier to read and understand the feelings of others.

Social skill, the ability to connect to others, build positive relationships, respond to the emotions of others, and influence others, is the final component of emotional intelligence. Leaders use social skills to understand interpersonal relationships, handle disagreements, resolve conflicts, and bind people together for a common purpose. The ability to build relationships is essential in modern team-based organizations, but is important for effective leadership in all organizations. Jerrold L. Miller, president of Earl Industries, Inc., a $35 million ship-repair business, explained that project managers who cannot handle relationships "really cost us a lot of money." When managers habitually say things to upset shipyard workers, Miller says, "the guys on the job are not as motivated to make this fellow look good . . . . They don't really care if his job is falling a little bit behind."[35]

The U.S. Army is helping its leaders develop emotional intelligence through a crash course they informally call "charm school."

LEADERSHIP SPOTLIGHT   THE UNITED STATES ARMY

At the U.S. Army's annual Brigadier General Training Conference, the select few who are promoted from colonel are pushed to make a mental and emotional leap and consider the Army and their command in a new way. One lecturer at a recent conference told the new generals to get in touch with the "inner jerk" and work on losing that aspect of their personalities. Another warned that the "first deadly sin of the general officer is arrogance. Bask in the glow—and get over it."

Much of the conference focuses on avoiding trouble and leading ethically and with heart. Lieutenant General John Keane, an infantry commander since 1966, stresses the importance of "leading from the front," to have empathy for soldiers on the front lines. "You've got to put yourself in harm's way to have moral authority," Keane says. "You must feel the horror they feel, the loneliness and despair they feel. . . ." Other sessions focus on problems such as sexual harassment, diversity issues, and improper use of power and privilege. New generals are advised to hone their social skills to interact effectively not only with insiders but with outsiders such as congressmen and journalists.

On the final day, the group finally hears from four-star General Dennis Reimer, Army Chief of Staff, who has spent most of the conference observing from the back row. After encouraging the generals to maintain balance to avoid burning out themselves and their staffs, Reimer adds this piece of advice: "Get your own coffee. It keeps you humble."[36]

Implications for Leadership

How is emotional intelligence related to effective leadership? For one thing, a leader's emotional abilities and understandings play a key role in charismatic leadership behavior, as described earlier in this chapter.[37] Charismatic leaders generally hold strong emotional convictions about their personal values and beliefs and are emotionally expressive in dealing with followers. In addition, these leaders exhibit self-confidence, determination, and persistence in the face of adversity.

A high level of self-awareness, combined with the ability to manage one's own emotions, enables a leader to display self-confidence and earn the respect and trust of followers. In addition, the ability to manage or temporarily restrain one's emotions can enable a leader to objectively consider the needs of others over his or her own immediate feelings. Giving in to strong feelings of anger or depression, for example, may intensify a self-centered focus on one's own needs and limit the ability of the leader to understand the needs of others or see things from other perspectives.

The emotional state of the leader impacts the entire group, department, or organization. Leaders who are able to maintain balance and keep themselves motivated are positive role models to help motivate and inspire those around them. The energy level of the entire organization increases when leaders are optimistic and hopeful. The ability to empathize with others and to manage interpersonal relationships also contributes to motivation and inspiration because it helps leaders create feelings of unity and team spirit.

Perhaps most importantly, emotional intelligence enables leaders to recognize and respect followers as whole human beings with feelings, opinions, and ideas of their own. Empathy allows leaders to treat followers as individuals with unique needs, abilities, and dreams. Empathic leaders can use their social skills to help followers grow and develop, see and enhance their self-image and feelings of self-worth, and help meet their needs and achieve their personal goals.

Emotionally intelligent leaders can have a positive impact on organizations by helping employees grow, learn, and develop; creating a sense of purpose and meaning; instilling unity and team spirit; and building relationships of trust and respect that allow each employee to take risks and fully contribute to the organization. Leaders who lead with the heart often can take the organization to a higher level of motivation and performance. In the final section of this chapter, we will focus on two key emotional categories and examine how leaders' emphasis on either *fear* or *love* impacts followers and the organization.

Leading with Love versus Leading with Fear

Traditionally, organizations often have been based on fear. An unspoken notion among many senior-level executives is that fear is a good thing and benefits the organization.[38] Fear does motivate people. When organizations were based primarily on people mindlessly doing as they are told, leading with fear often worked to meet the organization's needs.

However, especially today, an organization's success depends on the mind power and enthusiasm of everyone. The drawback of fear is that it often creates avoidance behavior, because no one wants to make a mistake, and this inhibits growth and change. Leaders can learn to bind people together for a shared purpose through more positive forces such as caring and compassion, listening, and connecting to others on a personal level. The emotion that attracts people to take risks, learn, grow, and move the organization forward comes from love, not fear. Jan Carlzon, president and CEO of Scandinavian Airline Systems Group, used love to turn the company around in an era of brutal competition.

> In my experience, there are two great motivators in life. One is fear. The other is love. You can manage an organization by fear, but if you do you will ensure that people don't perform up to their real capabilities. A person who is afraid doesn't dare perform to the limits of his or her capabilities. . . . But if you manage people by love—that is, if you show them respect and trust . . . in that kind of atmosphere, they dare to take risks. They can even make mistakes. Nothing can hurt.[39]

Showing respect and trust not only enables people to perform better, it allows them to feel emotionally connected with their work so that their lives are richer and more balanced. Executives can rely on negative emotions such as fear to fuel productive work, but by doing so they may slowly destroy people's spirits, which ultimately is bad for employees and the organization.[40]

Fear in Organizations

The workplace can hold many kinds of fear, including fear of failure, fear of change, fear of personal loss, and fear of the boss. All of these fears can prevent employees from doing their best, from taking risks, from challenging and changing the status quo. Fear gets in the way of people feeling good about their work, themselves, and the organization. It can create an atmosphere in which people feel powerless, so that their confidence, commitment, enthusiasm, imagination, and motivation are diminished.[41]

Aspects of Fear   One particularly damaging aspect of fear in the workplace is that it can diminish trust and communication. Employees feel threatened by repercussions if they speak up about work-related concerns. A survey of employees in 22 organizations around the country found that 70 percent of them "bit their tongues" at work because they feared repercussions. Twenty-seven percent reported that they feared losing their credibility or reputation if they spoke up. Other fears reported were lack of career advancement, possible damage to the relationship with their supervisor, demotion or losing their job, and being embarrassed or humiliated in front of others.[42] When people are afraid to speak up, important issues are suppressed and problems hidden. Employees are afraid to talk about a wide range of issues. These "undiscussables" can range from the poor performance of a coworker to concerns over benefits to suggestions for organizational improvement. However, by far the largest category of undiscussables is the behavior of executives, particularly their interpersonal and relationship skills. When fear is high, managers destroy the opportunity for feedback, blinding them to reality and denying them the chance to correct damaging decisions and behaviors.

Relationship with Leaders   Leaders control the fear level in the organization. We all know from personal experience that it is easier to report bad news to some people than to others. A boss or teacher who is understanding and caring is much easier to approach than one who is likely to blow up and scream at us. The relationship between an employee and supervisor is the primary factor determining the level of fear experienced at work. The legacy of fear and mistrust associated with traditional hierarchies in which bosses gave orders and employees jumped to obey "or else" still colors organizational life. Leaders are responsible for creating a new environment that enables people to feel safe speaking their minds. Leaders can act from love rather than fear to free employees and the organization from the chains of the past.

Bringing Love to Work

When leaders act from their own fear, they create fear in others. Organizations have traditionally rewarded people for strong qualities such as rational thinking, ambition, and competitiveness. These qualities are important, but their overemphasis has left many organizational leaders out of touch with their softer, caring, creative capabilities, unable to make emotional connections with others and afraid to risk showing any sign of "weakness." A leader's fear can manifest itself in arrogance, selfishness, deception, unfairness, and disrespect for others.[43]

Leaders can learn to develop their capacity for the positive emotions of love and caring. Former president Ronald Reagan was a master at leading with love, and the country responded. He openly showed his deep love for his wife and publicly displayed tender feelings on the beach at Normandy and at the funeral services for the dead astronauts following the *Challenger* disaster.[44] Isaac Tigrett built an international business, Hard Rock Cafe, based on love, as described in the Cutting Edge box.

We all know there are different kinds of love—for example, the love of a mother for her child, romantic love, brotherly love, or the love of country. Most of us have experienced at least one kind of love in our lives and therefore know the tremendous power it can have. Despite its power, the "L" word is often looked upon with suspicion in the business world.[45] However, there are a number of aspects of love that are directly relevant to work relationships and organizational performance.

Love as motivation is the force within that enables people to feel alive, connected, energized, and "in love" with life and work. Western cultures place great emphasis on the mind and the rational approach. However, it is the heart rather than the mind that powers people forward. Recall a time when you wanted to do something with all your heart, and how your energy and motivation flowed freely. Also recall a time when your head said you had to do a task, but your heart was not in it. Motivation is reduced, perhaps to the point of procrastination. Moreover, emotional attachments bind people together to jointly pursue a shared vision with creativity and enthusiasm. When leaders connect with their own emotions, they can connect with other people and create webs of relationships that release this emotional energy.

Love as feelings involves attraction, fascination, and caring for people, work, or other things. This is what people most often think of as love, particularly in relation to romantic love between two people. However, love as feelings is relevant in work situations. Feelings of compassion and caring for others are a manifestation of love, as are forgiveness, sincerity, respect, and loyalty, all of which are important for healthy working relationships. One personal feeling is *bliss*, best articulated for the general public by Joseph Campbell in his PBS television series and companion book with Bill Moyers, *The Power of Myth*.[46] Finding your bliss means doing things that make you light up inside, things you do for the sheer joy of doing rather than for the material rewards. Most of us experience moments of this bliss when we become so absorbed in enjoyable work activities that we lose track of time. This type of feeling and caring about work is a major source of charisma. Everyone becomes more charismatic to others when they pursue an activity they truly care about.

Love as action means more than feelings; it is translated into behavior. Stephen Covey points out that in all the great literature, love is a verb rather than a noun.[47] Love is something you do, the sacrifices you make and the giving of yourself to others. The feelings of compassion, respect, and loyalty, for example, are translated into acts of friendliness, teamwork, cooperation, listening, and serving others. Feelings of unity and cooperation in organizations by leaders or followers translate into acts of helping, cooperation, sharing, and understanding. Sentiments emerge as action.

Hard Rock Cafe

When he talks about the success of Hard Rock Cafe, founder Isaac Tigrett says, "All I did was put spirit and business together in that big mixing bowl and add love. I didn't care about anything but the people. Just cherish them, look after them, be sensitive to them and their lives. That important relationship with my staff is what made the Hard Rock, nothing else!"

Tigrett first got the idea for the Hard Rock when he witnessed the total separation of the classes in England after moving there from the United States in the 1960s. Not yet 20 years old, Tigrett decided to open an "absolutely classless" restaurant "where a baker and a banker could meet to talk." He personally hired every employee, which he referred to as his rainbow coalition because between them they spoke 25 different languages. He held daily and weekly "family meetings" to talk about things such as politeness, kindness, classlessness, friendliness, respect, and love. He paid everyone equally, even though women in London at that time were usually paid half of men's wages, and he instituted the first profit-sharing plan in a restaurant company in England. He often hired people who

couldn't get a job anywhere else. "Being one of the Hard Rock family was therapy for people. Even if they came from a violent home life, here they were loved, and they loved back in return. They always do. . . . Everybody loved the place, everybody felt bigger working there. Just walk into the place and this great energy hit you immediately."

That energy, and the success of the Hard Rock, couldn't be contained. The company opened successful restaurants in leading cities all over the world. After two decades of hard work, Tigrett sold the Hard Rock for around $107 million, an unheard-of selling price for the restaurant industry. He felt that the times had changed and that it was time for him to move on to new adventures. "Y'know," he said, "there are other things for me to do in this world." The Hard Rock has changed in many ways since it was founded in 1960s London. However, one thing remains the same. In every restaurant kitchen, in big brass letters, is the Hard Rock motto: "Love all, serve all."

SOURCE: Jack Hawley, *Reawakening the Spirit at Work: The Power of Dharmic Management* (San Francisco: Berrett-Koehler, 1993).

Why Followers Respond to Love

Leaders who lead with love have extraordinary influence because they meet five unspoken employee needs. Most people yearn for more than a paycheck from their jobs. The five unspoken requests are:

Hear and understand me.

Even if you disagree with me, please don't make me wrong.

Acknowledge the greatness within me.

Remember to look for my loving intentions.

Tell me the truth with compassion.[48]

When leaders address these subtle emotional needs directly, people typically respond by loving their work and becoming emotionally engaged in solving problems and serving customers. Enthusiasm for work and the organization increases. People want to believe that their leaders genuinely care. From the followers' point of view love versus fear has different motivational potential.

> **Fear-based motivation**: I need a job to pay for my basic needs (fulfilling lower needs of the body). You give me a job, and I will give you just enough to keep my job.

> **Love-based motivation**: If the job and the leader make me feel valued as a person and provide a sense of meaning and contribution to the community at large (fulfilling higher needs of heart, mind, and body), then I will give you all I have to offer.[49]

The many examples in the chapters on empowerment, culture, and learning organizations illustrated what happens when positive emotion is used. One management consultant went so far as to advise that finding creative ways to love could solve every imaginable leadership problem.[50] Rational thinking is important, but leading with love can build trust, stimulate creativity, inspire commitment, and create boundless energy in an organization.

Summary and Interpretation

Leaders use intellectual as well as emotional capabilities and understandings to guide organizations through today's turbulent environment and help employees feel energized, motivated, and cared for in the face of rapid change, confusion, and job insecurity. Leaders can expand the capacities of their minds and hearts through conscious development and practice.

Charismatic leaders use their minds and hearts to have a significant impact on followers. They create an atmosphere of change, articulate an idealized vision of the future, communicate clearly, inspire faith and hope, and incur personal risks to create change.

Five key issues important to developing a leader's mind are independent thinking, open mindedness, systems thinking, mental models, and personal mastery. Leaders should also understand the importance of emotional intelligence. Five basic components of emotional intelligence are self-awareness, managing emotions, motivating oneself, empathy, and social skills. Emotionally intelligent leaders can have a positive impact on organizations by helping employees grow, learn, and develop, creating a sense of purpose and meaning; instilling unity and team spirit; and basing relationships on trust and respect, which allows employees to take risks and fully contribute to the organization.

Traditional organizations have relied on fear as a motivator. While fear does motivate people, it prevents people from feeling good about their work and often causes avoidance behavior. Fear can reduce trust and communication so that important problems and issues are hidden or suppressed. Leaders can choose to lead with love instead of fear. Love can be thought of as a motivational force that enables people to feel alive, connected, and energized; as feelings of liking, caring, and bliss; and as actions of helping, listening, and cooperating. Each of these aspects of love has relevance for organizational relationships. People respond to love because it meets unspoken needs for respect and affirmation. Rational thinking is important to leadership, but it takes love to build trust, creativity, and enthusiasm.

Key Terms

capacity	mental models	empathy
charismatic leader	personal mastery	social skill
independent thinking	self-awareness	fear-based motivation
mindfulness	managing emotions	love-based motivation
systems thinking	motivating oneself	

Discussion Questions

1. How do you feel about developing the emotional qualities of yourself and other people in the organization as a way to be an effective leader? Discuss.

2. Do you agree that people have a capacity for developing their minds and hearts beyond current competency? Can you give an example? Discuss.

3. What do you consider the essential traits of a charismatic leader? Have you ever known a leader who uses emotional intensity for self-enhancement rather than group enhancement?

4. Discuss the similarity and differences between mental models and open mindedness.

5. What is the concept of personal mastery? How important is it to a leader?

6. Which of the five elements of emotional intelligence do you consider most essential to an effective leader? Why?

7. Consider fear and love as potential motivators. Which is the best source of motivation for soldiers during a war? For members of a new product development team? For top executives at a media conglomerate? Why?

8. Have you ever experienced love and/or fear from leaders at work? How did you respond?

Leadership Development: Personal Feedback

Emotional Intelligence

For each item below, rate how well you are able to display the ability described. Before responding, try to think of actual situations in which you have had the opportunity to use the ability.

Very Slight Ability		Moderate Ability		Very Much Ability
1	2	3	4	5

_____ 1. Associate different internal physiological cues with different emotions.

_____ 2. Relax when under pressure in situations.

_____ 3. "Gear Up" at will for a task.

_____ 4. Know the impact that your behavior has on others.

_____ 5. Initiate successful resolution of conflict with others.

_____ 6. Calm yourself quickly when angry.

_____ 7. Know when you are becoming angry.

_____ 8. Regroup quickly after a setback.

_____ 9. Recognize when others are distressed.

_____ 10. Build consensus with others.

_____ 11. Know what senses you are currently using.

_____ 12. Use internal "talk" to change your emotional state.

_____ 13. Produce motivation when doing uninteresting work.

_____ 14. Help others manage their emotions.

_____ 15. Make others feel good.

_____ 16. Identify when you experience mood shifts.

_____ 17. Stay calm when you are the target of anger from others.

_____ 18. Stop or change an ineffective habit.

_____ 19. Show empathy to others.

_____ 20. Provide advice and emotional support to others as needed.

_____ 21. Know when you become defensive.

_____ 22. Know when you are thinking negatively and head it off.

_____ 23. Follow your words with actions.

_____ 24. Engage in intimate conversations with others.

_____ 25. Accurately reflect people's feelings back to them.

Scoring

Sum your responses to the 25 questions to obtain your overall emotional intelligence score. Your score for self-awareness is the total of questions 1, 6, 11, 16 and 21. Your score for managing emotions is the total of questions 2, 7, 12, 17, and 22. Your score for motivating yourself is the sum of questions 3, 8, 13, 18, and 23. Your score for empathy is the sum of questions 4, 9, 14, 19, and 24. Your total score for social skill is the sum of questions 5, 10, 15, 20, and 25.

Interpretation

This questionnaire provides some indication of your emotional intelligence. If you received a total score of 100 or more, you are certainly considered a person with high emotional intelligence. A score from 50 to 100 means you have a good platform of emotional intelligence from which to develop your leadership capability. A score below 50 indicates that you realize that you are probably below average in emotional intelligence. For each of the five components of emotional intelligence—self-awareness, managing emotions, motivating one's self, empathy, and social skill—a score above 20 is considered high, while a score below 10 would be considered low. Review the discussion in the chapter of the five components of emotional intelligence and think about what you might do to develop those areas where you scored low. Compare your scores to those of other students. What will you do to improve your scores?

_____

SOURCE: Adapted from Hendrie Weisinger, *Emotional Intelligence at Work* (San Francisco: Jossey-Bass, 1998), 214–215.

Leadership Development: Case for Analysis

The USS Florida

The atmosphere in a Trident nuclear submarine is generally calm and quiet. Even pipe joints are cushioned to prevent noise that might tip off a pursuer. The Trident ranks among the world's most dangerous weapons—swift, silent, armed with 24 long-range missiles carrying 192 nuclear warheads. Trident crews are the cream of the Navy crop, and even the sailors who fix the plumbing exhibit a white-collar decorum. The culture aboard ship is a low-key, collegial one in which sailors learn to speak softly and peacefully share close quarters with an ever-changing roster of shipmates. Being subject to strict security restrictions enhances a sense of elitism and pride. To move up and take charge of a Trident submarine is an extraordinary feat in the Navy—fewer than half the officers qualified for such commands ever get them. When Michael Alfonso took charge of the USS *Florida*, the crew welcomed his arrival. They knew he was one of them—a career Navy man who joined up as a teenager and moved up through the ranks. Past shipmates remembered him as basically a loner, who could be brusque but generally pleasant enough. Neighbors on shore found Alfonso to be an unfailingly polite man who kept mostly to himself.

The crew's delight in their new captain was short-lived. Commander Alfonso moved swiftly to assume command, admonishing his sailors that he would push them hard. He wasn't joking—soon after the *Florida* slipped into deep waters to begin a postoverhaul shakedown cruise, the new captain loudly and publicly reprimanded those whose performance he considered lacking. Chief Petty Officer Donald MacArthur, chief of the navigation division, was only one of those who suffered Alfonso's anger personally. During training exercises, MacArthur was having trouble keeping the boat at periscope depth because of rough seas. Alfonso announced loudly, "You're disqualified." He then precipitously relieved him of his diving duty until he could be recertified by extra practice. Word of the incident spread quickly. The crew, accustomed to the Navy's adage of "praise in public, penalize in private," were shocked. It didn't take long for this type of behavior to have an impact on the crew, according to Petty Officer Aaron Carmody: "People didn't tell him when something was wrong. You're not supposed to be afraid of your captain, to tell him stuff. But nobody wanted to."

The captain's outbursts weren't always connected with job performance. He bawled out the supply officer, the executive officer, and the chief of the boat because the soda dispenser he used to pour himself a glass of Coke one day contained Mr. Pibb instead. He exploded when he arrived unexpected at a late-night meal and found the fork at his place setting missing. Soon, a newsletter titled *The Underground* was being circulated by the boat's plumbers, who used sophomoric humor to spread the word about the captain's outbursts over such petty matters. By the time the sub reached Hawaii for its "Tactical Readiness Evaluation," an intense week-long series of inspections by staff officers, the crew was almost completely alienated. Although the ship tested well, inspectors sent word to Rear Admiral Paul Sullivan that something seemed to be wrong on board, with severely strained relations between captain and crew. On the Trident's last evening of patrol, much of the crew celebrated with a film night—they chose *The Caine Mutiny* and *Crimson Tide,* both movies about Navy skippers who face mutinies and are relieved of command at sea. When Humphrey Bogart, playing the captain of the fictional USS *Caine,* exploded over a missing quart of strawberries, someone shouted, "Hey, sound familiar?"

When they reached home port, the sailors slumped ashore. "Physically and mentally, we were just beat into the ground," recalls one. Concerned about reports that the crew seemed "despondent," Admiral Sullivan launched an informal inquiry that eventually led him to relieve Alfonso of his command. It was the first-ever firing of a Trident submarine commander. "He had the chance of a lifetime to experience the magic of command, and he squandered it," Sullivan said. "Fear and intimidation lead to certain ruin." Alfonso himself seemed dumbfounded by Admiral Sullivan's actions, pointing out that the USS *Florida* under his command posted "the best-ever grades assigned for certifications and inspections for a postoverhaul Trident submarine." Some officers believe Commander Alfonso got a bum rap. One said, "My opinion is, the man in command is in command."

Questions

1. Analyze Alfonso's impact on the crew in terms of love versus fear. What might account for the fact that he behaved so strongly as captain of the USS *Florida*?

2. Which do you think a leader should be more concerned about aboard a nuclear submarine—high certification grades or high-quality interpersonal relationships? Do you agree with Admiral Sullivan's decision to fire Alfonso? Discuss.

3. Discuss Commander Alfonso's level of emotional intelligence in terms of the five components listed in the chapter. What advice would you give him?

SOURCE: Thomas E. Ricks, "A Skipper's Chance to Run a Trident Sub Hits Stormy Waters," *The Wall Street Journal*, November 20, 1997, A1, A6.

References

[1]Pamela Coker, "Let Customers Know You 'Love' Them," *Nation's Business*, August 1992, 9.

[2]Lester C. Thurow, "Peter's Principles," *Boston Magazine*, January 1998, 89–90; Michele Morris, "The New Breed of Leaders: Taking Charge in a Different Way," *Working Woman*, March 1990, 73–75; and Stanley Bing, "Executive Shelf Life," *Esquire*, June 1992, 69–70.

[3]Robert B. French, "The Teacher as Container of Anxiety: Psychoanalysis and the Role of Teacher," *Journal of Management Education* 21, No. 4 (November 1997), 483–495.

[4]This basic idea is found in a number of sources, among them, Jack Hawley, *Reawakening the Spirit in Work* (San Francisco: Berrett-Koehler, 1993); Aristotle, *The Nicomachean Ethics*, trans. by the Brothers of the English Dominican Province, rev. by Daniel J. Sullivan (Chicago: Encyclopedia Britannica, 1952); Alasdair MacIntyre, *After Virtue: A Study in Moral Theory* (Notre Dame, IN: University of Notre Dame Press, 1984); and Stephen Covey, *The Seven Habits of Highly Effective People: Powerful Lessons in Personal Change* (New York: Fireside Books/Simon & Schuster, 1990).

[5]Katherine J. Klein and Robert J. House, "On Fire: Charismatic Leadership and Levels of Analysis," *Leadership Quarterly* 6, No. 2 (1995), 183–198.

[6]Patricia Sellers, "What Exactly Is Charisma?" *Fortune*, January 15, 1996, 68–75.

[7]Ibid.

[8]Ibid.

[9]Charles A. Jaffe, "Moving Fast by Standing Still," *Nation's Business*, October 1991, 57–59.

[10]James M. Kouzes and Barry Z. Posner, *The Leadership Challenge: How to Get Extraordinary Things Done in Organizations* (San Francisco: Jossey-Bass, 1988), 270.

[11]Jay A. Conger, Rabindra N. Kanungo and Associates, *Charismatic Leadership: The Elusive Factor in Organizational Effectiveness* (San Francisco: Jossey-Bass, 1988); Robert J. House and Jane M. Howell, "Personality and Charismatic Leadership," *Leadership Quarterly* 3, No. 2 (1992), 81–108; Klein and House, "On Fire: Charismatic Leadership and Levels of Analysis."

[12]The following discussion is based primarily on Conger, et. al., *Charismatic Leadership*.

[13]Boas Shamir, Michael B. Arthur, and Robert J. House, "The Rhetoric of Charismatic Leadership: A Theoretical Extension, A Case Study, and Implications for Future Research," *Leadership Quarterly* 5, No. 1 (1994), 25–42.

[14]Richard L. Daft and Robert H. Lengel, *Fusion Leadership: Unlocking the Subtle Forces that Change People and Organizations* (San Francisco: Berrett-Koehler, 1998), 169.

[15]Sellers, "What Exactly Is Charisma?"

[16]Based on House and Howell, "Personality and Charismatic Leadership"; and Jennifer O'Connor, Michael D. Mumford, Timothy C. Clifton, Theodore L. Gessner, and Mary Shane Connelly, "Charismatic Leaders and Destructiveness: An Historiometric Study," *Leadership Quarterly* 6, No. 4 (1995), 529–555.

[17]O'Connor, et. al. "Charismatic Leaders and Destructiveness."

[18]Ellen Langer and John Sviokla, "An Evaluation of Charisma from the Mindfulness Perspective," unpublished manuscript, Harvard University. Part of this discussion is also drawn from Daft and Lengel, *Fusion Leadership*.

[19]T. K. Das, "Educating Tomorrow's Managers: The Role of Critical Thinking," *The International Journal of Organizational Analysis* 2, No. 4 (October 1994), 333–360.

[20]The Pike Syndrome has been discussed in multiple sources.

[21]James Gleick, *Genius: The Life and Science of Richard Feynman* (New York: Pantheon Books, 1992).

[22]Oren Harari, "Mind Matters," *Management Review*, January 1996, 47–49.

[23]Bernard M. Bass, *Leadership and Performance Beyond Expectations* (New York: The Free Press, 1985); and *New Paradigm Leadership: An Inquiry into Transformational Leadership* (Alexandria, VA: U.S. Army Research Institute for the Behavioral and Social Sciences, 1996).

[24]This section is based on Peter M. Senge, *The Fifth Discipline: The Art and Practice of the Learning Organization* (New York: Doubleday, 1990).

[25]Peter M. Senge, Charlotte Roberts, Richard B. Ross, Bryan J. Smith, and Art Kleiner, *The Fifth Discipline Fieldbook* (New York: Currency Doubleday, 1994), 87.

[26]Senge, *The Fifth Discipline*.

[27]Ian Mitroff, *Break-away Thinking: How to Challenge Your Business Assumptions* (New York: Wiley, 1988).

[28]Patricia Sellers, "Sears: In with the New," *Fortune*, October 16, 1995, 96–98.

[29]Senge, *The Fifth Discipline*.

[30]Sharon Nelton, "Emotions in the Workplace," *Nation's Business*, February 1996, 25–30 (quote on 25).

[31]This section is based largely on Daniel Goleman, *Emotional Intelligence: Why It Can Matter More Than IQ* (New York: Bantam Books, 1995), 289–290.

[32]Based on Goleman, *Emotional Intelligence*; Nelton, "Emotions in the Workplace"; and Lara E. Megerian and John J. Sosik, "An Affair of the Heart: Emotional Intelligence and Transformational Leadership," *The Journal of Leadership Studies* 3, No. 3 (1996), 31–48.

[33]Hendrie Weisinger, *Emotional Intelligence at Work* (San Francisco: Jossey-Bass, 1998).

[34]Alan Farnham, "Are You Smart Enough to Keep Your Job?" *Fortune*, January 15, 1996, 34–47.

[35]Nelton, "Emotions in the Workplace."

[36]Thomas E. Ricks, "Army's 'Baby Generals' Take a Crash Course in Sensitivity Training," *Wall Street Journal*, January 19, 1998, A1, A7.

[37]Based on Megerian and Sosik, "An Affair of the Heart."

[38]Kathleen D. Ryan and Daniel K. Oestreich, *Driving Fear Out of the Workplace: How to Overcome the Invisible Barriers to Quality, Productivity, and Innovation* (San Francisco: Jossey-Bass, 1991).

[39]George Gendron and Stephen D. Solomon, "The Art of Loving," interview with Jan Carlzon, *Inc.*, May 1989, 35–46.

[40]David E. Dorsey, "Escape from the Red Zone," *Fast Company*, April/May 1997, 116–127.

[41]This section is based on Ryan and Oestreich, *Driving Fear Out of the Workplace*; and Therese R. Welter, "Reducing Employee Fear: Get Workers and Managers to Speak Their Minds," *Small Business Reports*, April 1991, 15–18.

[42]Ryan and Oestreich, *Driving Fear Out of the Workplace*, 43.

[43]Donald G. Zauderer, "Integrity: An Essential Executive Quality," *Business Forum*, Fall 1992, 12–16.

[44]Marshall Manley, "Going Beyond 'the Issues'," *Newsweek*, January 18, 1988, 8.

[45]Jack Hawley, *Reawakening the Spirit at Work* (San Francisco: Berrett-Koehler, 1993), 55; and Rodney Ferris, "How Organizational Love Can Improve Leadership," *Organizational Dynamics*, 16, No. 4 (Spring 1988), 40-52.

[46]Joseph Campbell with Bill Moyers, *The Power of Myth* (New York: Doubleday, 1988).

[47]Stephen R. Covey, *The Seven Habits of Highly Effective People: Powerful Lessons in Personal Change* (New York: Fireside/Simon & Schuster, 1990), 80.

[48]Hyler Bracey, Jack Rosenblum, Aubrey Sanford, and Roy Trueblood, *Managing from the Heart* (New York: Dell Publishing, 1993), 192.

[49]Madan Birla with Cedilia Miller Marshall, *Balanced Life and Leadership Excellence* (Memphis, TN: The Balance Group, 1997), 76–77.

[50]Ferris, "How Organizational Love Can Improve Leadership."

13

Courage and Moral Leadership

- **Moral Leadership Today**   365

- **Becoming a Moral Leader**   369

- **Leadership Control versus Service**   371

- **Building an Ethical Culture**   377

- **Leadership Courage**   378

- **Sources of Personal Courage**   385

- **Leadership Spotlights:**
  Randall Tobias   366
  Malden Mills   376
  Ryder Systems   377
  Lawrence Fish   382

- **Leader's Bookshelf:** *Managing with the Wisdom of Love: Uncovering Virtue in People and Organizations*   368

- **Leadership Development: Personal Feedback**
  Moral Leadership   388

- **Leadership Development: Case for Analysis**
  The Boy, the Girl, the Ferryboat Captain, and the Hermits   390

Your Leadership Challenge

After reading this chapter, you should be able to:

- Combine a rational approach to leadership with a concern for people and ethics.

- Recognize your own stage of moral development and ways to accelerate your moral maturation.

- Apply the principles of stewardship and servant leadership.

- Know and use mechanisms that enhance an ethical organizational culture.

- Recognize courage in others and unlock your own potential to live and act courageously.

During the waning months of World War II, a young man climbed atop the roof of a train ready to start for Auschwitz. Ignoring shouts—and later bullets—from Nazis and soldiers of the Hungarian Arrow Cross, he began handing fake Swedish passports to the astonished Jews inside and ordering them to walk to a caravan of cars marked in Swedish colors. By the time the cars were loaded, the soldiers were so dumbfounded by the young man's actions that they simply stood by and let the cars pass, carrying to safety dozens of Jews who had been headed for the death camps.

Virtually alone in Hungary, one of the most perilous places in Europe in 1944, Raoul Wallenberg worked such miracles on a daily basis, using as his weapons courage, self-confidence, and his deep, unwavering belief in the rightness of his mission. His deeds inspired hope, courage, and action in many people who otherwise felt powerless. Wallenberg became a symbol of good in a world dominated by evil, and a reminder of the hidden strength of the human spirit. No one knows how many people he directly or indirectly saved from certain death, though it is estimated at more than 100,000.

Wallenberg was 32 years old in 1944, a wealthy, politically-connected, upper-class Swede from a prominent, well-respected family. When asked by the U.S. War Refugee Board to enter Hungary and help stop Hitler's slaughter of innocent civilians, Wallenberg had everything to lose and nothing to gain. Yet he left his life of safety and comfort to enter Hungary under cover as a diplomat, with the mission of saving as many of Hungary's Jews as possible. Wallenberg boldly demanded—and was granted—a great deal of latitude in the methods he would use, requesting the authority to use bribery, deception, and threats, and to invoke Swedish immunity as needed. He personally conceived the plan to use false Swedish passports and designed them himself as masterpieces of the formal, official-looking pomp that so impressed the Nazis. Later, as Wallenberg plunged into the midst of the struggle to free Jews from the trains and death marches, he convinced his enemies to accept such things as library cards and laundry tickets as Swedish passports. The Nazi and Hungarian Arrow Cross soldiers, accustomed to yielding unquestioningly to authority, yielded to Wallenberg on the strength of his character, personal authority, and courage.

Wallenberg never returned from Hungary, but apparently was captured as a suspected anti-Soviet spy, and died in a Soviet prison. He gave up his life fighting for a cause he believed in, and his actions made a real difference in the world. In the Avenue of the Righteous, a grove of trees planted in Israel to memorialize those who risked their lives to help Jews during the Holocaust, Wallenberg's medal summarizes his mission with the words, "Whoever saves a single soul, it is as if he had saved the whole world."[1]

Raoul Wallenberg emerged from a dismal period in human history as a courageous leader who made the ultimate sacrifice for what he believed. Most leaders never have the opportunity to save lives, and few leaders help as many people as Wallenberg did. In recognition of this fact, Congress made Wallenberg only the second person ever to be awarded honorary U.S. citizenship (the other was Winston Churchill). On that occasion, one television commentator spoke for millions when he said, "It is human beings such as Raoul Wallenberg that make life worth living." The principles of leadership he demonstrated are valuable to anyone who aspires to make a real and positive difference in the world.

One of the primary lessons from Wallenberg's life is that being a real leader means learning who you are and what you stand for, and then having the courage to act. Leaders demonstrate confidence and commitment in what they believe and what they do. A deep devotion to a cause or a purpose larger than one's self sparks the courage to act. In addition, Wallenberg's story demonstrates that leadership has less to do with using other people than with *serving* other people. Placing others ahead of oneself is a key to successful leadership, whether in politics, war, education, sports, social services, or business.

This chapter explores ideas related to courage and moral leadership. In the previous chapter, we discussed mind and heart, two of the three elements that come together for successful leadership. This chapter focuses on the third element, spirit—on the ability to look within, to contemplate the human condition, to think about what is right and wrong, to see what really "matters" in the world, and to have the courage to stand up for what is worthy and right. We will begin by examining the situation in which most organizations currently operate and the dilemma leaders face in the modern world. The next sections will discuss how leaders develop the capacity for moral reasoning and examine the importance of stewardship and servant leadership. We will then examine the ways in which leaders can create an ethical climate in their organizations. The final sections of the chapter will explore what courage means and how leaders develop the courage needed for moral leadership to flourish.

Moral Leadership Today

In recent years, numerous companies, including Prudential Insurance, Archer-Daniels-Midland, and Centennial Technology, have been charged with breaches of ethical or legal standards, including price fixing and insider trading. Columbia/HCA, the largest hospital company in the United States, is under federal investigation for possibly inflating the seriousness of patient illnesses to get larger Medicare and Medicaid payments. A $200 million suit against Baker & Taylor Books alleges that the company deliberately overcharged public libraries for trade books that were actually discounted by publishers. Widespread corruption in Bausch & Lomb's Hong Kong division included managers' faking sales, shipping products that customers never ordered, and accepting cash and third-party checks that may have indirectly helped launder drug money. In a Gallup poll asking about the perceived trustworthiness of six American institutions, only the U.S. government scored lower than U.S. corporations.[2]

The Ethical Climate in U.S. Business

Ethical and legal lapses occur at all levels of the U.S. workforce. A major study recently found that 48 percent of all workers admit to ethical violations on the job, ranging from abuse of sick leave to theft of cash or merchandise. If organizational leaders operate under principles of selfishness and greed, perhaps employees come to see unethical behavior as okay. At Bausch & Lomb, for example, managers say they resorted to corrupt practices because of intense pressure from top leaders to maintain sales and earnings growth. Companies that encourage their employees to do the right thing—and whose leaders model that behavior—have fewer ethical problems. Clark Construction Company of Lansing, Michigan, which operates in an industry known for litigation, has never sued or been sued in its 50-year history because leaders set and maintain high ethical standards.[3] In general, employees will be as ethical in doing their jobs as their leaders are in performing their own duties.

Virtually every survey about the qualities most desired in a leader reports honesty and integrity as the most important attributes.[4] Unfortunately, the public perception of business and political leaders is dismal. Fifty-five percent of the American public believe the vast majority of corporate executives are dishonest, and 59 percent believe white-collar crime occurs on a regular basis.[5] However, the news is not all bad. In an encouraging shift of public opinion, only 15 percent of U.S. workers believe dishonesty and selfishness are a necessary byproduct of business.[6] The public is tired of unethical and socially irresponsible business practices. Leaders are responsible for improving the cultures and systems that lead to ethical lapses. One example is how Randall Tobias's emphasis on respect, compassion, and integrity is changing the culture at pharmaceutical company Eli Lilly.

LEADERSHIP SPOTLIGHT   RANDALL TOBIAS

Randall Tobias believes there are financial as well as moral benefits to treating people with respect and dignity, and he is instilling that belief in employees throughout Eli Lilly, the Indianapolis-based multinational pharmaceutical company. In his first year on the job, Tobias experienced more personal and professional pain than most CEOs see in a lifetime. Yet, through it all he maintained a sense of integrity and caring for others that earned him respect from his employees.

Just after taking the job, he developed diabetes, his mother died, and his wife of 28 years was diagnosed with clinical depression. Life was tumultuous at work as well. Within weeks after taking the job, Tobias announced that the company would eliminate 3,000 jobs. Rather than giving out pink slips, however, Lilly offered early retirement options. Anyone accepting the early retirement offer received a year's pay as part of an early retirement package. This humane way of streamlining cost the company about $535 million, but demonstrated a concern for workers that gained the trust of those who stayed with the company. Tobias has also instituted flex time so workers with small children or aging parents have more flexibility in their schedules. He stresses that employees should take their vacations, enjoy their hobbies, and not work weekends, which Tobias believes is good for the company as well as for employees: "We perform better when our lives are not so consumed by work."

The CEO's ethical values are also reflected in Lilly's growing sense of social responsibility. Although not required to do so by law, the company is sharply cutting emissions of hazardous chemicals and has begun recycling in earnest. Company leaders quickly recalled four million bottles of antibiotics after four patients discovered small plastic caps inside the bottles. This $66 million cost was incurred even though there was no public outcry and no directive by regulators for a recall.

Tobias still faces considerable challenges in changing Eli Lilly's culture, but he is committed to the mission. "The way people behave with customers and with each other—the fundamental business culture—has a lot to do with the effectiveness of the strategy. As a human being, I think these issues are important. But they're also important for the bottom line."[7]

The Leadership Dilemma

Leaders shape the ethical choices and decisions of followers in the workplace. However, leaders may face a dilemma because of a perceived conflict between the realm of business and the realm of ethics. The domain of business is one of hard, mea-

EXHIBIT 13.1	COMPARING PERSONAL QUALITIES OF PURELY RATIONAL VERSUS ETHICAL LEADERS	
Rational Leader	**Ethical Leader**	
Concerned primarily with self and own goals and career advancement	Considers others equal to self, shows concern for development of others	
Uses power for personal gain or impact	Uses power to serve others	
Promotes own personal vision aspirations	Aligns vision with followers' needs and	
Denounces critical or opposing views	Considers and learns from criticism	
Demands decisions be accepted without question	Stimulates followers to think independently and to question the leader's view	
One-way communication	Two-way communication—listens to others	
Insensitive to followers' needs ers; shares recognition with others	Coaches, develops, and supports follow-	
Relies on convenient external moral standards to satisfy self-interests	Relies on internal moral standards to satisfy organizational and societal interests	

SOURCE: Jane M. Howell and Bruce J. Avolio, "The Ethics of Charismatic Leadership: Submission or Liberation?" *Academy of Management Executive* 6, No. 2 (1992), 43–54.

surable facts—market studies, production costs, managed inventory, stock value, profit and loss statements, and rational analysis. Ethics, on the other hand, is in the "soft," almost impossible to measure realm of human meaning, purpose, quality, significance, and values. Whereas the realm of business can be dissected, diagnosed, and compared, the realm of ethics doesn't lend itself to precise interpretation, comparison, and evaluation.[8] Modern society has created a forced separation between the two, but there is a growing recognition of the need to bring them back together. Business cannot be separated from the basic human issues of how people treat one another. The same moral and ethical questions that confront individuals also face businesses and other organizations. As Henry Ford, Sr. once said, "For a long time people believed that the only purpose of industry was to make a profit. They are wrong. Its purpose is to serve the general welfare."[9] The challenge for today's leadership is to merge the hard and the soft, the rational and the ethical, to create organizations that profit while truly "serving the general welfare." This chapter's Leader's Bookshelf argues for a spiritual foundation to business that can strengthen organizations and enrich the lives of employees.

Ethical leadership does not mean ignoring profit and loss, production costs, and so forth. Ethical leadership combines a concern for the rational measures of performance with a recognition of the importance of treating people right every day. Exhibit 13.1 compares the characteristics of leaders who follow a strictly ratio-

Managing with the Wisdom of Love: Uncovering Virtue in People and Organizations
Dorothy Marcic

The changes and challenges faced by today's organizations have spurred a new leadership paradigm based on concepts such as vision, commitment, empowerment, and accountability. All of these concepts, argues Dorothy Marcic, can become more than just words when leaders recognize that work—like life and personal relationships—is enriched by a spiritual foundation. Quoting extensively from major religious texts, Marcic illustrates the similar messages in a variety of religions and demonstrates the application of this spiritual wisdom to organizations. By citing figures of faith such as Buddha, Jesus Christ, and Baháulláh, the founder of the Baha'i tradition, Marcic distills five "new management virtues" that can provide a necessary balance among the physical, intellectual, emotional, volitional (willingness to change for the better), and spiritual dimensions of work.

New Management Virtues
These five virtues form a philosophical and spiritual foundation for the issues leaders struggle with every day and for the relationships between a leader and others.

- **Trustworthiness** This virtue corresponds to the organizational issue of accountability or stewardship. It means being honest, behaving ethically, and building relationships with customers and employees based on integrity.

- **Unity** Unity is the foundation for shared vision, commitment, and reciprocity. Unity in action means seeking unanimity in important decisions, satisfying customers, going from controlling to coaching.

- **Respect and Dignity** An attitude of respect and dignity is the basis for true empowerment. Leaders listen, act as coaches and mentors, create self-determining teams, and reward and appreciate workers for their contributions.

- **Justice** The virtue of justice corresponds to equal opportunity and profit sharing in organizations. Leading with justice means treating everyone fairly, eliminating barriers to equal opportunity, and providing equitable compensation and profit sharing.

- **Service and Humility** In organizations, service corresponds to the emphasis on quality and customer satisfaction. Truly serving others means being a servant to employees and customers. Leaders who embrace the virtue of service and humility share power, admit mistakes, and trust others.

Virtues at Work
When leaders go about their work and relate to others according to a spiritual foundation, they cultivate virtue in others by creating a balance in the work lives of organizational members. Marcic emphasizes that spirituality is not a quick fix but a process that takes time, commitment, and effort. Leaders can make a commitment to long-term organizational health and base their behavior on these five virtues to develop happier, more committed employees and stronger organizations.

Managing with the Wisdom of Love, by Dorothy Marcic, is published by Jossey-Bass.

nal self-interest approach with those who take an ethical approach. Rational leadership focuses primarily on self, whereas ethical leadership is about others. Ethical leadership is the primary route through which organizations become ethical. A first step toward developing into an ethical leader is recognizing the stages of moral development.

Becoming a Moral Leader

Is leadership moral or amoral? If leadership is merely a set of practices, with no association with right or wrong, it would be amoral. But all leadership practices can be used for good or evil and thus have a moral dimension. **Moral leadership** is about distinguishing right from wrong and doing right, seeking the just, the honest, the good, and the right conduct in its practice. Leaders have great influence over others, and moral leadership gives life to others and enhances the lives of others. Immoral leadership takes away from others in order to enhance oneself.[10] Leaders who would do evil toward others, such as Hitler, Stalin, or Cambodia's Pol Pot, are immoral, while Raoul Wallenberg typifies the height of moral leadership. Moral leadership uplifts people, enabling them to be better than they were without the leader.

Specific personality characteristics such as ego strength, self-confidence, and a sense of independence may enable leaders to behave morally in the face of opposition. Moreover, leaders can develop these characteristics through their own hard work. For example, Raoul Wallenberg made a concentrated effort to understand his enemies. His understanding of the Nazi's fear of those who displayed power gave him the self-confidence to act with authority even when he felt vulnerable.[11]

Viktor Frankl was in one of the death camps in Nazi Germany, and he learned that people have choices about whether or not to behave morally.

> We who lived in concentration camps can remember the men who walked through the huts comforting the others, giving away their last piece of bread. They may have been few in number, but they offer sufficient proof that everything can be taken from a man but one thing: the last of the human freedoms—-to choose one's attitude in any given set of circumstances. To choose one's own way.
>
> And there were always choices to make. Every day, every hour, offered the opportunity to make a decision, a decision which determined whether you would or would not submit to those powers which threatened to rob you of your very self, your inner freedom. . . .[12]

A leader's capacity to make moral choices is related to that person's level of moral development.[13] Exhibit 13.2 shows a simplified illustration of one model of personal moral development. At the **preconventional level,** individuals are concerned with receiving external rewards and avoiding punishments. They obey authority to avoid detrimental personal consequences. A person at this level is motivated solely by self-interest. Modern psychology believes that children who don't receive sufficient love and nurturing spend the rest of their lives filling that need by money, material goods, and over-achievement to gain the recognition of others. The basic orientation toward the world is one of taking what one can get. Someone with this

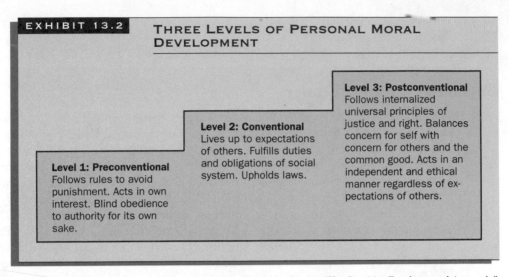

EXHIBIT 13.2

THREE LEVELS OF PERSONAL MORAL DEVELOPMENT

Level 1: Preconventional
Follows rules to avoid punishment. Acts in own interest. Blind obedience to authority for its own sake.

Level 2: Conventional
Lives up to expectations of others. Fulfills duties and obligations of social system. Upholds laws.

Level 3: Postconventional
Follows internalized universal principles of justice and right. Balances concern for self with concern for others and the common good. Acts in an independent and ethical manner regardless of expectations of others.

SOURCE: Based on Lawrence Kolhberg, "Moral Stages and Moralization: The Cognitive-Developmental Approach," in *Moral Development and Behavior: Theory, Research, and Social Issues*, ed. Thomas Likona (Austin, TX: Holt, Rinehart and Winston, 1976), 31–53; and Jill W. Graham, "Leadership, Moral Development, and Citizenship Behavior," *Business Ethics Quarterly* 5, No. 1 (January 1995), 43–54.

orientation in a leadership position would tend to be autocratic toward others and use the position for personal advancement.

At level two, the **conventional level,** people learn to conform to the expectations of good behavior as defined by colleagues, family, friends, and society. People at this level follow the rules, norms, and values in the corporate culture. If the rules are to not steal, cheat, make false promises, or violate regulatory laws, a person at the conventional level will attempt to obey. They adhere to the norms of the larger social system. However, if the social system says it is okay to inflate bills to the government, or make achieving the bottom line more important than integrity, people at the conventional level will often go along with that norm also. Often, when organizations do something illegal, many managers and employees are simply going along with the system.[14]

At the postconventional or **principled level,** leaders are guided by an internalized set of principles universally recognized as right or wrong. People at this level may even disobey rules or laws that violate these principles. These internalized values become more important than the expectations of other people in the organization or community. Raoul Wallenberg defied the formal authority and social system in Hungary to save Jews bound for death camps. Martin Luther King, Jr. broke what he considered unjust laws and spent time in jail to serve a higher cause of universal dignity and justice. Or consider the example of Gandhi, who went against prevailing customs to work with "untouchables" and broke British laws to facilitate Indian independence. When placed on trial for defying existing law, he told the presiding judge, "I am here therefore to invite and submit to the highest penalty that can be inflicted upon me for what in law is a deliberate crime and what appears to me to be the highest duty of a citizen."[15] A leader at this level is visionary, empowering, and committed to serving others and a higher cause.

Most adults operate at level two, and some have not advanced beyond level one. Only about 20 percent of American adults reach the third, postconventional level of moral development, although most of us have the capacity to do so. People at level three are able to act in an independent, ethical manner regardless of expectations from others inside or outside the organization. Impartially applying universal standards to resolve moral conflicts balances self-interest with a concern for others and for the common good. Research has consistently found a direct relationship between higher levels of moral development and more ethical behavior on the job, including less cheating, a tendency toward helpfulness to others, and the reporting of unethical or illegal acts, known as whistleblowing.[16] Leaders can use an understanding of these stages to enhance their own and followers' moral development and to initiate ethics training programs to move people to higher levels of moral reasoning. When leaders operate at level three of moral development, they focus on higher principles and encourage others to think for themselves and expand their understanding of moral issues.

Leadership Control versus Service

Assumptions about the relationship between leaders and followers are changing dramatically. Throughout this book we have referred to a number of shifts in thinking, such as from control to empowerment, from competition to collaboration, and from a focus on material things to people and relationships. All of these shifts mean that the concept of leadership is expanding and changing.

What is a leader's moral responsibility toward followers? Is it to limit and control them to meet the needs of the organization? Is it to pay them a fair wage? Or is it to enable them to grow and create and expand themselves as human beings? One CEO, who gave away his power to line workers, said, "It is immoral to prevent people from growing into all they can become."[17] He meant that his moral responsibility was to actively remove organizational limits and controls from employees so they could take as much responsibility as they could handle and could develop and use their own creative ability.

Much of the thinking about leadership today implies that moral leadership encourages change toward developing followers into leaders, thereby developing their potential rather than using a leadership position to control or limit followers. Exhibit 13.3 illustrates a continuum of leadership thinking and practice. Traditional organizations were based on the idea that the leader is in charge of subordinates and the success of the organization depends on leader control over followers. In the first stage, subordinates are passive—not expected to think for themselves but simply to do as they are told. Stage two in the continuum involves subordinates more actively in their own work. Stage three is stewardship, which represents a significant shift in mind-set by moving responsibility and authority from leaders to followers. Servant

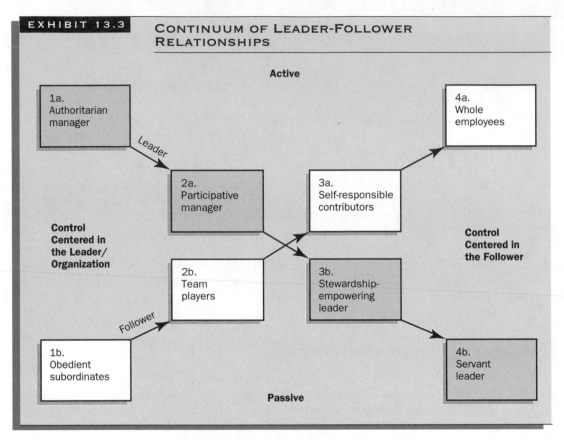

EXHIBIT 13.3 CONTINUUM OF LEADER-FOLLOWER RELATIONSHIPS

Active

1a. Authoritarian manager

Leader

2a. Participative manager

3a. Self-responsible contributors

4a. Whole employees

Control Centered in the Leader/ Organization

Control Centered in the Follower

2b. Team players

3b. Stewardship-empowering leader

Follower

1b. Obedient subordinates

4b. Servant leader

Passive

SOURCE: Based on Francine S. Hall, "Management Education by Design," *Journal of Management Education* 181, No. 2 (May 1994), 182–197.

leadership represents a stage beyond stewardship, where leaders give up control and make a choice to serve employees. In the following sections, we will discuss each stage of this leadership continuum.

Authoritarian Management

The traditional understanding of leadership is that leaders are good managers who direct and control their people. Followers are obedient subordinates who follow orders. In Chapter 3, we discussed the autocratic leader, who makes the decisions and announces them to subordinates. Power, purpose, and privilege reside with those at the top of the organization. At this level, leaders set the strategy and goals, as well as the methods and rewards for attaining them. Organizational stability and efficiency are paramount, and followers are routinized and controlled along with machines and raw materials. Subordinates are given no voice in creating meaning and purpose for their work and no discretion as to how they perform their jobs. This leadership mind-set emphasizes tight top-down control, employee standardization and specialization, and management by impersonal measurement and analysis.

Participative Management

Since the 1980s, many organizations have made efforts to actively involve employees. Leaders have increased employee participation through employee suggestion programs, participation groups, and quality circles. Teamwork has became an important part of how work is done in many organizations. The success of Japanese firms that emphasize employee involvement encouraged many U.S. organizations to try participatory management practices in response to increased global competition. One study, sponsored by the Association for Quality and Participation, revealed that over 70 percent of the largest U.S. corporations have adopted some kind of employee participation program. However, most of these programs do not redistribute power and authority to lower level workers.[18] The mind-set is still paternalistic in that top leaders determine purpose and goals, make final decisions, and decide rewards. Employees are expected to make suggestions for quality improvements, act as team players, and take greater responsibility for their own jobs, but they are not allowed to be true partners in the enterprise. Leaders are still responsible for outcomes, but they may act as mentors and coaches. They have given up some of their control, but they are still responsible for the morale, emotional well-being, and performance of subordinates, which can lead to treating followers as if they are not able to think for themselves.[19]

Stewardship

Stewardship is a pivotal shift in leadership thinking. Employees are empowered to make decisions and they have control over how they do their own jobs. Leaders give workers the power to influence goals, systems, and structures and become leaders themselves. **Stewardship** supports the belief that leaders are deeply accountable to others as well as to the organization, without trying to control others, define meaning and purpose for others, or take care of others.[20] In fact, stewardship has been called an alternative to leadership because the spotlight is on the people actually doing the work, making the product, providing the service, or working directly with the customer. Four principles provide the framework for stewardship.

1. *Reorient toward a partnership assumption.* Partnership can happen only when power and control shift away from formal leaders to core workers. Partners have a right to say "no" to one another. They are totally honest with one another, neither hiding information nor protecting the other from bad news. In addition partners (leaders and followers) are jointly responsible for defining vision and purpose and jointly accountable for outcomes.

2. *Localize decisions and power to those closest to the work and the customer.* Decision-making power and the authority to act should reside right at the point where the work gets done. This means reintegrating the "managing" and the "doing" of work, so that everyone is doing some of the core work of the organization part of the time. Nobody gets paid simply to plan and manage the work of others.

3. *Recognize and reward the value of labor.* The reward systems tie everyone's fortunes to the success of the enterprise. Stewardship involves redistributing wealth by designing compensation so that core workers can make significant gains when they make exceptional contributions. Everyone earns their pay by delivering real value, and the organization pays everyone as much as possible.

4. *Expect core work teams to build the organization.* Teams of workers who make up the core of the organization or division define goals, maintain controls, create a nurturing environment, and organize and reorganize themselves to respond to a changing environment and the marketplace they serve.

Stewardship leaders guide the organization without dominating it and facilitate followers without controlling them. Stewardship allows for a relationship between leaders and followers in which each makes significant, self-responsible contributions to organizational success. In addition, it gives followers a chance to use their minds, bodies, and spirits on the job, thereby allowing them to be more "complete" human beings.

Stewardship leaders can help organizations thrive in today's rapidly changing environment because they tap into the energy and commitment of followers. Although the ideas we have discussed may sound new, an early management thinker, Mary Parker Follett, captured the spirit of stewardship 80 years ago when she described the type of leader who motivated her.

The skillful leader, then, does not rely on personal force; he controls his group not by dominating but by expressing it. He stimulates what is best in us; he unifies and concentrates what we feel only gropingly and scatteringly, but he never gets away from the current of which we and he are both an integral part. He is a leader who gives form to the inchoate energy in every man. The person who influences me most is not he who does great deeds but he who makes me feel I can do great deeds.[21]

Servant Leadership

Servant leadership takes stewardship assumptions about leaders and followers one step further. **Servant leadership** is leadership upside-down. Servant leaders transcend self-interest to serve the needs of others, help others grow and develop, and provide opportunity for others to gain materially and emotionally. The fulfillment of others is the servant leader's principal aim.

The concept of servant leadership began with Robert Greenleaf and is described in his book, *Servant Leadership*. Greenleaf began developing his ideas after reading Hermann Hesse's novel, *Journey to the East*. The central character of the story is Leo, who appears as a servant to a group of men on a journey. Leo performs the lowliest, most menial tasks to serve the group, and he also cheers them with his good spirits and his singing. All goes well until Leo disappears, and then the journey falls into disarray. Years later, when the narrator is taken to the headquarters of the Order that had sponsored the original journey he encounters Leo again. There, he discovers that Leo is in fact the titular head of the Order—a great leader, not the lowly "servant" the travelers had thought him to be.[22] Hesse's fictional character is the epitome of the servant leader, and some question whether real human beings functioning in the real world of organizations can ever achieve Leo's level of selflessness in service to others. However, Greenleaf proposed that leaders can operate from the basic precepts of servant leadership:[23]

1. *Put service before self-interest.* Servant leaders make a conscious choice to use their gifts in the cause of change and growth for other individuals and for the organization. The desire to help others takes precedence over the desire to achieve a formal leadership position or to attain power and control over others. The servant leader calls for doing what is good and right for others even if it does not "pay off" financially. In this view, the organization exists as much to provide meaningful work to the person as the person exists to perform work for the organization.

2. *Listen first to affirm others.* The servant leader doesn't have answers; he asks questions. One of the servant leader's greatest gifts to others is listening, fully understanding the problems others face, and affirming his confidence in others. The servant leader tries to figure out the will of the group and then further it however he can. The leader doesn't impose his or her will on others. By understanding others, the leader can contribute to the best course of action.

3. *Inspire trust by being trustworthy.* Servant leaders build trust by doing what they say they will do, being totally honest with others, giving up control, and focusing on the well-being of others. They share all information, good and bad, and they make decisions to further the good of the group rather than their own interests. In addition, trust grows from trusting others to make their own decisions. Servant leaders gain trust because they give everything away—power, control, rewards, information, and recognition. Trust allows others to flourish. Max De Pree, former CEO of Herman Miller, Inc., once commented in a speech to hospital executives that one of the most wonderful letters he ever received came from a freelancer who designed a number of critical products for the company. In that letter was this sentence: "Your trust is the grace that enables me to be creative."[24]

4. *Nourish others and help them become whole.* Vaclev Havel, former playwright, dissident, and prisoner of the Soviet regime, who served as president of Czechoslovakia after the Soviet withdrawal, once said, "The salvation of this human world lies nowhere else than in the human heart, in the human power to reflect, in human meekness, and in human responsibility."[25] Servant

leaders help others find the power of the human spirit and accept their responsibilities. This requires an openness and willingness to share in the pain and difficulties of others. Being close to people also means leaders make themselves vulnerable to others and are willing to show their own pain and humanity.

Servant leadership can mean something as simple as encouraging others in their personal development and helping them understand the larger purpose in their work. At Web Industries, a Massachusetts manufacturer, for example, leaders give assembly line workers time off to read thought-provoking books to develop themselves.[26] An extreme case of servant leadership was Mother Teresa. She spent a lifetime serving the desperately poor and afflicted. Her devotion inspired hundreds of people to follow her and attracted millions of dollars in financial support. An example of devotion to workers in the corporate world was illustrated by Aaron Feuerstein of Malden Mills.

LEADERSHIP SPOTLIGHT   **MALDEN MILLS**

A faulty boiler started the December 1995 fire that destroyed a large portion of Malden Mills, of Lawrence, Massachusetts, and seriously injured several employees. Owner and president Aaron Feuerstein, age 70, was free to take the insurance money and retire. After all, the company faced intense competition from foreign mills and mills in the southern states, both of which had lower labor costs.

"No, I'll not weep," Feuerstein said of the catastrophe. "There will be a Malden Mills tomorrow." He gathered his employees together in the high school gym and told them he would continue paying their wages until the mill was rebuilt. It was an emotional meeting. Employees wept, hugged each other, and lifted Feuerstein onto their shoulders.

Feuerstein felt a responsibility to his employees and the community. He considered it unethical to kill the company and put 3,000 people out of work. He believes that people who work hard should make a good living and be able to retire comfortably. He says that the difference between his leadership philosophy and other American CEOs is that he considers employees as assets rather than expenses. His job is more than making money for shareholders, even though the shareholders of Malden Mills are his own family. He has always been generous with his earnings, such as arranging for several heart by-pass operations for employees. He will not replace permanent employees who earn $15 an hour with temporary employees who earn $7 an hour, or move his operation to a lower cost region. Such action would violate the spirit of trust he has established with his workers and would not serve the higher purpose for the community. For Feuerstein, leadership contains a strong moral component.[27]

Servant leaders truly value and respect others as human beings, not as objects of labor. To fully trust others relies on an assumption that we all have a moral duty to one another.[28] To make the choice for service requires a belief in a purpose higher than acquiring more material goods for oneself. Raoul Wallenberg made the choice for service when he exchanged a comfortable life of privilege for war-torn Hungary.

Organizational leaders can act from moral values rather than from greed, selfishness, and fear. Indeed, Greenleaf believed that many people have the capacity for servant leadership. He said the greatest enemy to organizations and to society is fuzzy thinking on the part of good, intelligent, vital people who "have the potential to lead but do not lead, or who choose to follow a nonservant."[29]

Building an Ethical Culture

Leaders who operate from the principles of stewardship and servant leadership are uniquely qualified to create ethical cultures within organizations. Because they demonstrate and act from high moral standards, they engender high standards in others. Despite the corporate realities of fear, greed, apathy, and divisiveness, these leaders act from their moral values and encourage others to bring their own ethical and spiritual values to work with them. Having the conviction and courage to stand up for one's beliefs is especially important in today's complex world where issues are seldom clear-cut.

All leaders face situations where right and wrong are hard to define. These ethical dilemmas often involve a conflict between the needs of the part and the whole—for example, the individual versus the organization, or the organization versus society as a whole. The way in which leaders approach ethical issues sets the tone for the rest of the organization. As we discussed in Chapter 7, leaders shape organizational culture, and cultural values exert a powerful influence on employee behavior. In ethical companies, employees believe that if they violate the ethical values they will not fit in or their jobs may be in jeopardy. Organizations such as Johnson & Johnson, General Mills, and Levi Strauss are known for setting high ethical standards as part of the organizational culture, and those high standards are based on the belief that organizations have an obligation to benefit society as well as themselves.

The leader's behavior is an important tool for shaping ethical values. Organizational leaders are models for the behaviors expected of others. At Eastman Kodak, for example, CEO George Fischer emphasizes the company's commitment to social responsibility by tying a portion of his own pay directly to social factors.[30] The single most important factor in ethical decision making in organizations is whether top leaders show a commitment to ethics in their talk and their behavior. Employees learn about the values that are important in the organization by watching leaders. Ryder Systems' Tony Burns puts ethical values into action to demonstrate the importance of giving something back to the community.

LEADERSHIP SPOTLIGHT   **RYDER SYSTEMS**

Two days after Hurricane Andrew swept through South Florida, leaving thousands homeless, Ryder Systems' corporate offices in Miami resembled command central on the edge of a war zone. Because United Way's power had been knocked out, they set up in Ryder's cafeteria. In the lobby, Ryder employees could sign up for on-the-spot interest-free company loans of up to $10,000. An army of volunteers sorted food and clothing, much of it to be delivered by the 500 yellow trucks Ryder loaned for free to various relief agencies.

At the heart of this humanitarian activity was M. Anthony Burns, Ryder's Chairman, President, and CEO. Burns himself delivered supplies to employees whose homes were destroyed and joined work crews going house to house repairing roofs. Employees volunteered to work half a day at Ryder and half a day in the community—seven days a week from sunup to sundown for three months. No one in the South Florida area was surprised by Ryder's contribution during the crisis. Burns has had a long-standing commitment to public service, which earned him the Humanitarian of the Year award from the Greater Miami chapter of the American Red Cross. He has also created an atmosphere for service within the company. Harvey Mogul, president of the United Way of Dade County, characterizes Burns as "very intense, very focused, and absolutely ethical. There's not a local cultural or social institution that has not been impacted by his leadership."

Burns modestly deflects the praise heaped upon him, and credits "a very good organization here at Ryder." However, he doesn't mind talking about his values and where they came from—Burns says he learned the values of hard work, integrity, service, and commitment as a boy growing up in a devout Mormon family in Nevada. His parents lived by the code of absolute honesty and integrity. Burns' commitment to helping others may have come from his grandfather, who "always thought the best thing you could do was giving service to other people." Burns deeply believes that a corporation has a responsibility to give something back to the community, and he also recognizes that doing so pays dividends. "I really think being a good citizen and offering opportunity to all people is not only the absolute right thing to do, it's also great business. Customers want to do business with you, and employees want to work here."[31]

Leaders like Tony Burns demonstrate the importance of serving people and society as well as the bottom line. Leaders are responsible for creating and sustaining a culture that emphasizes the importance of ethical behavior and service within the organization for all employees every day. They do this most clearly by behaving ethically themselves. There are a number of mechanisms leaders can also use to create an ethical organizational culture. Exhibit 13.4 lists ten ways to enhance ethical leadership.

Leadership Courage

Leadership demands courage. In particular, the moral leadership we have been discussing in this chapter requires that leaders reach deep within themselves and find the fortitude and courage to stand up for their beliefs. However, for many leaders, particularly those working in large organizations, the importance of courage is easily obscured—the main thing is to get along, fit in, and do whatever brings promotions and pay raises. In a world of stability and abundance, it was easy to forget even the *meaning* of courage, so how can leaders know where to find it when they need it? In the following sections, we will examine the nature of leadership courage

EXHIBIT 13.4 **TEN WAYS TO ENHANCE ETHICAL LEADERSHIP**

1. Establish a code of ethics or code of responsible business conduct.
2. Require all employees to verify that they've read and understand the code.
3. Integrate ethics into all performance evaluations.
4. Recognize and reward ethical behavior.
5. Establish a confidential ethics hotline or advisory service.
6. Incorporate ethics questions into employee opinion surveys.
7. Show and discuss videos that deal with ethical dilemmas.
8. Launch an ethics column in the employee newsletter.
9. Use on-line menu-driven answers to queries about ethical problems.
10. Hold open forums on ethics with top leaders.

SOURCE: The Canadian Clearinghouse for Consumer and Corporate Ethics, **www.interactive.yorku.ca/ethicscan/eem.html,** as published in Nancy Croft Baker, "Heightened Interest in Ethics Education Reflects Employer, Employee Concerns," *Corporate University Review* (May/June 1997), 6–9.

and discuss some ways courage is expressed in organizations. The final section of the chapter will explore the sources of leadership courage.

What Is Courage?

Many people know intuitively that courage can carry you through deprivation, ridicule, and rejection and enable you to achieve something about which you care deeply. Courage is both a moral and a practical matter for leaders. Years of stability and abundance misled American businesses into thinking that courage isn't needed in the business world. The lesson executives learned to advance in their careers was: "Keep your nose clean. Don't fail. Let someone else take the risk. Be careful. Don't make mistakes." Such a philosophy is no longer beneficial. Indeed, the courage to take risks has always been important for living a full, rewarding life, as discussed in the Living Leadership box. For today's organizations, things are constantly changing, and leaders thrive by solving problems through trial and error. They create the future by moving forward in the face of uncertainty, by taking chances, by acting with courage.[32] The defining characteristic of **courage** is the ability to step forward through fear. Courage doesn't mean the absence of doubt or fear, but the ability to act in spite of them.

Courage is not another word for fearless. In fact, if there were no fear or doubt, courage would not be needed. Raoul Wallenberg surely felt fear for his life as he threatened high-ranking Nazi officers. People experience all kinds of fears, including fear of death, mistakes, failure, embarrassment, change, loss of control, loneliness, pain, uncertainty, abuse, rejection, success, and public speaking. It is natural and right for people to feel fear when real risk is involved, whether the risk be los-

LIVING LEADERSHIP

Is It Worth the Risk?

To *laugh* . . . is to risk appearing the fool.
To *weep* . . . is to risk appearing sentimental.
To *reach out* . . . is to risk involvement.
To *expose feelings* . . . is to risk exposing your true self.
To *place your ideas and dreams before a crowd* . . . is to risk rejection.
To *love* . . . is to risk not being loved in return.
To *live* . . . is to risk dying.
To *hope* . . . is to risk despair.
To *try* . . . is to risk failure.

But risks must be taken, because the greatest hazard in life is to risk nothing.
Those who risk nothing
do nothing and have nothing.
They may avoid sufferings and sorrow,
But they cannot learn, feel, change, grow, or love.
Chained by their certitude, they are slaves; they have forfeited their freedom.
Only one who risks is free.

By an anonymous author.

ing your life, losing your job, losing the acceptance of peers, or losing your reputation. But many fears are learned and prevent people from doing what they want. True leaders step through these learned fears to accept responsibility, take risks, make changes, speak their minds, and fight for what they believe.

Courage means accepting responsibility. Leaders make a real difference in the world when they are willing to step up and take personal responsibility. Some people just let life happen to them; leaders make things happen. They do not expect others to tell them what to do or give them permission to act. Courageous leaders create opportunities to make a difference in their organizations and communities. Leaders also openly take responsibility for their failures and mistakes. Accepting responsibility in many of today's large, bureaucratic organizations seems nonexistent. In one large agency of the federal government, for example, the slightest mistake created a whirlwind of blaming, finger pointing, and extra effort to avoid responsibility. The absence of courage froze the agency to the point that many employees were afraid to even do their routine tasks.[33] At Quad/Graphics, on the other hand, leadership courage is reflected in employee courage, as described in the Cutting Edge box.

Courage means nonconformity. Leadership courage means going against the grain, breaking traditions, reducing boundaries, and initiating change. Leaders do not play it safe by following rules designed for an earlier time. They're willing to take risks and they encourage others to do so. At FedEx, leaders promote courage and risk-taking among all employees by encouraging them to work autonomously. Employees sometimes break the rules to satisfy customers, as when one worker loaded a dropbox into his van and delivered it to a central sorting facility because he had misplaced the key and didn't want the packages to be delayed. Silicon Graphics gives "spirit awards" annually to 50 employees who embody company values such as "encouraging creativity" or "seeking solutions rather than blame."[34] Going against the status quo is difficult. Most leaders initiating change find some cooperation and

ON THE CUTTING EDGE

Quad/Graphics

Harry V. Quadracci, founder and president of $600 million printing giant Quad/Graphics in Peewaukee, Wisconsin, has been called revolutionary because of his desire to help his employees, mostly high school graduates, "become something more than what they ever hoped to be."

Quadracci doesn't see anything revolutionary about it—he thinks doing things differently is the only way to survive. Doing things differently has enabled Quad/Graphics to boast average annual growth rates near 40 percent in an industry that is struggling just to achieve double-digit growth. Quadracci believes all of business is an experiment: "You try something and if it works, it works. If it doesn't work, you try something else. Quad/Graphics is a social experiment because we've . . . just tried to experiment with the way we can interact in the workplace as individuals and as responsible citizens." He runs his company with a minimum of rules and a maximum of indoctrination with values. For example, he thinks organizational charts limit people's responsibility. At Quad/Graphics, if you see something that needs to be done, you do it. There is no separation between management and labor. There are supervisors, but they wear the same uniform as their charges and do the same work. People and relationships are highly valued.

Quadracci admits his system takes a lot of trust, but, he says, "If you trust your employees, they'll trust you, and they'll rise to your level of belief in them." Quadracci celebrates employee mistakes, particularly what he refers to as "perfect failures." An example of a perfect failure is when two technicians spent a year and almost $800,000 developing a paper-folding machine that did not work. The company celebrated afterwards and even gave the workers a bonus for having the courage to try. Quadracci believes that when employees are afraid to make mistakes, the business is doomed. This belief has made Quad/Graphics a certifiable success, racing ahead of its competitors. When asked about his number one concern for the future, Quadracci speaks in terms of giving his employees continued opportunities to grow financially and personally, to continue to "become something more than what they ever hoped to be."

SOURCE: "Harry V. Quadracci," an interview with Craig Cox, *Business Ethics*, (May/June 1993), 19–21.

support, but they also encounter resistance, rejection, loneliness, and even ridicule. Taking chances means making mistakes, enduring mockery or scorn, being outvoted by others, and sometimes failing miserably. Courageous leaders are willing to disagree with the boss, persist with a new idea, and sacrifice the approval of others in the pursuit of a dream.

Courage means pushing beyond the comfort zone. To take a chance and improve things means leaders have to push beyond their comfort zone. According to Barry Diller, the former chairman of Paramount Pictures, Fox, Inc., and QVC, Inc., his secret to success is to "plunge into the uncomfortable; push, or be lucky enough to have someone push you, beyond your fears and your sense of limitations. That's what I've been doing . . . overcoming my discomfort as I go along." When Diller was 23 years old and working as assistant to the head of programming at ABC, he says his loftiest goal was "to be the best damn clerk in the world." One day his boss threw him a script and asked him to read it and tell the producer what he thought. Diller hated the script and pushed through his fear to say so. He got chewed out, but he had the courage to stand by his opinion.[35] Years later at Paramount, Diller helped select winning scripts for movies such as *Raiders of the Lost Ark*, *Trading Places*, and *Flashdance*. When people push beyond the comfort zone, they encounter an invisible "wall of fear." They may encounter it when about to ask someone for a date, confront the boss, break off a relationship, launch an expensive project, or change careers. Facing the invisible wall of fear is when courage is needed most.

Courage means asking for what you want and saying what you think. Leaders have to speak out to influence others. However, the desire to please others—especially the boss—can sometimes block the truth. Everyone wants approval, so it is difficult to say things when you think others will disagree or disapprove. Author and scholar Jerry Harvey tells a story of how members of his extended family in Texas decided to drive 40 miles to Abilene for dinner on a hot day when the car air conditioning did not work. They were all miserable. Talking about it afterward, each person admitted they had not wanted to go but went along to please the others. The *Abilene Paradox* is the name Harvey uses to describe the tendency of people to not voice their true thoughts because they want to please others.[36] According to Roger Enrico, president of Pepsi-Cola: "One of the things we look for when we are assessing people on their way up is 'Do they have a point of view? Do they have the guts to recommend what might be unpopular solutions to things?'"[37] Courage means speaking your mind even when you know others may disagree with you and may even deride you. Courage also means asking for what you want and setting boundaries. It is the ability to say no to unreasonable demands from others, as well as the ability to ask for what you want to help achieve the vision. When Ronald Shaw was hired as president of Pilot Pen, he insisted on autonomy in order to make the struggling company profitable. By asking for what he wanted, Shaw guided Pilot from sales of $1.2 million to sales of $81 million and a healthy profit.[38]

Courage means fighting for what you believe. Courage means fighting for valued outcomes that benefit the whole. Leaders take risks, but they do so for a higher purpose. Wallenberg did not risk his life just for the thrill of it; he risked it for a cause he deeply believed in: the dignity of human life. Taking risks that do not offer the possibility of valued outcomes is at best foolish and at worst evil. Courage doesn't mean doing battle to destroy the weak, trample the powerless, or crush things that are valued by others. It does mean doing what you believe is right, even when this opens you up to failure and personal sacrifice. One good example of a courageous leader in the business world is Lawrence Fish, who has experienced both failure and success by doing what he believes is right.

LEADERSHIP SPOTLIGHT   **LAWRENCE FISH**

Lawrence Fish, CEO of Citizens Financial Group, Inc., is a man who has known both success and failure as a result of his unconventional approaches and ethical beliefs. His effort to rescue the Bank of New England ended in defeat with the bank's sale to Fleet Financial Group. However, Fish's unconventional ideas have led to success at Citizens. He has more than doubled the Providence, Rhode Island, company's assets, snatched the biggest share of retail deposits in the state, and tripled earnings. According to Cornelius Hurley, a banking consultant in Boston, Fish has "put together a powerhouse." Yet when he talks about the company, Fish says, "If we just make money, we'll fail."

Before Fish left one top position, he donated half of his $2 million salary to Drake University in Iowa, his alma mater. When he was offered the job at Citizens Financial, Fish postponed taking it for three months so he could work in a shelter for abused kids—washing walls, feeding children, reading stories.

His approach at Citizens is to turn the conventional wisdom of banking on its head. Unlike most big banks, Citizens courts working-class customers and specializes in the human touch rather than promoting fancy electronic devices and new technology. Fish believes banking the old-fashioned way is the best way to long-term profitability. He gives local bank executives the freedom to decide how to make loans rather than insisting on approval from the home office. He makes a point of writing a thank you note to at least one employee a day, and he encourages his staff to spend part of their time caring for babies with AIDS. He is sometimes derided for "having too much heart" or "being too soft." However, Anat Bird, a banking consultant in New York, says Citizens' success shows there is still room for banks that execute efficiently but with a heart. She predicts the bank will outperform most of its regional competitors because the competition "can't compete with Citizens on the value they bring to the customer."

In the world of business, Fish believes there's more to life than material success. It's a belief that goes back to 1968, when he graduated from Harvard Business School. Rather than heading for Wall Street, the nonconformist Fish ended up at a remote ashram in northern India, where he lived as an ascetic for a year. "There are forces that brought me to India that are still with me," he says. "Ultimately, what matters is the good that we do."[39]

Moral Courage

Lawrence Fish is an example of the many people working in organizations who have the courage to be unconventional, to do what they think is right, to dare to treat employees and customers as whole human beings who deserve respect. Balancing profit with people, selfishness with service, and control with stewardship requires individual moral courage.

Moral leadership requires courage. To practice moral leadership, leaders have to know themselves, understand their strengths and weaknesses, know what they stand for, and often be nonconformists. Honest self-analysis can be painful, and acknowledging one's limitations in order to recognize the superior abilities of others takes personal strength of character. In addition, moral leadership means building relationships, which requires sharing yourself, listening, having significant personal experiences with others, and making yourself vulnerable—qualities that frighten many people. The quest for emotional strength requires people to overcome their deepest fears and to accept emotions as a source of strength rather than weakness. True power lies in the emotions that connect people. By getting close and doing what is best for others—sharing the good and the bad, the pain and anger as well as the success and the joy—leaders bring out the best qualities in others.[40]

One example of this in practice is when William Peace had to initiate a layoff as general manager of the Synthetic Fuels Division of Westinghouse. To make the division attractive to buyers, executives made a painful decision to cut any jobs not considered essential. Peace had the courage to deliver the news about layoffs personally. He took some painful blows in the face-to-face meetings he held with the 15 workers to be laid off, but he believed that allowing them to vent their grief and anger at him and the situation was the moral thing to do. His action sent a message to the remaining workers that, even though layoffs were necessary, leaders valued each of them as individuals. Because the workers recognized that layoffs were a last resort and the executive team was doing everything they could to save as many jobs as possible, they rededicated themselves to helping save the division. A buyer was found and the company had the opportunity to rehire half of those who had been laid off. Everyone contacted agreed to come back because the humane way they had been treated overcame negative feelings about the layoff.[41] For Peace, the courage to practice moral leadership gained respect, renewed commitment, and higher performance, even though he suffered personal rejection in the short run. Standing up for one's beliefs often entails great risk and tremendous courage. Nowhere is this more evident than in the case of ethical whistleblowing.

Opposing unethical conduct requires courage. **Whistleblowing** means employee disclosure of illegal, immoral, or unethical practices in the organization.[42] Although whistleblowing is more widespread in recent years, it is still risky for employees, who can lose their jobs, be ostracized by coworkers, or be transferred to lower-level positions. For example, when Mark Jorgensen exposed fraud in the real-estate funds he managed for Prudential Insurance Company of America, he was shunned by his supervisor and coworkers, accused by company lawyers of breaking the law, and eventually dismissed. He and his family suffered greatly for months, and even had to sell their home, but Jorgensen stood up for his principles. His willingness to fight for what he believed in won him the respect and admiration of some of Prudential's largest investors, and the company eventually offered him an apology and his job back (which he declined). Jorgensen became an industry hero, but this didn't alleviate the agony and despair he and his family suffered.[43]

Although some whistleblowers believe nothing bad will happen to them because they are "doing the right thing," most realize they may suffer financially and emotionally from their willingness to report unethical conduct on the part of bosses or coworkers.[44] They step forward to tell the truth despite a jumble of contradictory emotions and fears. As one professor put it, "Depending upon the circumstances, including our own courage, we can choose to act and be ethical both as individuals and as leaders."[45] Choosing to act courageously means conflicting emotions—whistleblowers may feel an ethical obligation to report the wrongdoing but may also feel disloyal to their boss and coworkers. Some may do battle within themselves about where their responsibility lies. Robert A. Bugai, who challenged college marketers on unethical business practices in the early 1980s, warns that there are considerable costs involved—"mentally, financially, physically, emotionally, and spiritually." However, when asked if he'd do it again, he says, "You bet."[46]

Sources of Personal Courage

How does a leader find the courage to step through fear and confusion, to act despite the risks involved? All of us have the potential to live and act courageously, if we can push through our own fears. Most of us have learned fears that limit our comfort zone and stand in the way of being our best and accomplishing our goals. We have been conditioned to follow the rules, not rock the boat, to "go along" with things we feel are wrong so others will like and accept us. There are a number of ways people can unlock the courage within themselves, including committing to a cause they believe in, connecting with others, welcoming failure as a natural and beneficial part of life, and harnessing anger.

Belief in a Higher Purpose Courage comes easily when we fight for something we really believe in. Service to a larger vision or purpose gives people the courage to step through fear. For someone to risk his life as Raoul Wallenberg did, or his personal safety as Gandhi did, requires a profound conviction that there is a greater good than the self. In organizations, too, courage depends on belief in a higher vision. A leader who is concerned only with his own career advancement would not be willing to report wrongdoing for fear of losing his position. On the other hand, after the 1986 *Challenger* explosion that killed seven crew members, concerns about the safety of astronauts was the higher purpose that led John W. Young, the chief of NASA's astronaut office, to publicly blow the whistle about safety-related problems in the NASA system.[47] Sometimes courage can increase simply by getting clear on what higher purpose you are seeking. V. Cheryl Womack, founder of VCW, Inc. in Kansas City, Missouri, tries to help employees find their own courage by asking each of them to write a personal mission statement which is reviewed annually and linked to company mission and goals.[48]

Connection with Others Caring about others and having support from others is a potent source of courage in a topsy-turvy world. Caring about the people who work with and for her was a source of courage for Cindy Olson, vice president of contract settlement in Enron's Capital and Trade Commercial Support Group. When Olson was asked to put the bulk of her job on the back burner and sign on as a leader with a major back-office reengineering project, she knew there were career risks involved. She was new in her position and hadn't yet mastered her duties. Everyone expected the reengineering effort would be difficult and thankless, and would result in lost jobs. She had the choice to say no; however, partly because she was concerned about the impact of reengineering on the people on the front line, Olson stepped forward and assumed the difficulties and additional responsibilities.[49] The support of others is also a source of courage. People who feel alone in the world take fewer risks because they have more to lose.[50] Being part of an organizational team that is supportive and caring, or having a loving and supportive family at home, can reduce the fear of failure and help people take risks they otherwise wouldn't take.

Welcoming Failure Thomas Moore, author of *Care of the Soul*, talks about the importance of "befriending a problem rather than making an enemy of it."[51]

Failure can play a creative role in work and in life. Success and failure are two sides of the same coin; one cannot exist without the other. A child learns to ride a bicycle by failing and trying again and again. Today, many people want success to arrive without difficulties, problems, and struggles. However, accepting failure enables courage. When people accept failure and are at peace with the worst possible outcome, they find they have the fortitude to move forward. Leaders know that failure can lead to success and that the pain of learning strengthens individuals and the organization. Both Walt Disney and Henry Ford had early business ventures go bankrupt. Anne Busquet, who is now executive vice president for consumer-card marketing at American Express, was once demoted for a bad-debt bombshell in the Optima Card unit. Thomas Ryder, who was her boss back then, refers to Busquet as "an example of someone whose career was stalled but who had the courage to [try again and] take on an incredibly difficult challenge."[52] There is evidence that with repeated practice, people can overcome fears such as a fear of flying or fear of heights. Practice also enables people to overcome fear of risk-taking in their work. Every time you push beyond your comfort zone, every time you fail and try again, you build psychological strength and courage.

Harnessing Frustration and Anger If you have ever been really angry about something, you know that it can cause you to forget about fear of embarrassment or fear that others won't like you. In organizations, we can also see the power of frustration at work. When someone has to be fired for just cause, a supervisor may put if off until some incident that makes her angry enough to step through the fear and act. Sometimes, outrage over a perceived injustice can give a mild-mannered person the courage to confront the boss head on.[53] Getting mad at yourself may be the motivation to change. Anger, in moderate amounts, is a healthy emotion that provides energy to move forward. The challenge is to harness anger and use it appropriately. After Glenn McIntyre was paralyzed in a motorcycle accident, he first used his anger to overcome thoughts of suicide and begin intensive physical therapy. His frustration at how poorly hotels served handicapped customers eventually led him to found Access Designs, a consulting firm that helps hotels such as Quality Suites and Renaissance Ramada become more usable for disabled travelers.[54]

Summary and Interpretation

This chapter has explored a number of ideas concerning moral leadership and leadership courage. People want honest and trustworthy leaders. However, leaders face a dilemma because modern society has created a separation between business and ethics. The world of business is one of rationality and hard measurable facts, whereas the realm of ethics concerns human meaning, purpose, significance, and values. But more and more ethics is being recognized as an essential part of business. For leaders to create ethical organizations requires that they themselves be honest, ethical, and principled.

One personal consideration for leaders is the level of moral development. Leaders use an understanding of the stages of moral development to enhance their own as well as followers' personal moral growth. Leaders who operate at higher stages of moral development focus on the needs of followers and universal ethical principles.

Ideas about control versus service between leaders and followers are changing and expanding, reflected in a continuum of leader-follower relationships. The continuum varies from authoritarian managers to participative managers to stewardship to servant leadership.

Leaders who operate from the principles of stewardship and servant leadership can help build ethical organizations. All leaders face ethical dilemmas. Leaders shape the ethical culture of the organization most clearly by their behavior. They can also use a number of formal mechanisms to create ethical organizations.

The final sections of the chapter discussed leadership courage and how leaders can find their own courage. Courage means the ability to step forward through fear, to accept responsibility, to take risks and make changes, to speak your mind, and to fight for what you believe. Two expressions of courage in organizations are moral leadership and ethical whistleblowing. Sources of courage include belief in a higher purpose, connection with others, experience with failure, and harnessing anger.

Key Terms

moral leadership	principled level	courage
preconventional level	stewardship	whistleblowing
conventional level	servant leadership	

Discussion Questions

1. If you were in a position similar to Raoul Wallenberg, what do you think you would do? Why?

2. Explain the dilemma between business and ethics. Do you feel a similar dilemma in your life as a student? As an employee?

3. If most adults are at a conventional level of moral development, what does this mean for their potential for moral leadership?

4. Do you feel that the difference between authoritarian leadership and stewardship should be interpreted as a moral difference? Discuss.

5. Should serving others be placed at a higher moral level than serving oneself? Discuss.

6. If you find yourself avoiding a situation or activity, what can you do to find the courage to move forward? Explain.

7. If it is immoral to prevent those around you from growing to their fullest potential, are you being moral?

8. Do you have the courage to take a moral stand that your peers and even authority figures will disagree with? Why?

Leadership Development: Personal Feedback

Moral Leadership

Think about situations in which you either assumed or were given a leadership role in a group or organization. Imagine your own courage and moral standards as a leader. To what extent does each of the following statements characterize your leadership?

1 = very little

2 = somewhat

3 = a moderate amount

4 = a great deal

5 = very much

_____ 1. My actions meet the needs of others before my own.

_____ 2. I create a sense of community.

_____ 3. I am a symbol of integrity and honesty.

_____ 4. I give people a lot of discretion.

_____ 5. I let others know my values and beliefs.

_____ 6. I give away credit and recognition to others.

_____ 7. I enable others to feel ownership for their work.

_____ 8. I encourage the growth of others, expecting nothing in return.

_____ 9. My choices reflect a larger moral purpose.

_____ 10. I display high moral standards and values for others.

_____ 11. I give up control to show that I trust others.

_____ 12. I risk substantial personal loss to achieve the vision.

_____ 13. I take personal risks to defend my beliefs.

_____ 14. I say no even if I have a lot to lose.

_____ 15. I am assertive about what I believe.

_____ 16. My actions are linked to higher values.

_____ 17. I often act against the opinions and approval of others.

_____ 18. I quickly tell people the truth, even when it is negative.

_____ 19. I speak out against organizational injustice, bureaucracy, complacency, or corruption.

_____ 20. I stand up to offensive people.

Scoring

Each of these questions pertains to courage and moral leadership. Calculate your total score by summing the scores for all 20 answers.

Interpretation

This questionnaire pertains to both courage and moral leadership. It provides some indication of the extent to which you infuse your leadership with moral values and risk-taking to uphold those values. If you received a score of 80, you would be considered a courageous moral leader. A score of below 40 indicates that either you have been avoiding moral issues or you have not been in situations that challenged your moral courage. A score of 40 to 80 means that you are using courage to assert moral leadership. Keep up the good work, but continue trying to improve. Is your score consistent with your understanding of your own strengths and weaknesses? Compare your score to that of other students. What might you do to improve your scores?

Leadership Development: Case for Analysis

The Boy, the Girl, the Ferryboat Captain, and the Hermits

There was an island, and on this island there lived a girl. A short distance away there was another island, and on this island there lived a boy. The boy and the girl were very much in love with each other.

The boy had to leave his island and go on a long journey, and he would be gone for a very long time. The girl felt that she must see the boy one more time before he went away. There was only one way to get from the island where the girl lived to the boy's island, and that was on a ferryboat that was run by a ferryboat captain. And so the girl went down to the dock and asked the ferryboat captain to take her to the island where the boy lived. The ferryboat captain agreed and asked her for the fare. The girl told the ferryboat captain that she did not have any money. The ferryboat captain told her that money was not necessary: "I will take you to the other island if you will stay with me tonight."

The girl did not know what to do, so she went up into the hills on her island until she came to a hut where a hermit lived. We will call him the first hermit. She related the whole story to the hermit and asked for his advice. The hermit listened carefully to her story, and then told her, "I cannot tell you what to do. You must weigh the alternatives and the sacrifices that are involved and come to a decision within your own heart."

And so the girl went back down to the dock and accepted the ferryboat captain's offer.

The next day, when the girl arrived on the other island, the boy was waiting at the dock to greet her. They embraced, and then the boy asked her how she got over to his island, for he knew she did not have any money. The girl explained the ferryboat captain's offer and what she did. The boy pushed her away from him and said, "We're through. That's the end. Go away from me. I never want to see you again," and he left her.

The girl was desolate and confused. She went up into the hills of the boy's island to a hut where a second hermit lived. She told the whole story to the second hermit and asked him what she should do. The hermit told her that there was nothing she could do, that she was welcome to stay in his hut, to partake of his food, and to rest on his bed while he went down into the town and begged for enough money to pay the girl's fare back to her own island.

When the second hermit returned with the money for her, the girl asked him how she could repay him. The hermit answered, "You owe me nothing. We owe this to each other. I am only too happy to be of help." And so the girl went back down to the dock and returned to her own island.

Questions

1. List in order the characters in this story that you like, from most to least. What values governed your choices?

2. Rate the characters on their level of moral development. Explain.

3. Evaluate each character's level of courage. Discuss.

References

[1]John C. Kunich and Richard I. Lester, "Profile of a Leader: The Wallenberg Effect," *The Journal of Leadership Studies* 4, No. 3 (Summer 1997), 5–19.

[2]Del Jones, "Doing the Wrong Thing: 48% of Workers Admit to Unethical or Illegal Acts," *USA Today*, April 4, 1997, 1A, 2A; Mark Maremont with Joyce Barnathan, "Blind Ambition: How the Pursuit of Results Got Out of Hand at Bausch & Lomb," *Business Week*, October 23, 1995, 78–92; and William J. Morin, "Silent Sabotage: Mending the Crisis in Corporate Values," *Management Review*, July 1995, 10–14.

[3]Jones," Doing the Wrong Thing."

[4]James M. Kouzes and Barry Z. Posner, *Credibility: How Leaders Gain and Lose It, Why People Demand It* (San Francisco: Jossey-Bass, 1993), 255.

[5]Al Gini, "Moral Leadership and Business Ethics," *The Journal of Leadership Studies* 4, No. 4 (Fall 1997), 64–81.

[6]Jones, "Doing the Wrong Thing."

[7]Dale Kurschner, "Interview: Randall Tobias," *Business Ethics*, July/August 1995, 31–34.

[8]Gini, "Moral Leadership and Business Ethics."

[9]Henry Ford, Sr., quoted by Thomas Donaldson, *Corporations and Morality* (Prentice-Hall, Inc., 1982), 57 in Al Gini, "Moral Leadership and Business Ethics," 64–81.

[10]Kouzes and Posner, *Credibility: How Leaders Gain and Lose It, Why People Demand It.*

[11]Kunich and Lester, "Profile of a Leader: The Wallenberg Effect," 15.

[12]Viktor E. Frankl, *Man's Search for Meaning* (New York: Pocket Books, 1959), 104.

[13]Lawrence Kolhberg, "Moral Stages and Moralization: The Cognitive Developmental Approach," in Thomas Likona, ed. *Moral Development and Behavior: Theory, Research, and Social Issues* (Austin, TX: Holt, Rinehart and Winston, 1976), 31–53; Jill W. Graham, "Leadership, Moral Development, and Citizenship Behavior," *Business Ethics Quarterly* 5,

No. 1 (January 1995), 43–54; and James Weber, "Exploring the Relationship between Personal Values and Moral Reasoning," *Human Relations* 46, No. 4 (April 1993), 435–463.

[14]Tom Morris, *If Aristotle Ran General Motors* (New York: Henry Holt, 1997).

[15]Keshavan Nair, *A Higher Standard of Leadership: Lessons from the Life of Gandhi* (San Francisco: Berrett-Koehler, 1994), 52.

[16]James Weber, "Exploring the Relationship Between Personal Values and Moral Reasoning," *Human Relations* 46, No. 4 (April 1993), 435–463.

[17]James A. Belasco and Ralph C. Stayer, *Flight of the Buffalo: Soaring To Excellence, Learning to Let Employees Lead* (New York: Warner Books, 1993).

[18]Peter Block, "Reassigning Responsibility," *Sky*, February 1994, 26–31; and David P. McCaffrey, Sue R. Faerman, and David W. Hart, "The Appeal and Difficulty of Participative Systems," *Organization Science* 6, No. 6 (November-December 1995), 603–627.

[19]Block, "Reassigning Responsibility."

[20]This discussion of stewardship is based on Peter Block, *Stewardship: Choosing Service Over Self-Interest* (San Francisco: Berrett-Koehler Publishers, 1993), 29–31; and Block, "Reassigning Responsibility."

[21]Mary Parker Follett, from *The New State* (1918), as quoted in David K. Hurst, "Thoroughly Modern—Mary Parker Follett," *Business Quarterly* 56, No. 4 (Spring 1992), 55–58.

[22]Robert K. Greenleaf, *Servant Leadership: A Journey into the Nature of Legitimate Power and Greatness* (Mahwah, N.J.: Paulist Press, 1977), 7.

[23]Based on Greenleaf, *Servant Leadership*, and Walter Kiechel III, "The Leader as Servant," *Fortune*, May 4, 1992, 121–122.

[24]Max O. DePree, "Leadership and Moral Purpose," *Hospital and Health Services Administration* 39, No. 1 (Spring 1994), 133–138.

[25]Parker J. Palmer, *Leading from Within: Reflections on Spirituality and Leadership* (Indianapolis: Indiana Office for Campus Ministries, 1990), 2.

[26]G. Pascal Zachary, "The New Search for Meaning in 'Meaningless' Work," *Wall Street Journal*, Eastern edition, January 9, 1997, B1, B2.

[27]T. Deal, "Not a Fool, Not a Saint," *Fortune*, November 11, 1996, 201–204; M. Ryan, "They Call Their Boss a Hero," *Parade* 4–5; M. Lee, "Corporate Focus; Malden Looks Spiffy in New England Textile Gloom," *Wall Street Journal*, November 10, 1995, B4.

[28]LaRue Tone Hosmer, "Trust: The Connecting Link between Organizational Theory and Philosophical Ethics," *Academy of Management Review* 20, No. 2 (April 1995), 379–403.

[29]Greenleaf, *Servant Leadership*, 45.

[30]*Corporate Ethics: A Prime Business Asset* (New York: The Business Roundtable, February 1988); "Best Moves of 1995," *Business Ethics*, January/February 1996, 23.

[31]John Grossmann, "A Whirlwind of Humanity," *Sky*, January 1997, 96–101.

[32]Richard L. Daft and Robert H. Lengel, *Fusion Leadership: Unlocking the Subtle Forces that Change People and Organizations* (San Francisco: Berrett-Koehler, 1998).

[33]Daft and Lengel, *Fusion Leadership*, 155.

[34]*Blueprints for Service Quality: The Federal Express Approach*, AMA Management Briefing, (New York: American Management Association Membership Publications Division, 1991), 29–30; Zachary, "The New Search for Meaning."

[35]Barry Diller, "The Discomfort Zone," *Inc.*, November 1995, 19–20.

[36]Jerry B. Harvey, *The Abilene Paradox and Other Meditations on Management* (Lexington, MA: Lexington Books, 1988), 13–15.

[37]Lester Korn, *The Success Profile: A Leading Headhunter Tells You How to Get to the Top* (New York: Simon & Schuster, 1988).

[38]Laurie Kretchmar, "Fortune People," *Fortune*, April 20, 1992, 185–186.

[39]Joseph Rebello, "Radical Ways of Its CEO Are a Boon to Bank," *The Wall Street Journal*, March 20, 1995, B1, B2.

[40]A.J. Vogl, "Risky Work," an interview with Max DePree, *Across the Board*, July/August 1993, 27–31.

[41]William H. Peace, "The Hard Work of Being a Soft Manager," *Harvard Business Review*, November-December 1991, 4007.

[42]Janet P. Near and Marcia P. Miceli, "Effective Whistle-Blowing," *Academy of Management Review* 20, No. 3 (1995), 679–708.

[43]Kurt Eichenwald, "He Told, He Suffered, Now He's a Hero," *The New York Times*, May 29, 1994, Section 3,1.

[44]Hal Lancaster, "Workers Who Blow the Whistle on Bosses Often Pay a High Price," *The Wall Street Journal*, July 18, 1995, B1.

[45]Richard P. Nielsen, "Changing Unethical Organizational Behavior," *The Executive*, May 1989, 123–130.

[46]Barbara Ettorre, "Whistleblowers: Who's the Real Bad Guy?" *Management Review*, May 1994, 18–23.

[47]Nielsen, "Changing Unethical Organizational Behavior."

[48]Charles Burck, "Succeeding with Tough Love," *Fortune*, November 29, 1993, 188.

[49]Jon R. Katzenbach and the RCL Team, *Real Change Leaders: How You Can Create Growth and High Performance at Your Company* (New York: Times Business/Random House 1995), 107–108.

[50]James M. Kouzes and Barry Z. Posner, *The Leadership Challenge: How to Get Extraordinary Things Done in Organizations* (San Francisco: Jossey-Bass, 1988).

[51]Thomas Moore, "The Soul of Work," *Business Ethics*, March/April 1993, 6–7.

[52]Patricia Sellers, "So You Fail. Now Bounce Back!" *Fortune*, May 1, 1995, 48–66.

[53]Ira Cheleff, *The Courageous Follower: Standing Up To and For Our Leaders* (San Francisco: Berrett-Koehler, 1995).

[54]Michael Warshaw, ed., "Great Comebacks," *Success*, July/August 1995, 33–46.

14

Followership

- **The Role of Followers** 396

- **Styles of Followership** 397

- **The Courageous Follower** 400

- **Sources of Follower Courage** 403

- **Developing Personal Potential** 404

- **Sources of Power** 406

- **Strategies for Effective Followership** 407

- **What Followers Want** 411

- **Building a Community of Followers** 411

- **Leadership Spotlights:**
  Lt. Colonel George Marshall 401
  Wes Walsh 409

- **Leader's Bookshelf:** *The Leadership Engine: How Winning Companies Build Leaders at Every Level* 413

- **Leadership Development: Personal Feedback**
  The Power of Followership 415

- **Leadership Development: Case for Analysis**
  General Products Britain 417

Your Leadership Challenge

After reading this chapter, you should be able to:

- Recognize your followership style and take steps to become a more effective follower.

- Apply the principles of courageous followership, including responsibility, service, challenging authority, participating in change, and knowing when to leave.

- Implement the strategies for effective followership at school or work.

- Know what followers want and contribute to building a community among followers.

When Dianne Martz asked her doctor to provide information about her asthma condition, he replied, "What is it you want to know? I don't have much time." Subsequently, she had a life-threatening asthma attack at an out-of-town conference that left her hospitalized for a week. As soon as she returned home from the hospital, she fired her doctor. Until this terrifying episode Martz had not realized she had been operating in such a state of isolation and vulnerability. She had the same feeling she had experienced in the mid-1960s when a pediatrician diagnosed her infant son with hemophilia and told her he might not live to the age of 17.

Martz says that, prior to her son's diagnosis, "It wasn't in my upbringing to challenge 'the system.'" Nevertheless, after her son was diagnosed, she made inquiries to clinics and support groups. She learned of options and choices that contradicted the pediatrician's grim prognosis. In 1969,

Martz contacted a manufacturer of a new clotting factor that she read about in a newspaper article. Her son, Kyle, became one of the first to use what later became the standard treatment. By the time he was 12, Kyle was administering the injections himself. Martz found herself in a role of influence in the hemophilia community, and even participated in lobbying the state legislature for the funding of hemophilia studies.

Martz's visibility and assertiveness landed her a sales job with a pharmaceutical company and she quickly became the top sales rep and eventually the sales manager. She also learned about the greed of her leaders and their practice of withholding information, which ultimately helped sales but not the customer. Then she discovered that HIV was present in the clotting factor, and that doctors and the pharmaceuticals industry had known this for two years without telling anyone, especially the patients who were at risk. Once again, Martz felt called upon to be an advocate for her son and others with his condition. To stay abreast of new information, she went to work for a clotting factor home delivery company.

However, when the company was purchased by one of the clotting-factor manufacturers who eliminated the sale and distribution of other competing treatment options, Martz saw a chance to serve those with hemophilia in a new way. She envisioned a company that would not only provide complete information on every treatment option available, but also offer meaningful employment for people with hemophilia or HIV. In 1988 she founded her own company, Hemophilia Health Services, which continues to offer every available treatment option, as well as workshops regarding the range of choices for those with hemophilia. Half of the company's 50 employees suffer from hemophilia or HIV. Kyle, now a grown man, is the director of operations.[1]

Until Dianne Martz became a leader of her own company, she was a follower, both personally and professionally. But even in the position of follower, she discovered that she could challenge the medical community, seek her own information, initiate change in the lives of others, and even reject the ways of the business world. And in the process Martz discovered the courage to think critically, act independently, and risk failure, becoming an authority on those matters that concerned her most. Her courage and initiative in changing the options and information available to the hemophilia community are the hallmarks of both effective followership and leadership.

Followership is an important consideration for both leaders and followers. In this chapter we will examine the nature of the follower's role, the different styles of followership that individuals express, and the definition of a courageous follower. This chapter also explores the sources of courage and power that are available to followers, and the strategies for effective followership. Finally, we will look at the consequential role of followers in building community within their organizations.

The Role of Followers

Followership is important in the discussion of leadership for several reasons. First, leadership and followership are fundamental roles that individuals shift in and out of under various conditions. Everyone—leaders included—is a follower at one time or another in their lives. Indeed, most individuals, even those in a position of authority, have some kind of boss or supervisor. Individuals are more often followers than leaders.[2]

Second, recall that the definition of a leader from Chapter 1 referred to an influence relationship among leaders and followers. This means that in a position of leadership, an individual is influenced by the actions and the attitudes of followers. In fact, the contingency theories introduced in Chapter 4 are based on how leaders adjust their behavior to fit situations, especially their followers. Thus, the nature of leader-follower relationships involves reciprocity, the mutual exchange of influence.[3] The followers' influence upon a leader can enhance the leader or underscore his or her shortcomings.[4]

Third, many of the qualities that are desirable in a leader are the same qualities possessed by an effective follower. In addition to demonstrating initiative, independence, commitment to common goals, and courage, a follower can provide enthusiastic support of a leader, but not to the extent that the follower fails to challenge the leader who threatens the values or objectives of the organization.[5] This is not very different from the role of leader. Both leader and follower roles are proactive; together they can achieve a shared vision. Chapter 9 discussed empowerment and described how organizations can benefit from having empowered employees. In a performance study of Navy personnel, the outstanding ships were staffed by followers who supported their leaders, took initiative, and did not avoid raising issues or concerns with their superiors.[6] The performance of followers and the performance of the leader and organization are variables that depend upon one another.

As organizations seek to empower their members to achieve superior performance, the process of followership will continue to be relevant, and the reciprocal partnership that makes up the leader-follower relationship will warrant increasing attention.

Styles of Followership

After extensive interviews with leaders and followers, Robert E. Kelley described five styles of followership.[7] These followership styles are categorized according to two dimensions, as illustrated in Exhibit 14.1. The first dimension is the quality of independent, **critical thinking** versus dependent, **uncritical thinking**. Independent thinking recalls our discussion of mindfulness in Chapter 12, independent critical thinkers are mindful of the effects of people's behavior on achieving organizational goals. They are aware of the significance of their own actions and the actions of others. They can weigh the impact of decisions on the vision set forth by a leader and offer constructive criticism, creativity, and innovation. Conversely, a dependent, uncritical thinker does not consider possibilities beyond what he or she is told, does not contribute to the cultivation of the organization, and accepts the leader's ideas without thinking.

According to Kelley, the second dimension of followership style is active versus passive behavior. An active individual participates fully in an organization, engages in behavior that is beyond the limits of the job, demonstrates a sense of ownership, and initiates problem solving and decision making. A passive individual is characterized by a need for constant supervision and prodding by superiors. Passivity is

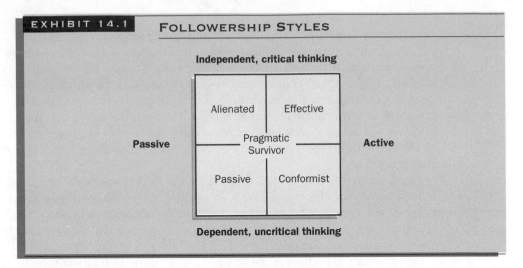

EXHIBIT 14.1	FOLLOWERSHIP STYLES

SOURCE: Adapted from *The Power of Followership* by Robert E. Kelley, 97. Copyright © 1992 by Consultants to Executives and Organizations, Ltd. Used by permission of Doubleday, a division of Bantam Doubleday Dell Publishing Group, Inc.

often regarded as laziness; a passive person does nothing that is not required and avoids added responsibility.

The extent to which one is active or passive, and is a critical, independent thinker or a dependent, uncritical thinker determines whether he or she is an alienated follower, a passive follower, a conformist, a pragmatic survivor, or an effective follower, as shown in Exhibit 14.1.

The **alienated follower** is a passive yet independent, critical thinker. Alienated followers are often effective followers who have experienced setbacks and obstacles, perhaps promises broken by superiors. Thus, they are capable, but they focus exclusively on the shortcomings of the organization and other people. Often cynical, alienated followers are able to think independently, but they do not participate in developing solutions to the problems or deficiencies they see. For example, Barry Paris spent over 10 years writing on and off for the *Pittsburgh Post-Gazette*, where he was known for his bad attitude and lack of enthusiasm and teamwork. Eventually Paris realized that he wasted that time ruminating over what he perceived as the hypocrisy of journalistic objectivity. "I could never resign myself to it," says Paris. Thus, rather than doing his best and trying to help others maintain standards of integrity, he allowed hostility and cynicism to permeate his work.[8]

The **conformist** participates actively in the organization but does not utilize critical thinking skills in his or her task behavior. In other words, a conformist typically carries out any and all orders regardless of the nature of those tasks. The conformist participates willingly, but without considering the consequences of what he or she is being asked to do—even at the risk of contributing to a harmful endeavor. A conformist is only concerned with avoiding conflict. Indeed, this style often results from rigid rules and authoritarian environments in which leaders perceive subordinate recommendations as a challenge or threat. When Kelley, the author who developed the two dimensions of followership, was consulted about how to improve employee creativity and innovation for an oil company, he discovered that each office was virtually identical, owing to strict company policies that prohibited individual expression, This is specifically the kind of environment that suppresses effective followership and leads to conformists.[9]

The **pragmatic survivor** has qualities of all four extremes—depending on which style fits with the prevalent situation. This type of follower uses whatever style best benefits his or her own position and minimizes risk. Pragmatic survivors often emerge when an organization is going through desperate times, and followers find themselves doing whatever is needed to get themselves through the difficulty. Within any given company, some 25 to 35 percent of followers tend to be pragmatic survivors, avoiding risks and fostering the status quo, often for political reasons. Government appointees often demonstrate this followership style because they have their own agenda and a short period of time in which to implement it. They may appeal to the necessary individuals, who themselves have a limited time to accomplish goals, and are therefore willing to do whatever is necessary to survive in the short run.[10]

The **passive follower** exhibits neither critical, independent thinking nor active participation. Being passive and uncritical, this type of follower displays neither initiative nor a sense of responsibility. Their activity is limited to what they are told to do, and they accomplish things only with a great deal of supervision. Passive followers leave the thinking to their leaders. Often, however, this style is the result of a leader who expects and encourages passive behavior. According to Red Auerbacher, president of the Boston Celtics, when followers are not creative, responsible, or innovative, typically it is not because of fear of making mistakes. Passive followers are often the result of leaders who are overcontrolling of others and who punish mistakes.[11]

The **effective follower** is both a critical, independent thinker and active in the organization. Effective followers behave the same toward everyone, regardless of their position in the organization. They do not try to avoid risk or conflict. Rather, effective followers have the courage to initiate change and put themselves at risk or in conflict with others, even their leaders, to serve the best interest of the organization.

Characterized by both mindfulness and a willingness to act, effective followers are essential for an organization to be effective. They are capable of self-management, they discern strengths and weaknesses in themselves and in the organization, they are committed to something bigger than themselves, and they work toward competency, solutions, and positive impact. For example, reorganization efforts led managers of a large commercial bank to devote their time to corporate clients in the field. The internal reorganization was delegated to rank-and-file staff members, despite the grave doubts of some managers. Nevertheless, the department followers successfully assumed responsibility and managed themselves through the turmoil. This required independent thinking, focus, skill, and self-control. The staff members were effective followers.[12] Effective followers are far from powerless—and they know it. Therefore, they do not despair in their positions, nor do they resent or

LIVING LEADERSHIP

Our Deepest Fear

Our deepest fear is not that we are
Inadequate, Our deepest fear is that we are
Powerful beyond measure.

It is our light, not our darkness, that most
Frightens us.

We ask ourselves, who am I to be brilliant,
Gorgeous, talented and fabulous?

Actually, who are you NOT to be?
You are a child of God.
Your playing small doesn't serve the world.

There's nothing enlightened about shrinking
So that other people won't feel insecure
Around you.

We were born to make manifest the glory . . .
that is within us.

It's not just in some of us; it's in everyone.
And as we let our own light shine, we
Unconsciously give other people permission
To do the same.

As we are liberated from our own fear, our
Presence automatically liberates others.

SOURCE: From the 1994 Inaugural Speech of Nelson
Mandela

---

manipulate others. The Living Leadership box provides highlights from a speech given by Nelson Mandela that underscores his meaning of effective followership.

The Courageous Follower

Recall the discussion of the importance of courage to leadership from Chapter 13. Courage is found in both effective leaders and followers. Indeed, a willingness to take risks, to challenge authority, and to believe one's own ideas are equal to or better than one's superior typically marks a follower as a future leader.[13] The role of followership includes responsibility, service, challenging authority, participating in change, and knowing when it is time to leave an organization.[14] All of these components of followership require courage.

Courage to Assume Responsibility

A courageous follower derives a sense of personal responsibility from the acknowledgment of ownership in the organization and the mission that the organization serves. By assuming responsibility for their own behavior and its impact on the organization, courageous followers do not presume that a leader or an organization will provide them with security, permission to act, or personal growth. Instead, courageous followers initiate the opportunities through which they can achieve personal fulfillment, exercise their potential, and provide the organization with the fullest extent of their capabilities. At Spartan Motors, for example, Larry Karkau and Tim Williams spent a year and a half tinkering over the production of a low-cost chassis for a high-end motor home. The project presented a number of difficulties with no quick solutions in sight, which had already led competing companies to give up on the idea, so company leaders discussed abandoning the project with Karkau and Williams. But Karkau insisted that their efforts be continued. "I was real candid about it. I knew this would work," says Karkau. Williams and Karkau had the courage to assume responsibility for the time and expense of their project and it paid off. Eventually, they had a product that cost $500,000 but reaped $30 million in sales in one year.[15]

Courage to Serve

A courageous follower discerns the needs of the organization and actively seeks to serve those needs. Just as leaders can serve others, as discussed in the previous chapter, so can followers. A courageous follower provides strength to the leader by supporting the leader's decisions and by contributing to the organization in areas that complement the leader's position. By displaying the courage to serve others over themselves, followers act for the common mission of the organization with a passion that equals that of a leader. For example, sales associates of Mary Kay Cosmetics support the company mission, which is to provide outstanding business opportunities to women. Gloria Hilliard Mayfield, who has a business degree from Harvard, left IBM to work for Mary Kay full time. This mission provides Mayfield ample defense against the incredulity of her Ivy League peers. She believes "it's no different from my having a Ford dealership. The Ford dealer is an independent entrepreneur. So am I."[16] Mayfield's service to her cause required courage on her part.

Courage to Challenge

Courageous followers do not sacrifice the purpose of the organization or their personal ethics in order to maintain harmony and minimize conflict. On the contrary, courageous followers take a stand against the leader's actions and decisions when that behavior contradicts the best interest of the organization, or their own integrity. They are not afraid of the consequences of their challenge, and they act according to the conviction that emotional reactions and conflict are worth risking to meet the needs of those served by the organization. Consider the following example.

LEADERSHIP SPOTLIGHT   **LT. COLONEL GEORGE MARSHALL**

In October 1917, General John J. Pershing criticized a military operation he had come to the field to observe. Lt. Colonel George Marshall felt Pershing's judgment was unfair and, although Pershing was his hero, he told the General on the spot, stating numerous facts to the contrary within earshot of many people. Normally a dutiful follower, Marshall, again in November 1938, shocked everyone at a presidential briefing with his sharp disagreement over President Roosevelt's illogical plan to build 10,000 warplanes. The president's program did not provide for such practical matters as servicing the planes. "I am sorry, Mr. President, but I don't agree with you at all," Marshall replied immediately when Roosevelt asked for his thoughts. Marshall confronted

Roosevelt publicly a second time in May 1940, during discussions of U.S. participation in the war in Europe. Marshall, by then Army Chief of Staff, felt the president was not listening to him, so he demanded three minutes and proceeded to delineate the army's deficiencies in rapid-fire frustration. He pointed out that everything was in short supply, and although weaponry was designed, it was not in production. Furthermore, the proposed number of soldiers to be deployed was grossly inadequate. His tirade took well over the three minutes he had requested.[17]

George Marshall had the courage to publicly criticize highly important people at crucial points in time. This courage rested upon two components. First, Marshall was confident in his convictions and had the knowledge to support them. Secondly, he saw himself as an equal to his leaders. Because he included himself in the circle of "legitimate" leadership, he had the courage to challenge others.[18]

Courage to Participate in Transformation

Courageous followers view the struggle of corporate change and transformation as a mutual experience shared by all members of the organization. When an organization undergoes a difficult transformation, courageous followers support the leader and the organization. They are not afraid to confront the changes and work toward reshaping the organization. David Chislett, of Imperial Oil's Dartmouth, Nova Scotia refinery, was faced with this test of courage. The refinery was the least efficient in the industry and the Board of Directors gave management nine months to improve the refinery's effectiveness. Chislett was asked to give up his management position and return to the duties of a wage earner as part of an overall transformation strategy. He and many others agreed to the request, and contributed to the success of the refinery's transformation.[19] The Cutting Edge box describes how courageous followers are helping lead the transformation of IBM.

Courage to Leave

Often organizational or personal changes create a situation in which a follower must withdraw from a particular leader-follower relationship. Courageous followers are not afraid to depart because they do not rely on their leaders or their organizations to provide them with self-worth. When courageous followers are faced with a leader or an organization unwilling to make necessary changes, it is time to take their support elsewhere. The opening case of this chapter provided an example of the courage to leave. Professionally, Dianne Martz could no longer contribute to the business ethic of her sales job, which paralleled the ethics of the pharmaceuticals industry that threatened the well-being of her son. So she quit and started her own business. Personally, she could no longer support her relationship with her autocratic physician, who obviously did not share her belief that information about her asthma condition was to be shared with her. So she left that relationship too.

ON THE CUTTING EDGE

IBM's Grassroots Transformation

The turnaround of Big Blue is one of the most unexpected comebacks in corporate history. When Lou Gerstner took over in 1993, IBM looked like a company bent on self-destruction. Although Gerstner has played a decisive role in IBM's comeback, no turnaround this far-reaching can be the work of a single leader. IBM's transformation is being driven by a network of followers—grassroots leaders who have made it their business to change the company.

For example, although Gerstner stressed the importance of IBM's presence on the Internet, the real pressure came from below. If you ask in-the-trenches IBMers who has really pushed the company onto the 'Net, the name you'll hear again and again is John Patrick. Patrick, a career IBM employee, has always been thinking about the future and tinkering with ways to get there. He saw early on the potential of the Internet and wrote a manifesto called "Get Connected," identifying six principles that would reshape industries and reinvent companies. The ideas are conventional wisdom today, but when Patrick first wrote them they were risky, exciting—even dangerous, especially in stodgy IBM. The paper got immediate results, firing up enthusiasm throughout the company. "People didn't know where I reported in the company, and they didn't care," Patrick says. "We shared a common vision that the Internet was going to change everything and that IBM should be a leader." Less than six months after "Get Connected" was distributed, IBM debuted with one of the first significant corporate Web sites in the world.

Meanwhile, Patrick was pushing further. Without authorization, he signed up IBM as a major participant in Internet World, an industry gathering scheduled for Washington, D.C. He networked to get the funding and other resources, and IBM dominated the show. In 1995, IBM finally created an Internet division responsible for defining the company's 'Net initiatives. Patrick became vice president and chief technology officer. He says he can feel a difference at IBM because of grassroots leadership at all levels. "Years ago," he says, you could hear a pin drop in the halls. Today, you can feel the excitement. Kids are building Java applets. People are in a hurry. We just have to keep moving faster."

SOURCE: Eric Ransdell, "IBM's Grassroots Revival," *Fast Company*, October/November 1997, 182-199.

Sources of Follower Courage

Personal courage is paramount to taking risks. The ability to consciously put one-self at risk requires a great deal of courage. Risk is often a necessary condition for effective efforts toward change. For example, research comparing urban schools revealed that the most effective schools had principals and teachers who assumed control without receiving authority from the district level, or who initiated change in their schools through direct insubordination.[20] Thus, the achievement of change is a process that entails risky behavior, such as challenging a leader, making a transformation, or leaving an unfulfilling situation. The courage to accept risk is derived from several sources, some of which were discussed in Chapter 13.

Effective followers find courage from numerous sources.[21] Individuals gain strength from their personal philosophical or religious beliefs. A vision of the

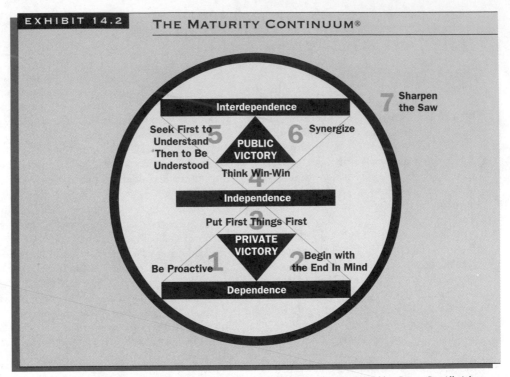

EXHIBIT 14.2 THE MATURITY CONTINUUM®

future—who and where they hope to be—can provide individuals with the courage to follow a difficult course of action. Often an event from the past that tested the courage of an individual makes future courageous behavior easier. The personal values of an individual can serve as a foundation for the courage to act. A commitment to peers and a deep concern for others can enable individuals to brave the risks demanding a change toward fairness. In the same vein, an outrage about injustice toward self or others can fuel the fire of a courageous act.

Developing Personal Potential

Followers can grow in courage when they develop and apply personal leadership qualities in both their private and work lives. One well-known and widely-acclaimed approach to helping people deal courageously with life's changes and challenges is Stephen Covey's *The Seven Habits of Highly Effective People*.[22] Covey defines a habit as the intersection of knowledge, skill, and desire. His approach to personal and interpersonal effectiveness includes seven habits arranged along a maturity continuum from dependence to independence to interdependence, as illustrated in Exhibit 14.2.

Each habit builds on the previous one so that individuals grow further along the maturity continuum as they develop these personal effectiveness habits.

In organizations, many people fall into a mind-set of dependency, expecting someone else to take care of everything and make all the decisions. The *dependent* person is comparable to the passive follower we described earlier, displaying neither initiative nor a sense of personal responsibility. Dependent people expect someone else to take care of them and blame others when things go wrong. An *independent* person, on the other hand, has developed a sense of self-worth and an attitude of self-reliance. Independent people accept personal responsibility and get what they want through their own actions. To be a truly effective follower—or a leader—requires a further step to *interdependence*, the realization that the best things happen by working cooperatively with others, that life and work are better when one experiences the richness of close interpersonal relationships.

From Dependence to Independence

Covey's first three habits deal with self-reliance and self-mastery. Covey calls these *private victories* because they involve only the individual follower growing from dependence to independence, not the follower in relationship with others.[23]

Habit 1: Be Proactive®.   Being proactive means more than merely taking initiative, it means being responsible for your own life. Proactive people recognize that they have the ability to choose and to act with integrity. They don't blame others or life's circumstances for their outcomes. Eleanor Roosevelt was talking about being proactive when she observed that, "No one can hurt you without your consent."[24] Proactive people know that it is not what happens to them but how they respond to it that ultimately matters.

Habit 2: Begin with the End in Mind®.   This means to start with a clear mental image of your destination. In Chapter 5 we discussed the importance of vision and strategy, whereby leaders set a course for the future and get everyone moving in the same direction. For each individual, beginning with the end in mind means knowing what you want, what is deeply important to you, so that you can live each day in a way that contributes to your personal vision. In addition to clarifying goals and plans, this habit entails establishing guiding principles and values for achieving them.

Habit 3: Put First Things First®.   This habit encourages people to gain control of time and events by relating them to their goals and by managing themselves. It means that, rather than getting tangled up dealing with things, time, and activities, we should focus on preserving and enhancing *relationships* and on accomplishing *results*.

Effective Interdependence

The first three habits build a foundation of independence, from which one can move to interdependence—caring, productive relationships with others—which Covey calls *public victories*. Moving to effective interdependence involves open communication (Chapter 6), effective teamwork (Chapter 10), and building positive relationships based on trust, caring, and respect (Chapters 12 and 13). No matter what position you hold in the organization, when you move to interdependence, you step into a leadership role.

Habit 4: Think Win-Win®. To think win-win means understanding that without cooperation, the organization cannot succeed. When followers understand this, they cooperate in ways that ensure their mutual success and allow everyone to come out a winner. Win-win is a frame of mind and heart that constantly seeks agreements or solutions that are mutually beneficial and satisfying.

Habit 5: Seek First to Understand, Then to Be Understood®. This principle is the key to effective communication, as we discussed in Chapter 6. Many people don't listen with the intent to understand; they are too busy thinking about what they want to say. Seeking first to understand requires being nonjudgmental and able to empathize with the other person's situation. *Empathic listening* gets inside another person's frame of reference so that you can better understand how that person feels.

Habit 6: Synergize®. In Chapter 5, we discussed synergy as an important aspect of organizational strategy. The same principle applies to relationships between people. **Synergy** is the combined action that occurs when people work together to create new alternatives and solutions. In addition, the greatest opportunity for synergy occurs when people have different viewpoints because the differences present new opportunities. The essence of synergy is to value and respect differences and take advantage of them to build on strengths and compensate for weaknesses.

Habit 7: Sharpen the Saw®. This habit encompasses the previous six—it is the habit that makes all the others possible. "Sharpening the saw" is a process of using and continuously renewing the physical, mental, spiritual, and social aspects of your life. To be effective followers and effective leaders requires living a balanced life.

Sources of Power

Another issue of concern is how followers gain and use power in organizations. Formal leaders typically have more power than followers do. Nevertheless, effective followers participate fully in organizations by culling power from the available sources. Even the lowest level follower has personal and position-based sources of power that can be used to generate upward influence, thereby impacting the organization, and establishing a mutually beneficial relationship with leaders.[25] Personal sources of power include knowledge, expertise, effort, and persuasion. Position sources of power include location, information, and access.

Personal Sources

A knowledgeable follower possesses skills and talents that are a valuable resource to the leader and to the organization. Such a follower is of real value, and his or her departure would be a loss. *Knowledge* is a source of upward influence. In addition, a follower who has a demonstrated record of performance often develops *expertise* and in this way can influence decisions. A record of successes and a history of contributions can garner expert status for followers, from which followers can derive the power to influence operations and establish themselves as a resource to the leader. The power to influence is also associated with the *effort* put forth by a follower. By demonstrating a willingness to learn, to accept undesirable projects, and to initiate activities beyond the scope of expected effort, a follower can gain power in an organization.[26] Tim Chapman was hired by Spartan Motors during his senior year of high school. By age 20, he was the head electrical engineer, troubleshooting and consorting with key vendors. "I guess I'm willing to learn," says Chapman.[27]

Persuasion is also a source of personal power that followers can utilize. *Persuasion* refers to the direct appeal to leaders in an organization for desired outcomes.[28] In addition to being direct, speaking truthfully to a leader can be a source of power for effective followers.[29] The earlier example in which George Marshall confronted his superiors illustrates how directness and honesty increased his power to influence others. Marshall's frank observations established his equal power based on knowledge, conviction, and persuasion.

Position Sources

Often the formal position of a follower in an organization can provide sources of power. For example, the location of a follower can render him or her *visible* to numerous individuals. A *central location* provides influence to a follower, because the follower is known to many and contributes to the work of many. Similarly, a position that is key to the *flow of information* can establish that position and the follower in it as critical—thus, influential—to those who seek the information. Access to people and information in an organization provides the follower in the position a means to establish relationships with others. With a *network of relationships*, a follower has greater opportunity to persuade others and to make powerful contributions to numerous organizational processes.

Strategies for Effective Followership

Most followers at some point complain about the leader's deficiencies, such as the leader's failure to listen, to encourage, or to recognize followers' efforts.[30] Perfection is impossible for leaders. However, followers can be effective in spite of their leaders by employing strategies that transform the greatest barrier to effective followership: the leader-follower relationship. Most relationships between leaders and followers are characterized by some emotion and behavior based on authority and

EXHIBIT 14.3	**WAYS TO INFLUENCE YOUR LEADER**

Be a Resource for the Leader	**Help the Leader be a Good Leader**
What are leader's needs?	Ask for advice
Zig where leader zags	Tell leader what you think
Tell leader about you	Find things to thank leader for
Align self to team purpose/vision	
Build a Relationship	**View the Leader Realistically**
Ask about leader at your level/position	Give up idealized leader images
Welcome feedback and criticism, such as "What experience led you to that opinion?"	Don't hide anything
	Don't criticize leader to others
Ask leader to tell you company stories	Disagree occasionally

submission. Leaders are authority figures and may play a disproportionately large role in the mind of a follower. Followers may find themselves being overcritical of their leaders, or rebellious, or passive. The relationships between leaders and followers are not unlike those between parents and children, and individuals may engage old family patterns when entering into leader-follower relationships.[31] Effective followers, conversely, may perceive themselves as the equals of their leaders, not inherently subordinate.[32] Exhibit 14.3 illustrates the strategies that enable followers to overcome the authority-based relationship and develop an effective, respectful relationship with their leaders.

Be a Resource for the Leader

Effective followers align themselves to the purpose and the vision of the organization. They ask the leader about vision and goals and help achieve them. They understand their impact on the organization's achievement. In this way, followers are a resource of strength and support for the leader. This alignment involves understanding the leader's position, that is, his or her goals, needs, and constraints. Thus, an effective follower can complement the leader's weaknesses with the follower's own strengths.[33] Similarly, effective followers indicate their personal goals and the resources they bring to the organization. Effective followers inform their leaders about their own ideas, beliefs, needs, and constraints. The more leaders and followers can know the day-to-day activities of one another, the better resources they can be for each other. For example, one group of handicapped workers took advantage of a board meeting to issue rented wheelchairs to the members, who then tried to move around the factory in them. Realizing what the workers faced, the board got the factory's ramps improved, and the handicapped workers became a better resource for the organization.[34]

Help the Leader Be a Good Leader

Advice from a leader can be helpful in cultivating followers' abilities. Furthermore, asking a leader for advice enables the leader to give advice. If a leader senses that his or her advice is well regarded, the leader is likely to give effective advice rather than unsympathetic criticism. Effective followers help their leaders be good leaders by simply telling their leaders what they need in order to be good followers.

A leader can become a better leader when followers compliment and thank their leader for things well done.[35] If a leader knows what followers appreciate, the leader is more likely to continue the appreciated behavior. Similarly, if ineffective or destructive actions are not congratulated, they may taper off. Thus, thanking leaders for helpful behaviors and being honest when leaders are counterproductive is an effective way to communicate the need for a leader to change. For example, an emergency room nurse who constantly confronted a temperamental doctor did not resist the tantrums he aimed at the nurses. After she began to thank him when he did not become angry, his temper flared less regularly.[36]

Build a Relationship with the Leader

Effective followers work toward a genuine relationship with their leaders, which includes developing trust and speaking honestly on the basis of that trust.[37] By building a relationship with a leader, a follower makes every interaction more meaningful to the organization. Furthermore, the relationship is imbued with mutual respect rather than authority and submission. Wes Walsh used mindful initiatives to create a relationship with his boss that maximized his own upward influence.

LEADERSHIP SPOTLIGHT   **WES WALSH**

When Wes Walsh came under an autocratic manager, his position predecessor warned him to either stay away from the infamously autocratic boss, or else be prepared to give up any influence over the unit operations. Walsh decided to ignore this advice. Instead, he started dropping by his boss's office on a regular basis to discuss production progress. Walsh also sought approval on very small matters because they were virtually impossible for his boss to oppose. Walsh continued these frequent, informal interactions over a lengthy period of time before moving on to more consequential matters.

Eventually, major projects had to be addressed. For example, an increase in the volume of materials processed had rendered Walsh's unit too slow and too limited to adequately serve the increased production. In response, Walsh first requested his boss to devote a couple of hours to him at some designated point in the near future. When the appointed time arrived, Walsh took his boss on a lengthy tour of the plant, pointing out the volume of material scattered about waiting to be processed. He supplemented this visual evidence with facts and figures.

The boss was compelled to acknowledge the problem. Thus, he asked for Walsh's proposal, which Walsh had carefully prepared beforehand. Although the boss had rejected identical proposals from Walsh's predecessor, this time the boss almost immediately approved the sum of $150,000 for updating the unit equipment.[38]

Walsh's conscious effort to interact and get his boss comfortable saying yes on small matters set a precedent for a pattern of respect that was not lost even on his autocratic superior.

Followers can generate respect by asking their leaders questions, such as about the leader's experiences in the follower's position and what the source was for given feedback and criticism. Followers can also ply the leader for company stories.[39] By doing so followers are getting beyond submissive behavior by asking leaders to be accountable for their criticism, to have empathy for the followers' position, and to share history about something both parties have in common—the organization. When Mary Kay Ash relates stories to her sales associates about her struggles prior to the founding of her cosmetics company, the associates repeat them to women all over the country. Women who have been underrated in the corporate world feel an immediate kinship because Ash is giving them the respect—and the opportunity— they are otherwise missing.[40]

View the Leader Realistically

To view leaders realistically means to give up idealized images of them. Understanding that leaders are fallible and will make many mistakes leads to acceptance. The way in which a follower perceives his or her boss is the foundation of their relationship. It helps to view leaders as they really are, not as followers think they should be.[41] For example, a follower must determine if he or she is reading the leader accurately. One employee believed for a long time that his boss disliked him because she was ignoring him. In reality, she believed him to be the most competent member of the department who did not require supervision like the rest of the crew.[42]

Similarly, effective followers present realistic images of themselves. Followers do not try to hide their weaknesses or cover their mistakes, nor do they criticize their leaders to others.[43] Hiding things is symptomatic of conforming and passive followers. Criticizing leaders to others merely bolsters alienation, and reinforces the mind-set of an alienated follower. Only positive things about a leader should be shared with others. It is an alienated follower who complains without engaging in constructive action. Instead of criticizing a leader to others, it is far more constructive to directly disagree with a leader on occasions relevant to the operation of the organization.

EXHIBIT 14.4	RANK ORDER OF DESIRABLE CHARACTERISTICS
Desirable Leaders Are	**Desirable Colleagues (Followers) Are**
Honest	Honest
Forward-thinking	Cooperative
Inspiring	Dependable
Competent	Competent

SOURCE: Adapted from James M. Kouzes and Barry Z. Posner, *Credibility: How Leaders Gain and Lose It, Why People Demand It* (San Francisco, CA: Jossey-Bass Publishers, 1993), 255.

What Followers Want

Research indicates that followers have expectations about what constitutes a desirable leader, as we discussed in Chapter 13.[44] Exhibit 14.4 shows the top four choices in rank order based upon surveys of followers about what they desire in leaders and colleagues.

Followers want their leaders to be honest, forward-thinking, inspiring, and competent. A leader must be worthy of trust, envision the future of the organization, inspire others to contribute, and be capable and effective in matters that will affect the organization. In terms of competence, leadership roles may shift from the formal leader to the person with particular expertise in a given area.

Followers want their fellow followers to be honest and competent, but also dependable and cooperative. Thus, desired qualities of colleagues share two qualities with leaders—honesty and competence. However, followers themselves want followers to be dependable and cooperative, rather than forward-thinking and inspiring. The hallmark that distinguishes the role of leadership from the role of followership, then, is not authority, knowledge, power, or other conventional notions of what a follower is not. Rather, the distinction lies in the clearly defined leadership activities of fostering a vision and inspiring others to achieve that vision. In fact, organizations that can boast of effective followers tend to have leaders who deal primarily with change and progress.[45] Followers do not want to find themselves subjected to authority that would make them alienated, passive, pragmatic, or conforming. They perceive their role to differ from their leader's primarily in terms of the leadership responsibilities of foresight and inspiration. The survey results in Exhibit 14.4 underscore the basis of this chapter—leaders and followers are acting in two different roles at any given moment, but effective behaviors often overlap.

Building a Community of Followers

Significantly, dependability and cooperation are necessary for the followers' role in building a sense of community. Leaders are often encouraged to achieve community in their organizations, especially if it is becoming a learning organization. Yet community building is firmly within the purview of followers too. The learning organization described in Chapter 8 depends on community, wherein all people feel encouraged, respected, and committed to a common purpose. In a community, people are able to communicate openly with one another, maintain their uniqueness, and be firmly committed to something larger than selfish interests. In short, a group of effective followers provides the basis for community. It is by no coincidence that effective followers and effective community members share certain characteristics. Historically, communities of all sorts were based on service, informed participation, and individual contributions.[46] Thus, the follower who has the courage to serve, who is an active, critical thinker, and who maximizes his or her contributions encourages a sense of community to develop in an organization.

Characteristics of a community include inclusivity, realism, and shared leadership.[47] Effective followers encourage these traits as they enact their followership roles.

Inclusivity   In a community, everyone belongs. Individuality and different points of view are encouraged. However, community focuses on the whole rather than the parts, and people focus on what binds them together rather than on what separates them. Effective followers are those who speak honestly when their convictions differ from others. This courage often stems from the belief in the inherent equality between themselves, other followers, and their leaders—that is wholeness. Effective followership facilitates an environment built on individual differences, which results in realism, and the equal worth of those differences, which leads to shared leadership.

Conversation   Conversation is how people make and share the meanings that are the basis of community. In a thriving community, conversation across traditional boundaries strengthens bonds of trust and commitment. As described in Chapter 6, one special type of communication, **dialogue,** means that each person suspends his attachment to a particular viewpoint so that a deeper level of listening, synthesis, and meaning evolves from the whole community. Individual differences are acknowledged and respected, but the group searches for an expanded collective perspective.[48] Only through conversation can people build collaboration and collective action so they move together on a common path.

Realism   By including the points of view of everyone, a community is realistic. A community includes people with very different perspectives and encourages people to speak up. Thus, community members appreciate the whole of any issue or problem, and the resulting conclusions are typically more sensible, creative, and well-rounded.

Shared Leadership   In a community, a leader is one among many equals. Decentralization is an essential aspect of true community, and decisions are reached by consensus. A community creates a "safe" place, so that anyone feels free to step for-

LEADER'S BOOKSHELF

The Leadership Engine: How Winning Companies Build Leaders at Every Level
Noel M. Tichy

In *The Leadership Engine*, Noel M. Tichy contends that winning companies win because they have leaders who nurture the development of other leaders, at all levels of the organization. Using examples from companies such as General Electric, PepsiCo, Intel, Compaq, and ServiceMaster, Tichy argues that consistently successful organizations are those in which leadership is shared by all members. Top leaders have a responsibility to develop leaders at all levels of the company. To do that, they need a teachable point of view.

A Leader's Teachable Point of View
Leaders share mistakes, communicate personally, and serve as role models to teach others how to act as leaders. In addition, they cultivate leadership potential by articulating a "teachable point of view," a set of business ideas and values linking success in the marketplace to strategy, products, services, customer segments, and so forth. There are four elements to a teachable point of view:

1. *Ideas.* Leaders have clear ideas about the purpose of the organization and how to best organize resources to achieve the purpose. They keep abreast of developments that impact the organization's ability to reach its goals and encourage others to generate new ideas.
2. *Values.* Successful leaders "see values as a competitive tool that allows their organizations to respond quickly and appropriately." Thus, they spend time instilling values such as honesty and integrity as

well as operational values of teamwork, risk-taking, and customer service. Leaders not only talk about values but embody them with their own behavior.
3. *Energy.* Effective leaders are high-energy people and they inspire positive energy in others. They like challenges, and they motivate others with their enthusiasm and action. They also set challenging goals that inspire the ambitions and energy of others.
4. *Edge.* Leaders demonstrate as well as teach "edge," the toughness to look at hard reality and make difficult decisions. Edge is courage, what Tichy calls "the willingness to sacrifice the security of today for the sake of a better future." Leaders with edge aren't deterred by risk, pain, or failure, and they support and reward others who take risks.

The Leadership Engine
These elements comprise a leader's teachable point of view. Leaders teach through example and through storytelling, so that others understand where the organization is going and how to help it get there. When a leader imparts these capabilities to followers throughout the organization and everyone operates according to the teachable point of view, the organization becomes a leadership engine, capable of sustained excellence.

The Leadership Engine, by Noel M. Tichy, is published by HarperBusiness.

ward as a leader. Like plugs of zoysia grass planted far apart that eventually meld together into a beautiful carpet of lawn, effective followers who share leadership throughout an organization meld together to make things happen.[49] The Leader's Bookshelf describes how strong leaders can cultivate the leadership abilities of others.

Summary and Interpretation

As organizations continue the trend toward empowering employees, the important role of followers can be recognized. People are followers more often than leaders, and effective leaders and followers share similar characteristics. An effective follower is both an active and an independent thinker. Being an effective follower depends on not becoming alienated, conforming, passive, nor a pragmatic survivor.

Courage is vital to effective followership. Effective followers display the courage to assume responsibility, to serve, to challenge, to participate in transformation, and to leave when necessary. Followers also are aware of their own power and its sources, which include personal and position sources. Strategies for being an effective follower include being a resource, helping the leader be a good leader, building a relationship with the leader, and viewing the leader realistically.

Followers want both their leaders and their colleagues to be honest and competent. However, they want their leaders also to be forward-thinking and inspirational. The two latter traits distinguish the role of leader from follower. Followers want to be led, not controlled. Conversely, followers want their peers to be dependable and cooperative. These features help develop community, which enables followers to prosper and to share leadership in organizations.

Key Terms

critical thinking	conformist	effective follower
uncritical thinking	pragmatic survivor	synergy
alienated follower	passive follower	dialogue

Discussion Questions

1. Discuss the role of a follower. Why do you think so little emphasis is given to followership compared to leadership in organizations?

2. Compare the alienated follower with the passive follower. Can you give an example of each? How would you respond to each if you were a leader?

3. Which of the five courageous actions of a follower do you feel is most important to an effective follower? Least important? How does a follower derive the courage and power to be effective? Discuss.

4. From what sources might a follower derive courage? Discuss.

5. Describe the strategy for effective followership that you most prefer. Explain.

6. What do the traits followers want in leaders and in other followers tell us about the roles of each? Discuss.

7. How might the characteristics of effective followership contribute to building community? Discuss.

8. Is the courage to leave the ultimate courage of a follower compared to the courage to participate in transformation? Which would be hardest for you?

Leadership Development: Personal Feedback

The Power of Followership

For each statement below, please use the six-point scale to indicate the extent to which the statement describes you. Think of a specific but typical followership situation and how you acted.

0   1   2   3   4   5   6

Rarely   Occasionally   Almost Always

_____ 1. Does your work help you fulfill some societal goal or personal dream that is important to you?

_____ 2. Are your personal work goals aligned with the organization's priority goals?

_____ 3. Are you highly committed to and energized by your work and organization, giving them your best ideas and performance?

_____ 4. Does your enthusiasm also spread to and energize your coworkers?

_____ 5. Instead of waiting for or merely accepting what the leader tells you, do you personally identify which organizational activities are most critical for achieving the organization's priority goals?

_____ 6. Do you actively develop a distinctive competence in those critical activities so that you become more valuable to the leader and the organization?

_____ 7. When starting a new job or assignment, do you promptly build a record of successes in tasks that are important to the leader?

_____ 8. Can the leader give you a difficult assignment without the benefit of much supervision, knowing that you will meet your deadline with highest-quality work and that you will "fill in the cracks" if need be?

_____ 9. Do you take the initiative to seek out and successfully complete assignments that go above and beyond your job?

_____ 10. When you are not the leader of a group project, do you still contribute at a high level, often doing more than your share?

_____ 11. Do you independently think up and champion new ideas that will contribute significantly to the leader's or the organization's goals?

_____ 12. Do you try to solve the tough problems (technical or organizational), rather than look to the leader to do it for you?

_____ 13. Do you help out other co-workers, making them look good, even when you do not get any credit?

_____ 14. Do you help the leader or group see both the upside potential and downside risks of ideas or plans, playing the devil's advocate if need be?

_____ 15. Do you understand the leader's needs, goals, and constraints, and work hard to meet them?

_____ 16. Do you actively and honestly own up to your strengths and weaknesses rather than put off evaluation?

_____ 17. Do you make a habit of internally questioning the wisdom of the leader's decision rather than just doing what you are told?

_____ 18. When the leader asks you to do something that runs contrary to your professional or personal preferences, do you say "no" rather than "yes"?

_____ 19. Do you act on your own ethical standards rather than the leader's or the group's standards?

_____ 20. Do you assert your views on important issues, even though it might mean conflict with your group or reprisals from the leader?

Scoring

Questions 1, 5, 11, 12, 14, 16, 17, 18, 19 and 20 measure "independent thinking." Sum your answers and write your score below.

Questions 2, 3, 4, 6, 7, 8, 9, 10, 13 and 15 measure "active engagement." Sum your answers and write your score below.

Independent Thinking Total Score = _____

Active Engagement Total Score = _____

Interpretation

These two scores indicate how you carry out your followership role. A score of 20 or below is considered low. A score of 40 or higher is considered high. A score between 20 and 40 is in the middle. Based on whether your score is high, middle, or low, assess your followership style below.

Followership Style	Independent Thinking Score	Active Engagement Score
Effective	High	High
Alienated	High	Low
Conformist	Low	High
Pragmatist	Middling	Middling
Passive	Low	Low

How do you feel about your follower style? Compare your style to others. What might you do to be more effective as a follower?

SOURCE: From *The Power of Followership: How to Create Leaders People Want to Follow and Followers Who Lead Themselves* by Robert E. Kelley, 89-97. Copyright © 1992 by Consultants to Executives and Organizations, Ltd. Used by permission of Doubleday, a division of Bantam Doubleday Dell Publishing Group, Inc.

Leadership Development: Case for Analysis

General Products Britain

Carl Mitchell was delighted to accept a job in the British branch office of General Products, Inc., a consumer products multinational. Two months later, Mitchell was miserable. The problem was George Garrow, the general manager in charge of the British branch, to whom Mitchell reported.

Garrow had worked his way to the general manager position by "keeping his nose clean," and not making mistakes, which he accomplished by avoiding controversial and risky decisions.

As Mitchell complained to his wife, "Any time I ask him to make a decision, he just wants us to dig deeper and provide 30 more pages of data, most of which are irrelevant. I can't get any improvements started."

For example, Mitchell believed that the line of frozen breakfasts and dinners he was in charge of would be more successful if prices were lowered. He and his four product managers spent weeks preparing graphs and charts to justify a lower price. Garrow reviewed the data but kept waffling, asking for more information. His latest request for weather patterns that might affect shopping habits seemed absurd.

Garrow seemed terrified of departing from the status quo. The frozen breakfast and dinner lines still had 1970s-style packaging, even though reformulated for microwave ovens. Garrow would not approve a coupon program in March because in previous years coupons had been run in April. Garrow measured progress not by new ideas or sales results but by hours spent in the office. He arrived early and shuffled memos and charts until late in the evening and expected the same from everyone else.

After four months on the job, Mitchell made a final effort to reason with Garrow. He argued that the branch was taking a big risk by avoiding decisions to improve things.

Market share was slipping. New pricing and promotion strategies were essential. But Garrow just urged more patience and told Mitchell that he and his product managers would have to build a more solid case. Soon after, Mitchell's two best product managers quit, burned out by the marathon sessions analyzing pointless data without results.

Questions

1. How would you evaluate Mitchell as a follower? Evaluate his courage and style.

2. If you were Mitchell, what would you do now?

3. If you were Garrow's boss and Mitchell came to see you, what would you say?

References

[1]Dianne Martz, "Hard Lessons, Well Learned," *Inc.*, December 1993, 29–30.

[2]Robert E. Kelley, "In Praise of Followers," *Harvard Business Review*, November/December 1988, 142–148.

[3]Bernard M. Bass, *Bass & Stodgill's Handbook of Leadership*, 3rd ed. (New York: Free Press, 1990).

[4]Ira Chaleff, *The Courageous Follower: Standing Up To and For Our Leaders* (San Francisco, CA: Berrett-Koehler, 1995).

[5]Ira Chaleff, "Learn the Art of Followership," *Government Executive*, February 1997, 51.

[6]D. E. Whiteside, *Command Excellence: What It Takes to Be the Best!*, Department of the Navy, Washington, D.C.: Naval Military Personnel Command, 1985.

[7]Robert E. Kelley, *The Power of Followership* (New York: Doubleday, 1992).

[8]Ibid., 101

[9]Ibid., 111–112

[10]Ibid., 117–118

[11]Ibid., 123.

[12]Kelley, "In Praise of Followers."

[13]Howard Gardner, *Leading Minds* (New York: Basic Books, 1995), 286.

[14]Chaleff, *The Courageous Follower: Standing Up To and For Our Leaders.*

[15]Edward O. Welles, "The Shape of Things to Come," *Inc.*, February 1992, 66–74.

[16]Alan Farnham, "Mary Kay's Lessons in Leadership," *Fortune*, September 20, 1993, 68–77.

[17]Gardner, *Leading Minds*, 148–149.

[18]Ibid.

[19]Merle MacIsaac, "Born Again Basket Case," *Canadian Business*, May 1993, 38–44.

[20]Kofi Lomotey and Austin D. Swanson, "Restructuring School Governance: Learning from the Experiences of Rural and Urban Schools," in *Educational Leadership in an Age of Reform*, Stephen L. Jacobson and James A. Conway, eds. (White Plains, NY: Longman 1990), 65–82.

[21]Chaleff, *The Courageous Follower: Standing Up To and For Our Leaders.*

[22]Stephen R. Covey, *The Seven Habits of Highly Effective People: Powerful Lessons in Personal Change* (New York: Simon & Schuster 1989). *The Seven Habits of Highly Effective People* are registered trademarks of Franklin Covey Co. Used with permission.

[23]This discussion of the seven habits is based on *The Seven Habits of Highly Effective People* by Stephen R. Covey. © 1989 Stephen R. Covey. All rights reserved. For more information call (800) 654-1776.

Also see Don Hellriegel, John W. Slocum, Jr., and Richard Woodman, *Organizational Behavior*, 8th edition (Cincinnati, OH: South-Western College Publishing, 1998), 350-352.

[24]Stephen R. Covey, *The Seven Habits of Highly Effective People* (New York: Fireside edition/Simon & Schuster, 1990), 72.

[25]David C. Wilson and Graham K. Kenny, "Managerially Perceived Influence Over Interdepartmental Decisions," *Journal of Management Studies* 22 (1985), 155–173; Warren Keith Schilit, "An Examination of Individual Differences as Moderators of Upward Influence Activity in Strategic Decisions," *Human Relations* 39 (1986), 933–953; David Mechanic, "Sources of Power of Lower Participants in Complex Organizations," *Administrative Science Quarterly* 7 (1962), 349–364.

[26]Peter Moroz and Brian H. Kleiner, "Playing Hardball in Business Organizations," *IM*, January/February 1994, 9–11.

[27]Welles, "The Shape of Things to Come."

[28]Warren Keith Schilit and Edwin A. Locke, "A Study of Upward Influence in Organizations," *Administrative Science Quarterly* 27 (1982), 304–316.

[29]Chaleff, *The Courageous Follower: Standing Up To and For Our Leaders.*

[30]Len Schlesinger, "It Doesn't Take a Wizard to Build a Better Boss," *Fast Company*, June/July 1996, 102–107.

[31]Frank Pittman, "How to Manage Mom and Dad," *Psychology Today*, November/December 1994, 44–74.

[32]Kelley, "In Praise of Followers."

[33]Chaleff, *The Courageous Follower: Standing Up To and For Our Leaders.*

[34]Christopher Hegarty, *How to Manage Your Boss* (New York: Ballantine 1985), 147.

[35]Ibid.

[36]Ibid., 107–108.

[37]Chaleff, *The Courageous Follower: Standing Up To and For Our Leaders.*

[38]Peter B. Smith and Mark F. Peterson, *Leadership, Organizations and Culture* (London: Sage Publications, 1988), 144-145.

[39]Pittman, "How to Manage Mom and Dad."

[40]Farnham, "Mary Kay's Lessons in Leadership."

[41]Hegarty, *How to Manage Your Boss.*

[42]Ibid., 49.

[43]Pittman, "How to Manage Mom and Dad."

[44]James M. Kouzes and Barry Z. Posner, *Credibility: How Leaders Gain and Lose It, Why People Demand It* (San Francisco: Jossey-Bass Publisher, 1993).

[45]Kelley, "In Praise of Followers."

[46]Juanita Brown and David Isaacs, "Building Corporations as Communities: The Best of Both Worlds," in *Community Building: Renewing Spirit & Learning in Business*, Kazimierz Gozdz, ed. (San Francisco: Sterling & Stone, Inc., 1995), 69–83.

[47]M. Scott Peck, *The Different Drum: Community Making and Peace* (New York: Touchstone, 1987).

[48]Brown and Isaacs, "Building Corporations as Communities"; Glenna Gerard and Linda Teurfs, "Dialogue and Organizational Transformation," in Kazimierz Gozdz, ed., *Community Building* (San Francisco: Sterling & Stone, Inc., 1995), 142–153; and Edgar G. Schein, "On Dialogue, Culture, and Organizational Learning," *Organizational Dynamics*, Autumn 1993, 40–51.

[49]Brown and Isaacs, "Building Corporations as Communities: The Best of Both Worlds."

PART SEVEN

Leading Change and Transformation

Chapter 15
Leading Change

Chapter 16
Leader Decision Making,
Power, and Influence

15

Leading Change

- **Change or Perish**   425

- **Transactional versus Transformational Leadership**   427

- **Leading Major Change**   429

- **The Focus of Change**   432

- **Creativity**   435

- **Leading Culture Change**   441

- **Culture Change Approaches**   443

- **Leadership Spotlights:**
  IBM PC Company   434
  IDEO Product Development   438
  General Electric's Work Out   444

- **Leader's Bookshelf:** *Leading Corporate Transformation: A Blueprint for Business Renewal*   433

- **Leadership Development: Personal Feedback**
  Are You a Change Leader?   448

- **Leadership Development: Case for Analysis**
  Southern Discomfort   449

Your Leadership Challenge

After reading this chapter, you should be able to:

- Recognize social and economic pressures for change in today's organizations.

- Apply the concepts that distinguish transformational from transactional leadership.

- Implement the eight-stage model of planned change.

- Expand your own potential for creativity and encourage creativity in others.

- Use techniques of communication, training, and participation to overcome resistance to change.

- Understand how to use concepts of organizational development and large-group intervention.

Royal Dutch/Shell has led the _Fortune_ Global 500 in total profits for three years in a row, operates in 130 countries around the world, oversees 54 refineries and 47,000 gas stations, and employs more than 100,000 people. In one recent year, the company earned a staggering $8.9 billion profit. By all the usual measures, the company is on top of the world. So why is Shell Chairman Cornelius Herkströter leading the company through its most dramatic transformation in 40 years?

When Herkströter and other top leaders considered the future of Shell, they realized the company was saddled with an insular corporate culture, a complicated and outmoded organizational structure, and a controversial public image.

Shell's structures, strategies, practices, and values were incompatible with the rapidly changing world in which the company operated. Managers rarely talked to rank-and-file employees, and top leaders at headquarters wrestled for power with the 100 or so influential CEOs who ran local operations in various countries. Shell's reputation in environmental matters had declined, and the company's association with the Nigerian dictatorship that executed environmental activist Ken Saro Wiwa sparked a global uproar. To meet the demands of a changing world, Herkströter wanted to create a fast, flexible, environmentally aware company that runs more efficiently, is more innovative, and is capable of moving Shell into profitable new businesses. Today, working with a cadre of consultants, he is putting his executives through a slew of workshops, team-building exercises, and self-analysis that includes taking personality tests and tracking their time to see if they're adding any value.

Even the most hallowed of Shell's practices and beliefs are being challenged as leaders push to change the bureaucratic, complacent, and arrogant corporate culture. Shell leaders are seeking a radical transformation that consultants warn could take 10 or more years to complete. Some employees are already resisting change and believe the pace is so overwhelming that Shell is on the verge of chaos. As Mac McDonald, who runs Shell's in-house corps of change agents, puts it, "Transformation is messy. We don't have this wonderful plan. [However,] if we don't change our leadership style, our behaviors and mind-sets, we aren't going to be able to get the results."[1]

Shell's leaders recognize that the company must change. Today, leaders throughout the United States and Canada face the formidable task of reinventing their organizations because of dramatic social and economic changes that have forever altered the playing field and the rules for success. Never before have so many companies across an array of industries simultaneously faced such a challenge. The patterns of behavior and attitudes that were once successful no longer work, yet new patterns are just emerging. As stated in one recent article, "Most managers today have the feeling that they are flying the airplane at the same time they are building it."[2]

Organizational leaders cite change as the most common problem they face.[3] Recall from Chapter 2 that the outcome of leadership is change—not efficiency or stability. Change always brings dislocation and discomfort. Every organization experiences stress and difficulty in coping with change, and the increased pace of change in today's world has led to greater challenges for leaders.

This chapter will explore how leaders guide change and transformation. We will first look briefly at the need for change in today's organizations. The next section will examine the concept of transformational leadership and its impact on followers and the organization. We will then examine a step-by-step model for leading major change in organizations and explore how leaders facilitate change by fostering creative people and organizations. The final sections of the chapter will focus on leading a change in culture. Culture plays an important role in facilitating all types of organizational change, so above all, leaders must influence culture to create improved, learning organizations.

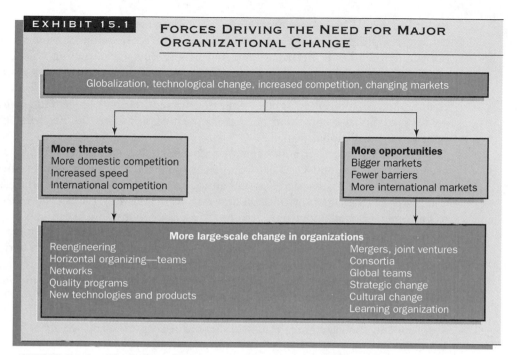

EXHIBIT 15.1   **FORCES DRIVING THE NEED FOR MAJOR ORGANIZATIONAL CHANGE**

Globalization, technological change, increased competition, changing markets

More threats
More domestic competition
Increased speed
International competition

More opportunities
Bigger markets
Fewer barriers
More international markets

More large-scale change in organizations

Reengineering
Horizontal organizing—teams
Networks
Quality programs
New technologies and products

Mergers, joint ventures
Consortia
Global teams
Strategic change
Cultural change
Learning organization

SOURCE: Based on John P. Kotter, *The New Rules: How to Succeed in Today's Post-Corporate World.* Copyright 1995 by John P. Kotter. Adapted with permission from The Free Press.

Change or Perish

As we discussed in Chapter 1, the world is changing more rapidly than ever before. Today's most successful organizations are changing fast. Their leaders recognize that internal changes must keep pace with what is happening in the external environment. As Jack Welch, chairman and CEO of General Electric once stated, "When the rate of change outside exceeds the rate of change inside, the end is in sight."[4] Organizations must poise themselves to change, not only to prosper but to survive in today's world. As illustrated in Exhibit 15.1, rapid technological changes, a globalized economy, and changing markets are creating more threats as well as more opportunities for organizational leaders.

Organizations face increased competition both domestically and internationally. In the 1980s, large companies such as Sears, IBM, and General Motors were seriously damaged by competition they did not see coming. August Busch III, CEO of Anheuser-Busch—still the dominant leader in its industry—admits his company was late in recognizing the threat of microbreweries: "If you had asked us 10 years ago whether there would be X-hundred little tiny breweries across this country who will end up with 3 percent of the market and 6 percent of the margin pool, we would have said no. . . . We were five years late in recognizing that they were going to take as much market as they did and five years late in recognizing we should have joined them."[5] Or consider the case of record store chains such as Camelot Music,

Record Giant, Wherehouse Entertainment, and Strawberries, all of which filed for bankruptcy protection. The whole nature of the record-selling business changed overnight when home electronics behemoth Best Buy started selling CDs for only about half what they cost in traditional music stores. Today, electronics stores like Best Buy and Circuit City sell more CDs than Sam Goody's and other record retail chains.[6] Yet, in addition to brutal domestic competition, both large and small companies face global competition on their home turf as well as the need to be competitive in international markets.

The ability to deliver goods and services quickly is another challenge for today's organizations. U.S. and Canadian companies have made dramatic improvements in quality over the past two decades, and although quality and cost are still important, competitive advantage now rides on how fast products and services can be delivered to customers as well. Companies use time-based competition to keep pace with and even stay ahead of their markets.[7] For example, 3M's giant electronics operation in Austin, Texas, cut its new-product development time from two years to about two months. Through aggressive use of new information technology, GTE Telephone Operations reduced the time it takes to complete a customer order from four days to less than two hours. Mattel perfected its new Top Speed toy car in just five months, as opposed to the usual 18.[8] Companies must do things faster than ever to keep up, and speed requires a transformation of corporate culture, technology, and structure.

Leaders initiate dramatic transformations, but change is not always successful. For example, many organizations are responding to global challenges by reengineering business processes, yet by one estimate nearly 70 percent of reengineering projects fail. The mid-1990s saw the greatest wave of mergers in American history, with more than 10,000 mergers taking place and more than $660 billion changing hands in 1996 alone. Boeing purchased McDonnell-Douglas, British Telecom bought MCI, and Gillette acquired Duracell. All of these "marriages" have the potential to be enormously successful, but half or more will be disappointing failures. As another example of the difficulties of change, the massive downsizing of the past decade has lowered costs and improved profits for many companies, but leaders are still struggling with the aftermath of more work with fewer resources.[9]

Other ways organizations are responding to external changes are by shifting to self-directed work teams or adopting structural innovations such as outsourcing functions to other companies. Some become involved in joint ventures, consortia, or virtual organizations to extend their operations and markets internationally. Leaders face an unending need for dramatic structural and cultural change and for rapid innovations in technology and products. Some are leading their companies to become learning organizations that continually learn and adapt to a chaotic environment. All of these changes provide potential for outright failure. The process of organizational change is complex and messy, and many times leaders stick with the known for fear of the unknown. As the head of one large U.S. corporation said, "The tragedy of top leadership . . . is that it is so much more reassuring to stay as you are, even though you know the result will be certain failure, than to try to make a fundamental change when you cannot be certain that the effort will succeed."[10]

However, most of today's leaders face serious threats to their company's very survival and are responsible for leading the way through the needed transformation.

Transactional versus Transformational Leadership

What kind of people can lead an organization through major changes? One type of leadership that has a substantial impact and can renew an organization is transformational leadership. Transformational leadership is best understood in comparison to transactional leadership.[11]

Transactional Leadership

The basis of **transactional leadership** is a transaction or exchange process between leaders and followers. The transactional leader recognizes specific follower desires and provides goods that meet those desires in exchange for followers meeting specified objectives or performing certain duties. Thus, followers receive rewards for job performance while leaders benefit from the completion of tasks. Leadership is a series of economic and social transactions to achieve specific goals. The exchanges involve goods that are specific, tangible, and calculable.

Transactional leaders focus on the present and excel at keeping an organization running smoothly and efficiently. They are good at traditional management functions such as planning and budgeting and generally focus on impersonal aspects of job performance. Transactional leadership can be quite effective. By clarifying expectations, leaders help build followers' confidence. In addition, satisfying the basic needs of subordinates may improve productivity and morale. However, because transactional leadership involves a commitment to "follow the rules," transactional leaders often maintain stability within the organization rather than promoting change. Transactional skills are important for all leaders, but when an organization needs change, a different type of leadership is needed.

Transformational Leadership

Transformational leadership is characterized by the ability to bring about significant change. Transformational leaders have the ability to lead changes in the organization's vision, strategy, and culture as well as promote innovation in products and technologies. Transformational leaders do not use tangible incentives to control specific transactions with followers. Instead, they focus on intangible qualities such as vision, shared values, and ideas in order to build relationships, give larger meaning to diverse activities, and find common ground to enlist followers in the change process. Transformational leadership is based in the personal values, beliefs, and qualities of the leader rather than on an exchange process between leaders and followers. Transformational leadership differs from transactional leadership in four significant areas.[12]

1. *Transformational leadership develops followers into leaders.* Followers are given greater freedom to control their own behavior. Transformational leadership rallies people around a mission and defines the boundaries within which followers can operate in relative freedom to accomplish organizational goals. The transformational leader motivates followers to take initiative and to solve problems, and helps people look at things in new ways. Developing courageous followers enables change to happen.

2. *Transformational leadership elevates followers' concerns from lower-level physical needs (such as for safety and security) to higher-level psychological needs (such as for self-esteem and self-actualization).* It is important that followers' lower level needs are met through adequate wages, safe working conditions, and other considerations. However, the transformational leader pays attention to each individual's need for growth and development. Therefore, the leader sets examples and speaks to followers' higher needs, as described in Chapter 9. Followers' abilities are challenged and linked to the organization's mission. Transformational leaders appeal to followers in a way that challenges and empowers them to change the organization.

3. *Transformational leadership inspires followers to go beyond their own self-interests for the good of the group.* Transformational leaders motivate people to do more than originally expected. They make followers aware of the importance of goals and outcomes needed for change and, in turn, enable them to transcend their own immediate interests for the sake of the organizational mission. Followers admire these leaders, identify with them, and have a high degree of trust in them. However, transformational leadership motivates people not to follow the leader personally but to believe in the need for change and be willing to make personal sacrifices for the greater purpose.

4. *Transformational leadership paints a vision of a desired future state and communicates it in a way that makes the pain of change worth the effort.*[13] The most significant role may be to find a transformation vision that is significantly better than the old way, and to enlist others in achieving the dream. It is the vision that launches people into action and engages the commitment of followers. Change can occur when people have a sense of purpose as well as a desirable picture of where the organization is going. Without vision, there will be no transformation.

Whereas transactional leaders promote stability, transformational leaders create significant change in both followers and organizations. Effective leaders exhibit both transactional and transformational leadership patterns, though in different amounts. Franklin D. Roosevelt, a political leader, reflected a balance of transactional and transformational leadership. His fireside chats, inspiring speeches, and remaking of the American landscape marked him as a consummate transformational leader. However, he was also quite skilled as a transactional leader in the give-and-take of political rewards to achieve his ends.[14] Larry Bossidy, CEO of Allied Signal, demon-

---

ON THE CUTTING EDGE

Helping Employees "See the Promised Land"

When Lawrence A. Bossidy took over as CEO of Allied Signal in 1991, the company was in dire straits. Cash was pouring out of the company and debt was 42 percent of capital. Within only 15 months, Bossidy had his transformation of the company well on its way. Today, the stock of this huge defense and auto parts conglomerate has nearly quintupled.

Bossidy began his transformation of the company by focusing on current problems and processes and paying close attention to cost control and short-term results. A restructuring plan chopped $225 million from capital spending, put eight small divisions up for sale, slashed 6,200 salaried jobs, and combined 10 data-processing centers into two. The plan helped put $225 million in the bag for Allied Signal the first year after Bossidy took over.

What made his plan so successful was Bossidy's ability to gain the commitment and enthusiasm of employees. Another aspect of Bossidy's transformation plan was to paint a picture of where the organization could be in the future and help employees see how to reach it. He created an inspiring statement of vision and values and outlined lofty goals so

folks could "see the promised land and know when they got there." He communicated the vision by regularly chatting with workers at all levels, refusing to be trapped by the old-style corporate hierarchy that separated employees from top leaders. A focus on teamwork and quality gave employees a sense of pulling together for a shared mission—the survival of the company—so that they were willing to temporarily make individual sacrifices for the greater good of the whole.

Today, Allied Signal workers feel good about themselves and where they have taken the company over the past few years. However, Bossidy knows the organization must continue to change. "What we did yesterday enabled us to survive," he says. "Now we'd like to set the table so we can prosper." Bossidy is using a combination of transactional and transformational leadership abilities to help Allied Signal grow and be prepared to meet new challenges.

SOURCE: Thomas A. Stewart, "Allied-Signal's Turnaround Blitz," *Fortune*, November 30, 1992, 72–76; and Geoffrey Colvin, "Larry Bossidy Won't Stop Pushing," *Fortune*, (January 13, 1997), 135–137.

---

strates both transactional skills and transformational qualities as an organizational leader, as discussed in the Cutting Edge box.

Leading Major Change

Major change does not happen easily. However, leaders do facilitate change and thereby help organizations adapt to external problems and opportunities. It is important for leaders to recognize that the change process goes through stages, that each stage is important, and that each may require a significant amount of time. Leaders are responsible for guiding employees and the organization through the change process.

Exhibit 15.2 presents an eight-stage model of planned change.[15] To successfully implement change, leaders must pay careful attention to each stage. Skipping stages or making critical mistakes at any stage can cause the change process to fail.

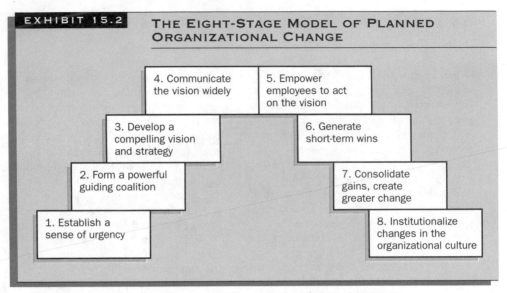

EXHIBIT 15.2 — THE EIGHT-STAGE MODEL OF PLANNED ORGANIZATIONAL CHANGE

SOURCE: John P. Kotter, *Leading Change* (Boston: Harvard Business School Press, 1996), 21.

1. At stage 1, leaders *establish a sense of urgency* that change is really needed. Crises or threats will thaw resistance to change. At IBM, for example, dramatically declining profits and stock prices in the early 1990s provided an undoubted sense of urgency. In many cases, however, there is no public crisis and leaders have to make others aware of the need for change. Leaders carefully scan the external and internal environment—looking at competitive conditions; market position; social, technological and demographic trends; profit and loss; operations; and other factors. After identifying potential crises or problems, they find ways to communicate the information broadly and dramatically.

2. Stage 2 involves *establishing a coalition* with enough power to guide the change process and then developing a sense of teamwork among the group. For the change process to succeed, there must be a shared commitment to the need and possibilities for organizational transformation. Middle management change will seek top leader support in the coalition. It is also essential that lower level executives become involved. Mechanisms such as off-site retreats can get people together and help them develop a shared assessment of problems and how to approach them. At MasterBrand Industries, transformation began with an off-site meeting of some 75 key managers who examined the need for change and discussed ways to remake MasterBrand into a team-based organization.[16]

3. Stage 3 requires *developing a vision and strategy*. Leaders are responsible for formulating and articulating a compelling vision that will guide the change effort, and developing the strategies for achieving that vision. A "picture" of a

highly desirable future motivates people to change. Jeff Campbell, president of Burger King, worked with other leaders to develop a vision to be the best convenience restaurant in America. Linda Wachner, CEO of Warnaco, created a vision to make the company's brands "the Coca-Cola of the intimate apparel business." Jack Sparks at Whirlpool had a vision that involved transforming the company from a conservative operation with some marketing skills into a marketing organization with some manufacturing and engineering skills, thus making it stronger in the face of new competition.[17]

4. In Stage 4, leaders use every means possible to widely *communicate the vision and strategy.* At this stage, the coalition of change agents should set an example by modeling the new behaviors needed from employees. They must communicate about the change at least 10 times more than they think necessary. Transformation is impossible unless a majority of people in the organization are involved and willing to help, often to the point of making personal sacrifices. At Siemens Rolm, a U.S. telecommunications company owned by Siemens AG of Germany, 600 managers attended a three-day institute where they learned about the new vision and were motivated to go back and mobilize commitment in their own units.[18]

5. Stage 5 involves *empowering employees throughout the organization to act on the vision.* This means getting rid of obstacles to change, which may require revising systems, structures, or procedures that hinder or undermine the change effort. People are empowered with knowledge, resources, and discretion to make things happen. For example, with the survival of the company at stake, labor and management at Rolls-Royce Motor Company revised narrow job categories that were undermining the change effort. Whereas Rolls-Royce once had hundreds of precise job descriptions, the new contract specified that all employees will do anything within their capabilities.[19] At this stage, leaders can also encourage and reward risk-taking and nontraditional ideas and actions.

6. At Stage 6, leaders *generate short-term wins.* Leaders plan for visible performance improvements, enable them to happen, and celebrate employees who were involved in the improvements. Major change takes time, and a transformation effort loses momentum if there are no short-term accomplishments that employees can recognize and celebrate. At one U.S. manufacturing company, the guiding coalition worked to produce a highly visible and successful new product introduction about 20 months after the start of its transformation efforts. This success boosted the credibility of the process and renewed the commitment and enthusiasm of employees.[20]

7. Stage 7 builds on the credibility achieved by short-term wins to *consolidate improvements, tackle bigger problems, and create greater change.* Leaders change systems, structures, and policies that do not fit the vision but have not yet been confronted. They hire, promote, and develop employees who can implement the vision for change. In addition, leaders revitalize the process

with a new round of projects, themes, or change agents. At this stage, leaders at Rolls Royce set up cross-functional teams with members cross-trained to perform one another's jobs. In addition, they implemented a "change team" concept throughout the company to get executives and shop floor workers communicating and developing new ideas together.

8. Stage 8 involves *institutionalizing the new approaches in the organizational culture.* This is the follow-through stage that makes the changes stick. Old habits, values, traditions, and mind-sets are permanently replaced. New values and beliefs are instilled in the culture so that employees view the changes not as something new but as a normal and integral part of how the organization operates. This stage also requires developing a means to ensure leadership development and succession so that the new values and behaviors are carried forward to the next generation of leadership.

Stages in the change process generally overlap, but each is important for successful change to occur. When dealing with a major change effort, leaders can follow the eight-stage change process as a roadmap to provide a strong foundation for success.

The Leader's Bookshelf box describes a similar approach to leading transformational change. Transformational change generally involves profound changes in all parts of the organization simultaneously. Change may also occur in only specific areas.

The Focus of Change

The eight-stage model of planned change applies particularly to top-down change inititatives, such as changes in organizational strategy and structure. **Strategy and structure changes** pertain to the administrative domain of an organization. These include changes in policies, reward systems, coordination, control systems, and so forth, in addition to changes in the organization's structure or strategic focus. This is one of four different types of change, as illustrated in Exhibit 15.3. Other types of change are technology changes, changes in products or services, and people and culture changes.

Technology changes are changes in an organization's production processes, including its knowledge and skill base, that enable distinctive competence. Technology changes, including changes in work methods, equipment, and work flow, are designed to make production more efficient or to produce greater volume. **Product and service changes** pertain to product or service outputs. New products are normally designed to increase market share or to develop new markets, customers, or clients. **Culture change** refers to changes in the values, attitudes, expectations, beliefs, and behaviors of employees. In the exhibit, the arrows connecting the types of change indicate that a change in one part may affect other parts of the organization. For example, a new strategic plan may lead to new products, which in turn

LEADER'S BOOKSHELF

Leading Corporate Transformation: A Blueprint for Business Renewal
Robert H. Miles

Robert Miles believes there are two initial requirements for successful organizational change:

1. The presence of a transformational leader.
2. A condition of substantial employee readiness and sufficient resources to support the process.

Transformation depends on a leader or leaders who believe in the need for profound change, have an ability to articulate their conviction in the form of a compelling vision, and can model what is required for transformation through a consistent pattern of words and behaviors. Transformational leaders help everyone in the organization recognize the need for change and find the motivation to work for it. In addition, they line up sufficient resources to support the transformation effort. When these two requirements are met, leaders can follow a framework for successful transformation.

The Transformation Framework
Miles outlines four basic elements that provide a leader with a platform for launching and implementing a successful corporate transformation.

Generating Energy. Miles emphasizes that it is easy to underestimate how much energy transformational change requires. Leaders must understand the personal dynamics of change, help people confront reality constructively, take steps to reallocate resources and set stretch goals, and overcome resistance to change.

Developing a Vision. Successful corporate transformation does not spring from energy alone. Leaders focus the energy on a clear, compelling vision of a highly desirable future. It is also important that leaders define the "critical path" to the vision state by identifying a limited number of initiatives around which to align energy and resources.

Aligning the Organization. Leaders take a total-system perspective and seek to move the organization boldly to the vision by simultaneously articulating all the major elements of the whole organization.

Orchestrating the Transformation. To orchestrate a total-system transformation means leaders put in place a process architecture to provide for continuous learning, coordination, and development. The architecture should include mechanisms for education and participation, coordination, communication and feedback, and consulting support.

Conclusion
With this framework and strong transformational leadership, Miles believes corporations facing a wide variety of challenges can be transformed. The second part of his book offers profiles of real-life corporate transformations in organizations such as National Semiconductor, Norrell Corporation, and the PGA Tour.

Leading Corporate Transformation, by Robert H. Miles, is published by Jossey-Bass.

require changes in technology. In addition, the exhibit shows that changes in culture provide the foundation for all other changes in the organization. Because all change depends on people and culture, we will discuss culture change in detail later in this chapter.

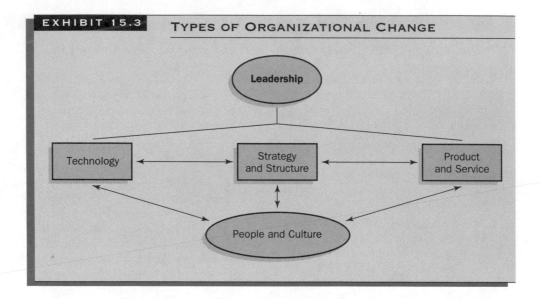

EXHIBIT 15.3   TYPES OF ORGANIZATIONAL CHANGE

Changes in strategy, structure, and culture are generally top-down, that is, initiated by top leaders, whereas product and technology changes usually come from the bottom up. The *bottom-up approach* means that ideas are initiated at lower levels of the organization and channeled upward for approval. Leaders know that employees at lower levels understand the technology and have the expertise to propose changes. For example, at Dana Corporation's Elizabethtown, Kentucky plant, two workers came up with an idea for automatically loading steel sheets into a forming press. This technology change saves the auto-parts maker $250,000 a year.[21] The bottom-up approach also applies to product and service changes. However, because products and services also must meet customer needs, these changes generally require expertise from several different departments simultaneously. Ideas originate at lower levels, as they do for technology change, but they also flow horizontally across departments. Leaders ensure horizontal coordination to facilitate success of product and service changes. For example, people in research, marketing, and manufacturing interact frequently to share ideas and solve problems. People in research inform marketing of new developments to learn whether they will be useful to customers. Marketing people pass customer complaints to research to use in the design of new products. Manufacturing informs other departments whether a new product idea can be manufactured within cost limits. IBM has used strong horizontal coordination to revive its PC division with new products.

LEADERSHIP SPOTLIGHT   **IBM PC COMPANY**

Once the overwhelming revenue leader in the personal computer market, IBM's PC division slid to No. 4 in the U.S. and to No. 2, behind Compaq, around the world. Products trickled out of development, and market forecasting was inept. While the industry was racking up double-digit revenue growth, IBM was writing off $700 million in obsolete inventory, with no potentially hot-selling new products to make up for it.

But Richard Thoman, head of the division, is working overtime to change that. A new approach to product development is key to Thoman's plans to bring new products out quickly, build them in sufficient volume at lower prices, and replace them before they become unsalable. New products are now created by teams from research, design, procurement, logistics, and manufacturing, all working side by side in Raleigh, North Carolina, rather than being spread out across the country in 9 different locations.

The cross-functional process has already produced some head-turning new products, the most promising of which is the Think-Pad 701 laptop, code-named Butterfly because of an innovative full-size keyboard that folds like the wings of a butterfly to tuck neatly into the compact 4½ pound subnotebook. Researcher John Karides, who came up with the idea for the Butterfly, and two colleagues joined a cross-functional design team in Raleigh and the product metamorphosed from idea sketch to finished product in a smooth 18 months. While this isn't particularly impressive in an industry with 9-month product cycles, the Butterfly is IBM's first on-time product in years and is a badly-needed smash hit. The division is now revamping the entire ThinkPad portable line to share the new keyboard as well as launching a new line of Aptiva home computers. IBM is counting on successful new-product development to help the division regain its position as market leader.[22]

Companies such as IBM, Dana, Rubbermaid, and 3M depend on lower level employees to develop new ideas for technology and product changes. However, all change requires active leadership. Leaders look for ways to encourage the development of new ideas. Dana, for example, offers classes on drumming up better ideas and holds award ceremonies for workers whose suggestions are implemented.

Creativity

In a fast-changing world, any company that isn't constantly developing new ideas will likely be out of business in a few years. Leaders find ways to promote creativity in the departments where it is most needed. For example, some organizations, such as hospitals, government agencies, and nonprofit organizations, may need frequent changes in policies and procedures, and leaders can promote creativity among administrative workers. For companies that rely on new products, leaders need to promote the generation and sharing of ideas across departments. In learning organizations, leaders want everyone to constantly be coming up with new ideas for solving problems and meeting customer needs. One of the best ways for leaders to facilitate continuous change is to create an environment that nourishes creativity. **Creativity** is the generation of new ideas that result in improved efficiency and effectiveness of the organization.[23] Creative people come up with ideas that may meet perceived needs, solve problems, or respond to opportunities and are therefore adopted by the organization. However, creativity itself is a process rather than an outcome, a journey rather than a destination. One of the most important tasks of leaders today is to harness the creative energy of all employees to further the interests of the organization.

Leading Creativity in Organizations and People

Leaders can create an environment that helps individuals as well as entire organizations or departments be more creative. Six elements of creative organizations are listed in the left-hand column of Exhibit 15.4 and each is described below.[24] These elements correspond to the characteristics of creative people, listed in the right-hand column of the exhibit.

Alignment For creative acts that benefit the organization to occur consistently, the interests and actions of all employees should be aligned with the company's purpose, vision, and goals. Leaders make clear what the company stands for, consistently promote the vision, and clarify specific goals. In addition, they make a commitment of time, energy, and resources to activities and initiatives that support the vision, and they hold employees accountable for decisions that affect key goals.

Self-initiated Activity Most people have a natural desire to explore and create, which leads them to want to initiate creative activity on their own. Unfortunately, this desire is sometimes squelched early in life by classroom teachers who insist on strict adherence to the rules. It is the responsibility of leaders to unleash deep-seated employee motivation for creative acts. For example, an effective system for responding to employee ideas and suggestions is essential to encouraging self-initiated activity. When employees feel that their ideas are valued, they begin to have more ideas.

Unofficial Activity Employees need to be able to experiment and dream outside of their regular job description. Leaders can give employees free time for activities that are not officially sanctioned. One study of creativity found that in almost every case the essence of the creative act came during the "unofficial" time period.[25] Dream time is what makes it possible for companies to go where they never expected to. The best-known example is 3M's Post-it Notes, one of the five most popular 3M products and one that resulted from an engineer's free time experiments with another worker's "failure"—a not-very-sticky glue. 3M lets employees spend 15 percent of their time on any projects of their own choosing, without management approval.[26]

Serendipity As originally defined by Horace Walpole in 1754, "serendipity combines a fortunate accident with sagacity."[27] Serendipity often seems like a magical occurrence and, thus, one leaders can do little to promote. However, leaders can encourage "fortunate accidents" by creating a culture that values risk-taking and exploration. They promote sagacity by helping employees develop their potential to think and solve problems so that they are able to recognize the potential value of an accidental discovery. Far from being magic, serendipity is present in every creative act, whether it is readily apparent or not.

EXHIBIT 15.4	CHARACTERISTICS OF CREATIVE PEOPLE AND ORGANIZATIONS
The Creative Organization	**The Creative Individual**
Alignment	Commitment Focused approach
Self-initiated activity	Independence Persistence Energy
Unofficial activity	Self-confidence Nonconformity
Serendipity	Playfulness Curiosity Undisciplined exploration
Diverse stimuli	Open-mindedness Conceptual fluency Enjoy variety
Within-company communication	Social competence Emotionally expressive Loves people

SOURCES: Based on Alan G. Robinson and Sam Stern, *Corporate Creativity: How Innovation and Improvement Actually Happen*, (San Francisco: Berrett-Koehler, 1997); Rosabeth Moss Kanter, "The Middle Manager as Innovator," *Harvard Business Review*, July–August, 1982, 104–105; and James Brian Quinn, "Managing Innovation: Controlled Chaos," *Harvard Business Review*, May–June 1985, 73–84.

Diverse Stimuli It is impossible to know in advance what stimulus will lead any particular person to come up with a creative idea. The seeds of the idea for Post-it Notes were planted when an engineer's bookmarks kept falling out of his church hymnal. However, leaders can help provide the sparks that set off creative ideas. Hallmark goes to extremes in this area, giving employees opportunities to explore wide-ranging interests at mountain retreats, workshops, sabbaticals, visiting lecture series, and other programs. Robert Hurlburt, a metal engraver for Hallmark, spent three months bent over a potter's wheel at a ceramics shop. "It's given me an opportunity to get back to thinking wild, crazy things," Hurlburt said.[28] Another simple way leaders can provide employees with diverse stimuli is by rotating people into different jobs. In addition, they can give employees opportunities to work with customers, suppliers, and others outside the organization, or give time off to participate in community volunteer activities.

Internal Communication Creativity flourishes when there is frequent contact with interdisciplinary networks of people at all levels of the organization.[29] Leaders can provide opportunities for employees who don't normally interact with one another to get together. Kodak, for example, offers Techfairs, which give employees the opportunity to learn about creative activities in other parts of the company.[30] In addition, leaders can make collaboration and widespread information sharing an integral part of the organizational culture.

Leaders can incorporate these six elements to spark creativity in specific departments or the entire organization. At IDEO Product Development, leaders have fostered a hothouse of creativity that has made the company the world's most celebrated design firm.

LEADERSHIP SPOTLIGHT   **IDEO PRODUCT DEVELOPMENT**

At IDEO, heavy doses of fun and freedom lead to radical new ideas that turn into important new products. About 250 people work in a network of offices stretching from San Francisco to London to Tokyo and create about 90 new products a year. Some of the products created by IDEO include Levelor blinds, Crest's Neat Squeeze toothpaste container, cutting-edge laptop computers, and virtual reality headgear. However, the company's ultimate creation may be the process of creativity itself. Employees continuously dream, experiment, and share ideas. The culture values playfulness, risk-taking, and nonconformity. Because some of the younger workers like to listen to loud music while they work, leaders created a special area called the Spunk Space, so that other workers wouldn't be disturbed by the noise.

Self-initiated creative activity is promoted because there are no "bosses" and the most important rule is to break the rules. One of the most valued company slogans is "fail often to succeed sooner." In addition, people are free to dream and experiment broadly (unofficial activity) because they aren't constrained by job titles, permanent work assignments, or job descriptions. Anyone can propose a new idea for further exploration and all work is organized into project teams that form and disband as needed to pursue new ideas. Brainstorming rooms have whiteboard covered walls and conference tables covered with butcher paper so people can doodle anywhere anytime the mood strikes them. Employees call a brainstorming session at the beginning of a new project or whenever they feel stumped, and a company-wide invitation goes out by e-mail. Although participation is voluntary, people from a mix of disciplines gladly participate because they want the same participation from others regarding their own ideas and projects.

"The most important thing I learned from big companies," says David Kelley, founder of IDEO, "is that creativity gets stifled when everyone's got to follow the rules. [IDEO] is in a state of perpetual experimentation. We're constantly trying new ideas in our projects, our work space, even our culture."[31]

To create this kind of environment, IDEO leaders naturally hire people who display some of the characteristics of creative individuals, as listed in the right-hand column of Exhibit 15.4. Creative people are often known for open-mindedness, a focused approach to problem solving, independence, persistence, self-confidence, nonconformity, a relaxed, playful attitude, and good social and interpersonal skills. Some people have more innate creativity than others and can help build creative organizations. However, each of us has the potential to be creative. This chapter's

LIVING LEADERSHIP

Five Myths that Stand in the Way of Our Creativity

There are a number of myths that stand in the way of recognizing and encouraging our own creativity.

Myth 1: Creativity requires an artistic temperament.
Culturally, we have learned to think of creativity by associating it with poets, painters, musicians, and other artists, but creativity should not be confused with talent.

Myth 2: Creativity happens in quantum leaps. It's the Eureka experience.
Creativity comes in all increments. Sometimes it is world-shaking and sometimes it is limited and modest.

Myth 3: You can't plan these things—inspiration just happens.
Thomas Edison tested several hundred different filaments before he hit upon the perfect one to light his fire. "Instantaneous creativity" is almost always the end result of hard work.

Myth 4: Some people are creative and some people aren't.
Research indicates that some people have more innate creativity than others, just as some people have more intelligence, height, or artistic talent. However, everyone has *some* creative potential—and the more they use it, the stronger it gets.

Myth 5: Creativity can't be taught.
A growing body of evidence confirms that in educational and work situations, creativity can be greatly enhanced through training.

SOURCE: First appeared in "Sure You're Creative—You Just Don't Know It," *Working Woman*, February 1997, 40. Written by Jim Frederick. Reprinted with the permission of MacDonald Communications Corporation. Copyright © 1998 by MacDonald Communications Corporation. For subscriptions call 1-800-234-9675.

Living Leadership box explores some of the myths about creativity. Individuals noted for their creativity include Edwin Land, who invented the Polaroid camera; Frederick Smith, who came up with the idea for Federal Express's overnight delivery service during an undergraduate class at Yale; and Swiss engineer George de Mestral, who created Velcro after noticing the tiny burrs caught on his wool socks. Each of these people saw unique opportunities in familiar situations. Leaders can foster environments that encourage both individuals and organizations to be more creative.

Stages in the Personal Creative Process

Creativity is not a mysterious talent of the select few. One important part of becoming more creative is understanding the stages of the creative process. One model of creativity is illustrated in Exhibit 15.5. Stages do not always occur in the same order and may overlap. In addition, if a person encounters a block at one stage, he or she may cycle back to an earlier stage and try again.[32]

Stage 1: Recognition of Problem/Opportunity Creativity often begins with the recognition of a problem that needs to be solved or an opportunity to explore. For example, the idea for Pringles brand potato chips (now owned by Procter & Gamble)

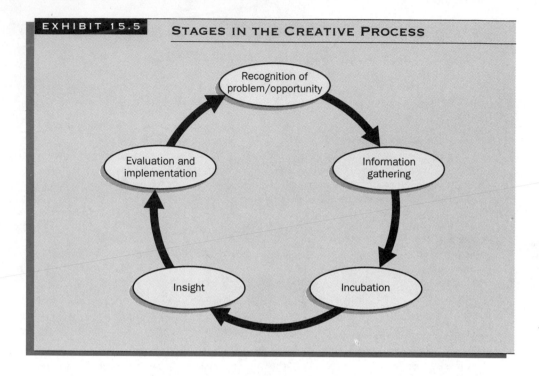

EXHIBIT 15.5 STAGES IN THE CREATIVE PROCESS

began when an employee at a small snack manufacturer started wondering how they could pack a large number of chips into a small package.[33]

Stage 2: Information Gathering The next step is to search for background information and knowledge about the problem or opportunity. This may involve reading in a variety of fields; attending professional meetings and seminars; traveling to new places; talking to anyone and everyone about the subject; scanning magazines, newspapers, and journals; and carrying a notebook to jot down useful information. It is also important to set aside time specifically for pursuing ideas and giving curiosity free rein.

Stage 3: Incubation This is the stage where a person allows the subconscious to mull things over. The incubation stage happens while the person is involved in activities totally unrelated to the subject—even during sleep. This is the period that really allows creativity to spring forth. Some helpful ideas for encouraging the incubation period are: engage in routine, "mindless" activities such as cutting the grass; get regular exercise; play and have fun; meditate; and try to relax on a regular basis.

Stage 4: Insight This is the stage that most people think of as "creativity." It is when the person hits upon an idea. The idea may occur while watching television, taking a shower, or reading the newspaper, or it may occur while one is thinking specifically about the problem. In most cases, the idea doesn't come as a bolt out of the blue, but in gradual increments. Ideas to speed up this stage include: daydream and fantasize about the project; practice your hobbies; keep a notebook by your bedside to record late-night or early-morning ideas; take regular breaks from working.

Stage 5: Evaluation and Implementation   This is the most difficult stage and requires courage, tenacity, and self-discipline. Creative people often fail many times before they succeed and have to cycle back through the information gathering and incubation stages. In addition, others may think the "brilliant" idea is crazy. Creative people don't give up when they run into obstacles. At 3M, the CEO five times tried to kill the project that led to the highly successful Thinsulate.[34] Some suggestions during this phase include: increase your energy level with proper diet, rest, and exercise; take note of your intuitive hunches; seek the advice of others; educate yourself in how to sell your ideas; and remember that you are facing challenges rather than problems.

Leaders of today's organizations have powerful reasons to encourage creativity. As we discussed in Chapter 1, many organizations are undergoing fundamental transformations to respond to new challenges. They need employees throughout the organization to contribute new ideas. In addition, creative people are less resistant to change because they are open-minded, curious, and willing to take risks. The success of change in any part of the organization depends on people's attitudes and culture. Because people are so important for any change effort, the remainder of this chapter is devoted to a detailed discussion of leading culture change.

Leading Culture Change

Organizations are shifting from cherishing stability to valuing change, from control to empowerment, from encouraging competition to supporting collaboration, and from an emphasis on machines and objects to an emphasis on people, ideas, and relationships. Many are striving to become learning organizations so that they quickly learn and adapt within turbulent environments. For organizations to transform toward becoming learning organizations, leaders must confront the "perplexing, annoying, distressing, and confusing" nature of changing people and culture.[35]

Why Do People Resist Change?

Leaders often see change as a way to strengthen the organization. However, employees often view it as disruptive and painful. Leaders need to put themselves in their followers' shoes and develop partnerships that make successful change possible. The underlying reason why employees resist change is that it violates the **personal compact** between workers and the organization.[36] Personal compacts are the reciprocal obligations and commitments that define the relationship between employees and organizations. They include such things as job tasks, performance requirements, evaluation procedures, and compensation packages. These aspects of the compact are generally clearly defined and may be in written form. Other aspects are less clear-cut. The personal compact incorporates elements such as mutual trust and dependence as well as shared values. Employees perceive that change violates the personal compact for several reasons.

Self-Interest   Employees typically resist a change they believe will take away something of value. Changes in job design, structure, or technology may lead to a perceived loss of power, prestige, pay, company benefits, or even an employee's job. For middle managers and lower-level supervisors, for example, a shift to empowered teams of workers can be quite threatening. Fear of personal loss may be the biggest obstacle to organizational change.[37]

Uncertainty   Uncertainty is the lack of information about future events. It represents a fear of the unknown. Employees often do not understand how a proposed change may affect them and may worry about whether they will be able to meet the demands of a new task, procedure, or technology. When leaders at Lands' End embarked on a dramatic effort to incorporate some of today's trends such as teams, peer reviews, and the elimination of guards and time clocks, employees balked because they liked the familiar "Lands' End Way" of doing things and were uncertain about how the changes would affect them.[38]

Different Assessments and Goals   Another reason for resistance to change is that people who will be affected by the innovation may assess the situation differently from those who propose the change. Sometimes critics voice legitimate disagreements over the proposed benefits of a change. Employees in different departments pursue different goals, and a change may detract from performance and goal achievement for some departments.

　　These reasons for resistance are legitimate and real. Leaders cannot ignore resistance to change, but can diagnose the reasons and come up with ways to gain acceptance of the change by employees.

Overcoming Resistance

Leaders can improve the chances for a successful outcome by following the eight-stage model discussed earlier in this chapter. In addition, leaders may use a number of specific implementation techniques to overcome employee resistance.

Communication and Training   Communication informs employees about the need for change and about the consequences of a proposed change, preventing false rumors, misunderstandings, and resentment. In one study of change efforts, the most commonly cited reason for failure was that employees learned of the change from outsiders. Top leaders concentrated on communicating with the public and shareholders, but failed to communicate with the people who would be most intimately affected by the changes—their own employees. It is also important that leaders communicate major change efforts face-to-face rather than through videos, memos, or company newsletters.[39] In addition, training is needed to help employees acquire skills for their role in the change process or their new responsibilities. Canadian Airlines International spent a year and a half preparing and training employees before changing its entire reservations, airport, cargo, and financial systems. This intensive training and communication effort, which involved 50,000 tasks, 12,000 people, and 26 classrooms around the world, resulted in a smooth implementation.[40]

Participation and Involvement Participation involves employees in helping to design the change. Although this approach is time-consuming, it pays off by giving people a sense of control over the change activity. Employees come to understand the change better and become committed to its successful implementation. A study of the implementation and adoption of new computer technology at two companies, for example, showed a much smoother implementation process at the company that introduced the change using a participatory approach.[41]

Coercion As a last resort, leaders overcome resistance by threatening employees with the loss of jobs or promotions or by firing or transferring them. Coercion may be necessary in crisis situations when a rapid response is needed. Coercion may also be needed for administrative changes that flow from the top-down, such as downsizing the workforce. However, as a general rule, this approach to change is not advisable because it leaves employees angry at leaders and the change may be sabotaged.

Culture Change Approaches

Leaders in numerous large organizations have undertaken some type of culture change initiative. Changing organizational culture fundamentally shifts how people think about their work and generally leads to renewed commitment and empowerment of employees and a stronger bond among workers and between the organization and its customers.[42] Two traditional ways leaders bring about culture change are through total quality management and organizational development programs.

Total Quality Management

The approach known as **total quality management** infuses quality values throughout every activity within an organization. By requiring organization-wide participation in quality control, TQM requires a major shift in mind-set for both leaders and employees. Workers must be trained, involved, and empowered in a way that is new for them and can be frightening. One way to involve workers is through quality circles, groups of 6 to 12 workers who meet voluntarily to analyze and solve problems. Another technique is benchmarking, a process whereby companies find out how others do something better than they do and then try to imitate or improve on it. Through research and field trips by teams of front-line workers, companies compare their products and service with those of their competitors and other companies. While the focus of total quality programs is on improving quality and productivity, TQM always involves a significant change in organizational culture.

Organizational Development

A more straightforward method of bringing about culture change is known as organizational development. In the 1970s, **organizational development** evolved as a separate field in the behavioral sciences focused on examining how work is done and how people who do the work feel about their efficiency and effectiveness. Rather than focusing on specific problems, OD became a process of fundamental change in an organization's overall culture.[43] Leaders use OD culture change interventions to improve organizational performance through trust, open confrontation of problems, employee empowerment and participation, the design of meaningful work, and the full use of human potential within the organization. One way to do this is to survey employees about their job satisfaction, attitudes, and quality of work relationships. Change leaders then use the data to stimulate a discussion of organizational problems and plan for changes. Off-site meetings can also be held to give people a chance to talk about problems and the change mission with limited interference and distractions. Another OD technique is team building. Team building activities bring people together to discuss conflicts, goals, communication, creativity, and leadership, and plan how to overcome problems and improve results.

Changing organizational culture is not easy, but organizational development techniques can help leaders smooth the process by getting people to think in new ways about human relationships.

Large-Group Interventions

Early work in organizational development focused on one or two groups or work teams at a time. In recent years, there has been a growing interest in applications to large-group settings which are more attuned to accelerating large-scale culture change in today's complex, fast-changing world.[44] The **large-group intervention** approach brings together participants from all parts of the organization—often including key stakeholders from outside the organization as well—to discuss problems or opportunities and plan for change. A large-group intervention might involve 50 to 500 people and last several days. The idea is to involve everyone who has a stake in the change, gather perspectives from all parts of the system, and enable people to create a collective future through sustained, guided conversation and dialogue. General Electric's Work Out program, a leadership initiative by CEO Jack Welch, is an excellent example of the large-scale intervention approach. It accelerates the eight steps in Exhibit 15.2 from years to months.

LEADERSHIP SPOTLIGHT   **GENERAL ELECTRIC'S WORK OUT**

The Work Out program is one of the ways Jack Welch reshaped General Electric's culture for renewed productivity and growth. The program was created out of Welch's desire to reach and motivate 300,000 employees and his insistence that the people on the front lines, where change had to happen, be empowered to create that change.

GE's Work Out began in large-scale off-site meetings facilitated by a combination of top leaders, outside consultants, and human resources specialists. In each business unit, the basic pattern was the same. Hourly and salaried workers came together from many different parts of the organization in an informal three- to five-day meeting to discuss and solve problems. Gradually, the Work Out events began to include external stakeholders such as suppliers and customers as well as employees. Today, Work Out is not an event, but a process of how work is done and problems are solved at GE. The format for Work Out includes seven steps:

1. Choose a work process or problem for discussion.

2. Select an appropriate cross-functional team (30 to 50 people), which may also include external stakeholders.

3. Assign a "champion" to follow through on recommendations.

4. Meet for several days and come up with recommendations to improve work processes and solve problems.

5. Meet with leaders, who are required to respond to recommendations on the spot.

6. Hold additional meetings as needed to implement the recommendations.

7. Start the process all over again with a new process or problem.

GE's Work Out process not only solves problems and improves productivity for the company but also gives employees the experience of openly and honestly interacting with one another without regard to vertical or horizontal boundaries. By doing so, Work Out has helped to create what Welch calls a "culture of boundarylessness" that is critical for continuous learning and improvement.[45]

Large-group interventions are a powerful tool for leaders, and are a significant social innovation compared to earlier OD concepts and approaches. Exhibit 15.6 lists the primary differences between the traditional OD model and the large-group intervention model of organizational change.[46] In the newer approach, the focus is on the entire system, which takes the organization's interaction with its environment into account. The source of information is expanded to include shop floor workers, customers, suppliers, community members, even competitors, and this information is discussed widely so that everyone has the same picture of the organization and its environment. The acceleration of change when the entire system is involved in a single retreat can be remarkable. In addition, learning occurs across all parts of the organization simultaneously, rather than in individuals, small groups, or business units. The end result is that the large-group approach offers great possibilities for fundamental, radical transformation of the entire culture, whereas the traditional approach creates incremental change in a few individuals or small groups at a time.

EXHIBIT 15.6	APPROACHES TO CULTURE CHANGE	
	Traditional Organization Development Model	**Large-Group Intervention Model**
Focus for action:	Specific problem or group	Entire system
Information **Source:** **Distribution:**	 Organization Limited	 Organization and environment Widely shared
Time frame:	Slow	Fast
Learning:	Individual, small group	Whole organization
	⬇	⬇
Change process:	Incremental change	Rapid transformation

SOURCE: Adapted from Barbara Benedict Bunker and Billie T. Alban, "Conclusion: What Makes Large Group Interventions Effective," *The Journal of Applied Behavioral Science* 28, No. 4 (December 1992), 579–591. Used by permission of Sage Publications, Inc.

Large-group interventions represent a significant shift in the way leaders think about change and reflect an increasing awareness of the importance of including the entire organization in any significant change effort.

Summary and Interpretation

The important point of this chapter is that tools and approaches are available to enable leaders to transform organizations. Change is inevitable in organizations, and the increased pace of change in today's global environment has created even greater problems for leaders. More organizations than ever face a need for fundamental, widespread transformation. Transformational leadership is one way leaders can renew entire organizations. Transformational leadership inspires followers to go beyond their own self-interest for the good of the whole, and it paints a compelling vision of a desired future that makes the pain of change worth the effort.

Despite the difficulties of major change, leaders can help ensure a successful change effort by following the eight-stage model of planned change—establish a sense of urgency; create a powerful coalition; develop a compelling vision and strategy; communicate the vision; empower employees to act; generate short-term wins; consolidate gains and tackle bigger problems; and institutionalize the change in the organizational culture. There are four types of planned change that can occur in organizations: strategy and structure changes, technology changes, product and service changes, and culture changes. Leaders can create an environment that nourishes creativity in particular departments or the entire organization to facilitate change in these areas. Six elements of creative organizations are alignment, self-initiated activity, unofficial activity, serendipity, diverse stimuli, and within-company comunication. These correspond to characteristics of creative individuals. Creative people are less resistant to change. The success of any change depends on people, and all types of change involve organizational culture.

Two traditional ways leaders bring about culture change are total quality management and organizational development programs. TQM focuses on improving quality and productivity, but leads to culture change by getting employees to think about work and human relationships in new ways. Leaders use OD interventions to promote trust, open confrontation of problems, employee empowerment and participation, and the full use of employee potential. A new approach is large-group interventions that hold great promise for rapid transformation even in large organizations.

Key Terms

transactional leadership
transformational leadership
strategy and structure changes
technology changes
product and service changes
culture changes

creativity
personal compact
total quality management
organizational development
large-group intervention

Discussion Questions

1. Of the eight stages of planned change, which one do you think leaders are most likely to skip? Why?

2. What advice would you give a leader who perceives an urgent need for a bottom-up change in work technology versus a leader who perceives a need for new products?

3. Do you think creative individuals and creative organizations have characteristics in common? Discuss.

4. What advice would you give a leader who wants to increase creativity in her department?

5. Why do employees resist change? What are some ways leaders can overcome this resistance?

6. Discuss the primary differences between large-group interventions and the traditional organizational development approach to changing culture. Why is the new approach more applicable in today's world?

7. Planned change is often considered ideal. Do you think unplanned change could be effective? Discuss. Can you think of an example?

8. Is the world really changing faster today, or do people just assume so?

Leadership Development: Personal Feedback

Are You a Change Leader?

Complete the following questions based on how you act in a typical leadership situation at work or school. For each item, circle the number that best describes you.

Disagree			**Agree**	
1	**2**	**3**	**4**	**5**

1. I have a clear sense of mission for change that I repeatedly describe to others.
   1   2   3   4   5

2. I signal the value of a change and improvement with various symbols and statements.
   1   2   3   4   5

3. One of my strengths is to encourage people to frequently express ideas and opinions that differ from my own.
   1   2   3   4   5

4. I always celebrate the "effort" to improve things, even if the final outcome is disappointing.
   1   2   3   4   5

5. I see my primary job as "inspiring" others toward improvement in their jobs.
   1   2   3   4   5

6. Sometimes I use dramatic flourishes—a brainstorming session, stop work, go to an off-site—to signal an important change to people.
   1   2   3   4   5

7. Often I take risks and let others take risks that could be a problem if the idea failed.
   1   2   3   4   5

8. I spend time developing new ways of approaching old problems.
   1   2   3   4   5

9. I always believe the "effort" to improve something should be rewarded, even if the final improvement is disappointing.
   1   2   3   4   5

10. I frequently compliment others on changes they have made.
    1   2   3   4   5

11. I am personally involved in several improvement projects at one time.
    1   2   3   4   5

12. I try to be a good listener and be patient with what people suggest, even when it is a "stupid" idea.
    1   2   3   4   5

13. I like to support change efforts, even when the idea may not work.
    1   2   3   4   5

14. I work at the politics of change to build agreement for ideas for improvement.
    1   2   3   4   5

15. I am able to get higher-ups to support ideas for improvement.
    1   2   3   4   5

Scoring and Interpretation

Add the numbers you circled for your total change leadership score. Your score indicates the extent to which you are a positive leader force for change. The questions represent behaviors associated with successful change leadership.

60–75: Great. A dynamo for leading change.

45–60: Good. A positive change leader.

30–45: Adequate. You have a typical attitude toward change.

15–30: Poor. You may be dragging down change efforts.

Go back over the questions on which you scored lowest and develop a plan to improve your approach toward change. Discuss your score and your ideas with other students.

Leadership Development: Case for Analysis

Southern Discomfort

Jim Malesckowski remembers the call of two weeks ago as if he just put down the telephone receiver: "I just read your analysis and I want you to get down to Mexico right away," Jack Ripon, his boss and chief executive officer, had blurted in his ear. "You know we can't make the plant in Oconomo work anymore—the costs are just too high. So go down there, check out what our operational costs would be if we move, and report back to me in a week."

At that moment, Jim felt as if a shiv had been stuck in his side, just below the rib cage. As president of the Wisconsin Specialty Products Division of Lamprey, Inc., he knew quite well the challenge of dealing with high-cost labor in a third-generation, unionized U.S. manufacturing plant. And although he had done the analysis that led to his boss's knee-jerk response, the call still stunned him. There were 520 people who made a living at Lamprey's Oconomo facility, and if it closed, most of them wouldn't have a journeyman's prayer of finding another job in the town of 9,900 people.

Instead of the $16-per-hour average wage paid at the Oconomo plant, the wages paid to the Mexican workers—who lived in a town without sanitation and with an unbelievably toxic effluent from industrial pollution—would amount to about $1.60 an hour on average. That's a savings of nearly $15 million a year for Lamprey, to be offset in part by increased costs for training, transportation, and other matters.

After two days of talking with Mexican government representatives and managers of other companies in the town, Jim had enough information to develop a set of comparative figures of production and shipping costs. On the way home, he started to outline the report, knowing full well that unless some miracle occurred, he would be ushering in a blizzard of pink slips for people he had come to appreciate.

The plant in Oconomo had been in operation since 1921, making special apparel for persons suffering injuries and other medical conditions. Jim had often talked with employees who would recount stories about their fathers or grandfathers working in the same Lamprey company plant—the last of the original manufacturing operations in town.

But friendship aside, competitors had already edged past Lamprey in terms of price and were dangerously close to overtaking it in product quality. Although both Jim and the plant manager had tried to convince the union to accept lower wages, union leaders resisted. In fact, on one occasion when Jim and the plant manager tried to discuss a cell manufacturing approach, which would cross-train employees to perform up to three different jobs, local union leaders could barely restrain their anger. Yet probing beyond the fray, Jim sensed the fear that lurked under the union reps' gruff exterior. He sensed their vulnerability, but could not break through the reactionary bark that protected it.

A week has passed and Jim just submitted his report to his boss. Although he didn't specifically bring up the point, it was apparent that Lamprey could put its investment dollars in a bank and receive a better return than what its Oconomo operation is currently producing.

Tomorrow, he'll discuss the report with the CEO. Jim doesn't want to be responsible for the plant's dismantling, an act he personally believes would be wrong as long as there's a chance its costs can be lowered. "But Ripon's right," he says to himself. "The costs are too high, the union's unwilling to cooperate, and the company needs to make a better return on its investment if it's to continue at all. It sounds right but feels wrong. What should I do?"

Questions

1. If you were Jim Malesckowski, would you fight to save the plant? Why?

2. Assume you want to lead the change to save the plant. Describe how you would enact the eight stages outlined in Exhibit 15.2.

3. How would you overcome union leader resistance?

SOURCE: Doug Wallace, "What Would You Do?" *Business Ethics*, March/April 1996, 52–53. Reprinted with permission from *Business Ethics*, P.O. Box 8439, Minneapolis, MN 55408. 612/879-0695.

References

[1]Janet Guyon, "Why Is the World's Most Profitable Company Turning Itself Inside Out?" *Fortune*, August 4, 1997, 120–125.

[2]Nicholas Imparato and Oren Harari, "When New Worlds Stir," *Management Review*, October 1994, 22–28.

[3]Eileen Davis, "What's on American Managers' Minds?" *American Management Review*, April 1995, 14–20.

[4]Quoted in *Inc.* (March 1995), 13.

[5]Gary Hamel, "Turning Your Business Upside Down," *Fortune*, June 23, 1997, 87–88.

[6]Tim Carvell, "The Crazy Record Business: These Prices Really Are Insane," *Fortune*, August 4, 1997, 109–115.

[7]George Stalk, Jr., "Time and Innovation," *Canadian Business Review*, Autumn 1993, 15–18.

[8]John A. Byrne, "Management Meccas," *Business Week*, September 18, 1995, 122–134; and Eric Schine, "Mattel's Wild Race to Market," *Business Week*, February 21, 1994, 62–63.

[9]David Whitford, "Sale of the Century," *Fortune*, February 17, 1997, 92–100; Bill Trahant, W. Warner Burke, and Richard Koonce, "12 Principles of Organizational Transformation," *Management Review*, September 1997, 17–21; and Jenny C. McCune, "Management's Brave New World," *Management Review*, October 1997, 10–14.

[10]Sumantra Ghoshal and Christopher A. Bartlett, "Rebuilding Behavioral Context: A Blueprint for Corporate Renewal," *Sloan Management Review*, Winter 1996, 23–36.

[11]The terms transactional and transformational leadership are from James MacGregor Burns, *Leadership* (New York: Harper & Row, 1978); and Bernard M. Bass, "Leadership: Good, Better, Best," *Organizational Dynamics* 13 (Winter 1985), 26–40.

[12]Based on Bernard M. Bass, "Theory of Transformational Leadership Redux," *Leadership Quarterly* 6, No. 4 (Winter 1995), 463–478, and "From Transactional to Transformational Leadership: Learning to Share the Vision," *Organizational Dynamics* 19, No. 3 (Winter 1990), 19–31; and Francis J. Yammarino, William D. Spangler, and Bernard M. Bass, "Transformational Leadership and Performance: A Longitudinal Investigation," *Leadership Quarterly* 4, No. 1 (Spring 1993), 81–102.

[13]Noel M. Tichy and Mary Anne Devanna, *The Transformational Leader* (New York: John Wiley & Sons, 1986), 265–266.

[14]Bernard M. Bass, *Leadership and Performance Beyond Expectations* (New York: The Free Press, 1985), 22, 26.

[15]The following discussion is based heavily on John P. Kotter, *Leading Change* (Boston: Harvard Business School Press, 1996), 20–25; and "Leading Change: Why Transformation Efforts Fail," *Harvard Business Review*, March–April 1995, 59–67.

[16]Patrick Flanagan, "The ABCs of Changing Corporate Culture," *Management Review*, July 1995, 57–61.

[17]Tichy and Devanna, *The Transformational Leader*, 122, 124; Charles Pappas, "The Top 20 Best-Paid Women in Corporate America," *Working Woman*, February 1998, 26–39.

[18]Gillian Flynn, "On Track to a Comeback," *Personnel Journal*, February 1996, 58–69.

[19]Charles Matthews, "How We Changed Gear to Ride the Winds of Change," *Professional Manager*, January 1995, 6–8.

[20]Kotter, "Leading Change: Why Transformations Fail," 65.

[21]Richard Teitelbaum, "How to Harness Gray Matter," *Fortune*, June 9, 1997, 168.

[22]Ira Sager, "The Man Who's Rebooting IBM's PC Business," *Business Week*, July 24, 1995, 68–72.

[23]Timothy A. Matherly and Ronald E. Goldsmith, "The Two Faces of Creativity," *Business Horizons*, September/October 1985, 8.

[24]The elements of creative organizations come from Alan G. Robinson and Sam Stern, *Corporate Creativity: How Innovation and Improvement Actually Happen* (San Francisco: Berrett-Koehler, 1997).

[25]Robinson and Stern, *Corporate Creativity*, 14.

[26]Gail Dutton, "Enhancing Creativity," *Management Review*, November 1996, 44–46.

[27]Robinson and Stern, *Corporate Creativity*, 192.

[28]Doug Glass, "Hallmark Feeds the Muse to Keep Workers Creative," *The Tennessean*, June 9, 1996, 2E.

[29]Cameron M. Ford, "Creativity Is a Mystery: Clues from the Investigators' Notebooks," in Cameron M. Ford and Dennis A. Gioia, eds., *Creative Action in Organizations: Ivory Tower Visions & Real World Voices*, (Thousand Oaks, CA: Sage Publications, 1995), 12–49.

[30]Robinson and Stern, *Corporate Creativity*, 234.

[31]Tia O'Brien, "Encourage Wild Ideas," *Fast Company*, April-May 1996, 82–88.

[32]This section is based on Donald F. Kuratko and Richard M. Hodgetts, *Entrepreneurship: A Contemporary Approach* (Fort Worth: The Dryden Press, 1998), 125–127.

[33]Magaly Olivero, "Some Wacko Ideas That Worked," *Working Woman*, September 1990, 147–148.

[34]Thomas A. Stewart, "3M Fights Back," *Fortune*, February 5, 1996, 94–99.

[35]Michael Hammer, *The Reengineering Revolution* (quoted in Anne Fisher, "Making Change Stick," *Fortune*, April 17, 1995, 122).

[36]Based on Paul Stebel, "Why Do Employees Resist Change?" *Harvard Business Review*, May–June 1996, 86–92.

[37]John P. Kotter and Leonard A. Schlesinger, "Choosing Strategies for Change," *Harvard Business Review*, March–April 1979, 106–114.

[38]Gregory A. Patterson, "Lands' End Kicks Out Modern New Managers, Rejecting a Makeover," *The Wall Street Journal*, April 3, 1995, A1, A6.

[39]Peter Richardson and D. Keith Denton, "Communicating Change," *Human Resource Management* 35, No. 2 (Summer 1996), 203–216; T. J. Larkin and Sandar Larkin, "Reaching and Changing Frontline Employees," *Harvard Business Review*, May–June 1996, 95–104.

[40]Rob Muller, "Training for Change," *Canadian Business Review*, Spring 1995, 16–19.

[41]Phillip H. Mirvis, Amy L. Sales, and Edward J. Hackett, "The Implementation and Adoption of New Technology in Organizations: The Impact of Work, People, and Culture," *Human Resource Management* 30 (Spring 1991), 113–139.

[42]Benson L. Porter and Warrington S. Parker, Jr., "Culture Change," *Human Resource Management* 31 (Spring/Summer 1992), 45–67.

[43]W. Warner Burke, *Organization Development: A Process of Learning and Changing*, 2nd ed. (Reading, MA: Addison-Wesley, 1994).

[44]This discussion is based on Kathleen D. Dannemiller and Robert W. Jacobs, " Changing the Way Organizations Change: A Revolution of Common Sense," *The Journal of Applied Behavioral Science* 28, No. 4 (December 1992), 480–498; and Barbara Benedict Bunker

and Billie T. Alban, "Conclusion: What Makes Large Group Interventions Effective?" *The Journal of Applied Behavioral Science* 28, No. 4 (December 1992), 570–591.

[45]Judy Quinn, "What a Work-Out!" *Performance* (November 1994), 58–63; and Barbara Benedict Bunker and Billie T. Alban, "Conclusion: What Makes Large Group Interventions Effective?" *The Journal of Applied Behavioral Science* 28, No. 4 (December 1992), 572–591.

[46]Bunker and Alban, "Conclusion: What Makes Large Group Interventions Effective?"

16

Leader Decision Making, Power, and Influence

- **Decision Making** 457

- **Leader Decisions** 461

- **Organizational Decision Making** 462

- **Decision Mistakes** 468

- **Power and Influence** 470

- **Leadership Spotlights:**
  Britt Technologies 464
  Gillette 467
  Crystal Manufacturing 473

- **Leader's Bookshelf:**
  The Nine Natural Laws of Leadership 460

- **Leadership Development: Personal Feedback**
  Personal Power Profile 478

- **Leadership Development: Case for Analysis**
  The Unhealthy Hospital 480

Your Leadership Challenge

After reading this chapter, you should be able to:

- Remember the constraints on rational decision making and begin to rely on intuition and experience in making complex decisions.

- Build coalitions for important decisions, particularly at the problem identification stage.

- Apply an experimental, trial-and-error process that solves complex problems in incremental steps.

- Use the five types of leader power and recognize other sources of power in organizations.

- Use the political tactics of building coalitions; expanding networks; legitimacy and expertise; information and analysis; symbolic action; and being assertive.

When *Casablanca* premiered in 1942, it made cinema history. The film won Academy Awards for best picture, best screenplay, and best director, and it is still considered a classic by film historians and the public alike. Ironically, until the filming of the final scene, no one involved in the production of the now-famous story even knew how it was going to end.

Everybody Comes to Rick's was not a very good play, but when it landed on Hal Wallis' desk at Warner Brothers, Wallis spotted some hot-from-the-headlines potential, purchased the rights, and changed the name to *Casablanca* to capitalize on the geographical mystique. A series of negotiations led to casting Humphrey Bogart as Rick, even though studio chief Jack Warner questioned Bogart's romantic appeal. The casting of Ingrid Bergman as Ilsa was largely by accident. A fluke had created an opening in her otherwise fully booked schedule. Now all the studio needed was the screenplay, which still had not been written.

Filming was chaotic. Writers made script changes and plot revisions daily. Actors were unsure of how to develop their characters, so they just did whatever seemed right at the time. For example, when Ingrid Bergman wanted to know which man should get most of her on-screen attention, she was told, "We don't know yet—just play it, well . . . in between." Scenes were often filmed blindly with no idea of how they were supposed to fit within the overall story. Because the cast typically received their scripts only hours before filming, they had trouble remembering their lines, causing more delays. Amazingly, even when it came time to shoot the climactic final scene, no one involved in the production seemed to know who would "get the girl"; a legend still persists that two versions were written. During filming, Bogart disagreed with director Michael Curtiz who wanted Rick to kiss Ilsa good-bye, and Hal Wallis was summoned to mediate.

Some industry analysts predicted disaster, but the haphazard process worked. Ingrid Bergman plays it "in between" just right. Bogart's characterization of Rick was perfect. The tale of love and glory and heartbreaking romance could not have been told better than it was in *Casablanca*. And fortuitous circumstances outside the studio contributed to the film's commercial success. Just 18 days before the film's premiere on Thanksgiving Day, 1942, the Allies invaded North Africa and fought the battle of Casablanca. Then, when the film opened nationwide, President Franklin D. Roosevelt and British Prime Minister Winston Churchill presided over the Casablanca Conference, a historical coincidence that was clearly a boon to the film, helping to push its initial gross to a then astounding $3.7 million.[1]

Making a major motion picture involves many decisions, including which script to shoot, who to cast, how to characterize the roles, how to shoot each scene, and how to end the picture. The production of *Casablanca* was not a systematic decision process that started with a clear problem and ended with a logical solution. Rather, some decisions were chance occurrences: the original script arrived just when Hal Wallis was looking for topical stories, and Bergman was surprisingly available to be cast in the role of Ilsa. Other decisions were marked by disagreement, such as whether Bogart was romantic enough to lead, or whether Rick should kiss Ilsa good-bye. These disagreements required consultations with production participants and key decision makers such as Hal Wallis himself. The unending script changes created uncertainty about the actors' roles, and decisions about how to play them were highly ambiguous. Finally, the outcome of all the decisions surrounding the film was influenced by world events, which put a positive spin on the film's subject matter. The impact of the outside world underscores the complex and uncontrollable situation leaders often face when making decisions.

Although decades have passed since the release of *Casablanca*, this story illustrates the central role of decision making in implementing a change or achieving a leader's vision. Despite great difficulties and uncertainty, leaders must make decisions and keep moving forward. Leaders decide the vision, strategy, and direction in which to take their followers. In addition, leaders use power and influence to implement decisions and achieve continuous improvement. The uncertainty, ambiguity, and ever-changing circumstances of today's environment require that leaders have the courage to make difficult decisions, many of which will not work out.

This chapter introduces the processes of leader decision making. We will examine decision making in the context of a complex environment, including the different stages and the types of decisions. We will examine when the logical, rational approach makes sense, and when to engage the social and political aspects of decision making. Additionally, we will compare decision making for individuals and for organizations. The role of power in the decision process is another important element that we will examine, as well as how power is used to influence others.

Decision Making

Leadership **decision making** is typically defined as the process of identifying and solving problems. Decision making typically involves two major stages: problem identification and problem solution. Moreover, leader decisions vary in complexity and can be categorized as programmed or nonprogrammed. We will discuss these two aspects of decision making in turn.

Two Stages of Decision Making

The two stages of decision making are the identification stage and the solution stage. In the identification stage, information about environmental and organizational conditions is monitored to determine if performance is satisfactory, to diagnose the cause of shortcomings, or to find an opportunity to pursue a new vision that exceeds current standards. Recognizing the need for a decision is often difficult, because it means integrating bits and pieces of information in novel ways. For example, some companies are trying a new approach to market research, called storytelling, to search for clues to customer needs and desires. Leaders at Kimberly-Clark asked customers and potential customers to tell real-life stories about their experiences toilet training their children and tried to listen and discern (Chapter 6) what people really want. The early recognition contributed directly to the success of Huggies Pull-Ups training pants.[2]

Before a solution can be developed, decision makers diagnose the situation: that is, they must try to understand what is happening and why. By examining events and their interconnectedness and outcomes, leaders may unravel the underlying causal factors associated with the decision situation.[3] Without a reasonable understanding of the decision situation, solution attempts are unlikely to be successful. For example, Greyhound Lines decided to address the problem of low profits with a decision to downsize the workforce. Unfortunately, the increased work load on the remaining employees contributed to declining customer service, and ridership on Greyhound buses plunged sharply.[4] Thus, the decision to cut the workforce only exacerbated the original problem.

Once the problem or opportunity has been recognized and diagnosed, decision makers begin the solution stage. This stage is to generate possible alternative solutions that will meet the needs of the situation and respond to the underlying causes. For example, Chrysler was faced with the problem of remaining competitive after the failure of the Omni and Horizon subcompact cars. Lee Iacocca and a dozen engineers decided the alternatives were to either abandon small car production, or try to produce a top-notch car at a rock-bottom price. They opted for the latter, and the resulting Dodge Neon helped revive the presence of U.S. automakers in the small car market.[5] Selecting the best alternative means choosing the solution that fits the overall goals and values of the organization and achieves the desired results using the fewest resources.[6] Chrysler's decision reflected the goal of being competitive and responding to the popularity of Japanese-made automobiles.

An alternative must not only be selected, it must also be implemented. The solution stage includes the implementation of the most promising course of action. Implementing a solution involves activities that ensure that the chosen alternative is carried out, similar to ideas for implementing change described in Chapter 15. Ultimate success depends on whether the choice is translated into action. Sometimes an alternative never becomes a reality because participants lack the resources, power, or influence to make it happen. Implementation often requires discussion with people affected by the decision. Communication, motivation, leadership, and change techniques are used to see that the decision is carried out. At Chrysler, the small car team leader built a coalition of managers who cooperated to design, build, and produce the Neon.

Two Types of Decisions

Organizational decisions vary in complexity and can be categorized as programmed or nonprogrammed.[7] **Programmed decisions** are repetitive and well defined, and procedures exist for resolving the problem. They are well structured because performance criteria are normally clear, good information is available about current performance, alternatives are easily specified, and there is relative certainty that the chosen solution will be successful. Examples of programmed decisions include decision rules, such as when to replace an office copy machine, when to reimburse employees for travel expenses, or whether an applicant has sufficient qualifications for a job as jet engine mechanic. Many companies adopt rules based on experience. For example, large hotels determine how many staff are needed for banquets with the simple rule that they need one server per thirty guests for a sit-down function and one server per forty guests for a buffet.[8] Programmed decisions do not require much leadership or risk taking.

Nonprogrammed decisions are novel and poorly defined, and no procedure exists for solving the problem. They occur when a leader or organization has not seen a problem before and may not know how to respond. Clear-cut decision criteria do not exist. Alternatives are fuzzy. There is uncertainty about whether a proposed solution will solve the problem. Typically, few alternatives can be developed for a nonprogrammed decision, so a single solution may be custom tailored to resolve the problem.

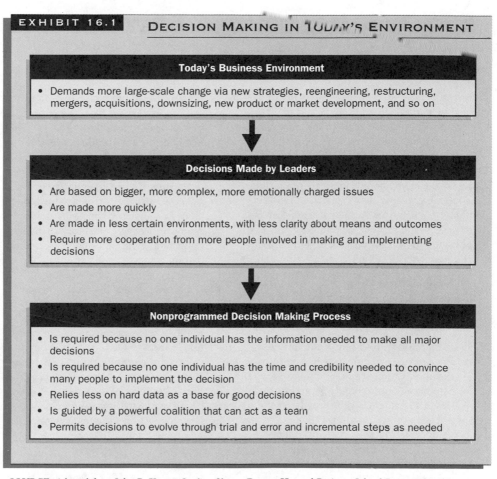

EXHIBIT 16.1 **DECISION MAKING IN TODAY'S ENVIRONMENT**

Today's Business Environment

- Demands more large-scale change via new strategies, reengineering, restructuring, mergers, acquisitions, downsizing, new product or market development, and so on

Decisions Made by Leaders

- Are based on bigger, more complex, more emotionally charged issues
- Are made more quickly
- Are made in less certain environments, with less clarity about means and outcomes
- Require more cooperation from more people involved in making and implementing decisions

Nonprogrammed Decision Making Process

- Is required because no one individual has the information needed to make all major decisions
- Is required because no one individual has the time and credibility needed to convince many people to implement the decision
- Relies less on hard data as a base for good decisions
- Is guided by a powerful coalition that can act as a team
- Permits decisions to evolve through trial and error and incremental steps as needed

SOURCE: Adapted from John P. Kotter, *Leading Change* (Boston: Harvard Business School Press, 1996), 56.

Today's leaders are dealing with a high percentage of nonprogrammed decisions. As outlined in Exhibit 16.1, today's environment has increased both the number and complexity of decisions that have to be made. One example of how the environment affects organizations is the recent increase in the minimum wage. Managers at Popeye's Chicken & Biscuits have estimated that paying the higher wage will decrease operating profits by 25 percent or more and are considering alternatives such as cutting jobs or raising prices to meet the new conditions. Or consider the effects from global competition. At Continental Airlines, new CEO Gordon M. Bethune decided to ground 41 planes, cut more than 4,200 jobs, and abolish cut-rate fares as part of his strategy to change the ailing airline into a profitable company again. Bethune and other top leaders had to analyze complex problems, evaluate alternatives, and make choices about how to pull Continental out of its slump without being certain what would work.[9] Leaders deal with uncertainty every day. This chapter's Leader's Bookshelf asserts that dealing with risk and uncertainty is one of the "natural laws" of leadership.

The 9 Natural Laws of Leadership
Warren Blank

Warren Blank contends that leadership is governed by natural laws. He applies principles of quantum physics to the contemporary business environment to arrive at nine laws that he believes hold true for all leaders. Using examples from real companies, this book explores what it means to be a leader, when and how leadership emerges, how leaders and followers influence one another, and how people can tap the unseen sources of leadership power. The book also includes practical action steps to help the reader develop leadership potential.

The Nine Natural Laws

To fully understand and gain mastery of the process of leadership, according to Blank, requires understanding nine fundamental laws.

1. **Leaders operate outside the boundaries of organizationally defined procedures.** Leadership is about change, not about maintaining the status quo. Leaders need courage to stir things up and keep things moving.

2. **Leadership involves risk and uncertainty.** Leaders live without a safety net. They accept that ambiguity and chaos are a natural part of the leadership territory.

3. **Leadership is a field of interaction.** Leadership is a relationship between leaders and followers. Leadership is not a person, a position, or a program but something that happens when a leader and followers connect.

4. **Leadership occurs as an event.** Leadership is not a continuous process. Leader-follower interactions happen as discrete occurrences, with each having a beginning, a middle, and an end. Thus, leadership occurs throughout organizations, with numerous leaders gaining followers in a variety of situations.

5. **Leaders use influence beyond formal authority.** Leadership influence does not extend from a person's position in the organizational hierarchy. Instead it is personal and arises from the interactions of a leader and followers.

6. **Not everyone will follow a leader's initiative.** All leaders face limits, and no leader will ever have everyone's support.

7. **Consciousness—the capacity to process information—creates leadership.** Leadership begins with an idea that might resolve a problem or exploit an opportunity. The ability to process information and create meaning from it is the underlying source of leadership power.

8. **Leadership is a self-referral process.** Leaders and followers process information from their own subjective, internal frame of reference. Leaders can expand their consciousness so that they operate from a more unified, enlightened state. If they are narrow-minded, their perception is limited and distorted.

9. **A leader has willing followers.** Voluntary followers are the underlying element that defines all leaders in all situations.

Developing Quantum Leadership

Blank calls his view of leadership based on natural laws "quantum leadership." To clarify his definition, he contrasts quantum leaders with classical managers. However, he emphasizes that managers can learn to be quantum leaders. Blank believes leadership development is primarily about expanding consciousness. Throughout the book, he offers action ideas to help the reader develop quantum leadership capacities, such as learning to deal with risk and uncertainty. The final chapter summarizes ideas and offers tips for initiating a plan for expanding consciousness and leadership potential.

The 9 Natural Laws of Leadership, by Warren Blank, is published by AMACOM, a division of American Management Association.

Leader Decisions

The rational approach to decision making stresses the need for systematic analysis of a problem followed by choice and implementation in a logical step-by-step sequence. When leaders are facing little difficulty and are dealing with well-understood issues, they generally use systematic procedures, market research, and computer-based data.[10] The rational decision process consists of the following steps.

Problem Identification	Problem Solution
Monitor the decision environment	Develop all alternative solutions
Define the decision problem	Evaluate each alternative
Specify decision objectives	Choose the best alternative
Diagnose the problem	Implement the chosen alternative

However, the ability of an individual leader to make the clearest, most rational decision is constrained by several factors. First, leaders have only so much mental capacity, that is, cognitive ability to process information, and this affects their ability to evaluate every goal, problem, and alternative.[11] In addition, decisions often must be made quickly. Time pressure, a large number of internal and external factors affecting a decision, and the nonprogrammed nature of many problems make systematic analysis virtually impossible. The attempt to be rational is limited by the enormous complexity of many problems in a rapidly changing environment. For example, Paula Cholmondeley, president of an Owens-Corning business unit, expedited a top-secret product initiative that required rapid, risky decisions. In order to have Miraflex fiber-glass on the shelves before competitors even knew of its development, she had to halve the development time and order production equipment after only a single trial.[12]

Big decisions are not only too complex to fully comprehend, but many other constraints impinge on the decision maker, as illustrated in Exhibit 16.2. The circumstances are ambiguous, requiring social support, a shared perspective on what happens, and acceptance and agreement. For example, a study of the decision making surrounding the Cuban missile crisis found that the executive committee in the White House knew a problem existed, but members were unable to specify exact goals and objectives. The act of discussing the decision led to personal objections and gradually to the discovery of desired objectives that helped clarify the desired course of action and possible consequences.[13]

Because the overwhelming number of factors limits rational decision making, intuition is often necessary for individual decisions. During **intuitive decision making,** experience and judgment rather than sequential logic or explicit reasoning are used to make decisions.[14] Intuition is not arbitrary or irrational; it is based on years of practice and hands-on experience, often stored in the subconscious mind. When leaders use their intuition based on long experience with organizational issues, they rapidly perceive and understand problems and develop a gut feeling or hunch about which alternative will solve a problem, speeding the decision making process.[15] Indeed, many universities are offering courses in creativity and intuition so business students can learn to understand and rely on these inner processes.

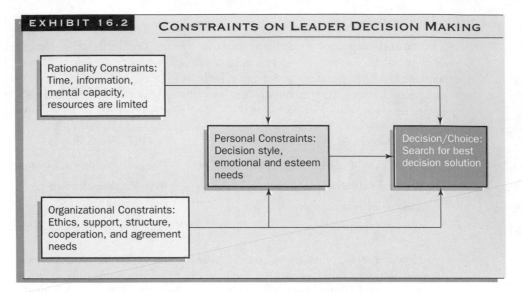

SOURCE: Adapted from Irving L. Janis, *Crucial Decisions* (New York: Free Press, 1989); and A. L. George, *Presidential Decision Making in Foreign Policy: The Effective Use of Information and Advice* (Boulder, CO: Westview Press, 1980).

In a situation of great complexity or ambiguity, previous experience and intuition incorporate intangible elements at both the problem identification and problem solution stage.[16] A study of manager problem finding showed that 30 out of 33 problems were ambiguous and ill defined.[17] Bits and scraps of unrelated information from informal sources resulted in a pattern in each leader's mind. The leaders could not "prove" which solution was best, but knew intuitively the right direction to take and trusted their instincts. Recall from *Star Wars* how Luke Skywalker shut off his targeting computer and trusted his intuition to know when to release the proton torpedo that destroyed the Death Star.

Examples in organizations of complex problems that might be resolved through informal, intuitive processes are the possibility of impending legislation against a company, the need for a new product, customer dissatisfaction, whether to start a new division, or a need to reorganize by creating new departments.[18] Given the constraints and complexity facing leaders, it is not surprising that in most organizations few leaders actually sit alone behind their desks and decide on alternatives to impose on the rest of the organization.

Organizational Decision Making

Organizations are composed of participants who make decisions using both rational and intuitive processes, but organization-level decisions are not usually made by a single leader. Many organizational decisions involve several people. Problem identification and problem solution involve many departments, multiple viewpoints,

EXHIBIT 16.3	RATIONAL VERSUS POLITICAL MODELS OF ORGANIZATION DECISION MAKING	

Organizational Characteristic	Rational Model	Political Model
Goals, preferences	Consistent across participants	Inconsistent, pluralistic
Power and control	Centralized	Decentralized, shifting coalitions and interest groups
Decision process	Orderly, logical, rational	Disorderly, characterized by push and pull of interests
Information	Extensive, systematic, accurate	Ambiguous, informal, limited
Beliefs about cause-effect relationships	Known, at least to a probability estimate	Disagreements about causes and effects
Decisions	Based on outcome-maximizing choice	Result of bargaining and discussion among coalition
Ideology	Efficiency, hierarchy of authority	Democracy

SOURCE: Based on Jeffrey Pfeffer, *Power in Organizations* (Marshfield, MA: Pitman, 1981), 31.

and even other organizations, which are beyond the scope of an individual leader. Research into organization-level decision making has identified a significant political process that engages leaders in both coalition building and the incremental decision approach.

Rational Choice versus Political Process

The rational choice model of organization is an outgrowth of the rational approach to decision making that individual leaders try to use when possible. The **rational choice model** suggests that leaders participate in an ideal sequence of decision steps undertaken in well-defined circumstances. Thus, behavior in a rational organization is not random or accidental, as illustrated in Exhibit 16.3. Goals are clear and choices are made in a logical way. When a decision is needed, the goal is defined, alternatives are identified, and the choice with the highest probability of achieving the desired outcome is selected. The rational model of organization is also characterized by extensive, reliable information systems, and emphasis upon efficiency, centralized power, and a norm of optimization. The uniformity of values assumed across groups leads to an absence of conflict in both problem identification and the selection of alternatives.[19]

The political model of organization is basically the opposite of pure rationality, as illustrated in Exhibit 16.3. The assumption is that uniformity and agreement do not exist. The **political model** assumes organizations are made up of leader coalitions that disagree about goals and have poor information about alternatives. The organization has groups with diverse interests, goals, and values. Disagreement and conflict are normal, so power and influence are needed to reach decisions. Groups engage in the push and pull of debate to decide goals and to reach decisions. Decisions are disorderly because information is ambiguous and incomplete. Bargaining and conflict are the norm because of the conflicting interests of the decision making coalitions.

The political model also applies to organizations that strive for democracy and participation by empowered workers. Purely rational procedures do not work in democratic organizations. In this sense, the political process refers to the relationships among leaders that constitutes the means by which decisions are reached and implemented. Whereas the rational choice model suggests an "ideal" decision making process, the political model closely resembles the real environment in which leaders and decision makers are operating. Consider the following example, in which leaders tried to make decisions rationally even though the situation demanded a political process.

LEADERSHIP SPOTLIGHT   **BRITT TECHNOLOGIES**

Britt Technologies was a new manufacturer of peripheral computer equipment, including tape and disk drives. The company's target was to sell equipment to manufacturers of complete computer systems. The strategy was working and the company was initially successful, but a problem surfaced.

The problem pertained to the extent to which products should be custom-designed for customers. A manufacturer might be interested in a tape or disk product, but only if it could be reengineered to change some operating characteristics. This reengineering was expensive and time consuming, and some managers felt it would be better to sell only what had already been designed. Indeed, almost every customer would ask for some modifications rather than accept the standard models.

The problem of custom design led to disagreement among leaders. The marketing vice president believed engineering and production should produce whatever the market demanded. The vice president of production disagreed, saying that efficiencies would never be achieved unless the company developed a standard production line. The controller agreed with the production vice president, because profit margins were reduced when redesigned units were produced. The engineering vice president was willing to redesign products so long as doing so did not result in engineering overload.

Rather than hammer out this problem among themselves, Britt's executives decided to retain an outside consultant. They believed an outside consultant would know how to rationally arrive at the correct answer, which each executive would accept. The consultant did some market research, competitive analysis, and strategic planning. A second consultant was hired to examine the manufacturing operations.

Unfortunately, the company was left in a state of drift while the consultants did their research for the perfect answer. Without a clear strategy, Britt Technologies was not excelling at either standard or custom-designed peripherals. Marketing would sometimes accept custom orders, but manufacturing would refuse to produce them. The consultants' reports arrived in due course and were very logical, but Britt executives still disagreed among themselves. A clear strategy was delayed. In this highly competitive industry, once the company fell behind the competition, bankruptcy was inevitable.[20]

Britt Technologies' leaders were searching for a logical, correct answer through an orderly decision process that used precise data. Executives tried to apply the rational model to a situation that required a political model. They needed to bargain, negotiate, use available information, talk to customers, and build a coalition among themselves. But they did not. The search for a rational answer was a futile, time-consuming process that caused the company's failure.

Coalition Building

Coalition building means that leaders actively build agreement for their complex decisions. A **coalition** is an alliance among several managers who agree about organizational goals and problem priorities.[21] It could include people from the line departments, staff specialists, and even external groups, such as powerful customers, bankers, or union representatives. The basis of this approach to organizational decision making comes from the work of Richard Cyert, James March, and Herbert Simon, who were all associated with Carnegie-Mellon University.[22] Their research provided new insights about organization decisions. Until their work, research in economics assumed that business firms made decisions as a single entity, as if all relevant information were funneled to the top decision maker for a choice. Research by the Carnegie group indicated that organization-level decisions involved many leaders and that a final choice was based on a coalition among those individuals.

Coalitions are needed during decision making for two reasons. First, organizational mission and goals are often ambiguous, and operative goals of departments are often inconsistent. When desired outcomes are unclear or inconsistent, organizational members disagree about problem identification and priorities. They must discuss problems and build a coalition around the question of which problem to solve. For example, months of discussion, bargaining, and planning took place before Chrysler decided not to abandon small-car production and began working on the Neon.[23]

The second reason for coalitions is that leaders intend to be rational but function with human limitations and other constraints, as described earlier. Individual leaders do not have the time, resources, or mental capacity to identify all dimensions and to process all information relevant to a decision. These limitations encourage coalition-building behavior. Participants exchange points of view to acquire information and reduce ambiguity. People who have relevant information or a stake in a decision outcome are consulted. Building a coalition will lead to a decision that is supported by interested stakeholders.

The process of building coalitions has several implications for organizational decision behavior. First, decisions are made to achieve a "satisfactory" rather than a so-called perfect level of performance, enabling leaders to integrate diverse people

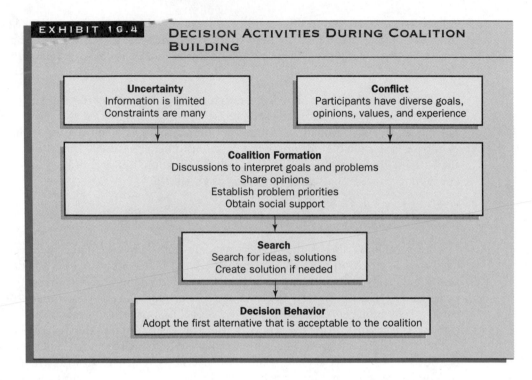

EXHIBIT 16.4 — DECISION ACTIVITIES DURING COALITION BUILDING

Uncertainty
Information is limited
Constraints are many

Conflict
Participants have diverse goals,
opinions, values, and experience

Coalition Formation
Discussions to interpret goals and problems
Share opinions
Establish problem priorities
Obtain social support

Search
Search for ideas, solutions
Create solution if needed

Decision Behavior
Adopt the first alternative that is acceptable to the coalition

and goals simultaneously. During decision making, the coalition will accept a solution that is perceived as satisfactory to all coalition members. Second, most people are concerned with immediate problems and short-term solutions. Leaders search in the immediate environment for a solution to quickly resolve a problem.[24] Leaders do not expect a perfect solution when the situation is ill defined and conflict laden. This contrasts with the rational-choice model, which assumes that analysis can uncover every reasonable alternative. The coalition approach says that people build agreement about a problem and a satisfactory solution. They want to keep things moving forward rather than suffer analysis paralysis. Third, discussion among stakeholders is especially important in the problem identification stage of decision making. Unless coalition members jointly perceive a problem, action will not be taken. The decision approach described in the coalition model is summarized in Exhibit 16.4.

Building agreement through a coalition is a major part of decision making. Discussion and coalition building are time-consuming, so the selected alternative typically satisfies rather than maximizes problem solution. If problems are programmed—are clear and have been seen before—leaders can rely on previous decisions and routines. Nonprogrammed decisions, however, typically require coalition building.

One of the best and most visible coalition builders of recent years was former President George Bush, who would seek a broad-based coalition at the start of an important decision process. During the decision process for the Persian Gulf War, President Bush kept up a barrage of personal calls and visits to world leaders to gain agreement for his vision of forcing Saddam Hussein from Kuwait and for shaping a "New World order."[25]

Incremental Decisions

Henry Mintzberg and his associates at McGill University in Montreal approached organizational decision making from a different perspective. They identified 25 decisions made in organizations and traced the events associated with these decisions from beginning to end.[26] Their research identified each step in the decision sequence. This approach to decision making, called the **incremental decision model,** places less emphasis on the political and social factors of coalition building, but tells more about the trial and error undertaken from the discovery of a problem to its solution.[27] While problem solution may be comprised of numerous small decisions, the decisions are connected steps that influence subsequent understanding and behavior of participants.[28]

Sample leader decisions in Mintzberg's research included choosing which jet aircraft to acquire for a regional airline, developing a new supper club, developing a new container terminal in a harbor, identifying a new market for a deodorant, installing a controversial new medical treatment in a hospital, and firing a star radio announcer.[29] The scope and importance of these decisions are revealed in the length of time taken to complete them. Most of these decisions took more than a year, and one-third of them took more than two years to implement. These decisions were nonprogrammed.

One discovery from this research is that major organizational choices are usually a series of small choices that combine to produce the major decision. Thus, many nonprogrammed organizational decisions are a series of nibbles rather than a big bite. Organizations move through several decision points and may hit barriers along the way. An interruption may mean leaders have to cycle back through a previous decision and try something new. Decision loops or cycles—trial and error—are how leaders learn which alternative will work. The ultimate solution may be very different from what was initially decided.

A second discovery is that many solutions are custom designed. This happens when the problem is novel (nonprogrammed) so that previous experience has no value. Mintzberg found that in these cases, key decision makers have only a vague idea of the ideal solution. Gradually, through a trial and error process, a custom-designed alternative emerges. Development of the solution is a groping, incremental procedure, building a solution brick by brick.

Nonprogrammed decision making is a dynamic trial and error process that may require a number of cycles before a problem is solved or an opportunity is fully taken. An example of incremental process and cycling that can take place is illustrated in Gillette's decision to create a new razor.

LEADERSHIP SPOTLIGHT   **GILLETTE**

A bright idea developed at Gillette Company's British research facility finally became the Sensor razor—13 years later. The bright idea was to create a thinner razor that would make Gillette cartridges easier to clean. The technical development cost for the idea ran $200 million.

The technical demands of building a razor with thin blades and floating parts to follow a man's face had several blind alleys. Engineers first tried to find established techniques, but none fit the bill. One idea called for the blades to sit on tiny rubber tubes, perhaps filled with fluid, but that was too costly and complicated to manufacture so it was back to the drawing board. Eventually, a prototype was built, and 500 men liked it. The next problem was manufacturing, which again required an entirely new process to laser weld each blade to a support.

Top management gave the go ahead to develop manufacturing equipment. Then a conflict arose between two groups of executives. One group wanted to orient the product toward an inexpensive disposable razor, whereas the other group fought for a heavier, more permanent razor. Then Gillette was threatened by an outside takeover, reducing the resources allocated to the project. A new executive vice president made the choice to deemphasize disposables.

The razor has been a smashing success, sliding off shelves, and Gillette recovered its huge investment in record time. Now Gillette is starting the process over again, experimenting with a curved blade and perhaps a new, ceramic blade.[30]

At Gillette, the decision process began because executives were aware of the need for a new razor and became aware of the idea for floating, thin blades. Leaders proceeded with a trial-and-error custom design. Some alternatives were found unacceptable, so Gillette recycled back to earlier steps until a workable product was created.

Combination of Coalition Building and Incremental Approaches

At the beginning of this chapter, decision making was defined as occurring in two stages: problem identification and problem solution. The coalition building approach is especially relevant for the problem identification stage. When issues are ambiguous, or if participants disagree about problem severity, then coalition building is needed. Once agreement is reached among relevant parties about the problem to be tackled, the organization can move toward a solution.

The incremental approach tends to emphasize the steps to achieve problem solution. After participants agree on a problem, the step-by-step process is a way of trying various solutions to see what will work. When problem solution is unclear, a trial-and-error approach may be needed.

The two approaches do not disagree with one another. They describe how organizations make decisions when either problem identification or problem solution is uncertain. The application of these two models to the stages in the decision process is illustrated in Exhibit 16.5. Leaders can facilitate either or both approaches, as needed. When both parts of the decision process are nonprogrammed, the organization is in an extremely difficult position. Decisions may require a combination of coalition building and incremental trial and error. Since important decisions typically are ill-defined, leaders can expect to spend time building coalitions and selecting new choices as things move forward via trial and error.

Decision Mistakes

Leader decisions produce many errors, especially when they are made under high uncertainty. In the course of leading change or creating a learning organization, lead-

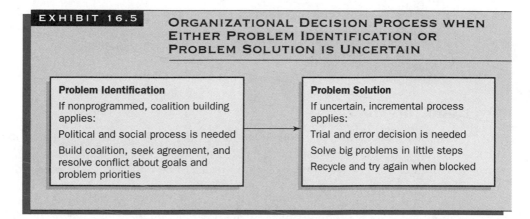

EXHIBIT 16.5

ORGANIZATIONAL DECISION PROCESS WHEN EITHER PROBLEM IDENTIFICATION OR PROBLEM SOLUTION IS UNCERTAIN

Problem Identification

If nonprogrammed, coalition building applies:

Political and social process is needed

Build coalition, seek agreement, and resolve conflict about goals and problem priorities

Problem Solution

If uncertain, incremental process applies:

Trial and error decision is needed

Solve big problems in little steps

Recycle and try again when blocked

ers cannot always determine or predict which alternative will solve a problem. In these cases, the leader or coalition must make the decision—and take the risk— often in the spirit of trial and error. If a choice fails, the organization can learn from it and try another alternative that better fits the situation. Each failure provides new information and learning. The point is for leaders to move ahead with the decision process despite the potential for mistakes. "Chaotic action is preferable to orderly inaction."[31] Especially when leaders want to create a true learning organization, they cannot shrink from the possibility of decision mistakes.

In some cases, leaders are encouraged to instill a climate of experimentation, even foolishness, to facilitate creative decision making. If one idea fails, another idea can be tried. Failure often lays the groundwork for success, as when technicians at 3M developed Post-it Notes based on a failed product—a not-very-sticky glue. Companies such as Pepsi-Cola believe that if all their new products succeed, they're doing something wrong, not taking the necessary risks to develop new markets.[32]

Only by making mistakes can leaders and organizations go through the process of decision learning and acquire sufficient experience and knowledge to perform more effectively in the future. Norm Brodsky's archive retrieval company, Citi-Storage, made no less than four major improvements as a result of choices that lost a huge customer account. The loss of the unhappy customer provoked CitiStorage to examine its remaining accounts a full 18 months before contract expiration, allow-ing Brodsky's staff plenty of time to fix any discovered problems. In addition to resulting in better business practice, the mistakes confirmed for Brodsky that the fault did not lie with his sales force, but within the company as a whole, for which he took responsibility. Thus, his response focused on learning from mistakes instead of laying blame.[33]

Consider the advice of Robert Townsend, who was president of Avis Corpora-tion and a champion of using decision mistakes to learn.

Admit your mistakes openly, maybe even joyfully. Encourage your associ-ates to do likewise by commiserating with them.

Never castigate. Babies learn to walk by falling down. If you beat a baby every time he falls down, he'll never care much for walking.

> My batting average on decisions at Avis was no better than .333. Two out of every three decisions I made were wrong. But my mistakes were discussed openly and most of them corrected with a little help from my friends.[34]

Power and Influence

The identification of a decision situation and the development of solution alternatives comprise decision making. However, decisions must be implemented, that is, transformed from a plan into a result, in order to be valuable.[35] The execution of a decision often requires power.

Power is an intangible force in organizations. It cannot be seen, but its effect can be felt. Power is often defined as the potential ability of one person (or department) to influence other persons (or departments) to carry out orders[36] or to do something they otherwise would not have done.[37] Other definitions stress that power is the ability to achieve goals or outcomes that power holders desire.[38] The achievement of desired outcomes is the basis of the definition used here. **Power** is the ability of one person or department in an organization to influence other people to bring about desired outcomes. It is the potential to influence others within the organization with the goal of attaining desired outcomes for power holders. Potential power is realized through the processes of politics and influence.[39] Power is essential for leaders to implement decisions or lead change.

In 1985, Steve Jobs, one of the co-founders of Apple Computer, found himself unable to achieve a desired outcome when he tried to oust then-CEO John Sculley from the computer company. Sculley was supported by the board of directors and senior management, so Sculley, not Jobs, effectively had power.[40] Shortly after, Jobs was forced from the company. In an interesting turnaround, in 1997 Jobs returned to save the faltering computer maker and once again runs Apple as "interim CEO," and this time with the power to decide who will help him run the company.

Five Types of Leader Power

Power is often described as a personal characteristic, but as described above, organizational position also influences a leader's power. Most discussions of power include five types that are available to leaders.[41]

Legitimate Power   **Legitimate power** is the authority granted from a formal position in an organization. For example, once a person has been selected as a supervisor, most workers understand that they are obligated to follow his or her direction with respect to work activities. Subordinates accept this source of power as legitimate, which is why they comply. Certain rights, responsibilities, and prerogatives accrue to anyone holding a formal leadership position. Followers accept the legitimate rights of formal leaders to set goals, make decisions, and direct activities. Most North Americans accept the legitimate right of appointed leaders to direct an organization.

Reward Power This kind of power stems from the authority to bestow rewards on other people. For example, appointed leaders may have access to formal rewards, such as pay increases or promotions. Moreover, organizations allocate huge amounts of resources downward from top leaders. Leaders control resources and their distribution. Lower-level followers depend on leaders for the financial and physical resources to perform their tasks. Leaders with **reward power** can use rewards to influence subordinates' behavior.

Coercive Power The opposite of reward power is **coercive power.** It refers to the power to punish or recommend punishment. Supervisors have coercive power when they have the right to fire or demote subordinates, criticize, or withdraw pay increases. For example, if Paul, a salesman, does not perform as well as expected, his supervisor has the coercive power to criticize him, reprimand him, put a negative letter in his file, and hurt his chance for a raise. Coercive power is the negative side of legitimate and reward power.

Expert Power Power resulting from a leader's special knowledge or skill regarding tasks performed by followers is referred to as **expert power.** When a leader is a true expert, subordinates go along with recommendations because of his or her superior knowledge. Leaders at supervisory levels often have experience in the production process that gains them promotion. At top management levels, however, leaders may lack expert power because subordinates know more about technical details than they do. Experts may use their knowledge to influence or place limits on decisions made by people above them in the organization.[42] Furthermore, specialized information may be withheld or divulged in ways designed to achieve particular outcomes desired by the leaders.[43]

Referent Power This kind of power comes from leader personality characteristics that command followers' identification, respect, and admiration so they wish to emulate the leader. When workers admire a supervisor because of the way she deals with them, the influence is based on referent power. **Referent power** depends on the leader's personal characteristics rather than on a formal title or position and is visible in the area of charismatic leadership as described in Chapter 12. The Living Leadership box talks about the far-reaching impact of referent power.

Other Sources of Leader Power

Legitimate power, reward power, and coercive power are derived from the leader's formal position in an organization. Expert power and referent power are derived from a leader's personal qualities. These five sources provide the basis for implementing many decisions and change projects. In organizations, however, additional sources of power and influence have been identified. The strategic contingencies theory identifies power sources not linked to the specific person or position, but to

---

LIVING LEADERSHIP

The Ripple Effect

Do you want to be a positive influence in the world? First, get your own life in order. Ground yourself in the single principle so that your behavior is wholesome and effective. If you do that, you will earn respect and be a powerful influence.

Your behavior influences others through a ripple effect. A ripple effect works because everyone influences everyone else. Powerful people are powerful influences.

If your life works, you influence your family.

If your family works, your family influences the community.

If your community works, your community influences the nation.

If your nation works, your nation influences the world.

If your world works, the ripple effect spreads throughout the cosmos.

SOURCE: John Heider, *The Tao of Leadership: Leadership Strategies for a New Age* (New York: Bantam Books, 1985), 107. © 1985 Humanic Ltd., Atlanta, GA. Used with permission.

---

the role a leader or group plays in the overall functioning of the organization. Three sources of power in this regard are dependency, centrality, and coping with uncertainty.

Organizational Dependency Many horizontal dependencies exist in organizations. Interdepartmental dependency is a key element underlying leader power. The power of department A over department B depends on the flow of resources between the two.[44] For example, materials, information, and resources may flow between departments in one direction. In such cases, the department receiving resources is in a lower power position than the department providing them.

In a cigarette factory, one might expect that the production department would be more powerful than the maintenance department, but this was not the case in a cigarette plant near Paris.[45] The production of cigarettes was a routine process. The machinery was automated. On the other hand, maintenance department workers and their leaders were responsible for repair of the automated machinery, which was a complex task, and they had many years of experience. Because maintenance workers and leaders had the ability to fix unpredictable assembly line breakdowns, production managers became dependent on maintenance, and maintenance leaders called the shots about machine repair and assembly line maintenance.

Organizational Centrality Centrality reflects a department's role in the primary activity of an organization.[46] One measure of centrality is the extent to which the work of the leader's department affects the final output of the organization. For example, production and marketing departments are more central and usually have more power than staff groups. Centrality is associated with more power because it reflects the contribution made to the organization. At the University of Illinois, for example, important resources come from research grants and the quality of students and faculty. Departments that provide the most resources to the university are rated as having the most power. Also, departments that generate large research grants are more powerful because the grants contain a sizable overhead payment to university administration.[47]

Coping with Uncertainty   We discussed earlier how the environment can change swiftly and create uncertainty and complexity for leaders. In the face of uncertainty, little information is available to leaders on appropriate courses of action. Departments that cope well with this uncertainty will increase their power.[48] When market research personnel accurately predict changes in demand for new products, they gain power and prestige because they have reduced a critical uncertainty. Consider the following example of Crystal Manufacturing Corporation.

LEADERSHIP SPOTLIGHT   **CRYSTAL MANUFACTURING**

A lthough union influence has been declining in recent years, unions are still seeking to extend their membership to new organizations. A new union is a crucial source of uncertainty for many manufacturing firms. It can be a countervailing power to management in decisions concerning wages and working conditions.

In 1990, the workers in Crystal Manufacturing Corporation voted to become part of the Glassmakers Craft Union. Management had been aware of union organizing activities, but it had not taken the threat seriously. No one had acted to forecast or prevent the formation of a union.

The presence of the union had potentially serious consequences for Crystal. Glassmaking is a delicate and expensive manufacturing process. The float-glass process cannot be shut down even temporarily except at great expense. A strike or walk-out would mean financial disaster. Therefore, leaders decided that establishing a good working relationship with the union was critically important.

The industrial relations department learned to deal with the union. This department was responsible for coping with the uncertainties created by the new union. Its leader helped the industrial relations group quickly develop expertise in union relationships. It became the contact point on industrial relations matters for managers throughout the organization. The industrial relations leader developed a network throughout the organization and could bypass the normal chain of command on issues she considered important. Industrial relations had nearly absolute knowledge and control over union relations.[49]

At Crystal Manufacturing Corporation, the industrial relations leader coped with a critical uncertainty. She was also more central to the company's mission, and other managers depended on her. She took action to reduce uncertainty after it appeared. This action gave both her and the industrial relations department increased power.

Asserting Influence

When leaders are in a position of power, the challenge is to use it to implement decisions, facilitate change, and pursue the shared vision. The use of power to influence others requires both skill and willingness. Much influence is interpersonal and one-on-one. This is social influence, which involves coalitions, rewards, and inspiration. Other influence has broader appeal, such as to influence the organization as a whole, or to influence those outside the organization. Sometimes leaders decide to join together to influence the broader society on important issues. The Cutting Edge box describes how a coalition of leaders is changing the way individuals, communities, and businesses think about society's interaction with the natural environment.

Politics involves activities to acquire, develop, and use power and other resources to obtain desired future outcomes when there is uncertainty or disagreement about choices.[50] Engaging in politics can be either a positive or negative force, depending on what a leader wants to accomplish. In a world of increasing change and complex decisions, most leaders find it essential to use politics to enable participants to arrive at consensus and make decisions that otherwise might be stalemated or unsolvable. Generally speaking, leaders can call upon various political tactics to get things done in an organization.

1. *Build coalitions.* Coalition building means taking the time to talk with followers and other leaders to explain problems and describe their point of view.[51] Most important decisions are made outside of formal meetings. Leaders consult with one another and reach a meeting of minds about a proposed change, decision, or strategy. Effective leaders are those who huddle with others, being willing to meet in groups of twos or threes to resolve key issues.[52] An important aspect of coalition building is to build positive social relationships. Social relationships are built on liking, trust, and respect. Reliability, trustworthiness, and the motivation to work with others to achieve desired future outcomes are the desired use of politics.[53]

2. *Expand networks.* A leader's network of contacts can be expanded by reaching out to establish contact with additional people and by co-opting dissenters. The first approach is to build new alliances through the hiring, transfer, and promotion process. Identifying people, or placing in key positions people who are sympathetic to the desired outcomes of the leader can help achieve the leader's vision.[54] The second approach, *co-optation*, is the act of bringing a dissenter into one's network or coalition. Dissenters can be influenced if they are brought into the group. One example of co-optation occurred at a university. Several female professors were critical of the tenure and promotion process. They were appointed to a university committee to review promotion and tenure procedures. Once a part of the administrative process, they could see the administrative point of view and learned that administrators were not as evil as suspected. They were able to work with administration to create procedures that satisfied the interests of everyone.[55]

ON THE CUTTING EDGE

The Natural Step

The Natural Step is a large-scale social and environmental movement based on a concept as simple as a circle: our environment is sustainable when what is taken out of the system for food, shelter, clothing, energy and other human uses is restored to the system in waste that can be reused. This is not, however, the way current societies operate. For the past 100 years or so, human beings have been converting resources to waste faster than nature can cope. A growing number of leaders throughout the world are trying to change that.

The Natural Step is an environmental organization that uses coalition building and four scientifically-based systems conditions to help guide communities, government agencies, academic institutions, and individuals toward sustainability. The movement, which now has national organizations in Sweden, Australia, the United States, Canada, Japan, and the United Kingdom, began when Karl-Henrik Robèrt, one of Sweden's leading cancer researchers, became concerned that people seemed to handle the problem of maintaining the environment by fighting instead of cooperating. He felt that there must be some way to reach consensus on how to change. Robèrt developed a draft list of scientific principles by which human beings could stop destroying the natural habitat. Setting a standard for cooperation, he sent the draft—21 times—to Swedish physicists, biologists, ecologists, economists, and cancer researchers, as well as to some doctors in the United States, inviting their comments, until the group had reached agreement on environmental principles consistent with science.

The Natural Step bases its work on a 4-system guide to thinking and acting in harmony with the earth's cyclical processes:

1. *Nature cannot withstand a systematic buildup of dispersed matter mined from the earth's crust.* This means that fossil fuels, metals, and other minerals must not be extracted at a rate faster than their slow redeposit back into the earth's crust.
2. *Nature cannot withstand a systematic buildup of substances produced by humans.* That is, substances must not be produced at a rate faster than they can be broken down in nature.
3. *Nature cannot withstand a systematic deterioration of its capacity for renewal.* This means we cannot harvest or manipulate ecosystems in such a way as to diminish their productive capacity or threaten the natural diversity of life forms.
4. *Therefore, if we want life to go on, there must be fair and efficient use of resources.* This means that basic human needs must be met with the most resource-efficient methods possible, including a just resource distribution.

More than 60 major corporations around the world, including Electrolux, IKEA, Scandic Hotels, McDonald's, Collins Pine, and Interface, Inc., are using The Natural Step principles as a part of their environmental programs. The Natural Step presents undisputed information in nonthreatening ways and invites listeners to open a dialogue in order to explore the issue of sustainability. As founder Karl-Henrik Robèrt describes the process: "First we educate business leaders, politicians, and scientists in the Four System Conditions, and then we ask them for advice. Instead of telling them what to do, we say, 'How could this be applied in your world?' This sparks creativity and enthusiasm into the process instead of defense mechanisms."

SOURCE: Based on "The Natural Step to Sustainability," *Wingspread Journal*, the quarterly publication of The Johnson Foundation, Inc., Spring 1997; Karl-Henrik Robèrt, *The Natural Step: A Framework for Achieving Sustainability in Our Organizations*, (Cambridge, MA: Pegasus Communications, Inc., 1997); and Ola Ivarsson, "The 'Environmental Dialogue' at Scandic Hotels—A Lot More than Just Talk," *At Work*, November–December 1997, 14-15. With thanks to The Natural Step U.S.A., San Francisco, California.

3. *Use Legitimacy and Expertise.* Leaders often exert the greatest influence in the areas in which they have recognized legitimacy and expertise. If a leader initiates a change that is within the task domain of a department, other departments will tend to comply. Leaders can also identify external consultants or other experts to support their cause.[56] Leaders use logical arguments and factual evidence to persuade others that a proposal is viable and can produce the desired outcomes.[57]

4. *Use Information and Analysis.* Information, and its ability to reduce uncertainty, is a source of influence. While it is true, as management guru Peter Drucker once said, that anyone over the age of 21 can find facts to support his or her argument, people do have faith in facts and analysis.[58] Although the world is often too chaotic and uncertain to make rational decisions, most people still desire the appearance of rationality. Thus, it is often important to gather facts and figures and do underlying rational analysis to enable broad support of a proposed course of action. For example, a financial vice president in a large retail firm wanted to fire the director of Human Resource Management. She hired a consultant to evaluate Human Resource Management projects undertaken by the director. A negative report from the consultant provided performance facts and figures compared to other retail firms. This was sufficient evidence to convince others that a new Human Resource Director was needed.

5. *Use Symbolic Action.* Influencing the underlying culture and values was described in Chapter 7. Leaders can use symbols, stories, heroes, slogans, and ceremonies to persuade others of the high purpose to be achieved with the desired course of action. "People are persuaded by reason, but moved by emotion."[59] It is a leader's job to help people want to do what they need or have to do to help the organization prosper, and symbolic leadership is a subtle yet effective way to help people do the right thing.[60] Symbols, ceremonies, heroes, and the like touch the heart rather than the mind. Symbolic action combined with other, more logical appeals can influence both the minds and emotions of followers.

6. *Use Assertiveness.* Leaders can have influence simply by being clear about what they want and asking for it. If leaders do not ask, they seldom receive. Political activity is effective only when the leader's vision, goals, and desired changes are made explicit so the organization can respond. Leaders can use their courage to be assertive, saying what they believe to persuade others. An explicit proposal may be accepted simply because other people have no better alternatives. Also, an explicit proposal for change or for a specific decision alternative will often receive favorable treatment when other options are less well defined. Effective political behavior requires sufficient forcefulness and risk-taking to at least try to achieve desired outcomes.[61]

Summary and Interpretation

Leaders achieve their desired future through decision making, power, and influence. Today's world is ambiguous and uncertain, with the environment changing at high velocity. Most decisions are nonprogrammed. When leaders make individual decisions, they often use intuition and experience. Decision making about large problems typically involves coalition building about the problem and potential solutions, and trial and error increments to ensure that the solution works. Nonprogrammed decision making is not a simple, rational process, but involves numerous increments, interruptions, dynamic factors, and cycles.

The implementation of desired choices requires power and influence. Power is the ability to influence others to reach desired outcomes. The best known sources of power are legitimate, reward, expert, referent, and coercive, which are associated with a leader's position and personal qualities. Contributing to the organization's purpose via dependency, centrality, and coping with uncertainty are also potential sources of power for leaders. Power can be exercised through political tactics such as building coalitions, expanding networks, legitimacy and expertise, information and analysis, symbolic action, and making preferences explicit. Leadership action depends on forming effective social relationships and achieving the desired future through agreements and cooperation in today's extraordinarily complex world.

Key Terms

decision making	coalition	expert power
programmed decisions	incremental decision model	referent power
nonprogrammed decisions	power	centrality
intuitive decision making	legitimate power	politics
rational choice model	reward power	
political model	coercive power	

Discussion Questions

1. Why is intuition used in leader decision making? Explain.

2. A professor once told her management class, "An individual decision maker should process all relevant information and select the economically efficient alternative." Do you agree? Why or why not?

3. Distinguish between the rational choice and political models of decision making. Which would you prefer to use as a leader? Why?

4. Which of the five political tactics would you be most comfortable with as leader of a study group? Of a work team?

5. For a decision to develop a new product for a large computer manufacturer, do you think coalition building or an incremental decision process would be more important? Why?

6. Would you tend to use a rational model or a political model for each of the following decisions: quality-control testing in a production department, budget allocation among major divisions, and deciding which division will be in charge of a recently-acquired plant? Why?

7. Why is decision making considered a fundamental part of being a leader?

8. Analyze three decisions you made over the past six months. Which were programmed and which were nonprogrammed? Did you use a different approach for the two types of decisions?

Leadership Development: Personal Feedback

Personal Power Profile

Below is a list of statements that describe behaviors that leaders in work organizations can direct toward their followers. Read each descriptive statement, thinking in terms of how you prefer to influence others. Mark the number that most closely represents how you feel. Use the following numbers for your answers.

1 = Strongly disagree

2 = Disagree

3 = Neither agree nor disagree

4 = Agree

5 = Strongly agree

To influence others, I would prefer to:

1. Increase their pay level
   1   2   3   4   5

2. Make them feel valued
   1   2   3   4   5

3. Give undesirable job assignments
   1   2   3   4   5

4. Make them feel like I approve of them
   1   2   3   4   5

5. Make them feel that they have commitments to meet
   1   2   3   4   5

6. Make them feel personally accepted
   1   2   3   4   5

7. Make them feel important
   1   2   3   4   5

8. Give them good technical suggestions
   1   2   3   4   5

9. Make the work difficult for them
   1   2   3   4   5

10. Share my experience and/or training
    1   2   3   4   5

11. Influence a pay increase
    1   2   3   4   5

12. Make working here unpleasant
    1   2   3   4   5

13. Make being at work distasteful
    1   2   3   4   5

14. Make them feel like they should satisfy their job requirements
    1   2   3   4   5

15. Provide them with sound job-related advice
    1   2   3   4   5

16. Provide them with special benefits
    1   2   3   4   5

17. Influence promotions
    1   2   3   4   5

18. Give them the feeling that they have responsibilities to fulfill
    1   2   3   4   5

19. Provide them with needed technical knowledge
    1   2   3   4   5

20. Make them recognize that they have tasks to accomplish
    1   2   3   4   5

Scoring:

Compute your scores from the 20 questions according to the following procedure: Reward power—sum your responses to items 1, 13, 16, and 17. Coercive power—sum your responses to items 3, 9, 11, and 12. Legitimate power—sum your responses to questions 5, 14, 18, and 20. Referent power—sum your responses to questions 2, 4, 6, and 7. Expert power—sum your responses to questions 8, 10, 15, and 19.

Scores: Reward = _____ Coercive = _____ Legitimate = _____ Referent = _____ Expert = _____

Interpretation:

A high score (16 and greater) on any of the five dimensions of power implies that you prefer to influence others by employing that particular form of power. A low score (8 and less) implies that you prefer not to employ this particular form of power to influence others. These scores represent your power profile.

SOURCE: Modified version of T.R. Hinkin and C.A. Schriesheim, "Development and Application of New Scales to Measure the French and Raven Bases of Social Power," *Journal of Applied Psychology* 74 (1989), 561–567, copyright © 1989 by the American Psychological Association, as appeared in Jon L. Pierce and John W. Newstrom, *Leaders and the Leadership Process: Readings, Self-Assessments, and Applications* (Chicago: Richard D. Irwin, 1995), 25–26.

Leadership Development: Case for Analysis

The Unhealthy Hospital

When Bruce Reid was hired as Blake Memorial Hospital's new CEO, the mandate had been clear: Improve the quality of care, and set the financial house in order.

As Reid struggled to finalize his budget for approval at next week's board meeting, his attention kept returning to one issue—the future of six off-site clinics. The clinics had been set up six years earlier to provide primary health care to the community's poorer neighborhoods. Although they provided a valuable service, they also diverted funds away from Blake's in-house services, many of which were underfunded. Cutting hospital personnel and freezing salaries could affect Blake's quality of care, which was already slipping. Eliminating the clinics, on the other hand, would save $256,000 without compromising Blake's internal operations.

However, there would be political consequences. Clara Bryant, the recently appointed commissioner of health services, repeatedly insisted that the clinics were an essential service for the poor. Closing the clinics could also jeopardize Blake's access to city funds. Dr. Winston Lee, chief of surgery, argued forcefully for closing the off-site clinics and having shuttle buses bring patients to the hospital weekly. Dr. Susan Russell, the hospital's director of clinics, was equally vocal about Blake's responsibility to the community, and suggested an entirely new way of delivering health care: "A hospital is not a building," she said, "it's a service. And wherever the service is needed, that is where the hospital should be." In Blake's case, that meant funding *more* clinics. Russell wanted to create a network of neighborhood-based centers for all the surrounding neighborhoods, poor and middle income. Besides improving health care, the network would act as an inpatient referral system for hospital services. Reid considered the proposal: If a clinic network could tap the paying public and generate more inpatient busi-

Abraham, David, 181
Adamson, James B., 319, 320
Alban, Billie T., 446
Albanese, R., 66
Alberthal, Les, 18–19
Alexander the Great, 157
Alfonso, Michael, 356–358
Alsop, Stewart, 127
Amerman, John, 169
Amin, Idi, 338
Anderson, Julie, 284
Andre, Rae, 325
Armstrong, David, 168
Arnold, Bill, 169
Ash, Mary Kay, 410
Auerbacher, Red, 399
Avolio, Bruce J., 307, 367

Baker, Kent, 160
aker, Nancy Croft, 379
ke, Dennis W., 259
dale, Jim, 167
n, Vic, 111–112
, Robert, 245
rnard M., 66, 103, 307, 341
Walter, 324
L., 321
ren, 271
rid, 455–456
lon M., 34, 459
icia Ward, 271
A., 240

99, 104,

Boyle, Gertrude, 40
Boyle, Richard, 284
Bradley, Betty, 248
Breland, Reed, 287
Brennan, Ed, 343–344
Brenneman, Gregory, 34
Brodsky, Norm, 161, 469
Bryant, Clara, 480
Brynes, Mary Ann, 3, 4, 17
Buckman, Bob, 219
Budner, Stanley, 27
Bugai, Robert A., 384
Bunker, Barbara Benedict, 446
Burns, Tom, 215
Burns, Tony, 165, 377–378
Busch, August, III, 425
Bush, George, 466
Busquet, Anne, 386

Calloway, Wayne, 194
Campbell, Jeff, 431
Campbell, Joseph, 351
Caotang, 164
Carlzon, Jan, 349
Carmody, Aaron, 357
Cassinelli, Ricardo Belmont, 19
Castle, Ted, 168
Chapman, Tim, 407
Chenail, Richard N., 310
Cheng, Mei-Lin, 284
Childress, Rusty, 159
Chislett, David, 402
Cholmondeley, Paula, 461
Churchill, Winston, 46, 337, 364, 456
Claizergues, Laurent, 310
Clark, Marsha, 20
Cleary, Thomas, 164, 319
Clinton, Bill, 4
Coker, Pamela, 331–332
Collins, James C., 133, 134
Colvin, Geoffrey, 429
Conger, Jay A., 337
Covey, Stephen R., 351, 404–405
Cox, Craig, 381
Cruikshank, Jeffrey L., 70
Curtiz, Michael, 456
Cyert, Richard, 465

Daft, Richard L., 48, 293
Dailey, Phillip, 216
Damphousse, Michael, 169
Danereau, Fred, 79
Davis, Jeff, 7
De Backer, Philippe, 105
de Geus, Arie, 241
de Mestral, George, 439
De Michele, Mark, 8
De Pree, Max, 42, 199
Deal, Terrence E., 225, 227
Deavenport, Ernest W., Jr., 273
Deitzer, Bernard A., 263
Deming, Edwards, 190
Den Hartog, Deanne N., 194
Deng Ming-Dao, 67
Denison, Daniel R., 194
DePree, Max, 375
Diller, Barry, 381–382
Disney, Walt, 129–130, 386
Doremus, Eric, 275
Drucker, Peter, 332, 476
Du Bois, W.E.B., 312
Dumaine, Brian, 39
Dunn, Keith, 107
Dunnigan, James, 157

Eckstein, Wendy, 230–231
Edmark, Tomima, 214–215
Elder, Irma, 43–44
Enrico, Roger, 23, 382

Faerman, Sue R., 257
Farkas, Charles M., 105
Farley, Ray, 256
Feuerstein, Aaron, 376
Feynman, Richard, 340
Fielder, Fred E., 94, 95–96, 97, 114
Fife, William J., Jr., 98
Fischer, George, 377
Fish, Lawrence, 382–383
Fishbein, Leslie, 158
Fisher, George, 198
Fisher, Jim, 324–325
Fleming, Stephen, 71
Fletcher, Philip B., 138
Follett, Mary Parker, 374
Ford, Henry, 367, 386

ness, it might be worth looking into. Blake's rival hospital, located on the affluent side of town, certainly wasn't doing anything that creative.

Questions

1. If you were Reid, would you choose to close or to maintain the clinics in the short run? Why?

2. What decision process would you use to resolve this dilemma over the long run? Explain.

3. What sources of power do you have? What influence tactics could you use? Discuss.

SOURCE: Based on Anthony R. Kovner, "The Case of the Unhealthy Hospital," *Harvard Business Review*, September–October 1991, 12–25.

References

[1]David Krouss, "Casablanca," *Sky*, November 1992, 82–91.
[2]Ronald B. Lieber, "Storytelling: A New Way to Get Close to Your Customer," *Fortune*, February 3, 1997, 102–108.
[3]C. Kepner and B. Tregoe, *The Rational Manager* (New York: McGraw-Hill, 1965).
[4]Robert Tomsho, "How Greyhound Lines Re-Engineered Itself Right Into a Deep Hole," *The Wall Street Journal*, October 30, 1994, A1.
[5]David Woodruff with Karen Lowry Miller, "Chrysler's Neon," *Business Week*, May 3, 1993, 116–126.
[6]Peter Mayer, "A Surprisingly Simple Way to Make Better Decisions," *Executive Female*, March—April 1995, 13–14; and Ralph L. Keeney, "Creativity in Decision-Making with Value Focused Thinking," *Sloan Management Review*, Summer 1994, 33–41.
[7]Herbert A. Simon, *The New Science of Management Decision* (Englewood Cliffs, NJ: Prentice Hall, 1960), 1–8.
[8]Paul J. H. Schoemaker and J. Edward Russo, "A Pyramid of Decision Approaches," *California Management Review* (Fall 1993), 9–31.
[9]Wendy Zellner, "Back to Coffee, Tea or Milk?" *Business Week*, July 3, 1995, 52–56.
[10]James W. Dean, Jr., and Mark P. Sharfman, "Procedural Rationality in the Strategic Decision-Making Process," *Journal of Management Studies* 30 (1993), 587–610.
[11]Stephan Wally and J. Robert Baum, "Personal and Structural Determinants of the Pace of Strategic Decision Making," *Academy of Management Journal* 37 (1994), 932–956.
[12]Justin Martin, "Tomorrow's CEO's," *Fortune*, June 24, 1996, 76–90.
[13]Paul A. Anderson, "Decision Making by Objection and the Cuban Missile Crisis," *Administrative Science Quarterly* 28 (1983), 201–222.
[14]Herbert A. Simon, "Making Management Decisions: The Role of Intuition and Emotion," *Academy of Management Executive* 1 (February 1987), 57–64; Daniel J. Eisenberg, "How Senior Managers Think," *Harvard Business Review* 62 (November–December 1984), 80–90.
[15]Wally and Baum, 1994; and Orlando Behling and Norman L. Eckel, "Making Sense out of Intuition," *Academy of Management Executive* 5, No. 1 (1991), 46–54.
[16]Thomas F. Issack, "Intuition: An Ignored Dimension of Management," *Academy of Management Review* 3, (1978), 917–922.
[17]Majorie A. Lyles, "Defining Strategic Problems: Subjective Criteria of Executives,"

Organizational Studies 8 (1987), 263–280; Majorie A. Lyles and Ian I. Mitroff, "Organizational Problem Formulation: An Empirical Study," *Administrative Science Quarterly* 25 (1980), 102–119.

[18]David A. Cowan, "Developing a Classification Structure of Organizational Problems: An Empirical Investigation," *Academy of Management Journal* 33 (1990), 366–390.

[19]Jeffrey Pfeffer, *Power In Organizations* (Marshfield, MA: Pitman, 1981).

[20]Adapted from Don Hellriegel, John W. Slocum, Jr., and Richard R. Woodman, *Organizational Behavior* (St. Paul: West, 1986); and Pfeffer, *Power in Organizations*, 339–341.

[21]William B. Stevenson, Joan L. Pearce and Lyman W. Porter, "The Concept of 'Coalition' in Organization Theory and Research," *Academy of Management Review* 10 (1985), 256–268.

[22]Based on Richard M. Cyert and James G. March, *A Behavioral Theory of the Firm* (Englewood Cliffs, NJ: Prentice-Hall, 1963); and James G. March and Herbert A. Simon, *Organizations* (New York: Wiley, 1958).

[23]David Woodruff with Karen Lowry Miller, "Chrysler's Neon," *Business Week*, May 3, 1993, 116–136.

[24]Cyert and March, *A Behavioral Theory of the Firm*, 120–122.

[25]Ann Reilly Dowd, "How Bush Decided," *Fortune*, February 22, 1991, 45–46.

[26]Based on Henry Mintzberg, Duru Raisinghani, and Andre Theoret, "The Structuring of 'Unstructured' Decision Processes," *Administrative Science Quarterly* 21 (1976), 246–276.

[27]Lawrence T. Pinfield, "A Field Evaluation of Perspectives on Organizational Decision Making," *Administrative Science Quarterly* 31 (1986), 265–288.

[28]Herve LaRoche, "From a Decision to Action in Organizations: Decision-Making as a Social Representation," *Organization Science* 6, No. 1 (January–February 1995), 62–75.

[29]Mintzberg, et al., "The Structure of 'Unstructured' Decision Processes."

[30]Keith H. Hammonds, "How a $4 Razor Ends Up Costing $300 Million," *Business Week*, January 29, 1990, 62–63.

[31]Karl Weick, *The Social Psychology of Organizing*, 2nd ed. (Reading, MA: Addison–Wesley, 1979), 243.

[32]Christopher Power, with Kathleen Kerwin, Ronald Grover, Keith Alexander, and Robert D. Hof, "Flops," *Business Week*, August 16, 1993, 76–82.

[33]Norm Brodsky, "A Whack on the Head," *Inc.*, November 1996, 31–32.

[34]Robert Townsend, *Up the Organization* (New York: Knopf, 1974), 115.

[35]Earle Hitchner, "The Power to Get Things Done," *National Productivity Review* 12 (Winter 1992/93), 117–122; John C. Philips, *Book Review*, Mortgage Banking 53 (January 1993), 82.

[36]Robert A. Dahl, "The Concept of Power," *Behavioral Science* 2 (1957), 201–215.

[37]W. Graham Astley and Paramijit S. Pachdeva, "Structural Sources of Intraorganizational Power: A Theoretical Syntheses," *Academy of Management Review* 9 (1984), 104–113; and Abraham Kaplan, "Power in Perspective," in Robert L. Kahn and Elise Boulding, eds., *Power and Conflict in Organizations* (London: Tavistock, 1964), 11–32.

[38]Gerald R. Salancik and Jeffrey Pfeffer, "The Bases and Use of Power in Organizational Decision Making: The Case of the University," *Administrative Science Quarterly* 19 (1974), 453–473.

[39]Earle Hitchner, "The Power to Get Things Done."

[40]Bro Uttal, "Behind the Fall of Steve Jobs," *Fortune*, August 5, 1985, 20–24; and Deborah C. Weise, "Steve Jobs versus Apple: What Caused the Final Split," *Business Week*, September 30, 1985, 48.

[41]John R.P. French, Jr. and Bertram Raven, "The Bases of Social Power," in *Group Dynamics*. D. Cartwright and A.F. Zander, eds. (Evanston, IL: Row Peterson, 1960), 607–623.

[42]Pfeffer, *Power in Organizations*.

[43]Erik W. Larson and Jonathan B. King, "The Systemic Distortion of Information: An Ongoing Challenge to Management," *Organizational Dynamics*, 24, No. 3 (Winter 1996), 49–61; Thomas H. Davenport, Robert G. Eccles, and Lawrence Prusak, "Information Politics," *Sloan Management Review*, Fall 1992, 53–65.

[44]Emerson, "Power-Dependence Relations."

[45]Michel Crozier, *The Bureaucratic Phenomenon* (Chicago: University of Chicago Press, 1964).

[46]D.J. Hickson, C.R. Hinings, C.A. Lee, R.C. Schneck, and J.M. Pennings, "A Strategic Contingencies Theory of Intraorganizational Power," *Administrative Science Quarterly* 16 (1971), 216–229.

[47]Jeffrey Pfeffer and Gerald Salancik, "Organizational Decision Making as a Political Process: The Case of a University Budget," *Administrative Science Quarterly* (1974), 135–151.

[48]Hickson, et al., "Strategic Contingencies Theory."

[49]Based on Aaron Bernstein, "The Unions Are Learning to Hit Where It Hurts," *Business Week*, March 17, 1986, 112–114; and James Worsham, "Labor Comes Alive," *Nation's Business*, February 1996, 16–24.

[50]Pfeffer, *Power in Organizations*, 70.

[51]Ibid.

[52]V. Dallas Merrell, *Huddling: The Informal Way to Management Success* (New York AMACON, 1979).

[53]Donald J. Vredenburgh and John G. Maurer, "A Process Framework of O Politics," *Human Relations* 37 (1984), 47–66.

[54]Ibid.

[55]Ibid.

[56]Ibid.

[57]Gary Yukl, "Leadership in Organizations" 3rd ed. (Englewo 1994), Chapter 8.

[58]Jeffrey Pfeffer, *Managing with Power: Politics and Influe* Harvard Business School Press, 1992), Chapter 13.

[59]Richard M. Nixon, *Leaders* (New York: Warner P

[60]Pfeffer, *Managing with Power*, Chapter 15.

[61]Richard L. Daft, *Organization Theory and D* College Publishing, 1998), Chapter 12.

Ba
Bar
Basha
Baro
Bass, B
Beacon,
Bennett,
Bennis, W
Bergman,
Bethune, In
Biederman, Gor
Bigley, Gregory
Bird, Anat, 383
Bishop, Sandy, 316
Blake, Robert R., 7
Blanchard, Kenneth H
114
Blank, Warren, 460
Blank, Humphrey, 455, 4
Bogart, E. Grady, 170, 173
Bogue, Lee G., 225, 227
Boller, David, 81
Bolman, Lee G., 74
Bonini, Jamie, 307
Bossidy, Lawrence A., 428–429
Bouw, Pieter, 65
Bowden, Bobby, 65
Bowen, Donald D., 84

Ford, Robert C., 257
Fottler, Myron D., 257
Frankl, Viktor, 369
Fulton, Bob, 268

Gadiesh, Orit, 335
Gandhi, Mohandas, 337, 370, 385
Gandz, Jeffrey, 194
Gannon, Timothy, 245, 246
Garrow, George, 417–418
Gates, Bill, 126, 156
Gendler, J. Ruth, 129
George, A. L., 462
Gerstner, Lou, 403
Gilmartin, Ray, 185
Goldin, Dan, 184–185
Goleman, Daniel, 346
Goodspeed, Bill, 173
Graen, George B., 79
Grant, Ulysses S., 157
Green, Richard F., 161
Greenleaf, Robert, 374, 375, 377
Grove, Andrew, 221
Guggiari, Tom, 217

Hale, Roger, 8
Hall, Douglas T., 84
Hall, Francine S., 84, 372
Halsey, William F. "Bull," 253–254
Handy, Charles, 10
Hart, David W., 257
Harvey, Jerry, 382
Havel, Vaclev, 375
Hawley, Jack, 352
Heider, John, 197, 211, 472
Helgesen, Sally, 301
Henderson, James, 51
Herkstreter, Cornelius, 423–424
Hersey, Paul, 99, 104, 114
Herzberg, Frederick, 244–245
Heskett, James, 187
Hesse, Hermann, 374, 375
Hesselbein, Frances, 43, 199
Hinkin, T. R., 480
Hitler, Adolf, 338, 369
Hitt, William D., 128, 140, 242
Hock, Dee, 221–222
Hofstede, Geert, 308
Hokoyama, J. D., 312–313
Holmes, Howard "Howdy," 137
Holpp, Lawrence, 257
Hooijberg, Robert, 194
Houghton, James R., 199
Howell, Jane M., 367

Hurlburt, Robert, 437
Hurley, Cornelius, 383
Hurst, David, 223
Hyatt, Joshua, 189

Iacocca, Lee, 49, 458
Ivarsson, Ola, 475

Jackson, Michael, 186
Jackson, Phil, 276, 277
Jago, Arthur G., 109, 111
Janis, Irving L., 462
Jiang Zemin, 64
Jobs, Steve, 470
Johnson, Jack, 102
Jones, Phil, 85–86
Jordan, Michael, 4, 124, 277, 336–337
Jorgensen, Mark, 384
Joseph, Moses, 21
Julius Caesar, 157

Kanter, Rosabeth Moss, 437
Kanungo, Rabindra N., 337
Karkau, Larry, 400–401
Kazarian, Paul B., 101–102
Keane, John, 348
Keating, John (fictional character), 340
Kelleher, Herb, 33–34, 35, 286, 335–336
Keller, Helen, 142–143
Keller, John J., 51
Kelley, David, 438
Kelley, Robert E., 397, 398, 399, 417
Kemp, Fred, 168
Kennedy, John F., 131, 283, 337
Kennedy, Robert, 283
Kent, Deborah S., 299–300
Kerr, Steven, 23, 252
Kierlin, Bob, 191–192
King, Martin Luther, Jr., 48, 153–154, 156, 164, 169, 336, 370
Knight, Phil, 123–124
Knoke, William, 289
Kolind, Lars, 209–210
Koopman, Paul L., 194
Kotter, John P., 39, 187, 425, 459
Kouzes, James M., 411
Krahl, Jack, 341
Kvasnica, Jean, 41

Lancaster, Patrick, III, 250–251

Land, Edwin, 45, 439
Larsen, Ralph, 133
Law, Andy, 182
Lee, Winston, 480
Lengel, Robert H., 48
Lewicki, Roy J., 84
Lewin, Kurt, 69
Lewins, Steve, 34
Lingyuan, 319
Loden, Marilyn, 303
Lombardi, Vince, 132
Lorenzo, Frank, 34

MacArthur, Donald, 357
McCaffrey, David P., 257
McCamus, David, 341
McCanse, Anne Adams, 75
McCarthy, Kevin, 117–119
McCarthy, Paul, 262–263
McClelland, David, 246
McCune, Jenny C., 316
McDonald, Mac, 424
McDonald, Paul, 194
McEnroe, John, 124
McGinn, Richard, 51
McGowan, Bill, 45
McGraw, Carole, 101
McIntyre, Glenn, 386
McPhee, Rob, 76
Mackey, John, 274
Madden, John, 132
Maidment, Fred, 231
Maleckowski, Jim, 449–451
Mamis, Robert A., 21
Mandela, Nelson, 400
Manson, Charles, 338
March, James, 465
Marcic, Dorothy, 308, 325, 368
Marshall, George, 401–402
Martinez, Arthur, 335, 343–344
Martz, Dianne, 395–396, 402
Martz, Kyle, 396
Maslow, Abraham, 243–244
Mason, Richard O., 204
Masterson, Daniel, 157
Matson, Eric, 284
Mavis, Mary, 171
Mayfield, Gloria Hilliard, 401
Mead, Margaret, 63–64
Mensah, Van, 189
Mercer, Lynn, 216–217
Miles, Robert H., 433
Miller, Herman, 199
Miller, Jerrold L., 347

Mills, Robert C., 176
Mintzberg, Henry, 36, 467
Mishra, Aneil K., 194
Mitchell, Carl, 417–418
Mitchell, Chuck, 188, 189
Mitroff, Ian, 343
Moeller, Mark, 92
Mogul, Harvey, 378
Moore, Thomas, 385–386
Morgan, James, 335
Morgan, Nicholas, 256
Morgan, Philip, 160
Morgan, Roy, 56–58
Morita, Akio, 142
Moskal, Brian S., 277
Moyers, Bill, 351
Muller, Robert, 7
Murphy, Dan, 256
Murphy, Tim, 306
Murray, Bill, 284

Nanji, Anil, 17
Neff, Peter, 196
Nemeth, Lane, 134
Newstrom, John W., 480
Nordstrom, Bruce, 191
Notebaert, Dick, 76
Noyce, Robert, 38
Nutt, Paul C., 27

Okum, Sherman K., 160
Olson, Cindy, 385
Oppenheimer, Robert, 68
Osborne, Tom, 65
Ostroff, Frank, 10
O'Toole, James, 199

Pagonis, William G., 69, 70
Paris, Barry, 398
Parker, Dory, 161
Parks, Rosa, 153
Pastiak, Grace, 305–306
Paterno, Joe, 65
Patrick, John, 403
Peace, William, 384
Perot, Ross, 17
Pershing, John J., 401
Peters, Tom, 162
Petrock, Frank, 194
Pierce, Jon L., 480
Platt, Michael, 187–188
Pol Pot, 369
Polese, Kim, 159
Ponchak, Robert, 45–46

Porras, Jerry I., 134
Porter, Lyman W., 240, 261
Porter, Michael, 142
Porter, Superintendent, 175–176
Posner, Barry Z., 411
Puffer, Shelia, 325
Purvis, Richard, 261–263

Quadracchi, Harry, 45
Quadracci, Harry V., 381
Quick, Alan F., 176
Quinn, James Brian, 437
Quinn, R. E., 194

Ransdell, Eric, 403
Ratcliffe, Jere, 141
Rawls, Jim, 204
Reagan, Ronald, 156, 351
Reeves, Paul, 113
Reid, Bruce, 480–481
Reimer, Dennis, 348
Reum, Earl, 44
Rice, Linda Johnson, 305
Ricks, Thomas E., 358
Rifkin, Glenn, 219
Ripon, Jack, 449, 450
Ritchie, J. B., 117
Robbins, Alan, 96–98
Robert, Karl-Henrik, 475
Roberts, Dorothy, 71
Robinson, Alan G., 437
Robinson, Jim, 57–58
Roddewig, Robert, 254
Roosevelt, Franklin Delano, 67,
    401–402, 428, 456
Rose, Pete, 280
Rosener, Judy B., 305, 314
Rost, Joseph C., 39
Row, Heath, 334
Rowe, Alan J., 204
Ruder, Brian, 168
Russell, Anne M., 16
Russell, Susan, 480
Ryder, Thomas, 386

Saddam Hussein, 466
Samuels, Ben, 85
Sandbrook, Judi, 258
Saylor, Michael, 127
Schacht, Henry, 50–51
Schein, Edgar, 163
Schillif, Karl A., 263
Schipke, Roger W., 102
Schlesinger, Arthur, 283

Schmidt, Warren, 69, 71
Schriesheim, C. A., 480
Schwarzkopf, Norman, 21, 156, 157
Sculley, John, 470
Seligman, Martin, 347
Senge, Peter, 132, 341, 342
Seuss, Dr., 91, 190
Sharp, Ron, 262
Sharpe, Tom, 306
Shaw, Ronald, 382
Sherman, Steve, 217
Siemens Rolm, 431
Silverman, Robin Landew, 253
Simon, Herbert, 465
Skywalker, Luke (fictional
    character), 462
Slaymaker, Patricia, 21
Sloum, Robert S., 158
Smith, Frederick, 167, 439
Sobol, Mark R., 158
Sokol, Marc, 221
Sparks, George, 41, 43
Sparks, Jack, 431
Stack, Jack, 161
Stalin, J., 369
Stalk, George, Jr., 213
Stalker, G. M., 215
Stanford, John H., 336
Steers, Richard M., 240
Stern, Sam, 437
Stevenson, Paul, 166
Stewart, Thomas A., 429
Stogdill, R. M., 65–66
Sullivan, Chris, 245
Sullivan, Jessie, 72–73
Sullivan, Paul, 357
Sweeney, E. J. (Bud), 272
Sztykiel, George, 50

Tannenbaum, Robert, 69, 71
Teerlink, Richard, 143, 163–164
Teresa, Mother, 4, 376
Terrill, John, 27–28
Thatcher, Margaret, 4, 64
Thibodeau, Dan, 91–92
Thoman, Richard, 435
Thomas, Kenneth, 287
Thompson, P., 117
Tichy, Noel M., 413
Tierney, Tom, 335
Tigrett, Isaac, 351, 352
Tobias, Randall, 366
Townsend, Robert, 469–470
Turner, Cal, 196

Turner, Ted, 4, 99, 142
Tyler, John, 204
Tyson, Donald, 221

Uhl-Bein, Mary, 79
Urban, Tammy, 284

Vaccaro, Sonny, 124
Van Fleet, D. D., 66
Van Gogh, Frank, 302
Van Muijen, Jaap J., 194
Veiga, John F., 205
Vroom, Victor H., 109, 111, 248

Wachner, Linda, 431
Wall, Bob, 158
Wallace, William "Scott," 22

Wallenberg, Raoul, 363–364, 369, 370, 379, 385
Wallis, Hal, 455–456
Walpole, Horace, 436
Walsh, Wes, 409–410
Walton, Sam, 142
Wang, Charles, 142
Warner, Jack, 455
Weigand, Principal, 176
Weinstein, Leonard "Boogie," 186
Weinstein, Rebekka, 126
Weisinger, Hendrie, 356
Welch, Jack, 4, 23, 38, 49, 247, 332, 425, 444
Wheatley, Margaret J., 12
White, Willis T., Jr., 345
Whyte, William, 301

Williams, Roy, 225
Williams, Tim, 400–401
Winfrey, Oprah, 4
Wiwa, Ken Saro, 424
Wolfe, Chip, 91–92
Wolfe, Michael P., 176
Womack, V. Cheryl, 385
Wong, Michele C., 158–159
Wright, Adam, 324

Yanouzas, John N., 205
Young, John W., 385
Young, Walter, Jr., 125
Yukl, Gary A., 86, 106, 118

Zaleznik, Abraham, 43
Zohar, Danah, 339

COMPANY INDEX

Access Designs, 386
Acme Electronics, 204–205
Acucobol, Inc., 331–332
Adidas, 124
Advanced Circuit Technologies, 220
AES, 258–259
Aetna, 19
Airstar, Inc., 56–58
Allied Signal, 428–429
Alvis Corporation, 117–119
American Express, 386
American Express Financial Advisors (AEFA), 213–214
Ameritech Corporation, 76
Amgen, 136
Andersen Windows, 220
Anheuser-Busch, 425
Apple Computer, 470
Archer-Daniels-Midland, 365
Arizona Public Service Company, 8
Armstrong International, 168
Asian Pacifics, Inc., 312–313
AT&T, 9, 19, 51, 219, 246, 284
ATI Medical, Inc., 166
Avis Corporation, 469–470
Bain & Company, 335

Baker & Taylor Books, 365
Bank of New England, 382
Barouh-Eaton Allen Corporation, 111
Bausch & Lomb, 365
Best Buy, 426
Betty Crocker, 137
Blake memorial Hospital, 480–481
Blue Bell Creameries, 270
Boeing, 198, 426
Borg-Warner Chemicals, 81
Boy Scouts of America, 141
BP Norge, 282–283
British Petroleum, 282
Britt Technologies, 464–465
Buckman Laboratories International, 219
Burger King, 47, 431

Cable Network News (CNN), 99
Cambridge Technology Partners, 284
Camelot Music, 425
Canadian Airlines International, 443
Canadian Auto Workers Union, 74
Carrefour, 303

Carrier, 258
Centennial Technology, 365
Center for Creative Leadership, 20
Cetus Scientific Laboratories, 293
Champion Enterprises, 125
Chase Brass Industries, 137
Chelsea Milling Co., 137
Chemical Banking Corporation, 198, 258
Chevron, 220
Chiat/Day, 182
Chicago Bulls, 276, 277
Childress Buick/Kia Company, 159
Chrysler Canada, 255
Chyrsler Corporation, 74, 273, 458, 465
Circuit City, 426
Citicorp, 124
CitiStorage, 161
Citizens Financial Group, Inc., 382–383
City Bank, 124, 126
Clark Construction Company, 365
Coca-Cola, 126, 300, 303, 431
Columbia Sportswear, 40
Columbia/HCA, 365

Com-Corp, 258
Compaq Corporation, 220, 413, 434
Computer Associates, 142
Computer Associates International, 221
ConAgra, 138
Consolidated Products, 85–86
Continental Airlines, 34, 459
Corning, 300
Corsair Communications, 4, 8, 17
Crescent Manufacturing, 269
Crystal Manufacturing, 473
Cummins Engine, 51

Dana Corporation, 434, 435
Denny's, 319–320
DGL International, 27–28
Digital Equipment Corporation, 303–304
Discovery Toys, 134
Disneyland, 129–130
Dollar General Corp., 196
Drucker Foundation, 43
Duncan Hines, 137
DuPont, 128, 241
Duracell, 426

Earl Industries, Inc., 347
Eastman Chemical, 273, 274
Eastman Kodak, 198, 377
Eaton Corporation, 190
Echo Scarves, 71
EDS (Electronic Data Systems), 17, 18–19, 20, 25
Edy's Grand Ice Cream, 273
Electrolux, 475
Eli Lilly, 366
Enron, 385
Erie Bolt, 137
Exxon, 268

Fairfax County Social Welfare Agency, 230–231
Fashion Fair Cosmetics, 305
Fastenal Co., 191–192
Federal Express, 167, 333, 334, 380, 439
Fernandes, Gary, 18
Flagstar Companies, 319, 320
Fleet Financial Group, 382
Flying Tiger Lines, Inc., 167
Ford Motor Company, 299–300, 303

Fox, Inc., 11, 381
Frito-Lay, 268–269

GE Lighting Co., 271–272
Genentech Corporation, 293
General Electric, 22, 23, 38, 56, 247, 332, 413, 425, 444
General Electric Plastics, 80–81
General Mills, 198, 377
General Motors, 17, 343, 425
General Products, Inc., 417–418
Gerber, 303
Giddings & Lewis, 98
Gillette, 300, 426, 467–468
Girl Scouts, 43
Giro Sport Design, 131
Glassmakers Craft Union, 473
Greyhound Lines, Inc., 14–15, 457
Gruntal & Co., 34
GTE, 198, 320, 426
GTO, Inc., 188, 189

Hallmark, 135, 437
Hampton Inns, 216
Hard Rock Cafe, 351, 352
Harley Davidson, 125, 143, 163
Harley Owners Group (HOG), 143
Harmon Auto Parts, 113
Harty Press, 187
Heineken, 289
Heinz, 168, 303
Hemophilia Health Services, 396
Herman Miller Company, 42, 375
Hewlett-Packard, 41, 198, 253, 284, 287
Hoffman-LaRoche, 293
Home Depot, 125
Honeywell, 275, 284

IBM, 111, 182, 308, 310, 401, 402, 403, 425, 430, 434–435
IDEO, 438
Ikea, 39–40, 475
Imperial Oil, 402
Intel, 38, 221, 413
Interface, Inc., 475
International Paper Company, 219

J.M. Huber Corporation, 173
Johnson & Johnson, 133, 198, 300, 377
Johnson Publishing Company, 305

Kacey Fine Furniture, 158

KFC, 23
Kimberly-Clark, 457
Kinko's, 112
KLM Dutch Airlines, 307
Kmart, 310
K'Netix, 219
Kodak, 182, 241, 437
Komatsu, 126
Korn/Ferry International, 16

Lamprey, Inc., 450
Lands' End, 442
Lantech Corporation, 250–251
Leadership Education for Asian Pacifics, Inc., 312–312
Levi Strauss, 190, 191, 377
LG&E Energy Company, 8
Lincoln Electric Co., 248
Lucent Technologies, 50–51, 217

McDonald's, 47, 137–138, 139, 272, 310
McDonnell-Douglas, 426
McGill University research, 467
McGuffey's, 107
Magnet Sales & Manufacturing, 17
Malden Mills, 376
Manco, 341
Marimba, 159
Mary Kay Cosmetics, 188, 401
Massachusetts General Hospital, 269, 279
MasterBrand Industries, 430
Matsushita Electric, 300
Mattel, 169, 426
MCI, 9, 45, 426
Medtronic, 40
Merck, 133–134, 185
Merrill Lynch, 161
Merry-Go-Round, 186, 187
MetLife, 347
Microsoft, 126
Microstrategy, 127
Mitsui, 241
Mobil Oil, 320
Monsanto, 475
Montague Corporation, 303
Morris Air, 34
Motorola, 22–23, 39, 133

Nabisco, 21
NASA, 131, 184–185, 385
NCR, 303
Nestlé, 82, 303

Nike, 123–124, 125, 131
Nordstrom, 189–190, 191
Northern Industries, 324–325
Northern Telecom, 198, 200, 303
Northrop Grumman, 275
Northrup Grumman, 200
Northwest Airlines, 307
Nucor Steel, 193

Omega Electronics, 204–205
Omnicom, 182
Oticon Holding A/S, 209–210, 213, 218
Otis Elevator, 310
Outback Steakhouse, 245–246
Owens Corning, 461

Paramount Pictures, 381–382
The Parlor, 261–263
People Express Airlines, 137
PepsiCo, 19, 23, 25, 194, 382, 413, 469
Philip Morris, 310, 335
Pilot Pen, 382
Plastic Lumber Company, 96–98
Popeye's Chicken & Biscuits, 459
Pratt & Whitney, 45–46, 56
Pre-Press Graphics, 187
Procter & Gamble, 190, 310
Prudential Insurance Company, 255, 365, 384

Quad/Graphics, 45, 341, 380, 381
Quaker Oats, 337
Quality Suites, 386
QVC, Inc., 381

Ralston Purina Company, 310
Record Giant, 426
Reebok, 124
Renaissance Ramada, 386
R.F. Moeller Jeweler, 92
Rhino, Foods, 168
Rhone-Poulenc, 195–196
Ritz-Carlton, 132
Rodel Inc., 20
Rolls-Royce Motor Company,

431–432
Rotoflow, 302
Royal Dutch/Shell, 423–424
Rubbermaid, 435
Ryder Systems, 165, 377–378

Safeco Insurance, 195
St. Luke's, 181–182, 196
Sam Goody's, 426
Scandic Hotels, 475
Scandinavian Airline Systems Group, 349
Schlage Lock Company, 128
Sears, 138, 335, 343–344, 425
Sequins International, Inc., 190, 237–238
ServiceMaster, 413
Sewell Village Cadillac, 142
Shell, 423–424
Shockley Semiconductor, 38
Siemens AG, 241, 310, 431
Silicon Graphics, 380–381
Sony Corporation, 126, 142
Southwest Airlines, 33, 35, 182, 191, 286, 335, 341
Spartan Motors, 50, 400–401, 407
Speedy Muffler, 190
Springfield Remanufacturing Corp. (SRC), 161–162, 220
Sprint, 9
Starbucks Coffee, 200
Sterling Information Group, 91–92
STET, 46
Strawberries, 426
Sunbeam-Oster, 101–102
Sunrise at Queen Anne retirement home, 161
Synergex, 158–159

Tellabs, Inc., 305–306
Tennessee Eastman Chemical, 273
Texaco, 320
Texas Instruments, 200, 289
3M, 133, 183, 219, 426, 435, 436, 441, 469
Time Warner, 11
TopsyTail, Inc., 214–215

Toshiba Corporation, 310
Total Quality Commitment, 306
Towers Perrin, 320
Troy Ford, 43–44
TRW, 3–4
Tyson Foods, 221

United States Information Agency (USIA), 267–268
UNR-Levitt, 137
UNUM Life Insurance Company of America, 315, 316
U.S. Army, 22, 172, 347–348
U.S. Army's National Training Center, 22, 172
U.S. Healthcare, 248–249
USS Florida, 356–358
USS Missouri, 254
USWest, 219

Valena Scientific Corporation (VSC), 293–294
VCW, Inc., 385
Visa International, 221–222
Volvo, 268

W. R. Grace, 241
Wal-Mart, 138
Walt Disney Co., 141
Warnaco, 431
Warner Brothers, 455
Web Industries, 376
West Coast Valet Service, 345
Westinghouse Electric Company, 273, 384
Wherehouse Entertainment, 426
Whirlpool, 431
Whole Foods Market, 274
Wilson Golf Ball, 273
W.L. Gore and Associates, 217, 255, 256

Xerox, 198, 255, 300, 320
Xerox Canada, 341

Zenith, 133

Abilene Paradox, 382
achievement culture, 194
achievement-oriented leadership, 104
acquired needs theory (McClelland), 246, 259
adaptability culture, 193–194
African Americans, 312, 313, 320
alienated follower, 398
alignment of creative acts, 436
alignment function, 40
anger, 345, 386
Asian Americans, 312–313
assertiveness, 287, 476
assessment, 170
Association for Quality and Participation, 373
athletic team interdependence, 279–280
authoritarian management, 372
authority-compliance management, 76
autocratic leader, 69, 71

bargaining/negotiating, 288–289
behavior
    of effective followership, 404–406
    motivation model and, 239
    path-goal theory on leader, 103–107, 248
    Pike Syndrome of, 340
    polarities of, 98
    primacy team, 283
    reward systems and, 252
behavior approaches, 69–77
behavior modification, 247
beliefs
    change and new, 432
    in higher purpose, 385
belongingness needs, 243
biculturalism, 312
"Black-Belt Boss" (Mamis), 21
Bold New World (Knoke), 289
boot camp values, 16
bottom-up approach, 434
box approach, 105
The Boy, the Girl, the Ferryboat Captain, and the Hermits, 389–390
Brigadier General Training Conference (U.S. Army), 347–348
"Building the Business" (PepsiCo boot camp), 23

Built to Last: (Collins and Porras), 134
bureaucratic culture, 195–196

The Caine Mutiny (movie), 357
capacity, 332
Care of the Soul (Moore), 385–386
Carnegie-Mellon University research, 465
"carrot and stick" approach, 246–247
"carrot and stick" controversy, 248–251
Carville City School District, 175–176
Casablanca (movie), 455–456
Center for Business Ethics study, 198
Center for Creative Leadership study, 13–14
centrality, 472–473
ceremony, 188
Challenger disaster, 351, 385
change
    ability to, 197
    creativity and, 435–441
    focus of, 432–435
    forces driving need for organizational, 425
    leading major, 429–432
    overcoming resistance to, 442–443
    or perish, 425–427
    resistance to, 441–442
    types of organizational, 434
    values-based leadership and, 199
    vision and, 131
    See also cultural change
change approach, 105
channel richness, 165–167
chaotic environment
    macro leadership in, 50–51
    micro leadership in, 49–50
    stable vs., 47
charismatic leaders, 334–338
clan culture, 195
clarity, 129
classroom leadership, 101
co-optation, 474
coalition building, 465–466, 468, 474
Code of Business Conduct (Northern Telecom), 198, 200

code of ethics, 198, 200
coercive power, 471
cohesiveness, 284–286
collaboration, 10–11
Coming of Age in Samoa (Mead), 63
command team, 270
commitment, 129
commitment probability (CP), 109, 111
commitment requirement (CR), 108, 111
communication
    by leaders, 155–156
    by team leader, 276
    conflict reduction through, 289
    described, **155**
    dialogue and, 162, 163, 412
    discernment and, 162–164
    feedback/learning and, 170–173
    internal, 437–438
    listening as, 159–162, 406
    nonverbal, 169–170
    open, 156, 158
    through stories and metaphors, 167–169
    to develop followers, 171–172
    to facilitate change, 442–443
    understanding and, 406
    of the vision, 431
communication champion, 155–156
communication channels, 164–167
community leadership, 412–413
competence, 333
competitive strategy, 218–220
competitive (team), 285
conflict
    defining, **286**
    handling team, 286–289
conflict management model, 287
conformist, 398–399
connection with others, 385
consequence, 170
consideration, 72, 73
contingency approach
    described, 93–**94**
    Fiedler's model of, 94–98
    path-goal theory and, 102–107
    situational theory and, 99–102
    substitutes for leadership in, 112–114
    Vroom-Jago Contingency Model of, 107–112

contingency theories
  described, 95–96
  development of, 49
controlling function, 35, 36
cooperation approach, 287–288
core competence, 136–137
core purpose, 133
core values, 133
corporate culture change, 318–320
  See also change
country club management, 76
courage
  defining, 379–383
  of followers, 400–405
  leadership, 378–379
  moral, 383–384
  sources of personal, 385–386
creative process stages, 440
creativity
  defining, **435**–436
  five myths standing in way of,
    439
  leading organizations/people to,
    436–439
  stages of personal process in,
    439–441
  See also decision-making
Crew Resource Management
  (CRM) program (Southwest Airlines), 286
Crimson Tide (movie), 357
critical team events, 283
critical thinking, 397
cross-functional teams, 270–272
Cuban missile crisis, 461
cultural change
  approaches to, 443–446
  leading, 441–443
  organizational, 432
  See also change
cultural characteristics, 309–311
cultural differences, 317
cultural gap, 187–188
culture
  achievement, 194
  adaptability, 193–194
  adaptive vs. unadaptive, 187
  building ethical, 377–384
  bureaucratic, 195–196
  changes in the organizational, 432
  changing corporate, 318–320
  clan, 195
  daily actions and, 191
  described, **183**

external adaptation and, 185–186
importance of, 184–186
of learning organizations,
  220–222
selection/socialization of,
  190–191
shaping, 188–192
social value systems and, 308–309
sociocultural environment,
  307–308
specialized language of, 190
symbols and, 190
team, 283–284
transforming unadaptive, 189
  See also diversity; values
culture change, 432
culture strength, 186–187
Czech Republic, 309, 310

Dallas Museum of Art, 126
Dead Poets Society (movie), 340
decision making
  by empowered employees, 255
  coalition building for, 465–466,
    468
  constraints on leader, 462
  defining, 457
  incremental, 467–468
  mistakes in, 468–470
  moral, 199
  organizational, 462–468
  political model for, 463–464
  power, influence and, 470–476
  programmed/nonprogrammed,
    458–459
  rational choice model for, 463
  rational process for, 461–462
  stages of, 457–458
  stewardship and, 373
  strategic, 140–143
  in today's environment, 459
  Vroom-Jago theory on, 108–112
  See also creativity; leaders
decision mistakes, 468–470
decisional roles, 36
deficiency needs, 244
delegating (S4) style, 99
democratic leader, 69, 71
deniability, 16
dependent person, 405
development, 170
dialogue, 162, 163, 412
directing function
  of management, 35, 36

management vs. leadership,
  39–40
directive leadership, 104
discernment, 162–164
disclosure mechanisms, 200
diversity
  cultural characteristics and,
    309–311
  defining, **302**
  from uniformity to, 13
  global, 306–311
  paradox of, 317
  reality of, 303–304
  stages of personal awareness of,
    321
  See also culture
**diversity awareness training,
  320**–321
diversity wheel, 303
"double-consciousness," 312
drive, 68–69
dyadic leadership approach, 78–82
dyadic theory, 78

Ebony magazine, 305
effective follower, 399
efficient performance, 210–212
emotional intelligence, 345–349,
  355–356
emotions, 345–346
empathic listening, 406
empathy, 70, **347**
employee morale, 285
employee ownership, 258
**employee-centered leaders,
  73**–74
employees
  characteristics of creative, 437
  ethical training of, 200
  leading creativity in, 436–439
  personal compact with, 441–442
  relationships between leaders
    and, 350
  using love vs. fear on, 349–353
  vision and, 129
  as whistle-blowers, 200, 371, 384
  See also empowerment; followers;
    motivation
empowered roles, 216–217
empowerment
  applications of, 255–256
  described, **251,** 253
  elements of, 254–255
  from control to, 10

empowerment *(continued)*
  implementing, 257–258
  reasons for, 253
  to act on the vision, 431
Era 1 leadership, 47–49
Era 2 leadership, 49
Era 3 leadership, 49–50
Era 4 leadership, 50
Ergonomics Project, 237
esteem needs, 243
ethical culture, 377–384
ethical leadership, 367, 379
ethical structure, 200
ethical values, 196–197
ethnocentrism, 311, 315, 322
ethnorelativism, 315
Everybody Comes to Rick's (play), 455
Everyday Revolutionaries: (Helgesen), 301
Executive derailment, 15
expectancy theory, 248
expert power, 471
expertise approach, 105
explicit statements, 284
external adaptation, 185–186
extinction, 247
extrinsic rewards, 239–240, 249

facilitating communication, 289
facilitating leader, 50
failure, 385–386
faith, 131
fear, 349–353, 382
fear-based motivation, 353
feedback
  on being a change leader, 448–449
  communication, 170–173
  culture preference inventory, 202–204
  on emotional intelligence, 355–356
  getting personal, 174–175
  on leader's strategic vision, 145–147
  on leadership orientation, 228–230
  on moral leadership, 388–389
  motivation and, 239
  on motivation assumptions, 260–261
  on personal power profile, 478–480

  on power of followership, 415–417
  on racial bias, 322–323
  on team cohesiveness, 291–293
feedback process, 171
Felton Elementary School, 72–73
femininity, 309
Fiedler's contingency model, 94–98
The Fifth Discipline (Senge), 19, 132, 341, 342
Flashdance (movie), 382
followers
  building community of, 411–413
  communication to develop, 171–172
  courage of, 400–405
  desirable characteristics wanted by, 411
  relationship continuum between leader and, 372
  role of, 396–397
  ways to influence leaders, 408
  See also employees
followership
  feedback on power of, 415–417
  seven habits of effective, 404
  strategies for effective, 407–410
  styles of, **397**–400
formal reporting systems, 217–218
forming stage of teams, 281–282
Fortune magazine, 40, 343
frame
  described, **224**
  human resource, 225–226
  political, 226
  structural, 224–225
  symbolic, 226–227
frustration, 386
functional team, 270
Fusion Leadership: (Daft and Lengel), 48

gainsharing, 258
"Get Connected" (IBM manifesto), 403
glass ceiling, 313
Glass Ceiling commission study, 304, 313
glass walls, 313
global diversity, 306–311
global teams, 289–290
goal congruence (GC), 109
The Golden Rule, 16

Great Man approach, 48–49, 51–52, **65**
Groundhog Day (movie), 284

Habits of Highly Effective People (Covey), 404
Hallmark's mission statement, 135
Harley Owners Group (HOG) rallies, 163
hierarchy of needs theory (Maslow), 243–244, 259
"high-high" leader theories, 76–77, 82
higher needs, 240, 242
Hispanics, 313
honesty/integrity, 67–68
hope, 131
horizontal organization structure, 213, 214
human assets approach, 105
human resource frame, 225–226
Hunterdon High, 256
hygiene factors, 244–245

"I Have a Dream" speech (Martin Luther King), 336
idealized influence, 306
ideals, 131
IDEO Product Development, 438
If I Ran the Zoo (Dr. Seuss), 91
Iliad (Homer), 48
imagination, 129
impoverished management, 76
In Search of Excellence, 169
in-group subordinates, 78–79
increase rewards, 103
incremental decision model, 467–468
independent person, 405
independent thinking, 338, 340
individual consideration, 306
individual rewards, 239–240, 249
individualism, 309
individualized leadership, 80
influence, 474–476
informational analysis, 476
informational roles, 36
initiating structure, 72
inspirational motivation, 306
integrators, 246
intellectual stimulation, 306
interactive leadership, 305
interdependence, 278–280, 405
internal communication, 437–438

International Campaign to Ban Landmines, 7
International Ladies Garment Workers' Union, 237
interpersonal roles, 36
intrinsic rewards, 239–240
"introspection training," 19
invisible corporate culture, 184
Iowa State University studies, 69, 72
iron fist, 16

Japan, 309, 311
Jet magazine, 305
job enrichment, 258–259
job-centered leader, 74–75
Journey to the East (Hesse), 374–375

knowledge, 407
Ko-Rec-Type, 111

large-group intervention, 444–446
law of effect, 247
Leader Behavior Description Questionnaire (LBDQ), 72, 73
leader capacity, 333
leader decision styles, 108–109
leader position power, 41, 95, 96
leader power
    sources of, 471–473
    types of, 470471
    See also power
leader-follower relationship continuum, 372
leader-member exchange (LMX), 79–80
leader-member relations, 95, 96
leaders
    asserting influence, 474–476
    autocratic, 69, 71
    becoming a moral, 369–371
    charismatic, 334–338
    charismatic vs. noncharismatic, 337
    communication by, 155–156
    as communication champion, 155–156
    comparison of male/female, 307
    democratic, 69, 71
    desirable characteristics of, 411
    employee-centered, 73–74
    facilitating, 50
    job-centered, 74–75
    of learning organizations, 222–224

learning stages to become, 24
major changes lead by, 429–432
nine personal attributes of, 334
path-goal theory on behavior of, 103–107, 248
personalized and socialized, 338
qualities/characteristics of, 41–44, 66, 67
relationships between employees and, 350
"Rushmorean," 199
search for new kind of, 16–17
strategic contribution by, 139–143
strategic impact of, 143–144
theories of "high-high," 76–77, 82
ways that followers influence, 408
within organizations, 17–19
women as, 305–306
See also decision making
leader's information (LI), 108
leadership
    behavior approaches to, 69–77
    business of living and, 7–8
    by women, 305–306
    in the classroom, 101
    community sharing of, 412–413
    compared to management, 37–46
    context of, 46
    contingency approach to, 93–119
    control vs. service, 371–377
    cultural awareness and, 310–311
    cultural/racial stereotypes of, 312–313
    defining, **5**
    emotional intelligence and, 345–349
    ethical, 367, 379
    evolution of management, 46–53
    five strategies for successful, 105
    from control to empowerment, 10
    importance of developing, 13–16
    individualized, 80
    interactive, 305
    introspection training for, 19–20
    learning, 20–24
    living company, 241
    macro, 47–49, 50–51
    micro, 47, 49
    mind-set of, 338–345
    moral, 365–369, 388–389

morality of today's, 365–369
motivation and, 238–242
nature of, 5–6
new reality for, 9
nine faces of, 334
nine natural laws of, 460
personal qualities of, 41–44
qualities no longer needed for, 16
quantum, 460
rational vs. ethical, 367
servant, 374–377
strategic, 124–126
team, 274–277
trait approach to, 65–69
transactional vs. transformational, 427–429
universalistic vs. contingency, 93
using love vs. fear, 349–353
values-based, 197–200
leadership continuum, 71
leadership courage, 378–379
Leadership Development Center (GE), 23
Leadership Dilemmas-Grid Solution (Blake and McCanse), 75
The Leadership Engine: (Tichy), 413
Leadership Grid, 75–76
Leadership Is an Art (De Pree), 42
Leadership and the New Science (Wheatley), 12
Leadership Orientation questionnaire, 228–230
leadership situation, 95, 96
leadership style, 94–95
leadership vision, 40, 126–133
leadership-management mix, 18
Leading Change: The Argument for Values-Based Leadership (O'Toole), 199
Leading Corporate Transformation: (Miles), 433
learning, 170–173
learning organizations
    competitive vs. linked strategy in, 218–220
    efficient performance vs., 210–212
    leaders of, 222–224
    leadership frames for, 224–227
    rigid vs. adaptive culture of, 220–222
    structure of, 212–215
    systems vs. networks in, 217–218
    tasks vs. roles in, 215–217

See also organizations
legitimate power, 470
linguistic pluralism, 309
listening, 159–162, 406
The Living Company: (de Geus), 241
"Loosening Up the Tie" memo
   (Honeywell), 284
love, 349–353
love-based motivation, 353
lower needs, 240, 242
LPC (lease preferred coworker)
   scale, 94–95, 98

macro leadership
   in chaotic world, 50–51
   micro vs., 47
   in stable world (Era 1), 47–49
   See also leadership
management
   authoritarian, 372
   compared to leadership, 37–46
   defining, **35**
   evolution of leadership in, 46–53
   functions of, 35–36
   the nature of, 35–37
   open-book, 218
   participative, 373
   strategic, 135
   styles of, 76
   top quality, 443, 447
Management by Storying Around
   (Armstrong), 168
"management by wandering around
   (MBWA)," 169–170
management communication, 155
management-leadership mix, 18
managerial roles, 36–37
managing emotions, 347
Managing with the Wisdom of Love:
   (Marcic), 368
masculinity, 309
Maslow's hierarchy of needs,
   243–244, 259
Maximum Leadership: (Farkas and
   De Backer), 105
mechanistic processes, 215–216
mediation, 289
Mega-Meal campaign (KFC), 23
mental models, 343–344
metaphors, 167–169, 284
micro leadership, 47, 49
middle-of-the-road management,
   76
mindfulness, 338, 340

minorities
   biculturalism and, 312
   challenges faced by, 311–313
   glass ceiling and, 313
   See also women
mission, 133–135
mommy track, 312
Montgomery Improvement Association, 153
moral choices, 369–370
moral courage, 383–384
moral development levels, 369–371
moral leaders, 369–371
moral leadership, 365–369, 388–389
morale, 285
motivating oneself, 347
motivation
   "carrot and stick" approach to,
      246–251
   feedback on, 260–261
   inspirational, 306
   leadership, **238**–242
   needs of people and, 242
   needs-based theories of,
      242–246, 259
   organization-wide programs pro-
      moting, 258–259
   reinforcement perspective on,
      247
   using love vs. fear for, 349–353
motivators, 244–245
Moving Mountains (Pagonis and
   Cruikshank), 70
multiculturalism
   current state of, 302–305
   leadership initiatives toward,
      314–321
   See also diversity

Nashville Humane Association,
   7
national value system, 308
The Natural Step environmental
   movement, 475
need for achievement, 246
need for affiliation, 246
need for power, 246
needs
   extrinsic rewards and lower, 249
   higher vs. lower, 240, 242
   motivation methods and, 242
   motivation theories based on,
      242–246
   within motivation model, 239

network expansion, 474
networks (dyadic approach), 81–82
neutralizer, 112, 113
The 9 Natural Laws of Leadership
   (Blank), 460
**nonprogrammed decisions,
458**–459
**nonverbal communication,
169**–170
norming stage of teams, 282
norms
   defining, **283**
   fast team cultural, 284

observations, 170
Odyssey (Homer), 48
Oh, The Places You'll Go (Dr. Seuss),
   190
Ohio State studies, 72–73, 75, 76,
   77
ombudsperson, 200
"On the Folly of Rewarding A
   While Hoping for B" (Kerr), 252
100 Best Companies to Work For in
   America (*Fortune* study), 40, 249
OPEC oil embargo (1972–73), 49
open communication, 156, 158
open mindedness, 340–341
open-book management, 218
organic processes, 215–216
"organization man" (Whyte), 301
organization structure, 212–215
organization-wide motivational programs, 258–259
organizational centrality, 472–473
organizational change, 434
   See also change
organizational culture, 183–186,
   432
   See also culture
organizational decision making,
   462–468
organizational dependency, 472
**organizational development
(OD), 444,** 447
organizational diversity, 304–305,
   314
organizational learning, 172–173
organizations
   changing realities for, 8–9
   characteristics of creative, 437
   circles of causality in, 342
   core competence of, 136–137
   core values/purpose of, 133

efficient performance vs. learning models of, 210–212
ethical values in, 196–197
fear in, 349–350
forces driving need for change in, 425
from competition to collaboration, 10–11
from control to empowerment, 10
from things to relationships, 11
from uniformity to diversity, 13
leaders within, 17–19
leadership solutions for, 317–321
leading creativity in, 436–439
mission of, 133–135
personal compact between employees and, 441–442
politics within, 474–476
quantum, 339
stages of diversity awareness by, 314–315
teams in, 268–269
See also learning organizations
organizing function, 35, 36
Organizing Genius: (Bennis and Biederman), 271
out-group subordinates, 78–79
Outcome functions, 45

paradigm
defining, **8**
human skills as part of, 14
new vs. old, 9
paradox of diversity, 317
participating (S3) style, 99, 102, 107
participative leadership, 104
participative management, 373
partnership assumption, 373
partnership building, 80
A Passion for Excellence, 169
passive follower, 399
path clarification, 102–103, 107
path-goal theory, 102–107, 248
pay for knowledge, 258
people and culture changes, 434
See also changes
people-oriented leadership, 113
performance (team), 285
performing stage of teams, 282
"peripheral vision," 341
personal attraction, 285
personal compact, 441–442
personal diversity awareness, 321

personal ethics, 197–198
personal leadership qualities, 41–44
personal mastery, 344–345
personal power profile, 478–480
personality clashes, 287
personalized leaders, 338
persuasion, 414
physiological needs, 243
Pike Syndrome, 340
planning function, 36
police department leadership, 147
political frame, 226
political model, 463–464
politics, 474–476
pooled interdependence, 279
position power, 41, 95, 96
Post-it Notes (3M), 436, 437, 469
power
effect of, 470
sources of, 406–407
team leader sharing of, 276
types of, 470–471
power distance, 308
The Power of Myth (Campbell and Moyers), 351
pragmatic survivor, 399
prejudice, 315–316, 322
primacy, 283
Principle Centered Leadership, 19
proactive behavior, 405
problem identification, 461, 469
problem solution, 461, 469
See also decision making
problem structure (ST), 108, 111, 112
problem-solving teams, 272
process-improvement team, 272
product and service changes, 432
programmed decisions, 458
punishment, 247

quality requirement (QR), 108, 111
quantum leadership, 460
quantum organizations, 339

racial bias quiz, 322–323
racism, 312, 319–320
Raiders of the Lost Ark (movie), 382
rational choice model, 463
rational decision process, 461–462
rational leadership, 367
rational manager leadership, 49, 51–52
reciprocal interdependence, 279

referent power, 471
reinforcement, 247
reinforcement theory, 247
relationship-oriented leader, 94, 96–98
relationships function, 40–41
reward power, 471
rewards
behavior resulting from, 252
intrinsic and extrinsic, 239–240, 249
for labor, 374
motivation model and, 239
path-goal theory on, 103, 106–107
which empower employees, 255
Rewiring the Corporate Brain (Zohar), 339
rich communication channels, 164–167
ripple effect, 472
risk of courage, 380
ROLAP (Microstrategy), 127
roles
empowered, 216–217
of followers, 396–397
tasks vs., 215–217
team leader's personal, 274–276
ROTC training, 104
"Rushmorean" leaders, 199

safety needs, 243
self-actualization needs, 243–244
self-awareness, 346–347
self-centeredness, 16
self-confidence, 66–67
self-directed teams, 214, 272–274
self-initiated activity, 436
self-reference, 132
selling (S2) style, 99
serendipity, 436
servant leadership, 374–377
Servant Leadership (Greenleaf), 374
shared mission/goals, 285
"sharpening the saw," 406
short-term wins, 431–432
situational theory, 99–102
social facilitation, 285
social skill, 347
social value systems, 308–309
socialized leaders, 338
sociocultural environment, 307–308
stable environment

stable environment *(continued)*
chaotic vs., 47
macro leadership in, 47–49
micro leadership in, 49
staffing function, 35, 36
Stanford Business School study,
168–169
Star Wars (movie), 462
stereotypes, 312–313, 315–316
stewardship, 373–374
stories
communication through,
167–169
culture shaped through, 188–190
storming stage of teams, 282
strategic approach, 105
strategic leadership, 124–126
strategic management, 135
strategic vision
action strategy and, 140
communicating, 431
feedback on leadership and,
145–147
leader impact on, 143–144
in learning organizations,
218–220
stimulating, 139–140
See also vision
strategy, 136
strategy formulation, 138
strategy implementation, 138
**strategy and structure changes,
432**
strategy/structure relationship, 139
structural frame, 224–225
subordinate conflict (CO), 109
subordinate information (SI), 109
subordinate in/out groups, 78–79
substitute, 112, 113
supportive leadership, 104
SWOT, 142
symbolic action, 476
symbolic frame, 226–227
symbols
of culture, **190**
of teams, 284
synergy, 137, 406
system-wide rewards, 239–240
systems (dyadic approach), 81–82
systems thinking, 341–342

T-P Leadership Questionnaire: An
Assessment of Style, 115–117

task structure, 95, 96
task-oriented leader, 94, 98
task-oriented leadership, 113
tasks, 215–217
team cohesiveness, 284–286,
291–293
team conflict, 286–289
team effectiveness, 276–278
team interaction, 285
team leadership, 49–50, 52,
274–277
team management style, 76
team performance, 285
team size, 278
teams
characteristics of, 278–280
culture of, 283–284
defining, **269**
development of, 280–283
global, 289–290
interdependence of, 278–280
organization built up by, 374
in organizations, 268–269
self-directed, 214, 272–274
types of, 269–274
technology changes, 432
telling (S1) style, 99, 102
**total quality management
(TQM), 443,** 447
Trading Places (movie), 382
trait leadership approach, 65–69
traits, 65
transactional leadership, 427
**transformational leadership,
427**–429
transnational teams, 289
two-factor theory (Herzberg),
245–245, 259

unadaptive culture, 187, 189
uncertainty, 473
uncertainty avoidance, 308–309
uncritical thinking, 397
University of Michigan studies,
73–75, 75, 76, 77
University of Texas studies, 75–76,
77
unofficial creative activity, 436

values
boot camp, 16
change and new, 432
as competitive tool, 413

core, 133
creating customer, **137**–138
ethical, 196–197
rank orderings of countries, 308
shaping, 192–193
social value systems, 308–309
team recognition of shared, 276
See also culture
values-based leadership, 197–200
Velcro invention, 439
**Vertical Dyad Linkage (VDL),
78**–79
vertical organization structure,
212–213
vertical team, 270
virtues, 368
visible corporate culture, 184
vision
communicating the, 431
defining leadership, **126**–133
destination described by, 40
during major changes, 430–431
peripheral, 341
personal mastery and, 344–345
strategic, 139–140
to manage conflict, 288
See also strategic vision
visionary leadership feedback,
145–147
**Vroom-Jago Contingency Model,
107**–112
Vroom-Jago decision tree, 110

"wall of fear," 382
The Way of the Warrior (Dunnigan
and Masterson), 157
welcoming failure, 385–386
whistle-blowing, 200, 371, 384
"white male" club, 317, 322
win-win frame of mind, 406
women
challenges faced by, 311–313
compared to male leaders, 307
glass ceiling and, 313
leadership by, 305–306
transformation by working, 301
See also minorities
Work Out program (General Electric), 444–445
Workers' Bill of Rights, 42
workforce diversity, 302
W.P. Wagner High school plan
(Canada), 76